PEDAGOGICAL PERSPECTIVES ON COGNITION AND WRITING

Lauer Series in Rhetoric and Composition
Editors: Thomas Rickert and Jennifer Bay

The Lauer Series in Rhetoric and Composition honors the contributions Janice Lauer has made to the emergence of Rhetoric and Composition as a disciplinary study. It publishes scholarship that carries on Professor Lauer's varied work in the history of written rhetoric, disciplinarity in composition studies, contemporary pedagogical theory, and written literacy theory and research.

Recent Books in the Series

Pedagogical Perspectives on Cognition and Writing (Rifenburg, Portanova, & Roen, 2021)

Feminist Circulations: Rhetorical Explorations across Space and Time (Enoch, Griffin, & Nelson, 2021)

Creole Composition: Academic Writing and Rhetoric in the Anglophone Caribbean (Milson-Whyte, Oenbring, & Jaquette, 2019). MLA Mina P. Shaughnessy Prize 2019-2020, CCCC Best Book Award 2021.

Retellings: Opportunities for Feminist Research in Rhetoric and Composition Studies (Enoch & Jack, 2019)

Facing the Sky: Composing through Trauma in Word and Image (Fox, 2016)

Expel the Pretender: Rhetoric Renounced and the Politics of Style (Wiederhold, 2015)

First-Year Composition: From Theory to Practice (Coxwell-Teague & Lunsford, 2014)

Contingency, Immanence, and the Subject of Rhetoric (Richardson, 2013)

Rewriting Success in Rhetoric & Composition Careers (Goodburn, LeCourt, & Leverenz, 2012)

Writing a Progressive Past: Women Teaching and Writing in the Progressive Era (Mastrangelo, 2012)

Greek Rhetoric Before Aristotle, 2e, Rev. and Exp. Ed. (Enos, 2012)

Rhetoric's Earthly Realm: Heidegger, Sophistry, and the Gorgian Kairos (Miller)
  *Winner of the Olson Award for Best Book in Rhetorical Theory 2011

Techne, from Neoclassicism to Postmodernism: Understanding Writing as a Useful, Teachable Art (Pender, 2011)

Walking and Talking Feminist Rhetorics: Landmark Essays and Controversies (Buchanan & Ryan, 2010)

For more titles, visit the series page: http://bit.ly/lauerseries

PEDAGOGICAL PERSPECTIVES ON COGNITION AND WRITING

Edited by J. Michael Rifenburg,
Patricia Portanova, and Duane Roen

Parlor Press
Anderson, South Carolina
www.parlorpress.com

Parlor Press LLC, Anderson, South Carolina, USA

© 2021 by Parlor Press
All rights reserved.

Printed in the United States of America
S A N: 2 5 4 - 8 8 7 9

Library of Congress Cataloging-in-Publication Data on File

978-1-64317-246-0 (paperback)
978-1-64317-247-7 (hardcover)
978-1-64317-248-4 (pdf)
978-1-64317-249-1 (epub)

1 2 3 4 5

Lauer Series in Rhetoric and Composition
Editors: Thomas Rickert and Jennifer Bay

Cover design by David Blakesley.
Cover image by Steve Johnson courtesy of Unsplash.

Printed on acid-free paper.

Parlor Press, LLC is an independent publisher of scholarly and trade titles in print and multimedia formats. This book is available in paper, cloth and eBook formats from Parlor Press on the World Wide Web at http://www.parlorpress.com or through online and brick-and-mortar bookstores. For submission information or to find out about Parlor Press publications, write to Parlor Press, 3015 Brackenberry Drive, Anderson, South Carolina, 29621, or email editor@parlorpress.com.

Contents

Foreword: Reflecting on and Learning from the
Past to Imagine the Future   *vii*
   Susan Miller-Cochran

Introduction: Promises and Perils of Cognition
and Writing Praxis   3
   J. Michael Rifenburg, Patricia Portanova, and Duane Roen

I Cognitive Theory and Writing Pedagogy   19

1 Readiness Redefined: Toward a Pedagogy of Here and Now   21
   Peter H. Khost, Wendy Ryden, and David Hyman

2 Metacognition: Crossing the Information
and Writing Thresholds   40
   Barbara J. D'Angelo and Barry M. Maid

3 What Do You Experience When You Read and Write?
Diversity in the Experience of Inner Speech   52
   Airlie Rose

II Classroom-Level Engagement   75

4 Recall, Reframe, Reflect: Threshold Concept Pedagogy and
Metacognitive Practice in First-Year Writing   77
   Gita DasBender

5 Cognitive Psychology and the *Framework for Success*:
Teaching Genre as a Design Problem   108
   Thomas Skeen

6 Creating a "Language" of Trauma: Exploring Trauma Theories
and Trauma Narratives in Multimodal Writing   134
   Courtney Patrick-Weber

7 Cognition and Community: Using the Habits of Mind to Engage Students in Community-Focused Writing   *149*
   Michelle Stuckey, James Toweill, Sean Tingle, Heather MacDonald, and Jessica Harnisch

III Program-Level Engagement   *173*

8 The Space Between: A Statewide Effort Using the *Framework for Success* to Bridge High School and College Writing   *175*
   Christine Cucciarre

9 A Metaphor-Based Curriculum: Fostering Inquiry, Metacognition, and Transfer   *187*
   Tonya Eick and Gregg Fields

10 Pedagogical Practices of the Habits of Mind   *210*
   Melvin E. Beavers, Subrina Bogan, Harold Brown, Caleb James, and Sherry Rankins-Robertson

11 The Effects of Metacognition on Student-Athletes' Academic Performance   *232*
   Martha A. Townsend

IV Writing Center Engagement   *249*

12 "This Is on You": When Responsibility as a Habit of Mind Informs Writing Center Consultant's Practice   *251*
   Morgan Gross and Kelsie Walker

13 The *Framework* Will Not Hold Without a Center   *280*
   William J. Macauley, Jr.

14 Writing Center Consultations as Emotional Experiences: How Different Learning Experiences Shape Student Perceptions of Agency   *303*
   Bronwyn T. Williams

Afterword: Considering Whiteness in the *Framework*'s Habits of Mind   *323*
   Asao Inoue

Contributors   *331*
Index   *339*

Foreword: Reflecting on and Learning from the Past to Imagine the Future

Susan Miller-Cochran

As I write this foreword, I am mindful that the *Framework for Success in Postsecondary Writing* has been an integral part of my professional experience and my understanding of writing instruction for an entire decade. As the "WPA Outcomes Statement for First-Year Composition" shaped my growing understanding of writing instruction in the 2000s, the *Framework* refined and challenged my practice as a writing instructor in the 2010s. When I imagine what the future might look like in my own writing classes, I draw on lessons learned from the "Outcomes Statement" and the *Framework*, illuminated by the kind of research in this collection and the critiques and recommendations made by teacher-scholars of writing over the past twenty years.

I was honored and humbled to be part of the group that drafted the *Framework*. I was invited by Linda Adler-Kassner, who was the president of the Council of Writing Program Administrators (CWPA) at the time. In her email invitation to me on March 31, 2010, she explained the purpose of the task force that was being formed:

> Last week, the Executive Committee of the Council of Writing Program Administrators endorsed a task force to create the CWPA Framework for Success in Postsecondary Writing. This framework, which will be derived from the WPA Outcomes, is an effort to have postsecondary writing instructors define what "college readiness" means, based on our expertise and scholarship.

The exigence behind the creation of the task force and the development of the *Framework* was to have a coordinated, broad-based, and knowledgeable response from teacher-scholars in writing studies to policies such as Race to the Top and the Common Core State Standards Initiative. Race to the Top had been introduced by the Obama administration in early 2009 to reward states that increased student achievement and graduation rates, among other factors (US Department of Education). Race to the Top emphasized STEM disciplines as the highest priority, and it called for nationwide standards and assessments of those standards. The Common Core State Standards were then ratified in early 2010 after a three-year development process (National Governors Association Center for Best Practices and the Council of Chief State School Officers), and the initiative's goal was to describe what those disciplinary standards would look like for K–12 education to ensure the "preparation of students for college and career" (O'Neill et al. 521).

The emphasis on STEM, standards, assessment measures, and nationwide norms raised red flags for many of us in writing studies, and Peggy O'Neill et al. have described in detail the ways these initiatives and concerns led to the development of the *Framework*. For postsecondary teachers of writing, it was of the utmost importance to participate in conversations about how standards were being defined, who was defining them, and how achievement was being measured. Because the goals of these initiatives were focused primarily on "college and career readiness" (US Department of Education 7), the CWPA, joined by the National Council of Teachers of English and the National Writing Project, felt it was imperative to respond from the perspective of teachers who would be working with students when they came to college.

According to the charge given to the *Framework* Task Force, we had three primary goals. The first defined goal was to, from our varied perspectives as twenty-three college writing teachers, "[outline] writing strategies and experiences essential for success in postsecondary writing courses" (Adler-Kassner). The second and third goals included (2) providing professional development resources to support the *Framework* and (3) conducting research on the *Framework*.

To meet the first goal, we started with the "Outcomes Statement" and built from it, identifying what would help students meet those outcomes and, ultimately, succeed as college writers. As the draft developed, it included clearer and more precise explanations of habits of mind that would help writers succeed in postsecondary contexts, a feature of the *Framework* that I have come back to time and time again. The eight habits of mind described in the *Framework*—curiosity, openness, engagement, creativity, persistence, responsibility, flexibility, and metacognition—provide students with a foundation to approach a range of writing contexts across disciplines and outside of college contexts, which is represented, for example, in the work by Barbara D'Angelo and Barry Maid and Michelle Stuckey, James Toweill, Sean Tingle, Heather MacDonald, and Jessica Harnisch in this collection.

In the years since the *Framework* was published, I have reflected on its implications for my own practice, and I have learned to approach writing instruction from a different perspective. Stacey Cochran points out that the habits of mind are closely connected to research on student well-being and that they resonate with models of human flourishing described by psychologists such as Martin Seligman. Seligman explains that to flourish, people need five foundational things: positive emotions, engagement, relationships, meaning, and accomplishment. In his earlier collaborative work, he describes character strengths that can help develop these foundational needs to flourish (Peterson and Seligman), and the eight habits of mind described in the *Framework* align—in many cases directly—with Christopher Peterson and Seligman's work (Cochran). The implication is that helping students develop those habits of mind/strengths can have potential positive implications for them far beyond my writing class.

By focusing solely on the achievement of outcomes in my classes, I was missing the broader picture. Having students identify their habits of mind/strengths and how to build upon them to develop as writers was a game-changer for me. It helped me move away from a deficit-based model, and in many ways, I've come full circle. I've returned to what researchers in applied linguistics, writing studies, and education have long understood: that students bring prior knowledge and experiences that can be beneficial to new tasks. The curiosity, openness, engagement, creativity, persistence, responsibility, flexibility, and metacognition that students bring to my class was developed in a range of experiences and contexts that are important for me to acknowledge, understand, and learn from. Helping students creatively repurpose (as Skeen describes in this collection) and draw upon those experiences and the resulting habits/strengths in new contexts is one of the greatest joys of teaching writing.

The work in this collection has given me new ideas while it has also caused me to question how I approach habits of mind in my writing classes. In doing so, it contributes to fulfilling the third and final part of that initial charge to the Task Force: developing research on the *Framework*. Of course, as should be the case, sound research often causes us to question our assumptions, including assumptions we had when we first wrote the *Framework*. Just as we questioned how standards were being defined, who was defining them, and how achievement was being measured back in 2010 when we responded with the *Framework*, we must now listen to the voices within our own discipline who are asking us to question the policies, practices, and assumptions that we have about writing, including the ideologies that have guided us in the past (see Inoue's Afterword in this collection).

When I imagine what writing instruction might look like in the next decade, the research collected here gives me profound hope and inspiration. As we continue to research and interrogate our own practices, we serve students more effectively because—to paraphrase what has been attributed to Maya Angelou—as we know better, we can do better.

Works Cited

Adler-Kassner, Linda. "Invitation to Participate in CWPA Framework for Success in Postsecondary Writing." Personal email, 31 Mar. 2010.

Cochran, Stacey. "Building Bridges: Exploring the Relationships between Student Well-Being, Habits of Mind and Threshold Concepts." 7th Biennial Threshold Concepts Conference, 14 June 2018, Miami University, Oxford, OH. Conference Presentation.

Council of Writing Program Administrators. "WPA Outcomes Statement for First-Year Composition (3.0)." CWPA, 2014, wpacouncil.org/aws/CWPA/asset_manager/get_file/350909?ver=552. Accessed 3 July 2020.

Council of Writing Program Administrators, National Council of Teachers of English, and National Writing Project. *Framework for Success in Postsecondary Writing.* CWPA, NCTE, and NWP, 2011, wpacouncil.org/aws/CWPA/asset_manager/get_file/350201?ver=505. Accessed 3 July 2020.

Inoue, Asao B. "2019 CCCC Chair's Address: How Do We Language So People Stop Killing Each Other, or What Do We Do about White Language Supremacy?" *College Composition and Communication*, vol. 71, no. 2, 2019, pp. 352–69.

Miller-Cochran, Susan. "Review: Beyond Typical Ideas of Writing: Developing a Diverse Understanding of Writers, Writing, and Writing Instruction." *College Composition and Communication*, vol. 62, no. 3, 2011, pp. 550–59.

National Governors Association Center for Best Practices and the Council of Chief State School Officers. *Reaching Higher: The Common Core State Standards Validation Committee, A Report from the National Governors Association Center for Best Practices and the Council of Chief State School Officers*. June 2010, www.corestandards.org/assets/CommonCoreReport_6.10.pdf. Accessed 2 Aug. 2020.

O'Neill, Peggy, et al. "Creating the *Framework for Success in Postsecondary Writing*." *College English*, vol. 74, no. 6, 2012, pp. 520–33.

Peterson, Christopher, and Martin Seligman. *Character Strengths and Virtues: A Handbook and Classification*. American Psychological Association/Oxford UP, 2004.

Seligman, Martin. *Flourish: A Visionary New Understanding of Happiness and Well-Being*. Free P, 2011.

US Department of Education. *Race to Top Program Executive Summary*. Nov. 2009, www2.ed.gov/programs/racetothetop/executive-summary.pdf. Accessed 2 Aug. 2020.

Pedagogical Perspectives on Cognition and Writing

Introduction: Promises and Perils of Cognition and Writing Praxis

J. Michael Rifenburg, Patricia Portanova, and Duane Roen

A human brain sits squarely in the middle of the cover of *National Geographic*'s February 2014 issue. *Nat Geo*'s well-known yellow border wraps around the cover on which the black silhouette of a human head sits against a muted grey-blue background. The brain matter is represented by a kaleidoscope of colors shooting off the page. The cover story title, "The New Science of the Brain," appears below the brain's stem, with the word *Brain* in larger type, drawing the reader's eyes to one of the most fundamental and puzzling human organs.

In this cover story, Carl Zimmer offers a history of the human brain: in the fourth century BCE, Aristotle described the brain as a refrigerator cooling the fiery heart; in the seventeenth century CE, Thomas Willis produced one of the first accurate maps of the brain; in the nineteenth century CE, we learned the brain is an electric organ. On and on these developments go. In the twenty-first century, we are surrounded by more understandings of the brain, facilitated by advances in technology so that Michael, one of the editors of this collection, can receive an MRI on his brain at 7:28 AM, as he did while we were working on this collection, and receive a call from his doctor at 11:31 AM with the results. Though the neurologist and radiologist and primary care physician, within hours of the completion of his routine MRI with sagittal axial and coronal images, have scores of pictures at their disposal of Michael's brain, they still had questions about a tiny spot of white matter in the left occipital region of his brain. The radiologist wondered if it was demyelination, an early indicator of multiple sclerosis. The neurologist ruled that out. Eventually, Michael received a diagnosis of ocular migraines. But the nagging question remains: what is that tiny white spot on Michael's brain? Knowledge of the brain, it seems, only produces more questions.

Our broadly sketched history and Michael's anecdote do not just serve those interested in histories of medicine, surgery, and anatomy. Reflecting on these developments, we (the editors of this collection) find that how humans think about the brain connects with how humans think about writing. As the *Oxford English Dictionary* reminds us, *cognition* comes from the Latin *to know*. What is writing but the representation of what we know—the internal—onto external material?

In the second and third century CE, physician and philosopher Galen understood human anatomy through Plato's threefold division of the soul. Roy Porter, in his highly readable and capacious *The Greatest Benefit to Mankind: A Medical History of Humanity*, writes that Galen approached the human body through the "Platonic doctrine of a threefold division of the soul" (77). Galen identified the liver, heart, and brain as the "three principal organs" (77) with the brain responsible for distributing spirits through nerves to "sustain sensation and movement" (77). Plato's threefold division of the body influenced how Enlightenment thinkers partitioned the brain into different compartments or faculties. Francis Bacon ascribed a genre to each mental faculty, and, a century later, as Scotland took center stage on the play that is western rhetorical history, George Campbell drew from the psychological traditions of faculty psychology and associationism to divide the mind into compartments. Fellow Scot, Alexander Bain, followed suit and later asserted the modes of discourse—the well-worn description, narration, exposition, argument, and poetry—aligned with mental faculties. As Sharon Crowley points out in *Methodical Memory: Invention in Current-Traditional Rhetoric*, such a view of the mind influenced approaches to invention, specifically, and writing and rhetoric, generally.

Making the large historical jump from nineteenth-century Scotland to the late twentieth-century US, John Hayes, Linda Flower, Sondra Perl, and other committed teacher-researchers implemented advanced methods for peeking into rhetors' brains as they sketched words across the page. Through administering think-aloud protocols to participants writing in response to the same prompt for the same length of time, researchers believed they could see where struggling writers encountered challenges. If these writers could externalize the internal actions completed while writing, then teachers could iron out querulous cognitive wrinkles. Perl wrote about this internal/external challenge after studying a struggling writer named Tony:

> Tony is a writer with a highly consistent and deeply embedded recursive process. What he needs are teachers who can interpret that process for him, who can see through the tangles in the process just as he sees meaning beneath the tangles in his prose, and who can intervene in such a way that untangling his composing process leads him to create better prose. (328)

For Perl, Tony didn't struggle because it was a challenge to sit down in the library for a set amount of time with a teacher peering over his shoulder, or because he was a twenty-year-old Puerto Rican ex-Marine. As we read Perl's findings, it appears she is able to put to the side Tony's age, ethnicity, and life-history and consider his cognitive moves as almost isolated phenomena. Like the work of the nineteenth-century Scots, cognitive models of writing dominant in the 1980s ascribed a great deal of agency to the individual mind and not to external factors impinging on the writing process.

Writing researchers now largely turn to ecological models of the writing process, studying the writer *in situ* and ascribing agency to external animate and inanimate objects crossing spatial and temporal boundaries (e.g., Micciche; Prior and Shipka; Rule). Researchers no longer limit the view of writing to the here-and-now perspective, the perspective of studying a writer in an artificial space for a constrained period. Again, this interest in ecologies of writing reflects larger trends in how we understand the brain, the ever-vexing organ that drives who and what we are—as writers and as people.

We are fascinated by connections between advances in the study of writing and advances in the study of the brain. This interdisciplinary comingling brings us to research like that undertaken by Richard L. Lamb, Brian Hand, and Sae Yeol Yoon, who, working across neuroscience, neuropsychology, and education, participate in what they term "Educational Neuroscience" (par. 3) by using functional near-infrared spectroscopy (fNIRS) to study students' brains while they completed science-writing assignments. fNIRS is a non-invasive imaging tool that captures hemodynamic responses in the prefrontal cortex. Through using fNIRS, the research team found that, for the student writers, "the summary task was characterized by greater intensity of activation with a larger number of activation sites" (par. 7). Summary writing is hard, not to be dismissed as a frivolous exercise. We have the brain images to show that. As teacher-scholars, we are committed to understanding better how writers write and the role of cognition during the physical act of pulling the pencil across the page, flinging the fingers across the keyboard.

We believe this collection comes at a *kairotic* moment because of renewed interest in cognition and writing among English Studies generally and Rhetoric and Composition/Writing Studies (RC/WS) specifically. To illustrate, we point to two exigencies for this collection: (1) the *Framework for Success in Postsecondary Writing*, a national consensus document jointly authored by the National Council of Teachers of English, the Council of Writing Program Administrators, and the National Writing Project that articulates eight habits of mind essential for strong writing and writers, and (2) the increased emphasis on writing researchers and teachers place on student metacognition, particularly the role metacognition plays in students successfully transferring the skills of knowledge of writing across contexts. Although we locate our exigencies in these two developments, this is not a collection about the *Framework*; this is not a collection about transfer. This is a collection that charts, through actual examples from classrooms, writing centers, and writing programs across the US, the pedagogical possibilities and attendant perils of cognition and writing praxis. In the section that follows, we unpack recent discussions of the *Framework* and metacognition to better frame our collection before you now.

FRAMING THIS COLLECTION

We see the *Framework* and the focus on metacognition as renewed interest in cognition and writing. However, English Studies, particularly within US English departments, has witnessed a steady decline in writing research exploring the long intersection between the written word and the human brain (Hayes). John Hayes, in his foreword to our previous collection, *Contemporary Perspectives on Cognition and Writing*, used Google Scholar to map citations of three different cognitive models of writing (i.e., Hayes and Flowers's 1980 model; Kellogg's 1996 model; and Hayes's 1996 model). All three models show a steady uptick in citations. Hayes and Flowers's model shows a steady rise in citations from 1980 to 2012 with only a slight decline in the late 1990s. However, and here is what we and Hayes find odd, these citations seem to represent international authors and fields outside of RC/WS. When Hayes focused just on articles published in *Written Communication* and drilled down to author and author's departmental home, he found a sharp decline in citations to cognitive models by scholars who identified their departmental home as either English, rhetoric, literacy, literature, or composition.

Despite the recent decline of published articles citing the work of Flower and Hayes, this current collection—focused more squarely on the *Framework* and pedagogy—links up with two important conversations currently animating RC/WS specifically and English studies generally. Both conversations signal renewed interest in cognition and writing. The first conversation speaks to the *Framework*, the national consensus document that, we believe, should help guide how K–16 educators think about and enact writing instruction. The *Framework* operates from two core beliefs. In a *College English* symposium on the *Framework*, Peggy O'Neill, Linda Adler-Kassner, Cathy Fleischer, and Anne-Marie Hall, who worked on the *Framework*, describe the two core beliefs of the Framework: writing instruction is a shared enterprise between K–16 educators and college readiness is a shared enterprise between secondary and postsecondary teachers. The *Framework* was released in 2011, at a time where many other policy documents on writing instruction surfaced. Bruce McComiskey, also writing in the *College English* symposium, confessed he "was unable to place it rhetorically (its audience, purpose, function, and so on) in the larger context of existing mandates and white papers, such as the Council on Writing Program Administration's Outcomes Statements and the more recent Common Core State Standards" (537). We nod along with McComiskey's struggle and place it in conversation with Kristine Johnson's 2013 *College Composition and Communication* article. Johnson, like McComiskey, places the *Framework* within the larger reform agendas promulgated by various educationally focused agencies and groups. These reform agendas, according to Johnson, define student success "in terms of students meeting standards" (517). But she believes the *Framework* doesn't look to standards but to "intellectual behaviors and educational experiences" (517).

The *Framework* positions eight habits of mind as essential for college readiness and college writing success: curiosity, openness, engagement, creativity, persistence, responsibility, flexibility, and metacognition. The executive summary of the *Framework* offers the following instruction to the habits of mind: "Habits of mind refer to ways of approaching learning that are both intellectual and practical and will support students' success in a variety of fields and disciplines" (1). Particularly helpful for the wide readership of the *Framework*, immediately following the introduction of the habits of mind, the executive summary leads into briefly capturing how teacher can foster the habits of mind through "writing, reading, and critical analysis" (1). Published in 2011, the *Framework* has enjoyed adoption across a wide-range of institutions, in a wide-range of classrooms, and for a wide-range of audiences. Many narratives on these various adoptions are captured in Nicholas Behm, Sherry Rankins-Robertson, and Duane Roen's collection *The* Framework for Success in Postsecondary Writing: *Scholarship and Application*, in which we learn how the *Framework* supports online writing courses (Brunk-Chavez), preservice teachers' preparation (Rodríguez), high-school writers (Powell), and our students' extracurricular literate practices (Kurtyka). With the emphasis on developing habits of mind in conjunction with, for example, rhetorical knowledge, the *Framework* in general and the habits of mind is one avenue into which we enter this important conversation on cognition and writing. How might we operationalize these habits of mind in our writing-intensive spaces?

Our second avenue leads to the role of metacognition, particularly its role in supporting successful writing transfer. Focusing on the role of metacognition in learning, education researchers still turn to psychologist John Flavell's 1979 definition of metacognition. Based on research on preschool and elementary school children, Flavell defines metacognition as "knowledge and cognition about cognitive phenomena" (906). He separates "phenomena" into four different classes: metacognitive knowledge, metacognitive experiences, goals, and actions (906). Following Flavell's work, psychologists often divide metacognition into a knowledge component and a regulation component. As writing teachers, we think of this delineation as one between writing *knowledge* and writing *skills*. Recently, researchers from across disciplines have investigated metacognition's role in academic writing development because, as educational psychologists Douglas Hacker, Matt Keener, and John Kircher argue, "writing is applied metacognition" (154). We now have research that links metacognition to a beginning academic writer's ability to develop rhetorical consciousness (Negretti), illustrating that metacognitive abilities separate strong and weak academic writers (Perin et al.), that metacognitive scaffolds form a cognitive bridge between extracurricular and curricular literacies (Rifenburg), and that teaching metacognition reinforces student agency in course-linked first-year courses (Winslow and Shaw). Coupled with these studies that focus, largely, on specific classes gathered over a semester or similar small segments of time, we have longitudinal studies that trace, over years, the successful development of metacognitive skills for high school upper secondary education students (Karlen et al.) and children (Harris et al.).

RC/WS scholars more directly enter this work on metacognition through our field's near two-decade-old interest in mapping and supporting writing-related transfer. This interest is most notably grounded in the Elon Research Seminar—and the subsequent position papers, articles, and edited collections coming from this seminar—and Kathleen Blake Yancey, Liane Robertson, and Kara Taczak's award-winning *Writing Across Contexts: Composition, Transfer, and Sites of Writing*. The Elon seminar brought together an international team of scholars for two years. This team drafted an "Elon Statement on Writing Transfer" position statement on transfer that includes various definitions and understandings of transfer and three concrete enabling practices that promote transfer in a writing class. This seminar led to various edited collections, journal articles, and book-length studies including Yancey et al.'s book—all three of whom were participants at the seminar. In their book, the co-authors offer a Teaching for Transfer curriculum that focuses students' attention to the knowledge and practice of writing. Of most significance to our collection is how the co-authors (and other transfer theorists) draw on the importance of metacognition, one of the *Framework*'s habits of mind. Using principles of metacognition and reflection as structural elements of the curriculum and foci of the four major assignments, the co-authors remind us of the inextricable link between cognition and writing.

In the wake of this scholarship, and many more individual articles populating our journals and the conversations driving our listservs; in the wake of our Cognition and Writing Standing Group increases in membership annually; in the wake of Asao Inoue offering a keynote address to roughly two thousand college writing teachers, researchers, and administrators in which he pointed to the whiteness of the *Framework*; in the wake of our neurodivergent colleagues calling for attention to ableist language that is a part of conversations on cognition and writing; and amid the promises and perils of this work, we offer this collection. As Linda Flower wrote in the afterword to *Contemporary Perspectives on Cognition and Writing* that "perhaps one of the most unusual things cognitive rhetoric affords is its direct transfer into teaching and learning" (336). This collection stands as a testament to Flower's assertion; we believe in this "direct transfer into teaching and learning," and we hold this assertion alongside the potential pitfalls of such work. In this collection, we move readers into pedagogical practices informed by cognitive theory; we move readers into the various writing spaces in which we labor and learn with writers.

We—the editors and authors—know we have more work to do. The 2019 CWPA conference took as its theme the title "More Seats at the Table: Radical Inclusion in Writing Programs." In the call for proposals, conference chair Mark Blaauw-Hara elaborated on the theme: "When we look closer to home . . . we also see a system that parses its participants into those who are at the table and those who are on the margins. Which students are college-ready? Whose languages are valued? Which faculty members have tenure and voting rights? . . . Whose ideas tend to be heard?" This conference theme came on the heels of Inoue's powerful 2016 CWPA keynote address in which he identified racism in writing program administration and his 2019 CCCC address in which he rightly pointed out that "18 or 19 of the members of the *Framework*'s designers were White." As we reflect on the work we undertake on cognition and writing, and as we reflect on this complete collection before you, we wonder who is missing. We wonder how theories and practices undergirded by cognitive science, neuroscience, the habits of mind, and the like can better consider the wide range of learners, instructors, and sites of learning in which we all collectively engage. Sociologist Tukufu Zuberi wrote that "Data do not tell us a story. We use data to craft a story that comports with our understanding of the world" (9). And we wonder about data provided by those working in cognition and writing: are these data just telling stories that relate to what we want to know and feel comfortable knowing about writers and how writing works. We wonder about the historical racism embedded in dangerous and faulty science, like phrenology, that used brain research to subjugate people groups. We wonder about the positivistic roots of cognitive theory, and we remember that indigenous researchers like Linda Tuhiwai Smith told us that positivism and empiricism are traits of colonialism, of people claiming definitive and universal knowledge. We wonder about Lamb, Hand, and Yoon's study of mapping one-hundred student brains while these students completed science writing assignments. We wonder where discussions are about who these one-hundred students are—the flesh and bones and beliefs and experiences that make them people. What are their ages, races, religions, and all the other identity markers that constitute life? Do we forsake important knowledge about embodiment and positionality when we take up cognitive models of writing? We wonder about the implications of this kind of work for our colleagues and students and community members and family who identify as neurodivergent? These are the hard questions we wrestle through as we do this work.

We don't presume to have the answers. As Leigh Patel points out in *Decolonizing Educational Research*, the research we undertake as committed teacher-scholars is "a fundamentally relational project" (48). Because we believe in "research as relational," to borrow from one of Patel's chapter titles, we seek more seats at the table of Cognition and Writing Praxis. Through increased attention to cognition and writing as exhibited by the *Framework* and by supportive metacognitive theories and practices, we look forward to continuing this work of supporting all the learners with whom we labor. To borrow from Susan Miller-Cochran's title of her foreword, cognitive approaches to composition is one avenue, we believe, for imagining and enacting better futures.

Chapter Summaries

Pedagogical Perspectives on Cognition and Writing carries readers through four sections that begin, briefly, with current RC/WS theories informed by cognitive developments and then delve more deeply into how these theories inform our work in writing-intensive spaces.

After a foreword by Susan Miller-Cochran, who was a member of the *Framework* Task Force and, at the time of this writing, is a past president of the CWPA, we offer our first section. In our lead chapter to this section, Peter Khost, who has established himself as a leading advocate of the *Framework* through his *English Journal* column, offers a co-authored chapter with Wendy Ryden and David Hyman. Their work complicates the pervasive ethic of college and career readiness as self-evidently good pedagogy and parenting. Barbara D'Angelo and Barry Maid spark a much-needed conversation between RC/WS and library information sciences to continue helping us think through metacognition's role in facilitating or stymieing writing transfer. We are then pleased to introduce Airlie Rose's voice. Rose pulls from a mixed methods interdisciplinary study on the experience of inner speech.

Section II brings the focus to classroom-level writing instruction. Gita DasBender continues her important scholarship on transfer by bringing our attention to metacognition as a threshold concept in a first-year college writing class. Next, Thomas Skeen draws on cognitive psychology and theories of design, and Courtney Patrick-Weber draws on cognitive theories of trauma and communication. By calling upon a variety of theories, Skeen and Webber broaden our understanding of what writing is, how it's accomplished, and how constructing connections—not walls—between disciplines better equips us for working with student writers. This section on classroom practices informed by cognitive theories of writing instruction concludes with the words of Michelle Stuckey, James Toweill, Sean Tingle, Heather MacDonald, and Jessica Harnisch. In their chapter, they provide rich qualitative data on the impacts of student engagement with metacognition in an online first-year writing class centered around community-focused writing.

In section III, we zoom out from the classroom and look at curricular and program-level work informed by cognitive theories of writing. Christine Cucciarre starts by writing how the state of Delaware used the *Framework* as a metaphorical bridge between high school and college writing. Tonya Eick and Gregg Fields describe a metaphor-based curriculum they developed at Arizona State University, one of the largest public universities in the US. This curriculum is explicitly grounded in the *Framework* and draws on a large data set to describe how students engaged with this curriculum. Melvin E. Beavers, Subrina Bogan, Harold Brown, Caleb James, and Sherry Rankins-Robertson describe a summer bridge program at their home university designed to prepare incoming first-year students for college-level work. The literacy component of this summer bridge program drew heavily on the *Framework*, and we are excited to offer their results in this collection. The next three chapters in this rich section draw more broadly on cognitive theories. We conclude this section with Martha A. Townsend's ongoing work with student-athletes at the University of Missouri. Townsend's qualitative study of student-athlete academic performance illustrates the importance of metacognition for individual literacy development.

Bringing our writing center colleagues into the conversation in the fourth section, Morgan Gross and Kelsie Walker share findings from an empirical study on a tutor-training workshop grounded in the habits of mind. William J. Macauley, Jr. articulates how writing centers facilitate agency and self-efficacy on the part of student-writers. Bronwyn T. Williams continues his work on literacy practices and agency by drawing from the Framework to consider the various dispositions student-writers bring with them to a writing center. Writing centers, as the intellectual and physical hubs of campus writing, are places of innovation, places where ideas and practices incubate and go forth across our campuses. We see the writing center space as a vital one in which writers from varied backgrounds and spaces and abilities come together to write and be in community. We believe the writing center, and the people that move through this space, will play a central role in developing and implementing classroom or curricular-level practices informed by cognitive theories of writing instruction.

This collection ends with remarks by Asao Inoue who, during his chair's address at the Conference of College Composition and Communication (CCCC), asked thousands of people packed into an auditorium in Pittsburgh to see and feel the whiteness embedded in the Framework. In his afterword, like in his work, Inoue pushes us to do and be better.

The chapters, foci, and contributors to this collection are varied—as they should be for collections seeking to represent the dynamic work of cognition and composition. However, from Miller-Cochran's foreword introduction all the way to the last sentence in Inoue's afterword, we weave a singular thread throughout the tapestry of the entire collection: the student-writer.

We thank all of the authors who contributed to this collection for their patience and goodwill during the publication process. We are grateful to Susan Miller-Cochran and Asao Inoue for their willingness to compose a foreword and afterword, respectively. Thank you to Thomas Rickert and Jennifer Bay, co-editors of the Lauer Series in Rhetoric and Composition. We also thank the wonderful team at Parlor Press; without the guidance and support of David Blakesley and Jared Jameson, this collection would not be possible.

Works Cited

Behm, Nicholas, et al., editors. *The* Framework for Success in Postsecondary Writing: *Scholarship and Application*. Parlor P, 2017.

Blaauw-Hara, Mark. "More Seats at the Table: Radical Inclusion in Writing Programs." 2019 CWPA Call for Proposals. Oct. 2018, www.cwpa2019.com/call-for-proposals. Accessed 12 Nov. 2019.

Brunk-Chavez, Beth. "The *Framework for Success* Goes Online: Integration of the *Framework* into Online Writing Courses." *The* Framework for Success in Postsecondary Writing: *Scholarship and Application*, edited by Nicholas N. Behm, et al., Parlor P, 2017, pp. 154–169.

"cognition, n." *OED Online*, Oxford University Press, March 2021, www.oed.com/view/Entry/35876. Accessed 6 Mar. 2021.

Council of Writing Program Administrators, National Council of Teachers of English, and National Writing Project. *Framework for Success in Postsecondary Writing*. CWPA, NCTE, and NWP, 2011, wpacouncil.org/aws/CWPA/asset_manager/get_file/350201?ver=505. Accessed 4 Apr. 2020.

Crowley, Sharon. *Methodical Memory: Invention in Current-Traditional Rhetoric*. Southern Illinois UP, 1990.

"Elon Statement on Writing Transfer." Elon University, 29 July 2013. www.elon.edu/ e-web/academics/teaching/ers/writing_transfer/statement.xhtml. Accessed 4 Apr. 2020.

Flavell, John H. "Metacognition and Cognitive Monitoring: A New Area of Cognitive-Developmental Inquiry." *American Psychologist*, vol. 34, no. 10, 1979, pp. 906–11.

Flower, Linda, and John R. Hayes. "A Cognitive Process Theory of Writing." *College Composition and Communication*, vol. 34, no. 4, 1981, pp. 365–87.

Flower, Linda. Afterword. "Reflection: What Can Cognitive Rhetoric Offer Us?" *Contemporary Perspectives on Cognition and Writing*, edited by Patricia Portanova, et al., Perspectives on Writing, The WAC Clearinghouse and UP of Colorado, 2017, pp. 331–47, wac.colostate.edu/books/perspectives/cognition/. Accessed 1 June 2020.

Hacker, Douglas J., et al. "Writing is Applied Metacognition." *Handbook of Metacognition in Education*, edited by Douglas J. Hacker, et al., Routledge, 2009, pp. 154–72.

Harris, Karen R., et al. "Metacognition and Children's Writing." *Handbook of Metacognition in Education*, edited by Douglas J. Hacker, et al., Routledge, 2009, pp. 131–54.

Hayes, John R., and Linda S. Flower. "Identifying the Organization of Writing Processes." *Cognitive Processes in Writing*, edited by Lee. W. Gregg and Erwin R. Steinberg, Lawrence Erlbaum, 1980, pp. 3–30.

Hayes, John R. *The Complete Problem Solver*. 2nd ed., Lawrence Erlbaum, 1996.

—. Forward. "Are Cognitive Studies in Writing Really Passé?" *Contemporary Perspectives on Cognition and Writing*, edited by Patricia Portanova, et al., Perspectives on Writing, The WAC Clearinghouse and UP of Colorado, 2017, pp. vii-xv, wac.colostate.edu/books/perspectives/cognition/. Accessed 1 Apr. 2020.

Inoue, Asao B. Plenary Speaker. "Racism in Writing Programs and the CWPA." Summer Conference for the Council of Writing Program Administrators. Raleigh, NC, July, 2016. Plenary speech.

—. "2019 CCCC Chair's Address: How Do We Language So People Stop Killing Each Other, or What Do We Do about White Language Supremacy?" *College Composition and Communication*, vol. 71, no. 2, 2019, pp. 352–69.

Johnson, Kristine. "Beyond Standards: Disciplinary and National Perspectives on Habits of Mind." *College Composition and Communication*, vol. 64, no. 3, 2013, pp. 517–42.

Karlen, Yves, et al. "The Effect of Individual Differences in the Development of Metacognitive Strategy Knowledge." *Instructional Science*, vol. 42, no. 5, 2014, pp. 777–94.

Kellogg, Ronald T. "A Model of Working Memory in Writing." *The Science of Writing: Theories, Methods, Individual Differences, and Applications*, edited by C. Michael Levy and Sarah Ransdell, Lawrence Erlbaum, 1996, pp. 57–72.

Kurtyka, Faith. "Messy but Meaningful: Using the Habits of Mind to Understand Extracurricular Learning." *The* Framework for Success in Postsecondary Writing: *Scholarship and Application*, edited by Nicholas N. Behm, et al., Parlor P, 2017, pp. 102–18.

Lamb, Richard L. et al. "An Exploratory Neuroimaging Study of Argumentative and Summary Writing." *Journal of Psychology and Brain Studies*, vol. 1, no. 1:3, 2017, DOI:10.1007/978-3-030-24013-4_5, Accessed 28 May 2020.

McComiskey, Bruce. "Bridging the Divide: The (Puzzling) *Framework* and the Transition from K-12 to College Writing Instruction." *College English*, vol. 74, no. 6, 2012, pp. 537–43.

Micciche, Laura. "Writing Material." *College English*, vol. 76, no. 6, pp. 488–505.

Negretti, Raffaella. "Metacognition in Student Academic Writing: A Longitudinal Study of Metacognitive Awareness and Its Relation to Task Perception, Self-Regulation, and Evaluation of Performance." *Written Communication*, vol. 29, no. 2, 2012, pp. 142–79.

O'Neill, Peggy, et al. "Creating the *Framework for Success in Postsecondary Writing*." *College English*, vol.74, no. 6, 2012, pp. 520–24.

Patel, Leigh. *Decolonizing Educational Research: From Ownership to Answerability*. Routledge, 2015.

Perl, Sondra. "The Composing Processes of Unskilled College Writers." *Research in the Teaching of English*, vol. 13, no. 4, 1979, pp. 317–36.

Perin, Dolores, et al. "The Academic Writing of Community College Remedial Students: Texts and Learner Variables." *Higher Education*, vol. 45, no. 1, 2003, pp. 19–42.

Portanova, Patricia, et al., editors. *Contemporary Perspectives on Cognition and Writing*. Perspectives on Writing, The WAC Clearinghouse and UP of Colorado, 2017, wac.colostate.edu/books/perspectives/cognition/. Accessed 4 Apr. 2020.

Porter, Roy. *Greatest Benefit to Mankind: A Medical History of Humanity*. Norton, 1999.

Powell, Rebecca. "Experiences, Values, and Habitus: Twelfth Graders and the *Framework*'s Habits of Mind." *The* Framework for Success in Postsecondary Writing: *Scholarship and Application*, edited by Nicholas N. Behm, et al., Parlor P, 2017, pp. 118–36.

Prior, Paul, and Jody Shipka. "Chronotopic Lamination: Tracing the Contours of Literate Activity." *Writing Selves / Writing Societies*, edited by Charles Bazerman and David R. Russell, The WAC Clearinghouse, 2002, wac.colostate.edu/books/perspectives/selves-societies/. Accessed 4 Apr. 2020.

Rifenburg, J. Michael. "Student-Athletes' Metacognitive Strategy Knowledge." *Composition Forum*, vol. 43, 2020, compositionforum.com/issue/43/student-athletes.php. Accessed 28 May 2020.

Rodríguez, Rodrigo Joseph. "Metacognitive Persistence and Cultural Knowledge: Application of the *Framework* with Preservice Teachers for Writing Instruction in Secondary Schools." *The* Framework for Success in Postsecondary Writing: *Scholarship and Application*, edited by Nicholas N. Behm, et al., Parlor P, 2017, pp. 204–22.

Rule, Hannah J. "Writing's Rooms." *College Composition and Communication*, vol. 69, no. 3, 2018, pp. 402–32.

Summerfield, Judith, and Phillip M. Anderson. "A Framework Adrift." *College English*, vol. 74, no. 6, 2012, pp. 544–47.

Tukufu, Zuberi, and Eduardo Bonilla-Silva, editors. *White Logic, White Methods: Racism and Methodology*. Rowman and Littlefield, 2008.

Winslow, Dianna, and Phil Shaw. "Teaching Metacognition to Reinforce Agency and Transfer in Course-Linked First-Year Courses." *Contemporary Perspectives on Cognition and Writing*, edited by Patricia Portanova, et al., Perspectives on Writing, The WAC Clearinghouse and UP of Colorado, 2017, pp. 191–211, wac.colostate.edu/books/perspectives/cognition/. Accessed 1 June 2020.

Yancey, Kathleen Blake, et al. *Writing Across Contexts: Composition, Transfer, and Sites of Writing.* Utah State UP, 2014.

Zimmer, Carl. "Secrets of the Brain." *National Geographic*, Feb. 2014, ngm.nationalgeographic.com/2014/02/brain/zimmer-text. Accessed 3 Sept. 2019.

I Cognitive Theory and Writing Pedagogy

1 Readiness Redefined: Toward a Pedagogy of Here and Now

Peter H. Khost, Wendy Ryden, and David Hyman

This chapter challenges the assumption that college and career readiness in writing is necessarily a wholly good pedagogical objective, at least insofar as readiness is commonly understood in this context. Praise for the ethic of readiness abounds in educational discourse at all levels these days, in both public and scholarly discourse, but seldom are its downsides considered. Of course, as theorists we acknowledge and as teachers we work to convey the benefits of preparing students for the writing they will do later and elsewhere in life, but we believe that too much emphasis on future/other occasions, for example through excessive attention to high-stakes tests, the college application essay, or even teaching for transfer, potentially diminishes attentiveness to the present moment. That, in turn, ironically risks detracting from a writer's rhetorical agency and effectiveness, as we will explain. Since writing is, as Thomas Skeen points out in this collection, an "ill-structured . . . always contextual" endeavor, our position is that writing-readiness fixation ignores and/or poorly engages students in the embodied, situational exigencies of authentic rhetorical situations, which occur to a significant degree in the here and now. To avoid or minimize these dangers, conventional secondary and postsecondary writing curricula should be balanced with cultivation of a rhetorical presence of mind, body, spirit, and environment.

The writing-readiness ethic manifests variously throughout United States' culture and is epitomized by high-stakes tests and test-prep practices (Khost, "The *Framework*"). But because the ubiquitous reality of testing remains largely beyond individual teachers' ability to control, our analysis here mostly focuses on more manageable curricular and pedagogical issues, which are nonetheless symptomatic of the bigger problem. Conventional US secondary and postsecondary academic writing instruction tends to focus so much on future-oriented (i.e., *deliberative*) and past-oriented (i.e., *forensic*) rhetorics that the rhetorical present moment (of which *epideictic* is not a comprehensive descriptor) has been prone to pedagogical neglect. We can define and distinguish these three branches of rhetoric and curricular categories from each other as, respectively, trying to influence pending outcomes, trying to understand prior discourse, and (in our expansive formulation) trying to perform effectively in contemporaneous social, if not necessarily synchronous, contexts that are mediated by language.

We admit that some of the key phrases we use here, such as "rhetorical present moment" and "here and now," are relatively unfamiliar theoretical and pedagogical terms, but that unfamiliarity factors into our concern and is something we hope to change for the better with this chapter. After laying out some background about the ethic of writing readiness in general, we explore some of its cognitive dimensions and ramifications, and we follow that with a call for an open and kairotic rhetoric of presence by way of contemplative scholarship that reconsiders the essential role of metacognition in writing pedagogy.

BACKGROUND

College readiness has been an implicit goal of US educational practices since the current system of sequential stages emerged in the US in the late nineteenth and early twentieth century. However, college readiness did not achieve hegemony as a guiding principle of secondary education until the last two decades, culminating in its articulation (along with career readiness) as key anchor standard of the Common Core State Standards Initiative in 2010 (Rothman). The emphatic importance of the concepts of college and career readiness in the CCSSI was accompanied by attempts to define the terms more precisely. David T. Conley defines college readiness as "the level of preparation a student needs to enroll and succeed—without remediation—in a credit-bearing general education course at a postsecondary institution that offers a baccalaureate degree or transfer to a baccalaureate program" (5). The ACT expands the definition to explicitly include postsecondary institutions that may find Conley's emphasis on the baccalaureate exclusionary: "The level of achievement a student needs to be ready to enroll and succeed—without remediation—in credit-bearing first-year postsecondary courses. By postsecondary we mean primarily two-year or four-year institutions, trade schools, and technical schools. Today, however, workplace readiness demands the same level of knowledge and skills as college readiness" (Mattern 5).

Such definitions have appropriately been criticized for several reasons: overreliance on standardized testing as a measure/predictor of college readiness, failure to focus on underlying social and economic factors, a reductive one-size-fits-all-students approach. These critiques link to broader criticism of standardization as producing inaccurate and unfair results: "When standardization is taken to mean universalization, the result may well be lower achievement for many students" (Noddings). Thus, the proposition that the current focus on readiness has improved the problems of inadequate student preparedness and achievement is at the very least questionable. There have been attempts to address these criticisms within the discourse of assessment, notably the *Framework for Success in Postsecondary Writing*.

While these criticisms challenge the validity and efficacy of current policies designed to promote college readiness, they accept the goal itself as a valid one. The paradigm of readiness remains intact; we are just going about it poorly. Who can object to the ideas that K–12 education should result in college-ready students, that introductory and remedial university coursework should strengthen and supplement this task, or that college should prepare students for their careers? But it is precisely those conventions that seem self-evident that pose dangers. An aura of indisputability cloaks them from the scrutiny of criticism, and thus any question marks they might provoke get straightened out into exclamation points of certainty. For example, when the Association of American Colleges and Universities (AAC&U) reports, roughly biannually, on its national survey of employers, the terms of debate will not appear very debatable to many readers: "both executives and hiring managers place the highest importance on the ability to communicate orally, but only 40% of executives and 47% of hiring managers rate recent college graduates as well prepared in this area" ("Fulfilling" 3), "More than three in four employers say they want colleges to place *more emphasis* on helping students develop five key learning outcomes" ("It Takes" 1), "Only one in four employers thinks that two-year and four-year colleges are doing a good job in preparing students for the challenges of the global economy" ("Raising" 1). Unsurprisingly, the AAC&U finds that "Students largely agree with employers on the importance of various learning outcomes for workplace success" ("Falling" 8). We teachers must take it upon ourselves, then, to scrutinize the implications of the term *readiness*.

This is especially true of current applications of college readiness as the standard by which to measure successful student writing, in which readiness is seen as the possession of a certain set of skills and experiences that are presumed to be essential for writing in college. The metaphor that comes to mind is that of an operator of a vehicle going through a series of systems checks before departure. Brainstorming? Check! Supporting evidence? Check! Conclusion? Check! The complex heuristics of composition are thus reduced to a series of measurable outcomes that can be, if not taught, identified as recognizable markers that can and must be documented in syllabi, curricula, and lesson plans. While this predictability makes the job of assessment easier, it comes at a price. The act of composing loses its connection to the moment and instead yokes itself to retrieval of the past (learned rules and strategies) and anxieties about the future (grades, achievement of expectations). The time is out of joint, and the notoriously heterodox chronotopes of classroom writing tend to become untethered from the here and now.

The Embodied Cognitive Rhetorical Present Moment

The resulting orthodoxy manifests itself subtly but profoundly in writing education through a de facto systemic approach to the rhetorical situation. Although writing classroom activities do sometimes enable students to encounter each other directly in real time, the most significant work they undertake—such as writing tests, major papers, college application essays—is directed neither to each other or to others they actually know, nor to anyone they would likely address if not forced to do so (Khost, *Rhetor Response* 147–70). Its value, sometimes amounting to nothing more than a numeric evaluation, is also often marked by deferment (and deference). That is to say, students typically write to un(der-)responsive, authoritative parties who are absent, abstract, and/or anonymous, whether invoked (Aristotle), invented (Ong), or partially both of these (Ede and Lunsford). Despite best efforts, teachers may receive little or no exemption here, as Susan Miller memorably argues:

> No matter how diligently we work to reduce the artificiality of the classroom situation, how adamantly we seek assignments whose responses will surprise or inform our genuine curiosity,

> or how rigorously we play the role of an intended audience, the student's 'reader' is always a fiction, purely if not simply no reader at all, but a teacher. And the student is no Author, but instead a 'writer' . . . Both parties—both the reader and the text—are always constrained by rhetoric's iron law of context, and, therefore, always doomed to attend dress rehearsals. (22)

Whether or not one takes the point to Miller's extreme degree, it seems clear at least that the written rhetorical occasions that matter the most and that occur most frequently in conventional educational settings center on hypothetical future or theoretical past discourse, or generally on contexts other than the actual here and now. That may be primarily attributable to inevitabilities that educators reluctantly resign themselves to, like the need to assign and assess a relatively uniform curriculum, but even more sympathetic aspects of the work of teaching writing may apply too, such as the ideal of transferability, whereby attention is directed to future situations for applying one's writing skills or to past situations from which to recall the same, through forward-reaching and backward-reaching transfer, respectively (Salomon and Perkins).

To an extent, drawing attention away from the present moment in writing and rhetoric instruction may be understandable and unproblematic; after all, written academic discourse usually involves parties who do not share each other's temporal or physical company. Furthermore, popular sentiment and valid research both maintain that education is instrumental to securing a more prosperous future. So, deferral is more or less baked into the whole enterprise, and accordingly, the great promise of college and career readiness pervades contemporary US culture so as to be seemingly indubitable. *Work hard now to be ready later*; this ethic constantly tells us literally from as early as preschool, where children now regularly practice reading and math "readiness," as such.

But decades of continuous adherence to future-oriented curricular norms and the cultural assumptions underwriting them may very well yield an unwitting and unwelcome byproduct of neglect for a simple but vital truth: that life is always, only lived here and now. In other words, by focusing too much on deferred situations one may very well miss the present moment, as a variety of commentators have tried to warn, from John Dewey to Ferris Bueller. Yet mainstream US educational culture seems increasingly intent on preparing students for a perpetually (im)pending future, while also fetishizing their pace of progress toward it, for example through advanced placement, dual enrollment, and influential speed-to-degree metrics (Keller presents a broad and deep account of this "acceleration" phenomenon; see also Tinberg and Nadeau).

Karen Uehling handily critiques this hurry-up-and-wait educational culture by pointing out the problematic underlying assumption "that one time of life is primarily preparation for the next" such that, in her admittedly exaggerated formulation, "If high school is preparation for college, then junior high is preparation for high school, and elementary for junior high; also college is preparation for grad school, and grad school, for a post doc perhaps, and a post doc for a career that probably has stages." Uehling concludes philosophically, "So . . . when are we there? When do we live and enjoy the now?" If we don't take deliberate counteractive action as instructors, then the answer to this question at least insofar as our classrooms are concerned may unfortunately turn out to be: rarely, at best.

Value and time, perhaps especially through deferment (e.g., the cost of college, delayed gratification), are often transparently entangled with each other in representations of education, sometimes to detrimental effect. Consider two pieces of evidence from institutional advertisements for summer classes posted at one of our campuses, which could be found at any college or university. The first shows students with wide smiles wearing sunglasses and reads in all caps: "THE COURSES YOU NEED . . . THE CREDITS YOU WANT." Isn't this an inversion of values and desire? Shouldn't students primarily want courses (i.e., learning)? Isn't the credit ascribed to their coursework secondary, a counterpart they may need but not necessarily desire? Desire exists, is embodied, becomes a motivating force in the here and now of the present moment; it pumps through our veins and fires across our neural networks. It is a fundamental, emotional, object-oriented element of human experience. Yet in this poster's formulation, which is metonymic for not only an institutional but also a cultural belief system, one's desire is supposed to be directed at such a deferred, abstract, and dehumanized concept as course credit. In this inverted scheme, the action might very well precede or even preclude the experience of desire that should have motivated the action in the first place, if it had naturally occurred.

The looseness of and perhaps laziness toward the metonymy of "course credit" enables a quantitative or commodifying (Gunner 119) attitude to creep into education and insidiously reify the inversion of values we have just critiqued. Another poster for accelerated summer courses that was hung at one of our campuses reads: "Earn 3 credits in

3 weeks." The word *credit* here, and often, means a value assigned to an action: in this case, passing a three-week course. But what is that value, really, and when and where does it accrue? Is it (in) the act itself or (in) the recognition of that by others, say, by means of a transcript (note the writing metaphor)? If both, then in what proportion to each other? It often seems as if the question of value—complicated by the ambiguous administrative/corporatized term *credit hour* (see Shedd)—gets subsumed by the matter of efficiency, as in the summer session poster under consideration. What supposedly makes this particular opportunity appealing to students is not the three-credit valuation per se, which, after all, goes for all equivalent courses, but the expeditiousness of earning them. In this light, we cannot help but think of another usage of the word *credit*, as in a credit card purchase, by which an acquisition can be made now and paid for later, with a penalty. It shouldn't be difficult to see the relevance of this tangent to the contemporary national student loan crisis, which we note to contend that what may appear to be microcosmic nitpicking of campus PR documents on our part is really a case in point for critiquing the macrocosmic hurry-up-and-wait ethic of readiness that shapes and is shaped by the culture at large through constant, subtle habituation.

Whenever human behavior is habituated—which is what happens to learners through constant writing and reading instruction from K–16 (and, incidentally, to curriculum and ideology builders through general immersion in the milieu)—a corresponding cognitive dimension exists in which patterns become "wired" into our brains. Much of this cognitive activity can thankfully remain unconscious and should do so, but some of it should be brought to awareness. Fortunately, most linguistic cognition happens unconsciously, for example, formation of words from letters, selection of most words in sentence building, and so forth; otherwise, communication as we know it would be prohibitively time-consuming. But writing instructors especially should be careful not to allow more significant components of linguistic behavior to be conditioned beyond our students' consciousness for the sake of efficiency or anything else (see Clark 177–85; Khost, "Researching"). Most notably, perhaps, this includes their reasons for writing, or the "exigence" without which a situation technically does not count as rhetorical, according to a strong theoretical tradition (see Bitzer). We consider rhetorical exigence to include not only a problem's existence and its potential to be positively influenced through discourse, as Lloyd Bitzer would have it, but also to subsume writers' active will to win over their audiences in such influencing, with mutually meaningful stakes, which accounts for the primary critiques of Bitzer's scheme (Consigny; Vatz). Lacking these elements of engagement, writers risk losing rhetorical agency, an effect that becomes normalized over time through repetition and reward.

So, the concept of *rhetorical present moment* that we wish to present involves a writer engaged through mind and body with an audience (including the attendant dynamics of intention and exchange, which some might call *spirit*) in which authentic exigence is realized (metacognition) in the here and now situation (environment). This is not to discount future outcomes of the transaction, of course, but only to try to avoid reducing its value to being all or mostly about those outcomes. What makes this worth considering from an explicitly cognitive angle (since nearly any human concern is implicitly cognitive in some respect) is how well our approach aligns with an emerging model of cognition as necessarily embodied and enactive, which raises our hopes of gaining real traction for our rhetorical agenda through association with that movement.

Over the past few decades, a gradual paradigm shift has been occurring in some areas of cognitive theory: roughly, from representational models to various embodied theories of human cognition. Putting aside many details that are relatively unimportant for current purposes (including that this movement has, of course, not been unanimous and cohesive), we might say that this shift generally entails moving away from a view of cognition as rule-governed mental computations representing a separate world to us, toward a view of cognition as a situational, enactive "brain-body-environment system" (Chemero 152) interacting in the world. To be further reductive, these respective theories can be said to regard meaning as being made of reality either by translation of information in mental categories or by enactment of embodied participation. For a simple example, people understand what a tree is, even in the absence of one, either because they have a word representing tree in their mind, which is a semantic process (i.e., the representational model), or because they can simulate the experience of a tree in their mind, which is a sensory-motor phenomenon; literally, visual and motor brain systems are activated despite the absence of a physical stimulus (i.e., the embodied model).

The subtle difference here that we wish to seize and focus on for pedagogical purposes is a difference in phenomenology: in our case, of the rhetorical experience. When students are assigned to engage audiences through writing, they are being asked to negotiate reality. So, we contend that teachers should be aware of their own and their students' underlying theoretical assumptions about the nature of this cognitive act; in other words, they should consider how they believe people negotiate reality in the first place. To maintain our reductive scheme: is writing of the ubiquitous argumentative essay, for example, primarily a semantic exchange of meaning played out across competing mental representations, or are bodies being activated in a shared rhetorical environment? When we factor in the element of habituation, it becomes easier to see the relevance of this question. Through years and years of essay writing in school, are students being implicitly trained to regard their rhetorical audiences as out-there, knowable *a priori*, and engaged primarily through logical persuasion, or as in-here, knowable *a posteriori*, and engaged through holistic negotiation?

Cognitive scientist Benjamin Bergen provides a helpful explanation of the embodied simulation hypothesis in lay terms, which we can take advantage of in developing our pedagogical application of this theory. Bergen explains that according to the embodied view of cognition, meaning is not a matter of definitions in mental symbols but a "creative process, in which people construct virtual experiences—embodied simulations—in their mind's eye," to which he adds, "If meaning is based on experience with the world—the specific actions and percepts an individual has—then it may vary from individual to individual and from culture to culture" (16). Herein lies the important difference we are trying to identify between competing cognitive assumptions about the rhetorical situation, which is by its nature a negotiation of differences in meaning: a universal approach grounded in the abstract realm of language or an individual approach grounded in applied experience of holistic presence.

We can identify provisional writing instructional analogues to the competing representational and embodied theories of cognition and their corresponding rhetorical attitudes. These might be called, respectively: modeling and responding. A model-based pedagogy treats rhetorical situations as predictable and best approached through preparation (a.k.a. readiness in the conventional sense): students practice at argumentation, rhetorical analysis, and so forth, all more or less as addressed to an abstract or completely unknown reader in a context that doesn't really exist. A response-based pedagogy (supplemental to or compatible, eventually, with genre and activity theories) treats rhetorical situations as unique, to which a more spontaneous approach is favored: students identify situations in which they are or wish to be engaged and refine their means of engaging real audiences in them.

A given rhetorical situation might look the same either way from an external view, but one's agency in the situation will differ according to which approach has been taken or emphasized. It's probably not controversial to propose that rhetoric has a cognitive dimension; after all, everyone knows it involves thinking, and many would acknowledge it sometimes includes affect. But if we accept that cognition is necessarily embodied and that rhetoric is necessarily social, then it seems advisable to teach rhetoric as at least first a matter of bodies transacting with other bodies in an environment (temporal and/or spatial) and then as a matter of linguistic strategies, as need be (which we disclaim because these may follow naturally from the former). Otherwise, being out of touch, literally and figuratively, with one's reasons for engagement in the transaction disadvantages the rhetor and the situation. Clay Walker makes a compelling similar case, following Lisa Blackman's view of literacy as something we do or become rather than have or are, for what he calls discursive readiness potential, "which accounts for how one's previous literate experiences emerge as potentials for action in a situation, and how cultivating and changing our sets of emergent potentials involves revising our connections among mind, body, and world" (2).

KAIROTIC TECHNE AS BODILY DISPOSITIONS

If writing and its teaching become more of a present-focused rather than "future-cast, assessed endeavor" (Peary 144), then what do such pedagogies look like that seek to foster strategies of being in the moment? To answer this question, we first consider the way pedagogies of presence might define or redefine our notion of techne from that of skill to that of disposition, or what Ehren Pflugfelder might call an "abstract" techne, which is "messier, less certain, and less precise" (46) than the "how-to" knowledge of specific technique. The groundwork for this shift is established in a concept of kairos as "immanent, embodied, mobile, non-rational" (Hawhee 68) and that incorporates related ideas of metis and tyche. Kairos, as a principle of timeliness, would seem indispensable to any discussion of readiness, as that is precisely the issue that the idea invites us to consider: what, in any given situation, are the circumstances at hand that afford response? A kairotic rhetoric and pedagogy, however, move the future-oriented focus of readiness away from how we can prepare for what will happen to how we can respond to what is happening. Through the concepts of metis and tyche, we can arrive at a kairotic understanding of techne as something not existing outside of ourselves to be deployed as demonstrable, detachable skill but rather as a bodily art, a way of being, to be cultivated in response to present and evolving circumstances.

Understood in its sense as "cunning becoming" (Hawhee 59), metis is techne inherently tied to the body, to the point where we might regard it as thinking through/with/as the body, as differing from detached dualistic conceptions of logic that can be separated and practiced apart from our physical selves. On this point scholars such as Debra Hawhee are insistent: metis is a corporeal art inhabiting the agent and exists as a kind of orientation, enmeshed in and manifest through circumstance rather than technique to be acquired independent of actualization. Rather than a future-oriented strategy that can be generally prescribed, metis exists "only at the moment of use" so that "general rules and strategies cannot be applied without regard to the particulars of a given situation" (Pflugfelder 107). Bringing the concept of metis into a discussion of dispositions invites us to think of dispositions then as not just habits of mind (or heart) but also habits of body or hexeis. This helps us prepare for a redefinition of readiness as being present and bodily-oriented. We can make an analogy here to athleticism. While the athlete must "have" and practices skills, such skills can never in and of themselves add up to successful performance. It is only in and through the moment of competition that the athlete actualizes his or her prowess in relation to evolving circumstances rather than static, controlled conditions.

Metis, then, is emergent in relation to tyche, the idea of chance or fortune. While tyche is associated with the unknowable and unpredictable, it is also associated with opportunity. As Janet M. Atwill describes it, "Tyche frequently refers to a point of indeterminacy that can be exploited by techne" (94). Thus, cunning exists only in relation to the openings that chance presents. The god Kairos is described as having hair on his face "For one who encounters . . . to grasp" but being bald on the back of his head, signifying lost opportunity and thus the elusive nature of chance (Hawhee 73). In this allegory, the principle of kairos is informed by the uncontrollable and unpredictable nature of circumstance, tyche, that can prove advantageous to one who is ready. But this kind of "readiness," metis, is predicated on being attuned to the right moment.

From this standpoint, the key questions of readiness become how to seize moments that we cannot completely prepare for, and what it means to teach once we accept this epistemological perspective. Rather than prefabricated strategies based on static reification of experience, a different techne might derive from attentiveness to what is present in the here and now as advocated by practitioners of mindfulness. As Keith Kroll suggests in "On Paying Attention: Flagpoles, Mindfulness, and Teaching Writing," "the responsibility of a writing teacher is, finally, to teach his or her students to pay attention—to their own lives and to the world in which they live" (69). Kroll laments the overall message sent to postsecondary students, especially at the community college level, "that speed and training are to be valued more than learning, intellectual engagement, and contemplation" (70). In our emphasis on preparing students for the practical work-a-day world, we are in reality, according to Kroll, promulgating "detachment and disengagement" (72). Kroll has found that personal narrative is still one of our most powerful tools for teaching engagement, and in implicit criticism of the profession's emphasis on rhetoric and transfer, concludes that writing must be "less about genre and rhetorical strategies and . . . more about the . . . expression of a writer's ideas" (74). In curricular attempts to ready writers by acquainting them with the art of rhetoric, our professional efforts may in fact be alienating students from the intuitive reason that we read and write: to connect with others (interpersonal) and with ourselves (intrapersonal).

It is this emphasis on the whole student, as promoted by David Schoem and others, that is precisely, perhaps in the name of efficiency, being given short shrift in bureaucratic understandings of readiness. But arguably, dissective views of readiness end up undermining their own goals through important omissions of developmental emphasis. Christy Wenger, in her use of yogic contemplative strategies in the writing classroom, makes this point about the nature of metacognition as deriving from the type of awareness promulgated through mindfulness practices: "the cultivation of mindfulness through contemplative practice has the potential to increase students' self-understanding and, in turn, provide them with the tools to better understand their cognitions, feelings and personal values" (134). Without the incorporation of this integrative concern, our conceptions of readiness are impoverished and compromised by a false binary metaphor of inner (self) and outer (world). It is the mission of contemplative practice to reveal and bridge this dichotomy. For Wenger, body awareness through yogic writing practice, "is a skill that can lead to more successful and generative writing sessions as well as a deeper understanding of the meaning-making process" (149). From this perspective, being ready means being present.

The connection between metacognition and mindfulness also is important in Alexandria Peary's critique of the pervasiveness of what she calls mind*less* writing practices and pedagogy. For Peary, the idea of "paying attention" emphasized by Kroll takes on a particular cast, as she, along with other mindfulness and contemplative practice advocates, emphasizes the power of presence. Peary identifies mindfulness as invention strategy that invites us to reshape our conception of metacognition to include it as an activity of presence rather than deferral (to the future) or reflection (on the past), the two paradigms that dominate writing studies' configuration, sometimes adversely, according to Peary, resulting in writing practice that is habitually mindless. Peary answers Robert Yagelski's question asked in *Writing as a Way of Being*, what if "we were to refocus writing instruction on the act of writing in the moment, rather than on the production of specific kinds of texts that are valued in academic settings?" (170) by asserting that "Writing becomes a markedly different experience if students think of it more consistently as part of a discrete now: every moment becomes an inventive moment due to the establishment of a calm, non-evaluative and observant outlook that promotes receptivity to new ideas and critical thinking" (24). This kairotic "receptivity" that Peary describes is in keeping with the precepts of metis and tyche that ask us to cultivate orientations and ways of being as strategies of readiness, to be attuned to what is unfolding and to feel our embodied responses to the moment at hand. Peary's pedagogy is based on "pairing awareness with language" (47) and features activities such as "Yoga for hands" (49), in which students write about their physical sensations of writing, and "mindful eating" writing assignments based on paying attention to what is often a mundane, thoughtless activity. In this way students immerse and train themselves in awareness.

In the spirit of Buddhist practice, Peary sees composing in the here and now as a means to release ourselves from the attachment of suffering associated with writing, what Nate Mickelson identifies as an iconic representation of writing as "discomfort" (x) that pervades our cultural view of composing. This sort of attachment exists in the prevalent academic readiness paradigm operational in much writing instruction, steeped as it is in hoarding product and anxiety about whether future selves and artifacts will measure up or be good enough. The view of those who adhere to mindful writing practices is that such anxiety is dysfunctional rather than productive. Mary Soliday and Jennifer Seibel Trainor associate such anxiety and discomfort that alienates students with the teaching of writing as part of a "literacy machine." Although Soliday and Seibel-Trainor do not explicitly reference tyche in their critique, they nonetheless lament the way outcomes-based culture discounts the accidental and the unplanned (128). They offer up the model of the *bricoleur* as a counter to the future-oriented readiness promulgated by the mechanized nature of outcomes education. *Bricolage* calls on us to respond to the affordances at hand and make use of what exists. As Claude Lévi-Strauss makes use of the term in *The Savage Mind*, *bricolage* contrasts with the planning and control of what we imagine is scientific discourse or what Pflugfelder might identify as "explicit" techne (46). While these characterizations create their own unfair and perhaps inaccurate dichotomy, Lévi-Strauss's division provides a useful heuristic nonetheless to distinguish between a methodology that encounters what *is* rather than one that seeks to control what cannot be completely known. And if it is not advisable or possible to completely eliminate aspects of "the literacy machine" that try to perpetuate such strategies of control, then we can certainly ask questions about the costs of pursuing such control and what we are excluding, in order to find ways to recuperate and encourage holistic praxis.

Indeed, purveyors of academic readiness culture might well appropriate the allegory of kairos to suggest that being ready to seize the moment is exactly what training in explicit techne will do by teaching students strategies that they can use to exploit future opportunities. But it is hubristic—and inaccurate—to imagine a tameable future in such terms. Kelly A. Meyers's expansion of the concept of kairos through the concept of *metanoia*—regret—is instructive here and a good adjutant to contemplative strategies that emphasize presence. Meyers revisits the depiction of the god to raise questions about how we define the notion of the opportune:

> When Opportunity appears, a person has that one moment—kairos—to seize the god by the hair. Any hesitation and Opportunity vanishes, the back of his head bald and ungraspable. Those who do not embrace Kairos reside with Metanoia. On the surface, the story creates a strict and foreboding distinction between the opportune and inopportune or seized versus missed moments . . . Looking more closely at metanoia's role, however,

invites ways to revise and expand the story and experience of opportunity. (386)

At first glance, the story here sounds like a cautionary tale that reinforces an aggressive, nonreflective view of readiness found in a skills-based narrative of preparedness: get your ducks in a row by learning the rules and middle-class values of diligence and industry that Lynn Bloom memorably identifies in the ethos governing writing instruction (self-reliance/responsibility, respectability, decorum/propriety, moderation/temperance, thrift, efficiency, orderliness, cleanliness, punctuality, delayed gratification, and critical thinking)—or suffer the consequences. But Meyers suggests another way of seeing what ensues when we appear to have missed the kairotic moment; the thing that did not happen. Rather than an end, we can expand our understanding of regret to see not just loss, but opportunity, a different if not new beginning that becomes possible through reconsideration of what was missed. In effect, Meyers extends the inventional reach of a kairotic principle of readiness to include recursive understanding of opportunity and generative failure. While Meyers's compositional process of what she terms *metanoic revision* focuses on past action, she nonetheless characterizes the nature of metanoic metacognition "as an active embrace of the remorseful turn" (391), thus construing it with mindful awareness.

Readiness and failure might seem like antithetical terms, but Asao Inoue has helpfully questioned our need to fetishize the avoidance of failure in the context of writing assessment, pointing to the way such practice perpetuates institutional racism in higher education and language performance ("Theorizing Failure"). The understanding of readiness implicitly critiqued in his call for a valuation of student labor is one that stems from an accommodationist notion of kairos, which stresses adaptation to prevailing conditions (see Hawhee 68). Certainly, the flexibility of adaptation is an advantageous, desirable faculty to cultivate. But when we only see kairos in these terms, as mastering what is forgone, our understanding of agency becomes debilitated, even ethically suspect, as we cede the range of possible action unquestioningly to authoritative discourses. Inoue has also critiqued such "progressive" models of readiness as the *Framework* and its accompanying habits of mind, suggesting that such documents are marred by inadvertent whiteness relating to a silently oppressive institutional habitus. Indeed, his critique principally targets the strain of control that runs through the educational enterprise masquerading under "student needs" rhetoric with regard to language that seeks in reality to enact hegemonic standards: "We must stop saying that we have to teach this dominant English because it's what students need to succeed tomorrow. They only need it because we keep teaching it!" ("Stop Killing"). In this we see the tautological conundrum of a readiness mill that is self-perpetuating and self-inflicting, something of an own goal.

Instead of seeing readiness in terms of normalization, Hawhee's alternate explication of kairos as "opening" is valuable here, a somewhat different sense than the "openness" identified among the *Framework*'s habits of mind. Referencing a hunting or battle image, Hawhee cites a meaning of kairos as the vulnerable opening on a body where an archer might aim, "a gap or softening in the otherwise protective skeleton, where the arrow can penetrate" (66–67). Certainly no one would wish to be the unlucky body at which the archer is aiming, but the notion of vulnerability here, of softness, offers a different slant on readiness than the paradigm in which we impregnably equip students with tools of self-interest to meet the challenges of the future. Instead of enameling students in readiness, what too often might be what Inoue references as the "steel cage" ("Stop Killing") of solipsistic whiteness perpetuating egoism at the expense of ethical action, we might think of opening or vulnerability as part of a kairotic moment that is invitational and receptive to possibility, a moment where something, someone can "penetrate" and possibly change us. As such, readiness becomes a synonym for receptivity and is large enough, "soft" enough, to encompass our failures and our regrets, as well as our relational selves. This kind of readiness is provocative enough to entertain uncertainty and risk, which ultimately are the factors, the qualities, that produce change—in ourselves and the world—if we are ready.

Works Cited

AAC&U. "Falling Short? College Learning and Career Success." Hart Research Associates, Jan. 2015, www.aacu.org/sites/default/files/files/LEAP/2015employerstudentsurvey.pdf.

—. "Fulfilling the American Dream: Liberal Education and the Future of Work." Hart Research Associates, July 2018, www.aacu.org/sites/default/files/files/LEAP/2018EmployerResearchReport.pdf.

—. "It Takes More than a Major: Employer Priorities for College Learning and Student Success." Hart Research Associates, Apr. 2013, www.aacu.org/sites/default/files/files/LEAP/2013_EmployerSurvey.pdf.

—. "Raising the Bar: Employers' Views on College Learning in The Wake of The Economic Downturn." Hart Research Associates, Jan. 2010, www.aacu.org/sites/default/files/files/LEAP/2009_EmployerSurvey.pdf.

Aristotle. *The Rhetoric and the Poetics of Aristotle*. Translated by W. Rhys Roberts. The Modern Library, 1984.

Atwill, Janet M. *Rhetoric Reclaimed: Aristotle and the Liberal Arts Tradition*. Cornell UP, 1998.

Bergen, Benjamin K. *Louder Than Words: The New Science of How the Mind Makes Meaning*. Basic Books, 2012.

Bitzer, Lloyd. "The Rhetorical Situation." *Philosophy & Rhetoric*, vol. 1, no.1, 1968, pp. 1–14.

Blackman, Lisa. *The Body: Key Concepts*. Berg, 2008.

Bloom, Lynn Z. "Freshman Composition as a Middle-Class Enterprise." *College English*, vol. 58, no. 6, 1996, pp. 654–75.

Chemero, Anthony. *Radical Embodied Cognitive Science*. MIT Press, 2009.

Clark, Irene. "Neuroplasticity, Genre, and Identity: Possibilities and Complications." *Contemporary Perspectives on Cognition and Writing*, edited by Patricia Portanova, et al., WAC Clearinghouse, 2017, pp. 169–87. wac.colostate.edu/books/perspectives/cognition/. Accessed 7 Mar. 2021

Conley, David T. "Redefining College Readiness." *Educational Policy Improvement Center*, 2007.

Consigny, Scott. "Rhetoric and Its Situations." *Philosophy & Rhetoric*, vol. 7, no. 3, 1974, pp. 175–86.

Dewey, John. "Self-Realization as the Moral Ideal." *The Philosophical Review*, vol. 2, no. 6, 1893, pp. 652–64.

Ede, Lisa, and Andrea A. Lunsford. "Audience Addressed/Audience Invoked: The Role of Audience in Composition Theory and Pedagogy." *College Composition and Communication*, vol. 35, no.2, 1984, pp. 155–71.

Gunner, Jeanne. "The Boxing Effect (An Anti-Essay)." *What is "College-Level" Writing?* edited by Patrick Sullivan and Howard Tinberg, NCTE, 2006, pp. 110–20.

Hawhee, Debra H. *Bodily Arts: Rhetoric and Athletics in Ancient Greece*. U of Texas P, 2004.

Inoue, Asao B. "2019 CCCC Chair's Address: How Do We Language So People Stop Killing Each Other, or What Do We Do About White Language Supremacy?" *College Composition and Communication*, vol. 71, no. 2, 2019, pp. 352–69.

—. "Theorizing Failure in US Writing Assessments." *Research in the Teaching of English*, vol. 48, 2014, pp. 330–52.

Keller, Daniel. *Chasing Literacy: Reading and Writing in an Age of Acceleration*. Utah State UP, 2013.

Khost, Peter H. "The *Framework for Success* as Rhetorical Common Denominator." *The Framework for Success in Postsecondary Writing: Scholarship and Applications*, edited by Nicholas Behm, et al., Parlor P, 2017, pp. 136–53.

—. "Researching Habits-of-Mind Self-Efficacy in First-Year College Writers." *Contemporary Perspectives on Cognition and Writing*, edited by Patricia Portanova, Michael Rifenburg, and Duane Roen, WAC Clearinghouse, 2017, pp. 271–89.

—. *Rhetor Response: A Theory and Practice of Literary Affordance*. Utah State UP, 2018.

Kroll, Keith. "On Paying Attention: Flagpoles, Mindfulness, and Teaching Writing." *Teaching English in the Two-Year College*, vol. 36. No. 1, 2008, pp. 69–78.

Lévi-Strauss, Claude. *The Savage Mind*. U of Chicago P, 1966.

Mattern, Krista, et al. "Broadening the Definition of College and Career Readiness: A Holistic Approach." *ACT Research Report Series*. 2014.

Meyers, Kelly A. "Metanoic Movement: The Transformative Power of Regret." *College Composition and Communication*, vol. 67, no. 3, 2016, pp. 385–410.

Mickelson, Nate. Introduction. *Writing as a Way of Staying Human*, edited by Mickelson, Vernon Press, 2019, pp. v-xvi.

Noddings, Nel. "Differentiate, Don't Standardize." *Education Week*, vol. 29, no. 17, 2010, pp. 29–31.

Ong, Walter J., S. J. "The Writer's Audience Is Always a Fiction." *PMLA*, vol. 90, no.1, 1975, pp. 9–21.

Peary, Alexandria. *Prolific Moment: A Theory and Practice of Mindfulness for Writing*. Routledge, 2018.

Pflugfelder, Ehren Helmut. *Communicating Mobility and Technology: A Material Rhetoric for Persuasive Transportation*. Routledge, 2017.

Rothman, Robert. "A Common Core of Readiness." *Educational Leadership*, vol. 69, no. 7, 2012, pp. 10–15.

Salomon, Gavriel, and David N. Perkins. "Rocky Roads to Transfer: Rethinking Mechanism of a Neglected Phenomenon." *Educational Psychologist*, vol. 24, no. 2, 1989, pp. 113–42.

Schoem, David. Introduction. *Teaching the Whole Student: Engaged Learning with Heart, Mind, and Spirit*, edited by David Schoem, Shristine Modey, and Edward P. St. John, Stylus, 2017, pp. 1–16.

Shedd, Jessica M. "The History of the Student Credit Hour." *How the Student Credit Hour Shapes Higher Education: The Tie That Binds*, special issue of *New Directions for Higher Education*, vol. 2003, no. 122, 2003, pp. 5–12.

Soliday, Mary, and Jennifer Seibel-Trainor. "Rethinking Regulation in the Age of the Literacy Machine." *College Composition and Communication*, vol. 68, no. 1, 2016, pp. 125–51.

Tinberg, Howard, and Jean-Paul Nadeau. "Contesting the Space Between High School and College in the Era of Dual Enrollment." *College Composition and Communication*, vol. 62, no. 4, 2011, pp. 704–25.

Uehling, Karen. "What's the Rush?" *Teacher-Scholar-Activist*. 26 July 2017, www.teacher-scholar-activist.org/2017/07/26/whats-the-rush/. Accessed 3 July 2019.

Vatz, Richard E. "The Myth of the Rhetorical Situation." *Philosophy & Rhetoric*, vol. 6, no. 3, 1973, pp. 154–61.

Walker, Clay. "Composing Agency: Theorizing the Readiness Potentials of Literacy Practices." *Literacy in Composition Studies*, vol. 3, no. 2, 2015, pp. 1–21.

Wenger, Christy I. *Yoga Minds, Writing Bodies: Contemplative Writing Pedagogy*. Parlor P, 2015.

Yagelski, Robert. *Writing as a Way of Being: Writing Instruction, Nonduality, and the Crisis of Sustainability*. Hampton, 2011.

2 Metacognition: Crossing the Information and Writing Thresholds

Barbara J. D'Angelo and Barry M. Maid

Writing Studies (WS) and Library and Information Science (LIS) have shared a longstanding and fruitful partnership and collaborative association to facilitate the teaching and learning of research and, more broadly, information skills. These partnerships are evident in the literature of both disciplines. In many ways, our own long collaboration is an example of this partnership. When we first started working together more than twenty years ago, Barbara D'Angelo was still a grad student working on her degree in LIS. Barry Maid was a professor of rhetoric and writing doing research on pedagogical possibilities in what were, then, new virtual environments. Over time, our work almost always gets us back to the nexus of WS and LIS in both academic and applied situations. In this chapter we focus specifically on recent developments related to threshold concepts, their relationship to transfer of learning, and the impact on pedagogical practices to help students learn and transfer their learning, with special attention to the role of metacognition.

Threshold Concepts

Threshold concepts were first proposed by Jan Meyer and Ray Land in 2003 based on research for the UK's Economic and Social Research Council's Teaching and Learning Research Programme. One of the characteristics of threshold concepts within a discipline or knowledge domain is that they are transformational. That is, threshold concepts transform an individual's way of thinking or interpreting something. Understanding and internalizing a threshold concept may be seen as analogous to crossing through a portal or doorway to a new world—in the case of threshold concepts, one enters into a new "world view" or perspective that can be seen as "thinking like . . . " a member of a discipline or group ("thinks like a lawyer," "thinks like a Democrat," "thinks like a scientist," etc.). Threshold concepts are also irreversible; once an individual crosses the threshold, they cannot reverse back to the previous way of thinking. Individuals adopt and comprehend threshold concepts at different rates; some may find the integration and comprehension to be simple and fast, others may resist or simply need time to comprehend. Building on the portal analogy, the passage through involves some degree of liminality. That liminal state represents an intermediary period in which the individual is learning the threshold concept but has not quite grasped it—or perhaps is resisting it due to previous experience or learning. Liminality may result in confusion, frustration, or resistance as the individual struggles with understanding and grasping the concept. Some may never pass through the portal; while for others, the passage may be facilitated by what we commonly call "ah ha" moments (or a light bulb going off). Indeed, crossing the portal may require some flexibility, openness, and reflective thinking that can be associated with the metacognition as a key component of learning and the ability to draw upon and adapt prior knowledge to new situations.

Since Meyer and Land's initial identification of threshold concepts, scholars within multiple disciplines have researched and identified them within their fields. In this chapter, we are specifically focused on the fields of WS and LIS. The interest in threshold concepts within WS is manifested in the collaborative work that led to the publication of *Naming What We Know: Threshold Concepts of Writing Studies*. This text identifies and proposes thirty-six threshold concepts for the discipline of writing studies based on the collective work of twenty-nine scholars in the field. Within LIS, the Association of College and Research Libraries' move from a standards-based document for information literacy to a framework was grounded on threshold concepts and metaliteracy. Similar to *Naming What We Know*, the *Framework for Information Literacy for Higher Education* (the *Framework for IL*) was developed through a collaborative process that intended to shift the focus of teaching, learning, and assessment away from the rigid approach imposed by standards towards an approach that emphasizes adaptability, curiosity, flexibility, critical thinking, and metacognition. As we and others have reported, the move towards the use of threshold concepts as a foundation for pedagogical practices and learning is remarkably similar in both the WS and LIS disciplines.

METACOGNITION: MOVING FROM NOVICE TO EXPERT

Metacognition has long been identified and recognized as key to learning. The 2000 research report from the National Academies of Science, *How People Learn*, identified metacognition as helping students to learn to take control of their own learning, to improve understanding and comprehension, and to achieve goals. In WS, metacognition (or reflection) has long been recognized as a way to help students articulate their learning and to facilitate their growth as writers (Yancey et al.). Indeed, best practices in portfolio assessment that incorporate Phase II scoring (White), reflect the use and importance of the cover (or metacognitive) statement in which students go beyond describing their portfolios to articulate their learning and application of that learning within the context of their coursework and programmatic outcomes. Importantly, the metacognitive cover statement asks students to describe the HOW and WHY of their learning in addition to the WHAT.

Further, in *How People Learn*, metacognition was identified as a key factor differentiating experts from novices—experts are able to monitor their understanding to identify gaps in information, integrate new information with previous knowledge, and draw upon and adapt previous knowledge to new situations through analogies (Bransford, Pellegrino, and Donovan). Seemingly, then, metacognition is tied to the idea of transfer.

Research within the field of LIS further supports the notion that metacognition differentiates experts from novices. Carol Kuhlthau, for example, found that lawyers (experts) drew upon previous experiences when engaged with the information search process and to apply those to facilitate the research needed to work on a current case. Further, lawyers exhibited a more open and flexible approach to the information search process that allowed them to formulate, construct, and adjust their process as it unfolded in reaction to what they found. Students (novices), on the other hand, expressed and exhibited more anxiety when approaching the information search process and were less open and flexible as they searched for the "right answer" rather than engaged in a process of exploration.

Similarly, Carl Bereiter and Marlene Scardamalia and Scaradmalia, Bereiter, and Rosanne Steinbach review relevant research on differences between expert and novice writers and ask, "what stands between the novice and expert competence" (277). They suggest it is the lack of executive structure to apply evaluative, diagnostic, and remedial abilities and that this executive structure can be developed to help novices think more like an expert. Hayes et al. indicated that the concept of revision was different in experts than in novices in relation to features of the text (experts focus on global issues, novices on surface features).

BRINGING IT ALL TOGETHER: INFORMATION LITERACY AND WRITING

If metacognition (or reflective writing) is the key to learning and to moving from novice to expert status, how do we help students learn to be metacognitive learners? Metacognition is not a threshold concept itself; instead, it can perhaps help novices to move through liminality and cross the threshold to expertise by prodding them to think about the HOW and WHY of what they have done as well as the WHAT. But metacognition is not an intuitive process; it must be developed over time as part of the pedagogical process of learning. As a result, it is important that we help students through this development and to learn the language needed to be metacognitive and to articulate their own metacognitive analyses.

The need to facilitate metacognition is supported by the research of Kathleen Blake Yancey, Liane Robertson, and Kara Taczak. This groundbreaking research on teaching for transfer highlights the need to help students to think metacognitively about their writing and to learn key terminology to articulate learning related to writing. Students cannot be *metacognitive* if they do not have the language with which to express how and why they have composed in a certain way.

Each discipline has its own discourse using language that has meaning and that is generally accepted by others in the field. Indeed, one of the characteristics of threshold concepts is that it is discursive; individuals who are crossing the portal master the language of the discipline and integrate it as part of their identity within the discipline. Learners who are new to a field do not know that field's language and associated discursive patterns; they must learn them. As Yancey, Robertson, and Taczak showed, doing so helps students to engage in metacognition and to transfer knowledge to other contexts. By having their first-year writing students begin to think like writers and think of themselves as writers, they assert that those students will be more likely to write successfully in other academic contexts.

Relevant to our discussion is the threshold concept "writing is (also always) a cognitive activity" from *Naming What We Know*. However, we must be mindful to distinguish between cognition and metacognition. As Howard Tinberg points out, metacognition and cognition are not the same thing. Cognition is the acquisition and application of knowledge; metacognition is the ability to think about and draw upon the processes and practices of application to assess which apply in new situations and which do not. Indeed, Tinberg claims that cognition—knowledge of subject content and rules of grammar and mechanics of writing—are not enough to produce successful writing; successful writing requires metacognition. Taczak further explains that it is the combination of cognition and metacognition that allows writers to recognize and build on prior knowledge—that is, the qualities identified as the difference between novice and expert. Thus, if achievement of expertise is associated with crossing a threshold (grasping a threshold concept) and metacognition is key to recognizing and building on prior knowledge to achieve expertise and transfer learning, then it can be assumed that adopting the behavior and language associated with being metacognitive is key to transfer.

Further, metacognition is a fundamental concept and disposition associated with metaliteracy as an underpinning of the *Framework for IL* along with threshold concepts to emphasize that, similar to writing, individuals must become metacognitive learners to become information literate—or move from novice to expert. Metacognition, then, has been clearly identified within LIS and WS as the key to moving students through liminality associated with comprehending threshold concepts. One could argue that this passage through liminality is also the passage from the state of being a novice to one of being an expert.

Moving from Concepts to Pedagogical Practice

Our interest in using metacognitive writing in the classroom began more than twenty years ago, and it was in many ways an accident. One of the authors (Maid) was teaching an upper-level/graduate class course called Technical Style and Editing. Technical editing courses have a reputation for being incredibly boring. It was a strange course for him to teach. He's the first to admit that he's not a particularly good editor, partly because he has an attention span that is shorter than that of most of his students. Still, he volunteered to teach it to help out the department.

Agreeing to teach this course, he was faced with developing a curriculum for a course that because of its content that most often focused on detailed, rule-bound acontextual information, like his students, he found quite boring. He decided to give it a few twists that he thought would interest him, engage his students, and provide them with a class experience that would translate into something they could carry with them into the workplace. He began by broadening the scope of the course into something it had not been before. He developed a curriculum that would have his students see the course as something that would not only work on their editing skills but also help prepare them to work as technical editors. With that as a theme for the course, since working technical editors often are responsible for the timeline and flow of a project, he included a unit on project management, and for the final assignment he asked them to choose an organization they knew and to write an in-house style manual for that organization. (They spent the last part of the course looking at in-house style manuals of businesses, government agencies, and non-profit organizations.)

Developing an in-house style manual can be a big job. It necessarily requires making decisions on what are sometimes seen as petty items. Still, those issues must be regularized for consistency's sake. As part of the assignment, he asked them to also write what he called a "cover paper." In the cover paper, they needed to explain every decision that went into the style manual. He developed the assignment to keep students focused and so they would not arbitrarily make things up (though sometimes the decision was arbitrary, and they needed to explain that). After several semesters, he realized that, since his students were looking closely at the decisions they were making in their writing process and of necessity articulating not only the decisions themselves but also the reasons for the decisions, the cover paper was the most important thing he had assigned in the course.

At some point he realized that because he was asking them to think about their own thought processes, the cover paper was an exercise in metacognition. He even started talking to his classes about what that meant and why he was having them do it. One of the things he discovered was that the cover paper had an impact on them. When he had them in later courses and asked questions about some of their assignments, they would respond and say things like "oh, you mean you want us to keep thinking like we did in the cover paper?" When he responded positively, they simply started doing it. It appeared that having the cover paper as a point of reference helped them understand what they needed to be doing in the future.

As a result of the fact that his students seemed to "get it" after doing a cover paper, he started using a similar assignment in most of the courses he was teaching. He wanted his students to not only turn in the assignment but also turn in a piece of writing where they demonstrated why their response to the assignment turned out the way it did. Sometimes the choices they wrote about were clearly based on decisions made after engaging in some kind of rhetorical analysis about the exigence for the document. Sometimes the choices were based on analysis of data. Sometimes the choices were, indeed, arbitrary. However, even when that happened, his students were able to comfortably acknowledge the arbitrariness and conclude it would be easy to make other decisions. All in all, he felt that his students were learning that writing was not just the act of putting words on paper (or some other kind of fixed or digital medium) but rather that it required a constant series of cognitive choices.

Fast forward a couple of decades. With this background, it was natural for Maid to include cover papers throughout the courses he developed for the program he built in Technical Communication at Arizona State University. Having the precedent of these assignments as part of the curriculum, it seemed quite natural that the other author (D'Angelo), who was also using metacognitive pieces as part of her own courses, move towards Phase II scoring for the program's Capstone Portfolios when she was revising the Capstone course. Requiring a reflective (metacognitive) piece in a program that was already using a similar kind of assignments in some of its classes was a good and seamless fit and also met disciplinary best practice for assessment. Of course, we recognize that our use of metacognition in our courses and in the Technical Communication Program was not unique to us. As we've indicated above, Yancey and others have been advocating for the use of reflection in writing pedagogy for decades.

Understanding this background, it is no wonder that when Maid heard Linda Adler-Kassner talk about threshold concepts in a presentation at the WPA conference in Savannah in 2013, he immediately thought about the years he had spent having students write cover papers and began to understand why it was an effective assignment. While he had been aware of the literature on reflection, he had never completely been committed to it. He had likely been in that liminal state that happens before passing through the portal. In many ways, listening to that presentation forced him to engage in the same metacognitive activities he was asking my students to do. He had crossed the threshold.

Returning home from the conference, he shared his newfound knowledge about threshold concepts with his colleague, Barbara D'Angelo. For more than a decade we had been looking at and writing about the "WPA Outcomes Statement" and the *IL Standards*. It seemed to both of them that the idea of threshold concepts was one that needed exploring. This need to better understand threshold concepts and their role in writing curriculum was compounded by the fact that the ACRL was at the same time looking at developing the *Framework for IL*. As we engaged with the scholarship and conversations ongoing within WS and LIS, we recognized how threshold concepts and the role of metacognition were beginning to fill in gaps in how we were shaping our curriculum, assessment practices, and what our students were gaining from the program.

For example, we had initiated a study to determine which skills being taught in their program had proven to be the most valuable to graduates. Though they interviewed a group of graduates with at least five years' experience beyond their degree, the results didn't show very much. Though the program's alums were generous in their comments about the program, they really didn't provide much information in the real questions we were interested in: Did the knowledge/information the students learn in the program transfer to their workplace responsibilities? In other words, had their work in the program helped them to transition from novice to expert?

After the fact, we realized that their series of interviews had produced inconsequential results because they had been asking the wrong questions. Indeed, the very fact that we are using the word *skill* to describe the study is a clue to just how wrong our questions were. How, then, to ask the right questions? As Annemaree Lloyd pointed out, no workplace research had shown that what was generally accepted as "information literacy" within academia was not consistent with workplace practices. After beginning to read the literature about threshold concepts, both by Meyer and Land and by the few WS and LIS scholars who had begun to venture in those lines, we began to realize we needed to start thinking, as Tinberg suggests, about metacognition instead of cognition. Perhaps, it should have been obvious since some of the program's courses were using metacognitive cover papers from the onset of the program and the program's capstone required a metacognitive paper for Phase II scoring. Still, sometimes the most obvious answer is the one that remains most elusive. Recognizing this, however, raises a more complicated question. Yes, we were using metacognition attempting to help students build the skills needed for transfer of skills and knowledge (and to learn the discourse of the discipline). But what about threshold concepts?

The real problem, then, becomes identifying the threshold concepts that are appropriate for students. The trend in both WS and LIS had been to focus on cognition—not metacognition. For all kinds of good reasons, the "WPA Outcomes Statement" focuses on cognitive not metacognitive behaviors. So, too, did the *IL Standards*. Cognitive behaviors can be assessed. It's more difficult to assess metacognitive behavior. In fact, while we often use metacognitive writing as a tool when we assess student work (for example in Phase 2 scoring of portfolios), we are not actually assessing the metacognitive thought but rather using the metacognitive writing as a way of assessing the greater cognitive body of student work. Of course, we are not alone in making this realization. We can see that the *IL Standards* and "WPA OS" were produced at the turn of the century. WS has since adopted the habitss of mind, and LIS has moved on to the *Framework for IL* incorporating six frames:

- Authority is Constructed and Contextual
- Information Creation as a Process
- Information Has Value
- Research as Inquiry
- Scholarship as Conversation
- Searching as Strategic Exploration

Likewise, Adler-Kassner and Wardle and the contributors to their collection posit five potential meta-threshold concepts for Writing Studies:

- Writing Is a Social and Rhetorical Activity
- Writing Speaks to Situations through Recognizable Forms
- Writing Enacts and Creates Identities and Ideologies
- All Writers Have More to Learn
- Writing Is (Also Always) a Cognitive Activity

Although it's possible to argue whether these are the only threshold concepts writers need to attain, they are a useful starting point. In many ways, when our students write their "persuasive statement," they are engaged in metacognitive activity that should help them understand why they make the decisions they do when they write. (In fact, much of this is similar to the three categories Gita DasBender finds at the end of her chapter in this collection.) That, by extension, should lead to transfer—from course to course and from academia to the workplace. The identification of threshold concepts—for IL and for WS—should provide us with a way to identify the language students need in order to move through the threshold and evolve from novice to expert.

So, where do we go from here? First of all, we think there needs to be a language we can use when talking about threshold concepts. Do we "attain" a threshold concept? Do we "learn" a threshold concept? Do we "cross" or "enter" a threshold concept? There are other possibilities, but none seem to consider what really happens. Once we have crossed the threshold, we have changed how we think about something. Is it possible to even teach someone how to change why they think? Especially in one course (or even in an entire degree program? In many ways, that's what often frustrates teachers. It's relatively easy to teach the what (facts) or to teach the how (skills). In fact, we can relatively easily test for the facts and skills. However, what seems to matter even more than the "what" of learning is the "why." It's the question Maid first asked his editing students over twenty years ago. As he told them, and still tells his students, that he is less concerned with having them respond to a normal workplace writing situation, for example, writing a report from an in-house template. He's more concerned with being able to create the appropriate template when none exists. To do so takes more than writing skills. It takes an understanding of why the report and future reports following the new template need to exist. On one hand, we might say it takes a thorough understanding of rhetoric, and that would be true. We could ascribe that to the first meta-concept that Adler-Kassner and Wardle name, writing is a social and rhetorical activity. However, it takes more. In fact, we might see how all five of their meta-concepts come into play in what might appear to be a simple workplace task.

So how do we get our students to progress through the threshold? We expect there is neither one answer nor an easy answer. However, it is clear we must ask our students to do more than simply show us they are capable of accomplishing certain tasks. Passing a test or writing an effective paper is not enough. Students need to understand why they were capable of passing the test and why they wrote a good paper and simply satisfying pieces of a rubric is not enough. Creating a pedagogical environment that forces students to engage in metacognitive activities about their own work not only helps students better understand their own response to a writing exigence and their own process. It also helps to prepare them when they are faced with a different context and exigence. The "cover paper" we mention gives students a start to this goal.

WORKS CITED

Adler-Kassner, Linda, and Elizabeth Wardle, editors. *Naming What We Know: Threshold Concepts of Writing Studies*. Utah State UP, 2015.

Bereiter, Carl, and Marlene Scardamalia. "Levels of Inquiry into the Nature of Expertise in Writing." *Review of Research in Education*, vol. 13, no. 1, 1986, pp. 259–82.

Bransford, John D., et al., editors. *How People Learn: Brain, Mind, Experience, and School:* Expanded Ed. National Academy Press, 2000.

Council of Writing Program Administrators. "WPA Outcomes Statement for First-Year Composition (3.0)." CWPA, 2014, wpacouncil.org/aws/CWPA/asset_manager/get_file/350909?ver=552. Accessed 3 Aug. 2020.

Dryer, Dylan B. "Writing Is (Also Always) a Cognitive Activity." *Naming What We Know. Threshold Concepts of Writing Studies*, edited by Linda Adler-Kassner and Elizabeth Wardle, Utah State UP, 2015, pp. 71–74.

Hayes, John R., et al. "Cognitive Processes in Revision." *Advances in Applied Psycholinguistics, Vol. 2: Reading, Writing, and Language Learning*, edited by Sheldon Rosenberg, Cambridge UP, 1987, pp. 176–240.

Kuhlthau, Carol. *Seeking Meaning. A Process Approach to Library and Information Services*. Libraries Unlimited, 2004.

Lloyd, Annemaree. "Trapped between a Rock and a Hard Place: What Counts as Information Literacy in the Workplace and How Is It Conceptualized?" *Library Trends*, vol. 60, no. 2, 2011, pp. 227–96.

Meyer, Jan, and Ray Land. "Threshold Concepts and Troublesome Knowledge (2): Epistemological Considerations and a Conceptual Framework for Teaching and Learning." *Higher Education*, vol. 49, no. 3, 2005, pp. 378–88.

Meyer, Jan, and Ray Land. *Threshold Concepts and Troublesome Knowledge: Linkages to Ways of Thinking and Practicing within the Disciplines.* ETL Project, Universities of Edinburgh, Coventry and Durham. Occasional Report 4. 2003.

Scardamalia, Marlene, et al. "Teachability of Reflective Processes in Written Composition." *Cognitive Science*, vol. 8, 1984, pp. 173–90.

Society for Technical Communication. "Technical Communication Body of Knowledge." 2016, www.tcbok.org/. Accessed 11 Nov. 2019.

Taczak, Kara. "Reflection Is Critical for Writers' Development." *Naming What We Know: Threshold Concepts of Writing Studies*, edited by Linda Adler-Kassner and Elizabeth Wardle, Utah State UP, 2015, pp. 78–79.

Tinberg, Howard. "Metacognition Is Not Cognition." *Naming What We Know: Threshold Concepts of Writing Studies*, edited by Linda Adler-Kassner and Elizabeth Wardle, Utah State UP, 2015, pp. 75–6.

White, Edward. "The Scoring of Writing Portfolios: Phase 2." *College Composition and Communication*, vol. 56, no. 4, 2005, pp. 581–600.

Yancey, Kathleen Blake, et al. *Writing Across Contexts: Transfer Composition, and Sites of Writing.* Utah State UP, 2014.

3 What Do You Experience When You Read and Write? Diversity in the Experience of Inner Speech

Airlie Rose

In his introduction to *Landmark Essays on Voice in Writing*, Peter Elbow sorts composition's multifaceted understanding of voice into five categories, hoping to make communication about this contested concept more productive. He used the term *audible voice* to describe the experience of reading a voiced text: "All texts are literally silent, but most readers experience some texts as giving more sense of sound—more of the illusion as we read that we are hearing the words sounded" (Elbow, "Introduction: About Voice and Writing" xxiv). I was intrigued by Elbow's audible voice and wondered about the relationship between style and the inner experience of language. My questions drew me to studies in psycholinguistics and psychology that explored the manifestation of voice during reading. When I began this work, I imagined that all readers were like me—that they experienced the sound of the text as if it were being read aloud in their mind whenever they read silently or were drafting. However, informal polls quickly revealed that not everyone experienced the sound of the text when reading. I realized that in order to understand the relationship between the features of a text and the experience of voice during silent reading, I would need to know the kind of variation possible in inner experiences of reading. I also wondered if the kind of variation that had been described in reading was also present in the inner experience of writing.

INTRODUCTION: GEERTZ'S BLURRED GENRES AND ELBOW'S MYSTERIES

Clifford Geertz published "Blurred Genres: The Reconfiguration of Social Thought" in 1980. It marked the start of a fertile period of interdisciplinarity as the exchange of genres in disciplines like sociology, anthropology, and linguistics created a mixing zone in the borderlands between the "hard sciences" and the humanities. As Dylan Dryer and David Russell note in the collection *Contemporary Perspectives on Cognition and Writing*, Elbow and Sondra Perl were particularly influenced by conversations in phenomenology that entered composition-rhetoric at this time, conversations that extend into the present as mindfulness and neurophenomenology (66).

Questions in composition-rhetoric are grounded in the praxis of teaching writing, and composition scholars' phenomenological stance is one of compassionate curiosity. In Elbow's "Three Mysteries at the Heart of Writing," he is curious about fundamental moves: (1) The generation of ideas, what he calls moving from "no words to words," (2) using Perl's "felt sense" to check whether the language we are producing matches our intention, and (3) crafting "Words that Give," the way that the human voice "entangled" in written text gives the reader access to meaning (Elbow, "Three Mysteries at the Heart of Writing"; Frost 670). As a skilled writer, he claims to find satisfaction in doing these things and is concerned that struggling students cannot access the intrinsic joy of writing: "If we can get students to make good progress on these three mysteries, they are far more likely to enjoy writing and to experience themselves as writers" (22).

When composition scholars read Elbow's phenomenological stance through today's critical lens, they tend to be uncomfortable. Our field's move to the social and deep interrogation of privilege makes us attuned to and rightly suspicious of someone assuming that their own experience can be used as a proxy for others. But, then, what can we do? How can we understand ways of experiencing the world that are different from our own? In the following sections, I will use current conversations in psychology and psycholinguistics to revisit Elbow's mysteries in the hope that a neurophenomenological approach may offer composition-rhetoric a less fraught path into Elbow's mysteries.

"Words that Give"—The Inner Experience of Voice

Russell Hurlburt is a psychologist in the neurophenomenological tradition. In "Can Inner Experience Be Apprehended in High Fidelity? Examining Brain Activation and Experience from Multiple Perspectives," he joins an interdisciplinary team of researchers in demonstrating that a mixed-methods approach with indirect data to supplement self-reports can be an accurate way of describing the inner experience of another human being. He and his colleagues define inner experience as, "phenomena (including seeings, hearings, inner speakings, thoughts, tickles, sensations, feelings, etc.) that naturally present themselves as ongoing and as directly apprehended (as 'before the footlights of consciousness') at particular moments" (Hurlburt et al. 2).

In the study described in this chapter, inner experience is the broad category that defines the phenomena being observed and described. Although we welcomed and described all inner experiences, I asked participants to pay particular attention to inner speech, one category of possible inner experiences. Our interest in audible voice narrowed our attention even further to the experience of inner speech during silent reading. In *Describing Inner Experience? Proponent Meets Skeptic*, Hurlburt reviews the troubled history of inner experience research in psychology and wrestles with a colleague, Eric Schwitzgebel, about the reliability of self-reported inner experience (Hurlburt and Schwitzgebel). Hurlburt developed the Descriptive Experience Sampling (DES) method that I modified for use in my study.

Variation in Inner Experiences of Language. Though notoriously difficult to study, variation in people's inner experience of language has been described in a variety of contexts. Robert Frost, a careful observer of audible voice, noted a difference between "eye readers" and people who clearly hear the sound of the language in inner speech when reading. He suggested that strong writers were ear readers (Barry 66).

In their review of theories of inner speech, Ben Alderson-Day and Charles Fernyhough emphasize Vygotsky's focus on the dialogic qualities of inner speech and his sense that it progresses from external conversations in childhood to internal conversations with the self in maturity (932). Although the developmental aspects of Vygotsky's theory are contested, the observation that individual experiences of inner speech vary is supported by several avenues of research (Alderson-Day and Fernyhough; Perrone-Bertolotti et al.). Researchers studying inner speech within the Vygotskian tradition developed the Varieties of Inner Speech Questionnaire (VISQ) to characterize their participants' everyday experience of inner speech and quantify incidents of these categories within the populations they study (McCarthy-Jones and Fernyhough). In their interdisciplinary review of inner speech, Marcela Perrone-Bertolotti and her colleagues noted evidence of varied experiences during silent reading (228) and concluded their review with a call for integrative research combining quantitative measures of inner speech with first-person, subjective accounts in order to better describe inner speech variation (Perrone-Bertolotti et al. 227–29, 236).

"No Words to Words"—Locating Hayes' Writing Processes in the Inner Landscape

In *Contemporary Perspectives on Cognition and Writing,* John Hayes and the editors describe the flash freeze of our field's understanding of cognition in the 1980s. Cognitive science has come a long way since then. Current models of cognitive activity in the brain are decentralized and dynamic. Rather than the stale image of a programming flowchart, imagine a skilled writer as a concert pianist who fluidly deploys "elementary mental processes" in the language centers of the brain, checks-in with their intended audience, and hopes for applause.

Hayes's "Elementary Processes." In 1981, Linda Flower and Hayes offered their cognitive process theory as an alternative to composition-rhetoric's stage theory, replacing fixed, linear stages with dynamic "elementary mental processes" that they emphasized "may occur at any time in the composing process" (Flower and Hayes 367–68). The field has resisted reducing the act of writing to a limited set of cognitive functions ever since (Bazerman; Pierstorff). The *Framework for Postsecondary Writing* uses the plural, "writing processes," to emphasize the need for students to be flexible in deploying activities like: "invention, research, drafting, sharing with others, revising in response to reviews, and editing" (CWPA et al. 12). These activities are all represented in the "process level" of Hayes's 2012 cognitive process model. However, Hayes reserves the term *writing processes* for four actions (proposing, translating, transcribing, and evaluating) that take place in the inner experience of an individual writer (Hayes and Olinghouse 482–83).

These "elementary mental processes" may be deployed by individual writers during stages such as drafting and revision. But they are not equivalent to them. They are the moments of cognitive action pointed to in Elbow's mysteries, and they manifest in our inner experience as the sensations Hurlburt describes in his definition. In contemporary psycholinguistics and cognitive neuroscience, Hayes's elementary processes can be observed using technologies that capture brain activity like EEG and fMRI. They have been timed, and some happen in milliseconds (Hagoort and Levelt 372). Without training in mindful pedagogies like Perl's "felt sense" curriculum, these fleeting sensations may be outside of the writer's awareness.

The "Inner Landscape." Kristie Fleckenstein's vision of embodied writing suggests resurrecting the body of the writer after the death of the author (Trimbur) and integrating it into the field's sociocultural worldview. Fleckenstein's "view from somewhere" and developmental biologist C. H. Waddington's image of an epigenetic landscape inspired my understanding of the "inner landscape," an imagined topography created by the interplay of biology and life experience. The inner landscape replaces the "tabula rasa" Fleckenstein rejects with a topography that shapes the inner experience of readers and writers (Fleckenstein 281; Gilbert). Attention and working memory are limited resources in this landscape, co-created and constrained by the material conditions and biological development of an individual writer. A corporeal representation of life experience, it holds Kathleen Blake Yancey's "The Prior" and grooved patterns of thought created by the accidental and deliberate cultivation of cognitive habits (Rose, *Audible Voice* 24–36).

An experienced writer is able to communicate their intention to their readers, in part, because they have taken the time to learn what works for them, and in doing so, have become skilled navigators of their own topography. Developing writers learn to improvise writing processes for different rhetorical situations by building a strategic toolkit one situation at a time. In this collection, William J. Macauley, Jr. discusses the way a writing center's individualized project-based learning supports developing writers in understanding the rhetorical situation and identifying, learning, and practicing the strategies they need to succeed. My study suggests that the most effective toolkits are ones that have been custom made for the writer's unique inner landscape.

Hayes's writing processes and the "inner landscape" look at writing from a fundamentally different perspective and scale than composition-rhetoric scholars are used to thinking about. In building a bridge into the sciences, I am compelled to use words in a more precise way and refer to elementary processes that, in theory, all human beings have in common. What we don't have in common is how we deploy and experience these processes. Some people experience the proposer as an inner movement when felt sense (our intention) takes shape and coalesces into the thing we are trying to say. During translation, somehow, the non-verbal becomes verbal, "no words to words." During transcription, we use technology (a pen, keyboard, or Dragon) to transcribe our words into their orthographic form. Hayes's fourth elementary mental process, evaluation, is the act of judging whether the language we are producing matches our intention. Evaluation can be deployed by the writer at any stage. We can evaluate what we are trying to express, possible wording for that concept, or the way we have expressed it (Hayes and Olinghouse 482–84). The results shared in this chapter suggest that some, but not all of us, experience transcription and evaluation as inner speech.

Using "Felt Sense"—The Elementary Process of Evaluating/Monitoring

The dominant cognitive models of spoken and written language production, respectively put forward by Willem Levelt and Hayes, have diverged over time. In his model, Levelt uses the term *monitor* for the "evaluator" and gives inner speech a role in the evaluation process[1] (Postma; Hagoort and Levelt; Levelt). In integrating the two models, I adopt Levelt's term because, in psycholinguistics, the term *monitor* is used in discussions about the relationship between inner speech and this function (Rose, *Can Hayes'*).

Toby Fulwiler explored what he called "the metaphorical notion of voice in writing—some identifying tone or timbre that makes us conscious of the author's presence, that lets us hear the person behind the sentences" (214). He proposed that the voice people claimed to hear in his writing was somehow embedded in the style that emerged as he imagined himself writing to his eighteen-year-old self. To quote Fulwiler,

> I do not remember sitting down and deliberately deciding to find a certain rhythm or tone or timbre or concreteness—yet I know that as I write and revise I am continually reading back to myself my sentences, to see if they sound right, to see if they are clear to me, and to see if they sound like me—the me I would like to have heard. (217)

Monitoring, as I use it here, is a judgment by an individual who, in that moment, draws on the whole of their being to answer Fulwiler's sound check: "Does it sound right?"—yes or no. Fulwiler experiences drafting and revision as activities that involve inner listening and the crafting of sound. The description of his inner experience reflects an almost naturalized understanding of these activities in our field. However, this chapter presents results that reveal diversity in the experience of inner speech, the psycholinguistic term for the voice Fulwiler hears as he writes and revises.

The Study

Audible Voice in Context was an IRB-approved study that systematically described the inner experience of seven participants when reading and writing. The goal of the study was to describe the phenomenology of audible voice in context, the context of a unique individual responding to a specific text. It was designed to explore the following questions: (1) What do readers hear or experience when they read silently? (2) What do writers hear or experience when they write?

Methods

Recruitment and Screening. In this study, I hoped to get a sense of the kinds of variation that might exist in a US classroom. Because diversity in the inner experience of language might be reflected in diversity in vocation and lifestyle, I recruited from Craigslist using an advertisement placed in several categories of "gigs." I then screened interested participants using an extensive background survey. I found two elements of the survey to be particularly useful in selecting for diversity in participants' response to voiced and unvoiced texts: activities that asked the participant to sample their own inner experience and the VISQ.

Out of more than sixty people who responded to the advertisement, seven made it through the enrollment, selection, and interview process. Each participant selected for the in-office session reported inner experiences of language that promised to be unique and, based on the background survey, their experiences of inner speech when reading appeared to range from a clear perception of audible voice to what I later called "slippery" perception.

My training in qualitative research led me to believe that my participants' introspection and descriptions of their inner experience would be more reliable if the participants saw themselves as co-researchers and felt personally invested in the work of the study. Therefore, I sought to recruit participants who were curious about their own inner experience and the experience of voice in writing in general. Recruitment materials and my stance during the interviews were designed to convey the sense that my participants and I were working together to understand a phenomenon that scholars knew little about.

In-Office Session: Interviews, "Implicit Prosody Quiz," and Inner-Experience Sampling. I invited the final set of participants to an in-office session that included two kinds of interviews, an "Implicit Prosody Quiz" ("IP Quiz") quantifying participants' ability to perceive implicit prosody, and a series of activities designed to sample the individual's inner experience of reading and writing.

The initial interview was semi-structured. I asked participants to reflect on their inner experience of language when reading, and I used genres they were familiar with to prompt their responses. I allowed myself to follow-up topics that seemed interesting and encouraged participants to ask questions.

The "IP Quiz" consisted of multiple-choice questions developed from previously published psycholinguistic materials. It was administered using software that recorded participants' response times. At the close of the quiz, I turned on the recorder and prompted participants to talk about their experience taking the quiz.

Finally, I led participants through a series of inner-experience-sampling activities. I presented them with a text on the computer and interrupted their reading with a beep randomly timed to go off after approximately one to two minutes. I prompted them with an open question: "What were you experiencing just before the beep?" and recorded their response. If they didn't mention the sound of language, I prompted them further with specific questions about sound.

Once they exhausted their memory of the details of their initial experience, we went through a three-page series of follow-up questions.

For the writing activity, I followed the reading experience-sampling procedure, but I asked participants to "write a letter to a friend" rather than read a text. I gave them unlimited time to think about the letter, and I started the timer when they began to type.

Compiling Descriptions of Participants' Inner Experience and Noting Broad Trends. Hurlburt's guidelines for DES suggest that my participants' descriptions of their experience immediately after the beep would be more accurate than their reflection on past experiences during the initial interview (Hurlburt and Schwitzgebel). I, therefore, used data from participants' immediate responses to form a core, initial description. I then "kneaded in" material from the background survey and initial interview and flagged moments when that material contradicted the core description. The complete results of the study (published online and excerpted below) include an overall summary of each participant's inner experience of language during reading and writing presented in the context of their lived experience as well as the text of the readings with examples of each participants' response to that reading.

When the summary descriptions for each participant were complete, I returned to the original transcripts and highlighted moments during the interviews that I found particularly interesting or thought might reflect broader trends in the data. I formalized those highlights into a coding scheme, coded the transcripts, and then recorded the presence or absence of coded phenomena in the experience of each participant during each activity. I then compiled this information and used it to describe broad trends in the final chapter of the study.

Summary of Results and Subsequent Support

My central questions were: What did my participants hear or experience when they read silently and what did they hear or experience as they wrote? During the in-office sessions, each participant heard some manifestation of audible voice at some point in the study. However, there was significant variation in the quality of these experiences. The experience of audible voice varied from reading to reading and when writing. Each participant's experience of inner speech and audible voice was distinct, with unique characteristics connected with their individual contexts.

Participants heard two kinds of audible voice when reading silently, one that they clearly identified as their own voice and one that they experienced as a distinct persona. In the study, I referred to this second category as a "personality voice." Personality voices were variable and seemed to be dynamic phenomena that were actively modified by the reader in response to cues from the text. They touched on qualities described by Elbow's categories of "dramatic voice" (xxviii) and "recognizable voice" (xxx) as well as "audible voice" (Rose 221–39). Participants also reported audible voice with mixed qualities.

Table 1. Guide to Participants and Results

Participant	Vocation	"IP Quiz" Score	Condensed VISQ Factor Score
Paula	poet, novelist	27	1.6
Maja	ESL teacher, aspiring novelist	26	1.6
Tom	physics student, pianist	24	5
Nancy	software engineer	20	3.2
Mark	jazz musician	20	3.8
Skyler	literature major, delivery driver	20	4.2
Gwen	editor, odd jobs	17	5.4

The published study is titled *Audible Voice in Context* because the mixed-methods approach made it possible to describe individual inner experiences of language within the context of participants' lived experience and the context of individual texts. This perspective was the primary goal of the study, so I did not aim for the large number of participants and representative sampling of the population required to rigorously describe broader quantitative trends. However, a few of the trends in the study were so clear that my scientific mentors in this work felt it would be misleading to leave them out.

In particular, my participants' ability to perceive prosody in inner speech (as reflected in their "IP Quiz" Scores) was negatively correlated with the extent to which they reported characteristics of condensed inner speech on the VISQ questionnaire. In other words, two independent quantitative measures supported my claim that the set of participants selected for my study reflect a spectrum where participants on one end of the spectrum clearly perceive the sound of inner speech when reading and writing while participants on the other end of the spectrum experience something closer to Vygotsky's description of condensed inner speech.

Tom was a notable exception to this trend. He was remarkable in that his ability to perceive prosody in inner speech was average while he reported the highest measure for condensed inner speech in the study. This exception suggests that this study only reveals the tip of the iceberg, and there are many mysteries yet to discover when it comes to people's inner experience of language.

Although the spectrum of ability to perceive the sound of inner speech roughly held true when writing, participants across the board seemed to find it easier to access the sound of the language of the text when writing than when reading. The experiences they reported during writing were less variable. All participants in the study, with prompting, reported hearing inner speech at the moment they began typing the words. When they heard this drafting or typing voice, they experienced it in their own voice as if they were saying the words, an experience that I categorized as the identity voice when reading. In this chapter, I have included excerpts from participants' inner experiences when reading a voiced text and when writing. Reading 1 was a first-person letter from a collection of letters written by soldiers on Armistice Day. It was chosen by Elbow as an example of a text with clear written intonation units. The complete descriptions and sample texts are published and available online (Rose).

Subsequent Support. I developed the "Implicit Prosody Quiz" with psycholinguists Mara Breen and Chuck Clifton to provide an indirect measure of my participants' abilities to perceive implicit prosody in inner speech. Sharon Geva and Elizabeth Warburton subsequently developed a "test battery" using a similar approach. Their study supports what I describe here: that there is variation in the ability to perceive implicit prosody in the general population, that this variation is quantifiable, and that this measurable variation may impact readers' experience of silent reading. Since I published *Audible Voice in Context* in 2015, studies using other methods have supported the broad categories of voice described in this study (e.g., Brouwers et al.; Alderson-Day et al.).

DIVERSITY IN INNER EXPERIENCES OF WRITING

In this section, I highlight results that seem most relevant to the teaching of writing. The excerpts discussed below illustrate the diversity in the inner experiences of my participants with a particular focus on variation in the inner experience of monitoring. I also note variations in participants' affect and flow. In the writing excerpts, I mark the text generated by participants during the writing activity with a box. I start with Paula.

> Dear R.,
>
> Thanks for your latest letter with the new poems and drawings. Sorry it's taken me so long to send the art paper you requested. I've been busy sending my novel to contests and preparing for my poetry book launch, which went well despite not having the books from the printer! I would love to send you a signed copy, but I don't know if the guards will let it through. Can you receive packages addressed from "<her company>" or should I send through Amazon only?

Figure 1. Paula's written text.

Paula's Evaluative Mode. A skilled and experienced reader and writer with a high "IP Quiz" score, Paula responded in a way that was similar to Fulwiler's description of his writing process. At the moment of the beep, Paula was in, as she put it, an "evaluative mode": "I was wondering if my sentences had too many, this or that, this and that. So, I was listening back through the sentence I was writing and thinking, should I put a comma there, should I make that two sentences?" Note that, like Fulwiler, she was reviewing her sentences and listening for a particular quality. She described a multilayered writing experience: "But, you know, so I was hearing it, I wasn't really looking up when I was typing. I was typing it and sort of hearing it in my mind. But then I'll sort of look and listen at the same time when I look back over it and see if it sounds syntactically interesting." Paula also described hearing the sound of the words as she was typing. Her checking for language that she called "syntactically interesting" was intertwined with inner speech while typing. In terms of Hayes's 2012 cognitive model, the inner experience she describes could include the goal setting, reading, and evaluating functions as well as the resource of the text-written-so-far. Inner speech appeared to be engaged as she was actively typing and while reviewing and monitoring text she had just written.

Skyler's Experience of Condensed Inner Speech when Monitoring. A participant whose "IP Quiz" score was low and condensed-inner-speech score high, Skyler was consistent in reporting an on/off quality in their[2] experience of inner speech when reading and writing. They had completed a two-year degree in literature, art, and music and seemed to be quite sensitive to written style. Their life experience suggested that they had a passionate love for literature but experienced some challenge in accessing reading (though not writing). At the time of the study, Skyler worked as a delivery driver and was able to listen to audiobooks for a significant portion of the day. During the interviews, Skyler mentioned using audiobooks in high school to support their reading and also mentioned that, when writing at home, they often read their writing aloud:

> Dear X,
>
> I've spent the last couple weeks making a list in my mind of the things you've done wrong. I know you can tell at least vaguely that I'm making this list because you know me really well. Let me get started. You were running out the door and were in a rush, so you threw your yogurt WITH the spoon in the garbage? Who does that?

Figure 2. Skyler's written text.

At the beep, Skyler was laughing and said they were considering three possible ways of expressing something all at the same time:

> SKYLER. I was thinking about how to like say three things at once without forgetting anything and trying to choose . . . what to write, like which of the three things to write.
>
> AIRLIE. So, like three ways of phrasing one idea or three topics or like three—
>
> SKYLER. Three ways of saying the same thing.
>
> AIRLIE. Okay. And how would you describe the way you hold that information—
>
> SKYLER. I feel like, like I said before, I don't think in sentences. I think in fragments. And it's almost like those fragments are images and I know right away like at the same time, like I have [it] very clear in my mind and then I have to figure out how to express it. It's, it's more like I think in like feelings or like, like little movements that are very abstract, like it's, like I don't know it's hard to talk about because I don't think I, I don't think it's like purely visual but it's also not sound. It's just something else . . . it's kind of spatial.

According to their reports, Skyler's experience evaluating potential language took place in a nonverbal mode. The monitor was still active. Skyler was still running potential phrasing by a judge; but sound seemed to have little to do with it. Skyler's description matches descriptions of someone whose inner speech is condensed, approaching Vygotsky's "thinking in pure meanings" (Alderson-Day and Fernyhough 932–33).

Skyler reported using images as prompts when drafting, and their thinking flowed from image to image:

> So, I was writing about how my roommate and friend, she was like in a rush and she just threw her spoon in the garbage. And so, I had an image of the yogurt and the spoon in the garbage that I took out of the garbage. So, there's that. And it was just like in my kitchen, the trash can. And then I had an image of myself earlier today thinking because like I've wanted to write something about this. So, I had an image of myself earlier just on a walk thinking about how I wanted to do this. And it was almost like a, like above my head like watching myself walk. And then the other images were of my friend reacting to me and me like being able to tell that she kind of knows how I feel.

Later, I prompted Skyler, asking if they heard sound at any point when writing: "Did I hear anything? No, I don't think so." At this point, Skyler started rereading what they wrote, and I commented on this:

> SKYLER. Because I'm just trying, I'm trying to remind myself of how I was thinking. I mean . . . I heard like my voice more than when I do when I'm reading. But it comes and goes, so.
>
> AIRLIE. So, as you're looking at what you wrote now, would you say any place that you think was louder than the other or like more, more accessible than the other?
>
> SKYLER. There was at the beginning like when I started writing, like the first words I was kind of writing.

Overall, as with Paula, at the beep, Skyler appeared to be in a moment of evaluation. Skyler also described an experience of drafting and appeared to be a fluid writer. But, unlike Paula, in each case, their inner experience of writing was dominated by experiences other than sound. At the beep immediately after reading 1, Skyler described struggling to focus and had paused, trying to imagine what the voice of the speaker sounded like. These descriptions, along with the quantitative data, support the idea that Skyler's experience of inner speech during reading and writing is "slippery," that their inner experience of language tends to be non-verbal during reading and writing. Skyler's description of monitoring suggests that the monitoring function may not rely on consciously processing the sound of language.

Tom's Vivid Imagery and Sparse Words when rafting. At the time of the study, Tom was a twenty-three-year-old undergraduate majoring in earth systems and physics with minors in music and geology. He plays piano semi-professionally. Vivid, multisensory imagery was a striking feature in his inner experience throughout the study. However, he said writing was a weak point for him. He wrote very little during the week, most of it physics homework:

> Dear X, How is your semester going? I know that we've only spoken a couple times

Figure 3. Tom's written text.

At the beep, Tom was deeply immersed in an image, a moment in time that he had spent with the friend he was writing to. Tom theorized that he needed this vivid, multi-sense image to "get enough information" to start writing. The contrast between this highly developed image (it incorporated kinesthetic sensations, weather, conversation, and visual imagery) and the sparse words it prompted was striking. It took some effort on my part to disengage him from his experience of that scene, kind of like waking someone up from a dream. When I did, though, he made a clear distinction between hearing himself saying the sound of the words when typing and hearing the sound of his friend's voice in the image. In terms of flow, it was interesting to compare Skyler's sequence of images with Tom's highly developed single image.

Tom's description of a person whose monitor was on overdrive seems familiar from my experience working with students:

> TOM. I heard my voice vaguely as I was like trying to find the words to, to say.
>
> AIRLIE. Okay, so talk just a little bit about that, yeah.
>
> TOM. It's mainly just me like trying to, I'm trying to put together these thoughts so that I could, whenever I write to people, like in, in letter form, I try to be as concise as possible. But it takes time for me to do that and so I try to do that but, you know, like I, I said before, I'm not satisfied like how . . . I . . . actually like pressed backspace several times over the course of

the writing experiment because I'm like, oh, no, that's not what I wanted to say. I wanted to say this—

* * *

TOM. My own voice, it's, it's unsure. It's, it's there, it's definitely there but it's just unsure. It's just me repeating the same thing over and over again. It's just each time was a little bit better than the last but it's, it's kind of like the think, think-before-you-talk type of deal.

AIRLIE. Uh-huh [affirmative].

TOM. Or, or say like you have something very difficult to say to someone and you want to like word it the right way.

AIRLIE. Yeah, yeah.

TOM. Except this is in writing and it's not something difficult but it's just, just because it's in writing, I need to word it the right way.

In his description of rehearsing language, Tom's process was similar to Paula's and Fulwiler's descriptions of saying the words and checking them against some ideal. However, there was a noticeable difference in affect between Tom versus Paula or Skyler, and his experience of the sound of the language was "vague." His attention seemed to be absorbed in his vivid imagery.

Mark's Free Style. Mark offers a different experience of monitoring and affect. A professional drummer and jazz enthusiast, Mark resisted layers or blocks to the flow of experience and his enjoyment when ideas and associations flowed freely was an important theme throughout our time together. He was trained in speed typing, wrote regularly, and was an experienced freewriter. In describing his inner experience, he used language almost word for word from typical freewriting instructions (Elbow, *Vernacular Eloquence* 148).

Dear C.,

Whats up man, hows Berkeee. That place is crazy. I can't believe you're going there. When are you coming home, I want to hang out. We should jam soon. I've been playing a lot of guitar and you need to give me some free lessons. How is your

---

Figure 4. Mark's written text.

At the beep, he was at a pause, a nonverbal sensation as he was trying to decide where to go next: "Yeah, it was like, what now, what now?" When I asked him to back up a little and think about when he had been drafting, he said he heard his voice, like he was speaking to his friend:

> AIRLIE: So just like you're kind of flowing out?
>
> MARK: Yeah.
>
> AIRLIE: And you kept talking about you were speaking to him, so like—
>
> MARK: Yeah, it was like I was talking to him directly. It wasn't, I don't know. I guess I, there wasn't any kind of analysis going on of what I was writing. I wasn't worried about the words or how they flowed together or like even if I spelt the words right at all. I wasn't worried about my grammar.

He described the process of drafting:

> AIRLIE: Okay. And so in terms of the sound during, in your mind, during the writing process, like did you hear anything?
>
> MARK: I guess I heard my voice.
>
> AIRLIE: Yeah.
>
> MARK: It was, yeah, it was like whatever I was thinking, I thought everything I wrote was a thought that I had had and like it was about like, it took me about as much time to, to get the sentence out as it does to get the whole thought out. It was like, I'll think the whole thing and I'll, I'll catch up with the, with the writing and then once I finish typing it, I'll have a new thought.
>
> AIRLIE: Okay.
>
> MARK: And then write that thought and then have a new thought and write that.

Summary of the Inner Experiences of Writing. Just as Fulwiler checks his sentences for three things—"to see if they sound right, to see if they are clear to me, and to see if they sound like me"—my participants describe focusing on particular things as they monitor their language when drafting. However, they do not all use sound to do so. Also, where Paula, Skyler, and Tom described monitoring the language they were producing, Mark talked about not monitoring his language. Freewriting is a practice that seeks to decrease deployment of the monitoring function, so Mark's experience with freewriting might be at play in this difference in the things they attend to.

Conscious Steering During Reading

In this section, I highlight two reports of steering during reading because these moments offer a glimpse into the agency of skilled readers and the kind of strategies for navigating diverse inner landscapes that may be possible in reading and writing. When coding for broad trends, I noticed that both Paula and Gwen described consciously shifting their attention from what their "IP Quiz" scores suggest might be their dominant inner experience of language to one that appears to be more difficult for them to access.

Paula Steers into Image in Reading 1. Paula's reading was driven by her quest for information, and she was drawn to the sound of the language, sound that she heard effortlessly. Sound-crafted language grabbed her attention. Paula also had a vivid visual imagination. However, to access it, she said she needed to take the time to slow down and build up the visual image. She talked about her experience with Reading 1:

> I have to kind of make a conscious effort to stop and visualize when I, when I read and not miss that because I'm so impatient. So around the part where he starts describing his first flight over the lines, then I start saying, okay, he's going to describe something visual now. I should stop and slow down and try to picture it before jumping on to the next bit of information.

Her experience of the male speaker's voice painting a picture of the landscape was unmarked in her description, effortless, and accessing a visual image of the landscape took conscious steering of her attention.

Gwen Steers into Sound in Reading 1. At the beep, Gwen was in editing mode, perhaps an easy mindset to fall into since she works as an editor. Note that she said, "I felt" and "I sensed"—not "I heard":

> I felt in the second paragraph, maneuvered was spelled wrong but then I sensed, so it raised a flag for me, and then I felt that

that was obviously probably a British spelling. And then also and then I confirmed it in that same paragraph with meter, and so I had kind of paused there and was mentally, I guess just going again with a feeling like it's okay. It's okay to keep on reading because that is, that is correct. And then I went back to reading. So, when I had stopped at those points, there was no words and I was sensing if things were correct. And then when I felt that things were okay, I kept on speaking out loud. I really, in this piece, I didn't get too many visual pictures. I, I have lived in Europe for a couple of years and so I had a somewhat inner picture of what flying over that land would feel like, and I, and that was kind of, kind of a, a really barely visual, visual that I had gotten as I was reading where, you know, the words weren't, weren't really doing anything. But I was kind of thinking of being nostalgic for Europe's, imagining what it would be like to fly over the land.

In her shift from editing mode to reading, Gwen seemed to move from a nonverbal experience of language to one of inner speech that she called "speaking aloud." This move was similar to what happened during the "IP Quiz" interview, when she talked about steering herself to tune-in to the sound to pay attention when reading directions and when she was required to focus on the sound by a problem on the "IP Quiz." In each case, she experienced inner speech as her voice, "saying it in my head."

Summary of Steering During Reading. Paula and Gwen's scores represent extremes in my participants' ability to perceive implicit prosody, and both work with text for a living. So, it makes sense that they have developed strategies for swimming upstream in the topography of their inner landscapes. Paula effortlessly perceives sound but slows down to access imagery. Gwen's inner experience is often occupied with nonverbal experiences of meaning and feeling, but she is able to tune into the sound of the language when she needs it to complete a task. This willful steering of attention is congruent with Chafe's discussion of attention during the flow of reading (53–54).

CONCLUSION: IMPLICATIONS FOR THE CLASSROOM AND WRITING CENTER

The participants who shared their experiences of reading and writing in this study all came to my office with a unique inner landscape. The questions I asked were important to several of them because they sensed that their inner experience of language was unusual, and it had created successes or challenges for them that they were trying to understand. Their stories of reading and writing in and out of the classroom suggest that some inner experiences of language are more compatible with success than others. They also suggest that a person's inner landscape is flexible, that whatever landscape life has shaped in us, we are capable of developing new habits of thought and adopting strategies that can help us navigate the world of language in the ways we aspire to.

Skyler, in their use of audiobooks for reading and speaking aloud when revising writing, seems to be an example of a person who has found ways to augment a "slippery" experience of inner speech. Despite being instructed not to, the two highest scorers on the "IP Quiz" nodded their head and shaped words with their mouth while taking the quiz, presumably supplementing their perception of implicit prosody with subvocalization. Both of these techniques are promoted by Elbow in *Vernacular Eloquence* to sharpen the writer's perception of written intonation when revising.

This study also suggests that people teaching in composition classrooms probably cluster on one end of the spectrum of the inner experiences described here, and therefore our assumptions about teaching and writing may rely on limited experiences of generating and crafting language. As instructors, the onus is on us to create an environment in which all students have the tools they need to satisfy their ambitions with language.

NOTES

1. The "evaluator" function in the 2012 revision of the Flower and Hayes model is analogous to the action described by "monitor" in Levelt's 1989 model of speech production. This may be confusing for readers familiar with Flower and Hayes's original use of the term that referred to the writer's executive functioning (Flower and Hayes 374). (See Alamargot and Chanquoy pp. 148–50 for an in-depth discussion.)

2. Skyler uses they/them pronouns and asked me to do the same when publishing this work.

Works Cited

Alamargot, Denis, and Lucile Chanquoy. *Through Models of Writing*. Kluwer Academic Publishers, 2001.

Alderson-Day, Ben, et al. "Uncharted Features and Dynamics of Reading: Voices, Characters, and Crossing of Experiences." *Consciousness and Cognition*, vol. 49, 2017, pp. 98–109.

Alderson-Day, Ben, and Charles Fernyhough. "Inner Speech: Development, Cognitive Functions, Phenomenology, and Neurobiology." *Psychological Bulletin*, vol. 141, 2015, pp. 931–65.

Barry, Elaine, editor. *Robert Frost on Writing*. Rutgers UP, 1973.

Bazerman, Charles. "What Does a Model Model? And for Whom?" *Educational Psychologist*, vol. 53, no. 4, 2018, pp. 301–18.

Brouwers, Vincent P. et al. "Pristine Inner Experience While Silent Reading." *Journal of Consciousness Studies*, vol. 25, nos. 3–4, 2018, p. 29–54.

Chafe, Wallace. *Discourse, Consciousness, and Time*. U of Chicago P, 1994.

Council of Writing Program Administrators, National Council of Teachers of English, and National Writing Project. *Framework for Success in Postsecondary Writing*. CWPA, NCTE, and NWP, 2011 wpacouncil.org/aws/CWPA/asset_manager/get_file/350201?ver=505. Accessed 1 Feb. 2020.

Dryer, Dylan B., and David R. Russell. "Attending to Phenomenology: Rethinking Cognition and Reflection in North American Writing Studies." *Contemporary Perspectives on Cognition and Writing*, edited by Patricia Portanova, et al., Perspectives on Writing, WAC Clearinghouse, UP of Colorado, 2017, pp. 57–76. wac.colostate.edu/books/perspectives/cognition/. Accessed 7 Mar. 2021.

Elbow, Peter. Introduction. "About Voice and Writing." *Landmark Essays on Voice and Writing*, edited by Peter Elbow, Hermagoras, 1994, pp. xi–xlvii.

—. "Three Mysteries at the Heart of Writing." *Composition Studies in the New Millennium: Rereading the Past, Rewriting the Future*, edited by Lynn Bloom et al., Southern Illinois UP, 2003, pp. 10–27.

—. *Vernacular Eloquence: What Speech Can Bring to Writing.* Oxford UP, 2012.

Fleckenstein, Kristie S. "Writing Bodies: Somatic Mind." *College English*, vol. 61, no. 3, 1999, pp. 281–306.

Flower, Linda, and John R. Hayes. "A Cognitive Process Theory of Writing." *College Composition and Communication*, vol. 32, no. 4, 1981, pp. 365–387.

Frost, Robert. *Collected Poems, Prose and Plays.* Library of America, 1995.

Geertz, Clifford. "Blurred Genres: The Refiguration of Social Thought." *The American Scholar*, 1980, pp. 165–79.

Geva, Sharon, and Elizabeth A. Warburton. "A Test Battery for Inner Speech Functions." *Archives of Clinical Neuropsychology*, vol. 34, no. 1, 2018, pp. 97–113.

Gilbert, Scott F. "Epigenetic Landscaping: Waddington's Use of Cell Fate Bifurcation Diagrams." *Biology and Philosophy*, vol. 6, no. 2, 1991, pp. 135–54.

Hagoort, Peter, and Willem J. M. Levelt. "The Speaking Brain." *Science*, vol. 326, 2009, pp. 372–73.

Hayes, John R., and Natalie G. Olinghouse. "Can Cognitive Writing Models Inform the Design of the Common Core State Standards?" *The Elementary School Journal*, vol. 115, no. 4, 2015, pp. 480–97.

Hurlburt, Russell T., et al. "Can Inner Experience Be Apprehended in High Fidelity? Examining Brain Activation and Experience from Multiple Perspectives." *Frontiers in Psychology*, vol. 8, Jan. 2017.

Hurlburt, Russell T., and Eric Schwitzgebel. *Describing Inner Experience? Proponent Meets Skeptic.* MIT P, 2007.

Levelt, Willem J. M. "CH12: Self-Monitoring and Self-Repair." *Speaking: From Intention to Articulation*, MIT P, 1989.

McCarthy-Jones, Simon, and Charles Fernyhough. "The Varieties of Inner Speech: Links between Quality of Inner Speech and Psychopathological Variables in a Sample of Young Adults." *Consciousness and Cognition*, vol. 20, no. 4, 2011, pp. 1586–93.

Perl, Sondra. *Felt Sense: Writing with the Body.* Heinemann, 2004.

Perrone-Bertolotti, Marcela, et al. "What Is That Little Voice inside My Head? Inner Speech Phenomenology, Its Role in Cognitive Performance, and Its Relation to Self-Monitoring." *Behavioural Brain Research*, vol. 261, 2014, pp. 220–39.

Pierstorff, Don K. "Response to Linda Flower and John R. Hayes, 'A Cognitive Process Theory of Writing.'" *College Composition and Communication*, vol. 34, no. 2, 1983, p. 217.

Portanova, Patricia, et al, editors. *Contemporary Perspectives on Cognition and Writing*. Perspectives on Writing, The WAC Clearinghouse and UP of Colorado, 2017. wac.colostate.edu/books/perspectives/cognition/. Accessed 1 Sept. 2020.

Postma, Albert. "Detection of Errors During Speech Production: A Review of Speech Monitoring Models." *Cognition*, vol. 77, 2000, pp. 97–131.

Rose, Airlie Sattler. *Audible Voice in Context*. 2015. University of Massachusetts Amherst, PhD dissertation.

—. "Can Hayes' Evaluator Follow Instructions? Freewriting as a Model System to Explore Monitoring During Writing." Writing Research Across Borders III. International Society for the Advancement of Writing Research. Universite Paris Ouest Nanterre La Defense, Paris, France. February 19-22, 2014. Poster presentation.

Trimbur, John. "Agency and the Death of the Author: A Partial Defense of Modernism." *JAC*, vol. 20, no. 2, 2000, pp. 283–98.

Vygotsky, Lev. *Thought and Language*. MIT P, 1962.

II Classroom-Level Engagement

4 Recall, Reframe, Reflect: Threshold Concept Pedagogy and Metacognitive Practice in First-Year Writing

Gita DasBender

In the past several years, composition scholars have begun to pay serious attention to threshold concepts as a broad theoretical framework for understanding student learning and its implications for writing transfer. As the discipline engages in efforts to identify threshold concepts in the field of writing (Adler-Kassner and Wardle; Wardle and Downs) and explores the relevance of such concepts to writing across the disciplines (Adler-Kassner et al.), there is increasing interest in ways of framing, situating, and establishing the declarative content of threshold concepts in first-year writing (FYW) and beyond. Linda Adler-Kassner's query in the Call for Program Proposals for the 2016 Conference on College Composition and Communication—"what are the core, or threshold, concepts of writing as a discipline? What . . . roles [do] these concepts play?"—not only highlights the field's growing focus on concept building and identification but encourages scholars to investigate how these concepts might function within particular instructional settings. Because threshold concepts are "more readily identified within disciplinary contexts where there is a relatively greater degree of consensus on what constitutes a body of knowledge" (Meyer and Land, "Introduction" 15), it becomes critical for the discipline of composition to develop a distinctive threshold concepts model of disciplinary knowledge that contributes to writing pedagogy and practices.

Although Elizabeth Wardle and Doug Downs organized the second edition of their textbook *Writing about Writing* around five sequenced threshold concepts, this chapter proposes a modified framework that integrates three of those concepts that are central to the development of writing knowledge in a FYW course. In Wardle and Downs's terms, they are: (1) Literacies: "*writing performance is informed by prior literacy experiences* . . . that our reading and writing past will shape our reading and writing present"; (2) Rhetoric: "good *writing is dependent on the situation, readers, and uses its being created for*"; and (3) Processes: "writing is *knowledge-making*, that making knowledge requires ongoing and repeating processes, and that *writing is not perfectible*" (vii). The network of relationships that exists among learner, learning situation, curriculum, and instructional methods is fairly complex as it is, and when writing concepts with threshold features are introduced, they can possibly further complicate teacher understanding and classroom practice. Because the curricular implementation of threshold concepts has to be accompanied with robust teacher training and development, this chapter emphasizes the construction of a threshold concept model and writing instruction that is directly informed by it. The proposed threshold framework articulates a critical relationship among the concepts: that development of writing knowledge rests upon a recognition of the constant dialogic interplay between the learner's awareness of prior writing experiences and new understandings of rhetorical and procedural knowledge. It also explains a fundamental premise underlying threshold concepts: that learning constitutes looking back at what was learned before (Recall), looking forward and reorienting oneself to what is to be learned (Reframe), and looking inward to make sense of both (Reflect). In this sense, this framework represents a three-dimensional model of learning, highlighting the multifaceted and metacognitive nature of threshold concept acquisition.

In considering ways of integrating the threshold approach in a composition course, this chapter focuses on three interrelated areas of inquiry: (1) Designing a threshold framework representing the relationship between stages of learning and threshold concepts in writing, (2) Applying the framework directly to writing instruction, and (3) Reporting on student responses to metacognitive tasks set up within the threshold framework. Aligned with the areas of inquiry are the following goals: to promote and engage writing-based threshold concepts in a FYW course; to enhance the value of threshold concepts as a curricular and pedagogical tool; to promote student awareness of writing knowledge through metacognitive tasks that advance writing transfer; and to situate threshold concepts within the growing body of disciplinary knowledge in composition studies.

Theoretical Background

A commonsense view of the enterprise of learning leans towards conceptions of straight-forward, linear, and mostly predictable pathways on which a learner proceeds, unhampered by obstacles, towards a clearly demarcated goal: the acquisition of new knowledge. Since their 2003 landmark publication "Threshold Concepts and Troublesome Knowledge," Jan Meyer and Ray Land have toiled over research in threshold concepts to reveal the complexities involved in the uptake of new knowledge by introducing a transformative model of learning that disrupts traditional perceptions of how people learn. Their early work on threshold concepts in economics opened the floodgates for an upsurge in scholarly investigation, intellectual inquiry, and research into the intersections of disciplinary knowledge, the nature of learning and engagement, and innovative pedagogical and instructional framework designs that contribute to new ways of understanding knowledge processing and transfer.

Meyer and Land's definition of threshold concepts as "akin to a portal, opening up a new and previously inaccessible way of thinking about something" ("Introduction" 3), establishes that fields of inquiry are grounded in foundational disciplinary concepts that perform a threshold function. In this sense, threshold concepts are aligned with boundary-crossing, representing moments of new understanding and intellectual discovery. However, they need to be differentiated from core concepts within disciplines in that they are "transformative" and engender a perceptible change in the learner's understanding of a previously perplexing idea. They are also "irreversible," becoming entrenched in the learner's knowledge repertoire, and "integrative," as they reveal the "previously hidden interrelatedness of something" (7). Also, as David Perkins notes, these conceptual abstractions are often challenging to novice learners and may be "troublesome" given that threshold concept knowledge appears in forms that are inert, ritualized, alien or tacit, and even counter-intuitive (Perkins, "Constructivism") and requires crossing over from a place of relative comfort and familiarity to new realms of knowledge and understanding that are unfamiliar, disorienting, and certain to produce a sense of instability in the learner.

At first glance, threshold concepts seem to be foundational disciplinary ideas and conceptual content—a product that a learner has to comprehend, and without which a learner cannot move forward to more advanced stages of learning. This "product" approach, tied to specific knowledge and content, is best understood when threshold concepts are associated with what Guy Walker calls a "particular state of expert knowledge" and the integration of cognitive ideas about knowledge and understanding (248). At the same time, as Meyer and Land have argued, threshold concepts are also aligned with transformative learning processes that produce "a significant shift in the perception of a subject" ("Introduction" 7) and can have a profound and irreversible effect on the learner. Thus, they can be conceived as both product and process, not only disciplinary content but also the procedural mechanisms by which such content is grasped, highlighting the essential pedagogical relevance of threshold concepts to learning in all settings. Given their obvious pedagogical implications, threshold concepts research has generated widespread inquiry into how these disciplinary concepts function in the academic sphere. In "Facilitating the Academy through Threshold Concepts and Troublesome Knowledge," Land makes clear that the thresholds approach "is now being used as a curriculum design tool, a mode of pedagogical research and an approach for the professional development of new academics" (26). It is also rapidly contributing to our "understandings of transformation, liminality, and students' experience of difficulty" (26), which are associated with the processes of threshold crossing. These innovative uses of disciplinary concepts with threshold features indicate the vast potential of threshold concepts application to writing studies.

A threshold concepts-based framework can be valuable to writing instructors as an initial stage of what Land and Meyer ("Dynamics") call a "*framework of engagement* that teachers may wish to construct to provide opportunities for students to gain important conceptual understandings and hence gain richer and more complex insights into the subjects they are studying" (75). Given that the framework maps stages of learning and students' encounters with what Perkins calls "troublesome knowledge," this chapter focuses on the association of threshold concepts with the state of liminality identified by Meyer and Land as "a suspended state in which understanding approximates to a kind of mimicry or lack of authenticity" ("Introduction"16). The liminal space that learners enter as they are introduced to threshold-based instruction is one where they engage with unfamiliar writing concepts and tasks representing varying levels of difficulty that pose serious challenges. As students begin their FYW course, prior literacy experiences inform students' understanding of writing and provide a space of security and perhaps confidence—a pre-liminal space defined by stable understandings. But they encounter shakier ground when introduced to specific threshold notions, such as *rhetoric* or *processes* that represent particular ways of thinking about how writing functions, and struggle with these notions during a liminal phrase where there is active and dynamic but unsettling engagement with new aspects of writing knowledge. At this stage, as Ray Land points out, it is critical for learners to "engage with and manipulate conceptual materials i.e. the physical means of describing, discussing, and exploring concepts" ("Facilitating" 25). Undoubtedly, this has significant implications for classroom practice.

Building a Threshold Concept-Based Instructional Framework

As threshold concept scholarship continues to flourish, for writing scholars and educators two important areas of consideration emerge that draw upon the current theories and ideas being proposed by threshold concept researchers. The first is the emphasis on curricular modification and the application of threshold features to pedagogy that can have a significant impact on direct instruction in the classroom. As noted in the preface of Land, Meyer, and Michael Flanagan's collection *Threshold Concepts in Practice*, a threshold concepts-based framework has garnered a great deal of attention and appeal because "it has explanatory and actionable potential . . . can provide a fresh analytic discourse and vocabulary to be applied to new contexts of practice . . . and addresses mainstream pedagogical and curricular issues" (xii). At a more granular level this refers to what Land and Meyer see as a conscious employment of "threshold concepts structurally as the foci for learning tasks at programme level" (75), which requires directly embedding such concepts into the course curriculum.

The direction, then, is toward developing strategies for applying disciplinary concepts and ways of thinking to teaching materials, establishing specific language for their delivery, and ensuring that these are executed with the larger course goals in mind. The second consideration is Land's call for "the need for *dynamic forms of assessment* which can capture a learner's progression through the liminal phase at different points" (27) and that are aligned with—and a critical component of—the curricular redesign and streamlined course content elements of such a framework. In the field of composition, from Downs and Liane Robertson's perspective, "teaching threshold concepts can help us achieve FYC's dual mission of helping students reconceive writing and transfer their learning to new contexts" (113). This points to the value and promise of establishing a framework that explicitly engages with threshold concepts in composition as a means of furthering writing knowledge and its transfer to writing situations beyond the writing course.

Additionally, Glynis Cousin has argued that the crossing of conceptual thresholds entails an ontological shift in the learner—from perceiving the self as learner to the self as "knower"—and thus, metacognition and reflection play a critical role in learning transfer where, as Kathleen Blake Yancey has aptly noted, "reflection becomes a habit of mind, one that transforms" (12). Thus, actively supporting and engaging metacognition as a habit of mind through writing activities built around specific threshold concepts, such as those related to rhetorical and epistemological knowledge, opens up opportunities for investigating the effect of prior literacy experiences on new writing experiences and on the transfer of writing knowledge. This chapter also presents and examines reflective writing tasks that, when set up strategically during specific writing assignments and as post-assignment meta-writing responses, can help learners probe into prior writing experiences; express their growing knowledge and understanding of rhetorical concepts such as situation, audience, exigence, and purpose; examine the process-oriented nature of writing; and, most importantly, articulate what they are learning about writing. The instructional element of this threshold-oriented framework makes it possible for instructors to review and assess students' reflective commentary to see how learners progress through the liminal space and to investigate emerging transformative qualities or new understandings of writing concepts evident in the meta-writing responses. Analysis of samples of reflective writing demonstrates the difficulties students encounter as they engage with the concepts in the framework, and findings suggest that their struggle is in itself indicative of a transformative process as they continue to develop as writers within new learning environments that present linguistic, rhetorical, and ultimately, ontological challenges.

THE STUDY AND METHODS

In the 2015 fall semester, I launched an IRB-approved research study on threshold concepts in a first-year composition class at a mid-sized private university in the northeastern region of the United States. The project was designed to understand how a threshold concepts framework that engages three concepts with threshold features identified in composition studies, namely literacy, rhetoric, and processes, can be used in a composition course to help students develop writing knowledge and promote transfer. For the purposes of my study, I recalibrated the existing syllabus to integrate these threshold concepts that would serve as a new frame for the work of the semester. I also aimed to understand what happens in the liminal space when students encounter "troublesome knowledge" and how metacognitive writing tasks can provide opportunities for students to recall previous literacy experiences, reframe new knowledge, and reflect upon the learning process. Relying on recent research on the curricular implications of using foundational disciplinary concepts, the study of a threshold concepts framework involving emergent concepts would, I hoped, contribute to the growing body of literature that focuses on the implementation of threshold concepts in the field of composition in particular and education research in general. Three research questions framed the study:

1. What are the effects of using a threshold concepts framework in instructing students in a FYW course?
2. What patterns are evident in students' uptake of the three threshold concepts—literacy, rhetoric, and processes?
3. What does metacognition as a habit of mind, when taught in the form of reflective writing, reveal about threshold concept instruction and student learning?

The study, approved in the fall semester of 2015, analyzes data drawn from two sections of Core English 1201, a required FYW course for incoming freshman (with SAT writing scores below 550), the majority of whom self-selected to place into the course through an online-directed self-placement survey process. A total number of thirty-three subjects participated in the study. All writing assignments, including three reflective writing responses written at the beginning, middle, and end of the semester were collected from students in the two participating courses. For the in-class reflective writing assignments, participants responded to a combination of Likert-scale and open-ended questions about how their prior writing experiences influenced the writing tasks in the course; what they were learning about the rhetorical terms *audience, genre, situation,* and *exigence*; and how writing processes such as sequenced writing tasks, revision, and self-review affected their relationship to writing. Written reports of conceptual difficulty with the three threshold concepts under investigation that were part of the reflective writing responses were also collected. Qualitative methods of data analysis that included grouping and coding of emergent categories and textual analysis were used to categorize and examine the data.

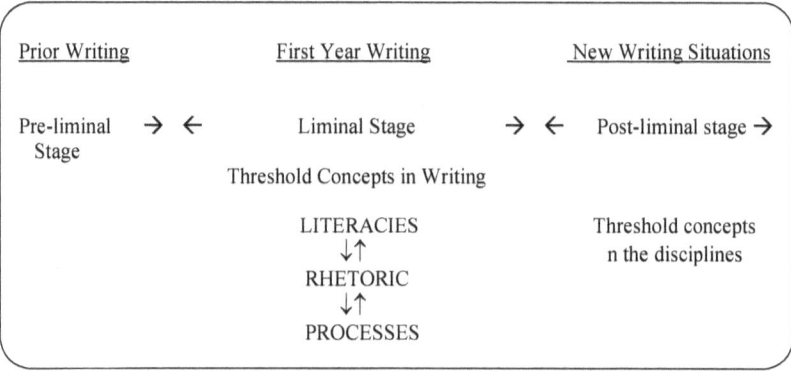

Figure 1: Writing concepts based threshold framework and stages of liminality.

Figure 1 establishes the general structure and integrative features of a writing concepts-based threshold framework and the stages of liminality that students are likely to encounter. Land and Meyer describe this interplay of struggle and achievement as the "dynamics of liminal variation" ("Dynamics" 63) and explain how the liminal space—a portal or "conceptual gateway" through which learners enter new knowledge situations—"is entered, occupied, negotiated and made sense of, passed through or not" (63). As learners enter a FYW course, they transition from a pre-liminal to a liminal stage as they engage with tasks that require explicit recall of skills and writing knowledge drawn from prior learning situations such as high school English classes and other educational and personal settings. Classroom instruction promotes further reflection upon *literacies*—prior reading and writing experiences—through individual and group discussions of reading and writing tasks, the levels of difficulty involved, and the expertise required to complete them. The term *rhetoric* is introduced, defined, and instantiated through specific reading materials, and its meaning as a process as well as a product is reiterated throughout the semester as students attempt to understand how rhetoric—and its various elements—function in texts they read and learn to develop rhetorical strategies in their own writing. Thus, *rhetoric* is a key term that is identified, described, emphasized, and engaged in each major writing assignment students complete during the semester. The third threshold concept—*processes*—is engaged throughout the semester in writing tasks that require revision, rethinking, self-review, and the knowledge that writing is not a linear but recursive act achieved through gradual, sequenced activities.

Prior Knowledge as a Threshold Concept

A critical prerequisite for developing writing competency and knowledge base is a simultaneous awareness of what a learner is already capable of doing. It entails not only the successful completion of writing tasks but also knowing which specific skills and knowledge contribute to that success and thus takes the form of declarative knowledge in which a learner expresses the ability to perform writing tasks. Engaging the threshold concept *literacies* requires a deliberate focus on recalling skills and knowledge that students bring to the writing course and metacognitive tasks that help them become conscious of the learning that occurs in the new writing situation. At the beginning of the term, as students wrote their first formal essay in which they analyzed a text of their choice (Gloria Anzaldua's "How to Tame a Wild Tongue," Al Gore's "Global Climate Change: Protecting the Environment," or Nicholas Carr's "Is Google Making Us Stupid") by applying several key concepts from Lloyd Bitzer's essay "Rhetorical Situation," they also responded to a separate set of questions about familiarity with specific tasks associated with the assignment: textual analysis, using ideas and concepts from one text to analyze another, and developing fresh and original ideas in response to texts.

Table 2
Prior Knowledge of Textual Analysis (N=33)

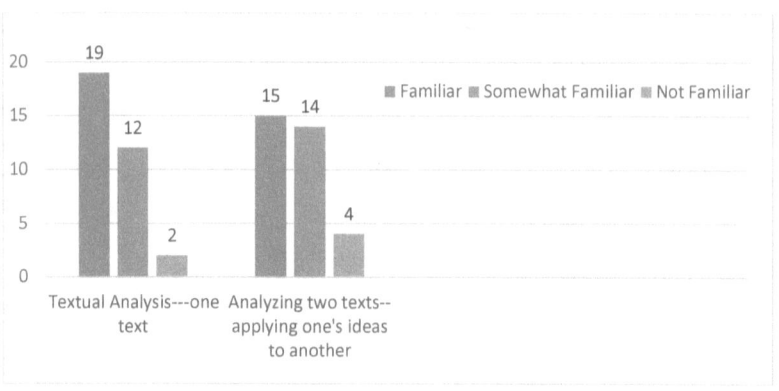

As table 2 depicts, when asked how familiar students were with textual analysis prior to writing the first essay, more than half of the subjects (n=19) admitted to having some understanding and skills related to analysis of one text when writing in response to Anzaldua's, Carr's, or Gore's essays. Yet, a significant number (n=12) also reported low levels of familiarity, and two reported no familiarity at all. Familiarity with analysis of two texts, which entailed examining the ideas of one text by applying the ideas of another and putting them into conversation with each other, dropped slightly, with more students (n=14) noting that they were less familiar with this skill and 4 students stating they had no prior experience with this skill. When queried about how the writing skills and strategies learned in prior settings affected students' ability to write the current assignment (table 3), several students commented on the usefulness of general writing skills learned in high school. But more strikingly, a greater number provided detailed comments on their lack of prior knowledge of textual analysis and proper integration of evidence, some even observing how previous knowledge interfered with learning in this new setting thus reflecting the phenomenon of negative transfer that, according to David Perkins and Gavriel Salomon, occurs when "learning in one context impacts negatively on performance in another" (4).

Table 3
Knowledge of Analytical Skills and Use of Evidence

HIGH LEVELS OF KNOWLEDGE

The idea of writing a long paper analyzing an essay or multiple essays was already an idea that I previously worked with in my junior and senior years of high school.

My skills properly acquired gave me the ability to effectively portray my ideas in this assignment as well as connecting it to the text.

My prior knowledge of introducing a quotation, transitions words and connecting my sentences helped me write my essay and make it flow well.

Having taken AP Literature in high school, I was taught a very general way to formulate a sufficient analysis on a given topic: by first making a claim, supporting the claim with textual evidence, then simply analyzing the heck out of it. I believe this formula helped enhance my writing in that it allowed my essay to be both coherent and cohesive.

LOW LEVELS OR LACK OF KNOWLEDGE

Coming into college, I lacked the ability of writing analytically because I failed to understand how to incorporate quote properly to back up my statements.

The main challenge was not being used to use textual evidence when critically analyzing the readings.

I had a general understanding of how to analyze a text. I wasn't educated on how to integrate quotes.

I had background knowledge of including quotes and phrases from other writings into my own; however, it wasn't actually analyzing anything, just simply adding a quote.

In high school most of the papers were opinion based, while this assignment was more of a response to someone else's work, which I have never really done.

In the past we were not taught how to really depict and work analytically with pieces of work like this.

The writing skills and strategies that I learned prior to this class were not up to par with what was expected from a college student. College writing is much different than prior writing.

The writing skills I learned prior made it more difficult for me to write this assignment. I've only written about nonfictional texts once before this in the past four years or so.

A lot of the writing skills learned in high school were useless for this essay because the basic five paragraph format is not how essays are supposed to be written in college.

Yet, students also wrote thoughtful responses to an open-ended question about task familiarity—"What aspects of Essay 1 felt new to you, that is, you don't recall practicing this type of writing before"—emphasizing three new areas of learning and textual engagement: Engagement with and analysis of two texts, synthesis of ideas from several texts and personal views, and integrating of evidence.

Table 4
New Areas of Learning

Engaging with two texts	Using ideas from one essay to analyze the ideas found in another was a relatively new idea.
	It felt new to me to use a definition, or ideas from one essay and apply it to a completely different essay to clarify the meanings in each. Using more than one text to strengthen my argument was also new to me in that fact that it forced me to really understand what each of them was saying.
	Integrating two different texts that were not very similar on the surface into a cohesive and coherent format was new to me.
	It was very unfamiliar to analyze multiple texts, especially looking at one through the lens of another.
Synthesizing Ideas	The aspects of Essay 1 that were new to me was writing in combination of my own thoughts, the authors thoughts, and expanding on both all together.
	Writing in a developmental way is new for me although it makes sense. An essay should not be the restating of facts, it should be the development of new ideas that lead to something different than what was originally given.
	Being able to narrate in first person, going back and forth between examples from the text and examples from your own life
	I was never told to define, explain, and apply.

Integrating Evidence	Using a lot of textual evidence and analyzing it. I never really used that many quotes in my writing during high school.
	A new aspect of writing for me that I never really practiced was quoting and citing my sources inside my essay. I knew that it was important to do this when writing but never fully understood how to do it correctly until this class.
	Having to properly use quotes to back up my statements.

Also, students' reflection in the narrative comments (table 4) align with their responses to a query about the level of achievability of tasks related to Essay 1 (table 5). The correlation between the sets of data here is high as a large number of students (n=27) report they were able to achieve the task for which they were required to do the least amount of analysis—developing their own ideas in response to a text. Although many students report high achievability with analysis of single (n=14) and multiple texts (n=20), the level of difficulty is clear, and a total of 18 students report that they were either somewhat or barely able to engage analytically with the rhetorical concepts in Lloyd Bitzer's essay.

Table 5
Troublesome Tasks

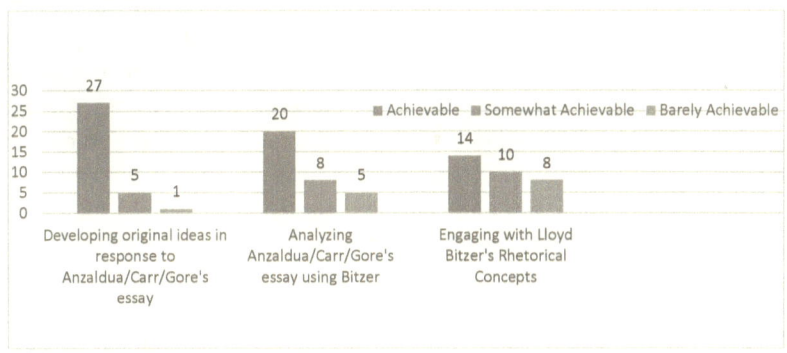

For this cohort of FYW students, early reports (table 2) indicate high confidence in analysis, or at least, a majority of students noted not only their familiarity with the term but also their ability to analyze texts. However, a closer look at other related data sets reveals interesting insights about this threshold concept. Students' familiarity with or prior knowledge of skills related to a concept (such as analysis) as reflected in responses to Likert scale answers do not provide sufficient insight into what students actually know or are able to do when engaged in tasks related to the concept. When such queries are answered through open-ended narrative responses where students have the opportunity to *reflect upon current task engagement in relation to prior knowledge,* that is, when students rely on their metacognitive abilities, the responses provide a richer portrait of how writing knowledge learned in prior settings actually impact learning in a new setting. Direct engagement with the writing task opens up a literacy landscape that helps students better map out areas of knowledge that are either previously well-explored or relatively unknown. In this study, students struggled the most with in-depth analysis of rhetorical concepts—through use of definition, explanation, and synthesis—and with the type of textual engagement necessary when putting multiple texts in conversation with each other, and students' reports reveal that they attribute the struggle with this form of troublesome knowledge to what they *did not learn* prior to the writing course.

Rhetoric as a Threshold Concept

If writing is always a social and rhetorical activity, then rhetoric as a method of engaging the power of language is necessarily embedded in writing situations such as college composition courses, writing across and within disciplines, and workplace and professional settings, and students have to be explicitly taught to recognize, comprehend, and directly work with rhetorical concepts and strategies. Kevin Roozen has noted that "while this concept may be troublesome, understanding it has a variety of benefits" (18). The threshold concept framework established for this course not only recognizes these benefits but was developed with the intention to immerse students in rhetorical concepts through each writing assignment and to track their growing understanding of and difficulties with the concept through meta-cognitive reflections. During mid-semester, after students had read and responded to Lloyd Bitzer's essay "The Rhetorical Situation" and written two essays that required rhetorical analysis, they responded to the questions "What is your understanding of the function of rhetoric, specifically rhetorical situation, exigence, and audience, in the texts you've read or the text you've written? What is still unclear or troubling?" A selection of responses (table 6) demonstrates that although several students were able to articulate what they understood to be the function of rhetoric, others admitted they continued to grapple with some of the aspects of the concept. In particular, students struggled to make sense of the meaning of the terms *situation* and *exigence* and continued to be vexed by how they could be applied to written discourse.

Table 6
Learning Rhetorical Concepts in the Liminal Space (Midterm)

Rhetoric is understandable	The function of rhetoric is to convince and audience of some issue and persuade them to assist in fixing the situation.
	The function of rhetoric is that it can be a written or spoken discourse in which the situation presents an exigence (problem) with a speaker that seeks for a change and an audience that can relate and helps to bring out a change.
	The purpose of rhetoric is to perform some type of discourse to encourage an audience of producing change.
	A rhetorical situation is a situation that leads to an exigence, or an issue that is urging the audience to change by influencing their thoughts and actions by the presence of a discourse.
	A rhetorical situation is a situation where there is a problem that has a pressing need. The rhetorical discourse is written or oral communication to help solve the exigence.
	If an author identifies an issue or the exigence he then can respond with rhetorical discourse which is an attempt to change the problem.
	The parts of rhetoric (rhetorical situation, exigence, and situation) allow the author to discuss a situation with an audience and allow them to share their thoughts and ideas about the situation and how they can improve the situation for the better.

Rhetoric is troublesome	Rhetoric is the act of persuasion in oral or written form. Sometimes I had trouble with the exigence, but it eventually became clear throughout Gore's essay and my own essay.
	Something that is still unclear is how to decide whether something is a rhetorical situation or not. I think I understand the idea of the rhetorical situation, I just don't see the point of it really. It could just be described as a situation with an issue, and an author trying to fix this issue that he sees.
	I'm still unclear of exactly what rhetorical situation and exigence is.
	Something that is still, somehow, unclear is what situations are rhetorical and which ones are not.
	It is still unclear as to the difference between situation and discourse, although if I consider it for a few minutes I often find the answer. I am also unsure of the support needed to make a rhetorical situation solid without fully comprehending the other parts that make up a situation.
	I have understood how to relate rhetorical situations to other texts and what it takes to have a rhetoric situation. I found it troubling on how to define it.

By the end of the semester, when students had completed the final writing assignment—an inquiry essay which included researched materials—they responded to a reflective writing prompt that included the question "What is your understanding now of how rhetorical discourse works to persuade readers? What is still challenging or troubling?" The majority of students noted how their writing was informed by the rhetorical elements they had been discussing all semester, demonstrating a deepening awareness and knowledge of a common vocabulary and conceptual structure connected to rhetoric. However, table 7 represents a selection of comments that reflects some self-doubt and uncertainty even in the face of new knowledge about rhetoric, indicating that rhetoric is indeed a threshold concept to novice writers. The data here suggests that while many students are able to comprehend the general meaning of rhetoric and thoughtfully explain some of the related terms, it remains a troublesome concept whose particular abstractions continue to pose difficulties for freshman writers.

Table 7
Learning Rhetorical Concepts in the Liminal Space (End of Term)

Rhetoric is understandable	Rhetorical discourse can be used to inform a reader about a problem and persuade the reader to take action to fix the problem. Rhetorical discourse can provide facts, statistics, and credible sources to persuade readers.
	Rhetorical discourse has an exigence that is in need of a solution and you have to provide evidence and use good sources to persuade your readers of the solution you want to do to fix your exigence.
	Rhetorical discourse is necessary for a paper to be intriguing and effective. There must be an exigence in which the writer wants to fix or change in some manner. The understanding of what proper rhetorical discourse is and how to use it effectively improved the conciseness of my writing tremendously.
	Rhetorical discourse addresses concerns to the public and sometimes provides ideas on how to fix the issue provided.
	Rhetorical discourse is a vital part of an essay that involves and audience. It helps craft the problems and the solution in an eloquent manner.
	A problem, exigence, is presented and you discuss the issue while also offering a solution to the problem. You analyze the problem to show people how large of a problem it is, and then fully convince them with your proposed solution.
	Rhetorical discourse works to persuade readers by establishing a problem and its effects. By stating a problem, it persuades readers to further read on how it can be fixed.
	Rhetorical discourse is a problem that has been brought to the attention of readers, with the intent for them to enact some form of change that will help resolve the problem.

Rhetoric is troublesome	Sometimes it is still challenging to understand how to bring my own ideas into the paper and have original thoughts on how to improve a situation.
	I still don't know what it means in detail. All I know is that it is writing used to persuade a reader and a call to change.
	Rhetorical discourse persuade people by providing factual information and bring out the solution to an exigence. However, I still have problem to distinguish between a rhetorical situation and the problem (exigence).
	Rhetorical discourse works to persuade readers by using persuasive language, I still have a hard time trying to explain what it is but I know when I've done it.

However, in conjunction with the narrative comments of table 7, responses to the question "To what extent do you see your writing in essay 3 as rhetorical discourse that has purpose, reflects and exigence, suggests a solution or argues for change, and has an audience you aim to convince?" (table 8) provide a more complete representation of students' knowledge and uptake of rhetoric not just as a threshold concept that has to be understood but as a set of strategies that can be consciously and deliberately employed in their own writing. By the end of the semester, the students who agreed that their writing engaged the concepts they had been learning all semester and thus qualified as rhetorical discourse had doubled from twelve to twenty-four. The number of students who only somewhat agreed fell by similar proportions, from eighteen to nine. Thus, while there was an increase in students' general understanding of rhetoric and its relevance to their own writing, some writers' view of rhetoric as a concept remained muddled and unclear.

Table 8
Recognition of Self-Produced Text as Rhetorical Discourse

WRITING PROCESSES AS A THRESHOLD CONCEPT

To generate strong, effective, and meaningful writing, students have to build an awareness of writing as a gradual, non-linear, recursive, and evaluative process that requires attentiveness to the developing text. They also have to learn to assess their own writing and develop the ability to rethink and revise within the context of the guidelines and requirements of the writing task. During the semester that this study was conducted, students were regularly required to engage with writing processes that involved, among others, two forms of procedural practices: short, sequenced writing exercises leading to a draft of a formal assignment and a self-review. An assignment sequence is a scaffolded prompt—often called a progression—that breaks down the required tasks (such as summary, analysis of a text, connecting ideas from two texts, synthesizing ideas, presenting a solution to a problem) into writing exercises of a page to two pages each (Appendix A) and progressively helps create a rough draft of the assignment. Of the various practices that were implemented to help students rethink and revise their writing—which included peer-review and extensive instructor feedback—sequenced writing and self-review practices were entirely new and unfamiliar to the majority of the student body. Yet each proved to carry significant benefits for the writers. Open-ended responses to a question about what students continued to learn about writing processes—specifically, shorter writing exercises and self-review—indicate that sequenced writing appears to have been the most helpful for brainstorming and generating ideas, focusing on idea development, and organizing, arranging ideas (table 9).

Table 9
Affordances of Assignment Sequencing

Idea development and focus	It helped me brainstorm and gather my thoughts. I highly recommend you keep this in the future.
	I very much appreciated having the writing exercises to help me develop my ideas.
	This makes it easier to develop my own thoughts rather than figuring it out all at once.
	This was very helpful in allowing me to focus on one source at a time. It also gave me more time to come up with ideas for my essay.
	These are really helpful because it gives you the opportunity to focus in specific aspects of the writing.
	They allow us to really focus in on one piece of the essay at a time. It allows us to really flush out our ideas, making them concise and clear.
	Shorter writing exercises allowed for complete focus on the individual assignment instead of writing everything at once. It also provided a clear structure for the essay.
	These are really helpful because it gives you the opportunity to focus in specific aspects of the writing.
Organizing text and ideas	This was a good way to practice writing transitions.
	They help break up and build on the specific ideas that need to be addressed. By introducing the mini-essays one at a time, students are not bombarded with an essay. We take little steps and walk our way to the big idea.
	I have struggled with research in the past and was therefore very grateful to have it broken up into smaller, more manageable pieces. With the shorter pieces, I could go back and refine what I had already written when I discovered a new way to approach the writing or the topic in a later exercise.
	I could add more detail to each assignment. If we were given one big prompt, details and information would have gotten lost.
	Very beneficial in creating a strong and cohesive final essay.
	They help make the essay easier and work to create fluidity. I learnt to organize these short pieces in a way that they could complement each other.

Noting the disjunction between contemporary efforts to establish a student and process-centered classroom and the role of student writers in assessing their own writing, Brian Huot observes that "a crucial missing element in most writing pedagogy is any experience or instruction in ascertaining the value of one's own work" (67). He calls for a "pedagogy of assessment" that enables us "to rethink what it means for our students to evaluate the way writing works and to relate these decisions about writing quality to the process of writing itself" (69). Huot's assessment pedagogy, which he labels *instructive evaluation*, is reflected in what I call the *self-review*, a term more easily understood by students who are already familiar with the companion feedback mechanism "peer review." Once students produce a rough draft, in addition to participating in peer-review workshops, they also complete a self-review (see Appendix B) by writing questions, comments, thoughts, ideas, and corrections on an electronic copy of the draft. The purpose of a self-review is to allow writers to take a closer, more holistic look at their work, evaluate it according to the guidelines of the assignment, and be able to engage in some revision and rethinking before handing it in for instructor feedback.

The self-review as a threshold concept-based instructional practice emphasizes how writing processes can provide affordances that engage students in learner-initiated and self-directed learning related to their writing. Three important categories emerge here: audience awareness, reflection and review, and error correction (table 10). As students reflected upon their drafts, they developed increasing awareness of how to read as an "audience member," from a "different standpoint" and to "critique from an outside perspective." While noting the importance of maintaining writerly authority while revising, a large number of students also reported their ability to gain greater distance from their writing, which they claim led to deeper engagement with revision—to literally re-see their writing. Charles Bazerman and Howard Tinberg have emphasized this point arguing that, "becoming aware that the text exists outside the writer's projection and must convey meaning to readers is an important threshold" (62) for developing writers. The self-review thus provided a richer, more reflective approach that allowed for closer scrutiny of ideas, restructuring of thought and error correction, and helped build a foundation for learner-initiated assessment that is a critical part of the instructional framework for this particular threshold concept. As a method, then, the self-review is a concrete instantiation of writing process evaluation through activities that, according to Peggy O'Neill, are "more formalized, such as a structured protocol for a self-assessment of a text" (68). Students' responses to the usefulness of these practices were overwhelmingly positive, (table 11) and for this study both sequenced writing and the self-review seemed to provide students with opportunities for experiencing revision as a deeper, more complex, and generative activity.

Table 10
Affordances of Self-Review

Audience awareness	The self-review helped me in reading my work form an audience perspective.
	The self-review allowed me to look at my writing as an audience member instead of as a writer because most writers are biased towards their writing. Without the self-review, a writer could not interpret their writing from another perspective and add details that would complete the essay.
	The self-review gave me an opportunity to step back from my writing and give myself honest feedback.
	I enjoyed it because it was another set of eyes looking at my work.
	I was looking for things that professors and teachers are usually looking for which made it like I was reading it from a different standpoint and definitely helped point out the flaws of my essay.
	Allowed me to work on my writing as a reader and not a writer. It was helpful in showing how someone with no previous knowledge of the topic will understand the ideas that I was attempting to portray.
	It allowed me to view and critique my work from an outside perspective. I am accustomed to reading my writing from my own point of view but when I had to read my writing objectively I felt like I had a greater sense of what made my essay good as well as my essay's flaws.

Reflection and review (beyond proofreading)	It really helped me reflect on my writing. What helped me the most was being to ask questions throughout my essay.
	It allowed me to ask questions about my writing in a more personal manner.
	Self-review, rather than simple proof reading, allowed me to see past what I normally look at when fixing an essay.
	I am able to see things I can improve on by reflecting on the different things I have learned. There is something new to learn in every class that can help make my essay better.
	This was very interesting because it made me question every sentence and the reason behind the placement of that particular sentence in that particular situation.
	It also allowed deeper corrections to be made rather than superficial grammatical errors.
Error correction	Paying close attention to my own work helped me with grammar mistakes and making sure that my sentences were accurate for what I wanted to express.
	Self-review helped me notice things that did not belong in my essay, small grammar mistakes, and how I did some things well and others poorly.
	It can make a major difference in the outcome of my work for the better. It helps me see my own mistakes and helps me fix structural issues.
	It has helped me because it's a good way to go over the work and learn from your errors and then hopefully not make the same mistakes again.
	The self-review helps me to see what mistakes I've made in my essay and helps me see what I should explain more or what I don't need to have in the essay.

Table 11
Sequenced Writing, Self-Review, and Revision

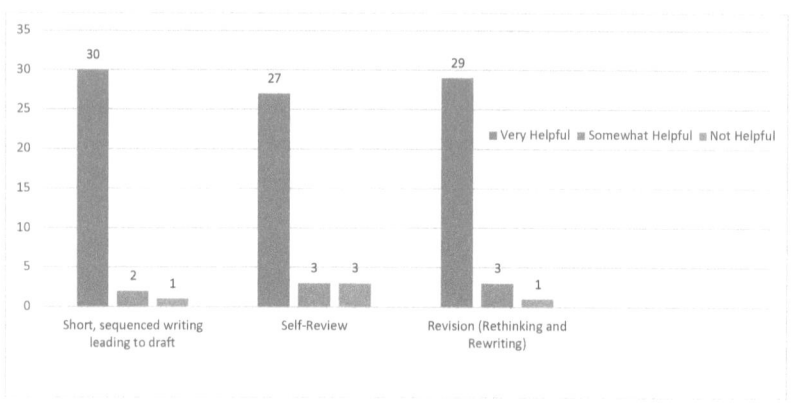

Discussion

The instructional framework utilized for the study presented in this chapter included strategic opportunities for students to both engage directly in writing tasks that bore threshold features and reflect upon the learning process by considering the affordances and challenges of the tasks presented. While responses to Likert scale-based questions provided important clues to students' measurement of prior knowledge of writing skills, their ability to accomplish difficult and often unfamiliar analytical tasks, and to produce rhetorical discourse, the more open-ended, narrative style questions produced more detailed and revelatory information about each of these threshold areas. Reflection-based metacognitive writing associated with the threshold framework yielded more meaningful insights into students' uptake of each of the threshold concepts engaged in the study, and more critically, about the level of difficulty associated with them. Additionally, findings reveal that the theoretical concept of rhetoric and the particular features associated with it appear to be most troubling, with the concept coming into view for some students but also disappearing into a fog of confusion for others. Students also grappled with prior knowledge and literacy experiences as it became clear that writing analytically in a new context (a composition classroom) not only presented greater challenges than they had expected but also led to new writing knowledge. In her discussion of a related threshold concept "All Writers Have More to Learn," Shirley Rose observes that "encountering difficulty in a writing situation is an indication that [students] are ready to learn something new about writing" (61). The threshold concept associated with writing processes involving short, sequenced writing and self-review led to the perception of revision as a meaningful, productive, and valuable activity to the majority of students. This finding holds significant implications for the development of instructional strategies for revision as it reveals students' greater ability to comprehend this concept when provided with carefully conceived tasks and conditions for generating, reviewing, and reconceiving written work.

In this early phase of threshold concept development in writing studies, a flexible and dynamic approach to threshold concept theory—and inevitably, its practice—is vital for finding effective ways of designing, implementing, and assessing curriculum and pedagogy that lead to enhanced student learning and transfer of writing-based knowledge and concepts into other learning settings and situations. The approach employed in this study focused on three threshold concepts that seemed most relevant to the instructional setting—a FYW course—and reflects a conscious effort to be selective about the concepts for the purposes of the particular writing context. Best practices in threshold concept pedagogy, to which this chapter aspires to contribute, promotes the view that this framework is neither prescriptive nor exhaustive but a heuristic that opens up possibilities for further exploration of—and experimentation with—the growing body of knowledge associated with threshold concepts and its deep intersections with the value of metacognitive writing. If, as Meyer and Land argue, threshold concepts "lead not only to transformed thought but a transfiguration of identity and adoption of an extended discourse" ("Epistemological" 375), instructional frameworks built to integrate writing studies concepts can provide students with opportunities to develop a discursive repertoire that will not only influence their future engagement with writing but have an indelible and irreversible impact on their writerly identity.

WORKS CITED

Adler-Kassner, Linda, et al. "The Value of Troublesome Knowledge: Transfer and Threshold Concepts in Writing and History." *Composition Forum*, vol. 26, 2012, compositionforum.com/issue/26/troublesome-knowledge-threshold.php.

Bazerman, Charles, and Howard Tinberg. "Text is an Object Outside of Oneself That Can Be Improved and Developed." *Naming What We Know: Threshold Concepts of Writing Studies*, edited by Linda Adler-Kassner and Elizabeth Wardle, Utah State UP, 2015, pp. 61–62.

Cousin, Glynis. "An Introduction to Threshold Concepts." *Planet*, no.17, 2006.

Downs, Doug, and Liane Robertson. "Threshold Concepts in First Year Composition." *Naming What We Know: Threshold Concepts of Writing Studies*, edited by Linda Adler-Kassner and Elizabeth Wardle, Utah State UP, 2015, pp. 105–21.

Huot, Brian. *(Re)Articulating Writing Assessment for Teaching and Learning*. Utah State UP, 2002.

Land, Ray. "Facilitating the Academy through Threshold Concepts and Troublesome Knowledge." *On Facilitation of the Academy*, edited by Elias Westergaard and Joachim S. Wiewiura, Sense Publishers, 2015, pp. 17–29.

Land, Ray, et al. *Threshold Concepts in Practice*. Sense Publishers, 2016.

Land, Ray, and Jan H.F. Meyer. "Threshold Concepts and Troublesome Knowledge (5): Dynamics of Assessment." *Threshold Concepts and Transformational Learning*, edited by Jan H.F. Meyer, Ray Land, and Caroline Baillie, Sense Publishers, 2010, pp. 61–79.

Meyer, Jan H. F., and Ray Land. "Threshold Concepts and Troublesome Knowledge—Linkages to Ways of Thinking and Practising." *Improving Student Learning: Theory and Practice—Ten Years On*, edited by Chris Rust, OCSLD, 2003, pp. 1–16

—. "Threshold Concepts and Troublesome Knowledge (2): Epistemological Considerations and a Conceptual Framework for Teaching and Learning." *Higher Education*, vol. 49, no. 3, 2005, pp. 373–88.

—. "Threshold Concepts and Troublesome Knowledge: An Introduction." *Overcoming Barriers to Student Understanding: Threshold Concepts and Troublesome Knowledge*, edited by Jan H. F. Meyer and Ray Land, Routledge, 2006, pp. 3–18.

—. "Threshold Concepts and Troublesome Knowledge: Issue of Liminality." *Overcoming Barriers to Student Understanding: Threshold Concepts and Troublesome Knowledge*, edited by Jan H. F. Meyer and Ray Land, Routledge, 2006, pp. 19–32.

O'Neill, Peggy. "Assessment is an Essential Component of Learning to Write." *Naming What We Know: Threshold Concepts of Writing Stud-

ies, edited by Linda Adler-Kassner and Elizabeth Wardle, Utah State UP, 2015, pp. 67–68.

Perkins, David N. "Constructivism and Troublesome Knowledge." *Overcoming Barriers to Student Understanding: Threshold Concepts and Troublesome Knowledge*, edited by Jan H.F. Meyer and Ray Land, Routledge, 2006, pp. 33–47.

Perkins, David N., and Gavriel Salomon. "Transfer of Learning." *International Encyclopedia of Education 2*, Pergamon, 1992, pp. 3–13.

Roozen, Kevin. "Writing is a Social and Rhetorical Activity." *Naming What We Know: Threshold Concepts of Writing Studies*, edited by Linda Adler-Kassner and Elizabeth Wardle, Utah State UP, 2015, pp. 17–19.

Rose, Shirley. "All Writers Have More to Learn." *Naming What We Know: Threshold Concepts of Writing Studies*, edited by Linda Adler-Kassner and Elizabeth Wardle, Utah State UP, 2015, pp. 59–61.

Yancey, Kathleen Blake. *Reflection in the Writing Classroom*. Utah State UP, 1998.

Walker, Guy. "A Cognitive Approach to Threshold Concepts." *Higher Education*, vol. 65, no. 2, 2013, pp. 247–63.

Wardle, Elizabeth, and Doug Downs. *Writing About Writing: A College Reader*. Macmillan, 2014.

Appendix 1: Assignment Sequence

Analytical Essay: Understanding Rhetorical Discourse

Readings:
Gloria Anzaldua's "How to Tame a Wild Tongue"
Nicholas Carr's "Is Google Making Us Stupid"
Al Gore's "Global Climate Change: Protecting the Environment"
Lloyd Bitzer's "The Rhetorical Situation"

Goal:
For this assignment you will craft an essay in which you analyze the rhetorical elements of an assigned text by engaging with several rhetorical concepts. While the task of the essay is to demonstrate a nuanced understanding of the function of rhetorical discourse, you are also expected to

develop an elegant, compelling essay that offers a commentary on the particular situation that led to the creation of the discourse and develop an argument in response to it.

Writing Exercise 1
Now that you have read three essays (Gore, Carr, Anzaldua), choose one whose ideas you find to be particularly important. None of the essays is "easy" so make your selection based upon the ideas the writer presents and the extent to which you find these ideas meaningful, valuable, or provocative.

In this first writing exercise you will analyze how and why the author develops these ideas. To do this, **summarize** the main ideas and purpose of the essay you are analyzing.

This exercise should be about one page in length.

Writing Exercise 2
Define the key terms **rhetorical situation, exigence, audience,** and analyze the particular **situation** that gives rise to the selected reading. Describe the background and context that the writer is responding to by writing the essay (or speech). Who is the author's **audience**? What is the "**exigence**" (Bitzer 7) that gives rise to the essay and what **action or change** do you think the author would like to see? How can you tell? Use brief direct quotes from your main text as well as Bitzer's essay as you develop your analysis. Your essay will not be convincing without proper *evidence* to support them.

This assignment should be about two pages in length, double-spaced.

Writing Exercise 3
For this exercise, *respond to the rhetorical situation* in the selected reading. To do this you should focus on a particular idea or argument that the author develops. Find pieces of evidence that represent this argument and examine them carefully. Why is this argument important? Focus on the underlying purpose of the essay and deepen our understanding of its implications by developing your own idea or response to the exigence. As you conclude your essay present an original argument that builds upon and extends the author's ideas or is different from the author's.

As you put Ex. 1 and Ex. 2 together, think of the "parts" of your essay—the analysis of the text, inclusion of Bitzer's ideas, your response to the ideas of the text, and development of your own argument. You may re-organize these sections of your writing as you wish but keeping in mind that your essay should be cohesive and well-organized in structure and compelling in its subject and style.

This assignment should be at least two pages in length, double-spaced.

Essay 1—Rough Draft
The goal of this essay is for you to be able to analyze the rhetorical situation in an essay of your choice and develop an interesting argument from this analysis. The ideas of the published essay should be your springboard, a place of interest or curiosity from which you launch your own ideas. The essay you're writing should leave the reader with new thoughts and questions and not merely the ideas of the published essay.

Put together all the writing you have done (writing exercises 1, 2, and 3) in the form of a rough draft and use brief quotes from the text as supporting evidence.

Please create an interesting and descriptive title for your draft. Your draft should be at least five to six pages long. Please attach your rough draft as a Word document.

APPENDIX 2: SELF-REVIEW GUIDELINES

Self-review is a reflective practice which goes beyond simple proof-reading, that is, merely making surface-level corrections related to grammar, punctuation, and spelling errors, and involves textual annotation. It requires you to become aware of yourself as a writer and critical thinker and reflect on your *writing process* so you can plan and strategize, make important changes to your writing, begin to understand the composing process, and develop a deeper sense of what it means to be a writer. Simply put, self-review helps you *become* a writer.

As you write the self-review by annotating your draft, try out these ways of reflecting upon and responding to your own writing:

- Consider whether—and to what extent—you have completed all the requirements of the assignment
- Ask open-ended questions of yourself as well as the reader
- Rethink, be open to, and try out new ideas or ways of thinking
- Proofread and make grammatical and sentence-level corrections. If necessary, make editorial notes and comments
- Consider the Self-review as the beginning of a dialogue with another reader

You may ask direct yes/no questions about your writing in the self-review but take this opportunity to also have a conversation with yourself, test out some of your theories about writing, and engage your audience in a conversation about your essay. Write comments or notes that will help you move forward and further revise your writing. In my written feedback to the self-reviewed draft, I will respond to many of your questions and comments but not necessarily all of them. You will still certainly benefit from practicing the skills involved in closely examining your writing in order to improve it.

As you complete the self-review, keep these writing requirements and guidelines in mind and annotate your writing by checking against these criteria.

1. *Introduce* authors and the titles of their essays.
2. *Define* the key terms from Bitzer's essay.
3. *Explain* the key terms in your own words.
4. *Discuss* these aspects of rhetorical discourse by *analyzing* parts of the essay. (What is the rhetorical situation that leads to this particular discourse? What is the exigence? Who is the audience?)
5. Use *direct quotes* (textual *evidence*) as you analyze the essay. Avoid making general claims about the text that are not supported by evidence.
6. Offer concrete solutions to the problem (problem-solving) if you are so inclined.
7. Introduce quotes and *integrate* them into your sentences as much as you can.
8. Always analyze texts in present tense.

9. Make sure your essay has a compelling beginning and thoughtful ending.
10. Follow 2016 (8th edition) MLA style format for in-text citations and works cited list.

5 Cognitive Psychology and the Framework for Success: Teaching Genre as a Design Problem

Thomas Skeen

In "Writing as an Unnatural Act," Joseph Petraglia draws from the work of cognitive psychologist Walter Reitman to critique General Skills Writing Instruction (GWSI), which Petraglia defines as "a set of rhetorical skills that can be mastered through formal instruction" and "as skills that transcend any particular content and context" ("Introduction" xi). Petraglia uses Walter Reitman's theories of *well-structured* and *ill-structured* problem solving to explain how writing is not a well-structured set of procedures that lead to an invariant result in pursuit of an unambiguous goal; rather, writing is ill-structured because the procedures and the aims of writing are always contextual, making them ambiguous and uncertain ("Writing" 81). To support this assertion, Petraglia outlines the ways in which the field of writing studies understands writing as "instrumental," "transactional," and "rhetorical"; that is to say that writing helps people do things through exchanges with others and that the act of writing is strategic, meaning that the rhetorical problems a writer faces do not have clear procedures or end states. Complicating its ill-structuredness, Petraglia explains, is the field-dependent nature of writing: audience, language, domain knowledge, and other factors are highly situational and do not lend themselves to particular strategies or end-states.

This, Petraglia argues, makes writing incompatible with classroom instruction, which lends itself to well-structured problem solving ("Writing" 87). In Petraglia's view, GWSI is a form of highly generalized, well-structured problem solving that grows out of the context of schools and assessment, meaning that students will not be able to participate in "just any rhetorical practice" (90). GWSI assignments include a variety of predictable features so that they can be taught and assessed in a well-structured way: fictitious parameters for a rhetorical situation; a predictable and consistent audience (the teacher) as opposed to highly inconsistent and unpredictable audiences of the real world; rules that homogenize the writing for the purpose of consistent student development and evaluation but do not correspond to real-world writing (91). The result of this disjuncture between lived contexts and classrooms is that choices students have to make in the classroom "bear little resemblance" to choices they might make in real-life situations, even if class work is meant to model real situations (86). Thus, Petraglia's argument anticipates an important question for this collection: To what extent can cognitive psychology assist writing teachers in helping learners gain new writing skills and apply them outside the classroom, especially considering the *Framework for Success in Postsecondary Writing*? In Petraglia's view, cognitive psychology tells us that the transfer of classroom writing skills to real-world contexts is, to use his language, "inimical" at best ("Introduction" xiv).

Like Petraglia, Elizabeth Wardle uses cognitive psychology's framework of well-structured and ill-structured problem solving to approach writing instruction. Wardle questions the ability to teach general skills by challenging her own readers to simply write "in general" ("You Can Learn"). Unlike Petraglia, who focuses on the development of general skills that are assumed to transcend context but really do not—thus rendering school-based writing instruction inapplicable for real-world application—Wardle focuses more on helping learners develop adaptive capacities that could help them grapple with ill-structured problem solving, including problems of context and adaptation. With that teaching problem in mind, a more recent (and hopeful) treatment of well-structured and ill-structured problem solving can be found in Wardle's "Creative Repurposing for Expansive Learning: Considering 'Problem Exploring' and 'Answer-Getting' Dispositions in Individuals and Fields." In that introduction to the fall 2012 issue of *Composition Forum*, Wardle argues that writing instruction should focus on what she calls *creative repurposing*—the capacity to adapt previous knowledge and find workable solutions to complex, messy, ill-structured problems. To achieve that, she explains, a learner must adopt a "problem-exploring" disposition, as opposed to an "answer-getting" disposition: The first "incline[s] a person toward curiosity, reflection, consideration of multiple possibilities, a willingness to engage in a recursive process of trial and error, and toward a recognition that more than one solution can 'work'"; the second "seek[s] right answers quickly and [is] averse to open consideration of multiple possibilities" ("Creative Repurposing" par. 13). If transfer is the end goal of writing instruction, Petraglia's treatment of GWSI corresponds to well-structured problem solving in that it encourages a learner to eschew open-ended answers necessary to make rhetorical choices. One might imagine what such a curriculum might do to a learner: Drawing from Anastasia Efklides, Wardle makes the point that a learner's exposure to particular ways of knowing can affect disposition in profound ways, including a learner's willingness to learn and/or willingness to regulate that learning over time ("Creative Repurposing" par. 34). Whereas Petraglia's articulation of GWSI might encourage learners to think of writing in terms of one size fits all because it discourages thinking about writing as a varying problem to be solved, Wardle's conception of a problem-exploring disposition does the opposite.

The *Framework* provides a way to address the cognitive problem of well-structuredness in the writing classroom and prepare learners for ill-structured problem solving. Paralleling Wardle, the principles and guidelines in the *Framework* can help learners build capacities through a reciprocal relationship between its two parts: its habits of mind and its recommended "Experiences with Writing, Reading, and Critical Analysis." The habits of mind—with dispositions such as curiosity about the world, openness to new ways of approaching problems, flexibility and persistence in dealing with problems, and metacognitive awareness about the writer's own thought processes—could foster what Wardle would call creative repurposing ("Creative Repurposing"). As the writers of the *Framework* note, classroom "Experiences with Writing, Reading, and Critical Analysis" also help build and expand the habits of mind through practice with rhetorical concepts as they compose in different genres for different audiences. In other words, the *Framework* offers a capacity-building approach that emphasizes conceptual understanding, opportunities for practice, appropriate dispositions, and metacognitive awareness could help learners develop capacities that help meet the intended ends of composition courses: the ability to apply and repurpose knowledge for later writing and communication tasks.

With this background, I would like to explore genre as a key component of writing instruction, especially to prepare learners for the ill-structured problem solving they would face in their writing endeavors inside and outside of school. I see genre as a central component of teaching writing not only because others have argued that it is a key component to transfer (see Linda Adler-Kassner et al.; Irene Clark and Andrea Hernandez) but also because it touches (and perhaps encompasses) many of the other items listed in the *Framework*'s "Experiences with Writing, Reading, and Critical Analysis." If a genre grows out of a recurring occasion, the recurrence of audience, purpose, and context are tied directly to genre. While a writer would likely adjust language, style, conventions, arguments, and other rhetorical considerations while writing different artifacts within the same genre, changes in genre often require writers to make significant rhetorical adjustments. Writing in diverse genres requires critical thinking and decision making about writing, multiple approaches to writing processes, consideration of a range of conventions because what might be "correct and appropriate" for an audience in one genre might not be for another, and genres occur in multiple technological environments. From a cognitive perspective, it is clear that writing in a genre is a form of ill-structured problem solving, especially given the many variables listed above. Teaching learners about genre and having them practice genres provides at least a partial answer to Petraglia's critique of GWSI because writing in different genres requires multiple approaches, and there are degrees of appropriateness rather than well-structured, right-or-wrong answers. However, a more nuanced approach to ill-structured problem solving can offer our learners additional conceptual understanding of genre that may enable them to pursue the creative repurposing that they need to approach novel (and sometimes not so novel) writing situations that they will inevitably face.

In this chapter, then, I will draw from cognitive psychology to add to our discipline's discussion of classroom experiences that will expand learners' capacities to deal with ill-structured writing problems. Following a review of literature on problem solving in writing studies and cognitive psychology, this chapter will have three focal points. The first is that studies on expertise show that experts can recognize meaningful "chunks" of information in ways that enable them to perform better than novices. Thus, providing learners with a framework that enables them to develop the capacity to find meaningful chunks could help them expand their capacity to write in new genres they encounter. The second is that a more nuanced framework for ill-structured problem solving can inform the teaching of genre. While Petraglia's critique of writing instruction based on the ill-structured nature of writing itself is certainly warranted, educational psychologist David H. Jonassen provides a nuanced understanding of ill-structured problem solving by identifying several different types of ill-structured problem solving and placing writing in the category of *design problems* ("Toward"). The third focal point is a sample lesson plan, along with further classroom-level assignment suggestions, for teaching genre as a design problem. It relies on Jonassen's concept of *design problem solving* and his recommended pedagogical practices that fit that particular type of ill-structured problem solving, these suggestions follow pedagogical practices that may enable learners to adapt to new genres on their own and thus respond to the particular ill-structured problem solving that writing demands.

Importantly, we already have a range of literature that provides guidance on the development of a curriculum and teaching for transfer. Kathleen Blake Yancey, Liane Robertson, and Kara Taczak review a range of curricular approaches to transfer by several authors, including the Writing About Writing (WAW) curriculum as expressed by Doug Downs and Wardle, as well as Debra Dew, which emphasizes a conceptual focus on writing and rhetoric; Yancey et al.'s own Teaching for Transfer (TFT), which provides a full curriculum complete with metacognitive assignments and writing assignments in various genres; Rebecca Nowacek's "concurrent" approach emphasizes writing transfer between courses in which students are concurrently enrolled; and Doug Brent explains a "naturalized" approach that emphasizes students drawing from their rhetorical education as a whole (Yancey et al. 44). All of these approaches provide guidance for a curriculum—what to teach and how to teach it. For example: Yancey et al. provide a full syllabus, complete with assignments, for teaching for transfer. In light of this important work, what I present here is not meant to serve as an ersatz curriculum, but rather a suggestion for classroom pedagogy to complement approaches that already exist.

Problem Solving in Cognitive Psychology: Some Background

In cognitive psychology, problem solving and expertise are closely associated, so it is important for us to attend to expertise in our classroom practices in writing studies. The book *How People Learn* offers several attributes that experts in a given area tend to have, while also taking the argument that because experts are effective problem solvers in their domains, studies in expertise help us understand successful learning. Among other things, expert knowledge helps experts readily notice meaningful patterns of information that novices do not, includes a great deal of content knowledge that is organized conceptually in a discipline-specific way, consists of contextualized knowledge based on its applicability rather than isolated facts, and allows experts to retrieve knowledge without requiring careful attention. For example, in a well-known study of chess players called "Skill in Chess," expert players were more adept recalling the placement of chess pieces after seeing a brief view of a chess game than novices were (Simon and Chase). The experts were more accurate because they grouped chess pieces according to their relationship to each other within the game, whereas the novices could only try to memorize where each piece was on the board. In another study, experts and novices grouped physics problems differently; experts grouped different problems based on principles in physics that could be used to solve them, whereas novices grouped the same problems according to whether they "look the same" on the surface (Chi et al.).

It would follow that the same differences between experts and novices apply to writing; different genres of writing arguably have different types of meaningful patterns that an experienced writer would recognize in a particular type of writing. For example, an experienced grant writer might notice immediately if a particular part of a grant proposal were missing or poorly argued in the context of grant writing, but one might not expect the same level of detail from a beginning grant writer. Not only might a grant writer recognize those patterns quickly, but she would also have meaningful patterns of knowledge organized around the process of grant writing itself, including social contexts and sub-genres of grant proposals. How, then, should we teach genre, given that writers "carry" genres with them from old contexts to new ones (Bazerman, "The Life of Genre") and that genre knowledge accrues, shifts, and deepens as a writer continues to gain diversified experience (Rounsaville)?

Given the advantages that experts have outlined above, the authors of *How People Learn* suggest that teachers provide learners with experiences that help them recognize "meaningful chunks" of information and help them organize it (24, 36). For writing—especially in general writing courses that are meant to serve learners early in their academic careers, but also in more specialized writing courses—this might mean teaching them to "see" writing in terms of genre and providing them with a conceptual framework that will help them organize genre knowledge. It is within this context of problem solving that I would like to offer a conceptual model of genre that helps learners build their adaptive capacities. In an effort to set our learners on the path to expertise, I submit that a particular approach to teaching genre will provide learners with a tool that can help them continue their path toward expertise as an accomplished novice. Namely, special attention to genre can help learners begin to recognize patterns of content, structure, and style—a form of writing expertise that will enable them as they use genres to respond to writing situations outside of the classroom. Situations that, as Petraglia reminded us, are never exactly the same.

Helping Learners "See" Genres through ROCSS

In keeping with the recommendation in transfer literature by Wardle and others to help learners gain conceptual experience; our goal is not to teach particular genres because we cannot anticipate what genres students might need to learn in the future. Rather, our goal is to help learners gain experience with genre conceptually through practice. If genres have meaningful patterns, recognizing them can be complicated, and the indeterminate nature of genre poses a problem for teachers. The main goal for teaching genre is to help them learn to analyze genres on their own later, so providing learners with a framework for learning about analyzing genres can be helpful. After reviewing some of the literature about the often-inchoate nature of genres, this section of this chapter provides two very different pieces of writing in the same genre (two music reviews by Sasha Friere-Jones) and demonstrates how a conceptual framework based on a Bakhtinian theory of genre can help explain how those two artifacts can belong to the same genre. Lastly, this section offers a student-friendly articulation of Bakhtin's theory of genre and offers ideas about how it can be supplemented in the classroom with other content from writing courses (such as tools for developing ideas and organizing writing).

The Complexity of Genre

In the classroom, students need individual genres with which to practice, but Anis Bawarshi and Mary Jo Reiff argue that such a complex understanding of genre challenges researchers in rhetoric (specifically, rhetorical genre studies, or RGS) "to consider how genre knowledge is acquired, and raises questions as to whether genre knowledge can be taught explicitly" (82)—an assertion that again parallels Petraglia's claim that writing is ill-structured and thus can't be taught ("Writing"). Thus, in a writing classroom, genres might be represented by individual artifacts with which students must be familiar if they are to produce an effective piece of writing in that genre, but individual artifacts bring with them a variety of variables to which there are no formulaic answers or ways to get the desired results. As Maria Antonia Coutinho and Florencia Miranda argue, the gap between a genre as a theoretical abstraction and an example of the same genre in the form of a written artifact is difficult to bridge. They explain that "the multiplicity of facts and criteria that may intervene in this descriptive work" is very difficult to apply to particular artifacts because of "the changing nature that characterizes genres" themselves (35). Deciding what counts as a representative artifact for a genre can also be difficult, thus also making it difficult to teach genre. There is no discrete catalog of artifacts for a particular genre that we may develop or maintain because the artifacts we collect may have significant differences on the basis of social contexts or the caprice of individual authors.

Two music reviews, for example, might be quite different from each other, even though they're written within the same context—by the same author for the same publication. Suppose a writing instructor wants learners to write a music review. Collecting what might be considered good samples of reviews and then helping learners decipher the elements of a music review can be very difficult. While there might be reviews that seem more standard and straightforward, there will also be those that push the boundaries of what the genre of music review is. Consider two examples from Sasha Frere-Jones, a former music critic for the *New Yorker* who sometimes wrote reviews that were wildly different from each other. The first review, "Diamond Dancers," is about a Van Halen concert at Madison Square Garden during the band's comeback tour featuring David Lee Roth. In this review, Frere-Jones provides a brief history of the band while discussing its musical history, its breakup, and later comeback. The review dwells on David Lee Roth's largely mediocre performance and describing him as a circus ringmaster from the vaudeville era—as a figure that attempted (but failed) to mimic the captivating, energetic vivacity of his younger years on stage. By contrast, Frere-Jones explores how the rest of the band—guitarist Eddie Van Halen, drummer Alex Van Halen, and bassist Wolfgang Van Halen (Eddie's son) still carry the show musically and make up for Roth's shortcomings.

The second review, "U2's Forgettable Fire," is about the band's *Songs of Innocence* album, which was also released automatically by Apple on all iPhones at the time. The U2 review exhibits elements of a review much more subtly. After commenting briefly on the album's rather glitchy release to all iTunes libraries and surmising that Tim Cook (the CEO of Apple) and U2 wanted to tap into the same "organic delight" that Beyoncé did when she made the sudden announcement that she was releasing an entire album on iTunes, Frere-Jones reviews the album in what reads as a roast. He lists each of U2's eleven songs, one by one, and provides a brief but scathing critique: "The track sounds like seventeen different bands averaged out in Yelp and turned into an Active Rock Smoothie" ("The Forgettable Fire" par. 5) or "Not necessarily clear if anybody from the band attended the recording of this song" (par. 11). Each of the eleven tracks also received a comparison to a corresponding (by number) track on Beyoncé's "Beyoncé": "Not as good as 'No Angel'" (par. 7) or "Don't even compare this to 'Partition'" (par. 8).

Categorically, the U2 review might be an outlier in the genre of music reviews (or maybe it really does belong outside it). As a reader, I had trouble deciding whether it was really a review. (Is it really just a roast in the music section of the *New Yorker*?) However, in some ways it could be, depending on what framework we might use to analyze it as an instance of the genre. Cases like this can help us (and our students) decide what the "boundaries" of a particular genre might be as we seek to recognize the components of a genre we would like to write in.

A Conceptual Framework from Bakhtin

One framework our discipline has to offer—one that can help our learners organize writing conceptually and thus enable them to see meaningful chunks—is Mikhail Bakhtin's theory of genre. For guidelines on describing a genre, we can turn to Coutinho and Miranda, who drew from Bakhtin to help us understand the "relatively stable" attributes of a genre. As they explain, Bakhtin offered a three-part framework for identifying and describing genres: that they can be distinguished by thematic subject, composition, and style. For Bakhtin, the thematic subject would be what we might call exigence. The thematic subject is the occasion that, at least for us, prompts a writer to deploy a particular genre. Importantly, not just single instances of an occasion but rather the recurrence of occasion and thus a "typified rhetorical action" is what produces a genre (Miller). Coutinho and Miranda explain that the composition is the "text substructure"—the elements that include things like the organization of the text and the sequencing it uses (such as narrative or argument)—to advance ideas. The composition is the set of structural elements that prompt a writer to develop the text and make it cohesive. Lastly, Coutinho and Miranda explain two definitions of style, in which the plural version "styles" includes the "phraseology of a social group," and the singular version of style in which an individual invokes his or her own version of the social group's discourse (36–37). In an attempt to make this framework more straightforward and accessible for my learners, I use the acronym "ROCSS" (Recurring Occasion, Content, Structure, and Style) to provide them with a framework for describing genres.

Although it is clearly impossible to describe a particular genre in full using Bakhtin's framework, a teacher of writing must at least make an attempt to help learners articulate genre and provide opportunities for practice by offering invention or other strategies that might help learners adapt to different genres. Some of those strategies can come from the genres a teacher decides to use for practice, especially if the same strategies might be adaptable to other genres. For instance, the recurring occasion that prompts reviews is the emergence of a new or revised product, performance, service, or other consumable that leaves an audience deciding whether they would like to partake in the experience or purchase and/or consume the product. To that end, stasis theory can be helpful. The content of a review relies strongly (but also either implicitly or explicitly) on the stasis of evaluation or quality (see, for example, Fahnestock and Secor; Ramage), where the product, performance, or service is measured against a typical set of standards for the class of item under review. Both the Van Halen review and the U2 review rely on this stasis, although the U2 review relies on standards that are so implicit that the reader has to do a great deal of work (or be very familiar with the discourse of the music industry and the artists in question) to interpret what those standards might be. Depending on the type of review and the author's inclinations, reviews might be structured not only around standards and measures of quality, but also around narratives or other organizational schemes. Frere-Jones's (2012) "Diamond Dancers" provides two loose narratives: the first is a brief history of Van Halen that roughly approximates chronological order, while the second is Frere-

Jones's observations from the concert at Madison Square Garden that isn't necessarily in chronological order. Lastly, each review is written in a popular style expected in many publications where one might find music reviews, though some aspects of style might be unique to the publication in question (the *New Yorker*) and the author.

My rendition of ROCSS may seem sweeping or incomplete, and it may even tempt instructors and learners to try to distinguish genres exclusively by their form, but the pedagogical value is that it can frame genre for learners in a flexible, dynamic way that meshes well with a variety of rhetorical concepts and strategies. For example, a recurring occasion consists of important threshold concepts in writing such as audience and purpose. Recurring occasions bring purposes, audiences, writers, motives, rhetorical recurrence, and other aspects of context into conversation with each other, thus creating a set of exigencies that a particular genre of writing meets (see Carolyn Miller's "Genre as Social Action"). To meet those exigencies, writers must develop particular content that might be expected, find ways to structure that content in an acceptable way, and find ways to present it through an appropriate style befitting the genre and context in question. Throughout a semester with ROCSS as a centerpiece, then, teachers can help learners get used to "decoding" recurring occasions and adapt strategies for content, structure and style. From there, they can also offer strategies from a variety of resources (such as textbooks or our various encyclopedia of rhetorical terms). For content, teachers can help learners practice various forms of invention to help learners generate content adaptively (such as stasis theory and other systems of invention), various strategies for structuring writing (such as narrative, classical argument, and placing old information before new information) and various strategies for style (including adding levels of formality or practicing various voices that seem to accompany different genres). Thus, genre becomes an operationalized term that could enable learners to read their way into unfamiliar genres and then draw from various strategies that could then help them meet the expectations for those genres.

Adding Nuance to Ill Structuredness: Genre as a Design Problem

Even with a framework, though, a writing teacher cannot reproduce all the dimensions that help create a "mental model" for a given genre that an experienced writer would have. Experienced writers of any stripe spend a lot of time working within the recurring occasion of the genre(s) they write, which gives them several advantages: first, they have regular social interaction with others in relation to the type of writing they do. Additionally, they have a lot of experience both reading and writing in the genre and, like experts in other areas like chess, can recognize meaningful chunks of their specialty genres just by virtue of their vast experience. We cannot expect to recreate this type of experience for students, and thus we need to find ways to develop cognitive skills that might speak to the type of knowledge students need to adapt to new genres—despite the necessity of taking an ill-structured cognitive task like writing and translating it into the well-structured environment of the classroom.

Thus, we can turn our attention again to ill-structured problem solving and explore a nuanced discussion of it by David H. Jonassen. Jonassen argues that, although problem solving outside of school is almost always ill-structured while school-based instruction is well-structured, ill-structured problems still vary in terms of the skills and knowledge they require. Jonassen recommends a "typology" for ill-structured problems, naming eleven different types (*Learning* 11). The requirements for each type vary in terms of how they are represented (both internally by the problem solver and externally), as well as the activities one must undertake to approach each one in the classroom ("Toward" 65). Further, much in line with previous research on transfer, Jonassen explains that a problem solver's mental representations of ill-structured problems come from prior knowledge and experience, and problem solvers apply their existing schemas to new problems or instances of similar problems. While experts have well-developed problem schemas, novices must rely on general strategies that might not apply (66). Importantly, Jonassen's work has much in common with our discipline's concept of genre because he develops a very robust definition of *problem schema* that takes into account not only individual problem solving activities such as creating artifacts or fixing broken equipment, but also the social frameworks that support those problem solving activities. (Jonassen variously uses at least two other terms for *problem schema*: "problem space" and "mental model." I am using problem schema for the sake of simplicity.) It is my intention in this section to explain what Jonassen calls design problem solving, under which he categorizes writing, to draw connections between our concept of genre and ill-structured problem solving. To help explain how design problem solving works, I will contrast it with another type of ill-structured problem solving that Jonassen calls "troubleshooting" before linking design problem solving to writing in specific genres.

Fortuitously for us, Jonassen describes problem solving in a way that parallels our understanding of genre—that "as problems become more ill-defined, their solutions become more socially and culturally mediated. What becomes a problem arises from the interaction of participants, activity, and context" (*Learning* 2–3). Additionally, the way Jonassen and Henning describe problem schemas sounds suspiciously like the way our discipline would describe genres of writing. These authors argue that a problem schema is a dynamic cognitive construction of a problem that has at least four dimensions: activity-based knowledge, or knowledge of the social and material circumstances (and how to work within those circumstances) of a given problem; social/relational knowledge, or the identity the problem-solver must adopt within the problem-solving context; conversational/discursive knowledge, or the "social negotiation of meaning" through exchanges of discourse within the problem solving context; and artifactual knowledge, or knowledge of the material artifacts around which the problem is centered (Jonassen and Henning 40–41). However, they also admit that "[problem schemas] are theoretical constructs [that] do not exist in any reified form," leaving us "[un]certain how they develop" (38). Drawing from Jean Lave (1988), who believes that "cognition and thinking are shaped by activity, and that learning is represented as the centripetal movement toward the center of a community of practice," Jonassen and Henning think of problem solving in much the same way that the field of rhetoric and writing sees genres: for them, knowledge of a problem is "embedded in the activities and processes that people engage in, the social relations and identities of the actors, and in the conversations or social discourse they use to make meaning of the activities and events" (40).

Although various ill-structured problems have ambiguous goals or procedures, Jonassen also notes the need to develop a typology because ill-structured problems vary in the degree of ill-structuredness. To illustrate, Jonassen and Henning's example of repair work on refrigeration systems would be classified as troubleshooting (Jonassen, *Learning*) in which the end-goal might be fairly stable (to identify and fix a "fault state" that is keeping the system from reaching a goal, such as cooling to thirty-five degrees Fahrenheit), but the process of reaching that goal might have ambiguous paths because refrigeration systems are complex systems that have a variety of treatment options (Jonassen, "Toward," 75). The example Jonassen and Henning provide comes from their work studying the problem schemas for refrigeration systems as conceptualized by novice and expert repair technicians. They describe these technicians' knowledge as a sort of interplay between what they conceptualize as individuals ("knowledge in the head") and what demands and conceptualizations come from the social context ("knowledge in the world"). The technicians they studied had to have knowledge of the components of refrigeration systems (like compressors and pipes), but they also had to work within social relationships contextualized within a supermarket and with other technicians; participate in their context through their identities as refrigeration repair specialists (as outsiders in the context of the supermarket, but as insiders with other technicians); engage in conversations and storytelling about the problem and other similar problems with a variety of people in the context(s); and use their senses (along with their tools) to become familiar with the refrigeration systems themselves—their artifacts (40–41).

By contrast, Jonassen describes a design problem with criteria such as the need for a great deal of *problem structuring*—continual revision of the problem schema—on the part of the problem solver; vague goals with few stated constraints; vague or unstated criteria for evaluation; limited or delayed feedback; high degrees of freedom for the problem solver; and solutions that are only better or worse, rather than wrong or right (Jonassen, "Toward"). Additionally, design problems have several other characteristics: the need to integrate multiple knowledge domains; high levels of domain knowledge; goals and intentions instead of procedures and solutions; the need to produce artifacts that function independently of the designer; multiple, highly subjective criteria for evaluation that change over time or are unknown to the designer; and highly heterogeneous interpretations of the problem with multiple (yet legitimate) solutions (Jonassen, "Toward"; Jonassen and Hung). Design problems ask problems solvers to apply domain knowledge and strategic knowledge to make an artifact. Whereas troubleshooting involves finding solutions that will result in better performance of a system or an elimination of the fault state, design problem solving requires that designers themselves must deal with criteria for a solution that might not be apparent.

To apply the characteristics of design problem solving to writing, consider my own experience writing this chapter. I have dealt with many difficulties that writers face: the original CFP and follow-up conversations with the editors have included references to the *Framework*, but the only instruction has been that it should be used as a starting point; I have had to decide who my readers are without ever talking to them, and then assess their previous knowledge of things like writing, transfer, cognitive psychology, problem solving, and the like; and I have had to decide on the best conceptual ideas from writing studies and cognitive psychology to frame my discussion, and then find a way to organize those ideas without an established template for those ideas. Although there may be more leeway for structure in a book chapter such as this one than there would be in an article that presents empirical research (with its introduction, review of literature, methods, results, and discussion), even genres with more established structures and expected content can demand a high degree of guesswork from their authors in terms of exactly what literature to review, what methods to use, how to present results, and so on.

Although we could speculate that an expert writer (or "design problem solver") like music critic Frere-Jones can write reviews more or less automatically because he has extensive experience and practice within the domain of review writing (and thus intimate knowledge both of the genre and the subject matter), designers with less experience and expertise need to spend more time developing their problem schemas of written artifacts, in the form of particular genres, as well as the situations out of which they derive, the subject matter they should use, and so on. What Bakhtin's theory of genre (and my framework of ROCSS) does for writers is provide them with a way to begin developing a problem schema for themselves—it provides them with a place to begin as they tackle design problem solving. Cueing in to the recurring occasion, content, structure, and style of a genre will provide them with an approach that helps them identify a genre they may need to use, gain insight into the typified situation in which that genre might be used, discern some typical characteristics of the genre (while understanding that both situation and characteristics are variable), and then approximate that for the writing problem of their own while revising their understanding of it (their problem schema vis-a-vis the genre).

Because design problems are different from other ill-structured problems, Jonassen also argues that the way they are taught should also differ. From a pedagogical perspective, Jonassen's typology for ill-structured problems can assist us, as he also offers recommendations for teaching each type of design problem. Using his framework for design problem solving involves relying on his recommendations. Thus, I recommend teaching genre by adapting Jonassen's ("Research Issues") recommendations for teaching design problems so that the pedagogical problems unique to design problem solving help maximize learning for students. What follows is a lesson plan about genre that makes that adaptation.

TEACHING GENRE AS A DESIGN PROBLEM

The following is a sample set of classroom exercises about genre that I often use in my classes. Importantly, it is one of several similar lesson plans (to provide learners with ongoing and varied practice periodically throughout a course) that ask learners to adapt to new genres and reflect on both the concept of genre and decisions they make. To the extent possible in one lesson plan, it attempts to incorporate a variety of the case and scaffold types that Jonassen recommends for design problems. For the purposes of classroom instruction, Jonassen refers to *cases* and *scaffolds* as instructional support, and particular combinations of cases and scaffolds help learners with different types of problems. A case is a particular instance of a problem type that can be studied and manipulated for the learner's benefit. However, rather than focus on traditional case-based learning, Jonassen focuses on the function and purpose of cased-based learning. Thus, cases for Jonassen help learners consider a problem (or problems) from a variety of angles. He identified seven different case types (*Learning* 150). Scaffolds, as Jonassen sees them, should help learners analyze relationships among components of a problem ("Research Issues" 7). He identified seven different types of scaffolds (12). However, Jonassen does not apply all types of cases or all types of scaffolds to all problem types. For design problems, Jonassen recommended combinations of *problems, prior experiences,* and *alternative perspectives* for the cases and *causal, argumentation,* and *modeling* scaffolds (12).

In the material that follows, I will share a lesson plan I use to teach genre. It consists of seven different prompts and relies on the framework for genre (recurring occasion, content, structure, and style) that I presented earlier. At the same time, I will connect each prompt to Jonassen's recommended teaching strategies for design problem solving. The main focus of this lesson plan is a problem case (in which students write in the genre of a dictionary entry using ROCSS). Of course, this lesson plan does not represent all that could be done, and some lesson plans could emphasize some of Jonassen's other types of cases and scaffolds over others—any of them could be used as the central focus of a given lesson, while others provide support.

Prompt One

Prompt one reviews previous knowledge students may have gained from their participation in the course: "Group: Make a list of as many different types of writing (genres) as you can. Examples: texts, e-mails, business proposals, birthday cards." This prompt contextualizes the day's tasks by asking them to name a variety of genre types. It also helps learners review one of the main focal points of the course, which is to gain practice writing in different genres. Given previous class discussions about the need to adapt to various genres, asking learners to make a list reinforces the idea for them that genres vary widely.

Prompt Two

The second prompt continues the review by focusing specifically on ROCSS: "Individual: Please define the four elements of ROCSS. Recurring Occasion, Content, Structure, Style." Because this is an individual exercise, the framework is reinforced for all learners in the classroom by asking each one to recall this knowledge. In conjunction with the first prompt, the second can be used to reinforce memory and provide a conceptual framework for the day's activities.

Prompt Three

The third prompt reads: "Group: analyze a typical dictionary entry. What are the Recurring Occasion, Content, Structure, and Style?" This prompt entails a brief example of prior experiences. Not to be confused with the prior knowledge or experience that an individual learner might already have, Jonassen and Henning recommend providing students with similar design problems to the one being taught and then adapting those cases to fit the problem students are working on, providing them with enough background information to do a task (8–9). For the purposes of this lesson plan, that might mean exposing learners to a variety of dictionary entries from different types of dictionaries (perhaps medical dictionaries, the *Urban Dictionary*, a glossary at the back of a technical manual, and so on). Exposing students to a range of samples and a range of approaches could also be very important for helping them develop a problem schema of a given genre and teaching them to seek out multiple examples on their own would be beneficial. Given that this lesson plan covers only one class period and is meant to help learners practice adapting to new genres, I only included one sample, that I wrote myself. However, in preparation for a major assignment that requires learners to write in a genre (such as a review, a commentary, grant proposal, or other lengthier type of writing), I would assign several varying examples of that genre for reading.

Sample Dictionary Entry

practice   [prak' - tis]

noun

1. Systematic repetition of a skill with the aim of maintenance or improvement.
Ex. *With enough practice, one can become a skilled chess player.*

verb

1. To incorporate performance into a daily routine.
Ex. *Shaolin monks practice Kung Fu four hours per day.*

2. To apply specialized knowledge professionally.
Ex. *Some undergraduate students study to practice law.*

Figure 1. A case of prior experiences for design problem solving. This lesson plan draws from the genre of a dictionary entry to provide "prior experience" before students "design" their own dictionary entry.

Prompt Four

The fourth prompt employs the problem variant of Jonassen's case types, which Jonassen and Henning define as a representation of an authentic problem (7). For writing, this could mean providing a writing scenario to which students should respond:

> Individual Scenario: Help Your Parents
>
> Suppose you are having a discussion during the summer with your parents, and they throw some shade. Suppose you say, "Stop throwin' shade," but they don't know what it means. You decide that a dictionary of slang terms for your parents would be a good idea.
>
> Instead of continuing the conversation, you decide to start this project and open your own Website. Kind of like Urban Dictionary, but with parents as an audience. You need a starter definition so that others can contribute to your dictionary, so your first sample entry is *throwin' shade*.
>
> Create a dictionary entry that is similar to what one might find in a regular dictionary but adapt it for parents as an audience. Make sure to adjust your writing for content, structure, and style. Make yours look like a dictionary entry, too; like many types of writing, dictionary entries have a visual structure and not just a textual one.

This prompt asks learners to engage with design problem solving by writing their own dictionary entry for a slang term (throwin' shade) with their parents as an audience. Although the scenario I supplied might not be authentic in the sense that it is real, it has some authentic elements (such as a real audience that learners could address), a motive that learners might find plausible and familiar (a misunderstanding between parents and children), and a genre that arguably exists (a dictionary of slang terms for the uninitiated—*Urban Dictionary*) and could be adapted to the scenario. In some cases, I might strive for an even higher degree of authenticity.

Prompt Five

The fifth prompt covers two scaffolds on Jonassen's list—alternative perspectives and causal reasoning:

> Individual Reflection: How effective do you think your entry for throwin' shade would be, given parents as an audience? Would a dictionary for parents with entries like yours help improve communication between young adults and parents? Why or why not? Given our scenario, what are some other genres of writing that could be used to interact with parents? What would their advantages and disadvantages be?

Alternative perspectives introduce students to alternative ways of thinking about a problem ("Research Issues" 9). The first question for this prompt—which asks learners to choose a different genre to communicate with parents—gets at one of the fundamental aspects of communication (to choose a genre that can best be used to communicate with an audience) by prompting learners to make choices about the best genre to use in a recurring occasion. In other words, given the open nature of design problem solving, it's asking learners to contemplate how they would solve the same design problem differently. In the second question in the fifth prompt, students would study the relationships of cause and effect among variables in the problem, which could help the student make predictions or infer potential causes ("Research Issues" 10). In a writing course, asking learners how a particular audience might react and whether the writer would accomplish her goal is a central question about writing that requires causal reasoning: how will the writing affect the audience?

Prompt Six

The sixth prompt asks students to engage in Jonassen's scaffold of argumentation: "Group: Our dictionary entries are effective for an audience of parents. Believe it / doubt it." Here, students must justify decisions they make in their solution of a problem ("Research Issues" 11); this believe it and doubt it exercise (Elbow, 14–15) requires learners to think through the strengths and weaknesses of writing.

Prompt Seven

The seventh (and last) prompt in this classroom-based lesson plan asks students to reflect on their experience adapting their writing to a specific genre:

> Draw a hand-made word cloud that represents your experience adapting to a new genre. Use it to represent how important you think different elements of the task were. For example: some terms might be larger because you think they played a more important role, while others might be smaller because they did not play as dominant of a role. Use the following terms to create your word cloud: 1. Audience; 2. Content; 3. Genre; 4. Structure; 5. recurring occasion; and 6. Style.

In this prompt, students rely on Jonassen's scaffold of modeling, which requires them to develop their own representations (models) of components and relationships in their problem ("Research Issues" 11). There are many different ways to ask students to represent their work, and this one asks them to review key writing terms and prioritize them in relation to their experience with the scenario. It also includes a wordle (see figure 2) as a visual cue.

Conclusion: Expanding Capacities

In light of the important recommendations for teaching for transfer in the "Elon Statement on Writing Transfer," which emphasizes the need for conceptual learning about writing, varied practice on the basis of that conceptual learning, and metacognitive reflection, Jonassen's framework for design problems and his recommendations for teaching them overlap well with important pedagogical focal points from our discipline. For example—some aspects of my lesson plan above conform to both Jonassen's framework and a metacognitive framework outlined by Gorzelsky et al., who recommend evaluation of one's own work as an important focal points of metacognition (among others). What Jonassen adds, from the perspective of cognitive psychology, is a nuanced understanding of ill-structured problem solving that enables us to see writing as design problem solving, thus offering further direction about how to provide learners with the practice they need for that type of problem solving. Jonassen provides us, at least, with suggestions that can help us construct

Figure 2. A wordle as a visual cue.

helpful classroom activities on a day-to-day basis. Although the *Framework* offers suggestions we can use to develop a curriculum, a syllabus, and assignments, I find Jonassen's theory most useful directly at the classroom level in support of principles our discipline has already established. At the same time, a nuanced approach to ill-structured problem solving, as well as the use of conceptual learning with the aim of transfer, may also supplement approaches provided in this book. We might consider how design problem solving and a strong conceptual understanding of genre might help learners with metacognitive reflection in online environments (Stuckey et al., this collection) or how they might fit within a curriculum framed through threshold concepts (DasBender, this collection).

However, this is not to say that we should expect our learners to become full-fledged experts with the expectation that they can "solve" any writing problem successfully, or even that we should characterize our expectations for them through the lens of "expertise." Yancey et al. frame their discussion of their Teaching for Transfer curriculum partly through a particular attitude toward expertise that they recommend we foster in our learners—one that is very much about capacity building and problem solving. Also drawing from *How People Learn*, Yancey et al. explain the difference between the assumption of expertise and that of an *accomplished novice*: learning can be short-circuited by the assumption of superior expert knowledge and a possession of all the answers, whereas accomplished novices recognize the usefulness of their previous experiences while also acknowledging that they can still learn more (40–41). Teaching genre as a design problem may expand learners' capacities in the way I outlined at the beginning of this chapter, and using it as a supplement to already established pedagogies may benefit students in writing transfer.

Works Cited

Adler-Kassner, Linda, et al. "Assembling Knowledge: Threshold Concepts in Facilitating Transfer." *Critical Transitions: Writing and the Question of Transfer*, edited by Chris Anson and Jessie Moore, Perspectives on Writing, WAC Clearinghouse and UP of Colorado, 2016, pp. 17–48.

Bakhtin, Mikhail. *Le Marxisme et la Philosophie du Langage*. Minuit, 1977.

Bawarshi, Anis S., and Mary Jo Reiff. *Genre: An Introduction to History, Theory, Research, and Pedagogy*. Parlor P, 2010.

Bazerman, Charles. "The Life of Genre, the Life of the Classroom." *Genre and Writing: Issues, Arguments, Alternatives*, edited by Wendy Bishop and Hans Ostrom, Boynton/Cook, 1997, pp. 19–26.

Bergmann, Linda S., and Janet Zepernick. "Disciplinarity and Transfer: Students' Perceptions of Learning to Write." *WPA: Writing Program Administration*, vol. 31, no. 1–2, 2007, pp. 124–49.

Brent, Doug. "Crossing Boundaries: Co-op Students Relearning to Write. *College Composition and Communication*, vol. 63, no. 4, 2012, pp. 558–92.

Chi, Michelene T. H., et al. "Categorization and Representation of Physics Problems by Experts and Novices." *Cognitive Science*, vol. 5, 1981, pp. 121–52.

Clark, Irene L., and Andrea Hernandez. "Genre Awareness, Academic Argument, and Transferability." *The WAC Journal*, vol. 22, 2012, pp. 65–78.
Council of Writing Program Administrators, National Council of Teachers of English, and National Writing Project. *Framework for Success in Postsecondary Writing*. CWPA, NCTE, and NWP, 2011, wpacouncil.org/aws/CWPA/asset_manager/get_file/350201?ver=505. Accessed 18 Jan. 2020.
Coutinho, Maria Antónia, and Florencia Miranda. "To Describe Genres: Problems and Strategies." *Genre in a Changing World*, edited by Charles Bazerman, Adair Bonini, and Débora Figueiredo, Parlor P, 2009, pp. 35–55.
Downs, Doug, and Elizabeth Wardle. "Teaching about Writing, Righting Misconceptions: (Re)envisioning 'First-Year Composition' as 'Introduction to Writing Studies." *College Composition and Communication*, vol. 58, no. 4, 2007, pp. 552–84.
Efklides, Anastasia. "Metacognition, Affect, and Conceptual Difficulty." *Overcoming Barriers to Student Understanding: Threshold Concepts and Troublesome Knowledge*, edited by Jan H.F. Meyer and Ray Land. Routledge, 2012, pp. 48–69.
Elbow, Peter. *Writing without Teachers*. Oxford UP, 1973.
"Elon Statement on Writing Transfer." Elon University, 29 July 2013, www.elon.edu/e-web/academics/teaching/ers/writing_transfer/statement.xhtml. Accessed 13 Sept. 2019.
Fahnestock, Jeanne, and Marie Secor. "Teaching Argument: A Theory of Types." *College Composition and Communication*, vol. 34, no. 1, 1983, pp. 20–30.
Frere-Jones, Sasha. "Diamond Dancers: The Sparkly World of Van Halen." *The New Yorker*, 19 March 2012. Rpt. in John Trimbur, *The Call to Write*, Brief 6th ed, Wadsworth/Cengage, 2013.
—. "U2's Forgettable Fire." *The New Yorker*. 2014, www.newyorker.com/culture/sasha-frere-jones/u2s-forgettable-fire. Accessed 13 Mar. 2019.
Gorzelsky, Gwen, et al. "Cultivating Constructive Metacognition: A New Taxonomy for Writing Studies." *Critical Transitions: Writing and the Question of Transfer*, edited by Chris Anson and Jessie L. Moore, Perspectives on Writing, WAC Clearinghouse and UP of Colorado, 2016, pp. 217–49.

Jonassen, David. H. "Toward a Design Theory of Problem Solving." *Educational Technology, Research, and Development*, vol. 48, no. 4, 2000, pp. 63–85.

—. "Research Issues in Problem Solving." *11th International Conference on Education Research: New Educational Paradigm for Learning and Instruction*, Sept. 29–Oct. 1, 2010.

—. *Learning to Solve Problems: A Handbook for Designing Problem-Solving Learning Environments*. Routledge, 2010.

Jonassen, David. H., and Philip Henning. "Mental Models: Knowledge in the Head and Knowledge in the World." *Educational Technology*, vol. 39, no. 3, 1999, pp. 37–42.

Jonassen, David H., and Woei Hung. "All Problems are not Equal: Implications for Problem-Based Learning." *Interdisciplinary Journal of Problem-Based Learning*, vol. 2, no. 2, 2008, pp. 6–28.

Lave, Jean. *Cognition in Practice: Mind, Mathematics, and Culture in Everyday Life*. Cambridge UP, 1988.

Miller, Carolyn. "Genre as Social Action." *Quarterly Journal of Speech*, vol. 70, 1984, pp. 151–67.

Novacek, Rebecca. *Agents of Integration: Understanding Transfer as a Rhetorical Act*. Southern Illinois UP, 2011.

Petraglia, Joseph. "Introduction: General Writing Skills Instruction and Its Discontents." *Reconceiving Writing, Rethinking Writing Instruction*, edited by Joseph Petraglia, Lawrence Erlbaum, 1995, pp. xi–xvii.

—. "Writing as an Unnatural Act." *Reconceiving Writing, Rethinking Writing Instruction*, edited by Joseph Petraglia, Lawrence Erlbaum, 1995, pp. 79–100.

Ramage, John. *Rhetoric: A User's Guide*. Pearson, 2006, New York.

Reiff, Mary Jo, and Anis Bawarshi. "Tracing Discursive Resources: How Students Use Prior Genre Knowledge to Negotiate New Writing Contexts in First-Year Composition." *Written Communication*, vol. 28, no. 3., 2011, pp. 312–37.

Reitman, Walter. *Cognition and Thought: An Information Processing Approach*. Wiley, 1965, New York.

Rounsaville, Angela. "Selecting Genres for Transfer: The Role of Uptake in Students' Antecedent Genre Knowledge." *Composition Forum*, vol. 26, 2012, compositionforum.com/issue/26/selecting-genres-uptake.php. Accessed 16 Sept. 2019.

Simon, Herbert, and William G. Chase. "Skill in Chess." *American Scientist*, vol. 61, 1973, pp. 394–403.

Wardle, Elizabeth. "Understanding 'transfer' from FYC: Preliminary Results from a Longitudinal Study." *WPA: Writing Program Administration*, vol. 31, no. 1–2, 2007, pp. 65–85.

—. "Creative Repurposing for Expansive Learning." *Composition Forum*, vol. 26, 2012, compositionforum.com/issue/26/creative-repurposing.php. Accessed 16 Sept. 2019.

—. "You Can Learn to Write in General." *Bad Ideas about Writing*, edited by Cheryl Ball and Drew Loewe, West Virginia University Libraries Digital Publishing Institute, 2017, pp. 30–33.

Yancey, Kathleen Blake, et al. *Writing Across Contexts: Transfer, Composition, and Sites of Writing.* Utah State UP, 2014.

6 Creating a "Language" of Trauma: Exploring Trauma Theories and Trauma Narratives in Multimodal Writing

Courtney Patrick-Weber

In my first year as an assistant professor at Bay Path University, one of my first-year students wrote an essay for my class about the time her neighbor raped her when she was in middle school. I didn't purposefully assign a trauma narrative; all I asked was for my students to write about a time in their lives that changed them in some way. My hope was for them to find confidence as writers in that first assignment since so many of them felt they weren't good writers. I was fresh off my PhD in Rhetoric, tons of composition theorists' work sharp in my mind, and as I sat with her paper in my hand, I realized that I had no idea how to respond to this paper. It was visceral, raw, honest, and rough around the edges. It needed revision, but how do I ask my student to revisit this paper and work on her comma splices? After speaking with the student, I was shocked at her honest desire to receive critical feedback. She wanted me to ask questions, to excavate the emotional bones of her work and bring them to the light. She wanted to share her story, and she wanted people to read it. I did what I could to help her but felt woefully unprepared and angry at my ignorance. This moment revealed a gap in my learning and, consequently, a gap in our scholarship. To help fill in the blanks, I consulted trauma theorists and memoir writers. I read Louise

DeSalvo's *Writing as a Way of Healing* and studied cognitive theorists in our field. But there is much more work to be done in this vital area.

The First-Year Writing (FYW) course is a vulnerable eco-system. For so many in-coming students, it is the first (and perhaps only class) during that vital first year that is small enough for instructors to actually know their students' names. Because college is such a powerful crossroads in so many students' lives, FYW courses that give students that one-on-one attention missing from many other courses open up a seam for emotional writing to seep into the class, regardless of whether the instructor overtly advocates it. Many instructors may assign a seemingly simple personal narrative as the first writing assignment with the hope to ease students into the college writing process, only to find themselves face-to-face with complicated trauma narratives to begin the semester. Even if an instructor doesn't assign an essay under the genre of "personal" essay, these stories still trickle into the essay.

We wonder what to say in response to these papers, if we should say anything at all, and we wonder why a student, a virtual stranger at this point, feels comfortable enough with us to recall a painful event from the past onto a page. But before we respond, or simply cut the paper from the curriculum, it's imperative for us to learn the process students make leading up to the day they hand in their trauma narratives. If we understand more about the current cognitive theories around trauma and writing, then perhaps we can be more prepared for this inevitable event and learn how to retool the traditional personal narrative assignment to be better equipped to help students navigate their need to write about a trauma in the classroom-setting. The personal narrative is a powerful and important writing assignment, one that should not be removed because of our fear of a student writing about a traumatic event.

Before I examine trauma theory and its ties to writing, I first want to advocate for the personal narrative as a legitimate assignment in the FYW classroom. There are many arguments against assigning a personal narrative, but for the purpose of this chapter I will focus on two of the main arguments that surface when this topic is broached by academics in our field. The first argument is that "those who teach the personal essay engage in inappropriate and intrusive relationships with their students—and they promote an individualistic view of authorship that is naive and ultimately disempowering" (Newkirk 36). To this argument I ask, "What is wrong with knowing our students on a personal level?" Indeed, it is by knowing and understanding who students are on an individual basis that ultimately helps with retention. When our students enter our FYW classroom, many of us assume they are just like we were when we were that age. This is assumption is wrong:

> Politicians, administrators, and even faculty must accept that. . . college students today are not the type of students that many of us probably were—a fact that is too often used by some to scorn or shame students. They face challenges that are often far removed from the daily lives of their professors. Their lives are different, their needs are different, and as a result, the paths they must take to earn their degrees are different. (Webb-Sunderhaus 115)

The best way to learn about their lives is through their writing where they reveal to us their struggles and their goals. While, on the surface, we might know basic information about our students, it is only through personalized writing assignments that we can see "other, less quantifiable problems, such as mental health issues, histories of abuse, and addiction, which can also impact their college careers" (Webb-Sunderhaus 116–17). Their writing, especially their personal writing, reveals to us who they are and the struggles they face every single day. We know their names, but we know so much more.

The second major argument against assigning the personal essay in the FYW classroom is that the type of writing needed for the personal essay is not the same (and is not as important) as the kind of writing associated with academic writing. While on the surface, this argument is accurate as the personal essay does tend to use a less formal approach to language than that of an academic essay, the former assignment can ultimately help students succeed with the latter. All writing, regardless of genre, is personal because it comes from a person with emotions and individual experiences. For a student to succeed in an academic discourse, they must first feel confident in their ability as a writer, and this confidence can be garnered through the personal essay. Indeed, personal writing can "be a way to teach students how to use writing as a tool for thinking and a way for students to learn how to generate writing and familiarize themselves with acts of writing" (Rysdam 287). And "[w]hile teaching form and academic literacy cannot be ignored, some aspects of expressivism, like low-stakes writing, can meet the demand for increasing students' academic literacy, while simultaneously valuing the multiple discourses and knowledge they bring to the classroom" (Rysdam 286).

There is one more argument, that of the fear of being forced into the role of a therapist, that I will tackle later on in this chapter. For now, it's important for us to see the value of assigning the personal narrative in the FYW classroom and how it can tie to issues of retention as well as how the assignment can translate into success in the academic writing arena.

Engaging in trauma theory/writing and creating a language of trauma directly ties into the abits of mind in *The Framework for Success in Postsecondary Writing* by addressing Openness and Responsibility. By reading trauma narratives in various formats, and questioning the role of language in those narratives, students "consider new ways of being and thinking in the world," a move that is followed by the responsibility of the student to take this new knowledge and "act on the understanding that learning is shared among the writers and others" as trauma narratives must not only be written but experienced by a receptive audience (CWPA et al. 4–5). In his study on personal narratives, Thomas Newkirk notes that the personal essay, especially one based on a traumatic event, can ultimately help students become "co-theorists" of their own life and to share those findings with readers. After sharing some excerpts from one of his students' essays, he notes that the student made an "attempt to take agency and assert that she has made constructive use of [her] experience, while acknowledging that she still lives with the trauma of those years . . . [b]y claiming a positive outcome she finally becomes an agent in her own story" (45). Personal narratives that examine a trauma often try to find some "meaning" behind the darkness, revealing to readers how the writer reassesses their place in the world after the trauma.

There are currently two main cognitive theories regarding trauma and memory that can inform our understanding of trauma writing, particularly why students may choose to write about a traumatic event and why that decision is such a difficult one to make for the student. These two theories disagree on how survivors of traumatic events remember those traumas, with one camp advocating that survivors repress traumatic memories to protect the psyche (only to have those memories come to the surface due to some sort of spark/recognition from the outside world) while the other camp believes that these memories are never repressed—that we remember the details of a traumatic event more vividly than any other type of memory. The two camps also disagree regarding the role of the therapist in working through these traumatic memories. The first camp is helmed by trauma scholar Judith Herman and leans towards the belief in repressed memory. Often, the survivor needs a trained therapist to negotiate the complex recovery stages (safety, remembrance/mourning, and reconnection) once that traumatic connection is made (Herman 156). Since these memories are often repressed, "[t]he therapist's first task is to conduct a thorough and informed diagnostic evaluation" in order to name the problem (Herman 156–57). Once the problem is named, and can then be controlled in some way, the therapist works to create a safe environment for the patient to remember their trauma (157). Before the therapist and the patient delve into the details of the traumatic memory, Herman reminds us of the potency of traumatic memories:

> At this point, especially after a single acute trauma, the survivor may wish to put the experience out of mind for a while and get on with her life. And she may succeed in doing so for a time. . . But traumatic events ultimately refuse to be put away. At some point the memory of the trauma is bound to return, demanding attention. Often the precipitant is a significant reminder of the trauma—an anniversary, for instance—or a change in the survivor's life circumstances that brings her back to the unfinished work of integrating the traumatic experience. (174)

Even if the patient is reluctant to remember, the memory of trauma is more often than not just below the surface and will be triggered at some point. Due to this reluctance, Herman warns that the recovery process is anything but linear, which is important to remember when I talk about traumatic memory itself—which is also reluctant to follow a linear pattern. Usually, the recovery process ebbs and flows; the patient's advancement through the stages of recovery can be out of order, or a patient can regress to earlier stages, depending upon the severity of the memory.

The second stage of recovery focuses on remembrance and mourning, and Herman constantly reminds us of the importance of the therapist in the patient's recovery during this stage. It is true that the "choice to confront the horrors of the past rests with the survivor," but "the therapist plays the role of witness and ally, in whose presence the survivor can speak of the unspeakable" (Herman 175). The therapist, then, holds a lot of power in the process; indeed, Herman notes later that the therapist must play a "validating role" for the patient (Herman 179). No idle listener, the therapist cannot remain neutral and must be a witness for their patient, a position that leads many to question exactly how much influence the therapist has on the patient. Herman warns against this influential possibility, asking therapists to refrain from being "detectives."

As the second stage progresses, the patient comes face to face with their trauma as the therapist guides them through the memory recall. Once the memory is revealed, in detail, the patient needs to grieve for the loss of their old self, the self before the trauma (Herman 195). The mourning is perhaps the hardest, and most necessary, part of the healing process. What makes mourning difficult is because it doesn't really ever end for the survivor: "She will never forget. She will think of the trauma every day as long as she lives. She will grieve every day. But the time comes when the trauma no longer commands the central place in her life" (195).

The other main theory regarding trauma and memory comes to us primarily from Richard McNally. While Herman's camp believes survivors repress traumatic memories, McNally is critical of the concept of repressed memory in general, arguing that "[p]eople with PTSD [post-traumatic stress disorder] remember trauma all too well" (125). Citing numerous studies, McNally believes that memory issues in trauma survivors aren't necessarily linked to trauma and that survivors may already suffer from memory issues regardless of the trauma. He also argues that "patients remember their trauma all too well, but have difficulty remembering other parts of their past in detail" (134). For McNally, survivors do not suppress these memories because, at the time of the event, they do not consider it a traumatizing moment. Also, to suppress these memories directly goes against human survival mechanisms:

> To be sure, being haunted by memories of trauma is a singularly unpleasant experience. But natural selection does not care whether we are happy. The painful capacity for remembering trauma may be the price we pay for possessing memory mechanisms that allow us to remember dangers, survive, and reproduce. (McNally 62)

Although I agree with McNally's points about traumatic memory's refusal to be repressed, I disagree with his overall critique of the role of language in recalling these memories. In *The Body Keeps the Score*, author Bessel van der Kolk examines what happens to the brain during a traumatic flashback. In his studies, van der Kolk learns that when a flashback is triggered, the patient's Broca's area, a major speech center of the brain, goes "offline" (43). This important observation encourages van der Kolk to declare that "all trauma is preverbal" and "[t]rauma by nature drives us to the edge of comprehension, cutting us off from language based on common experience or an imaginable past" (43). In 1995, van der Kolk made a similar observation that McNally was quick to discount:

> [Stating that trauma has no language] makes no sense. The subjects *themselves* provided the narrative accounts of their traumatic experiences . . . [w]hatever the explanation for the deactivation of Broca's area, it cannot be attributed to the subjects' inability to narrate what happened to them. (McNally 153).

McNally gives language too much credit. Just because a survivor can put a trauma story into words doesn't mean that the words are an accurate depiction of what happened. Language has never been able to truly represent those images that flicker in our minds, regardless of whether or not we are recalling a traumatic event. Marian MacCurdy addresses this disconnect in her book *The Mind's Eye* when survivors describe how a traumatic event left them "speechless": "[survivor's inability to put experience into words] does not mean that survivors do not remember their experiences or cannot put words to them. It does mean that the iconic nature of the traumatic image often takes precedence over language, which can make it difficult to both 'feel' the image and construct a narrative about it at the same time" (21). Indeed, van der Kolk calls these traumatic narratives a "cover story" meant to help share with others some imperfect example of what happened to them (43). These "cover stories" are usually what we tend to encounter in the classroom.

But how do these theories and how we remember (or don't remember) trauma tie into the narratives we tend to assign in FYW? When a student writes about a traumatic event, it's important that we understand the cognitive steps that a student went through to come to a place where they feel comfortable and competent enough to try to write their stories. We also need to understand that survivors need to tell their stories; they look backwards for clues to the traumatic event, pieces that at the time seem insignificant but, in the shadow of trauma, serve as a threat for our narrative of the event. Telling these stories helps survivors make sense of and feel in control of the trauma. Upon learning about Broca's area's status during a flashback, we realize that "part of trauma's corrosive power lies in its ability to destroy narratives" but "stories, written and spoken, have tremendous healing power both for the teller and the listener" (Morris 17). But language is a poor, and seemingly only, outlet to tell these stories. David Morris, who primarily writes about PTSD in veterans, writes that survivors struggle to communicate to non-veterans, leaving the survivor in a liminal space between what is considered "normal" and "abnormal": "It is, as so many veterans have noted, as if they no longer speak the language of their countrymen. This language barrier, this inability on the part of the untraumatized to understand the existence of a place like No Man's Land, further alienates the survivor . . . [i]t's the language barrier that makes an unbloodied suburbanite ask a veteran whether or not he'd killed anyone in Iraq" (127). The language barrier is felt on both ends of communication as the survivor also struggles to make sense of their trauma through the inadequacy of language. Pat Barker writes in *The Regeneration Trilogy* of a WWI veteran, Charles Manning, with PTSD and his struggles to tell his story to the famous psychologist William Rivers. When Rivers suggests that the communication struggles may be because Manning doesn't think Rivers and others who have not experienced war first-hand would understand Manning's experiences, Manning answers, "It's ungraspable...I don't mean *you* can't grasp it because you haven't been there. I mean, *I* can't grasp it and I *have* been there" (Barker 525).

Trauma also resists language on a more social level as non-survivors of a traumatic event often ignore or shy away from a survivor's narrative. Susan Brison, herself a survivor of sexual assault and attempted murder, notes that "[w]e lack the vocabulary for expressing appropriate concern, and we have no social conventions to ease the awkwardness . . . we do not learn—early or later in life—how to react to a rape" (2). Brison goes on to describe how close relatives, including her own parents, shied away from contacting her after her rape because they feared saying the "wrong" thing or causing her more pain, a silence she believes is rooted in "misguided caution" (12). Not only do survivors struggle with telling their stories, but non-survivors struggle with listening to these stories. However, the stories need to be told, and they need to be heard if we want this disconnect between survivors and non-survivors, language and silence, to shrink. These stories also help people on both sides of the narrative understand what happened and why it happened.

Usually, the personal narrative essay is assigned at the beginning of a new semester as a low-stakes writing that allows students to write what they know while, simultaneously, serving as a writing sample for instructors to gauge the current writing ability of each student—and to plan for the semester ahead. What may seem like a simple assignment can immediately turn into a heart-wrenching essay if a student uses the opportunity to write about a traumatic event. The personal essay is the perfect genre for these difficult topics because of the inherent intimacy of the essay. Instructors should always be aware of this possibility and welcome it, but also not require students to write about something traumatic.

It's also important to remember that regardless of the essay's topic, personal essays can be complicated because the writer (the student) is complicated. Candice Spigelman explains, "We recognize that individuals are fragmented and fragmentary. In fact, theorists today use the word *subject* rather than *individual* to emphasize the formations that 'subject,' or structure, human identity and thinking" (39). Just as the writing classroom is a vulnerable place, "writing teachers are particularly vulnerable to the eruption of personal experiences into educational contexts, just by the nature of what we do . . . trauma is all too often an intimate part of [our students'] lives, and all they need is the real or perceived opportunity to express it" (MacCurdy 47). We are taking a risk when we assign a personal narrative, especially since this assignment takes place in a vulnerable first-year writing course. That doesn't mean we should abandon the personal essay, even though many of us have done exactly that.

The personal essay is risky, but the first-year writing course is a risky place, perhaps more so after 9/11. After that day, "students' needs changed" in ways we never imagined (Murphy et al. 69). These needs changed even more as the potential for a mass shooting haunts school campuses. Students needed to feel safe in secondary school campuses and still need to feel safe on college campuses. It's important for us all to remember that "[i]f we claim to offer a rhetorical education that is relevant to students' academic, professional, and civic lives, we must engage them in discussions that challenge their understanding of local, national, and international events. During times of national tragedy, this can only be accomplished after students have been able to address one of their most basic needs—the need to feel secure" (Murphy et al. 81). With today's social media landscape, perhaps more than ever students have the ability to experience tragedies directly, blurring the line between public and private traumas. When bombs exploded during the Boston Marathon, Twitter users bombarded feeds with graphic photos of the victims. When a truck driver crushed a crowd in France on Bastille Day in 2016, videos surfaced online immediately of the gory aftermath. Our students come to us with memories not only personal traumas but public traumas, and many of them want and need to write about it to make sense of what happened since "*trauma* can only be tackled/approached/grappled with discursively; it is not until it is spoken/written that trauma is made present" (Goggin and Goggin 31). Writing is risky, and it is our job to teach it. Jeffrey Berman writes, "The writing teacher's task is to help students express themselves on a wide range of subjects, some of which may be risky" (34).

Part of the risk is the very real fear we may have that we will be placed in the awkward position of therapist to a student, a position that carries with it genuine personal and political concerns. But this fear is really unfounded. Students are aware that we are not therapists. When a student chooses to write about a traumatic event for an assignment, that student usually wants the instructor to remain firmly in the role of a writing teacher. It's important to remember that "[m]ost students know what to reveal and what to conceal, and they remain sensitive to their audience, not wishing to burden classmates with more than they can endure" (Berman 70). bell hooks echoes a similar concept regarding her own students: "There are times when I walk into classrooms overflowing with students who feel terribly wounded in their psyches (many of them see therapists), yet I do not think that they want therapy from me. They do want an education that is healing to the uninformed, unknowing spirit" (19). Whether we realize it or not, the writing classroom is very similar to a therapist's office. We encourage personal connections, we dissect student sentences and paragraphs, trying to diagnose the thought process behind a piece of writing. We often ask them, "Why did you decide to say this instead of that?" or "How could you explain this point better?" We encourage self-efficacy by our methods, much like therapists encourage self-efficacy in patients. Berman agrees:

> A pedagogical model of classroom self-disclosure has many elements in common with therapeutic models . . . teacher-student and therapist-patient relationships both involve relational situations in which affective and cognitive issues are discussed from a variety of theoretical perspectives...teachers and therapists both seek to empower their students and patients . . . investigations of point of view, plot, character, symbolism, language, irony, and ambiguity are central to both writing teachers and therapists. (48)

Also, when students are at the place emotionally to write about a traumatic event, the writing process can facilitate perceived self-efficacy—especially if we give examples of trauma writing for students to read. Sharing trauma narratives written by others can give students a social model to follow—a realization that they are not alone and the belief that their story needs to be told. Telling their stories can help students feel more in control of the narrative as well.

Because of the direct connections between therapist and instructor, writing and self-disclosure, it's important for us to remember the dangers of the therapist's role (mentioned above) and for us to lean more toward Herman's position of a therapist as not neutral but also not pushing a student to disclose something they are not ready to disclose—or to play the role of detective, looking and pushing for clues that simply are not there. To help us balance this tricky space, MacCurdy suggests that we first validate the importance of the topic a student writes about *before* tackling that paper as we would any other paper. She also suggests that we remember the main components of a personal essay that "make it work" and reminds us that "we do not have more insight into the student's life than the student . . . but we may have insight into what makes a text work and what inhibits it" (72). It is our job to teach students how to communicate effectively to a variety of audiences, and sometimes the topic of that communication is traumatic. But, as mentioned above, these stories need to be told by survivors and heard by non-survivors—and this complicated relationship usually happens in the writing classroom whether we want it to or not. We must also remember that students who choose to self-disclose a traumatic event in a college paper want us to grade the papers as we would any other paper on a more benign topic. Many of my own students encouraged me to ask questions for clarification and genuinely wanted my help to make their message clearer for their readers. Newkirk noticed the same pattern in his own experiences, claiming that "students who choose to write about traumatic issues are, almost without exception, not asking us to be therapists" but instead "to be sensitive and curious readers who help them elaborate and explore topics they have chosen to write about" (50).

Based upon what we know about language and traumatic memories, it comes as no surprise that creative writing methods can only help survivors tell their stories to a certain point before the language fails to truly communicate the survivor's message to the audience. While "[n]arrative is the chain that links our moments together . . . image is what we see in the dark of night, what we wake up with from dreams . . . it is image that burns itself into our minds whether we want it to or not, and image that can free us from a past if we can look straight at the pictures that live behind our eyes and communicate them with others" (MacCurdy 53). Where language fails, perhaps images and more multi-modal venues can succeed. As Herman points out, "[t]raumatic memories lack verbal narrative and context; rather, they are encoded in the form of vivid sensations and images" (38). MacCurdy adds to the conversation that "[t]raumatic memories retain their imagistic quality precisely because they are not coded into a meaning scheme" (25). Instead of trying to translate these images into a language, which may prove too difficult and overwhelming to do, it might be best to include the images in the composing process of a personal narrative.

Using images and other non-textual methods of communication in the composition classroom isn't a new idea. As digital devices permeate our students' lives, the way we communicate has changed substantially, ushering in a new composing era where we send complex messages to each other using only emoticons and memes. In an effort to keep up with the new literacy of our students, many composition scholars have endorsed the use of multimodal assignments (digital and non-digital). In the 2004 Conference on College Composition and Communication chair's address, Kathleen Blake Yancey declared that "[l]iteracy today is in the midst of a tectonic change" and that writing includes "students who write words on paper . . . but who also compose words and images and create audio files on Web logs (blogs)" (Yancey 298). Pamela Takayoshi and Cynthia L. Selfe reiterate Yancey's statement: "In a world where communication between individuals and groups is both increasingly cross-cultural and digital, teachers of composition are beginning to sense the inadequacy of texts—and composition instruction—that employs only one primary semiotic channel (the alphabetic) to convey meaning. In internationally networked digital environments, texts must be able to carry meaning across geo-political, linguistic, and cultural borders, and so texts must take advantage of multiple semiotic channels" (2).

Digital composition is not the only avenue we encourage students to follow when integrating alphabetical text with images to meet where our students (and society) currently communicate. Jody Shipka explores using more tangible methods of communicative images outside of the digital realm in her book *Toward a Composition Made Whole*. In this book, she recalls students crafting essays with physical objects, like a garbage can or ballet shoes, helping students navigate the rhetoricity of objects they use every day (often without thinking twice). Like multimodal/digital composition scholars, Shipka also sees the value in non-alphabetical texts as a way to communicate effectively in a global world. But these multimodal methods are also a valuable way for survivors of a traumatic event to communicate their own experiences. Regardless of the medium, the message remains the same: alphabetical text can only represent a traumatic event so far. The rest must be done via imagery of some kind, be it digital in nature or not.

In lieu of a personal narrative that follows the traditional essay format, (knowing what we now know about trauma, memory, and language) we might consider crafting the assignment into a self-representation visual project. The word "project" immediately tells students that this assignment is not a traditional language-based essay, and the phrase carries with it the connotation of something more hands-on and tangible than an alphabetical essay. Also, the lack of the word "narrative" rejects the idea that one can write about oneself in a linear, concrete fashion. "Self-representation" is relative and open to each student's interpretation of what it means to represent one's self. Students can create something that reflects their identity and aspirations in the form of some type of visual representation. The medium is open and is part of the representation; if part of a student's identity is a painter, then they are encouraged to create a painting or a collage. If a student is more comfortable with digital environments, they can make an iMovie trailer or a mini film. The main message of the project is not for a student to tell her entire life story but instead to examine her values and how those values tie into her identity—a mini-memoir in a medium of student's choice.

Through the use of visual communication, perhaps we can begin to mine a language of trauma from the wreckage of our students' trauma narratives. Even if we do not encourage self-disclosure, our students often feel comfortable enough to self-disclose without any prompt from us. This generation is more in-tune and unashamed of their identities than any one before it. We need to adjust to the cognitive and emotional demands our students place on us as teachers of communication. We need to remember the complex path a survivor takes to reach the point where they can write their traumas—and we need to respect and encourage that journey as scholars of communication if we want to help our culture create a language of trauma and start to take the steps towards healing and true empathy.

Works Cited

Barker, Pat. *The Regeneration Trilogy*. Penguin, 1998.
Berman, Jeffrey. *Risky Writing: Self-Disclosure and Self-Transformation in the Classroom*. U of Massachusetts P, 2001.
Brison, Susan J. *Aftermath: Violence and the Remaking of a Self*. Princeton UP, 2002.
Council of Writing Program Administrators, National Council of Teachers of English, and National Writing Project. *Framework for Success in Postsecondary Writing*. CWPA, NCTE, and NWP, 2011, wpacouncil.org/aws/CWPA/asset_manager/get_file/350201?ver=505. Accessed 18 Jan. 2020.
Goggin, M. Peter, and Maureen Daly Goggin. "Presence in Absences: Discourses and Teaching (In, On, and About) Trauma." *Trauma and the Teaching of Writing*, edited by Shane Borrowman, SUNY P, 2005, pp. 29–51.
Herman, Judith. *Trauma and Recovery*. Basic Books, 1997.
hooks, bell. *Teaching to Transgress*. Routledge, 1994.
MacCurdy, Marian. *The Mind's Eye*. U of Massachusetts P, 2007.
McNally, Richard J. *Remembering Trauma*. Belknap Press of Harvard UP, 2005.
—. "Searching for Repressed Memory." *True and False Recovered Memories: Toward a Reconciliation of the Debate*, edited by Robert F. Belli, Springer, 2012, pp. 121–47.
Morris, J David. *The Evil Hours: A Biography of Traumatic Stress Disorder*. Houghton, 2015.
Newkirk, Thomas. "Selfhood and the Personal Essay: A Pragmatic Defense." *Critical Expressivism: Theory and Practice in the Composition Classroom*, edited by Tara Roeder and Roseanne Gatto, WAC Clearinghouse, 2014, pp. 33–53.
Rysdam, Sheri. "The Economy of Expressivism and Its Legacy of Low/No-Stakes Writing." *Critical Expressivism: Theory and Practice in the Composition Classroom*, edited by Tara Roeder and Roseanne Gatto, WAC Clearinghouse, 2014, pp. 281–288.
Shipka, Jody. *Toward a Composition Made Whole*. U of Pittsburgh P, 2011.
Spigelman, Candice. *Personally Speaking: Experience as Evidence in Academic Discourse*. Southern Illinois UP, 2004.

Sullivan, Patrick. "The UnEssay: Making Room for Creativity in the Composition Classroom." *College Composition and Communication*, vol. 67, no. 1, 2015, pp. 6–33.

Takayoshi, Pamela, and Cynthia L. Selfe. "Thinking About Multimodality." *Multimodal Composition: Resources for Teachers*, edited by Cynthia L. Selfe, Hampton, 2007, pp. 1–12.

van der Kolk, Bessel. *The Body Keeps the Score*. Viking P, 2014.

Webb-Sunderhaus, Sara. "'Life Gets in the Way': The Case of a Seventh-Year Senior." *Retention, Persistence, and Writing Programs*, edited by Todd Ruecker, et al., Utah State UP, 2017, pp. 114–31.

Yancey, Kathleen Blake. "Made Not Only in Words: Composition in a New Key." *College Composition and Communication*, vol. 56, no. 2, 2004, pp. 297–328.

7 Cognition and Community: Using the Habits of Mind to Engage Students in Community-Focused Writing

Michelle Stuckey, James Toweill, Sean Tingle, Heather MacDonald, and Jessica Harnisch

In the 2017 collection *Contemporary Perspectives on Cognition and Writing*, John Hayes refutes the notion that cognitive approaches to writing were a passing fad that fell out of favor in large part due to the lack of attention to social, political, and historical context. He makes clear that the decline of work in this area occurred in a subfield of writing studies—in English departments primarily—while cognitive approaches continued to be widely used in the fields of education and psychology, for instance. The renewed interest in cognition by scholars in the rhetoric and writing studies over the last decade, as the editors of this collection also speak to, has stemmed in part from research on learning transfer that emphasizes reflection and metacognition and builds on the ongoing work of educational psychologists.

Hayes's brief piece, as well as others in the collection, make important advances in bridging the gap between social and cognitive work in the field. He asserts the need to "recognize that both social/cultural and cognitive factors are essential for understanding writing" (xi-xii). Hayes makes the case that cognitive-focused research on writing can, and often should, account for the social, political, and/or historical context of the writer. For our purposes here, understanding the context of the learner—the social, historical, even technological environment in which the student is writing and composing—is essential for understanding how we can best support the cognitive practices and habits to help them transfer learning related to writing. Specifically, we consider the context of online writing instruction in our first-year composition (FYC) courses to help us better understand the relationship between cognition and community-focused writing.

In online courses, the social or community element of learning has often been defined in deficit terms, which can be particularly challenging for writing instruction because social and collaborative engagement is central to developing strong rhetorical practices. Specifically, students often view and experience online learning as solitary and isolating. Since the early years of online writing instruction, students have described their experience in the online classroom as "feeling isolated" (Woods 379). This sentiment has not changed significantly, despite much research on the subject. In fact, "faculty members, on average, appear to underestimate the level of disconnect that students experience in the online environment" (Otter et al. 30). Ken Gillam and Shannon R. Wooden explain, "(students) may do their coursework alone, situated within rudimentary text-based course management systems (CMS) designed to facilitate content delivery and assessment of information mastery, interacting with others mainly in the form of disembodied typed comments sent in the silence of email" (25). Although there have been new teaching strategies introduced into the online learning space within the last decade, the sense of disconnect is still palpable. Recent research has attempted to identify ways to improve the togetherness and sense of unity that students feel with each other in the online classroom, and this "sense of being in a place and belonging to a group" is certainly crucial (Picciano 22), both to student learning and to student persistence. Both the Council of Writing Program Administrators (CWPA) and the National Council of Teachers of English (NCTE) "have indicated that online FYW cannot accomplish what occurs in face-to-face environments" (Litterio 2). The connection to community is challenging to re-create in the online classroom, and this issue still dominates much of the discussion of online learning.

Furthermore, online students can also feel disconnected from the communities they inhabit—they often lack the connection to others living, working, and playing in their communities. Yet this is not a problem experienced only by online students; in "Writing to Assemble Publics," Laurie E. Gries suggests that college students in general feel increasingly disconnected from political and civic structures and institutions.

We recognize that students are not just isolated from their online peers, but often also from these larger community institutions and networks. We engage students in community-focused writing in order to address the unique challenges of the online learning context. We also hope to help students better understand their own social contexts in which they are learning, by helping them reconnect and reassemble communities through inquiry, research, writing, and reflection. We draw on Gries, who extends previous notions of service learning such that students are challenged to

> take sole responsibility for inventing their own organizations, identifying their own community needs and organizational goals, and putting their own bodies and self-designed discourse into circulation in order to assemble a larger public around shared matters of concern . . . If we think of service learning projects as writing *with* publics, we might call this pedagogical approach writing *to assemble* publics. (331)

As Gries suggests, opening students up to the possibility of the fluidity of communities as they are constantly assembled and reassembled is a powerful tool for learning. She argues that assemblage is not just textual but ontological—that "communities are assembled and reassembled from within" (332), by writers and by readers, and "acquire rhetorical force" in relation to other assemblages (335). As students exchange and share their community-focused research among their peers across the US and even internationally, they can forge new understandings of their own communities, and themselves as participants in both the communities they are researching and the community of the classroom. Through the research process, students' understanding of their communities, ideally, is transformed, while their understanding of their communities themselves are re-assembled through both the production of their multimodal textual projects and their presentation of those projects to their classroom communities.

In this piece, we hope to show how our curriculum extends this methodology by incorporating cognition and reflection as tools to help students re-imagine their communities and their own agency within them. We engage students with the habits of mind from the *Framework for Success in Postsecondary Writing* at the beginning of the class. They reflect on these habits of mind in relation to their writing as well as the "WPA Outcomes Statement" throughout the course. Through metacognition and reflection, students can come to understand the way their writing reshapes their own *knowledge* of their communities, their location within their communities, as well as others' understanding of the community. It is the focus on communities that we propose helps students metacognitively navigate between their physical space in the world (their towns, cities, states, etc.), the not-so-tangible space of digital media, and the digital classroom. In turn, students are able to view their experience in the online writing classroom as less transactional, and the classroom becomes a shared space in which a multitude of ideas and perspectives contributes to a re-embodied and re-assembled space.

Online Learning and Learners

Perhaps one of the most significant impacts on colleges and universities in the last two decades has been the expansion of online education. A 2018 Babson Survey Research Group report indicates that between Fall 2018 and Fall 2016, the number of students enrolled in online education courses increased by 5.6% to 6,359,121 students, or 31.6% of all students enrolled in post-secondary education; 14.9% of students are enrolled in fully online programs (Seaman et al.). At the same time, the report shows the number of on-campus students, which includes students who are not enrolled in any online courses and those taking a combination of online and on-campus classes, is down by more than one million, representing a 6.4% decrease. Arizona State University (ASU), where we teach, had 43,547 online students as of August 22, 2019, according to ASU's Fall 2019 21st Day Enrollment Reports.

The Babson report also reveals that the majority of students (68.9%) taking online classes are enrolled in public institutions (Seaman et al.). Public institutions also experienced the highest level of growth in online students compared to private non-profit and private for-profit institutions, increasing by 299,855. Interestingly, the majority (56.1%) of online-only learners enrolled in institutions located in the state where they reside. However, ASU is among a handful of institutions where the majority of online learners reside out of the state. As of Fall 2016 at ASU, 61,080 online-only students resided in Arizona, while 205,740 students, or 77.1%, lived out of state (Seaman et al.). Our program, the Writers' Studio, serves more than three thousand online students who reside across the country every semester.

ASU's online students are primarily nontraditional learners, with the majority between the ages of 21 and 35. Research indicates that nontraditional students often manage family and job responsibilities and demands on their time (Thompson et al.). Cheryl Hawkinson Melkun, in "Nontraditional Students Online: Composition, Collaboration, and Community," outlines some of the unique challenges of working with nontraditional students, as follows:

> Because most nontraditional students have been away from academia for years or even decades, and their writing skills have often atrophied. Furthermore, the nontraditional student population tends to be more diverse particularly in relation to writing skills than the traditionally aged student population, and this diversity is evident in online composition courses. The nontraditional student population contains a full spectrum of students with vastly different life experiences from single parents with a GED to working professionals who are simply getting their "ticket" punched so that they can climb further up the corporate ladder. Some of these students are basic writers, while others are published authors. (33–34)

Demographic information is sometimes used to try to predict student readiness for and likelihood of success in online courses. However, research by Linda Boynton and Lisa M. Litterio has shown that despite a wealth of materials about the kinds of students who might succeed in online courses, it is still unclear what demographics of students do well in online courses. Yet, we do know from past research that student habits play an important part in their success, both in face-to-face and online contexts. In a study conducted by William West et al., faculty compared responses from sixty students in sections of online courses in scientific/technical writing with those in face-to-face sections. They discovered that online students' assignments averaged half a grade above those of face-to-face students. What's more, they determined that "it was students' behaviors or study habits that were the primary influencer of their success, rather than personal characteristics or learning environments" (300). This finding indicates that primary motivators for success in student learning in an online writing course are very similar to those in face-to-face classes: student motivation and responsibility external to an environment or the instructor.

Indeed, Beth Brunk-Chavez suggests that the outcomes and guidelines that structure curricular decisions in online classes need not be different than those for face-to-face courses. In "The *Framework for Success* Goes Online," Brunk-Chavez maps the habits of mind to the Illinois Online Network's characteristics of successful online students to argue for the utility of the habits of mind in supporting student success. Specifically, the author asserts the importance of both instructors and students engaging with the habits of mind throughout the course, as instructors are vital to the development of attitudes and behaviors that will help students to succeed in post-secondary education as online learners. Indeed, according to R. J. Maxfield and Gary Noll, "Metacognition is important to the adult learner. After reflecting on [their] vast reservoir of experience, the adult student if given the right instructions and tools, can understand [their] unique learning processes" (52). Our curriculum, which helps students practice metacognition through reflective writing, supports all learners in the online environment grow as writers through community-engaged writing projects.

COMMUNITY-ENGAGED WRITING

Much of the literature about FYC and public communities frame community engagement in terms of service and civic participation and posits that transferable skills and the use of habits of mind are embedded in these processes. This literature assumes that writers are assembled in and write from discrete communities and that the divide between academic and extra-academic "public" space is permeable. Broadly, this literature "define[s] the civic university as teaching citizens the Habits of Mind and civic actions" to prepare students to participate in democratic structures (Ryder 240). While much of this scholarship does not explicitly address the habits of mind as a larger framework for these models of community interaction, this work assumes many habits are an embedded part of the process for writing for and within public or academic communities. For instance, in their influential essay *Community Literacy*, Wayne Campbell Peck, Linda Flower, and Lorraine Higgins note the importance of a pedagogical model that recognizes difference but asks people within a community to work together productively. The habits of engagement and metacognition figure prominently in this process, as does the role of reflection. Invoking the habit of metacognition, the authors note the necessity of bringing a "strategic approach" to community literacy and "to openly acknowledge not only the difficulty of empathy and the history of failed conversations, but to purposefully examine the genuine conflicts, assumptions, and practices" (207).

Not surprisingly, engagement, as a sense of investment and involvement with community, continues to be a habit that figures prominently in this literature. Susan Murphy discusses the connections between "linked learning communities" and civic engagement, noting that "elements of this civic engagement focus can be translated to other programs if they have a similar focus on the uses of writing that serve social aims and issues, including argument and argument analysis" (120). Lauren Esposito writes that placed-based community writing "offers students a more dynamic engagement with audience, purpose, and context" and "place engages students in real writing tasks to reach communal goals" (74).

In the Writers' Studio, we have drawn on this body of work to develop our own community-engaged curriculum. In our courses, students identify their communities, whether civic or professional, and conduct research into various aspects of these communities through multiple writing projects. For example, they might profile an organization within their local physical community; rhetorically analyze social media profiles of a well-known public individual in their community; analyze an issue in their community; or propose a solution to a problem in their community. Students employ a number of research methods, including observation, interview, rhetorical analysis, and secondary research. As we engage them with their external communities, they have significant control over what it is they choose to write about, as well as who they choose to engage with outside of class. While all students focus on engaging with and practicing the learning outcomes defined by the Council of Writing Program Administrators, specifically, rhetorical knowledge, critical thinking and composing, processes, and conventions, each student is able to personalize that experience around a topic that is nearly entirely of their own choosing. We also introduce students to multimodal composition, as a way to help them develop digital literacy skills and practices. For the multimodal components of their projects, students might compose infographics, fliers, or public service announcements. This aspect of the project helps them to practice their rhetorical knowledge as they adjust their message to a different audience, for a different purpose.

Much of the scholarship on community-engaged writing assumes a face-to-face classroom as the default, although recently scholars have given more attention to the ways writers conceive of and engage with communities using digital or online classrooms as a starting point. Christine Blair and Cheryl Hoy analyze the way online classrooms complicate the idea of "virtual community" as a social metaphor, and prompt us to consider the most effective forms of communication and community-building in digital classrooms (33). This can be in conflict with the motivations of students. As Nicole Thompson, Nicole Miller, and Dana Pomykal Franz's work reveals, often students say they prefer self-paced learning for the convenience and find daunting the social and collaborative requirements such as discussion boards and peer reviews. However, "Social interaction with the instructor, other students, and other communities of learning is particularly important when delivering courses via the Internet" (Maxfield and Noll 51). Susan Gallagher-Lepak, Janet Reilly, and Cheryl Killion note that having a "strong sense of community" and identity within an online classroom also contributes to better student performance (133). Using inquiry and research to generate and share knowledge about their communities with their classmates can also help to increase understanding and a sense of connection and engagement among students within online writing courses.

Although some nontraditional students may express a preference for asynchronous learning, research suggests that nontraditional students generally "want and need to use their lived experience and incorporate reflection into their learning schemas" (Maxfield and Noll 50). For example, one Writers' Studio student, Zyvo, noted in their post-course reflection:

> Using Twitter to talk with classmates and [my professor] was also a huge help for me in staying engaged in the course. Being connected to people who were working on the same things and dealing with the same kinds of hurdles helped me stay on track with the work and kept me active in the course outside of the coursework itself. I learned that engagement and persistence really are habits of mind, and are something that go beyond just how you engage with the work of writing itself.

Because writing is an inherently social act, these moments of collaboration allow for important learning opportunities. As Zyvo's reflection suggests, through their participation in the writing community of the classroom, students can observe what other students are writing about.

This enables them to expand their perspectives on both their own communities as well as on the communities of their peers.

Another student, Selena, shared their experience with choosing a topic about their community and how it helped them connect more deeply with the work they were completing in class. This topic was a particularly difficult and sensitive one for Selena to write about, involving going to school on a US compound in Saudi Arabia. Writing to those in school leadership, they addressed concerns with student behavior and extreme punishment for breaking rules they may not have been made aware of properly. A careful balancing act of navigating cultural differences, legal hurdles, and a need to not rock the boat due to parental employment hanging in the balance, Selena struggled quite a bit through the process but was determined to triumph. They reflected that

> writing about an issue that was so personal to me and that had previously impacted my friends and people within my community was what engaged me so deeply with this project. Without this sense of engagement and investment, I would likely have not written as passionately and my letter would not be persuasive. Although being so emotionally invested in the issue made it difficult to write in an unbiased manner, I believe that it was what pushed me to identify and discuss the most feasible solution to the problem that I identified.

While they clearly identify a connection between researching and writing about their community and developing the habit of engagement, their reflection also suggests the importance of persistence. Due to this persistence, not only were they able to successfully complete all course assignments, but they found true meaning throughout the process. Through discovering the importance of choosing an issue important to their community, they were able to pair their experience with effective reflection and connect their FYC learning with knowledge making through their research on their community.

Because many of our online students are "multilocal," coming to ASU from locations outside the Phoenix Metro area or internationally, the communities and topics they choose to discuss in their coursework are typically personally meaningful. One student, Kenna, quite literally lives the idea of multilocal, as they are constantly on the move and traveling to new destinations all over the globe every few days. They work on various yachts as part of crews, taking the meaning of community to a unique level. In exploring an issue regarding a specific visa restriction and how it limits yacht crew members in various international ports, they were able to connect more deeply with not only crews they work with personally, but all crews throughout the industry:

> The issue . . . can be seen impacting the lives of everyday yachties. Researching this topic also helped me learn so much about how the yachting industry affects the places that I visit every year (and puts into perspective how much they would suffer if the industry were to decline in some areas). Through these projects I now have a greater understanding of how the yachting community is engaged with the communities it resides in.

The student's reflection speaks to a growing awareness of the complexity of community—the professional yachting community as a community that impacts smaller local communities around the world—and the way their understanding of their professional community was transformed by their research.

Thinking about an audience's perspective is crucial to success as well, and having a diverse group of peers can provide many opportunities for these varying perspectives to come up in discussion or review. While many students may not know much about their classmates' topics and communities, they can still provide support and assistance in the peer review process. Furthermore, they can also offer varying perspectives in discussion boards, offering viewpoints their classmates may not have considered previously. This all allows for students to help develop their own skills, particularly when it comes to their comfort with practicing the various habits of mind. Again, Selena reflected on her learning as follows:

> Instead of telling myself that my work wasn't good or satisfactory, I could reference these principles to determine what about my creative elements was ineffective, and also received feedback on my peer reviews that directly pointed out specific elements I could work on. Using these principles was an extremely effective way for me not only to create multimodal components of my project that I was proud of, but to be critical of my work in a productive way, which resulted in really great feedback from my peers and instructors.

Selena discovered how to more productively engage with feedback and view their own writing, while improving on an area they had identified as a personal weakness—creativity, especially regarding an understanding of visual design principles.

COMMUNITY-ENGAGED WRITING, METACOGNITION, AND TRANSFER

Phyllis Mentzell Ryder emphasizes the role of transfer between academic and public writing, and the role of metacognition in this process, noting "the moves of academic writing are not so divergent from the moves of other public writing" (219), and ultimately advocates for "a pedagogy that brings together multiple publics, that allows students to compare their different experiences with public spaces and public rhetorics and that offers an analytical method for multiple components of public formation" (225). One might easily see the habits of mind serving as an analytical framework for these components. Indeed, metacognition and reflection are important in Ryder's conception of public community formation. She observes that public writers "invoke a sense of interdependence" through reflective activities, such as "referencing their own past accomplishments, telling historical stories of a similar public's accomplishments, and showing how past citizens were transformed by working together" (221). In their reflections, Writers' Studio students draw specifically on the habits of mind to discuss the connections between their coursework and their local communities. One student, Marco, reflected on the responsibility they felt toward their military community, which was also their intended audience for a project discussing veterans' mental health issues: "I felt this was my responsibility to get this project correct. To me this was more than just an assignment for a grade. I had an obligation to get this right out of respect to all my fallen brothers and sisters in arms. There was no way I was going to just dial this in or not to give this project my fullest of attention." Here, we can see how community obligations can become embedded in the processes of composing and can help students generate meaningful skills and experiences that connect to their lived contexts.

James Dubinsky, Marshall Welch, and Adrian Wurr also suggest the necessity for reflection and thinking-about-thinking in writing pedagogy that involves service learning and public engagement. They note that "service-learning provides opportunities for "reflective thought" and learning through civic engagement (168). The authors also discuss the role of creating such opportunities in online contexts, noting that ePortfolios "when integrated into courses as both a tool and a text, can facilitate the process of writing and the recursive movement between service and learning" (168). Recent scholarship, by Kathleen Blake Yancey in particular, has emphasized the value for reflection and ePortfolios in facilitating learning transfer. The term *transfer*, in writing studies, is used to discuss writers' application and adaptation of previous knowledge to new learning situations or experiences. As we know, the pervasiveness of the FYC requirement in post-secondary education suggests these courses are widely considered to be essential for students to develop writing knowledge and skills they can apply in other classes and in other composing situations. Scholars began to be interested in transfer when research revealed little integration of learning from first-year writing classes to courses in the disciplines or professional settings (Downs and Wardle).

In bringing together community-engaged writing with metacognitive practices and habits, our curriculum design helps students assemble and re-assemble their communities, as well as their own understanding of how their growth as writers impacts their own possibilities for engaging with those communities. Students reflect on the "Outcomes Statement" as well as the eight habits of mind (Curiosity, Openness, Engagement, Creativity, Persistence, Responsibility, Flexibility, and Metacognition), which are our course learning outcomes, in relation to their community-focused research and writing. Reflective activities are central to the learning students undertake in our FYC courses and enhance their engagement with and understanding of their communities.

In the first week of class, students are introduced to the learning outcomes, the habits they need to be successful learners, as well as the value of reflection for transfer. Students also become familiar with the concept of "transfer" in the first week, to encourage them to think of their learning as "knowledge to go," as Anne Beaufort frames it. This helps them imagine how they might take the learning they are doing with them to other contexts, by connecting writing tasks and activities in the class with those outside the class, in other courses, as well as to co-curricular and lived experiences. As Thomas Skeen discusses in this collection, applying the habits of mind to specific composing skills and practices can help prepare learners for "ill-structured problem solving" related to writing, which can then be adapted more easily to other contexts.

The Writers' Studio curriculum is informed by Yancey's work on reflection and portfolios. Yancey has argued for the value of cumulative, rather than summative, reflection for learning transfer ("The Social Life of Reflection"). In the Writers' Studio, reflection is designed into the curriculum from the outset and sustained throughout the course. Students compose a pre-course reflection as their initial writing assignment during the first week of class. They compose a mid-course reflection halfway through the class, and a final reflection at the end of the class. The reflective writing assignments as well as drafts of major projects and select invention work are housed in students' digital portfolios. The curriculum also includes smaller reflective writing assignments related to peer review, multimodal composing, and revision. Thus, students have ample opportunities to examine their own learning. This allows instructors in our program to also understand each student's perceptions about their writing development throughout the course, enabling them to evaluate student work based on how each student has improved from where they began.

The use of reflection in writing courses has expanded significantly over the last forty years as a means of self-assessment, yes, but also as a way to foster metacognition and deepen learning. Yancey's recent theorizing of reflection draws on the work of John Dewey to articulate a deeper understanding of reflection as a "synthetic knowledge-making activity tied to uncertainty" (*The Rhetoric of Reflection* 8). For Dewey, reflection offers the learner an opportunity to connect understanding about an experience to other experiences and ideas. This meaning making is ignited by a confrontation with uncertainty and ambiguity. Systematic and rigorous reflection, according to Dewey can facilitate the transformative aspect of learning. For Dewey, experience is interaction between an individual and the world, whether physically or mentally. That interaction is dialectical—it changes individuals and those they interact with. The goal of our curricular focus on both reflection and community-engaged, experiential research and writing is for us to enable students to experience this transformation through uncertainty.

As part of the reflections students compose in the Writers' Studio, they discuss their Theory of Writing, which includes reflection on how their identity as writers might have changed. In developing this assignment, we have drawn in part on Yancey, Liane Robertson, and Kara Taczak's work in *Writing Across Contexts*. In their post-course reflection, one student discusses the ways in which their sense of self as a writer had changed by the end of the course and the ways that this process has helped to transform their professional experience, as well as the social aspects of composing through collaboration. Sheila writes:

> At the end of this course, I really feel like a much more accomplished writer. I feel more comfortable using different genres, focusing in deeply on my target audience, and really working through a composing process. Currently, I'm in charge of the master presentation for an upcoming event . . . I'm pulling together several presentations and working through a process to ensure a smooth show flow. My team and I are managing this process through Trello [a productivity software] to help keep us on track and make our work visible to one another. I feel really pleased to be able to transfer my skill from this class into my day to day.

As the reflection above suggests, reflection in the writing classroom can foster the transfer of composing knowledge and practices from the academic to the professional context, for example.

One multimodal project assignment used in the Writers' Studio asks students to propose and develop solutions to a problem in their local communities or workplaces. Through this process, students transfer existing knowledge and experiences between the online space and their local communities, sometimes transforming both in the process. Frequently, students note direct and concrete instances of transfer between Writers' Studio courses and their workplace experiences. In their post-course reflection, Sheila discusses the connections they made between the course and their professional experience, directly referencing the habits of mind in the process:

> So, one of the things that I am happy to report is that I made a conscious effort to work on my Curiosity and Creativity and Transfer those outside of this class. While my Project 2 ended up being a formal letter (which was not the most creative genre), I was able to incorporate a couple curious and creative things into my day job! For Curiosity, I sought out some team building ideas for my newly re-aligned team at work, and one of my managers came up with something brilliant! We were divided into teams and had the challenge of building something out of pipe cleaners that would uniquely represent what we each bring to the team.

Although it is clear that the student has had previous experience with professional communication, the habits of mind and the space of the online learning community all allow the student to process this experience in a new, more explicit way. In this case, we see the student taking ideas and insights gained through the process of composing and moving beyond direct application of the finished product. As a result, we might see the habits of mind operating as threshold concepts, or "portal[s], opening up a new and previously inaccessible way of thinking about something" (Meyer and Land).

Examples of Student Work

In all three of the courses we offer—English 101, 102 and 105—the projects are designed to not only expose students to the requirements of the curriculum, but to engage them in real-world critical writing and thinking. In the sections below, we will discuss three specific student projects that exemplify the affiliations students forge through community-engaged writing, as well as the cognitive transformations that reflective writing enables in their understanding of their communities.

Diana. In one assignment, an analysis paper, students choose an issue in their community that needs addressing; students can focus on their civic or professional communities. They then spend time completing primary and secondary research, including interviewing strategically selected stakeholders in their chosen community. They first analyze the issue and present it to a chosen audience, explaining the importance of this issue and the need for it to be addressed. In a subsequent assignment, they compose a proposal where they present one effective solution to a carefully selected audience in the community—a person or group of people who may be able to make this solution a reality. This allows students to share an important facet of their civic or professional lives with one another, creating opportunities for them to learn more about their diverse classmates and provide support throughout this challenging process. Although student topics can vary greatly, all students in the class undertake the same writing process at the same time, offering plenty of opportunities for mutual support despite topical differences.

In the process of learning from others, students are also able to better understand themselves, their communities, and how they fit into those communities. One student, Diana, wrote about a topic and community to which they were both personally and professionally connected.

Specifically, the student, who was both an enthusiast and a professional instructor, explored sexual assault and harassment in the ski industry. They had first-hand experience with the issue, and even though they knew quite a bit about the topic already, they still discovered a lot about themselves through the research process. In a reflective assignment, the student wrote:

> My purpose again changed after I dove further into my research. I worked with [a] human rights lawyer . . . to discuss her experience prosecuting sexual abuse and harassment in front of juries, and our conversation led me to realize that what the PSA really needed to be about was not just exposing that there was a problem, but to humanize that problem so that it became relevant to the many people who do not want to see or notice that a problem with sexualized behavior exists in our industry.

Through the research process, Diana connected with resources in their community, such as a human rights attorney. This research helped them to better understand not only the issue but also their audience—to think rhetorically about how to present this issue to their community.

Diana also discussed applying their curiosity to the topic themselves, as well as sparking curiosity in others in the field: "When I first began to ask the questions, and I got the huge scary blowback, I was really shocked and saddened. Then, I realized, we as an industry have to get curious. We need to wonder, ask and be open to the answers we get." This curiosity did expose Diana to some serious pushback, even leading them to being attacked by close friends in the industry due to a lack of openness in exploring the topic further. This, in turn, made Diana worry about continuing to practice openness themselves, yet they write that they were able to overcome this concern and "adopt all of the openness that was missing from those who interpreted my initial survey as threatening on behalf of those who are being injured by the current climate where no one is asking." This push for remaining open also allowed Diana to continue with persistence, and after gaining high-level support in the industry, they were able to "know that whatever people may be saying, that's their problem, not mine, and I have a project to finish." By the end of this experience, Diana had this to say: "I learned that my morals, ethics, and standing up for what is right is much more important to me than ignoring the issue in order to stay on top of the industry."

Stephen. In another of our courses, students profile a local community organization. This assignment requires that students conduct primary research, either observation or interviews. One student chose to profile a local community group, the Tempe Community Action Agency, that provides resources and support for community members living in poverty. Before we discuss their specific project, we will first examine their pre-course reflection. In this reflection, students discuss their previous experience with the "WPA Outcomes Statement," and the habits of mind they feel confident in and those they need to improve. In this reflection, Stephen wrote that one of the learning outcomes they especially wanted to strengthen in the course was "experiencing the collaborative and social aspects of the writing process." Interestingly, many of the examples of previous composing experiences the student draws on in this reflection relate to group or collaborative projects. One such example is especially intriguing, as they discuss collaborating with a high school colleague to compose a letter in response to a policy change for a Catholic retreat. The new policy meant less student autonomy for the student-led retreat, and according to Stephen, "a removal of some of the trust and intimacy involved in a student led retreat for other students." In their reflection, Stephen quotes the letter to the administration they wrote with a fellow student as follows:

> Students were placed in a situation where we were silenced from expressing our true opinions and instead forced to share only positive feedback. Specifically, on the issue regarding adult leaders. The focus of the meeting was not on feedback but on adult leaders being brought into every small group session. And while we were hoping this was up for discussion, we were silenced from expressing any "rebuttal" to this.

Additionally, they write the following of their previous experiences with the social and collaborative aspects of composing:

> While I have worked on group writing pieces before, it is not always easy. Hearkening back to the excerpt from the letter I co-wrote in point two of the [C]WPA outcomes, it was difficult to work collaboratively at times. Different people have different ideas and figuring out a happy medium or sacrificing pride can be difficult for me.

This example signals that early in the course, the student was already considering how they have used written communication to engage critically—transform, even—their community and their given role in it.

The student's profile project focused on the Tempe Community Action Agency, as Stephen was interested in issues of poverty and employment in the Tempe community. In reflecting on their final project, they wrote,

> This project made me go much deeper into a topic, one that I was not familiar with, and do a lot of behind the scenes work to create my final piece. I think that all of that extra work has helped to create something that I can be proud of though. There is something special about being the one to actually conduct the interviews, to sit down and listen to recordings, and to interact with experts in a subject rather than grabbing information off the internet. While I did incorporate sources from the internet and it serves as a vast resource for writing and pretty much anything you can think of, it is harder to get the personal element from those sources, and it is difficult to get specific answers for specific groups if that information is not already out there. Without conducting interviews, my profile would not even be close to having all of the substance and value that it does, and I am proud of that. I am now much more comfortable reaching out to experts, or those close to, a subject and it is something that I would like to do in the future when researching a topic. I am past the fear of doing so because I had such a positive experience with those I spoke to.

In this passage, Stephen indicates that their learning was transformed by the processes of conducting research in the community—that they learned information about the organization from speaking directly with employees that could not be gained from text-based research alone.

In their post-course reflection, Stephen discusses their learning throughout the semester, providing examples of how they transferred or applied that learning to other learning contexts. They write,

> This class has taught me a lot about communication, gathering research and synthesizing information for many different situations, and in many different mediums. Throughout the semester we have been exposed to a lot of different writing scenarios that range from news articles, self-reflections, shared reflects, peer

> responses, peer reviews, correspondence with professionals and more. I really have had to tackle a very diverse range of different writing styles with a very broad range of audiences, and I think it has been great practice for future writing and have seen some of the skills developed here bleed over into my other subjects.

Stephen uses metacognition to identify learning experiences throughout the course and begin to identify ways that the community-based research methods they practiced during the class will be transferable to other writing contexts in the future. They go on to discuss the way they applied this learning to a presentation for his biomedical engineering course, that Stephen made to two different audiences. Stephen explains how they incorporated feedback from peers and their professor, and how they approached making rhetorical changes to present to potential investors versus peers.

Rocky. In another profile of a community group, Rocky chose to profile an organization called the Sons of Italy, a cultural appreciation and heritage group whose chapter is based in Central California. In the Mid-Course Reflection, Rocky provided an excerpt from the rough draft, making an important connection between the student's role as a composer and the group's role in the local community:

> The Sons of Italy Enrico Caruso Lodge's members are deeply involved with the Valley Children's Healthcare Foundation. "The foundation treats children with Endocrinology & Diabetes, Cancer & Blood Disorders, Gastroenterology issues, Fetal Care, Orthopedics, heart conditions, Neonatal problems, Neurological disorders, and performs Pediatric surgeries" (Valley Children's Foundation 2019). Those are just some of the services they provide to the children of the Valley. With the aid of the foundation, research is carried on, and those children whose families cannot afford specialized care for their children. Valley Children's Hospital is critical to our community. I, myself, was cared for at the Hospital. I suffered from a Gastroenterological disorder, and they helped me, and maybe even saved my life.

Rocky then illustrates how the research process helped them develop skills in Rhetorical Knowledge, a key outcome in the CWPA "Outcomes Statement":

> The excerpt from above was developed after hours reading about the SOI [Sons of Italy], researching various sites, deciding on a direction the project should take. I chose charity because almost any audience would be interested in charitable acts of any group. I must admit though that I wanted the charity as my main focus after the input of my instructors and peers helped guide me in that direction. I used emotion or empathy to attract my audience in the example above. **Rhetorical Knowledge** was not an area I initially believed I needed to strengthen in my Pre-Course Reflection, but it did require some tweaking. It went from healthy to stronger after I started Project 1.

Rocky clearly relied on feedback from his class community to identify an organization that would be interesting to a wide audience. Later in the reflection, Rocky demonstrates progression in the habits of mind, in particular, how the habit of Persistence was a mental compass on the journey of completing the project. Once again, feedback was important to the growth Rocky identified in his learning.

> I claimed **Peristance** [sic] as a strength in my Pre-Course Reflection, and that did not change. Just ask my poor instructors. I pursued them with questions the entire course. No matter how many failures on each assignment I kept plugging along. Whenever they or my peers criticized or made suggestions, I did not get mad or discouraged. I took their ideas and bravely went forward. I am still doing that today and will continue to do so. Two examples I will put forward right now is a contrast from my rough draft and final draft. You can see that there were several changes. The changes took quite a while, and that illustrates **Persistence.**

Incidentally, Rocky's local chapter actually extended an invitation to present the completed profile at an upcoming meeting, once the project had been scored. Rocky's development is indicative of how the habits of mind can be transferred to arenas outside the digital writing classroom, and also of the strong connections that can be made when students are engaged in writing tasks that allow them to venture out into their physical spaces, and think critically about their role in those spaces.

Conclusion

While the individual goals of the assignments reflected in the student examples here differ, the underlying scaffolding of engaging and understanding roles in one's community and transforming cognition through the "WPA Outcomes Statement" and habits of mind remains the same. In Diana's case, their goal as a composer shifted through the experience of completing the community problem analysis, the very real issue of sexual assault in a community was identified and explored, and the student's ability to practice the habits of Curiosity and Openness, both as a human and a writer, were further developed. Stephen's work in the community group profile assignment allowed the student to rethink notions about collaboration and come to a new understanding of the value of feedback in the writing process, and even transferring that learning to another composition. In addition, Stephen expanded their ideas about what defines research, realizing the utility of engaging with primary sources in the community in order to compose a meaningful profile. Finally, Rocky was afforded the opportunity to re-evaluate skills that once appeared developed, in particular Rhetorical Knowledge, and put those skills to the test in a real-world setting. Through Persistence, Rocky was also able to explore a particular community, realize the growth and change that comes with Persistence, and deliver the findings to the very community being profiled.

In providing these examples, we hope we have provided some insight into the way community-engaged writing can help students examine their affiliations within their communities and transform their own understandings of their communities and their place within them. Through community-focused writing and research projects, online students can actively and purposefully locate their writing through the community affiliations they assert. Our goals are akin to those described by Gillam and Wooden, particularly in their overall goal of re-embodying the online writing classroom experience:

> By focusing on the common beliefs undergirding our efforts to facilitate a social construction of knowledge, to demonstrate the interconnected multivalence of communication situations, and to deliberately build learning communities in a disembodied space, we may reconceptualize elements of the course so as to productively pursue all of these goals simultaneously. (25)

We aim to accomplish this through teaching and learning that fosters collaboration and engagement with issues directly affecting one or more student communities; student research and writing focuses on their communities—professional, civic, or personal—by employing a number of research methods: observation, interview, rhetorical analysis, secondary research.

By using sustained reflection throughout the course, at each major milestone of the writing process, and asking students to directly consider how they do or might transfer their learning to other contexts, community-engaged writing can frame the metacognitive work students do to also transform their own understanding of themselves as writers. This framework for approaching writing communities can lead students to consider and apply frameworks like the habits of mind in new and unexpected ways.

Works Cited

Beaufort, Anne. "Reflection: The Metacognitive Move Toward Transfer of Learning." *A Rhetoric of Reflection*, edited by Kathleen Blake Yancey, Utah State UP, 2016, pp. 23–41.

Blair, Christine, and Cheryl Hoy. "Paying Attention to Adult Learners Online: The Pedagogy and Politics of Community." *Computers and Composition*, vol. 23, no. 1, 2006, pp. 32–48.

Boynton, Linda. "When the Class Bell Stops Ringing: The Achievements and Challenges of Teaching Online First-Year Composition." *Teaching English in The Two-Year College*, vol. 29, no. 3, 2002, pp. 298–311.

Brunk-Chavez, Beth. "The *Framework for Success* Goes Online: Integration of the *Framework* into Online Writing Courses." *The Framework for Success in Postsecondary Writing: Scholarship and Applications*, edited by Nicholas N. Behm, et al., Parlor P, 2017, pp. 154–68.

Council of Writing Program Administrators. "WPA Outcomes Statement for First-Year Composition (3.0)." CWPA, 2014, wpacouncil.org/aws/CWPA/asset_manager/get_file/350909?ver=552. Accessed 3 Aug. 2020.

Council of Writing Program Administrators, the National Council of Teachers of English, and the National Writing Project. *Framework for Success in Postsecondary Writing*. CWPA, NCTE, and NWP, 2011, wpacouncil.org/files/framework-for-success-postsecondary-writing.pdf. Accessed 10 Oct. 2019.

Dewey, John. *How We Think*. Heath, 1910.

Downs, Doug, and Elizabeth Wardle. "Teaching About Writing, Righting Misconceptions: (Re)Envisioning 'First-Year Composition' as Introduction to Writing Studies. *College Composition and Communication*, vol. 58, no. 4, 2007, pp. 552–84.

Dubinsky, James M. M., et al. "Composing Cognition: The Role of Written Reflections in Service-Learning." *Service-Learning and Writing: Paving the Way for Literacy(ies) through Community Engagement*, Brill, 2012, pp. 155–80.

Esposito, Lauren. "Where to Begin? Using Place-Based Writing to Connect Students with Their Local Communities." *English Journal*, vol. 101, no. 4, 2012, pp. 70–76.

Gallagher-Lepak, Susan, et al. "Nursing Student Perceptions of Community in Online Learning." *Contemporary Nurse*, vol. 32, nos. 1–2, 2009, pp. 133–46.

Gillam, Ken, and Shannon R. Wooden. "Re-Embodying Online Composition: Ecologies of Writing in Unreal Time and Space." *Computers and Composition*, vol. 30, no. 1, 2013, pp. 24–36.

Gries, Laurie E. "Writing to Assemble Publics: Making Writing Activate, Making Writing Matter." *College Composition and Communication*, vol. 70, no.3, 2019, pp. 327–55.

Hayes, John R. "Forward. Are Cognitive Studies in Writing Really Passé?" *Contemporary Perspectives on Cognition and Writing*, edited by Patricia Portanova, et al., Perspectives on Writing, The WAC Clearinghouse and UP of Colorado, 2017, pp. vii-xv, wac.colostate.edu/books/perspectives/cognition/.

Litterio, Lisa M. "Uncovering Student Perceptions of a First-Year Online Writing Course." *Computers and Composition*, vol 47, 2018, pp. 1–13.

Maxfield, R. J., and Gary B. Noll. "Epistemology and Ontology: The Lived Experience of Non-Traditional Adult Students in Online and Study-Abroad Learning Environments." *Journal of Organizational Psychology*, vol. 17, no. 6, 2017, pp. 48–60.

Meyer, Jan, and Ray Land. *Threshold Concepts and Troublesome Knowledge: Linkages to Ways of Thinking and Practising Within the Disciplines*. ETL Project Occasional Report 4, Edinburg, 2003.

Murphy, Susan Wolff. "Apprenticing Civic and Political Engagement in the First Year Writing Program." *Going Public: What Writing*

Programs Learn from Engagement, edited by Shirley Rose and Irwin Weiser, Utah State UP, 2010, pp. 110–21.

Melkun, Cheryl Hawkinson. "Nontraditional Students Online: Composition, Collaboration, and Community." *The Journal of Continuing Higher Education*, vol. 60, no. 1, 2012, pp. 33–39.

Otter, Ryan R., et al. "Comparing Student and Faculty Perceptions of Online and Traditional Courses." *The Internet and Higher Education*, vol. 19, 2013, pp. 27–35.

Peck, Wayne Campbell, et al. "Community Literacy." *College Composition and Communication*, vol. 46, no. 2, 1995, pp. 199–222.

Picciano, Anthony G. "Beyond Student Perceptions: Issues of Interaction, Presence, and Performance in an Online Course." *Journal of Asynchronous Learning Networks*, vol. 6, no. 1, 2002, pp. 21–40.

Ryder, Phyllis Mentzell. *Rhetorics for Community Action: Public Writing and Writing Publics*. Lexington Books, 2011.

Seaman, Julia E., et al. *Grade Increase: Tracking Distance Education in the United States*. Babson Survey Research Group, 2018, www.onlinelearningsurvey.com/highered.html.

Thompson, Nicole L., et al. "Comparing Online and Face-to-Face Learning Experiences for Nontraditional Students: A Case Study of Three Online Teacher Education Candidates." *Quarterly Review of Distance Education*, vol. 14, no. 4, 2013, pp. 233–51.

West, William, et al. "How Learning Styles Impact e-Learning: A Case-Comparative Study of Undergraduate Students who Excelled, Passed, or Failed an Online Course in Scientific Writing." *Journal of Administrators of Electronic Learning*, vol. 3, no. 4, 2006, pp. 533–41.

Woods, Robert H., Jr. "How Much Communication is Enough in Online Courses? Exploring the Relationship Between Frequency of Instructor-Initiated Personal Email and Learners' Perceptions of and Participation in Online Learning." *International Journal of Instructional Media*, vol. 29, no. 4, 2002, p. 377–94.

Yancey, Kathleen. *A Rhetoric of Reflection*, E-book, Utah State UP, 2016.

—. "The Social Life of Reflection: Notes Toward an ePortfolio-Based Model of Reflection." *Teaching Reflective Learning in Higher Education: A Systematic Approach Using Pedagogic Patterns*, edited by M. E. Ryan, Springer International, 2015, pp. 189–202.

Yancey, Kathleen, et al. *Writing Across Contexts: Transfer, Composition, and Sites of Writing*, Utah State UP, 2014.

III Program-Level Engagement

8 The Space Between: A Statewide Effort Using the *Framework for Success* to Bridge High School and College Writing

Christine Cucciarre

This is a story about students believing in their identities as student writers. These identities aren't determined by the scores students get in standardized testing, or academic benchmarks they reach during a term; this story is about the effort to persuade middle and secondary school writers, so often told that they can't write, that they are writers because of their lived practices and habits. It isn't the more common story of a typical secondary and post-secondary partnership limited to a focus on the aptitudes student writers need on their first day of college. It is a narrative that illustrates what most readers of this book already know about how writing improves: by having faith in the dedicated practice and habits of writing. I argue that identifying and cultivating shared beliefs in K–16 education, spreading those beliefs to stakeholders beyond the schools themselves, and encouraging students to identify as writers is a powerful path toward change.

The story demonstrates the range of contexts and perspectives educators bring to the table, the inconsistent terminology we use, and the situations we commonly face as teachers of writing. I offer a new and broader definition of *metacognition* that links to identity change to foster students' understanding of what it means to be college-ready. Building on the argument that Peter Khost, Wendy Ryden, and David Hyman articulated earlier in this collection, the story here challenges the conventional understanding of college readiness and offers an alternative.

Like any other state, Delaware has diverse needs and a wide range of proficiencies in its K–12 education system. However, the state's small size allows Delaware to gather all key stakeholders: representatives from all state higher education institutions and twenty-two education districts, and a K–12 literacy cohort comprised of leaders from each of Delaware's three counties. In 2016, the Delaware Office of Higher Education formed a committee of these cross-state educators, charging it with eliminating remedial, non-credit-bearing classes in the state's institutes of higher education. To do so, the "P-20 Committee" would need to confront the challenge of improving the readiness of the state's young people for college.[1]

Like most states, Delaware has major urban areas (Wilmington and Dover), which are surrounded by suburban communities, with a state that is otherwise rural. Consequently, despite its size, Delaware faces the same challenges germane to jurisdictions across the country that arise socio-economic disparities coupled with the challenges of inequitable educational experiences in urban and rural areas. High schools are hamstrung by state-mandated proficiency requirements and are often viewed as "teaching to the test": Advanced Placement exams, the SAT (that is given free of charge to every senior in Delaware's high schools), Common Core Standards (CCSS) and Smarter Balance assessments. For many, successful K–12 education is measured simply and exclusively by the demonstrated success of these instruments.

Moreover, high schools have felt the pressure to offer courses that count for college credit through AP Credit and programs such as dual enrollment. Still, while these courses provide college credit content, they often do not provide college proficiency. Students often earn these credits in classrooms where there are more students, less time, fewer resources, and lower expectations than they would enjoy in post-secondary settings. Moreover, the pressure to offer college credit in these secondary—and sometimes even middle schools draws students who may lack the requisite emotional and intellectual maturity for key components of an effective writing curriculum: guided drafting, peer workshops, and meaningful revision. Kristine Hanson and Christine Farris challenged the trend of earned credit in their well-researched book *College Credit for Writing in High School: The "Taking Care of" Business*, where they conclude that expectations for advanced credit threatens the effective teaching of writing to school-aged children. In sum, developmentally and now institutionally, it is getting more difficult to instill in high schools the values of writing emphasized by the authors in this book.

Carol Severino, in her response to the *Framework for Success in Postsecondary Writing*, asks "how high school English teachers can do any more to prepare their students for college than they are already doing—teaching five classes and 100-plus students whose literacy skills range from college level to minimal" (533). Unsurprisingly, high school teachers often rely on prescribed and formulaic means of writing; in doing so, however, they compromise the degree to which their students become college-ready. This debate isn't new, and indeed, Janet Alsup et al. and Howard Tinberg and Jean-Paul Nadeau and many others have explored, challenged, and argued how high school curricula should prepare students for college. As the debate continues, pressure grows from the private sector and local, state, and federal governments to address the challenge.

It is evident that we are far from solving this challenge. Indeed, there is growing tension between efforts to expand college readiness, and to lessen college course loads by gaining credit in high school. Caught in the middle are those students who didn't earn college credit before matriculation and are not college ready. These remedial students must take courses for which they pay tuition but do not earn college credit.

But like the story I am telling now, Melanie Burdick and Jane Greer write "Much of the existing literature [on these issues] is anecdotal" (83). They argue that despite efforts to define and improve college readiness, "these calls for collaboration among secondary and postsecondary writing teachers, it is surprising that researchers in writing studies and writing program administrators (WPAs) have not explored how high school teachers understand their roles in preparing students for college writing" (83). Burdick and Greer recognize how many "inharmonious stakeholders" have their hands in this issue (85). And given the freely available evidence of what people deem "good" or "bad" writing, much of the public believes they know what's best.

Having the *Framework* as a guiding document from our discipline's leading organizations helps. Meant to bridge high school and college writing, it's no wonder that many states are using it to guide discussions about curriculum. The Nicholas Behm, Sherry Rankins-Robertson, and Duane Roen edited collection, *The* Framework for Success in Postsecondary Writing: *Scholarship and Applications* references state-wide efforts such as in Maine and Tennessee. Delaware started its work with the Framework because of a state mandate to end what they consider all remedial, non-credit-bearing classes on the college level. My first meeting at the State Board of Education was in the Fall of 2016. The day's agenda stated, "To identify changes in policies and practice across high school and post-secondary to eliminate remediation for all Delaware students entering the state's higher education institutions credit-bearing English courses." The key question on the agenda was "What must a student be prepared to do in their 1st year college English course?" (P20 Council Subcommittee). We discussed revising the Foundations of College English course, a course that was designed to prepare struggling students who scored below a 480 on their PSAT in their final years of high school. During that meeting, we also had a presentation on the College Board's assessments and reviewed the "SAT Suite of Assessments: Alignment to Delaware." This document assessed that Delaware state standards alignment was "strong to very strong" with the suite of SAT aptitudes. But that good rating wasn't translating into the expectations of what a prepared student body looks like to colleges and universities. The data from 2015 showed that one quarter of all graduating students in Delaware required "remediation" in both English and math (P-20 Report Draft).

In subsequent meetings, we drafted a memo of understanding (MOU) to be signed by higher education institutions across the state saying they would no longer offer remedial, non-credit-bearing classes. It further stated that secondary schools would revise the eleventh grade "Foundations of English" course to better prepare students for twelfth-grade and first-year writing, something that the State assessed that the current class was not doing. All but one of the institutions of higher education in Delaware, Delaware College of Art and Design, accepted the memo. Delaware State University, Delaware Technical Community College, Wesley College, and Wilmington University signed the document; Goldey-Beacom College and my institution, the University of Delaware, signed the document although neither offer any remedial classes in writing. The MOU was also signed by the three school districts: Brandywine, Laurel, and Woodbridge, who are piloting the new Foundations of English course. The agreement to pilot the new eleventh-grade class and end remedial classes was, I think, the easy part of our committee's charge. Our discussions after that revealed the rift between writing and literacy instruction in the high schools and the expectations colleges had for incoming students. The universities were advocating process, drafting, active reading, and higher-level writing strategies while the high schools were constrained by the Common Core and other curricular expectations. The six post-secondary representatives were in general agreement of advocating process and classroom habits. And the high school representatives agreed, but noted that the benchmarks they needed to achieve, the number of students they taught, and the more basic needs of high schoolers prevented them from working toward these goals. Although everyone engaged eagerly in these meetings, the skepticism of the high school educators was clear and "you just don't understand" was said at least twice. The truth was, I didn't understand. Having never taught high school, I cannot appreciate the demands and pressures put on secondary teachers. We were just beginning to work with one another during this first set of meetings, and we had to recognize the variety of backgrounds and educational settings from which we came. We realized that what higher education representatives advocated were ideals that just weren't possible in most high school settings.

This impasse, as the conditions that created it, was the very reason that the University of Delaware had decided to stop accepting dual and concurrent enrollment credit from other universities and ended our own offerings of those high school classes in writing. It was an unpopular move given that, like national trends, concurrent classes were successful in encouraging Delaware students to attend college after high school. We didn't come to our decision easily, but having little control over the quality of dual enrollment, our writing program's main value is that writing must be practiced consistently in a setting with other college students and guided by college instructors. Accepting dual enrollment (sometimes from students who our records showed took a dual- or concurrent-enrollment course during the sophomore or junior years of high school), all but guaranteed that Delaware's first-year students would not be practicing writing. It also ensured that students would not take part in any small, academic seminar where the professor would know their names during their first year in college. Those things were antithetical to the way we thought about writing: as process, as community, as a way to learn. We also knew that our first-year writing class teaches much more than strategies of writing; it teaches students how to manage projects, how to research, how to work with other writers, how to provide feedback on writing, that writing can lead to discovery, and maybe most of all, how to think of themselves as writers.

The University of Delaware's decision on dual enrollment informed my approach to the P-20 subcommittee. At the very center of our belief is that writing is not a set of skills, but an ongoing plan for cognition and thinking. Those at the committee meeting table also firmly held this belief. We all knew that if not practiced, writing and thinking habits would atrophy. With that starting point, we began defining and sketching what students needed to know about writing on their first day of college. But we kept the disparity of settings and resources that separated what could be practiced in high schools with what was possible in college at the forefront of our discussions.

In many of those early P-20 subcommittee meetings and the working groups within that committee, we struggled to agree on terminology. As Dylan Dryer argues, not only do the scholars in writing studies contest what the keywords *mean*, we contest what the keywords of our discipline *are*. In exploring a "Corpus [that] consists exclusively of research articles" from 2005–2017 in our field (217–218), Dryer admits in his conclusion that "Since academics have vested interests in speaking easily and comfortably with the peers with whom they share assumptions and research priorities, there is no obvious or natural counter to this trend" (250). Dryer's research is magnified when the audience is widened to middle and secondary teachers, those very educators that comprise the P-20 subcommittees. Linda Adler-Kassner and Elizabeth Wardle's *Naming What We Know*, also addresses the bigger concepts that many in our field hold to be true in writing studies, but within those concepts, the terms we use are often challenged. And they should be. Contested meanings of words is at the heart of many of the concepts such as "writing is a social and rhetorical activity," ideas about reader reconstruction of writing, and words that get their meanings from other words. Our discipline should thrive on these disparities and the local contexts of meaning. Bringing high school teachers and university writing program administrators together complicates the work, which is further confounded when we also include high school administrators, parents, and students.

During these meetings, I found myself pushing against efforts to use abstract and reductive terminology in favor of including action verbs that suggested sustained action that still assured the learning outcomes. For example, I would argue that the language that we used needed to favor the routines of writing such as "practicing" or simple changes that privileged the action rather than the product such as "writing" over "written." What struck me was the disconnect between my own language in talking about writing and those of my colleagues both in higher education and secondary education. We often debated the terms, revising and restating a committee member's contribution to the conversation by repeating it with the terms that we believed were needed, rather than the ones they used. I witnessed this happening, and I did it myself to my colleagues sitting around me. These subtle shifts seemed calculating, but words' definitions became more consistent, our discussions evolved, and our conversations shifted into consensus.

Between the entire P-20 subcommittee and the individual working groups we met, either in person or virtually, almost every month. As we got to know and trust each other, our differences no longer felt insurmountable. Putting the student at the center of our conversations helped turn us to the *Framework*, and, in particular, to the habits of mind. We talked about the lack of any sort of writing in their classes and that students don't think of themselves as writers. Looking back, our dialogue about student identity was a key moment in our progress. It made us think about identity and the gap between high school and college writing as the important part of this story. The space between twelfth grade and a student's first year in college could represent the real or figurative time between graduating and becoming a college freshman; it could represent summer learning loss; it could be the stark difference between the rules and mandated outcomes in postsecondary education defined by the state; or it could be the adoption of a national set of rules and the bureaucratic freedoms of college. However we want to use the metaphor, it was clear that students themselves occupied that space. If we helped to shape their identities as writers, we could buoy them to get to the other side.

The foreword to *The* Framework for Success in Postsecondary Writing: *Scholarship and Applications*, argues this too. In the foreword, Peggy O'Neill et al., all members of the task force charged with authoring the *Framework*, write,

> By focusing on habits of mind rather than discrete outcomes, the *Framework* suggests that college and career readiness in writing depends on broader understandings of those activities. And because we positioned it as a border-crossing kind of document, based in ideas that came from educators at multiple levels, we hoped that it would lead to important conversations about ideas that are too often taken for granted, particularly what knowl-

edge, competencies, and experiences are needed for success in college writing. (xi)

Focusing on student writing habits, cognitive and physical, allows us to look more holistically at the practice of writing. We concerned ourselves less with the destination and more with the journey and who was taking it. Once our group began talking about students' practices and routines rather than outcomes, we found more solid common ground. As we were all once students and some still practicing writers, we know the most effective habits of strong writers. Getting students to accept these practices early and dispel the myths of the lone, inspired writer who completes writing in one sitting, those struggling writers who are often shamed into silence might begin believing in themselves and identifying as writers.

Of course, the *Framework* was drafted for the sole purpose of secondary and post-secondary collaborating on a "living" set of expectations. What Delaware, I think, is doing differently, is targeting a wider audience to push the message and foster the habits. The *Framework* itself says that its audience goes beyond the teachers of writing "because writing is of concern for those inside and outside education, audiences beyond the classroom—including parents, policymakers, employers, and the general public—also can use this document" (CWPA et al). But using the *Framework* beyond the actual classroom, became a place where most all of the educators on the committee could agree. Instead of thinking primarily as teachers, professors, and writing program administrators, we began looking at our committee's charge and the *Framework* as parents, thinking about what could be nurtured and encouraged in the home. This is where our committee united.

We began talking about writing, habits, and process in the way Severino discusses the *Framework*, "although the eight habits [of mind] refer mainly to individuals' cognitive skills, social skills are included in terms of the influence of 'others' under the habits of openness, engagement, persistence, and responsibility" (535). Akin to the way Martha A. Townsend in this collection uses athletic practice as an analogy for the practice of writing, the idea of teamwork, community, persistence, and responsibility to those beyond oneself, our conversations shifted to the coaches and practice spaces in this analogy. We moved our focus to those who support students such as administrators in how they talk to parents, parents in how they encourage their children, and in the students themselves as they define themselves as writers. We talked about the environments where these habits of mind can take hold, and the students who are offered a way of thinking about writing that is manifested through their daily activities as students. Just as Patrick Sullivan writes in "Essential Habits of Mind for College Readiness," we embraced the habits of mind and shifted to an audience beyond the teachers; we moved from proficiencies to the ways writers think, their mindset, and in short, their individual character (547). We may not have said it aloud, but we were crafting an identity for student writers and expanding the definition of metacognition as a way for each student, their family, their school, and the administration to think about who they are.

The prefix "meta" works on a number of levels here in considering this habit for statewide change. Defined in the *Framework* as "the ability to reflect on one's own thinking as well as on the individual and cultural processes and systems used to structure knowledge," we are also looking at the prefix in its other meaning: transformation. We are asking educators and parents to revise what they believe about writing and thinking. And we are asking students to transform into writers based on their habits.

The teaching implications of this effort expand the idea that students are *college-ready*, a term that suggests that students have the necessary skills to succeed in college. This misnomer perpetuates the broader public beliefs that students have the content knowledge and a set of aptitudes that prepare them. Most college educators would agree that content knowledge and skill sets may be part of what make a student able to excel, but writing scholars are acutely aware that the best writers are those that have approaches to learning and the habits defined in the *Framework*. These fundamental practices of writers are not at odds with the state mandated requirements; thus, they do not add new curriculum to already overburdened secondary teachers. The changes would occur in the home, and in spaces beyond the classroom. What would be brought to the classroom is students' understanding of self and their identity as writers.

As a result, our efforts in Delaware shifted. We began drafting a document that promotes the *Framework*'s habits as the primary avenue to achieve the more conventional competencies expected. Dispelling the myth that writing is a skill that is achieved, our document envelopes each writing strategy with behaviors and ways of thinking to illustrate that writing is an ongoing practice.

Delaware's "College Student Readiness Framework" was drafted for all parents, students, teachers, and administrators, but our main audience is the families of middle school and high school students. The document begins, "Being ready for any type of education or training after high school requires preparation. Good grades and test scores will help you to get into the program, but to complete the program, students must have the skills and behaviors listed below. We have created this guide to help you get ready for success after high school." At the time of this book's printing, Delaware is still in the process of drafting this document. Currently, the table is made up of two sections "Reading and Writing Strategies," and "Habits of a Successful Student Signs of Readiness." In each of those sections, we have a list of strategies and habits. Each row that lists a strategy and habit has two corresponding rows that list "Questions to Ask" and "Ways to Get Ready." In our drafting, we reminded ourselves frequently to use accessible language for a wide range of readers. Each strategy is paired with a series of questions that a parent might ask a student or the student might ask of themselves. We have yet to draft the "Ways to Get Ready" column. But like the strategies and their affiliated questions, these preparation suggestions will be underscored with the habits of mind.

In the "Habits of a Successful Student" section, the column "Signs of Readiness" is where the *Framework*'s habits of mind are most explicit. I've copied the list in the first column and added its corresponding habits:

> "Manage time/organize tasks"—Responsibility
>
> "Locate and understand information"—Curiosity
>
> "Persist/demonstrate sustained effort"—Curiosity and Persistence
>
> "Follow directions, complete assignments on time with creativity and care"—Responsibility and Creativity
>
> "Know how to provide thoughtful discussion in and out of class"—Engagement)
>
> "Live with flexibility, patience and perseverance"—Openness, Persistence, and Flexibility
>
> "Practice professional, kind and respectful conduct"—Responsibility

I would argue that the consideration of each of these habits of mind make up the idea of metacognition, thus completing the *Framework*'s list. The *Framework* provided us a way to begin thinking about the college student on day one. Thinking as parents as well as educators allowed us to think about how a student identifies as a writer. While the "teaching" of metacognition is accomplished by assignments and practices in the classroom as described by the *Framework*'s own language, "Metacognition is fostered when writers are encouraged to . . ." (CWPA et al. 5), Delaware's effort sees this encouragement extending beyond the school, to curricular discussions, board of education meetings, to the students while they revise, and to the home. With a nod to Asao Inoue's scholarship on the labor of writing, this approach promotes the consideration of the whole student, encourages instilling these characteristics, and illustrates that the work of writing and the habits we consistently practice are what makes writing improve.

If metacognition is one of the ways that most effectively enables transfer in writing as Gwen Gorzelsky et al. claim in "Cultivating Constructive Metacognition," then Delaware's effort to foster behaviors and awareness in students might help to reshape the student's writerly identity. Educators' beliefs about which student is a writer and which student isn't, is often conflated with our judgments of who are good students. If the efforts in Delaware work, all students will think of themselves as practicing writers, and if even a few of the habits of mind are instilled, we might see a significant shift across all levels of education.

Note

1. The P-20 Committee was so named because the group works on issues that cover pre-school through college. It works primarily through two sub-committees: math and language arts.

Works Cited

Alsup, Janet, et al. "Seeing Connections, Articulating Commonalities: English Education, Composition Studies, and Writing Teacher Education." *College Composition and Communication*, vol. 62, no.4, 2011, pp. 668–86.

Burdick, Melanie, and Jane Greer. "Paths to Productive Partnerships: Surveying High School Teachers about Professional Development

Opportunities and 'College-Level' Writing." *Writing Program Administration*, vol. 41, no. 1, 2017, pp. 82–101.

"SAT Suite of Assessments: Alignment to Delaware." College Board, Oct. 2016. https://reports.collegeboard.org/pdf/2018-delaware-sat-suite-assessments-annual-report.pdf. Accessed 7 Mar. 2021

Dryer, Dylan. "Divided by Primes: Competing Meanings among Writing Studies' Keywords." *College English*, vol. 81, no. 3, 2019, pp. 214–55.

Gorzelsky, Gwen, et al. "Cultivating Constructive Metacognition: A New Taxonomy for Writing Studies." *Critical Transitions: Writing and the Question of Transfer*, edited by Chris M. Anson and Jessie L. Moore, Perspectives on Writing, WAC Clearinghouse and UP of Colorado, 2017, pp. 215–46.

Hansen, Kristine, and Christie R. Farris, editors. *College Credit for Writing in High School: The "Taking Care of" Business*. NCTE, 2010.

Inoue, Asao B. *Labor-Based Grading Contracts: Building Equity and Inclusion in the Compassionate Writing Classroom*. Perspectives on Writing, The WAC Clearinghouse and UP of Colorado, 2019, wac.colostate.edu/books/perspectives/labor/

O'Neill, Peggy, et al. Foreword. "The and Now, Reflections on the *Framework* Six Years Out." *The* Framework for Success in Postsecondary Writing: *Scholarship and Application*, edited by Nicholas Behm, et al., Parlor P, 2017, pp. ix-xxi.

"P20 Council Subcommittee Agenda." Department of Higher Education, State of Delaware, Dec. 14, 2016.

"P20 Committee Report Draft." Department of Higher Education, State of Delaware, Oct. 2017.

Severino, Carol. "Responses to the *Framework*: The Problems of Articulation: Uncovering More of the Composition Curriculum." *College English*, vol. 74, no. 6, 2012, pp. 533–36.

Sullivan, Patrick. "Essential Habits of Mind for College Readiness." *College English*, vol. 74, no. 6, 2012, pp. 547–53.

Tinberg, Howard, and Jean-Paul Nadeau. "Contesting the Space between High School and College in the Era of Dual-Enrollment. *College Composition and Communication*, vol. 62, no.4, 2011, pp. 704–25.

9 A Metaphor-Based Curriculum: Fostering Inquiry, Metacognition, and Transfer

Tonya Eick and Gregg Fields

> *Metacognition—the ability to reflect on one's own thinking as well as on the individual and cultural processes and systems used to structure knowledge.*
> —*Framework for Success in Postsecondary Writing*, p. 5

> *Structural metaphors allow us to do much more than just orient concepts, refer to them, quantify them, etc. . . . ; they allow us, in addition, to use one highly structured and clearly delineated concept to structure another.*
> —Lakoff and Johnson, p. 61

Introduction

As many in this collection have noted, the *Framework for Success in Postsecondary Writing* and its habits of mind act as a "disciplinary document" (Gross and Walker, this collection) or mission statement for writing teachers and scholars to say, "what is important and how to make it work" (Macauley, Jr., this collection). Unfortunately, though, both in spite of and because of the very practical nature of the eight habits of mind, it can sometimes be challenging to think of them as more than the status quo, the habits that many writing instructors have simply internalized and come to practice. Not many would argue the need to embed more creativity or persistence or responsibility into the writing classroom in the current culture of college writing, yet, as found in this collection, scholar-practitioners continue to challenge, nuance, articulate, re-invent, and re-contextualize different aspects of the framework to grow and enhance our discipline. Essentially, the *Framework* has become its own "system . . . to structure knowledge" (5). Using aspects of the *Framework* as a guide to inform structure, the following chapter lays out a curriculum for first-year college composition that reinforces habits of mind like curiosity and engagement through the metacognitive processes of what we term a *metaphor-based curriculum* (MBC).

This metaphor-based curriculum has multiple components that work in tandem to reinforce the development of the habits of mind, and we will return to each of these components more substantially throughout the chapter: however, to begin building that conceptual system or curricular blueprint of the course for our readers, we will define the foundations for a few of these components.

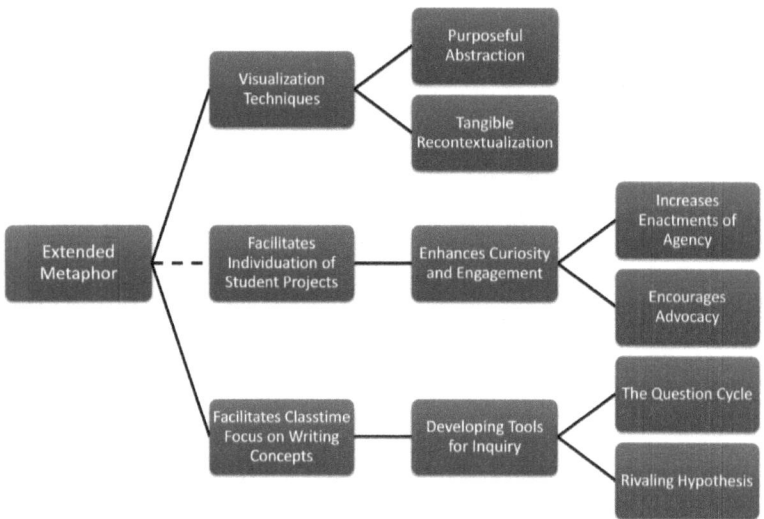

Figure 1. Mapping key components for metaphor-based curriculum.

The primary component for the course was an extended metaphor that we constructed across fifteen weeks as a system within which we could anchor or hang curricular content. This metaphor directly facilitated visualization techniques that helped concretize the sometimes more abstract metacognitive work by encouraging students to "examine processes" (CWPA et al. 5) within the context of the metaphor to understand the alternate contexts of the students' own writing processes. We created a cognitive bridge aiding their understanding of these new concepts and strategies by using metaphorical language students were already familiar with (through the image-based metaphor) to mediate the newly introduced writing concept or strategy terminology that students may not have been exposed to before this course. The tangibility of the metaphor helped demystify those abstract ideas introduced in first-year composition (FYC).

The metaphor also indirectly facilitated more individuated student projects that in turn provided students with a greater "sense of investment and involvement" (CWPA et al. 4). Further, the MBC provided room for students to develop tools for inquiry that include techniques like the Rivaling Hypothesis (Flower, Long, and Higgins) and the Question Cycle (Eick, "A Response"; "It's All About Timing"). By being equipped with these toolkits, students could then become more engaged with their own topics and local contexts for agentive writing.

The MBC was implemented at a large public university in the United States by two instructors across four sections of English (ENG) 102, the second in a sequence of two FYC courses required for all undergraduate students. This chapter draws on research from an IRB-approved embedded mixed methods ethnographic study with a substantial variety of data types. For this study, 67 out of 86 students across four sections consented to participate. For qualitative data analysis, we examined one-on-one conferences, group conferences, class session recordings, and peer review activities. Whereas, quantitative data were gathered through pre- and post-course positioning surveys and a corpus analysis of reflective essays and in-class synchronous free-writing activities. We used this approach to the study because, initially, we were unsure in what form the habits of mind might become apparent.

With the metaphor-based curriculum, instruction can support sustained inquiry and problem solving while respecting the wide range of values and commitments that students bring with them to (and refine for themselves while in) college (Hairston 186; Flower, Long, and Higgins 300).

Extended Metaphors

Comparisons, allusions, and metaphors have played a central role in conversations on cognition and the classroom for many years (James "Teaching" 156; Lakoff and Johnson 97–9), and metaphors specifically continue to be an area of study in second language writing by scholars such as Mark A. James and Wan Wan. A metaphor can be particularly effective as a vehicle for learning because "metaphor or analogy . . . is an analytical thought structure which . . . exposes and extends relationships by linking the unfamiliar to the familiar" (Schor 123). Further, according to Wan, using metaphors for writing enhances students' metacognition because working with metaphors necessitates that students "practice thinking critically about their own writing" (66). In most classroom situations however, metaphors are used in individual moments; like hyphenated adjectives, metaphors act as temporary constructions to facilitate situated uptake and then become forgotten (Carter and Pitcher 584). However, extended metaphors, those that are refreshed across a longer period of time, tend to be remembered and used to recall prior knowledge because the context they connect to remains alive in students' minds.

While we already used metaphors in our courses, these were being used in that more singular, independent, and forgettable mode to describe individual ideas in the classroom. However, with these things in mind, we chose to develop a single extended metaphor across a fifteen-week semester to establish and maintain a cognitive system made tangible through the metaphor upon which we could "hang" curricular content (e.g., aspects of writing, rhetoric, and research). We chose to prepare this course-length metaphor because we hypothesized that, when content is placed within a system as previously described, the metaphor could act as a way of creating cognitive *save points* for students through the metacognitive work of purposeful abstraction and recontextualization. This *transfer-appropriate processing* (TAP) (Lightbown 57) helps the student to re-enact the analytical processes of writing in diverse contexts rather than a contextually-locked theme. TAP scaffolds creativity where analytical processes are habitualized by the student. They are using the new information inside a framework of knowledge they are already familiar with or understand. The work they do is, then, more readily recalled and repeated by these save points (Tomlinson 367). Thus, a metaphor allows students a frame to 'hang' writing concepts on, and an extended metaphor allows them to continue co-constructing that same system over time as they work through their various individual writing projects. Once writing concepts and strategies are situated in this larger metaphor system, students are more disposed to using these concepts and strategies beyond an individual assignment, leading to more sustained engagement.

MBC AND INSTRUCTOR-BASED THEMES

For similar reasons, some teachers may choose a more traditional theme-based approach, where a single theme or topic is used to focus the course for all students. Comparably, themed courses also have the benefit of a single guiding structure that can be effective for enhancing students' uptake of the course content while also encouraging deeper study of a single subject. However, themed courses tend to drive class time, reading, and essay assignments; and more importantly, according to Maxine Hairston, courses like these can impose the instructor's ideology on the course and the students, diminishing opportunities for student curiosity and engagement. For these reasons, the theme-based curriculum was not aligning with the values of inquiry, student curiosity, and agency that we hoped to encourage through our various assignments. Beyond these habits of mind, while sometimes engaging students through the use of culturally relevant topics, a traditional themed course has been challenged for drawing focus away from the actual content of writing, leading some scholars to even adopt a "No Vampires Policy" (Adler-Kassner 132). Choosing the MBC instead of a traditional themed course opened up our options for course design to include student-initiated inquiries while class activities utilized the metaphor structure to incorporate writing concepts. Developing a greater meta-awareness of the web of processes behind those concepts through the more tangible metaphor system, class time then became focused not on any one given topic but on how to apply strategies across topics, projects, and contexts. Thus, once students are situated in this metaphoric system, they are more disposed and better positioned for using these concepts and strategies beyond the assignment (Yancey et al. 152).

The work then became focused on students' ability to write more deeply meaningful compositions. The students had a point of commonality for the class, in using the structure and in talking about their own topics, but in a way that did not distract from writing content from their own unique perspectives. Although it might seem as if there were no limits to the topics of the classroom, it proved to be just the opposite. The metaphor system acted as the boundary building that students need before they are aware of what concepts like analysis mean or entail. Linda Adler-Kassner's "No Vampires Policy" ideal is then supported in this design, giving the students the tools they need to engage in writing through visual abstraction, not just with the contexts in which they are already familiar.

Visualization

One of the key reasons for building the MBC was to find a way of internalizing the writing strategies that we wanted students to adopt and develop because metaphors can be a form of strategic encoding. Supporting this idea that metaphors help encode, Patsy M. Lightbown talks about content-based language teaching in a way that harkens back to psychological research and regards teaching strategies that allow for knowledge to be operationalized through working memory with mechanisms that promote strategic *encoding* (56). By creating structures through visualized metaphor that allow for this internalized, encoded knowledge, we also aid in creating the cognitive pathways that increase working memory retrieval (Lightbown 57). The more active these pathways to the encoded knowledge, the more readily students are able to retrieve the writing concepts and practices that we are asking them to employ.

Further, metaphors tend to tap into cognitive processes of mental visualization that many students already use to digest language and alphabetic text , and through metaphors, linguistic repertoires are then given a more tangible space (Tomlinson 358; James, "Teaching" 156). Therefore, in the same way that George Lakoff and Mark Johnson (58) describe visualizing sentence structures and writing constructions more tangibly, actual visualizations of the metaphor can help to develop thought and scaffold students' critical analyses, strengthening students' awareness and use of writing strategies by learning to engage with instructor- and student-created visualizations of the extended metaphor of writing concepts (Tomlinson 369–370; Gee 47–48). Again, the students' ability to put any topic into the metaphor-based framework draws from linguistic tools. Lightbown describes this as a necessary step where "we internalize not only that which we intend to learn but also some aspects of the contextual features that were present and the cognitive processes we used when we learned it" (57). The metaphor curriculum repositions multiple texts around any given topic. As students work through topics, the metaphor does three important things: (1) establishes the urgency or intensity of a topic, (2) identifies the nuances of relationships, and (3) positions those interconnected, interrelated stakeholders in a visualized space. Therefore, this overarching framework allows students to create a practice space for conducting awareness-building while engaging in analysis.

While we use the term *abstraction* to describe the visualization of concepts in terms of the metaphoric frame of the course, this abstraction and visual recontextualization serves to make those concepts and strategies of writing more explicit in practice. The vast majority of readers (or listeners, for that matter), visualize and create worlds as we engage with a text (Tomlinson 366-67). Through metaphor, instructors are able to engage in analysis with students and 'show' how to read a text, how to break apart the appeals used in a text, test their effect, and then create a text of their own through the constructed metaphor.

CURIOSITY, ENGAGEMENT, AND ADVOCACY

It is one thing to talk about how decision makers should listen and should allow citizens to participate (they should!). It is an entirely different project to structure as part of the everyday practices of a given institution research designed to facilitate user/citizen participation as legitimate knowledge producers and decision makers.

—Grabill and Simmons, p. 437

The metaphor (as opposed to an instructor-initiated theme) allows students to develop individualized projects while keeping actual class time and content-delivery focused on aspects of composition itself rather than instructor-themed content. This sort of inquiry-to-action objective is meant to promote student curiosity and engagement. Further underscoring these habits of mind, we wanted to address the issue of students connecting to the strategies and concepts of writing while also finding meaning and situating themselves in a topic relevant to their own lives and interests. The course, then, is meant to act as a crucible for inquiry where students are action-makers who learn to build agentive expertise and analyze meaningful phenomena in their worlds in a connected way. Kathleen Blake Yancey, Liane Robertson, and Kara Taczak described this idea as an agency-driven "GPS" that allows students to create texts within multi-genre contexts that the phenomena live within (41). In the end, the MBC acts as an effective compromise to enhance engagement and curiosity, help the course maintain focus on concepts of writing and rhetoric, and allow students to "participate as legitimate knowledge producers and decision makers" (Grabill and Simmons 437). Further underscoring these habits of mind, we wanted to address the issue of students connecting to the strategies and concepts of writing while also finding meaning and situating themselves in a topic relevant to their own lives and interests.

This relevancy became a priority. We are told as FYC instructors, over and over again, that we are the professors and instructors with whom students often build their first face-to-face and meaningful college relationships. We get to know students, how they position themselves within a topic, and even how they position themselves in the world. Our own experiences as students left us less inclined to adhere to a specific theme or too narrow a topic for the course. As scholars, we are writing about the topics we are interested in writing about—be that composition, language acquisition, rhetoric, course design, or pedagogy. While we may revel in the foundation of thought and analysis as the tenants of our own expertise, our students may not share this same passion. If students cannot see themselves in the topic, their personal sense of agency is diminished (Flower et al. 66; Yancey et al. 5). By presenting the concepts within such a curricular framework, students are allowed to choose the pathway, the actions, and the urgency expressed in their writing. In writing conferences, many students expressed both their excitement and insecurity at following their own interests. We may forget that our students are pursuing fields removed from our own as writing and language specialists. In other words, while they may find that they can position themselves within any topic, it may be beneficial for students to understand what it feels like to do so in a topic they have an existing investment in before asking them to be committed to a topic or theme or new set of ideas in which they have absolutely no reason to continue in after the course. The students then can become owners of their own writing and see how it fits into a world that they already exist within. The writing for the course provides students with the opportunity to become active (rather than passive or temporary) participants in these contexts.

Rivaling Hypothesis

The MBC design, which gave the students a framework for inquiry and the introductory concepts of analysis, was initially inspired by Linda Flower, Elenore Long, and Lorraine Higgins' *Rivaling Hypothesis* (*RH*) and Long's later 2015 study related to *RH* and teacher cognition. *RH* was a call that challenged composition specialists to create curriculum frameworks that guide students from inquiry to application. This foundation helped us to create the curricular arch in the MBC design to equip students with "toolkits for inquiry" that could be utilized beyond the initial point of instruction (Gee). The inquiry portion of this curriculum positioned the students to focus content upon their own interests, sustaining curiosity and personal engagement (through advocacy design and proposals students put into real-world contexts), while also incorporating techniques like *Rivaling* (Flower et al.) to teach varied perspectives for approaching a given issue. *Rivaling* in and of itself is a concept that supports the habits of curiosity, engagement, and responsibility. Working at both the individual and group levels, this framework allowed the students to adapt the metaphor to the needs of their chosen subject matter, both in the FYC classroom and in applications beyond the classroom with those three habits of mind. Meaning that while they used the strategies within the confines of the classroom, they were building cognitive resources that left with them when they completed the course.

As this design came from *RH*, these were tools of inquiry-to-action. In *RH*, students are to challenge (rival) existing knowledge, their own or others, in order to act upon the information in an expanded context. This student-centered, student-initiated call to action is seen by Flower, Long, and Higgins as an opportunity to advocate through their writing in a socially engaged way. *Rivaling* is a foundation that begins to "equip" students to do the work of writing, no matter the context or focus. But specifically within the MBC framework, the *RH* creates an inquiry-based feedback loop with the visualization aiding students in giving meaning to form. For Lakoff and Johnson, this spatial assignment of language gives meaning to a given piece of writing. Students position their writing as a way to engage with the world around them supporting *Rivaling* application.

Question Cycle

The *Question Cycle*, like the MCB, is also a response to the *Rivaling*. Part of the premise of *RH* is that inquiry is what Flower, Long, and Higgins describe as an "experimental way of knowing"(51), where all phenomena are open to hypothesis, and in our own interpretation students are tasked to test their hypothesis *through* questioning. The construction of the *Question Cycle* was meant to be a visual tool students could *see* as they, first, analyze materials for class and, then, as they write. Regardless of the course activity, from free-writes to the larger writing projects, this visual was meant as an explicit means of operationalizing curiosity as a habit of inquiry, again connecting back to Lightbown's idea of *encoding* (55–57). The Question Cycle structure itself allows for practice of the eight habits of mind of the *Framework*.

The *Question Cycle* becomes one of the habitual tools students use to support curiosity in context and engagement with any phenomena. The *Question Cycle* as a strategy is also based on James Paul Gee's concept of *make a strange tool* where, when analyzing a given set of discourse, we should consider both what is being said and the context (or contexts) in which the discourse is in use (11–12). This concept, inherent in the *Question Cycle*, asks us to challenge what we are listening to and challenging the status quo of the given context. In the case of an FYC classroom, the application of the *Question Cycle* occurs within the writing context the student has chosen to enter into with their topic selection.

The *Question Cycle* itself is a sequence of steps. Students first begin with a phenomenon. This could be a lens text, claim, argument, or general topic. Then the students can develop their own initial questions about that phenomenon. They are encouraged to ask questions that look at the phenomenon in a meaningful way; for example, how or why did this phenomenon come to be? Once they have spent some time with research or discussion, they have the beginning of an analytical answer, one that can oftentimes form an initial thesis. From here, students begin asking more detailed, follow-up questions to expand their analysis and understanding of the phenomenon. As a final step, the students then reconnect their analysis to the original phenomena to confirm the answer to their initial question, thereby closing the loop on the cycle.

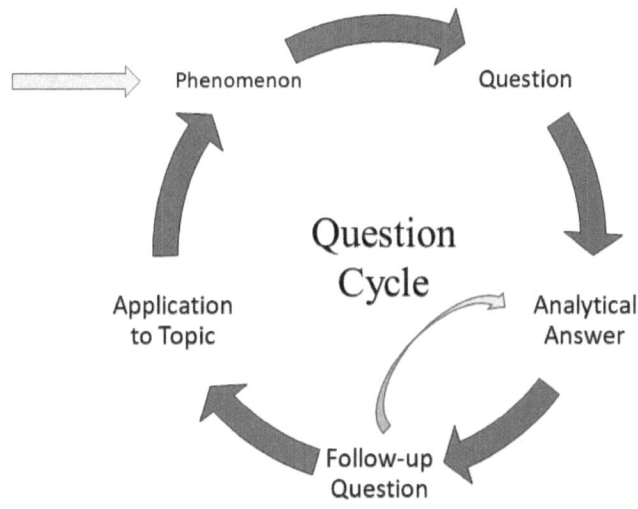

Figure 2. Eick's *Question Cycle* representation.

Connecting the ideas that are generated back to the original phenomenon students engage with also has had the added benefit of helping students develop the flow or the cohesiveness of their entire piece of writing. Whether they started with a thesis statement or research question, the *Question Cycle* is designed to help keep the generation of ideas open and yet constrained in order to sustain the students' attention to the topic. The students themselves are also allowed within this structure to engage in and pursue the lines of questioning about their topic that they personally feel are relevant. Coupled with the MBC in the course, students now have two tools at their disposal: metaphor-based meta-language to talk about writing concepts they are still in the process of acquiring and using that meta-language, a structure of inquiry to apply to the contexts they are writing about through the *Question Cycle* (as a structure of inquiry).

IMPLEMENTATION

Now that we have established the various elements of the MBC behind our application of the *Framework*, we will move to our development, implementation, and reflection on the effectiveness of two specific metaphors: space/the solar system and camping. Each action and entity of the space-based "universe" and later "solar systems" are given a designation relevant to the course design. The initial interest of the student is connected, for example, to a moment in time—their "big bang"—which could be an actual event that brings their attention to a topic. Comparatively, with the campfire metaphor, stakeholders could be analyzed for their proximity to the fire (the rhetorical situation), their interaction with the fire, their position compared to others, and their research as finding kindling. (More information, including color versions of tools and student work, can be found here: https://tinyurl.com/y6nuzsat)

STUDENT COGNITION: POSITIONING IDEAS OF INQUIRY WITHIN A VISUALIZATION

By presenting the concepts within such a framework, students are allowed to choose the pathway, the actions, and the urgency expressed in their writing. To connect this to what we discussed above, we wanted students to have ownership and investment in their chosen topics, so that writing concepts are locked into place experientially. In conferences, many students expressed both their excitement and insecurity at following their own interests. The metaphor framework allows students to reflect on these experiences and develop their strategic competencies. It frees the instructor to vary the classroom topics and provide opportunities for students to apply writing strategies to contexts most relevant to their writer development. This means that there was a certain consideration for the diverse backgrounds, personalities, and priorities that needed to be made in any course design we considered. Part of the research then was an anticipation of and a confirmation from students (through needs analysis) of the students' writing experiences and perceptions. A metaphor-based curriculum has the potential to offer both students and instructors the opportunity for creativity and practical application beyond the classroom. As many students have reported, this extends to both academic and non-academic analysis of the 'work' in the world around them. In terms of ENG102, the metaphor-based curriculum would allowed students the opportunity to spend the semester digging deeply into subjects of their own choosing with relevance unique to each student, and the students' projects became sites where writing concepts could be applied without the student being unduly influenced by the expressed opinions of the instructor. It allows for them to think about their analysis in a dynamic fashion.

The FYC classroom became the system that connects these skills, concepts, and strategies indicative to FYC course objectives within such a meaningful framework. Visualizations and illustrative means developed in our teaching. Prior to this application of the framework, similes and more relevantly metaphors were already in play in the lessons, yet these were periodic, episodic, and independent modes to describe one particular idea in the classroom. When placed within the "system" as previously described, the metaphor acts as a "save point," it allows the students to "hang" their analysis on that framework to continue to build on and come back to as they work through a given topic. It is here that one aspect should be made clear and should become even more apparent with the later student-generated metaphor work, the metaphor used is not particularly relevant, though it should be grounded in shared cultural knowledge (Lakoff and Johnson 232). Yes, the metaphor should be one that can house the system of strategies, concepts, and activities needed to address the objectives of a composition course; however, we each envision our own design, our own associations to these metaphor systems. We wanted most of all for our metaphors, as well as the visualized metaphors our students would later independently create, to be functional, facilitating a creative, reflective process that enabled students to explain how they understood the course content and how they addressed engagement with the course outcomes.

Apart from outcomes, student response can often be mixed with any curricular innovation (especially one that students are aware of). To determine student reactions to the best of our ability, we incorporated freewrites throughout the course asking for feedback on how students were using the metaphor in the drafting process, and we created a more formal end-of-semester survey where students could provide feedback on different aspects of the course.

The survey included free response questions to discuss the effectiveness of the metaphor curriculum. Of the students who consented to share their survey responses, about three quarters of students indicated the metaphor-based curriculum's helpfulness and reinforced some aspect of its effectiveness. They praised the metaphor for its ability to help them re-see and sometimes redefine their writing, topic, or problem as part of a larger whole instead of a single lone essay, writing assignment, or piece of knowledge uniquely contextualized. Some students explicitly mention how the very fact that they remember course content because of the metaphor as a criterion for the curriculum's effectiveness. Further, students also regularly noted that it aided their ability to understand the complexity of their chosen issue more effectively. These sorts of considerations were in response to questions asking students to evaluate the metaphor's ability to help the students think about their work and their writing processes across multiple assignments. Further, it was not uncommon for students to use the metaphor as a reference point for communication and understanding, not just their own projects or the instructor-created assignments but as a way of working with fellow students and giving feedback. The metaphor became a linguistic vehicle for understanding.

When presenting the students with a lens text, for example, in the rhetorical analysis project introduction we had the opportunity to practice using the *Question Cycle* from the start. By using a simple text like a short article, image, or video, an instructor can present an argument for analysis without necessarily providing background or setting up a particular text or topic. Introducing the process of rhetorical analysis using the meta-language of the MCB goes hand in hand with the *Question Cycle*. One moment in the study comes to mind, when using a text students may or may not have readily paid attention to before: an advertisement for an anxiety treatment program. The advertisement used for this activity sparked a greater conversation about anxiety because of the treatment of the condition (anxiety) as demonstrated by the wording, presentation, and design of the document. The class had discussed the *Question Cycle* in the prior week and the instructor had walked through several readings while modeling the strategy to the students (instructor-generated questioning, student generated analysis). Students realized that in the process of answering the questions, a large amount of analysis and potential writing content had been generated and cohesively constructed. The first step in the *Question Cycle* is always to identify and interpret the phenomenon: what is the message or purpose of the text? Who are the authors/creators/speakers and what are they trying to get you as the reader or consumer to do? How does this matter in the context of the community in which the text is situated? During this conversation, the students used the metaphoric terminology that was relevant to the concepts, especially when they were not sure how the rhetorical concepts applied to the analysis they were engaging in, in real time.

Stepping forward from the modeling activities to the students engaging their chosen lens text, the instructor allowed the students to create their own collective progression of questioning in the same way this strategy had been modeled. In doing this as a class or in a group, this visual text was more effective than originally planned. The pop art style of the anxiety advertisement seemed to have the opposite effect than the designer likely intended. Using the universe metaphor, we discussed the factors in 'orbit' around the 'star' of the given situation: which of those factors has the most "gravitational pull" in the system (agency/power), how do aspects of the problem form the different bodies (planets, comets, stars, moons, etc.) within the evolving solar system (positioning/genre/purpose/rhetorical appeals)?

Students found that the comic book style art and message of easy treatment for anxiety sparked a conversation where students' different levels of experience with the condition came into play. Some felt that the advertisement was a great way to connect to sufferers of anxiety (those in orbit around the issue) and the message was one of hope that anxiety could easily be treated. However, a deeper set of questions came from two students who felt it was important to point out that anxiety is not something easily treated and there are cyclical moments of good and bad that this art style seemed to trivialize. As sufferers of anxiety, they had a perspective and a message of their own for their fellow classmates: your own experience is not enough, and you must question how the intended audience would actually receive this message. This text, in terms of the metaphor in use (the Space Metaphor), was the students' 'big bang'; it was the moment when they began to engage with a problem. While, as an instructor, this was one of those gratifying moments where you watch the entire class have that light-bulb, aha!, eureka-style realization, it was also the first big test for the MBC and the *Question Cycle* structure. The visualizations they created to demonstrate how they viewed their selected topics inside of the metaphor made the analysis tangible. When working on the problem analysis, they were able to draw on interactional relationships in the metaphors to talk about those of their given problem-based topics.

As we progressed through the course content using the MBC and *Question Cycle*, the instructors could take a step back and let students initiate and drive the production of ideas and practice applying it to their own assignments and larger project topics. Student survey responses further reinforce the effectiveness of the multisensory stimulus in connection with the cognitive recontextualization of the metaphor. Students began linking analytical concepts connected to writing like stakeholders because they "physically saw the lines and relationships" in "a web or galaxy," they were activating mental-visual associations not unlike mnemonics and other memory techniques, and they were doing this not simply as a memorization technique but as they make a practical application of the stakeholder concept within a situated context.

STUDENT CONSTRUCTION IN THE METAPHOR

One of the ways the design allowed for student-initiated engagement was to ask them to use the metaphor to complete process work in each project through visualizations. Class time was used to model these visualizations, and then allow them the autonomy to adapt the visualizations. In Instructor A's curriculum, pre-draft conferencing was used to collaborate with the student, mediated by their visualizations. For example, for a student in a section using the Campfire Metaphor, the visualization he created was another tool used to talk through their perceptions of the rhetorical analysis project in these pre-draft conferences. In the conference, the student was able to show what topics made up the main social issue, 'the logs' making up the central 'campfire' the student would position stakeholders around later in the Problem Analysis.

For a student in a section using the Space Metaphor, their 'big bang' was the central identified social problem and the celestial bodies surrounding that central theme were the features that coalesced as their problem's 'universe' formed. It may be noted that the students used obviously different modalities to create their visualization, and this was done purposefully. The content and how they discussed the features of their visualization was the objective, not the creation of tiddy process document. The visualizations are meant, as we continue to reinforce, to be tools in the messy process of idea generation and process writing. Seeing their visualizations helped us answer the questions: How are they using the metaphorical language to describe concepts and writing processes? How are the metaphors themselves aiding students in acquiring the competencies that are the objectives of the course? How do the students understand the objectives through the metaphor? Do the metaphors actually help them develop the meta-linguistic, reflective language needed to talk about their writing? Often students could not name the concepts as they are named in pedagogical literature. Making these concepts nearer to their points of reference by using the metaphoric language made the initial introduction accessible. Gradually over time and with practice that connected the concept, they began to better understand what that concept meant and looked like in practice because of the metaphor that they associated with that concept.

We would use free-writes in class regularly, having students reflect on different aspects of the writing process while using the terminology of the metaphor: During multiple sessions, students were asked to anchor yet unlinked writing concepts or aspects of their own writing process to the metaphor. Doing this allowed students the opportunity to build salient portions of their own writing experiences into the metaphor system sketched out by the instructor and practice the metacognitive habit of purposeful abstraction. One notable discovery surrounding this activity was how students in the same class would make different personal connections to the same metaphorical item. For instance, during one of these brainstorm sessions in a space metaphor section, aliens and black holes (previously unmentioned by the instructor) became popular novelties of the metaphor. One student connected aliens to "the fluff" in a student's paper (Student AE); whereas, another student used aliens to describe a research article on her topic that she had not yet read fully because, for her, there was some mystery surrounding the content and appropriateness of the article for her topic (Student AA). Other students compared black holes to procrastination and writer's block (Student AF and AE), presumably because these sucked time away from productive writing, and yet another student described black holes as "a part in your paper that isn't really related or needed" (Student AR) like digressions or going off on a tangent. This supports what Carter and Pitcher say, describing the importance not of the item in the metaphorical system as much as the connection made within the mind of the individual (581).

In-class free-writes reflected that 'toolkit' language in which the concepts were initially delivered to the students. It got them started with a set of prompts, as in the examples below. In the beginning of the semester, these questions (and often a modeled start point for the *Question Cycle* activities) were very much instructor-centered, instructor generated. As the semester progressed, the students were given less specific guidance prompts to shift to co-created content and, finally, student-centered, student generated work within the metaphor. In group conferences later in the semester, the students collectively took it upon themselves to expand the metaphors. 'Camp Fire' students likened peer review to 'lost hikers' trying to find the path back to the main idea, or 'Park Rangers' making sure campers around their fire were following the conventions of the writing assignment.

Still, throughout the semester, some students did express confusion or discomfort with the metaphor through group work, free-writes, or conferences with instructors. However, these moments where the metaphor seemed to misfire for individuals also became opportunities for further teaching because the metaphor acted as a common language to talk through the writing concepts being taught. Further, the students (mis) understanding of the metaphor in these moments often linked to a deeper-rooted misunderstanding of the writing concept as well. By having the student explain their interpretation of the metaphor, we were able to better understand the breakdown in the uptake of the writing concept.

Some of the misfires did persist through to the end of the semester and resurfaced with interesting results in the work of a few students' end-of-semester surveys and even in their final reflections. In the survey there were a handful of students' negative sentiments toward the various aspects of the curriculum or implementation. One student stood out, as we will detail in the section below, by completely rejecting the metaphor-foundation, yet still presented his own metaphor with exceptional skill.

The Reflective Process: Student Conceived Metaphor Development (Final Reflections)

In this course design, we were focused on framing strategies as tools that were part of a toolkit. Throughout the semester we maintained the continuity of the instructor metaphors and modeled how to purposefully abstract. We even had students help brainstorm along the way about ways to add to the instructor metaphor to help them practice the act of recontextualizing the knowledge they were gaining. Still, we wanted to close the semester with a final reflective writing, but we wanted to foreground the metacognitive function of this bread-and- butter aspect of FYC. So, for their final reflection project, we gave students the opportunity to build their own framework for writing where they were recontextualizing their knowledge by creating the structure, connecting the dots, and articulating the relationships between writing concepts learned throughout the course in a metaphor of their own making. This way, they were not just working within the activity system that we had created through the instructor metaphors of space and camping. This final assignment acted in a doubly metacognitive way through the reflective nature of the writing, first, because students needed to draw back on the knowledge and experiences of the semester, and second, through the active creation of the new cognitive system of their own metaphor. This could be considered a variant on what some teaching-for-transfer scholars are doing when they have students create their own theory of writing (Yancey et al. 35). Our version asks students to further anchor their theory to a more tangible, everyday system that makes sense to that individual student.

Students were asked to connect at least eight aspects of writing, rhetoric, or academic research in their final metaphor project; students were also given the opportunity to experiment with visualizing their metaphor as well. We received a variety of final products, from MLA formatted essays to PowerPoint presentations to Prezis to posters with each aspect described, explained, and reinforced by the presentation. These projects connected writing concepts to a variety of topics that students found relevant, including *Dungeons & Dragons (D&D)*, *Pokémon Journeys*, theatre productions, basketball games, and even train wrecks.

The student who created the *D&D* final reflection had the image in his mind from an early point in the class. Along with their final reflection essay, they created a large-scale map visualization that went along with the essay with features on the map corresponding to aspects of writing and rhetorical devices. As the instructor and student engaged with both the course metaphor and their personally-constructed metaphor over the length of the semester, it was clear the course metaphor worked. However, the student wanted to reanalyze and reinterpret the concepts into a metaphor of their own liking aligning with the final course reflection assignment. In this realignment, the student literally created a map. In addition to using their visualization, they likened the roles of game construction, player responsibilities, and the interactions of a *D&D* role playing game to the course concepts and strategies effectively. As they had constructed this design and reflected on the purpose of using metaphor, they appreciated the opportunity to prove their understanding in a design that thoroughly appealed to their own aesthetic: "Much like me, I feel like my fellow classmates saw the value in the metaphor and no doubt had minimal trouble with using it. But the fact is that we are all different in the fact that we analyze topics differently, and the metaphors will be skewed to fit the thought processes of the writer using them" (Student CG). Once the student was able to work within the course metaphor, they tailored the concepts to their own *D&D* design, often using the additional metaphor in class discussion.

Additionally, the students did use the metaphor course reflection as an opportunity to express their perceived limitations of the MBC. One particular student was resistant to the MBC, stating, "I did not like this project at all because I hate abstract thinking. I'm not entirely sure if I'm supposed to be relating to my experience with the campfire metaphor or create [sic] a new metaphor for the same purpose as the campfire metaphor" (Student DA). However, when they were trying to be critical of the MBC in a class discussion they called the process of trying to work with the MBC a train wreck. It gave the instructor a chance to make a teachable moment for the student, proving that their negative image was still an image of their own design. For their final reflection assignment, the student expanded course concepts from this temporary construction of the train wreck to images of a train, an impending collision, and the passengers and witnesses of the crash. While preparing this final course reflection in conferences, the student admitted that while they did not like using the metaphor, it was effective in describing concepts they were unfamiliar with or had limited exposure to in previous writing contexts. They and other students were able to use this final reflection as an opportunity to acknowledge and articulate what they had acquired in the course. One of the outcomes of this sort of course is that students don't just acquire reflection or metacognition as a habit of mind, but that they develop the tacit practice of adapting what they know about writing to new contexts through the metaphor course reflection.

Conclusion and Implications

While using metaphor in the classroom is not particularly novel, using an extended metaphor as a foundation and guiding structure for a course designed to develop curiosity through inquiry has desirable benefits. Over the fifteen-week implementation across four sections of ENG 102 of the metaphor-based course design, we observed students internalizing and habitualizing key aspects of the *Framework*—specifically metacognition, curiosity, and engagement—in multiple aspects of the course from daily freewriting and brainstorming to final polished course reflections. Further, students appear to have successfully abstracted and recontextualized key aspects of the writing content, even when reacting negatively to the structure of the curriculum. With this act of purposeful abstraction and then reconceptualization of course content by creating their own metaphor and metaphoric visualization, students are required to explore their own understanding of the writing concepts. This meta-reflective process gives the writer the responsibility for both articulating the concepts in a new metaphor and testing of their own reinterpretation, reinforcing the habits of curiosity and engagement with the process of writing and reflections on their writing. Through our Metaphor-Based Curriculum, students developed broader processes of engaged inquiry to enhance curiosity—through the rivaling hypothesis and question cycle—and enhanced reflection on more personally meaningful writings that supported student engagement and developed metacognition. While this chapter focused on a single semester of our study, the curriculum possesses traits that many scholars link to more effective transfer of course content (James, "Teaching," "'Far,'" "An Investigation"; Reiff). Often when students could not name the concepts as they are named in pedagogical literature nearest to the point they were introduced in the course, they could use the metaphoric language (Bawarshi "Tracing"; DePalma and Ringer's "Toward," "Adaptive"), and these potential connections warrant further longitudinal study.

To elaborate on these potential connections, the MBC utilizes bridging techniques that could lead students to habitualize bridging or far-transfer techniques (James, "Teaching" 152), making the act of far transfer a practice and turning the practice of far transfer into a more automated near transfer activity. Further, Mary Jo Reiff and Anis Bawarshi highlight how, "based on research into high-road transfer, . . . comfort with reformulating and transforming existing resources may serve students well in accessing and adapting to future writing contexts" (330), so when we ask writers to reflect on systems and processes or develop metaphors as a way of structuring their knowledge around these systems, we could be helping them develop more effective transfer as a skill or practice. Further, the MBC helps emphasize engagement by encouraging students to "build on existing meanings as a result of new connections" (CWPA et al. 4), and the curriculum can coax writers to be "'boundary crossers' . . . who engaged in . . . transfer as they repurpos[e] and reimagin[e] their prior . . . knowledge for use in new contexts" (Reiff and Bawarshi 325).

Works Cited

Adler-Kassner, Linda. "The Companies We Keep or the Companies We Would Like to Try to Keep: Strategies and Tactics in Challenging Times." *WPA: Writing Program Administration*, vol. 36, no. 1, 2012, 119–40.

Carter, Susan, and Rod Pitcher. "Extended Metaphors for Pedagogy: Using Sameness and Difference." *Teaching in Higher Education*, vol. 15, no. 5, 2010, 579–89.

Council of Writing Program Administrators, National Council of Teachers of English, and National Writing Project. *Framework for Success in Postsecondary Writing.* CWPA, NCTE, and NWP, 2011, wpacouncil.org/aws/CWPA/asset_manager/get_file/350201?ver=505. Accessed 18 Jan. 2020.

DePalma, Michael-John, and Jeffrey M. Ringer. "Toward a Theory of Adaptive Transfer: Expanding Disciplinary Discussions of 'Transfer' in Second-Language Writing and Composition Studies." *Journal of Second Language Writing*, vol. 20, no. 2, 2011, pp. 134–47.

—. "Adaptive Transfer, Writing Across The Curriculum, and Second Language Writing: Implications For Research." *WAC and Second-Language Writers: Research Towards Linguistically and Culturally Inclusive Programs and Practices*, edited by Terry Myers Zawacki and Michelle Cox, WAC Clearinghouse, 2014, pp. 43–67.

Eick, Tonya. "A Response to the 'Rivaling Hypothesis': The Question Cycle." *ASU Composition Conference*, 2016, Arizona State University, Tempe, AZ. Conference Presentation.

—. "It's All about Timing: Pre-draft Conferencing as Negotiative Practice." *Symposium on Second Language Writing*, 2016, Arizona State University, Tempe, AZ. Conference Presentation.

Flower, Linda, et al. *Learning to Rival: A Literate Practice for Intercultural Inquiry.* Lawrence Erlbaum, 2000.

Gee, James Paul. *How to Do Discourse Analysis a Toolkit.* Routledge, 2011.

Grabill, Jeffrey T., and W. Michele Simmons. "Toward a Critical Rhetoric of Risk Communication: Producing Citizens and the Role of Technical Communicators." *Technical Communication Quarterly*, vol. 7, no. 4, 1998, pp. 415–41.

Hairston, Maxine. "Diversity, Ideology, and Teaching Writing." *College Composition and Communication*, vol. 43, no. 2, 1992, pp. 179–93.

James, Mark Andrew. "Teaching for Transfer in ELT." *ELT Journal*, vol. 60, no. 2, 2006, pp. 151–59.

—. "'Far' Transfer of Learning Outcomes from an ESL Writing Course: Can the Gap Be Bridged?" *Journal of Second Language Writing*, vol. 18, no. 2, 2009, pp. 69–84.

—. "An Investigation of Learning Transfer in English-for-General-Academic-Purposes Writing Instruction." *Journal of Second Language Writing*, vol. 19, no. 4, 2010, pp. 183–206.

Lakoff, George, and Mark Johnson. *Metaphors We Live By*. U of Chicago P, 1980.

Lightbown, Patsy M. *Focus on Content-based Language Teaching*. Oxford UP, 2014.

Reiff, Mary Jo, and Anis Bawarshi. "Tracing Discursive Resources: How Students Use Prior Genre Knowledge to Negotiate New Writing Contexts in First-Year Composition." *Written Communication*, vol. 28, no. 3, 2011, pp. 312–37.

Schor, Sandra. "Revising: The Writer's Need to Invent and Express Relationships." *The Writer's Mind: Writing as a Mode of Thinking*, edited by Janice N. Hays, et al., National Council of Teachers of English, 1983, pp. 113–26.

Tomlinson, Brian. "Seeing What They Mean: Helping L2 Readers to Visualize." *Materials Development in Language Teaching*, edited by Brian Tomlinson, Cambridge UP, 2011, pp. 357–78.

Wan, Wan. "Constructing and Developing ESL Students' Beliefs about Writing through Metaphor: An Exploratory Study." *Journal of Second Language Writing*, vol. 23, no. 1, 2014, pp. 53–73.

Yancey, Kathleen Blake, et al. *Writing Across Contexts: Transfer, Composition, and Sites of Writing*. Utah State UP, 2014.

10 Pedagogical Practices of the Habits of Mind

Melvin E. Beavers, Subrina Bogan, Harold Brown, Caleb James, and Sherry Rankins-Robertson

Introduction

During the revision of this book, the country witnessed as George Floyd was pinned to the ground under the knee of white police officer, Derek Chauvin, and suffocated as Floyd called out for mercy, "I Can't Breathe." As a result of Floyd's death, cities from coast to coast held Black Lives Matter marches in protest. Communities within the academia responded by writing antiracist statements, developing taskforces, and promoting Black scholars. Within a few months, calls to action from national organizations occurred. Vershawn Young, (then) Chair of CCCC, assembled a taskforce of BIPOC colleagues to develop the CCCC statement entitled, "This Ain't Another Statement! This is a DEMAND for Black Linguistic Justice." The Special Committee on Composing a CCCC Statement on Anti-Black Racism and Black Linguistic Justice, Or, Why We Can't Breathe! (July 2020) asserted, "We cannot say Black Lives Matter if decades of research on Black Language has not led to widespread systemic change in curricula, pedagogical practices, disciplinary discourses, research, language policies, professional organizations, programs, and institutions within and beyond academia! We cannot say that Black Lives Matter if Black Language is not at the forefront of our work as language educators and researchers!" (Introduction). This kairotic moment in our discipline has been an opportunity to stop and reflect on our own experiences as teachers and to ask ourselves to reframe our thinking about the teaching of writing to all students through values and cultures that do not belong to "White Mainstream English " (Baker-Bell 2). This moment calls for a correction in our pedagogical training in the disciplined that has not made "Black linguistic consciousness" a more dominant frame when consider the demographics of learners in our classrooms (Baker-Bell 48). This chapter examines the habits of mind as core tenants of our discipline's foundational document the *Framework for Success in Postsecondary Writing* through the pedagogical experiences of part-time contingent faculty members teaching in a summer program to a community of predominately Black students. This chapter proposes habits of mind connected to the histories and realities of Black students and faculty.

While writing faculty have used the habits of mind as dispositions for student learning, the habits can (and should) be intentionally integrated into pedagogical practices. Examining our approaches to teaching writing toward a curriculum and pedagogy that foster the habits of mind allowed us to rethink how we felt about these expectations and what it means in relation to our practices. Moreover, adopting this problem-exploring disposition prompts us "toward curiosity, reflection, consideration of multiple possibilities, a willingness to engage in a recursive process of trial and error, and toward a recognition that more than one solution can 'work'" (Wardle). Thus, the habits of mind are instrumental in informing and shaping instructor attitudes toward teaching writing as much as the habits have been used to discuss students' readiness for learning to write well and succeed at the college level.

As we came together when we planned and drafted this chapter, we interrogated the habits of mind as a type of framework for pedagogy. At the same time, because of the positionality of this author team, we found it important to call out those who are regularly charged with classroom instruction and materials development for the composition classroom. Collectively, we nod to the idea that our professional identity is maintained through our classroom praxis as much as our scholarly work; however, part-time contingent faculty often lack the resources or time to cultivate their professional identities as teachers and scholars. Penrose questions, "can faculty see themselves as professionals if they must adhere to curricular goals defined by others?" (p. 110). And through the work of the CCCC Special Committee and the scholarship of April Baker-Bell's *Linguistic Justice: Black Language, Literacy, Identity, and Pedagogy*, we push the question of whose voice determines curriculum further:

how have teachers and students from minoritized populations been suppressed to support white academic writing norms. Therefore, to foster this much needed support, this chapter offers voices from a community of contingent faculty as we examine our habits of mind with a focus on developing professional identities through pedagogical practices.

The purpose of this chapter is to reflect on our collective uses of the habits of mind while teaching in the literacy portion of the summer bridge program, which was developed using the habits of mind as the curricular foundation. In this chapter, authors offer short discussions on their habits of mind with a community of students who were labeled as "unprepared" for college. As Peter Khost, Wendy Ryden, and David Hyman explore, in their chapter within this collection, we consider and problematize the "kairotic opening" that determined the students' levels of "readiness" for college; for students in our program readiness was as dictated by the institutional infrastructures (i.e., the summer bridge program, the students' public school system, standardized test scores, our university's admissions standards, and the federal courts) with particular focus on the complications for teachers and students of color. We look particularly at the habits of mind we most closely identify with from the *Framework* and the habits that we would argue should be considered—if not included—to support the success of minority student populations.

Common Ground

Our commonality is that we are five faculty members who taught a diverse group of writers, predominately Black learners, in literacy courses, often identified as developmental, offered within a summer bridge program held on our university's campus. The program was originally established in 2013 with the support of private donors and then expanded in 2014 with federal desegregation funds; the federal funds were used to develop a pipeline to bring underrepresented students into college from a specific school district with the purpose of growing knowledge and skills for matriculation toward college graduation. The summer program expanded over the years that followed to include students in grades 9–12 and Saturday programming throughout the academic year; however, this chapter draws only on our experiences teaching students who had graduated high school the weeks prior to the program and were potential (and hopeful) incoming freshman.

The summer program is a residential, two-week program that aims to strengthen students' readiness for college and develop skills in the areas of mathematics, reading, and writing; however, one clearly stated goal (via the funding agreement) was to help students achieve admission into college through preparation for test taking and knowledge development. Many students in the program used this opportunity to make themselves eligible for admission. All students who participate in the program had low test scores on standardized college admissions tests in one of the three academic areas; however, some students needed development in all three areas.

Much like students in any given semester, students come to this program with various levels of preparation in the areas of reading and writing. Students came to the program with little hope of being able to persist into a college classroom because their test scores were so far away from the admissions scores; additionally, a lack of identity as a college student resulted from the community and home narratives they heard. Many students (and sometimes their parents) clearly told us that they "did not belong in college" or they "would not make it" here. However, as authors of this chapter, we want to call out the decades of exclusion and elimination of Black language in Pre-K–College classrooms; the message has been clear, you do not feel you belong because the social structures have told you that you do not belong as a Black language speaker and writer. Nearly all of the students were the first students from their families who would come to college. One of the motivational forces for students to persist through the summer program was that upon completion of the summer bridge program each student would receive $10,000 (funding that came from the desegregation grant) spread over the four year period to attend either our public metropolitan state university or our sister institution—a private, religiously affiliated HBCU.

The literacy portion of the summer program was designed using the habits of mind because the *Framework* is a curricular model that suggests "ways of approaching learning that are both intellectual and practical—are crucial for all college-level learners" (CWPA et al.). When we discuss the eight habits of mind, we are not discussing curriculum prescriptions. These are not standards but attitudes and mindsets we would like our students to practice both for the duration of their college experience as well as beyond the walls (or discussion boards) of our classrooms and in their personal and professional lives: "Attitudes have two components: cognition and affect. An attitude is a combination of what you believe or expect of a certain object and how you feel about these expectations" (Perloff 95). In the summer programming, for over five years we positioned the habits of mind as approaches for any reading, research, and writing situation. The habits employ critical thinking through, interactions with, and reflections on meaning making. While master curricular planning occurred and materials were selected and aligned with the *Framework*, faculty were invited to use pedagogies and theories (along with any supplemental materials) they deemed appropriate for the learners in the classroom. Teachers were not restricted to only these materials, but they were asked to ensure all curricula reflected the values stated in the eight habits of mind. Additionally, we had a book that all students read, which changed each summer.

Like other summer teaching environments where timelines are too tight and students' needs drastically vary, this summer program shared those attributes, but it differed because the program contained only eight teaching days and four evening sessions—each spanning two full hours—that focused on literacy development for not only "college readiness" but also, in most cases, college admission. The agreements with the federal courts required us to engage students in standardized testing preparation so that students could increase test scores to become admissible to college and/or eliminate the need for developmental coursework. We surrendered a significant portion of our weekly instructional time to prepare students with test-taking strategies—even though test preparation content and material included on standardized tests do not align with our general views for knowledge students need to be successful in a college composition classroom—and teach content that was missing throughout the students' previous educational preparation.

In some cases, we could see that students had the skills and knowledge that was not reflected by the test score; simply put, many students do not test well. However, in other cases we encountered students who had reading comprehension issues, and we were tasked with developing years of experience and knowledge in less than twenty-four instructional hours—and the feat wasn't possible. The emotional burden for the WPA to discern if we were helping or hurting each student for long-term success was laborious. Each Friday was dedicated to students' participation in Compass testing through the campus testing services, and then Saturday mornings and Sunday evenings were filled with testing and then test preparation in immediate response to students' test results. Each summer the demographics divided differently, but most summers nearly all students' scores showed growth was needed in writing and between one half to one third of students needed instruction in reading. It was made clear to us that, ultimately, if students weren't admissible to college, then the reports to the federal courts showed the summer programming was not meeting the stated expectation "to pipeline students into college," and students who might have had access would no longer receive the opportunity to come to college.

Teaching from the Trenches: The "Most Vulnerable Stakeholders in Higher Education"

Some of us have taught each summer in the bridge program for the past five years, since its inception, while others of us have taught only one or two summers. Four out of five authors were contingent faculty during the time they taught in the summer bridge program; the fifth author was the writing program administrator. One author was beginning his MA journey, while the other four authors had master's degrees in Rhetoric and Composition. Three of the authors hold doctoral degrees with emphasis or concentration in Rhetoric and Composition. While each of the five of us has had coursework in composition theory and knowledge of disciplinary documents for teaching first-year writing, we use the space within this chapter to call attention to the fact that workload demands are heavy and resources are limited for many faculty members working in contingent positions to stay on top of the current scholarship of our field who have not had similar disciplinary backgrounds.

It is widely known that contingent faculty are typically charged with the teaching of first-year writing courses. Faculty members working in contingent positions have steadily continued to rise over the last decade (Nelson; Kezar and Maxey). Low wages, inadequate working conditions, and employment instability are just a few of the markers that tend to characterize the labor associated with contingency. As noted in the "Indianapolis Resolution: Responding to Twenty-First-Century Exigencies/Political Economies of Composition Labor," more focus is warranted on the working conditions of contingent faculty (Cox et al., 40). However, from first-hand experiences we can say we often feel vulnerable about the lack of stability of our positions, the lack of professional development, and low pay. As discussed by Katie Kalish et al. in "Inequitable Austerity: Pedagogies of Resilience and Resistance in Composition," contingent faculty, as the "most vulnerable stakeholders in higher education" face "uncertainty"... among other things:

> With limited support, financial resources, and time, the reflective process and higher-order thinking that enables self-assessment and understanding that define growth and competence as a teacher is at best extremely difficult. Under austerity, instructors are limited in the ability to implement change in their classrooms, because revisions require higher degrees of agency that are often stifled situationally, while other habits of mind are essentially required. (275)

The following snippets bring forward stories of praxis from the four faculty members who worked in contingent positions within our summer bridge program. These stories share their quests to reflect on the habits of mind in their own teaching in the summer bridge program against the odds of the positions in which they serve. Narratives of metacognition, openness, and freedom are situated within the larger context of teaching along with their positionality as part-time contingent labor in writing programs.

Employing Metacognition Through Modeling Instruction: Caleb's Story

Throughout my development as a writing teacher, I've established instructional modeling as a regular practice in my own teaching. At the core of modeling writing processes are the habits of mind that are outlined in the *Framework*. Specifically, the habits of mind I strive to foster in my students are engagement, responsibility, and metacognition. By intentionally modeling the thinking and writing processes that I go through when I write demonstrates to students that writing isn't always successful in its first attempt, but effective writing usually takes effort and attention through multiple messy processes. Of course, this modeling often makes me feel vulnerable because it may include problems I face when I write, including my false starts, my word choice, and a list of other challenges. However, modeling revision and editing for students shows that we can address our individual challenges with writing through conscious reflection to be successful in our writing and learning. I've developed this practice through reflecting on my own challenges and successes in the classroom as well as conversations with and observations of other educators.

While teaching in the summer bridge program, I was assigned to teach two sections of writing, both for students whose test scores indicated they did not need developmental coursework. After my first day's lesson, an introduction to rhetoric, I realized my students had a better grasp on these basic rhetorical concepts than many typical first-year students who sit in my classes each fall and spring; additionally, many of the students had already decided on a major. In the following class meetings, we had discussions on what the students would find valuable for the course, and I offered a discipline-specific research and writing guide, which I adapted from Todd Peterson's assignment contribution to the WAC Clearinghouse. The students agreed the assignment would be helpful for their future writing preparations.

The assignment required students to identify several research resources specific to their majors in the categories of people, library, and online resources. For instance, the people category asked students to identify their department chairs and other faculty or staff; the library category asked them to identify online databases and key journals associated with their discipline's research aims; and, the online category asked students to identify Web resources that would help them be successful during college and in their careers, such as job posting boards or professional email lists. Their finished research guide was to include an introduction that oriented readers, which we imagined as other new students to their majors. In short, the assignment gave them flexible parameters on what types of resources to include, and the guide's purpose was to help the students navigate their discipline with an emphasis on research writing.

The assignment was useful in fostering students' habits of mind in the areas of engagement and responsibility. That is, students are invested in the assignment because it is specific to their majors, and they are actively involved in the invention process, which also requires selection of material based on their current or anticipated needs. Second, the process of assessing students' needs after the class had started and negotiating a new assignment gave me a valuable opportunity to model the habits of mind in a real situation. For this particular activity, within the limited timeframe I had to teach, the habits of engagement, responsibility, and metacognition seem to be especially necessary for students (and the instructor) when we assess students' goals and analyze course materials to make a change.

At the crux of the process of redesigning curriculum during a course—and thereby enacting these three habits of mind I have discussed—is *modeling*. Demonstrating for students ways of engaging with course documents has the potential to demystify course expectations and requirements. Students understood the function of the learning goals and the assignments as being representative of their ability to demonstrate their meeting programmatic goals successfully. The important point is that the materials for a course—the syllabus, the assignments, the schedule, etc.—provide real texts with which students can engage. Students and the instructor have an inherent investment in the documents that detail their learning outcomes, how they can demonstrate their learning, and when they are to have completed tasks. Therefore, offering these documents as sites for negotiation models engagement with real documents for students.

The habit of responsibility is also inherent in the process of being flexible with curriculum in a course. Again, the instructor and students had an inherent investment in the curriculum, yet the instructor is the expert in the classroom and, therefore, the responsibility of the curriculum is primarily theirs, especially when redesigning a set curriculum after a course has started. However, this responsibility and leading a discussion about alternative assignments including the rationale for the alternatives effectively models responsibility as outlined by the *Framework*. Students, though, also have a stake in a redesigned curriculum, and their input should be valued in discussions whose outcomes will affect them.

Metacognition has an important relationship with engagement and responsibility in all cases, but especially when students and instructors engage in discourse to rethink curriculum. In other words, cognition/metacognition is the mechanism by which we can examine current course materials in relation to learning objectives, and then rethink alternatives to assignments and their parameters. Making explicit the learning objectives invites the cognitive activity of analysis of the individual and cultural processes for how they were developed. Again, using course documents as artifacts for analysis and discussions led by the instructor creates a site to model metacognition for students with real documents in which they have an inherent investment. Further, beyond the documents is the student at the center of the conversation to be empowered in their education and engage in a community of learners through their ability to understand others who do not come from similar educational and cultural backgrounds. In Carol Severino's "The Problems of Articulation," she argues, "both Habits and Experiences sections seem to favor reasoning and problem solving over the empathy and creation of social ties so important in composition" (535). However, empathy seems to be a habit that ties into Ratcliffe's concept of *rhetorical listening*—a way to "facilitate cross-cultural dialogues about any topic"—that is undoubtedly useful for fostering empathy in a community of learners (196). For that reason, I would argue the habits should be expanded to include empathy, which stretches beyond openness to new ideas or experiences in the cultural sensitivity to be inclusive.

During the process of modeling engagement, responsibility, and metacognition in the context of course design, students practice those habits, as they ponder the perceptions, ideas, opinions, ethics, and goals of the course. In reflection, I'd like to offer a couple points. First, during the course, I didn't make the habits of mind explicit in our discussions. My thoughts are the result of reflecting after the course had ended and considering my experience in the context of the habits of mind. Therefore, activities focused on course documents would be more effective for fostering the habits of mind if those habits had been made explicit to students. I wonder, though, how others in the profession teach toward these habits. Do they identify the habits for students? Does the *Framework* assume these habits of mind are to be made explicit in writing instruction? That is, do students need to be informed that when course activities or assignments ask them to "make connections between their own ideas and those of others; find meanings new to them or build on existing meanings as a result of new connections; and act upon the new knowledge that they have discovered," we are fostering their habit of engagement (CWPA et al. 4)? My own view is that these habits don't have to be named for students to develop them. In my courses, I attempt to foster the habits as attitudes or dispositions implicitly through the activities and assignments that align with my course goals. However, in my reflections on this instance of curricular redesign, I recognize that naming the habits may have been more effective than not, because the habits became the learning objectives of the activity.

My second reflection is that the course was a two-week course designed to bridge students from high school to college, which made it easier to change an assignment because we only had time to complete one major assignment. Although changing curriculum during a full-semester course might be more challenging, there is more space and time for explicitly discussing habits of mind within the context of course design, which may prove to be more effective for students developing those habits further and adding to the habits those that resonate with students.

In my experience of redesigning this course curriculum after the course began, the themes of engagement, responsibility, and metacognition were at its core. Students found these discussions valuable and respectful because they consider their goals and past experiences and contribute to their development as successful college students. Finally, my experience has led me to reconsider how I use instructional modeling with students. Although typically I incorporate a think-aloud protocol to model my writing processes and dilemmas as a writer, I wonder now what practices I can adopt to better model the habits of mind for students whose success depends on them.

Cultivating a Pedagogy of Freedom: Subrina's Journey

What does it mean to teach someone how to write? As a composition instructor, I have done more soul searching on this subject than I care to admit, and to be honest, I still find myself searching for answers. I often tell my students writing is baring one's soul onto a page. It's about taking risks. I ask students to take a monumental leap, to be open and write about things that are important to them. I ask them to trust me and their peers, complete strangers, with their innermost thoughts and personal experiences. I talk to them about writing with a sense of openness, a habit of mind that I display with my students in my "performative act" of teaching (hooks 11). To be open so not to fear others' opinions or comments—and I must foster a learning environment where opinions and comments from all participants are thoughtful and helpful.

The first thing I do in my classroom is to establish a safe place for writing to happen. This means I have to build a sense of trust with all of my students. I believe this can happen when I encouraged them to see me as a "real person." This means that I have to be open with them about my own struggles as a writer and how I overcame (and continue to manage) them. Being honest about my own writing challenges has broken down barriers many times in the classroom—these barriers often come from students' notions that the instructor "knows all" or "doesn't struggle with writing." Those barriers when left unspoken are sometimes associated with making students feel inferior about their writing. By adjusting the student/teacher dynamics with my openness, I could see and feel the classroom environment changing for the better. I formed a partnership with my students. This partnership consisted of my giving them the opportunity to share their ideas about writing assignments. I wanted them to become invested in their own learning and take responsibility for it. In many cases, students of color often feel invisible when it comes to writing about what matters to them. Their stories have broken my heart and at times have made me stand and cheer for them. I have read about the loss of parents, brothers, sisters, and best friends to the "streets." I have read stories about "rising from the ashes" to fulfill a desire to create a better life through the pursuit of a college education. They have taught me lessons of resilience.

Resilience, as a habit of mind should be included in the *Framework* because students of color have faced situations that many of us will probably not face in our lifetimes. Resilience reaches beyond the habit of persistence. As managing to get through all of those hurdles foster the willingness and ability to move forward in spite of past or present circumstances. In her book *Teaching to Transgress*, bell hooks reminds us that students should have the freedom to think and to grow as writers and also the role of the instructor in this process. She says

> When education is the practice of freedom, students are not the only ones who are asked to share and to confess. This type of pedagogy (engaged) does not seek simply to empower students. Any classroom that employs a holistic model of learning will also be a place where teachers grow and are empowered by the process. That empowerment cannot happen if we [instructors] refuse to be vulnerable while encouraging students to take risks. (21)

Students often expect the instructor to provide writing prompts for impromptu writing sessions at the beginning of class, provide the topic for the writing project, and lead the class discussions; however, when students are given the opportunity to decide his or her own topic to write about a sense of panic seems to spread over them, paralyzing the thought process in its midst because students have oftentimes not been empowered to be at the center of their educational process. Freedom can feel like a double-edged sword for student writers.

Faculty have a responsibility to cultivate a safe haven to foster creative freedom for students. The freedom that I speak of is the freedom to express their own culture, as illustrated in the CCCC statement on students' right to use their natural way of speaking and writing in the classroom. The CCCC text "Students' Right to their Own Language" argues, "We affirm the students' right to their own patterns and varieties of language—the dialects of their nurture or whatever dialects in which they find their own identity and style. Language scholars long ago denied that the myth of a standard American dialect has any validity. The claim that any one dialect is unacceptable amounts to an attempt of one social group to exert its dominance over another . . . We affirm strongly that teachers must have the experiences and training that will enable them to respect diversity and uphold the right of students to their own language" (CCCC 711). While offering instructions in standard written English may help students in future endeavors, it also may result in students' loss of identity, particularly those who come from marginalized backgrounds.

Further, the CCCC Statement on Students' Rights alerts educators at all levels to, "uncover and examine some of the assumptions on which our teaching has rested. Many of us have taught as though there existed somewhere a single American 'standard English' that could be isolated, identified, and accurately defined. We need to know whether 'standard English' is or is not in some sense a myth. We have ignored, many of us, the distinction between speech and writing and have taught the language as though the talk in any region, even the talk of speakers with prestige and power, were identical to edited written English" (710). When faculty focus on teaching students to write correctly, teachers may lose sight of the individuals who come with a rich history of lived experiences that include dialects and language influences.

Freedom in student writing should be embraced by the academic community as a way of providing inclusion instead of exclusion. Writing is not just the act of putting words on a page—especially for writers who do not know how to "invent the university" (Bartholomae) or perform standard written English. Language is the commodity we use to communicate our life experiences. When the freedom to use our "native" language is taken from us, what is left is a shallow impersonation of the writer and his or her experiences? While the argument for teaching students to use Standard Written English may serve our society's expectations with an effort to teach students to be a productive member of society, there is also a place for the inclusion of various dialects. In *Other People's English*, Vershawn Ashanti Young makes the case for the use of one's own language. He states:

> The argument that good writing cannot occur except in Standard English does not hold water either. The use of multiple language varieties is a hallmark of American literature. Would it really make *Huckleberry Finn* a better book if it were written entirely in Standard English? Because language is closely tied to individual identity and personal experience, great writers know that the use of undervalued varieties is often the best way (if not the only way) to accurately convey specific ideas, experiences, and emotions. (22)

As Young points out, the use of one's native language does not lessen the writer's message. It adds to it. I want my students to feel comfortable writing in his or her "mother tongue.". When students are able to use their native language in composition classrooms, a benefit for all participants of the classroom community is an opportunity to openly share cultural and linguistic histories and realities.

Discovering Academic Realities, Languaging Identity Through Shifts and Meshes, and Honoring the First Voice that Is Your Own: Harold's Realization

The Boondocks, one of my favorite animated television shows of all time, represents the spectrum of how black people exist in all of their complex intersectionalities that occur while in traditional white spaces. The show comments on just about every aspect of blackness that is up for critique: education, pimp culture, incarceration, socioeconomic status, as well as the portrayal of blatant and subtle racism. My approach to all of my classes typically starts with a conversation inspired by this animated show. I'm constantly asking myself what background and experiences my students are bringing into the classroom. Understanding their lives outside of the classroom can better equip teachers to incentivize, encourage, and reward students appropriately and effectively. My practice of teaching is a bit reflective of my writing: slightly unorthodox, passionate, relatable, but impactful all the same. At this point in my career, as a novice writing instructor and (self-proclaimed) nerd, I provide opportunities to have conversations about race with peers and students because the conversation is evolving and perspectives are able to grow through this evolution. By using this conversation about identity through race and gender, and sometimes orientation, I began creating a safe space for my students to start understanding who they want to become without the projections from others.

The structure and systems in place for traditionally white spaces needs to be challenged. I agree with Subrina Bogan's sentiments (expressed in the section above) that faculty must create safe spaces for our students' creativity. I think most faculty members don't understand how powerfully the language used in the classroom can impact our students. In his TedX talk "Reality Pedagogies," Christopher Emdin mentions that the transformative power of words is lost because instructors attempt to speak over students' heads. By acting as guardians of the academy at such an early stage of our students' academic careers, we are keeping students from expressing and discovering things about themselves and prohibiting opportunities for them to become more experienced in writing.

My instruction is woven with the tweeds of collaborative, reality, and Pentecostal pedagogies with an eye toward the habits of mind. Employing these pedagogies has proven helpful because they afforded my students the opportunity to find their voice, provided me the opportunity to explore authenticity in instruction, and offered the privilege of exploring the merger of language both in their own writing and the world beyond our classroom. I make it a point to create safe spaces for my students because those spaces are so few and far between for them outside of my classroom. I tell them that I never forget what it's like to sit in their chairs for two reasons: (1) to remove the pressure and expectations they have placed upon me as their instructor, and (2) to allow space for them to develop ideas that are authentically theirs. Students of color don't have the opportunity to explore their own self-discovered values and ideas because they are too busy switching in and out of codes. It's interesting because even though I'm trying to create this safe space for my students' creativity and expression, I find myself code-switching in the beginning of every class until I can gauge the balance of academic superiority and social inferiority. As a student, my favorite faculty were those who taught from their honest perspectives and allowed me to bring my authenticity to the table and discuss topics from my perspective, so I aim to model that; however, I was viewed as an instructor who didn't identify with their experiences outside of the classroom. I immediately understood that they were under the impression that I was faking my experiences. I came off as the instructor trying to insert himself into a life that wasn't authentically his own—or as Riley from *The Boondocks* would say, "game recognize game" (McGruder). This statement indicates that individuals respond to authenticity.

Those expectations come with certain performances that I had to enact. There's a pressure to speak eloquently, forget the language I would use with family, and disregard my mother tongue. Jacqueline Joyce Royster describes the pressure and silent expectations that students of color feel. Her scene two perfectly explains why my students are upset. She describes, "Trespass vision," the vision that comes from intellect and imagination but not actually living (Royster 34). I have taught students who were frustrated because they had faculty who tried to know their experiences without any conversation with them. I see this manifest in my students who carry anger and rage that they do not know how to express; I have students who decide to act out in the classroom as opposed to learning. Furthermore, those students who perform as the class clowns seemingly make it their mission to hinder the learning of others.

In my experience of teaching underrepresented students, student performance has been something that I have had to monitor in my classroom. Students who pursue an education due to parents' wishes tend to be not as bought into the process as someone who is genuinely pursuing an education for themselves. I've found that having honest conversations about their lived experiences allow them to not only discover their voice but to also honor that authentic voice. Through the lens of learner-centered theory, I funnel my conversations with students by unpacking the responsibility of learning. In my conversations with students, I often ask a series of investigative questions that mold students' self-interests in their education. Most times, I have built relationships with students that allow me to not only understand why a student is in college but also increase my means for motivating my students. I've concluded that allowing students to actually write with the first voice that they hear proves to be impactful. It validates their thoughts, feelings, and ideas. As novice writers, they just need to know their experiences hold meaning and value. In my classroom, I make it a point to tell them that they must write from their perspectives and not anyone else's. Their stories matter. Their experiences matter. Their voices matter.

In an effort to foster deeper learning, I propose utilizing levels of vulnerability, a habit of mind not identified in the *Framework*, as this is a habit I believe is critical to students and faculty of color. In Asao Inoue's CCCC's 2019 opening address, he calls into question the language and inclusivity of minority representation used to describe the habits of mind. Inoue argues that the language used to codify the habits of mind from the *Framework* are reinforcements of a structure meant to keep people of color outside of academic spaces. While some may desire to lump vulnerability in with openness, I argue from a cultural perspective these two habits cannot be conflated. The habits I exercise in the classroom have allowed me to, as Emdin deems, engage in "co-generative dialogues" (10:19–11:23). By exercising vulnerability from both a student and instructor point-of-view, I create relationships where students not only want to understand who it is that they wish to be but also empowering students to be advocates for their classmates on journey of self-discovery. I realized that my willingness to be vulnerable in the classroom not only jolts this idea of me being a guardian but also empowers my students to become true authors of their own experiences.

Once students assume authority, our conversations regarding identity through the lens of race, class, and gender become more intentional and less chaotic. Those conversations allow students to practice the same vulnerability that I display when sharing my experiences. Vulnerability allows students to form deeper bonds of trust and respect for the content of the class as well as in each other. Vulnerability allows students to feel safe when exploring who they are and who they want to become. Vulnerability allows students to relive their experiences on the page as authentically as they can, and what's more powerful than that in a composition classroom?

Considering Openness: Melvin's Reflection

Currently working in a full-time non-tenure-track position, I have had opportunities to serve my department and seek out professional development training that a part-time faculty member may not. As a result of professional opportunities and funding to support these engagements, such as attending and presenting at national and regional conferences or receiving online writing instructional training, I have continued to research and develop my teaching craft. However, when I taught as a part-time faculty member, I had limited access to professional development opportunities beyond my formal education.

As a part-time instructor, my goal is for my students to practice their writing. Many students come into the classroom with apprehension and anxiety about their writing abilities. Learning to write well was an arduous process; like any skill, it takes practice to improve. The way I attempted to help students improve was to entrench them in the "unplanned and uncensored freewriting" (Elbow 5), which gave my students permission to play in the realm of ideas and thoughts before harnessing those thoughts into clear, coherent, and more effective prose. Accordingly, I wanted my students to understand writing was messy, time-consuming, but also a rewarding process. These approaches to writing were no different for me when I taught in the summer bridge program, which centered on the habits of mind.

I think of the eight habits of mind as the groundwork or foundation in which the outcomes stand. Although I was introduced to the "WPA Outcomes Statement" ("OS") before the eight habits of mind, much of what is presented in the "OS" has close ties to the eight habits of mind. The habits of mind reflect ideas about learning that speak to our students' diverse backgrounds and ethnicities in multiple ways. We are better informed if we think about our habits of teaching and what that may mean for our students. Still, we cannot ignore that many of the decisions made about curriculum leave out a large portion of those actually doing the teaching of it and how to help them when they face difficulties.

As a part-time faculty member, I remember constantly searching for materials to aid my instruction; I was not sure what, if anything, was sticking with my students. While I understood what my goals were for the course, I spent many days searching for materials and pedagogical practices to engage my students. While I had a pretty solid handle on maintaining the process model within the classroom, I felt something was missing. This missing component became evident to me during a particular student conference; one of my students came to meet me without a completed draft for feedback and discussion. Instead the student wanted to use the time to discuss the assignment and talk about what to write. I was perplexed. We had spent several days discussing the assignment, and I had allowed for in-class time to "just write" and created space to discuss their work. Yet, this was not enough for this student; the student needed more. I instructed the student to think about the writing task and just get words on the paper. Once our conference ended, I sat at my desk in the shared part-time faculty office (yes, the institution provided office space; many do not) and thought about the loneliness and feelings of self-doubt that writing often engenders. During our meeting, the student broke into a chorus of tears, admitting to having a terrible time digesting some of the course readings and feeling stymied because of reading comprehension issues.

As a result of this interaction, I began to question my own knowledge on how to address reading comprehension in the classroom. I did not have a solid background in reading theories and the classroom praxis that follows. Unfortunately, given the constraints on my time, I was not able to devote much time to collecting resources and increasing my understanding about how to approach students displaying reading problems. I decided to talk to other part-time colleagues and get their view, so we could share ideas and discuss ways to address reading problems. I remember we all agreed that reading comprehension was a problem for many of our students. There was not any sense of deep reading from our students. Some colleagues suggested finding more relatable texts and others said we should allow students to collaborate and read together. All were good ideas and I liked the conversations we shared about our various classroom approaches.

As a result of my student encounter, I recognized the problem many of my students face. Yet, I lacked a clear sense of what to do, where to go, or who to ask for help, which may speak to both the outsider and insider structure that prevails within some departments. I imagined this is a common experience among many part-time faculty members. Based upon my own experiences, I did not feel like an outsider within my department; in fact, the department in which I worked for the majority of my part-time status supported me through multiple professional opportunities. Still, after my student conference, I felt like an imposter and in some ways an outsider within my discipline. The constraints of my job ultimately dictated my response to my student's needs. Through reflection and engagement with my peers, I was able to explore my understanding of student reading comprehension issues. I have come to learn of the call for expansion of deep reading theories in our field and Ellen Carillo's and Alice Horning's calls, as indicated in their chapters included in *The* Framework for Success in Postsecondary Writing: *Scholarship and Applications*, to integrate reading more heavily into the habits of mind—along with the "OS." In retrospect, I question whether I displayed an openness to my students and to myself. Although I practiced the tenets of openness, they were passive approaches.

PRACTICING WHAT WE PREACH: INSTRUCTOR EMBODIMENT OF HABITS OF MIND

As we close this chapter, we support Christine Cucciarre's argument in her chapter "The Space Between: A Statewide Effort Using the *Framework* to Bridge High School and College Writing," toward a more common conversation that moves beyond test scores to focus on identities of K–16 writers using programming and partnerships rooted in the *Framework*; like our campus' summer bridge program, she has developed partnerships that bridge students into college writing environments. More so we have focused this chapter on an expansion of the habits of mind from student learning outcomes to pedagogical practices. We embrace Patrick Sullivan's argument that the list of the habits of mind is not complete, and we argue for inclusivity of habits that promote teachers and students of color, particular Black language speakers, to include empathy, resilience, and vulnerability. We have aimed to make space for the voices of contingent part-time faculty, as Kalish et al.'s call in "Inequitable Austerity" to further refine the *Framework* (275) to be inclusive of the students who occupy our learning spaces and account for the cultural and linguistic values of those who facilitate learning in first-year composition classrooms—let alone their contingent positions.

WORKS CITED

Baker-Bell, April. *Linguistic Justice: Black Language, Literacy, Identity, and Pedagogy*. Routledge, 2020.

Bartholomae, David. "Inventing the University." *Journal of Basic Writing*, vol. 5, no. 1, 1986, pp. 4–23.

Carillo, Ellen. "A Place for Reading in the Framework for Success in Postsecondary Writing: Recontextualizing the Habits of Mind." *The Framework for Success in Postsecondary Writing: Scholarship and Applications*, edited by Nicholas Behm et al., Parlor P, 2017, pp. 39–53.

Conference of College Composition and Communication. "Anti-Black Racism and Black Linguist Justice, Or, Why We Cain't Breathe!" CCCC, 2020, cccc.ncte.org/cccc/demand-for-black-linguistic-justice. Accessed 15 Sept. 2020.

Conference of College Composition and Communication. "Students' Right to Their Own Language." *College English*, vol. 36. no. 6, 1975, pp. 709–26.

Council of Writing Program Administrators. "WPA Outcomes Statement for First-Year Composition (3.0)." CWPA, 2014, wpacouncil.org/aws/CWPA/asset_manager/get_file/350909?ver=552. Accessed 3 July 2019.

Council of Writing Program Administrators, National Council of Teachers of English, and National Writing Project. *Framework for Success in Postsecondary Writing.* CWPA, NCTE, and NWP, 2011, wpacouncil.org/aws/CWPA/asset_manager/get_file/350201?ver=505. Accessed 15 June 2019.

Cox, Anicca, et al. "The Indianapolis Resolution: Responding to Twenty-First-Century Exigencies/Political Economies of Composition Labor." *WPA: Writing Program Administration*, vol. 68, no. 1, 2016, pp. 38–67.

Elbow, Peter. "Voice in Writing Again: Embracing Contraries." *College English*, vol. 7, no. 2 2007, pp. 168–88.

Emdin, Christopher. "Reality Pedagogy" *TedX Teachers College*, 2012, youtube/2Y9tVf_8fqo. Accessed 15 June 2019.

hooks, bell. *Teaching to Transgress.* Routledge, 1994.

Horning, Alice. "Enhancing the Framework for Success: Adding Experiences in Critical Reading" *The* Framework for Success in Postsecondary Writing*: Scholarship and Application*, edited by Nicholas Behm, et al., Parlor P, 2017, pp. 54–68.

Inoue, Asao B. "2019 CCCC Chair's Address: How Do We Language So People Stop Killing Each Other, or What Do We Do about White Language Supremacy?" *College Composition and Communication*, vol. 71, no. 2, 2019, pp. 352–69.

Kalish, Katie, et al. "Inequitable Austerity: Pedagogies of Resilience and Resistance in Composition." *Pedagogy: Critical Approaches to Teaching Literature, Language, Composition, and Culture*, vol. 19, no. 2, 2019, pp. 261–81.

Kezar, Adrianna, and Daniel Maxey. "Missing from the Institutional Data Picture: Non-Tenure-Track Faculty." *New Directions in Institutional Research*, vol. 155, 2012, pp. 47–65.

McGruder, Aaron, creator. *The Boondocks.* Sony Pictures, 2005–2014.

Nelson, Cary. "Solidarity vs. Contingency." *Inside Higher Ed*, 2010, www.insidehighered.com/views/2010/09/07/solidarity-vs-contingency. Accessed 7 Sept. 2019.

Penrose, Ann. "Professional Identity in a Contingent Labor Profession: Expertise, Autonomy, Community in Composition Teaching." *WPA: Writing Program Administration*, vol. 35, no. 2, 2012, pp. 108–26.

Perloff, Richard M. *The Dynamics of Persuasion: Communication and Attitudes in the 21st Century*. Routledge, 2017.

Peterson, Todd. "Research Guide to the Major." Course assignment. Pennsylvania State University.

Ratcliffe, Krista. "Rhetorical Listening: A Trope for Interpretive Invention and a 'Code of Cross-Cultural Conduct.'" *College Composition and Communication*, vol. 2, no. 51, 1999, pp. 195–224.

Royster, Jacqueline. "When the First Voice You Hear Is Not Your Own." *College Composition and Communication*, vol. 47, no. 1, 1996, pp. 29–40.

Severino, Carol. "The Problems of Articulation: Uncovering More of the Composition Curriculum." *College English*, vol. 74, no. 6, 2012, pp. 533–53.

Sullivan, Patrick. "Essential Habits of Mind for College Readiness." *College English*, vol.74, no. 6, 2012, pp. 547–53.

Wardle, Elizabeth. "Creative Repurposing for Expansive Learning: Considering 'Problem-Exploring' and 'Answer-Getting' Dispositions in Individuals and Fields." *Composition Forum*, vol. 26, 2012.

Young, Vershawn Ashanti, et al. *Other People's English: Code-Meshing, Code-Switching, and African American Literacy*. Teachers College P, 2014.

11 The Effects of Metacognition on Student-Athletes' Academic Performance

Martha A. Townsend

> *The heart directs you where to go, the brain tells you how to get there.*
>
> —Wide Receiver and Biology Major

College students' participation in sport in the United States is different from most other countries in that the US integrates sport into higher education; the US system of intercollegiate athletics considers teams from one school competing against teams from other schools to be an integral aspect of the educational experience. We tell ourselves that sport and academic pursuit go hand in hand—that they mutually reinforce one another and make for a better educational experience. Or, as virtually any American academic in higher education would put it, we *try* to integrate sport into higher education. The National Collegiate Athletic Association (NCAA) oversees college students' participation in sport in an attempt to keep things fair, aligned, and running smoothly. And several independent national organizations, most notably the Knight Commission on Intercollegiate Athletics, work to ensure that the educational purpose of college sports is maintained. Many US citizens take intercollegiate sports as a given; they can't imagine college without football or basketball or many of the other Olympic sports in which people participate. How well we accomplish that integration and how effective the NCAA is are matters of considerable dispute, but those are not the concern of this essay.

The problem this essay addresses is that in the US, especially at large universities with "big-time" sports programs, student-athletes who are involved in the "money sports"—those sports that generate significant revenue, specifically football and men's basketball—are subject to a decades-old stereotype that permeates the culture of US higher education: "dumb jocks" are not highly regarded. Myles Brand, a philosophy professor who served as president of both Indiana University and the University of Oregon before becoming president of the NCAA colorfully notes that, "the idea persists that college athletes are little more than knuckle-dragging Neanderthals incapable of being real college students." He traces the stereotype back, at least, to the 1927 Broadway production of *Good News*, a popular musical at the time but now largely forgotten that tells the story of a college football player at a fictional university falling in love with his tutor. The dumb jock myth, Brand says, "has stuck to college sports like corruption has stuck to American politics." Although exceptions to the stereotype exist, and although some institutions hold student-athletes to a higher academic standard than their non-athlete peers, student-athletes are often derided, discriminated against, and criticized for their unpreparedness for college study.

A favorite target of the popular press, student-athletes are the frequent focus of negative publicity. One article's headline, for example, reads, "CNN Analysis: Some College Athletes Play Like Adults, Read Like Fifth-Graders" (Ganim). Labeling the news article an "analysis" suggests an in-depth, substantive examination of athletes' reading acumen. Yet the story is little more than a rehash of previously reported information about problems at one school coupled with limited new data the reporter was able to obtain through open records requests. Only later does the reporter acknowledge that the sample is small and that this "is not an exhaustive survey." Moreover, as is often the case, as the story is picked up by subsequent news outlets, newer headlines strike even more strident tones. One source from within higher education itself—and which should therefore be less sensationalistic—opts for this headline: "CNN Finds Athletes Who 'Read Like 5th Graders'" (Jaschik). Gone is the qualifier "some." And added to the first line of the new story is the label "investigation," suggesting a level of detailed inquiry and systematic examination that belies the original account. The CNN story and others like it occupy the national mindset on a regular basis.

At my own Division 1 university, faculty have questioned student-athletes' usurping seats in classrooms that could otherwise go to "more deserving" students. Some resent special admissions policies that, in faculty's perceptions, allow coaches to recruit less qualified students. Others, not without just cause, question the scandalous amounts of money that institutions spend to support athletic programs in what has rightly come to be called an "athletics arms race" as sports programs' budgets grow exponentially in comparison to academic expenditures. One of the more dramatic critiques comes from Rutgers University English professor Richard Miller. Alluding to the Wallace Stevens' poem, Miller's stunning pictorial essay "13 Ways of Looking at a Football Stadium" uses historic bird's-eye-view photographs to trace the growth of the Rutgers's football stadium from its earliest days to present time. The facility is just one part of a program that at the time of Miller's essay had the dubious distinction of draining more money from public coffers into athletics than any other public university's in the US.

Another example comes from Louisiana State University, which recently unveiled a $28 million dollar state-of-the-art football facility complete with "all of the bells and whistles," individual sleeping pods, and meals prepared by a professional executive chef (Machlin "LSU Football"). Machlin writes that "LSU has to keep raising the bar to go toe-to-toe with the likes of Alabama, Clemson, and others" ("LSU Football"). LSU officials addressed the inevitable backlash by touting four recently renovated academic and student buildings (Machlin "LSU Responds"). Administration's defense is insufficient for one student, however, who posts pictures of LSU's leaky library, with water on the floor encroaching on file cabinets pulled away from a damaged wall.

Given the well-known conflicts between athletic and academic priorities and given the common perception of student-athletes' unpreparedness for college study, I was surprised when the head football coach at my own university announced a few years ago that *all* of his large senior class was going to graduate at the end of the spring term. Some players, he claimed, had already graduated and were enrolled in graduate courses. This claim seemed all the more surprising given attrition rates for college graduates in general. Pleased but somewhat skeptical about the team's academic success, I proposed a formal study that might discern how that happened. The athletic director, with whom I had worked on several committees, supported my proposal.

A larger study, still in progress, "The Literate Lives of Athletes: How a Division I Championship Football Program Graduated 100% of Its Senior Players" from which the metacognitive and embodiment data is drawn, is an IRB-approved qualitative case study of twenty-six football players, all of whom did graduate within the NCAA's five-year eligibility period. Eligibility refers to the maximum amount of time student-athletes may receive institutional scholarship support to complete their academic degrees. Using a protocol of twenty generative questions, I interviewed all twenty-six players and the head coach, along with select support personnel, teachers, and administrators. Interviews lasted between forty and sixty minutes and produced some 550 pages of professionally transcribed text. I also examined other artifacts including the athletes' official academic records (transcripts), syllabi from representative courses, and various written assignments the players provided voluntarily. One article, on findings related to the players' reading acumen, is already in print (Townsend); another on the players' performance in writing-intensive courses is in progress. The data on metacognition and embodied knowledge constitute a third subset of the findings from the *Literate Lives* project.

The connection between the football players' metacognition and their academic performance is surprisingly relevant for this collection, particularly considering the degree to which these athletes as a category have been stereotyped, as shown above. Each was asked to name one or two qualities from football that helped them succeed in the classroom. Their swift and plentiful replies (elaborated below) are exemplified in a comment by the team's wide receiver, a biology major, foregrounded at the top of this chapter as an epigraph.

The MU 26, as I have come to call the cohort, are remarkable in their diversity. Their level of achievement in high school, their scores on college entrance exams, and their preparedness for college study vary widely. They come from a mix of small rural high schools, suburban high schools with sophisticated college-prep curricula, and large urban high schools capable of offering curricula for every type of student. Fifteen (58%) of the players are white; eleven (42%) are African American. Some have parents who went to college; many are first-generation college students. A few come from comfortable socioeconomic backgrounds, others fit squarely into the American middle class, and a few come from economically disadvantaged backgrounds. Twenty-two (85%) are first-time college students; four (15%) are two-year college transfers. Twenty-two hold athletic scholarships: four are walk-on non-scholarship players. Theirs is a large senior class (the following year's is smaller by a third). Twenty of them took the ACT college entrance exam, earning composite scores ranging from 12 to 30, with an average of 21. (The four players who transferred were not required to submit ACT scores; one took the SAT.) By contrast, the average ACT composite score for all MU students in 2003, the year before most of the MU 26 entered MU, was 25.3. Their high school graduation rankings range from a low of 27% to a high of 98%. Ten (38%) finished in the upper quarter of their high school graduation classes; twelve (46%) finished in the lower half. Three were inducted into the prestigious National Honor Society, whose members are selected on the basis of scholarship, leadership, service, and character.

By the time the MU 26 graduated, their cumulative college GPAs ranged from 2.0 (the minimum allowed) to 3.6 on a 4.0 scale. Several cycled on and off academic probation when their semester grades fell below the minimum allowed. Based on the university's formula for predicting students' first-year success, twenty-one of the twenty-two freshmen in the cohort (i.e., the non-transfer students) finished their first year with higher-than-predicted GPAs (Scogin). All took courses during the summer session. They earned degrees in eleven different academic areas, spread across four colleges.

The research may be categorized as a qualitative, reciprocal, and disciplinarily responsive case study. Bill Gillham says a case study examines "a unit of human activity embedded in the real world; [it] can only be studied or understood in context; [and] exists in the here and now" (1). Likewise, Gillham notes that multiple sources of evidence and lack of *a priori* theory to explain the phenomena being studied are key characteristics of the approach (2). The larger *Literate Lives* project is a "bounded" case study in that it has finite qualities: a specific number of participants (twenty-six football players), located in a particular place (the University of Missouri), at a specific point in time (the conclusion of their undergraduate education), all of which, according to Robert Stake, comprise "a specific, complex, functioning thing" (qtd. in Merriam 178). As Stake notes, case studies constitute one form of scientific method; however, their purpose is "not to represent the world, but to represent the case" (245): outcomes can lead to valid generalizations if modifications are made to fit particular instances.

Within the qualitative tradition, the project is indebted to the theory and methods espoused by Egon Guba and Yvonna Lincoln, especially to their notions of "fairness, openness, and involvement in the inquiry process . . . open and democratic nature [compared to conventional, scientific inquiry] . . . and axiomatic assumption of intense and nonmanipulative trust" between researcher and those being researched (133–34). In Guba and Lincoln's thinking, "truth" is a matter of consensus rather than "objective" reality and is discovered through a hermeneutic, ongoing dialectic between researcher and those being researched. Significant emphasis is placed on ethics so as to foster trust between the subjects and the researcher.

Integrated into these principles is the concept of *reciprocity*, as defined by Elaine Lawless. Reciprocal research treats participants as collaborators in the study. So, in the *Literate Lives* study, the MU 26 hold the right to verify and clarify what I write about them. Former Senior Associate Athletic Director and IRB Co-Principal Investigator Brian Maggard represents the cohort, or when the MU 26 are available, I go directly to them. "Disciplinarily responsive" refers to my adhering to the CCCC Guidelines for Ethical Conduct of Research in Composition Studies: "When conducting studies in sites outside the classroom, [researchers] give primary consideration to the contexts of [their] research and to the fair treatment of all participants" (CCCC).

For this study, "senior" refers to the players who in the 2008–2009 academic year had achieved senior status as defined by the NCAA. It does not refer a group of student-athletes who entered the university together as a single cohort in the same year. In other words, some players who started with some of the MU 26 did not stay with the team or at the university long enough to become seniors. Fifteen of the MU 26 took an NCAA-permitted "redshirt year," giving them five years instead of the traditional four to complete their degree. Most of the MU 26 enrolled in 2004; others came in 2005, 2006, or 2007. All graduated in 2008 or 2009.

The overall finding of the larger *Literate Lives* study is that the MU 26 earned their degrees by the same standards that their general population (non-athlete) peers were held to. There were no "athletes only" classes, no special deals, no "clustering" of athletes into "easy" degree programs, nor any exemptions granted that would have made their graduating more likely than any other student. That finding includes the Writing Intensive classes every student is required to take and for which the university's curriculum is known. Likewise, reading and writing scores from college entrance exams for the MU 26 indicate that the cohort is commensurate with their general population peers. In other words, the MU 26 fulfilled the same graduation requirements as did their non-athletic peers, thus substantively countering the prevailing dumb jock stereotype.

One possible explanation for the MU 26's academic success comes from considering the interview data related to players' use of metacognitive and embodied knowledge. As researchers at Columbia University's Embodiment Lab explain, "embodiment theories attempt to understand the mind as a set of physical processes derived throughout the brain and body of a human, that ultimately serve his/her action in the physical world" (Davis). It is now readily accepted that not only does the mind influence the body, but that the body also influences the mind. The student-athletes who comprise the MU 26 cohort spend dozens of hours each week, hundreds of hours over a season, and thousands of hours over their lifetimes as they acquire the knowledge needed to execute football plays. For high profile college football players, this involvement typically begins well before high school, often around age ten or eleven if not earlier, and continues steadily from then on. By virtue of this learning, which occurs through physical repetition in practice; body and verbal commands from their coaches; and close reading, memorization, and interpretation of complex written playbooks, the knowledge of their sport becomes an embodied, integral aspect of who the MU 26 are and how they live their lives.

One interview question in particular elicited insight into the metacognition that players bring to their academic performance: "Can you name one or two qualities you learned from football that helped you succeed in the classroom?" All but one (who I inadvertently neglected to ask) of the twenty-six answered this question quickly, spontaneously, and without the further prompting that some of the other questions had required. The degree to which they found this question easy to answer is revealing. The athletes were highly self-conscious of the effect of their sport on their academic performance. They spoke about this influence convincingly and authoritatively.

Kristie Fleckenstein, Julie Cheville, Debra Hawhee, Kevin Roozen, and J. Michael Rifenburg are among composition researchers who contributed to the literature on students' literate practices, metacognition, and embodied knowledge. A decade and a half ago, Fleckenstein lamented that our philosophical perspectives on writing rely on conceptual or epistemological frameworks that disregard physical bodies. "[A]n embodied discourse," she argues, is essential for addressing "the tragedies and victories that play out in our classrooms, our lives, and our worlds" (281). Not long after, Cheville's ethnographic study of women basketball players showed how these athletes' ways of knowing and doing their sport "embody cognition," but also that this knowledge goes unrecognized in the classroom—and therefore unappreciated and untapped for learning purposes. Hawhee, like Cheville an athlete herself, reconnected rhetoric with athletic endeavors in ancient Greece, showing that "The three Rs of athletic training—rhythm, repetition, response—lie at the very heart of Isocrates's conception of [rhetorical] training" (144) and that he uses the same word (*epimeleias* "diligent attention" or "care") to refer to both athletic and rhetorical training. Roozen's longitudinal ethnography of one basic writer's rich extracurricular life shows that "the writer's school tasks are profoundly shaped by [his] extensive network of non-school practices, artifacts, and activities" (95).

Most recent among the compositionists to attend to this theme, Rifenburg specifically explores the connection between football players and cognition. He carefully explicates a sample play from Auburn University's football playbook to show how it "and hundreds like it, are run and embodied endlessly in practices" (par. 18) as well as games. Rifenburg convincingly argues that, "football is a complex literate activity imbued with a great variety of multimodal literacy practices beyond the enactment of the playbook" (par. 23). His larger project aims to demonstrate to college writing instructors that college football plays can teach us a great deal about multimodality in our classrooms.

All of these composition researchers attend to the ways that students' literate activities in the composition classroom are influenced by physical phenomena outside the classroom. I suggest that these scholars' thinking can be extended beyond the composition classroom, to the many other kinds of classrooms and learning situations in which the MU 26 found themselves. My project has less to do with the embodiment of football plays as they relate to the composition classroom, than with how the embodiment of learning and playing the game relates to players' academic success—or potential for academic success—more broadly.

Understanding the Metacognitive and Embodied Knowledge Components

When asked to name one or two qualities they learned from football that helped them succeed in the classroom, each of the MU 26 identifies at least two and up to eight specific characteristics, which they believe help to account for their academic accomplishments. In each case, with each mention, the athletes' replies describe qualities they learned, developed, and had reinforced from their involvement with football, whether from their coaches, teammates, parents, or from the game itself, all of which they claim have affected their academic performance. The qualities they cite, along with the number of times they mention each one, fall into the six overlapping categories below.

Unlike the tutors that Morgan Gross and Kelsie Walker write about in this collection who were explicitly taught one habit of mind from the *Framework for Success in Postsecondary Writing*, the MU 26 rely entirely on their own language to describe the characteristics to which they attribute their academic success. Nonetheless, it is possible to discern a correspondence between their own descriptions and the *Framework*'s habits of mind. What the MU 26 describe in Category #1, *Being disciplined*, and Category #4, *Time management*, carry strong connotations to the habit of mind of *Responsibility*. Likewise, the way the MU 26 describe Category #2, *Work Ethic*, relates closely to the habit of mind of *Engagement*. And their explanations for Category #3, *Perseverance/Mental Toughness*, bear a close relationship to the habit of mind of *Persistence*. In this Category, notice especially the mechanical engineering major who refers explicitly to needing the "right frame of mind." Implicitly, these student-athletes describe having acquired habits from sport that are very similar to those the *Frameworks* document espouses. Finally, the closing example below, in a catch-all category labeled *Other*, addresses the habit of mind of *Metacognition* explicitly. This wide receiver and biology major's statement provides the powerful epigraph for this chapter: "The heart directs you where to go, the brain tells you how to get there."

Being Disciplined / Consistent / Committed

This category often manifests with players describing their "passion" for the game. They refer to their need in football to be accountable to their teammates, coaches, program, and institution. Presumably, this quality translates to being accountable to their classroom teachers and academic advisors as well. They speak about needing to keep their "priorities straight" and to focus on "the big picture." For the MU 26, the big picture includes not just winning games but also finishing their time at the university with a degree, a commitment and a priority established as early as the head coach's visit in their homes with their parents during the recruitment process. As one player, an offensive lineman with a General Studies major, puts it, "I was just not one to have to go back home without a degree or to have to worry about this when I'm thirty."

WORKING HARD / HAVING A GOOD WORK ETHIC

This category of response is often characterized by players who invoke the need to "just get the job done." Again, the principle that applies to practicing for and winning games presumably is also applied to getting homework done, tests prepared for, and papers submitted on time, in compliance with the head coach's mantra of "No Excuses" for everything they do in the sport. Consistent with the "No Excuses" mantra, players seem to have embodied the concept that if hard work is necessary for achieving success on the field, hard work is also necessary for success in the classroom. Likewise, many of them invoke lessons taught by parents and grandparents on the value of working hard to get what they want. "You've got to try hard if you want to succeed . . . You always have to have that kind of same thing off the field, in the classroom, going to meetings," says one. Or as another, a Hotel and Restaurant Management major and tailback, answers simply, "Work ethic. I just try to work hard at what I do."

PERSEVERANCE / NOT GIVING UP / MENTAL TOUGHNESS

Admittedly, overlap exists between these responses. Being disciplined (#1), working hard (#2), and not giving up (#3) seem closely related. Coding players' responses into categories, however, is not entirely arbitrary. Often, responses can be distinguished by the examples the MU 26 give as they describe what they mean by each one. With regard to mental toughness, one player, a mechanical engineering major who served a tour of duty in Iraq before joining the team, notes, "It takes a lot of drive to keep yourself on the right track, you know, [in the] right frame of mind." Another, an agriculture major who went on to a career in the National

Football League, describes mental toughness by saying, "I mean if you're strong-minded, I mean you can win, [you can] do anything. I mean on football, it's . . . 90% mental, 10% physical . . .[Y]ou take that same thing to the class . . . [S]ome days I didn't want to go to class, but I showed up . . . it took me a while to go, but within 10 to 15 minutes . . . I was more opened up, asking questions." For this athlete, persevering through the inevitable tiredness that all players suffer, struggling to get to an early morning class pays off by becoming engaged within a short time. Referring to his position as the team's back-up quarterback, a biology major speaks poignantly about perseverance and "sticking through things that are tough." Through perseverance, he channels the frustration that comes from maintaining football skills that are rarely used into completing not only his biology degree but also dental school. He is now a dentist in his hometown.

Time Management / Being Organized / Being on Time

Collegiate football athletes live tightly scheduled lives. The responses in this category reflect the rigid timetables they maintain, so that workouts, practice, travel, games, required community service work, and school work are completed on time each week. No player expresses regret for his choice to become a scholarship athlete; all are grateful for the opportunities afforded them. But several do express regret about not having more time to devote to their academic studies. Recreational reading, professional internships, and family and personal relationships are also among things they regret not having more time for. That some of them performed as well as they did academically is due, they say, to the ability to manage their time, be organized, and be on time—all skills acquired, they say, through the sport. "You gotta plan out when you have assignments due . . . write everything down. I started using a planner," says a hotel and restaurant management major, an offensive lineman. The team's lead quarterback, a business major, says, "The main thing that helped me throughout college is being organized and being almost obsessive compulsive with everything having to be right. That's how it is with every quarterback." "Just being on time," says another agriculture major and a strong safety, "that's number one . . . Be on time to anything. A meeting, practice, study hall, anything. I learned [to be] in class five minutes before it starts."

Another managed to tie three categories—working hard, persevering, and time management—into one response. A finance and banking major who played defensive back, he replies to the question of football's influence on his academic life by saying he has "a strong will, never to give up . . . 6:00 AM workouts, then class, then back to football . . . I just pretty much gained the ability to have a routine and get stuff done, work hard, be strong willed about everything, just go into everything and try my hardest, no matter if I'm tired just try to get everything done, so things get accomplished."

ABILITY TO FOCUS AND CONCENTRATE / ATTENTION TO DETAILS

One player, an agriculture major and linebacker, connects the source of this quality to more than just football: "I've been an athlete my whole life, so just athletics in general, but now in the context of football—being able to focus. That was something on the football field. If you can't focus you can't do anything, 'cause there's always a lot going on. There's people yelling and formation shifts and . . . all kinds of crazy stuff going on . . . . You got to be able to focus." The team's placekicker, a plant science major preparing to go into his family's landscaping business, echoes the attention to detail theme (along with accountability). He remarks, "By instilling those characteristics . . . that you learned from football, that translates to everything you do in life, so not necessarily just into academics, but just whatever you're doing in life . . . You learn a lot here from the athletic department and from the coaching staff about how to be successful, and actually that carries over into academics and in life." Another player, a defensive linebacker and agriculture major, also claims that the ability to concentrate he acquired in football transfers not just to the classroom but beyond: "I just transfer everything that I learned on the football field, like paying attention to little details—like if you have to do on certain plays and applied it to like small things in the book that I've read and stuff that I need to focus on that I know might be on a test. They're all just plays. Football is just like life. So, it all plays out."

Desire for Self-Improvement / Wanting to Show Leadership

The last category that elicits multiple responses relates to players self-consciously seeking to be better at what they do, whether footfall or academics. Closely related is their sense of being leaders and wanting to demonstrate leadership ability, whether on the playing field or off. An agriculture major and wide receiver says, "One [thing I learned from football that I applied to schoolwork] is being ambitious, going for what I want, knowing what I want to accomplish, knowing my goals in life." A tight end, another of the hotel and restaurant management majors, attributes this lesson to his father: "My dads taught me ever since I was young, if you're gonna . . . do something, do it to the best of your ability until it's done...You just gotta care about what you're doing." The military veteran also invokes the importance of "the will to want to do [something]" and "to want to make yourself better." And the offensive lineman majoring in general studies notes, "[P]ractice wasn't fun every day, but it's somethin' you had to do to get better. It's the same thing with class."

Other

Responses with fewer mentions, and thus not plentiful enough to constitute a category beyond "Other" include having a "happy spirit," not being shy, and having faith in God. The player who invokes the "happy spirit" quality, a defensive back and agriculture major, believes that the sense of humor and "right attitude" he initially honed through the game applies equally well in the classroom. The defensive end majoring in interdisciplinary studies (a psychology/sociology combination) believes that his small-town upbringing where he "knew everybody" contributes to his being shy and less communicative when meeting new people. The teamwork required in football leads to his feeling more confident when doing group projects and team presentations in class. Several players refer to the role of faith in connection to their football ability; one, in particular, believes his faith also helped him persevere through difficult situations off the field. One final response grouped in the Other category may, in fact, belong in a category by itself. This wide receiver and biology major makes an explicit metacognitive connection between football and academics in this reply:

By far, confidence [is what I've taken from football to the classroom]. The mind is the most amazing part of your body. The heart directs you where to go, the brain tells you how to get there. So, I sit there [in class] and I believe I can do anything . . . that's just the confidence I have that I didn't have when I first got here. I didn't have fight . . . Just the amount of confidence that I've had in myself to overcome any of life's unforeseen challenges is the greatest strength and attribute that I could ever [have]. I've attained that at this university.

MINDSET, LEARNING, AND ENABLING ALL STUDENTS—ATHLETIC AND OTHERWISE

One possible explanation for the MU 26 cohort's ability to apply these embodied, football-derived lessons in the classroom may be a *mindset* the athletes possess. Mindset, according to psychologist Carol Dweck, whose work is referenced by several other authors in this collection and who has been studying the mindset concept for nearly four decades, refers to the student's view of his or her own intelligence and abilities. Mindset, Dweck says, falls into two categories: "fixed" and "growth" (qtd. in Doyle and Zakrajsek). A student with a fixed mindset believes that intelligence is a fixed trait; the student who doesn't do well in a given area—math for example—thinks it's because he isn't "smart" in math to begin with and, no matter what, simply isn't ever going to do well in it. Conversely, a student with a growth mindset believes that intelligence grows as he adds new knowledge and skills. So, students with this mindset value hard work, challenges, and practice, thinking that failure is a reason to try again and that performance can improve with continued effort. These students believe that practice can make a significant difference in whatever they're doing. According to Dweck, these views of intelligence begin to form in middle school when more stringent academic work appears in the curriculum (Doyle and Zakrajsek). Coincidentally, this is also about the same time that many football athletes begin learning and playing their sport in earnest.

Another possible explanation may come through the work of English professor Cathy Davidson. Her thinking about how the brain science of attention is changing the way students live and learn has led her to Columbia University clinical neuropsychologist Yaakov Stern. From Stern's research comes a list of mentally stimulating activities anyone can use to "pump up our cognitive reserves": continue one's education;

engage in meaningful and enjoyable work, pleasurable leisure activities, physical exercise, and social interactions; learn a new language, or other new skills, especially computer skills; play video games; and interact on social networks. As Davidson points out, what Stern calls cognitive reserves, she calls "learning." With the possible exception of learning a new language, many of the items on Stern's list are among the activities that most of the MU 26 engage in on a daily basis. The correspondence between Stern's activities for building cognitive reserves, Davidson's "learning," and football players' daily activities seems to indicate connections and relationships that may help explain how the embodied knowledge from football helps to account for the MU 26's success in their academic courses.

Neither Dweck's nor Davidson's models fully address *how* embodied knowledge from football influenced the MU 26's successful academic performance. Clearly, other factors that exist must also be considered. But the fact that the MU 26 were highly aware of having learned lessons from the sport that they strongly believe contributed to their academic performance, and the degree of confidence with which they articulated this influence, should give us reason to keep looking for better explanations for how the phenomenon occurs. Moreover, if the phenomenon occurred for the MU 26, it is likely occurring for athletes in other sports as well. If we can better understand the phenomenon, classroom instructors can tap into that knowledge and apply its lessons to our teaching. Compositionists as well as educators beyond our discipline could help ensure improved academic performance not only for the student-athletes we too often unfairly stereotype as "dumb jocks," but for all students as well.

Acknowledgements

I wish to thank Michael Alden, former Director of Athletics, University of Missouri; Bryan Maggard, Director of Athletics, University of Louisiana Lafayette; Joe Scogin, Sr. Assoc. Athletics Director and Asst. Provost, U of Tennessee; Briana Fields, Assoc. Director of Compliance, Ohio State University; and, especially, the MU 26 cohort.

Works Cited

Brand, Myles. "The 'Dumb Jock' Myth is Dumb," *Huffington Post*, 2011. www.huffpost.com/entry/the-dumb-jock-myth-is-dum_b_133322. Accessed 1 Aug. 2019.

Cheville, Julie. *Minding the Body: What Student Athletes Know About Learning*. Boynton/Cook, 2001.

Conference on College Composition and Communication. "CCCC Guidelines for the Ethical Conduct of Research in Composition Studies." CCCC, 2015. www.ncte.org/cccc/resources/positions/ethicalconduct. Accessed 11 Nov. 2019.

Davidson, Cathy. *Now You See It: How the Brain Science of Attention Will Transform the Way We Live, Work, and Learn*. Viking, 2011.

Davis, Josh I. Embodiment Lab. *Columbia University*, (n.d.), www.embodimentlab.com/ Accessed Apr. 3, 2012. Paywall protected.

Doyle, Terry, and Todd Zakrajsek, editors. *The New Science of Learning*, Stylus, 2014.

Fleckenstein, Kristie S. "Writing Bodies: Somatic Mind in Composition Studies." *College English*, vol. 61, no. 3, 1999, pp. 281–306.

Council of Writing Program Administrators, National Council of Teachers of English, and National Writing Project. *Framework for Success in Postsecondary Writing*. CWPA, NCTE, and NWP, 2011, wpacouncil.org/aws/CWPA/asset_manager/get_file/350201?ver=505. Accessed 18 Sept. 2020.

Ganim, Sara. "Some College Athletes Play Like Adults, Read Like 5th Graders." *CNN*, 2014, Jan. 8, www.cnn.com/2014/01/07/us/ncaa-athletes-reading-scores/index.html. Accessed 11 Nov. 2019.

Gillham, Bill. *Case Study Research Methods*. Continuum, 2000.

Guba, Egon, and Yvonne Lincoln. *Fourth Generation Evaluation*. Sage, 1989.

Hawhee, Debra. *Bodily Arts: Rhetoric and Athletics in Ancient Greece*. U of Texas P, 2004.

Jaschik, Scott. "CNN Finds Athletes Who Read Like 5th Graders." *Inside Higher Ed*, 2014, Jan. 8, www.insidehighered.com/quicktakes/2014/01/08/cnn-finds-athletes-who-read-5th-graders. Accessed 11 Nov. 2019.

Lawless, Elaine J. "'Reciprocal' Ethnography: No One Said It Was Easy." *Journal of Folklore Research*, vol. 37, no. 2/3, 2000, pp. 197–205.

Machlin, Tzvi. "LSU Football Has Unveiled an Insane New Facility," 22 July 2019, thespun.com/sec/lsu/lsu-football-has-unveiled-an-insane-new-facility. Accessed 11 Nov. 2019.

—. LSU Responds to Criticism of Its New Football Facility." 24 July 2019, thespun.com/sec/lsu/lsu-football-facility-criticism-response. Accessed 11 Nov. 2019.

Merriam, Sharan, and Associates, editors. *Qualitative Research in Practice: Examples for Discussion and Analysis*. Jossey-Bass, 2002.

Miller, Richard. "Thirteen Ways of Looking at a Football Stadium." 31 Jan. 2012, web.archive.org/web/20140220114030/http://text2cloud.com/2012/01/thirteen-ways-of-looking-at-a-football-stadium/. Accessed 26 July 2019.

Rifenburg, J. Michael. "Writing as Embodied, College Football Plays as Embodied: Extracurricular Multimodal Composing." *Composition Forum*, vol. 29, 2014, compositionforum.com/issue/29/writing-as-embodied.php.

Roozen, Kevin. "Journalism, Poetry, Stand-up Comedy, and Academic Literacy: Mapping the Interplay of Curricular and Extracurricular Literate Activities." *Journal of Basic Writing*, vol. 27, no. 1, 2008, pp. 5–34.

Scogin, Joseph. *Predicting First Year Academic Success of the Student-athlete Population at the University of Missouri*. 2007. University of Missouri, PhD dissertation.

Stake, Robert E. "Case Studies." *Handbook of Qualitative Research*, edited by Norman Denzin and Yvonne Lincoln, Sage, 1994, pp. 236–46.

Townsend, Martha. "High Profile Football Players Reading at a Research University: ACT Scores, Interview Responses, and Personal Preferences." *Across the Disciplines*, vol. 10, no. 4, 2013, wac.colostate.edu/docs/atd/reading/townsend.pdf.

Townsend, Martha. *The Literate Lives of Athletes: How a Division I Championship Football Program Graduated 100% of Its Senior Players*, in progress.

IV Writing Center Engagement

12 "This Is on You": When Responsibility as a Habit of Mind Informs Writing Center Consultant's Practice

Morgan Gross and Kelsie Walker

The habits of mind, as an intellectual and practical approach to learning, is an untapped resource in writing center tutor education. The *Framework for Success in Postsecondary Education*, jointly developed by the Council of Writing Program Administrators (CWPA), the National Council of Teachers of English (NCTE), and the National Writing Project (NWP), surprisingly does not mention writing center professionals (WCPs), graduate writing center professionals, or under/graduate writing consultants as a potential audience, although, to be fair, some WCPs (Carolyn Calhoon-Dillahunt, Richard Selfe, and Kirsten Jamsen) and former WCPs (Linda Adler-Kassner, Darsie Bowden, and Susan Miller-Cochran) had a hand in creating the document as members of these organizations. The work of writing center consultants, however, is to support students' learning about and through writing. They interact with a variety of student clients across disciplines, helping them to become better writers and successful college students; thus, the *Framework* can be used to inform writing center work. We believe the habits of mind, specifically, can enhance consultants' tutoring toolbox, giving them another way to think about the work they do and how they approach their clients. Our research, then, investigated this assumption by analyzing how consultants in one writing center talked about their work after participating in a habits of mind-centered consultant development workshop. We wondered, following this consultant development, do consultants actively think about the habits of mind as they consult with clients? And if so, how do they implement what they have learned to promote cognitive habits to clients?

This chapter reports on an IRB-approved empirical study at a mid-sized Midwestern university in which we (1) implemented locally developed instruction on the habits of mind for writing center consultants and (2) tracked consultants' perceptions of their practices before, soon after, and several weeks after the consultant development had taken place. As a result of the consultant development workshop, the consultant participants in our study seemed to acquire additional ways to discuss tutor and client responsibilities and roles, which in turn helped them attend to responsibility as a habit of mind in their sessions. We suggest this indicates the usefulness of the habits of mind as a tutor education heuristic.

Current Conversations About the *Framework* and Habits of Mind

The *Framework* acts as a disciplinary document that defines "the rhetorical and twenty-first-century skills as well as habits of mind and experiences that are critical for college success" (1). Furthermore, the authors of the document—from high schools and two- and four-year colleges and universities—identify eight "Habits of Mind" that "[refer] to ways of approaching learning that are both intellectual and practical and that will support students' success in a variety of fields and disciplines," as well as draw on the WPA's "Outcomes Statement" (1). These habits are curiosity, openness, engagement, creativity, persistence, responsibility, flexibility, and metacognition. As evidenced by the publication date of the *Framework*, the habits of mind are a fairly recent development in conceiving of "college readiness" and ways to approach writing, thinking, and doing. Despite the habits of mind's novelty, some rhetoric and composition scholars have considered it in their work, most often praising the habits of mind or discussing them in meta-conversations within larger educational contexts (O'Neill et al.; Sullivan; Newcomb; Johnson). On the other hand, Jonathan Alexander and Daniel M. Gross take a critical approach to the privileging of "success," inquiring instead about the productive potential of failure. They write, "We like to be just as positive as anyone else, just as optimistic. We also fear failure, and we understand that failure is, shall we say, not the most fundable project in these times and places" (274). Failure, though, according to Alexander and

Gross, is not unproductive as it, too, can lead to growth and learning (see also Williams's discussion on emotion and persistence in this collection).

The *Framework* is trending in disciplinary conversations, a point this collection confirms, and Alexander and Gross's piece sheds light on some of its controversial aspects; however, because of the *Framework*'s newness, scholarship on it and the habits of mind are still emerging in writing center studies. The *Framework*, as the document states, is intended for a primary audience of instructors who teach or implement writing in their courses, as well as an audience of parents, schools, and policymakers. As we mentioned before, WCPs are not specifically identified or included in this audience, and the International Writing Centers Association (IWCA) organization is not listed as a contributor or author. Perhaps this ambiguity reflects the tension in writing center scholarship about whether consultants are in fact "teaching" writing or just supporting writing through peer feedback. As we reflected on our own writing center work, we concluded that while writing center consultants may not hold traditional "teacher" positions, may not design lesson plans in advance or evaluate students' writing with letter grades, teaching (and learning) indeed happens in writing center consultations. Thus, we concluded that the work of the writing center is concerned with writing and the teaching of writing (Lerner). We can say, then, that writing centers are ideal contexts within the institution in which to apply knowledge of the habits of mind, and we argue that the writing center is a site of learning, a site of inquiry, and a site where writing and learning (and learners) converge. The question follows, if the writing center is a site of learning, how can it incorporate the habits of mind? We suspect, and our research supports, that the habits of mind, when used to inform consulting practices, can be beneficial to consultants and students.

Research Methods

Our qualitative, empirical study responds to the call within writing center scholarship for more replicable, aggregable, data-supported (RAD) research (Driscoll and Perdue; Grutsch McKinney). The research questions, which rely on consultants' perceptions, guiding our project were

1. To what extent—if any—does locally crafted instruction on the habits contribute to writing center consultants' repertoire of con-

sulting tools and/or affect their practice as they work with students writers?
2. And how do writing center consultants see the habits affecting students' experiences in the tutoring session?

Our participants, whom we refer to using pseudonyms (some of which were participant-selected), were consultants in one writing center at a mid-sized Midwestern university with varying levels of experience with writing center work. The participants were split nearly evenly between undergraduate and graduate student consultants, and two of the graduate students held administrative positions in the writing center at the time of our study. At the beginning of our study, thirteen consultants responded to our pre-workshop survey (see Appendix A); twelve of those thirteen were present for the workshop we taught on "responsibility"; only seven attended the focus group session we held two weeks after the lesson; from those seven consultants, we invited two to participate in follow-up interviews.

After securing permissions from IRB and the institution's writing center director, we surveyed consultants, asking them about their previous training or consultant development, consulting experiences, and knowledge and use of the habits of mind as individual units in their consulting practice (see Appendix A). In the pre-workshop survey, consultants were asked to circle the individual habit of mind they engaged students in *most often* during their sessions; we then developed a workshop on *responsibility*, the habits of mind participants reported being least likely to use in their consulting practice—instead of trying to provide an overview of all of them. Retrospectively, we might have selected one of the habits of mind to focus on based on what participants said they wanted to know the most about instead. We also discovered from the survey that, despite consultants' varied levels of experience and field knowledge, none of them were familiar with the habits as a framework before we introduced it—likely because of its newness at the time.

During the habits of mind's workshop, we worked with consultants to develop a definition for responsibility—by having them first either illustrate what responsibility looked like to them or describe a moment from their experiences in which they were cultivating responsibility in their own lives. After sharing their experiences, they formed small groups to write working definitions of the term. We then synthesized these to form a single (albeit complex) definition. After comparing what we wrote to the definition for responsibility offered in the *Framework* document, we remained satisfied with our generative one (see "Findings and Analysis" or Appendix B). Next in the workshop, we provided the consultants, in small groups, with different writing center session scenarios (Appendix C), crafted intentionally for the lesson and informed by our own consulting experiences. We asked them to come up with a plan for how they would respond as the consultant in the scenario, keeping the goal of developing students' responsibility in mind. From consultants' responses to the scenarios, we noted the consulting strategies they discussed on the board. These are catalogued in the handout that we made as a result of what happened during the workshop (specifically for the consultants who were not able to attend the meeting), also available in Appendix B. We concluded the workshop by encouraging consultants to take what they learned from our workshop/discussion into their tutoring practice.

Two weeks later, we held a forty-minute, audio recorded focus group with the majority of the consultants who were present for the workshop. The questions we asked consultants during the focus group (see Appendix D) focused primarily on how the workshop had influenced their consulting practice since then and, if so, in what ways, as well as how their clients seemed to be responding to those changes in particular. We transcribed the recorded focus group session, and then coded it independently, but discussed patterns and noteworthy moments. We did not attempt to streamline our codes at this point; instead, we were granted a lab time session at the International Writing Center Association Collaborative @ the Conference on College Composition and Communication (Houston, Apr. 6, 2016), a new session format in which researchers collaborate with other WCPs to get help with data collection or analysis. In the lab time session, we asked other conference attendees with qualitative coding experience to serve as peer de-briefers, providing their own codes for emergent themes in the focus group transcript as verification that our findings were valid. John Creswell states that peer debriefing can contribute to the validity of a study, when the researchers' interpretation of their data "resonate[s] with [other] people" (192). Indeed, much of our discussion in the lab time session focused on patterns in the data that both we and our peers had noted, although they also pointed out some topics in and approaches to the research that aligned with their own interests but went beyond the scope of what we were willing to explore for this limited study. The peer debriefing activity, then, both helped us confirm some of the themes we had previously identified *and* helped us reaffirm our commitment to our methods and purpose.

After returning from the conference and having sat with our preliminary analyses of the focus group data for a few weeks, we selected two consultants with whom to conduct brief in-person, follow-up interviews to gather additional information. Specifically, we wanted to hear more from two of the undergraduate participants: Cassidy, about her thoughts on the ways in which her positionality influenced the consulting strategies she used, and Apryll, about her use of "waiting" as a strategy to encourage clients to take responsibility. Like the focus group, the interviews were audio recorded, transcribed, and coded, and it was at this point that we went through our individually developed codes and decided on a schema that accounted for both sets, which can be seen in the findings and analysis section of this chapter.

The primary limitation of the study is its small sample size. We worked with consultants from only one writing center, and all of the consultants had previous consulting experience. This makes it difficult to draw generalizations from our findings, although their ideas and our analysis provide a starting point for other WCPs interested in using the habits for tutor education or conducting further research on the topic. Furthermore, we explicitly taught only one of the habits due to time constraints, and we did not collect any data from student clients about their experiences working with consultants who consciously promoted responsibility. In the section on future research, we discuss some of the ways these limitations could be addressed.

Findings and Analysis

We found two prominent, noteworthy themes emerging from our data: (1) the many definitions and ways of conceiving of both clients' and consultants' responsibility in the writing center and (2) the various strategies consultants used to engage student clients in acts of responsibility, including factors that influenced their use of those strategies.

Developing/Diverging Definitions of Responsibility

The *Framework* defines responsibility as "the ability to take ownership of one's actions and understand the consequences of those actions for oneself and others." The definition our participants generated during the workshop on responsibility is more disjointed and complex:

(self) accountability; meeting others' expectations (and your own), yet (how to) balance these two; self-reflective choices; awareness of being self-motivated and prepared; awareness of sacrificial nature of responsibility—obligations; taking care of yourself (what are you (not) capable of?); having qualities of organization and resourcefulness.

Our participants' definition is similar to the *Framework*'s in that both mention accountability, are action-oriented, and recognize that responsibility (or lack of it) affects others as well as oneself. The participants' definition goes further by describing how responsibility works and how it is connected to qualities such as good decision-making, motivation, preparedness, balance, organization, and resourcefulness.

Participants further expanded this already lengthy definition as they brought an awareness of responsibility to their consulting work over the weeks following the workshop. One of the consultants, Brandon, came to realize, in fact, that all of the habits of mind are interconnected: they "weave together." Reflecting on this in our focus group discussion, Brandon stated, "I think one thing that's interesting about the habits of mind is how they kind of play off each other. Like, to what extent do you have a *responsibility* to be *open*?" Brandon has made connections between various habits of mind that seem to make his understanding of responsibility more complex and concrete.

One of the most interesting points of observation that came from listening to the consultants discuss their ideas about responsibility is that they couldn't help but attend to their own responsibilities, rather than the students' responsibilities alone. One of the consultants, Ellen, when explaining why she chose not to mark on the pre-workshop survey "responsibility" as a habit of mind in which she regularly engages students, said, "I have a tendency to see all of the responsibility being on me because I'm paid to do this."

Furthermore, Susan admitted, "when I first heard the word 'responsibility,' I actually thought more like what responsibilities do I, myself, have as someone who the student has gone to for help? So, I didn't think about it in reference to the student; I thought about it in reference to myself." Ellen agreed, saying she had the exact same thoughts at first. After initially thinking about responsibility only in terms of herself as a consultant rather than in terms of clients, however, Ellen began to reflect on instances of client responsibility. She shared with us during the focus group that "[English Language Learners (ELLs)] sometimes write in their own language . . . [If] you give them a chance to do all of the writing on that paper you're helping them connect themselves to the work a little bit closer." Here we found Ellen moving from a singular definition of responsibility to one that involved the client. Similarly, Linda recounted a time when "[she] realized there was something the student needed to do herself that [she] could not really do for her or with her. So [she] said, 'I'm gonna leave it on you to do this.'" Linda continued her anecdote by reflecting on how she believes some clients react to this: "And I think sometimes the students appreciate that 'cause you're not forcing them to do it right now and you're also not telling them how to do it; you're saying, 'this is your task.'" For additional discussion of the connection between responsibility and student agency (see Macauley, Jr.'s chapter in this collection).

Consultants in our study reported, despite initially having a hard time relinquishing their own sense of responsibility, the workshop on responsibility-as-a-habit helped them to realize that responsibility "is a two-way street" (Ellen). They came to understand the fact that student clients have responsibilities, too—ones that impact their learning—and one of their own responsibilities as consultants is to help students figure out how to take on those responsibilities, which might, by extension, ease the consultants' unnecessarily assumed burdens. Table 1 includes our summary of the ways in which our participants discussed responsibility post-workshop, for example, in the focus group and individual interviews.

The participants, however, also maintained an awareness of and commitment to their own responsibilities as consultants throughout our discussions. They mostly identified those responsibilities as consulting tasks, such as helping students learn to research, plan, and edit; teaching students about plagiarism; "waiting" on students when they need time to think or are disengaged; and recommending that students make follow-up appointments when appropriate. Interestingly, Cassidy, also discussed responsibility as allegiance: She claimed to have a responsibility to both students and the writing center, and she identified herself as occupying, at least in the writing center, a "really messy gray area between teacher and student," commenting that because consultants in this writing center are students, both graduate and undergraduate, they are all still learning, too.

Table 1
Participants' Evolving Definitions of Responsibility

Responsibility is . . .	Students are responsible for. . .	Responsibility leads to. . .
foundational to learning professionalism	reading materials (e.g. emails) about on-line appointments showing up to on-line appointments being prepared for their sessions taking notes about what's discussed in a session putting effort into their work taking next steps after a session owning their writing their grades using knowledge gained in a session (i.e., transfer)	a student's pride in their work

Broadly, the participants' definitions of responsibility evolved to account for their everyday consulting experiences, incorporating much more practical application, as well as specific examples. They pointed out a number of ways in which issues with responsibility appeared in their sessions, and, more importantly, they named their consulting values and practices in response to particular instances. Over the course of the research project, then, consultant participants developed a complex and evolving definition of responsibility, and they discussed the different ways in which both consultants and student clients have responsibilities. In the focus group session, they took time to reflect on their consulting practice, which seemed to help them articulate tutors' and students' nuanced roles in the writing center. As a result, some consultants reported feeling more comfortable/confident articulating those roles to students during their consultations.

Strategies for Helping Students Cultivate Responsibility

As with their definition of "responsibility," our participants also identified and continued to expand on their strategies for cultivating responsibility in clients throughout our study. Initially, in the workshop, the consultants suggested using the following strategies in response to the scenarios we gave them for practice:

- Offer strategies (such as pre-writing, advice about editing their work based on patterns of error you've identified, and contacting the professor for more information), not solutions
- Encourage students to tap into their own knowledge/expertise
- Frame yourself as a reader, so the client is "responsible" to you and your response to their text
- Give gentle reminders to students about their role in the session
- Pose scaffolded questions that guide the client to resolve the issue in their text
- Point clients to additional resources

During the focus group session and follow-up interviews, after consultants had a chance to work with real student clients rather than contrived scenarios, they reported using strategies (see table 2) that diverge quite a bit from the original strategies above. Some of these strategies feel more forceful in comparison to the workshop-generated strategies: for example, instead of giving "gentl[e] remind[ers]" to students about their responsibilities, consultants reported directly explaining those responsibilities. They also discussed the multiple material and interpersonal factors that were connected to their practices, such as the session's format and technological availabilities, as well as the consultant's positionality. These post-workshop strategies indicate to us that once participants had developed collaborative definitions of responsibility and strategies for cultivating it in students, they continued to think about responsibility and ways to put it into action after the workshop took place.

Table 2
Participants' Strategies for Cultivating Clients' Responsibility

Strategies	Examples
Direct explanation about students' responsibilities	Consultants (Ellen, Apryll) "interrupt" their sessions to explain, very explicitly, that the client has a responsibility to "make sure [they] get to where [they] need to go."
Shift in tone (more subtle than direct explanation)	"I use a lot of emoticons" in online sessions, "but when I need to get serious I leave them off" (Cassidy).
Empathy/ relating to the client/ modeling desired behavior	"I actually used my personal experience, like, you're allowed to come in with your article and have notes off in the margins" (Cassidy, speaking about her experience with taking the writing proficiency exam.) "It's always about me making myself relatable and then, like, showing them how I'm responsible in hopes that they listen and maybe want to be [responsible] too" (Apryll).
Guided instruction (with technologies)	"Before, when I know that they have not talked to their professor, I have actually helped them write an email, showing them . . . like what they would say in the email" (Cassidy). "I use the iPads a lot to pull up things and do research . . . I see a lot of people help their clients plan out their papers using, like, the whiteboards."
Physical redistribution of responsibility	Consultants (Ellen, Cassidy) "nudge" pens and paper toward clients to indicate that they have a responsibility to engage in the session.
Wait time	"I'm the queen of waiting . . . My suggestions become, like, comments, or my comments become questions . . . [to] make it a more thought provoking process for them" (Apryll, from focus group). "So, to be honest, so I give my clients space to if they are thinking, think. If they are waiting for me to respond, give them the opportunity to know that I'm not going to" (Apryll, from interview).

With respect to session format, undergraduate consultants Cassidy and Ellen and graduate consultant Susan all stated their belief that it's more challenging to foster students' responsibility in online sessions when they can't make use of physical strategies like "nudging," or moving the student's paper closer to their person. In contrast, Apryll contributed that online sessions are a good context for using wait time and questioning as alternatives. Both Cassidy and Apryll reported using student-centered practices—Cassidy, for example, by softening a directive with an emoji, and Apryll by trying to ascertain the reason behind a client's silence.

Most prominently, consultants indicated in focus group and interview discussions that their own positionality was a significant factor influencing their strategy choices. In the focus group, we noticed that peer undergraduate consultants and graduate teaching assistants (TAs) working as consultants had differing levels of authority guiding their engagement with students. When sharing her own reluctance to call out a student for their lack of responsibility, even calling such moments "awkward," Cassidy (a senior undergrad) explained, "I don't like messing with authority" because, she felt, it disrupts the "community" vibe of the writing center, "but," she conceded, "sometimes you have to." Cassidy also shared her feelings from observing consultants in different positions: "I've heard graduate assistants use, like, what they would say to their students, but I just don't have that, or not yet." Linda, a graduate TA confirmed Cassidy's observation about the effects of consultants' positionality: "I feel like becoming a teacher has made me more bold as a tutor in some ways 'cause I feel like I've read so many student papers and I've done this for so long that when I see something that I think the student should do—I just feel like I can tell them that and I don't feel as hesitant about it as I would maybe three years ago."

In addition to positionality, consultants' unique personalities and dispositions may also influence which strategies they use and when. The interesting, different approaches of undergraduate consultants Cassidy and Apryll demonstrate this point. Where Cassidy insists on her "peerness" in consulting, Apryll observes, "some tutors . . . don't want to be bossy or reinforce rules or stuff that the client should know. I don't care about being bossy." Despite this evidence, we hesitate to make a generalizable claim about the extent to which consultants' personalities matter in their use of consulting strategies, as this is the only example from our study that we could rely on to prove the point. However, our experiences with Apryll and Cassidy, in and out of the study, and our social intuitions lead us to believe there is more to study and write on this point in future research.

DISCUSSION

When we began this research project, we wanted to know about the value, if any, of using the habits of mind to inform consultants' writing center work. We also began with the beliefs that writing centers are important institutional spaces for students' learning and that the habits of mind offer ways to foster that learning. Our study revealed that consultants found learning about responsibility useful and that they used what they had learned about responsibility to inform their consulting practices. We also found that that their definitions of responsibility and the strategies they used to cultivate responsibility in their clients continued to develop and become more nuanced as a result of the workshop, but, more importantly, as a result of the opportunity to reflect on their experiences. Specifically, consultants reflected on how responsibility informed their tutoring strategies and how various factors impacted their ability to apply those strategies to their tutoring practice. While we were able to make some limited claims about our findings, the descriptive nature of our study actually affords us the opportunity to discuss two major implications: the potential benefits of using the habits of mind in tutor education and the future research possibilities that were opened up as a result of this exploratory research.

THE HABITS OF MIND AS A HEURISTIC FOR TUTOR EDUCATION

Knowing that we undertook this study because we believed in the potential of the habits as a heuristic for tutor education, we investigated if and how scholars had been discussing individual habits of mind prior to the development of the *Framework*. As such, we found that scholars primarily discussed individual habits of mind as qualities that consultants have or should have, such as in Jennifer Nicklay's article where she discusses the role of guilt in consultants' practice, noting *flexibility* as a useful and important quality for consultants to have when navigating a session. Additionally, Lisa Zimmerelli makes the case for community *engagement* in the form of service-learning tutor education as a way to promote social justice. Furthermore, we found that a few tutor education sourcebooks reference individual habits, again, apart from the habits of mind. Lauren Fitzgerald and Melissa Ianetta's book, for example, mentions one of the habits of mind when it addresses "Authoring Processes" and "encourage[s] reflection and *metacognition*" (90; emphasis added).

These instances point to both a scholarly interest and trend in issues related to cognition in the writing center context, which lends credibility to our study and call for additional research.

With tutor education in mind, we wanted to hear what the participants thought about the instruction we crafted for them and the value they saw in the habits of mind, as well. In the focus group session, we explicitly asked consultants to give feedback on this. Generally, participants easily bought into the purpose of the study; the habits of mind; and, of course, writing center work. One consultant, Ellen, however, responded with some hesitation. She stated her belief that the habits of mind were a good topic for continued education for consultants with experience, but not as much for the preparation of new consultants: "I think if I were learning how to tutor, and I was faced with this kind of stuff, it might be too abstract to understand . . . It makes a lot more sense to me because actually being able to think about past experiences and being able to jump right into using it, without also having to deal with the struggles of also learning how to tutor itself." Indeed, all of the participants in our study did have at least some prior consulting experience.

We empathize with Ellen's point that new consultants are often preoccupied with very practical matters. However, in *The Everyday Writing Center: A Community of Practice* Anne Ellen Geller et al. offer a different perspective on consultant preparation, in particular when they discuss the concept of the *trickster*, or a being who functions as a boundary-crosser, a breaker of societal rules, a personification of chaos. The authors attempt to "cultivate a Trickster mind" in themselves and tutors, "one that can be awakened to and can awaken moments of discernment about uncertainty" (16). Accordingly, they also lament the "tendency toward technical rationality" in consultant preparation (21) that betrays Ellen's comment. Tutor training textbooks, for example, can "[limit] tutors' meaningful participation in their own learning" (21). The authors discuss the ways in which consultant preparation might close off consultants from their own creativity, flexibility, and intuition, as well as the importance of a Trickster mentality to consulting practices:

> Familiar memes—don't write on the paper, don't speak more than the student-writer, ask non-directive questions—get passed among cohorts of writing tutors as gospel before they even interact with writers in an everyday setting . . . These mindsets may actually discourage tutors from admitting or even noticing that on-the-ground practices contradict implicit or explicit writing

> center "policy" . . . Ingesting sound bites, axioms, and policies is easy; it is learning to unlearn, learning to be flexible in the face of newness, and learning deep listening that is hard . . . Staff education practices that welcome a Trickster state of mind are even more important than we thought. (21)

Applying a Trickster approach to tutor education can help consultants to handle new situations in their practice with flexibility and thoughtfulness. Similarly, we contend, using the habits of mind as a framework for tutor education has the potential to help consultants develop methods for handling practical issues (as well as grapple with abstract pedagogical concerns) without situating those matters as the focal point of their work. They would be encouraged to act from what they know rather than follow a pre-established doctrine. For example, one would not need to direct a consultant to refrain from marking on a student's paper during a session because an understanding of responsibility as a habit of mind would make the consultant aware that a student begins to take responsibility for their writing and their learning when they physically mark the changes brought up in consultant/client conversation.

Another point worth making is the importance of offering consultants opportunities for reflection as a part of tutor education. Gita DasBender and Martha A. Townsend, contributors to this collection, likewise point out the importance of reflection as metacognitive work as they discuss students' learning and the transfer of knowledge, respectively. Our participants confirmed this claim when they commented on the significance of how frequently they reflected on responsibility or other habits of mind, whether because we asked them to or not, over the duration of our study. Cassidy, for example, in her interview, stated, "The follow-up focus group thing, and then having the details from our meeting [the handout]—in the writing center we get those like bonus points if we read those and comment on them, and I did that and was able to reflect more on it on my own. I think that helped." To collect data for our research, we needed participants to reflect continually on responsibility and tutoring. This reflective work they were doing seems to have yielded an increased awareness for them about both our research topic and their consulting practices, in general. Cassidy's comment, at least, suggests that, in the context of tutor education, consultants benefit from revisiting concepts they've learned.

The participants in our study, then, have confirmed our belief that the habits of mind offer a valuable way to teach consultants about writing center consulting work. The habits of mind shift the focus of a session away from practical/technical, how-to matters and toward an emphasis on student clients' learning, especially when consultants are given ample opportunity to reflect on the habits of mind and their consulting practices. Consultants can use the habits of mind to inform the practical and pedagogical decisions they make while tutoring, developing in them a flexible, reasoned tutoring practice. In this way, writing center consultants reinforce the idea of the writing center as a site where learning happens. Future research should test these claims from a variety of contexts. The next section offers suggestions for ways to extend our study and this research topic.

Questions Raised and Opportunities for Future Research

Our research provided insight into the many ways consultants define responsibility as well as the factors that influence how responsibility manifests in consultants' sessions. It also prompted us to ask more questions and inspired additional ways to study the habits in a writing center context. One question raised was how do we look beyond the individual responsibilities of student clients and consultants in the writing center to the responsibilities of writing centers as entities for student learning, as well as to institutions of higher education? Not doing this could play into a bootstraps mentality in which students, solely, are blamed for their failings when systemic forces also need to be interrogated. During our study's focus group, Apryll commented, "Sometimes it's hard for [students] to have that responsibility because a lot of teachers will spoon-feed you what they want." Apryll's comment shifts the notion of responsibility—from students to teachers—and prompts us to consider further what responsibility the institution has to/for students. To/for consultants? To/for the writing center? If new college students are underprepared to take responsibility for their learning, is that their fault, considering they may have been educated within a system that has not properly encouraged them to act as agents in knowledge construction? Alexander and Gross pose similar questions in "Frameworks for Failure," in which they argue against "plac[ing] the burden of action and consequence on the individual" (291). Furthermore, they seek to disrupt the conception of failure as wholly negative, suggesting instead that a "responsible pedagogy" views some failures as productive and even necessary for growth. While this issue of institutional and public responsibility lies outside the scope of our study, we believe it no doubt impacted our study's participants and the clients with whom they worked and should, therefore, continue to be grappled with in theory and pedagogy.

In terms of future research, one possibility lies in further studying how clients were affected by consultants' use of strategies during sessions. Thus, including clients as participants would allow a researcher to understand clients' experiences during a session as well as gain insight into the expectations they had for a session. In our focus group, consultants reported clients' mixed reactions to strategies that required active learning and shared responsibilities on the part of both consultant and student. Typically, clients were surprised or resistant. Linda reflected on a seemingly rocky session that ended in a client leaving:

> I was trying to ask her questions to get her to, like, talk about it and everything, but she didn't seem like she really was into brainstorming about it and I realized, I thought, she kind of wanted me to tell her what to say, and I told her twice, like, "I can't write this for you." And eventually she got really mad and she left. I was like, "Hm. I'm not gonna sit here and feel bad about this because I know that it's not my responsibility, and it would be like unethical for me to tell her what to write.

Additionally, Apryll commented on the surprise reactions students have when she hands them pens: "I'm like, 'You should write this.' Like I do that, and then they're like, 'Why are you?' And I'm like, 'You should write it down 'cause I don't think you're gonna understand if I write it.'" These responses seem predictable to people who have worked in writing centers before. Clients' expectations for how a writing center session will go often clash with consultants' expectations and intentions. But what is missing in these scenes is the clients' voices. We imagine our research would have been richer if we had included follow-up interviews with clients, or even if we had been present during sessions to observe the tutoring dynamics. Additional data like this would have allowed us to triangulate our findings and perhaps allow others to build on the findings we present in order to make different and more robust claims about the habits of mind and tutor education.

In this collection, William J. Macauley, Jr. points out that student writers expressing their agency make the choice to put habits into practice when they know what options exist and find value in them. Future research that includes client voices, then, may provide an understanding of how clients conceive of their own responsibility—without reliance on tutors' perceptions. The implications for this understanding could impact not only what WCPs tell tutors about how clients perceive sessions but also how the writing center markets itself to the university.

Another opportunity for future research is to expand the pool of consultant participants. Our study included consultants who all had previous writing center experience either at the site of the study or at other writing centers. We imagine our findings might have changed somewhat if we had novice consultants who were still "figuring out" the fundamentals of their consulting work; a future study, of course, would help us understand how novice consultants negotiated the habit of mind as a heuristic for consulting, a helpful understanding given our earlier recommendation that the habits of mind be used in the context of tutor education. In addition to studying different participant populations, future research could also study other habits of mind singularly (such as metacognition *or* curiosity) or in combination with each other (such as metacognition *and* curiosity). Our study focused on responsibility, only one of eight total habits of mind. Studying additional habits would also be helpful in knowing how the habits of mind as a whole concept might function in tutor education and how clients respond to consulting that's informed by the habits of mind. We also see the possibility of taking up several of these future research possibilities and combining them, for example in a study that teaches all eight habits of mind as part of tutor education and that includes both consultants and clients as participants, leading to complex insight about the impact of the habits of mind in a writing center.

Conclusion

Responding to the novelty of the habits of mind (and the *Framework*), this study set out to describe what happened when one of the habits of mind was explicitly taught and promoted within one writing center context. We found that as a result of our workshop and the moments of reflection via the focus group and interviews, consultants in our study engaged in making definitions and strategies. That is, explicitly talking about responsibility prompted consultants to define "responsibility" for themselves and collectively as a group—a definition that was complex and multifaceted—which then informed strategies that several consultants reported using in their sessions with clients. Furthermore, because we asked our participants to see their consulting through the lens of responsibility, many reported seeing their role and the client's role in different ways than they previously did. We sensed that these new roles helped consultants do their work with more confidence and with new strategies—strategies that were not prescribed to them but were instead generated during sessions as a result of seeing their work through a lens of responsibility. We argue that the habits of mind are valuable for writing centers and for tutor education inasmuch as they require consultants to think through and about their work according to productive habits that foster learning, instead of through a technical, step-by-step method. We are eager to see this value tested and extended as the habits of mind gain prominence in the field of rhetoric and composition and in writing center studies.

Works Cited

Alexander, Jonathan, and Daniel M. Gross. "Frameworks for Failure." *Pedagogy*, vol. 16, no. 2, 2016, pp. 273–95.

Council of Writing Program Administrators. "WPA Outcomes Statement for First-Year Composition (3.0)." CWPA, 2014, wpacouncil.org/positions/outcomes.html. Accessed 18 Jan. 2020.

Council of Writing Program Administrators, National Council of Teachers of English, and National Writing Project. *Framework for Success in Postsecondary Writing*. CWPA, NCTE, and NWP, 2011, wpacouncil.org/aws/CWPA/asset_manager/get_file/350201?ver=505. Accessed 18 Jan. 2020.

Creswell, John W. *Research Design: Quantitative, Qualitative, and Mixed Methods Approaches*. Sage, 2008.

Driscoll, Dana Lynn, and Sherry Wynn Perdue. "Theory, Lore, and More: An Analysis of RAD Research in *The Writing Center Journal*, 1980–2009." *The Writing Center Journal*, vol. 32, no. 1, 2012, pp. 11–39.

—. "RAD Research as a Framework for Writing Center Inquiry: Survey and Interview Data on Writing Center Administrators' Beliefs about Research and Research Practices." *The Writing Center Journal*, vol. 34, no. 1, 2014, pp. 105–33.

Fitzgerald, Lauren, and Melissa Ianetta. *The Oxford Guide for Writing Tutors: Practice and Research*. Oxford UP, 2015.

Geller, Anne Ellen, et al. *The Everyday Writing Center: A Community of Practice*. Utah State UP, 2007.

Grutsch McKinney, Jackie. *Strategies for Writing Center Research*. Parlor P, 2015.

Johnson, Kristine. "Beyond Standards: Disciplinary and National Perspectives on Habits of Mind." *College Composition and Communication*, vol. 64, no. 3, 2013, pp. 517–41.

Lerner, Neal. "Writing Center." *A Guide to Composition Pedagogies*, edited by Gary Tate et al., Oxford UP, 2013, pp. 301–15.

Newcomb, Matthew. "Sustainability as a Design Principle for Composition: Situational Creativity as a Habit of Mind." *College Composition and Communication*, vol. 63, no. 4, 2012, pp. 593–615.

Nicklay, Jennifer. "Got Guilt? Consultant Guilt in the Writing Center Community." *The Writing Center Journal*, vol. 32, no. 1, 2012, pp. 14–27.

O'Neill, Peggy, et al. "Creating the 'Framework for Success in Postsecondary Writing.'" *College English*, vol. 74, no. 6, 2012, pp. 520–24.

Sullivan, Patrick. "Essential Habits of Mind for College Readiness." *College English*, vol. 74, no. 6, 2012, pp. 547–53.

Zimmerelli, Lisa. "A Place to Begin: Service-learning Tutor Education and Writing Center Social Justice." *The Writing Center Journal*, vol. 35, no. 1, 2015, pp. 57–83.

Appendix A: Pre-workshop Survey

Your responses to this survey will help us, Kelsie Walker and Morgan Gross, decide which of the eight habits of mind to teach in a writing center consultant development meeting soon to come in spring 2016. Please also see the attached consent form to learn more about our research project, "Requests and Outcomes: Teaching the Habits of Mind to Tutors for Their Practice," and indicate whether you wish to be included as a participant in the study.

1. Please select your age:
    a. 18–24
    b. 25–31
    c. 32–38
    d. 38 and up
    e. prefer not to answer

2. What is your gender identity?

3. What is your ethnicity?

4. What year are you at BSU [Ball State University]?
    a. first-year
    b. sophomore
    c. junior
    d. senior
    e. graduate student

5. How many semesters have you worked in the BSU writing center?

6. Please describe any experience you have working in a writing center or other kind of tutoring center or teaching environment in or out of BSU.

7. How long did you work in the writing center, tutoring center, or teaching environment?

8. What kinds of tutoring preparation and/or ongoing consultant development have you participated in (e.g., practicum courses, bi-weekly meetings, reading groups, etc.)?

9. Describe one of your tutoring strengths.

10. Describe one of your tutoring weaknesses.

11. Have you ever conducted and/or presented research in and/or about a writing center or writing center studies?
    a. Yes
    b. No

12. If you answered yes to question 11, please briefly describe the research you conducted and/or presented on.

13. Are you familiar with the habits of mind defined in the *Framework for Success in Postsecondary Writing*?
    a. Yes

b. No
c. Maybe/Somewhat

14. If you answered yes to question 13, briefly describe what you know about the habits of mind, including where you encountered them.

15. The habits of mind, according to Council of Writing Program Administrators, are "ways of approaching learning that are both intellectual and practical and that will support students' success in a variety of fields and disciplines." Of the eight habits of mind listed below, which habits do you attempt to engage students in during writing center tutoring sessions **most** often? Circle the letters for all that apply.
    a. Curiosity – the desire to know more about the world.
        i. Example: Inspiring or encouraging clients to ask questions about their writing, their writing topic, or the writing process
            1. Briefly describe your experience(s).
    b. Openness – the willingness to consider new ways of being and thinking in the world.
        i. Example: Engaging clients in interrogating their race, class, gender, sexuality, age, or ability in order to understand opposing or differing perspectives for an argument assignment
            1. Briefly describe your experience(s).
    c. Engagement – a sense of investment and involvement in learning.
        i. Example: Making space for student clients to take initiative for the development of a writing center session and make decisions about their writing
            1. Briefly describe your experience(s).
    d. Creativity – the ability to use novel approaches for generating, investigating, and representing ideas.
        i. Example: Asking clients to arrive at an idea by doing an activity such as free-writing, making a visual map, or altering the layout of ideas in a project
            1. Briefly describe your experience(s).
    e. Persistence – the ability to sustain interest in and attention to short- and long-term projects.
        i. Example: Discussing with clients the goals and plans

they have for completing their project; encouraging clients to stick to their plans
   1. Briefly describe your experience(s).
f. Responsibility – the ability to take ownership of one's actions and understand the consequences of those actions for oneself and others.
   i. Example: Making clients aware and asking clients to acknowledge the consequences of their procrastination on a project
   1. Briefly describe your experience(s).
g. Flexibility – the ability to adapt to situations, expectations, or demands.
   i. Example: Helping students to rhetorically analyze and respond to their situation for a given writing assignment, which entails distinguishing it from other kinds of writing assignments
   1. Briefly describe your experience(s).
h. Metacognition – the ability to reflect on one's own thinking as well as on the individual and cultural processes used to structure knowledge.
   i. Example: Reflecting with clients about the decisions they have made while composing and how those decisions affect (and are affected by) the author and the audience
   1. Briefly describe your experience(s).

Appendix B: Workshop Handout

Cultivating Responsibility with/in Student Writers

The Habits of Mind (from the Council of WPAs) aim to develop students' rhetorical knowledge, critical thinking, writing processes, knowledge of conventions, and ability to compose in multiple environments. They are ways of approaching learning to support students' success in a variety of disciplines, and they are fostered in reading, writing, and analysis.

curiosity ⁕ openness ⁕ engagement ⁕ creativity ⁕ persistence ⁕ **responsibility** ⁕ metacognition ⁕ flexibility

Responsibility is the habit of mind that tutors in our Writing Center have reported being least likely to engage students in during their sessions. *What does responsibility mean to you?*

 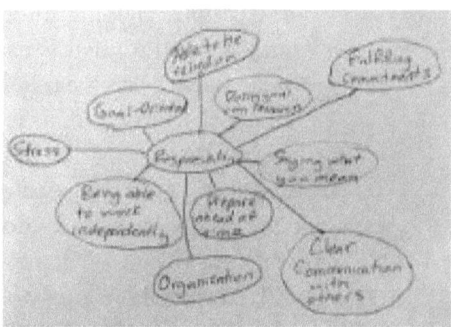

Images 1 & 2: Tutor-made representations of responsibility from brainstorming activity in workshop (February 26, 2016)

Definitions of Responsibility

- (self) accountability
- meeting others' expectations (and your own)
   - yet (how to) balance the two
- self-reflective choices
- awareness of being self-motivated and prepared
- awareness of sacrificial nature of responsibility
   - obligations
- be responsible to yourself by taking care of yourself
   - what are you capable/not capable of?
- qualities of a responsible person: resourceful, organized

From the Framework for Success

Responsibility is "the ability to take ownership of one's actions and understand the consequences of those actions for oneself and others."

Habits of Mind Workshop | Morgan Gross & Kelsie Walker | February 26, 2016

> How does "responsibility" manifest in your writing center sessions?

What are some strategies tutors can use to foster students' responsibility?
- offer strategies, not solutions
    - free writing, outlining, contacting the professor--in order to understand the assignment better
- encourage student to tap into their own knowledge/expertise about the course/course content (as a way to help the client take responsibility of their learning)
- frame yourself (the tutor) as a reader/audience member so the client is "responsible" to you to listen to suggestions
- gentle reminders to clients about their role in the session
- pose "leading" questions that guide the client to resolve the issue/problem/question in their text
- offer the client strategies, tips that they can use on their own time
    - point our patterns of error and teach a quick lesson on the grammar/punctuation rule that they can apply later
- point clients to resources they can access after the session

APPENDIX C: WRITING CENTER SESSION SCENARIOS FROM WORKSHOP

SCENARIO 1

Alex is a third-year undergraduate student studying psychology. She made a face-to-face appointment with the writing center and brought in an assignment sheet for her PSYC 350 course because she remembers the writing center tour given by a tutor earlier in the semester and that the writing center "helps writers in all stages of the writing process." She has no idea how to start the assignment or where to begin. She begins the session frustrated and somewhat resistant to the tutor's questions about what she already knows about the assignment. Alex comments that she "just wants someone to tell her how to do it." How would you engage with/respond to Alex?

Scenario 2

Andrea is a first-year undergraduate student studying English—creative writing. She made an online appointment to work on a rough draft of her screenplay because her instructor has offered extra credit for doing so. She is excited about the assignment and satisfied with what she has written already. She begins the session by chatting with the tutor about the assignment and the screenplay. When the tutor makes suggestions about where Andrea could take the plot, the student appears to ignore the tutor's suggestions by "resolving" any questions or comments the tutor makes in the Google Doc. How would you engage with/respond to Andrea?

Scenario 3

Gerry is a second-year undergraduate student studying biology. He made a face-to-face appointment to work with a tutor on a research report that's based on research he has conducted. He has been to the writing center before for help on lab reports, so he thinks the writing center can help him with his research report. He identifies that he wants feedback on grammar and the overall sound of the report. When the tutor asks him questions about the origin of his sources and the clarity of his citations, he says, "that's just what they do in Biology," and then continues reading the report. How would you engage with/respond to Gerry?

Scenario 4

Liz, a non-native English speaker, is a third-year PhD student working on her dissertation proposal. She asks her tutor for help editing/proofreading the 38-page paper, which is due to her dissertation chair tomorrow. Unfortunately, Liz has a lot of mistakes with local issues in her writing, especially word choice and sentence structure, that make the paper confusing and unclear in places. You recognize early in the session that you won't be able to discuss the entire paper with her in your allotted time together, but Liz consistently and desperately pressures you to work faster *and* point out every error. How do you handle this?

Appendix D: Focus Group Questions

1. Based on the initial surveys we asked you to fill out, we identified that "responsibility" was the habit of mind that most of you were least likely to engage student clients in during their writing center sessions. We didn't ask *why* that is. Please speak to it now if you can.
2. Have we discussed the habits of mind, as an approach to student learning, adequately so that you understand what it is? If so, have you bought into the idea that the habits of mind are a useful tool for writing center tutors? Please explain.
3. What did you learn from our workshop on "responsibility"? (What do you remember from it? What stood out to you as helpful, informative, or interesting to consider?)
4. Has the instruction on "responsibility"—or our discussions on the habits of mind, more generally—had an impact of any kind on your personal tutoring practice? (Has it had an impact on your own approach to learning/writing?) If so, how do you see it affecting what you do?
5. If you believe instruction on "responsibility" as a habit of mind has impacted your tutoring practice, what are the consequences, from your own perspective, for the clients with whom you work? (Recall specific moments or stories with details, if possible.)
6. Would you like to have additional consultant development or continued support about tutoring with the habits of mind? If so, what kind of support would be most helpful to you?
7. We mentioned at the end of the "responsibility" instruction that "openness" was the habit of mind that was next, after responsibility, for least likely to be used by tutors in sessions, and we encouraged you all to think about what openness means as an approach to learning and how you might engage students strategically in openness when you work with them on their writing. Have any of you been able to do this, and would you speak to your ideas/experiences?
8. We didn't have time to teach all of the habits of mind, which is why we selected one, responsibility, to focus on previously. Are

there any other habits of mind you would like to spend a few minutes discussing now, though? (curiosity, openness, engagement, creativity, persistence, responsibility, flexibility, metacognition)
9. Is there anything else you'd like to add to this discussion, something we haven't asked about directly, for our research?

Appendix E: Interview Questions

Cassidy

1. Since our focus group session, have you had even more instances of encouraging student clients to develop responsibility for their learning in your consultations? If so, please tell me about those moments.
2. In the focus group, you shared an interesting story about how you used personal experience to make it easier to have the "awkward" conversation about a student needing to do more to prepare for his upcoming writing proficiency exam. It seems to me that a tutor's position (as undergrad, grad TA, etc.) might play a role in the strategies they use to encourage students' growth in terms of their use of the habits of mind. Do you think this is true? Can you talk more about strategies, especially as they relate to positionality?
3. As someone who has been working in the writing center for a while now, can you share your thoughts on the responsibility consultant development workshop Kelsie and I facilitated? How useful was it to you, in terms of both content and delivery, compared to other preparation/development activities you've participated in? Why do you think that is?
4. Has your understanding of responsibility as a habit of mind changed since we worked collaboratively on a definition for it? If so, how and why? (Here is what we came up with previously:
    a. (self) accountability
    b. meeting others' expectations (and your own)
        i. yet (how to) balance these two
    c. self-reflective choices
    d. awareness of being self-motivated and prepared
    e. awareness of sacrificial nature of responsibility
        i. Obligations

            f. be responsible to yourself by taking care of yourself
                i. what are you capable/not capable of?
            g. qualities of a responsible person: resourceful, organized)
    5. You mentioned in the focus group that it might be "harder" to use certain, e.g. physical, strategies to cultivate students' responsibility in online sessions. Do you want to elaborate on this idea now?
    6. Do you have any additional thoughts you want to share on our research project or stories you want to tell that are related to it? Anything about the habits of mind for use in consulting? About students' responses to that? About consultant development?

APRYLL

1. Since our last focus group meeting, how have you seen responsibility playing out in your sessions with students?
2. Has your definition of responsibility changed since the focus group? If so, how has it changed? Can you point to moments in your tutoring that have shifted/altered/built your definition or understanding of responsibility?
3. In the focus group, you talked about a session where the client was resistant at first but then they came up with a plan to "freewrite and put things together and then come back to [their] introduction when [their] thoughts were more clear," which you commented was a good thing. What other strategies that promote responsibility have you promoted or have you seen students engaging with?
4. You also said during the focus group that you are the queen of waiting, and I think you were referring to online sessions. Can you talk more about this? Do you also use this in f2f sessions?
5. You commented, too, that students are often "spoon-fed" through their education. Can you speak to this phenomenon? Why do you think it's the case and how does it affect tutoring? What, then, is the tutor's role in helping students cultivate responsibility?
6. Do you have other ideas, questions, or thoughts about the habits of mind in general or about responsibility?

13 THE *FRAMEWORK* WILL NOT HOLD WITHOUT A CENTER

William J. Macauley, Jr.

The *Framework for Success in Postsecondary Writing*, even in its title, argues that writing at the college-level is different. The Council of Writing Program Administrator's "Outcomes Statement for First-Year Composition" ("OS") and the *Framework* read *fait accompli*, except wicked problems (Rittel and Webber). One such problem is what precipitated the *Framework*, which is that post-secondary writing requires change at fundamental of thinking. These changes are neither simple nor easy, but they are all the responsibility of the student writers themselves. No one can make these changes for them. That leads to another wicked problem, which is how to facilitate these very different kinds of thinking and practice in classrooms that will seem, especially to new college students, all too familiar and seldom evocative of these new expectations. A third wicked problem in the *Framework* and the "OS" is that, for these kinds of intensive and impactful changes within individual minds, depending on classrooms alone is not going to work. The process articulated between the *Framework* and the "OS" can seem complete, or at least closed, but how can it be so without including expanded learning opportunities for the kinds of expanded learning anticipated? How can this happen without the active participation of the primary agent whose writing is the focus of the entire process—the student writer? Students learning new ways must have opportunities to practice where risks aren't discouraged, where mistakes are part of the learning process, where they can speak to and about their individual questions and concerns. Individual habits of mind are acquired, so individuals must be supported in their unique processes of development. What the *Framework* needs and doesn't include is writing centers and the agentive, self-efficacious writers that result from the important and unique work writing centers do. Differentiated, individual changes simply cannot be accomplished by undifferentiated, collective means.

In the rest of this chapter, I make a case for writing centers empowering individual agentive student writers. Writing centers facilitate what I see as the *Framework*'s three primary habits of mind essential to agentive student writing anticipated by the *Framework*: engagement, persistence, and responsibility. I will describe the importance of student writer agency in each habit of mind, what writing centers do that facilitate them, and what the results can be in terms of students not only adopting but successfully deploying these habits of mind.

Writing Centers, Agentive Student Writers, and Fulfilling the Promise of the Framework

It was an oversight on the part of the *Framework* developers to exclude writing centers from a document framing experiences for success in postsecondary writing. Every day, writing centers support student writing, reading, and critical analysis. Writing center environments facilitate habits of mind through developing student writer thinking, reading and writing with knowledgeable, prepared consultants. Scholars argue that writing centers are the only resources to this important role based on at least one-to-one attention and freedom from disciplinary bias (Waldo).

Writing centers grew out of the nineteenth century United States' realization that (1) direct/differentiated instruction is a most productive writing pedagogy and (2) institutions of higher education simply could not provide such attention to every student within the confines of the traditional classroom (Lerner). Tutors had been a part of Western higher education long before then, going back at least as far as the fourteenth century in western Europe, always providing individualized attention to students as a complement to institutional resources (De Ridder-Symoens 132). Tutoring variations have in large part been responsive to the students and contexts that it served. In the era of open admissions, Stephen North's "The Idea of a Writing Center" had to establish that writing centers had a richer purpose than what faculty were then seeming to assume. North writes,

> in a writing center the object is to make sure that writers, and not necessarily their texts, are what get changed by instruction.

> In axiom form it goes like this: Our job is to produce better writers, not better writing. Any given project—a class assignment, a law school application letter, an encyclopedia entry, a dissertation proposal—is for the writer the prime, often the exclusive concern. That particular text, its success or failure, is what brings them to talk to us in the first place. In the center, though, we look beyond or through that particular project, that particular text, and see it as an occasion for addressing our primary concern, the process by which it is produced. (438)

Tutoring (and writing centers) has constantly adapted and changed; North was fighting the idea of remediation in the mid-1980s and, by the mid -1990s, tutors had become a status symbol in the US (Jordan "Private," "Tutors"). Many who have been in writing centers since then, like me, will share stories of the marvelous changes that have brought writing centers out from under staircases in the back corners of forgotten buildings and into the mainstream of campuses and writing curricula. Writing centers simply don't have to be "dirty little secrets" anymore (Boquet). The history of tutoring in general, and writing centers particularly, is one of focusing on the development of the individual learner rather than on demonstrated collective learning. This means, in reference to the *Framework*, that writing centers are readily visible and available, well-suited, well-positioned, and well-prepared to support active, agentive student writers' essential habits of mind.

Two ways that writing centers contrast most with more traditional academic settings are where they start and how they proceed. Standard practice in writing centers includes building rapport through introductions and discussion before diving into any text (Gillespie and Lerner). When students in the classroom or lab do this kind of context development in small groups or one-on-one, it is often seen as being off-task because they haven't jumped straight to the task at hand. This is a luxury that is built into common writing center practice but too often absent in the writing classroom.

From there, consultants will often ask open-ended questions to get the students talking about their work, to get a sense of where the writer is in relation to the writing they have done and to get a better idea of writers' challenges in thinking, process, and product. Together, based on dialogue, consultants will then collaboratively set an agenda for the consultation, which ensures writers' interests are responded to while allowing the consultant to bring their expertise to the session in meaningful ways (Macauley, Jr.). It may be most essential that, in these early stages of the consultation, the focus is on higher-order or content concerns—not accuracy or correctness but content and thinking (McAndrew and Reigstad). This validates the writer as a thinker while it allows the consultant to find out if the "problems" in the piece are about knowledge or expression or both.

There are reasons why writing centers can accomplish some of these goals, while it is much more difficult and sometimes impossible for writing classrooms to do so. One explanation sees the writing center as a unique space, as what Hakim Bey calls a "temporary autonomous zone." A TAZ is characterized by is temporality, its liminality; in short, it is not sustained or continuing. A TAZ is also characterized by the autonomy one experiences there; a student in a consultation will never have exactly the same experience twice and can have so much more control and authority over their work than in a teacher-led classroom.

Bey was also very careful to use the term *zone* rather than location or space. This is significant because it is not about *where* it happens as much as *that* it happens or *what/how* it happens. TAZ is an experience rather than a location, as is a writing center. Elizabeth Bouquet asks whether a writing center is a space or an illusory "temporality" (464). The answer is yes—it can be both. Students can certainly visit a writing center, and students can be equally creative in repurposing spaces for writing, acts of both agency and self-efficacy. Edward Soja describes more extended examples as "thirdspace," spontaneous and unplanned activity in a space designed for other purposes. Students can speak with consultants almost anywhere; there are no furnishing requirements. Thus, not only are writing centers apt theoretically and pedagogically for supporting agentive student writers and the *Framework*, but they can do so almost anywhere, anytime and actually be expressions of student writer agency and self-efficacy as "pop-ups" of those writers' own making.

My background in writing centers colors my thinking more than I sometimes realize. I don't think this grounding is a bad thing, of course, because my writing-centeredness sensitizes me to students as owners of their work, to their roles as active learners, and to just how empowering the teaching of writing can be when it respects both. As a consultant, there has been real excitement when I could see writers actively negotiate what they *have to do* in writing with what they *want to do* with their ideas. As a teacher with this kind of background, I have been particularly interested in stepping back so student writers can make decisions about what they want their writing to accomplish, as opposed to their passively fulfilling my requirements or producing textual objects that too often seem isolated and evaluated based on arbitrary peeves. These interests and experiences make the *Framework* a particularly engaging document for its ambitions and potentials.

A reason for this emphasis on writing centers in support of the *Framework* is the centrality of student writer decision-making in writing center practice. Key scholarship that both developed and sustains writing center practice emphasizes the importance of guiding student writers, facilitating their decision-making, rather than making decisions for them (Gillespie and Lerner; McAndrew and Reigstad; Ryan and Zimmerelli). Thus, writing center scholarship has always embraced the idea of "making better writers," possibly to the degree that it has become a foregone conclusion in most centers. Even at the most fundamental and functional levels, the assumption of respecting student writer decision-making is emphasized through practices such as asking open-ended questions about the work at hand, collaborative agenda-setting, and guided planning for what happens after the consultation. Ideally, a student writer cannot participate in a writing center session without being agentive (a recognized decision-maker) and self-efficacious (acting on that role). Thus, writing centers are prime locations for both understanding what student writer agency and self-efficacy might look like and what conditions contribute to amplifying them.

Not unlike ancient Western teachers (e.g., Plato, Cicero, Quintilian), the emphasis is on the person/mind first and the practices/products afterward. This makes writing centers potentially important locations in the discussion of student writer agency and self-efficacy. This brings us to looking at writing centers in two ways. First, student writers typically interact with writing center consultants in ways that call for articulation and decision-making (and provides practice with both) about writing processes, goals, and options. Student writers assume and deploy a great deal of agency and self-efficacy in writing centers because writing centers "put student writers in the driver's seat" (Ryan and Zimmerelli).

The writing center is also an essential location for understanding student writer agency and self-efficacy because of reduced teacher authority/evaluation. Consultations rely on student representations of teacher expectations, as well as writer interests. This is not to suggest that faculty instructions or feedback are ignored but, rather, that the student writer makes all of the decisions about how to respond while the consultant simply asks questions and provides options. Because the teacher cannot play a role separate from teacher and because, within a consultation, the student is forced to make decisions, writing center staff are trained explicitly not to make decisions for writers (and shouldn't).

These interactions can result in a great deal of understanding of agentive student writers. There are other factors that contribute to knowing students who take first-year composition (FYC). Much scholarship on young adult psychology focuses on young adults' seemingly high propensity for risk-taking (Blakemore and Robbins; Males). Recent scholarship shows that the segments of the brain/mind responsible for emotion develop earlier than do those focused on executive or decision-making functions (Nagel). Dobbs argues this might be considered an evolutionary transition from childhood to adulthood and, thus, a time when rules and regulations are tested not out of arbitrariness or oppositional thinking but out of working to become successful adults. One important potential function of a writing center might be the opportunity to explore decisions in a low-stakes setting absent authority figures. In writing classrooms, students can often be more risk-averse if they worry that their risk-taking will be graded.

Susan Ambrose et al. summarize the literature on the development of thinking in young adults in a pattern that moves roughly from dualities (good/bad) to multiplicity (everyone has an opinion) to relativism (all opinions can be evaluated and not all opinions are equal) to commitment (provisionally choosing to develop further thinking). Sprague and Stuart offer another continuum that runs from unconscious incompetence to conscious incompetence to conscious competence to unconscious competence. In the former paradigm, a student's development is understood in relation to the ability to deal with ideas and concepts that may or may not fit neatly into available categories. In the latter, the development is more about awareness and facility. Together, these schemas provide a complex representation of young adults not only developing in terms of their internal cognitive habits but external processes of becoming more adept at what they do. This parallels nicely the relationship between agency and self-efficacy, as well as the acquisition of new habits of mind, which could arguably be presented as internal conditions with external expressions of those conditions. Thus, in terms of adding the eight habits of mind advocated by the *Framework*, it seems reasonable that both must be attended to with some care and diligence.

These transitions are further complicated by societal conditions. Alina Tugend and Carol Dweck each argue that Western cultures do not generally deal productively with errors, which are essential to this kind of learning. Dweck is well-known to argue that we tend much more toward a "fixed mindset," which would likely interpret mistakes as indicators of having run into a cognitive capacity threshold, than we do toward a "growth mindset," which is more likely to see mistakes as part of the learning process, as indicators of continued development. Much of this discussion also depends on "locus of control" (Rotter); if the locus of control is external (the teacher, the parent, the principal, etc.), the fixed mindset is more likely because the roles and responsibilities for change are understood as external. The growth mindset tends to be much more associated with an internal locus of control because the freedom to see mistakes as development is closely associated with one's internal sense of ongoing learning.

So, why does all of this matter for our discussion of habits of mind, agentive student writers, and writing centers in relation to the *Framework*? Well, as is the case with so many constructs designed at a global level for local uses, the *Framework* treating the students as a unified whole to which we can respond singularly is problematic. Inoue has argued that when writing assessments start from homogeneity rather than diversity, we necessarily lose many of the essential details of the learners we seek to support. Working, for instance, from teachers toward their courses makes sense in terms of creating a document that is broadly focused and articulate at the curricular level, but it can also be misunderstood to imply that all students will or should come to our classes similarly prepared or matured. Thus, it seems wiser to think very thoroughly about our end beneficiaries—students—when we strive to inform the *Framework* in these ways. Writing centers, as complements to classroom instruction and internal student developments, can provide learning experiences that allow for levels of individuation that cannot be accomplished in large classroom settings.

It could be argued that more academic reward for appropriate risk-taking could be helpful, especially if those risk opportunities were couched in better understanding outcomes and future successes. Helping students to work progressively from dualities through a process of reflecting on and through their intellectual development would be advisable, even if only to get students conscious of the decisions they are making and the ways they are thinking about those decisions. Then, after lunch . . .

This is quite a charge for one person, teacher or student, to take on. In fact, it is not realistic to expect any instructor to be this aware and conscious of each individual student in any course, let alone feel confident that their students are developmentally ready for this. However, unlike the way that the *Framework* is construed, this is not the work of any student or teacher alone. It is a shared mission with student writers and, I would argue, other writing resources on most campuses, most especially writing centers.

AN AGENTIVE WRITER HAS TO BE ACTIVATED IN THE FRAMEWORK

The agentive student writer is the most essential participant in any plan such as the *Framework* and, thus, should be emphasized as the activator of the "foundations for success in writing in college-level, credit-bearing courses" (CWPA et al. 2). It is student writers who must have, develop, and apply the "Habits of Mind and experiences that are critical for college success" (CWPA et al. 1). It is student writers who not only do the writing, reading, and critical analyzing but do all three consciously. They eventually apply those activities intellectually and textually to the production of documents that are evaluated and assessed for the recommended results of FYC in both the *Framework* and the "OS." In many cases, the students themselves are evaluated on the bases of their successful demonstration of these outcomes. In truth, no one else can do this work. There is an assumption of agency and self-efficacy inherent in the building of these systems, even if there are not always the resources and emphasis to enable them.

"Agency" here is based on Albert Bandura's 1989 foundational definition. Agency is acknowledging that one has at least the potential for an active relationship with a task or practice. In some ways this is reflective of what Rotter has deemed an "internal locus of control." Self-efficacy, on the other hand, is not an internal condition or sense as much as a combined understanding/action based on them. Agency is seeing oneself as an actor, and self-efficacy is acting on that sense. According to Bandura, self-efficacy is based on agency and includes intention, forethought, self-reactivity, and self-reflectivity: what one would like to do, how one might go about it, how one has gone about doing similar tasks in the past, and how what one has done in the past has worked out. This combination, agency and self-efficacy, is largely internal because it is about getting to action rather than what the actions themselves are. These "getting tos" can include habits of mind such as engagement, responsibility, and metacognition, as well as the other habits of mind (CWPA et al. 4–5). An "agentive student writer" is both agentive and self-efficacious, recognizes both their active role in a writing activity and decides for themselves whether and how to act on it. An agentive student writer decides what they want to do with their writing and pursues that outcome. The acquisition of new habits of mind become reflexive. In this construction habits of mind can be predictive and reflective; they can respond to inquiries and requirements; they can develop in response to assignments and inform required writing as a product of deeper thinking.

Ellen Usher and Frank Pajares identified four kinds of experiences that promote agency and self-efficacy (mastery, vicarious, social, and physiological). Any of these experiences can be relevant to student writing at the post-secondary level, but our focus here will be student writers striving for mastery of the qualities and processes of writing recommended in both the *Framework* and the "OS." In a very overt way, I am equating "success in postsecondary writing" with mastery. Bandura ("Toward") also notes three different types of agency (individual, proxy, and collective); each is developed and expressed in very different contexts and toward very different purposes. The *Framework* seems less accommodating to writer advocates ("proxy agency") or collaborative writers ("collective agency") as the focus of its efforts so, for our purposes here, we will focus on individual agency. Agency is no panacea, however; it is not always positive or purposeful. One can have agency without acting (*not* acting is a choice, too). One can act decisively in what might be described by others as unproductive ways. One cannot act or choose not to act without agency or self-efficacy, though. The risk of encouraging agency and self-efficacy is that the choices and means of activating them are more or less in the hands of the agent. Teachers who seek specific recognizable and/or consistent processes or outcomes may not want to encourage individual agency or self-efficacy. They may want to keep the "locus of control" external to their students (Rotter). The more agency and self-efficacy students have and deploy, the less control and consistency will likely be available to teachers.

Agency and self-efficacy are means. Agentive student writers are not immune to mistakes. They are, after all, learning. Mistakes and missteps are part of the process, but they have to be understood and managed in ways that limit if not exclude damage to student writers' senses of their confidence. Agency and self-efficacy, in relation to the *Framework* are about students occupying writerly roles and taking on the challenges of being writers, as active participants who are learning and communicating through writing for the writers' purposes. Mistakes will be made, and those mistakes have to be available as positive contributions to the larger developmental goals of "making better writers" or, to be more accurate, agentive student writers participating in their own becoming more successful post-secondary writers. Dweck would characterize this thinking as a "growth mindset" for the writers, as a mindset that sees errors as part of learning.

We must take care not to objectify or homogenize student writers as it is these varied young people who are in the processes of becoming successful post-secondary writers, who take on the experiences of trying and erring. These are people whose concepts of themselves and of their own abilities are being challenged in the present and future (but never without the context of their pasts in academics). That needs to be taken very seriously. Those students should not be misled, neither into thinking that they have no significant role to play in their learning nor into believing that they are alone in it. I benefited from having been told neither.

I was a nontraditional student, at least four years older than most of the others in my classes, self-supporting, commuting, working full-time, and attending university full-time as well. I was eager for any kind of confirmation that I knew something that counted, but I also understood that I was there because I didn't know much more. I wasn't as afraid of my mistakes as I was of being discounted or found out as an imposter. I knew I had the support of knowledgeable faculty who seemed to care about what happened to me. I felt that; I knew that because they took the time to get to know me, to talk with me about how I was thinking and how to get through the challenges I was facing in my schoolwork. I often recall, even now, a book Steve Rowe had us read in a Philosophy class: William Barlett's *The Illusion of Technique*. Bartlett stays with me particularly in one quote:

> The teacher may give us certain quite simple and mechanical rules to get started. But if the pupil persists and develops, he eventually reaches a point where the teacher has to tell him he is on his own, and there is no prescribed technique that will paint his picture for him. (22)

Even now, some forty years later, they remember me and I them. Even though I wouldn't have then known to think about it in this way, it was an ideal balance of autonomy and support, of agency and community.

While Bartlett describes the end of a teacher's instruction, Brenda Ueland describes that same point of departure from a different point of view when she writes "you must freely and recklessly make new mistakes—in writing or in life—and do not fret about them but pass on and write more" (101). In both cases, agency is required of the student/writer, not because they have to do it all alone but because there is learning that must be acquired through taking on the risks and tasks oneself, because there is a point at which the learning is so personalized and unique to each learner that the generalizable just doesn't work anymore. Certainly, an assignment could be designed and completed wherein student writers might complete a set of documentable steps that an instructor decides represents agentive decision-making, but that may not represent anything more than compliance with an assignment. Thus, because the thinking and skills/practices in the *Framework* must be choices made and valued individually, the agent making those choices must be supported in them individually, as an agentive student writer. Because the processes that the *Framework* expects are intrusive and cumulative, sequential and active, they cannot be prescribed generically because each student will encounter them differently, respond to them differently, and handle them differently. If the *Framework* purports to encroach on students' minds and shape their writing, the students must be directly and deliberately involved in those processes. That said, agentive student writers require support and resources that allow them to thoughtfully and individually develop their habits of mind, writing, reading, critical analysis, toward the recommended objectives outlined in the *Framework* and in the "OS," and the classroom represented in the *Framework* is not going to be sufficient.

Habits of Mind and the Agentive Student Writer

Before getting into where this work needs to be done, it is important to articulate more thoroughly what that work will be. Habits of mind are neither readily accessed nor easily understood, let alone changed. Studying and understanding what goes on in the minds of student writers has continued to present significant challenges. Janet Emig's 1971 *The Com-*

posing Processes of Twelfth Graders was one of the earliest studies to gain any insight into the working minds of student writers. The results were revelatory in the sense that no prior studies had been able to gather such useful and insightful data. Although the innovation and importance of Emig's research can't be overstated, speak-aloud protocols captured only a part of what writers might have been thinking. More recent research suggests that the mind is thinking at somewhere between three and six times the speed of average speaking (assuming that a sentence represents a thought) (Sasson). This doesn't even consider the filtering that participants may have been doing to ensure what they said was "good" in any way. Others like Linda Flower and John Hayes and many after, have continued to explore these questions, and we have made strides, no doubt, but the bulk of research on student writer agency and self-efficacy has happened in other fields. Within Writing Studies, we discuss agency with some ease even while we have, within our own field, only relatively recently begun to explore it in depth.

All eight of the *Framework*'s habits of mind rely in some essential way on a student writer's agency and self-efficacy. First, there is no question that all eight habits of mind require a first assumption that the student is the one acting on learning. None of these are passive constructs; none of these habits of mind are entirely unconscious if they are being fostered or taught or amplified by teaching or experiences in the classroom. They are choices, choices about what role the student writer wants to play in relation to learning, using information, and applying what is learned. In short, students are trained into these habits or choose these habits, and to choose them, they must understand and believe that the choices are available. These are not genetically indicated or geographically sourced—they are taught and/or learned, chosen and/or practiced.

Second, for these practices to become habitual, they must be valued by the student. As Dr. Phil often says, we only keep doing what is rewarded. For students to believe in them, these habits of mind must result in positive outcomes. In some cases, where students' agency is weak or where a fixed mindset is too thoroughly established, change can only come when the limitations of the former ways of thinking are revealed as high-cost and the successes of the new options clearly and/or more consistently positive. In some important ways, curiosity for instance, must act as a kind of extreme optimism, a belief that one cannot only look into things that are not familiar without benefitting significantly by doing so. This may be one of the places where the claim of young adults' predilections for unnecessary risk-taking is contradicted (Blakemore and Robbins; Dobbs; Males). In my experience, first-year composition (FYC) students have been much less willing to take risks with their writing because of their perceptions of norms that discourage doing so. This may be an apt example of perceived social norming taking precedence over individual choices, of social or collective agency overruling mastery or individual agency. In any event, it is clear that instruction is not enough; these habits of mind must be adopted consciously, highly rewarding, and reiterated positively in practice with some frequency.

Third, each of the habits of mind must be confirmed as valuable and valid by respected educational mentors, and the more the better. When a student is enrolled in four classes where reviewing the PowerPoint slides for the next quiz is the primary teaching and learning activity and the fifth class wants them to be curious and explore their thinking about writing as self-expression, the cognitive dissonance will be deafening. I have been teaching FYC since 1989 and, to be frank, a lot of the work I have done over the years in that course has been dissuading students from their formulas and forms for successful academic writing, which they guard with incredible zeal and determination. They have to see that a change in their writing makes a difference in their grade way before they will even start to consider that a change in the way they think will make a difference in the way they write. Truth be told, first-semester and first-year students are often overwhelmed. They have a lot on their plates in just learning how to be in college and take care of themselves and manage their social lives and hold jobs and do their laundry and . . . So, it's no small feat to convince them that a new way to think about their writing in school is going to be better, unless they can see results pretty quickly.

But many students do acquiesce. Many do try on new ways of thinking about their writing. Sometimes they try new ways of thinking about their writing because they don't like the grades they are getting. Some don't like the way they have to kill themselves to get their writing done. Some want the writing to work better. Some visit the writing center and find that process more pleasant and productive and want to allow more time for consultations. Some really like writing and want to get better. But, in all of these scenarios, for all of these and a million other reasons, these student writers are recognizing that they can choose differently and then act on those choices. These are agentive student writers who are engaging in habits of writing mind.

Instead of examining all eight of the *Framework*'s Habits of Mind in detail, I will focus on three that are primary to agentive student writing: engagement, persistence, and responsibility. These three are primary for a couple of reasons. First, they represent the most fundamental commitments to writing—investing in the writing, sustaining interest in the writing, and taking ownership of the writing. Second, without these three habits of mind solidly in place, the others are not available. Without a sense of investment, curiosity cannot be sustained; without persistence, there is no need to be open to new ways of being or thinking; without responsibility, adaptation is unnecessary, and metacognition is not useful. However, all of that said, in the discussion of these three primary habits of mind and their relationships to agentive student writing and the activation of the *Framework*, I will also articulate how the secondary habits of mind are enabled.

ENGAGEMENT

Sometimes, the best we can hope for in our teaching is providing students with opportunities to become involved. We have all seen those students who are clearly not paying attention, not engaged in discussion, not responding to feedback, not active in group work. These are often described as social issues, but if we believe that students can choose them, we have to also believe that students do choose them. I think this is what the *Framework* means by engagement, "a sense of investment and involvement in learning" (4). We all make decisions every day about what we engage with and what we do not. Students and learning are no different, with the caveat that their prior academic experiences could have discouraged or encouraged individualized interests. It may be that some students need only trust that engagement is a viable option while others have decided that it is not, which would be an unfortunate possible outcome of agency and self-efficacy.

Curiosity, another habit of mind, depends on engagement because curiosity is both sustained by and dependent on it. It is sustained in the sense that it means being able to confidently pursue tangents, to look into something that may turn out to be nothing, to look around at other options and ideas even while you know where you are already planning to go. Curiosity can also mean finding out what others think, maybe even those you know will disagree. This all takes time, and that time is a result of engagement. Curiosity is also dependent for all of these reasons, because it is always beginning from, contingent upon, related to the engagement that a writer has with the project at hand. Curiosity without purpose can sometimes be productive, but curiosity with engagement can much more often become productivity. Openness, another habit of mind, is a big result of engagement and curiosity because being open to new ideas and avenues of inquiry for oneself makes being open to others all the more appealing and comfortable. Engagement means curious and open on some levels anyway, doesn't it?

Persistence

Persistence in the *Framework* is "the ability to sustain interest in and attention to short- and long-term projects" (5). Persistence is a choice, but not a choice made in isolation. While ultimately we all have to choose to persist or not, it must be acknowledged that this decision is not made in a vacuum and can be influenced by any number of variables. That said, though, the person who persists is the one who chooses to do so. Recognizing one's decision-making role relative to persistence is a hallmark of the successful college student, and the student's recognition of their ability to make those choices is essential. When students see their educations as happening to them and their work as valuable only in terms of what others think and say, those students are on a path that makes persistence increasingly difficult.

Persistence is probably one of the most overtly conscious of the habits of mind because it is so easy to choose otherwise. To persist, one must be creative. If you are writing a paper and the argument is just not working, you must find another way—and it is creativity that allows you to consider what that other way might be. If the sources you are finding simply don't support the conclusions you want to reach, a flexible thinker and writer is better able to come up with alternatives that could range from taking a different position based on what the research is showing to scrapping the topic and starting over with something else. This is the agent—who has a role to play—self-efficaciously/persistently pursuing their objectives through creativity and flexibility.

Responsibility

Responsibility is a curious phenomenon. In some ways it is externalized, in the sense that, if one seems responsible, options may become available that are not there for those deemed less so, not responsible, or irresponsible. However, the *Framework*'s emphasis on responsibility is internal: "the ability to take ownership of one's actions and understand the consequences of those actions for oneself and others" (1). It does not seem entirely reasonable to expect this kind of predictive capacity given that young adults are building their decision-making reserves and have so frequently had limited experience with these responsibilities. Especially considering that the *Framework* is built to reveal (and therein acknowledges) a new set of habits of mind necessary to success in writing at the post-secondary level. The *Framework* would be better acclimated to the young adults it intends to support by arguing not for the demonstration of responsibility but for its development. In either case, there seems little question that agency and self-efficacy are key.

Responsibility is so often something seen in plans looking forward and actions reviewed, which is why metacognition, while a separate habit of mind in the *Framework*, is such an integral part of responsibility. Reviewing one's thinking is key to reflection and improvement. Just as the *Framework* begins with habits of mind, so would any process of development and progress begin with the thinking that underlies it. Metacognition can contribute at all stages throughout a writing project, for instance, especially for an agentive student writer, and that contribution can be particularly rich in the stages that Usher and Pajares call "self-reactivity" and "self-reflection," key components to self-efficacy. Both are metacognitive and responsible participation in ongoing development of mind and practice.

Agentive student writers engage the habits of mind listed in the Framework as they develop and act in their roles as thinker, decision maker, reader, critical analyst, process developer, writer, researcher, and any number of other tasks and responsibilities they take on when they are writing in the post-secondary environment. But they cannot be expected to pick up all of these responsibilities on their own, without support (or all in FYC, for that matter). Within the *Framework*, students have only minimal "fostering" from teachers somewhere in the middle of a process that could take semesters or longer, and there is no reason to leave them largely to their own devices like that. There is a resource that only a very few campuses don't have, and it has been designed with exactly these purposes in mind. The writing center can not only help to fulfill the promise of the *Framework* but provide the support and resources that developing agentive student writers need to actively and successfully participate in the demanding processes outlined for success in postsecondary writing.

Conclusion

Rhetorical education in the classical period valued greatly both practice and learning, but the goals were never pedagogical, and as rhetorical education continued to develop, teachers seemed more and more willing to acknowledge that the results of their teaching were individualized and subject to the abilities, dispositions, and characters of their students. Thus, the focus was seldom on pedagogy except in terms of effectiveness in producing and/or provoking agentive and self-efficacious rhetors (Cicero; Plato; Murphy). This is where things get interesting because this is where we can glean information, based in cognitive sciences research, that can help us to encourage our student writers' agency and self-efficacy, not to mention their writing performance. We have to be careful here not to overestimate what this kind of inquiry can provide; neither do we want to ignore any insights or outcomes that can help us to encourage our student writers' sense of writing agency and self-efficacy.

Multiple studies have confirmed the relationship between student writer views and experiences with writing and performance in writing, based on, for example, incoming literacy skills, gendered approaches to writing, goal-setting, and perceptions of writing's utility (Daly; Daly and Miller; Faigley et al.; Jones et al; Pajares; Pajares and Cheong; Pajares and Johnson; Pajares et al.; Pajares and Valiante; Piazza and Siebert; Zimmerman and Bandura). Responses to these consistencies have varied. For instance, Frank Pajares and Giovanni Valiante found that girls' approaches to writing were more adaptive while boys' orientations were enhanced when escorted by female peers. Christy Teranishi Martinez, Ned Kock, and Jeffrey Cass found that students who wrote for leisure tended to experience lower levels of writing anxiety. Lindy Woodrow found that writing self-efficacy could disrupt the relationship between writing anxiety and performance. Inviting students to imitate a successful writerly identity, as opposed to imitating forms or processes, was more powerful in positively impacting student writer agency and self-efficacy (Brooke). Writing about concerns prior to an exam helped students to perform better on those exams (Ramirez and Beilock). Social opportunities to gather and activate both local and general knowledge are productive in terms of student writer agency and self-efficacy (Foertsch). Teachers using motivating strategies improve student motivation (McCarthy et al.) and performance in written work (Lam and Law). Students' beliefs and self-perceptions may not be borne out by writing performance but adding self-efficacy to students' options and the expansion of self-evaluation can both improve writing performance (Lam and Law; Magogwe et al.; McCarthy et al.; Prat-Sala and Redford). These more social constructs seem to consistently impact student writers positively. They could encourage help-seeking, which James Williams and Seiji Takaku found correlated with writing performance. They might facilitate a more transactional understanding of writing, which Mary Jane White and Roger Bruning found more conducive to student writing than a transmissional stance. These options seem especially appealing in light of the limited impact of sanctions in discouraging bad behavior (Ogilvie and Stewart).

What seems consistent in this body of literature is that student writers can associate both positive and negative experiences and perceptions with their writing. They can hang themselves up in their writing just by emphasizing one kind of experience or another. However, it also seems that the more the learning is social within a social learning environment, the better. The more interactive, expressive, and engaged the interactions seem to be, the better. These ideas complement all too clearly recent trends in writing pedagogy. However, it is also important to note that these studies not only span a number of grade levels but also focus almost exclusively on classrooms. Writing centers have much to offer that departs from the typical classroom and resonates with what these studies recommend and, as such, promise to provide a new set of additional opportunities and supports for developing and supporting agentive student writers.

The *Framework*'s ambitious effort to outline and articulate the elements necessary to succeed in post-secondary writing is a good start but incomplete. It does not accommodate the wide array of individuation, preparation, and situation that different students bring to higher education, let alone accommodate the numerous audiences, levels of education, and disciplines that the *Framework* itself includes. Most importantly, the scale of demand made on student writers by the *Framework* can only be taken on by an agentive student writer who is supported by a state-of-the-art writing center. That agentive student writer must be able to not only engage with the significant demands of the *Framework* but consciously respond to them and act on them with aplomb and confidence. To do so, that agentive student writer must have adequate and readily available support that can respond effectively to all facets of the *Framework*'s rigorous project, and only writing centers are ready and able to do so. Their histories, theories, pedagogies, and practices have been developed specifically for these roles, even though they have evolved independent of the Framework and the "OS." The *Framework* sets forth an incredibly demanding set of expectations for first-year writing students, but they are not demands that are out of reach for agentive student writers with the support of quality, modern writing centers. Thus, to accurately articulate what is necessary for success in post-secondary writing now and in the near future, the *Framework* must overtly include the development and support of active student writer agency and self-efficacy and the support of both through an engaged writing center. Otherwise, this *Framework* will remain incomplete and the results disappointing.

Works Cited

Ambrose, Susan A., et al. *How Learning Works: 7 Research-Based Principles for Smart Teaching.* Jossey Bass, 2010.

Bandura, Albert. "Toward a Psychology of Human Agency." *Perspectives on Psychological Science*, vol. 1–2, 2006, pp. 164–180

Bandura, Albert. "Human Agency in Social Cognitive Theory." *American Psychologist*, vol. 44, no. 9, 1989, pp. 1175–84.

Bartlett, William. *The Illusion of Technique.* Anchor Books, 1978.

Bey, Hakim. *TAZ: The Temporary Autonomous Zone, Ontological Anarchy, Poetic Terrorism.* 2nd ed., Autonomedia New Autonomy Series, 2003.

Blakemore, Sarah-Jayne, and Trevor W. Robbins. "Decision-Making in the Adolescent Brain." *Nature Neuroscience*, vol. 15, no. 9, 2012, pp. 1184–91.

Boquet, Elizabeth H. "'Our little secret': A History of Writing Centers, Pre- to Post-Open Admissions." College Composition and Communication, vol. 50, no. 3, 1999, pp. 463–82.

Brooke, Robert. "Modeling a Writer's Identity: Reading and Imitation in the Writing Classroom." *College Composition and Communication*, vol. 39, no. 1, 1988, pp. 23–41.

Cicero. *De Oratore Books I-II.* Translated by E. W. Sutton and H. Rackham, Harvard UP, 1979.

Council of Writing Program Administrators, the National Council of Teachers of English, and the National Writing Project. *Framework for Success in Postsecondary Writing.* CWPA, NCTE, and NWP,

2011, wpacouncil.org/files/framework-for-success-postsecondary-writing.pdf.

Council of Writing Program Administrators. "WPA Outcomes Statement for First-Year Composition (3.0)." CWPA, 2014, wpacouncil.org/aws/CWPA/asset_manager/get_file/350909?ver=552. Accessed 14 July 2020.

Daly, John A. "Writing Apprehension and Writing Competency." *The Journal of Educational Research*, vol. 72, no. 1, 1978, pp. 10–14.

Daly, John A., and Michael D. Miller. "Further Studies on Writing Apprehension: SAT Scores, Success Expectations, Willingness to Take Advanced Courses, and Sex Differences." *Research in the Teaching of English*, vol. 9, no. 3, 1975, pp. 250–56.

De Ridder-Symoens, editor. *A History of the University in Europe Volume 1: Universities in the Middle Ages*. Cambridge UP, 1992.

Dobbs, David. "Beautiful Brains." *National Geographic*, vol. 220, no. 4, 2011, pp. 36–59.

Dweck, Carol S. *Mindset: The New Psychology of Success*. Ballantine Books, 2007.

Emig, Janet. *The Composing Processes of Twelfth Graders*. Research Report No. 13, National Council of Teachers of English, 1971.

"Engagement Indicators." *National Survey of Student Engagement*. Indiana University School of Education, 2016, nsse.indiana.edu/html/engagement_indicators.cfm/. Accessed 11 Nov. 2019.

Faigley, Lester, et al. "The Role of Writing Apprehension in Writing Performance and Competence." *The Journal of Educational Research*, vol. 75, no. 1, 1981, pp. 16–21.

Flower, Linda, and John R. Hayes. "A Cognitive Process theory of Writing." *College Composition and Communication*, vol. 32, no. 4, 1981, pp. 365–87.

Foertsch, Julie. "Where Cognitive Psychology Applies: How Theories About Memory and Transfer Can Influence Composition Pedagogy." *Written Communication*, vol. 12, no. 3, 1995, pp. 360–83.

Gillespie, Paula, and Neal Lerner. *The Allyn and Bacon Guide to Peer Tutoring*. Allyn and Bacon, 2000.

Inoue, Asao B. Plenary Speaker. "Racism in Writing Programs and the CWPA." Summer Conference for the Council of Writing Program Administrators. July 2016, Raleigh, NC. Plenary speech.

Jones, Lisa Øen, et al. "Reading and Writing Self-Efficacy of Incarcerated Adults." *Learning and Individual Differences*, vol. 22, no. 3, 2012, pp. 343–49.

Jordan, M. "Private Tutor Newest of Status Symbols Education: Parents Seek Extra Help to Give Their Children an Edge." *Los Angeles Times*, 22 May 1994, www.latimes.com/archives/la-xpm-1994-05-22-mn-60691-story.html/. Accessed 11 Nov. 2019.

Jordan, Mary. "Tutors Give Suburban Kids Something Extra/Help Newest Status Symbol For Kids." *Houston Chronicle*, 29 May 1994, 11.

Lam, Shui-Fong, and Yin-Kum Law. "The Roles of Instructional Practices and Motivation in Writing Performance." *The Journal of Experimental Education*, vol. 75, no. 2, Winter 2007, pp. 145–164.

Lerner, Neal. *The Idea of a Writing Laboratory*. Southern Illinois UP, 2009.

Macauley, Jr., William J. "Setting the Agenda for the Next Thirty Minutes." *A Tutor's Guide: Helping Writers One-to-One*, 2nd ed., edited by Ben Rafoth, Heinemann, 2005, pp. 1–8.

Magogwe, Joel M., et al. "Developing Student-Writers' Self-efficacy Beliefs." *Journal of Academic Writing*, vol. 5, no. 2, 2015, pp. 20–28.

Males, Michael. "Does the Adolescent Brain Make Risk Taking Inevitable? A Skeptical Appraisal." *Journal of Adolescent Research*, vol. 24, no. 1, 2009, pp. 3–20.

Martinez, Christy Teranishi, et al. "Pain and Pleasure in Short Essay Writing: Factors Predicting University Students' Writing Anxiety and Writing Self-Efficacy." *Journal of Adolescent and Adult Literacy*, vol. 54, no. 5, 2011, pp. 351–60.

McAndrew, Donald A., and Thomas J. Reigstad. *Tutoring Writing: A Practical Guide for Conferences*. Heinemann, 2001.

McCarthy, Patricia, et al. "Self-Efficacy and Writing: A Different View of Self-Evaluation." *College Composition and Communication*, vol. 36, no. 4, 1985, pp. 465–71.

Murphy, James J., editor. *Quintilian on the Teaching of Speaking and Writing: Translations from Books One, Two, and Ten of the Institutio Oratoria*. Southern Illinois UP, 1987.

Nagel, Bonnie. "The Neural Substrates of Emotional Attention and Inhibition Across Adolescence." The Dana Foundation, 2016, www.dana.org/grant/the-neural-substrates-of-emotional-attention-and-inhibition-across-adolescence/. Accessed 11 Nov. 2019.

North, Stephen. "The Idea of a Writing Center." *College English*, vol. 46, no. 5, 1984, pp. 433–46.

Ogilvie, James, and Anna Stewart. "The Integration of Rational Choice and Self-Efficacy Theories: A Situational Analysis of Student Misconduct." *Australian and New Zealand Journal of Criminology*, vol. 43, no. 1, 2010, pp. 130–55.

Pajares, Frank. "Self-Efficacy Beliefs in Academic Settings." *Review of Educational Research*, vol. 66, no. 4, 1996, pp. 543–78.

Pajares, Frank, and Yuk F. Cheong. "Achievement Goal Orientations in Writing: A Developmental Perspective." *International Journal of Educational Research*, vol. 39, no. 4–5, 2003, pp. 437–55.

Pajares, Frank, and Margaret J. Johnson. "Self-Efficacy Beliefs and the Writing Performance of Entering High School Students." *Psychology in the Schools*, vol. 33, no. 2, 1996, pp. 163–75.

—. "Confidence and Competence in Writing: The Role of Self-Efficacy, Outcome Expectancy, and Apprehension." *Research in the Teaching of English*, vol. 28, no. 3, 1994, pp. 313–31.

Pajares, Frank, et al. "Gender Differences in Writing Self-Beliefs of Elementary School Students." *Journal of Educational Psychology*, vol. 91, no. 1, 1999, pp. 50–61.

Pajares, Frank, and Giovanni Valiante. "Gender Differences in Writing Motivation and Achievement of Middle School Students: A Function of Gender Orientation?" *Contemporary Educational Psychology*, vol. 26, no. 3, July 2001, pp. 366–81.

—. "Grade Level and Gender Differences in the Writing Self-Beliefs of Middle School Students." *Contemporary Educational Psychology*, vol. 24, no. 4, Oct. 1999, pp. 390–405.

—. "Self-Efficacy Beliefs and Motivation in Writing Development." *Handbook of Writing Research*, edited by Charles A. MacArthur, Steve Graham, and Jill Fitzgerald, Guilford, 2006, pp. 158–70.

Piazza, Carolyn L., and Carl F. Siebert. "Development and Validation of a Writing Dispositions Scale for Elementary and Middle School Students." *The Journal of Educational Research*, vol. 101, no. 5, 2008, pp. 275–85.

Plato. *Phaedrus*. Translated by W. C. Helmbold and W. G. Rabinowitz, Macmillan, 1956.

Prat-Sala, Mercè, and Paul Redford. "Writing Essays: Does Self-Efficacy Matter? The Relationship between Self-Efficacy in Reading and in

Writing and Undergraduate Students' Performance in Essay Writing." *Educational Psychology*, vol. 32, no. 1, 2012, pp. 9–20.

Ramirez, Gerardo, and Sian L. Beilock. "Writing About Testing Worries Boosts Exam Performance in the Classroom." *Science*, vol. 331, no. 6014, 2011, pp. 211–13.

Rittel, Horst W., and Melvin Webber. "Dilemmas in a General Theory of Planning." *Policy Sciences*, vol. 4, no. 2, 1973, pp. 155–69.

Rotter, Julia. B. "Generalized Expectancies for Internal versus External Control of Reinforcement." *Psychological Monographs: General and Applied*, vol. 80, no. 1, 1966, pp. 1–28.

Ryan, Leigh, and Lisa Zimmerelli. *The Bedford Guide for Writing Tutors.* 5th ed., Bedford St. Martin's, 2010.

Sasson, Remez. "How Many Thoughts Does Your Mind Think in One Hour?" *Success Consciousness: Skills for Success, Positivity, and Inner Peace*, www.successconsciousness.com/blog/inner-peace/how-many-thoughts-does-your-mind-think-in-one-hour/. Accessed 10 Oct. 2019.

Soja, Edward W. *Thirdspace: Journeys to Los Angeles and Other Real-and-Imagined Places*. Blackwell Publishers, 1996.

Sprague, Jo, and Douglas Stuart. *The Speaker's Handbook*. Harcourt Brace, 2000.

Tugend, Alina. *Better by Mistake: The Unexpected Benefits of Being Wrong*. Riverhead Books, 2011.

Ueland, Brenda. *If You Want to Write: A Book about Art, Independence, and Spirit*. Graywolf P, 2007.

Usher, Ellen L., and Frank Pajares. "Self-Efficacy for Self-Regulated Learning: A Validation Study." *Educational and Psychological Measurement*, vol. 68, no. 3, 2008, pp. 443–63.

Waldo, Mark L. *Demythologizing Language Difference in the Academy: Establishing Discipline-Based Writing Programs*. Lawrence Erlbaum, 2004.

White, Mary Jane, and Roger Bruning. "Implicit Writing Beliefs and Their Relation to Writing Quality." *Contemporary Educational Psychology*, vol. 30, 2005, pp. 166–89.

Williams, James D., and Seiji Takaku. "Help-Seeking, Self-Efficacy, and Writing Performance Among College Students." *Journal of Writing Research*, vol. 3, no. 1, 2011, pp. 1–18.

Woodrow, Lindy. "College English Writing Affect: Self-Efficacy and Anxiety." *System*, vol. 39, no. 4, 2011, pp. 510–22.

Zimmerman, Barry J., and Albert Bandura. "Impact of Self-Regulatory Influences on Writing Course Attainment." *American Educational Research Journal*, vol. 31, no. 4, 1994, pp. 845–62.

14 Writing Center Consultations as Emotional Experiences: How Different Learning Experiences Shape Student Perceptions of Agency

Bronwyn T. Williams

It is an encounter familiar to anyone who has worked in a writing center. A student sits down for a consultation, looks uncertainly at a draft, and says, "I'm not a good writer." Though the exact words may vary, time and again writers begin their conversations with consultants by explaining that they feel they are not "good writers" or that they know the draft in front of them is "bad writing." The emotions they convey in such moments range from anxiety to resentment to despair to weary resignation. What is common, however, is that the writers have had negative experiences with writing in school that have led them to develop and internalize negative emotions when faced with a writing assignment. The initial site of grading rubric can be discouraging, like spotting a flat tire, well before the content of the assignment is discussed in detail. These emotions, in turn, shape students' sense of identity as writers, and their sense of agency in responding effectively to writing situations, both in and out of school.

We may want to blame these negative experiences on poor teaching, institutional pressures, or outside influences. Regardless of the source, however, the point is that students bring to writing dispiriting and often debilitating emotional dispositions. Such emotional dispositions play a significant role in the ability of students to write effectively and successfully. Whether a student encounters writer's block or has difficulty dealing with response or struggles with authorial position is determined in part by the emotional dispositions the writer has developed over the years. Research in psychology and neuroscience offers insights into the ways that internal responses and social contexts create patterns that shape these emotional dispositions and, in turn, perceptions of agency. Additionally, such research demonstrates that emotions play a significant role in how we learn and reason. As we attend to issues of cognition in writing pedagogy, then, it is important not to overlook the important role the cognitive processes of emotion play in how all writers perceive and respond to writing situations.

Indeed, a number of the central qualities noted in the *Framework for Success in Postsecondary Writing* carry with them implied connections to emotional dispositions that enable students to *feel* open, engaged, creative, flexible, and persistent as they also demonstrate such qualities in their learning and writing. Although the *Framework* emphasizes intellectual and practical aspects of "the Habits of Mind and experiences that are critical for college success" (CWPA et al.), such experiences and habits are never disconnected from emotion. Developing and sustaining a productive, internalized habit—of any kind—is as dependent on a series of positive emotional experiences as it is on practices of reasoning and metacognition. Practices experienced as disempowering, harsh, or uncaring, make us unlikely to want to repeat them, in any context for any reason.

For many students, however, writing center consultations offer emotional experiences distinct from what they have encountered, year after year, in classroom settings. Writing center consultations, by emphasizing dialogic learning, open-ended timelines, and avoiding graded assessment (Bouquet; Geller et al.), offer learning experiences that are different emotionally from many previous experiences with writing in school. Writing center consultations are typically individualized, patient, and often less explicitly hierarchical. As a result, students can leave writing center appointments not just with a stronger draft, but also a stronger sense of confidence and agency.

In this chapter I will draw from a research project focused on student writers and their perceptions of agency, as well as my experiences as the director of a University Writing Center, to discuss how writing center experiences influence student confidence about whether they can write successfully in a given context. The research involved interviews and observations with both undergraduate and graduate student writers at our university writing center that focused on questions of what, in their writing experiences in or out of school, had facilitated or obstructed a perception of agency, a sense that they could write and read effectively in a given context. Many factors shape perceptions of agency in literacy practices (Williams, *Literacy Practices*), but in this chapter I use recent research in psychology and neuroscience to explore how the simultaneously intimate, but public, reality of emotion influences how we understand literacy experiences and construct literate identities. I discuss the inseparable connection between emotion, cognition, and learning. If we know more about how emotion works, both cognitively and socially, we'll understand how such processes form attitudes and dispositions that frame and mediate how students approach the habits of mind we want them to employ in their literacy practices. I conclude by offering strategies for both writing center consultations and classroom pedagogy that can recognize and respond productively to their emotional contexts in ways that facilitate the habits of mind outlined in the *Framework*, as well as student writers' perceptions of agency.

Emotion as Integral to Cognition and Learning

There has been a resurgence of interest in recent years in the role emotion plays in writing and pedagogy, particularly drawing from conversations in rhetorical theory (Cooper; Campbell; Leake) and classroom pedagogy (Belli; Kurtyka; Micciche; Newkirk). The ongoing interest in the field in how social contexts influence writing has shaped the focus of much of the discussions of how universities reproduce larger cultural ideologies and conceptions of emotion. Cultural codes concerning definitions and performances of emotion are constructed around the dominant cultural subject positions, meaning that conventions of what is acceptable in terms of emotion, and what is "too emotional," are interpreted and evaluated in terms of these normalized, dominant ideologies. Many of the performances of emotion that are regarded as inappropriate for the college classroom, such as sentimentality or anger, are also used to mark individuals as part of groups that are not part of the dominant cultural subject position, such as women or people of color.

At the same time, there has been a renewed interest in issues of cognition and writing, as evidenced by this collection and others. While attending to the social context of theories of cognition, this scholarly conversation has engaged more directly recent research in neuroscience and psychology to explore our understanding of how writing, and learning to write, happens. Yet, this renewed interest in cognition and writing has also been focused more on what would be considered the "rational" parts of cognition, such as critical reasoning and metacognition. In many of the recent articles exploring new directions in cognition and writing pedagogy, emotion is not explicitly addressed, or even mentioned, including in many of the chapters in this collection. I do not, of course, expect every article to address emotion. That said, the still somewhat limited engagement with emotion, particularly with the interactions between neuroscience and social contexts, is indicative of the reality that emotion remains a subject, or a reality, regarded with suspicion by many in the academy. The goal of many schools and writing programs, often enshrined in their mission statements, is to promote critical thinking and rational discourse, both of which are regarded as antithetical to the broader cultural conceptions of emotion. In an institution dominated by the sciences and empiricism, dispassionate analysis and discourse are the standardized conventions of most disciplines, including ours. Emotion, by contrast, is typically perceived as extreme responses, such as anger, sentimentality, or sadness and is frowned upon in both speech and writing. Student writers are often warned that what is coded as explicit emotion in writing is evidence of manipulation or a lack of rigor. Also, many instructors view emotion warily as something that will be impossible to assess and so elide it in their assignments and grading rubrics.

What we are missing, when we approach cognition and learning from this perspective, however, is that cognition, learning, and emotion are inextricable. Conventional attitudes toward emotion, which define it as moments of extreme and noticeable feelings, such as anger or disgust or compassion, are flawed in understanding of the constant presence and central role of emotion in every moment of our lives. The definition of emotion I use describes the "embodied meaning-making" process that connects bodily responses with social interpretation and performance (Wetherell). While some people prefer the term *affect*, I have chosen to use *emotion* because it brings together more effectively the threads of biological, social, and rhetorical scholarship being discussed in various fields, and it is a more familiar and accessible term for students and teachers alike. Emotion entwines the internal and the social through ongoing, recursive interactions. A given stimulus, a loud sound or change in our circumstances, results in immediate physiological processes that we feel in our bodies. For that moment to make sense as an emotion, however, it is compared against similar moments from our past (Barrett) and interpreted in terms of social and cultural contexts. The ways in which we learn to define emotions are socially constructed. Making a public mistake may be learned as shame in one culture, embarrassment in another, and, depending on the mistake, stoic resilience in a third. What's more, our minds are *always* experiencing, monitoring, and categorizing emotions, not just at the moments when we note we feel joyful or distressed. Rational and disinterested demeanors, though often described as an absence of emotion, are, in fact, also emotional states and performances. Like the weather, we notice emotions more when they are unusual—stormy or brilliant—but they are always present. We experience and understand emotion, then, through an ongoing, fluid process of recognition, interpretation, and retrieval. (Barrett; Reddy; Scherer; Wetherell). Each emotional experience is added to cognitive patterns established by earlier, similar experiences. Eventually, similar sets of emotional experiences are internalized and normalized into dispositions that regulate how we feel, and how we understand our identities. I become a person who likes to swim or hates to wait in line. Or I become a person who loves—or hates—to read and write.

In terms of writing pedagogy and cognition, it is also important to understand the crucial connections between emotions and learning. The influence of emotion on motivation to learn, and to achieve, has been the focus of a substantial body of scholarship. One influential line of research has been Carol Dweck's work on whether students have an incremental conception of intelligence—rather than a static "entity" conception—(Dweck), that focuses on the process of learning, rather than the grade, and allows them to deal more effectively with difficulty and struggle. Another area of study has focused on "achievement emotions" (Daniels et al.; Goetz et al.; Postareff et al.), demonstrating that things such as hopefulness and mastery goals are connected with a sense of enjoyment and achievement in student learning, and that helplessness predicts boredom and lower achievement. Research illustrates that predictive relationships between student goals and achievement are mediated by students' emotions (Daniels et al.). In addition, further longitudinal research indicates that such emotional experiences form dispositions toward learning that can have long-term effects on student learning (Pekrun et al.). Research focused on dispositions toward learning and achievement is connected to ongoing research on motivation that demonstrates that internal motivations, rather than instrumental rewards such as money or grades, are more powerful in helping individuals overcome obstacles and take on new challenges (Wrzesniewski et al.). What's more, internal motivations are most common, and strongest, when a task or project provides individuals with elements such as a sense of control, a sense of meaning, or the development of relationships (Norton et al.; Ryan and Deci; Wilson). The student responses in *The Meaningful Writing Project* illustrate how important those student writers found a sense of meaning or the development of mentoring relationships to be to the work they found the most fulfilling during their university careers (Eodice et al.). Meanwhile, conditions that limit or diminish these elements, and increase a sense of futility in the purpose of project, quickly reduce internal motivations (Ariely et al.). How our emotional experiences have created dispositions toward learning, toward writing, then will influence how confident or anxious we will feel when we next encounter a writing situation, in school or out (Williams, *Literacy Practices*).

Yet emotions have other influences on cognition and learning beyond how we feel about particular writing circumstances. Research indicates that emotions, both positive and negative, influence the availability of our cognitive resources. Emotions such as anxiety or anger, that are unrelated to learning activities, create demands on our cognitive load that leave fewer resources for learning (Ellis and Ashbrook; McConnell and Eva). In addition, positive emotions can increase cognitive flexibility that allows individuals to connect diverse ideas or elements (Isen). Daniel Kahnemann points to a substantial body of research that indicates that the intensity and timing of an experience shapes how we remember it in terms of both cognition and emotion. If we, as writing studies scholars and teachers, want to engage in the current important research on cognition and learning, we need to be mindful of the integral and inextricable role emotion plays in these processes.

Emotion and the Framework for Success

Reading the *Framework*, with the perspective of the research on emotion, motivation, and learning in mind, reveals how integral emotion is in the qualities and goals of the project. Although the word "emotion" never appears in the document, some of the habits of mind described are often used to describe emotional states, such as curiosity, flexibility, openness, and persistence, while others, such as creativity and engagement are dependent or entwined with emotions. Habits of mind and experiences are also always going to be connected to emotional patterns, stances, and emotional experiences. The *Framework* describes habits of mind as "ways of approaching learning that are both intellectual and practical" that enable students to "approach learning from an active stance." Research on emotion demonstrates that all such practices also result in emotional experiences that create emotional patterns and dispositions. If, for example, we do not find a practice meaningful, and if we don't have some sense of control over it, we are unlikely to make it a habit. What's more, implied in the description of these habits of mind is an expectation that they will result in writers who are more confident, less anxious, and feel a stronger sense of agency, an "active stance" if you will, when faced with a writing situation.

More specifically, the habits of mind call to mind a number of key emotions that students may feel, or need to feel, to engage successfully in them when writing. Creativity, for example, is often dependent on a sense of safety that allows for risk, and possible failure. Openness connects to trust, generosity, and empathy. Persistence often depends on patience or stubbornness. Even metacognition, which is often summarized as "thinking about thinking," can be connected to emotions. Our thinking, regardless of the subject, never takes place outside of our ongoing emotional mediation. Consequently, if we reflect on feedback that focuses on error, we may feel embarrassed or angry as we do so, and, if we receive a more constructive, respectful response to writing, our metacognitive process may be shaped by confidence and reassurance. Such responses suggest interrelations between metacognition and emotion that regulate and shape the willingness, and ability, to engage in metacognitive processes. Anastasia Efklides notes, for example, that surprise and curiosity, are emotions that can arise when there may be discrepancies, inconsistencies, or interruptions of metacognitive processes of reflection (4).

Yet, when writers come in for appointments to our University Writing Center, the emotions they describe, in terms of their writing experiences, may be just the opposite of those necessary for the habits of mind in the *Framework*. The following quotations were from IRB-approved research. Students chose their own pseudonyms. Take a few examples.

They may feel deeply averse to risk if they fear the possibility of a failing grade. Katrina, an undergraduate Business major described how she was approaching final papers in her courses, "In these last two weeks, this pressure, feeling like I needed to produce something that ends up being fine, is all I can think about. Who knows? Maybe I could write something creative, but I feel like I don't necessarily have the freedom to do anything but be careful."

They may lack trust in the audience of the instructors they are writing for, which limits their curiosity or their willingness to be open and empathetic. Hannah, an English major, talked about an instructor who said, on the first day of a first-year writing course, "'If you're used to getting an "A" in high school, that could be a "C" here.' It's like, 'I'm used to getting an "A," what if I get a "C"?' I was really traumatized. I thought, what's the point of trying for this person if I'm going to fail?"

They may not have the patience to believe that a writing assignment will have meaning for them and be less inclined to persist in engaging in the kinds of revision that will require them to struggle and be flexible. Dwayne, an undergraduate criminal justice major said, he felt that, in many of his courses, "I knew what they wanted. I knew how to get a good grade. I just did that. I knew the formulas. I didn't even study. I had skimmed the entire book. I knew the places that I needed to pull out for quotes. I passed."

Their ability to engage in effective reflection and metacognition may be short-circuited by harsh and punitive responses to their writing that focus on error and deficits. Jason, an undergraduate Engineering major, said, "I would get panic attacks about the judgment. It was never a problem of doing the reading for assignments. Writing was always this very stressful situation because I knew when I turned it in, they would look at it and tell me whether they thought it was good or bad and I'd get a grade and all of that would really drive me nuts."

The stories these writers tell, and the emotions they have patterned and internalized through experience, will be familiar to any writing teacher or tutor. Yet we all want students, when they leave our classes or writing center consultations, to feel more confident, more capable of taking the active stance in their writing that the *Framework* envisions.

Our Work in the Writing Center

I believe that, if we want more confident students who can establish the *Framework*'s habits of mind, then we need to create different emotional experiences along with the pedagogical experiences. At our University Writing Center we approach our work in terms of not only working with the draft and the writer's writing and rhetorical abilities, but also with engaging writers' dispositions that shape when people feel they can, or cannot write effectively. We keep in mind that every writing center consultation is an emotional experience, and that, sometimes, those experiences can reshape, or reinforce dispositions that are integral to cognition and learning. We talk about how certain pedagogical values we hold in the writing center, learning from the writer, building trusting relationships, taking long timelines toward learning, starting from where the writer is, and dialogic and flexible response, also can result in different emotional experiences from what writers have in other courses and other parts of the university (Williams, "Making Sense"). These same values and approaches connect to the habits of mind articulated in the *Framework* and, potentially, find ways to enhance or push them further.

OPENNESS AND HOSPITALITY

Openness, what the *Framework* defines as "the willingness to consider new ways of being and thinking in the world," is, in many ways, central to the mission, and to the success of a writing center. When the *Framework* discusses the ability to listen and reflect on the ideas and responses of others, and to consider and connect to other perspectives, it is describing what typically happens in a successful writing center consultation. The goal of writing center appointments is often to get the writer to rethink, and revise, a draft through a constructive dialogue that enables the writer to make the decisions about possible revisions. To accomplish this, the writer must be willing to consider other perspectives and listen and reflect carefully to the consultant's questions and suggestions.

The reality, however, is that some students have not had a great deal of practice in engaging in such dialogue in an educational setting. For years, they may have had classes where they are given content, and response in the way of grades, directly and they receive it fairly passively. Providing an opportunity to practice openness is something that we can do in a writing center setting. This begins when we simply describe for the writer how an appointment will unfold, and why we approach teaching this way. But, more important, are the ways we model openness for the writer. The stance we take, the emotional disposition we perform, in a consultation is an important aspect of what takes place. We draw from Richard Haswell and Janis Haswell's conception of *hospitality* in teaching in framing how we understand these tutor-student encounters. In traditional cultural concepts of hospitality, strangers and their hosts shared shelter and work through customs of respect and reciprocity. Brought to teaching and learning, Haswell and Haswell see hospitality as an approach to education that foregrounds openness and reciprocity and "welcomes and makes room for new ideas coming from any direction, including students, and undercuts the fatal expectation that knowledge transfer is a one-way street" (8). In writing center consultations, such an approach highlights the dialogic exchange of ideas in which both sides make themselves open to learning and change. By being clear that we are open to learning from the writer and the draft, even as we have things to teach in return, allows us to model a stance of response and teaching that is more collaborative and less hierarchical. The Habits of Mind of openness are grounded in the give and take that Haswell and Haswell describe, and which we have all experienced with collaborators or mentors. Such encounters also require honesty and trust, as they can involve difficult truths and the risk of opening ourselves up to critique—an approach of hospitality is not just about positive comments. Yet, hospitality, does model the kind of open, reflective, and thoughtful stance that the *Framework* advocates in the principle of openness.

CREATIVITY AND RISK

Approaching consultations through a disposition and framework of hospitality and openness is a crucial step toward creating a relationship of trust between the consultant and writer. Trust, in this context, often means the understanding that both writer and consultant can try out different ideas and responses and that the other person will consider and respond to the ideas honestly and respectfully. In such an environment of trust, writers can feel safe in testing ideas without worrying that a failure of an idea will mean a failing grade. The *Framework* emphasizes that creativity is grounded in circumstances in which people can "take risks by exploring questions, topics, and ideas that are new to them." Research in psychology illustrates connections between positive moods and trust, and creativity, in terms of perceptions and experimentation (Baas, et al.; Davis). Without the safety to try, maybe fail, and try again, writers will not generate new ideas and approaches to their work. Writing centers, as places where we don't grade writing, offer spaces where writers can experiment and foster habits of creativity.

Creating a safe space for risk taking can take a variety of forms. To begin with, we remember that students may have previous experiences that make them reluctant to risk failure, and we reassure them that we can try different approaches until we find one that works. We also, when appropriate, try a range of creative approaches during consultations. We may put the draft aside and brainstorm or sketch out ideas—including images and diagrams—on a whiteboard or encourage language play in revising sentences. Though we believe in the importance of play in learning, not every moment of creativity is playful. For example, we are talking about creativity when we talk with writers about ideas such as learning new genres, and how, when doing so, we often need to experiment with how we connect our antecedent genre knowledge with the new genres they are trying to master. We explain that learning the new genre may require experimenting and experiencing some setbacks, but it will lead to eventual success.

Perhaps most important, we draw from Dweck in how we talk with writers about the reality that creativity and the ability to write well are achievable, rather than inherent. We tell them that all writers have to keep learning, struggle, fail, and succeed to be able to learn how to write in new circumstances. As Dweck has pointed out, students who regard abilities as learnable, rather than inherent, do better at dealing with, and navigating through, obstacles. Many writers in the writing center have internalized a judgment that they are, inherently, bad writers. What we encourage is the possibility, and the need, to try and experiment, in ways that will help them learn.

It is also worth noting that in teaching our new consultants, I also talk about the importance of their experimenting, and possibly failing and trying again, during their appointments with writers. I tell them it is acceptable to try something they think might work, and if it doesn't, explain that to the writer and try again. Not only does this offer consultants the freedom to create, it creates a model for student writers of attempt, reflection, and trying again.

Persistence and Long Timelines

One of the central benefits of many writing centers is that they are not bound by the limits of a single semester. Many writing centers work on the principle of long timelines, in which writers can come in multiple times, not just during a semester, but over their academic careers. Being able to take the long view helps writing centers work with writers on habits of persistence. If writers know they can continue to work and improve their writing in many contexts, they can be more willing to return to do such work. The approach of writing centers allows us to talk about learning as an ongoing, sometimes recursive, process. Yet again, it is an opportunity talk about literacy as achievable, not inherent. A number of studies have demonstrated that a message to students that achieving a goal may be a challenge and require hard work, but that the teacher or tutor has confidence in the students' abilities to meet the challenge, results in increased levels of internal motivation, optimism, and willingness to revise and persist in working on a project (Wilson). In addition, finding meaning in a project often takes time, and response, and a longer timeline offers more possibilities to find a way to make a project meaningful (Wegner).

When we think about longer timelines in working with writers, we talk about it in terms of more than a writer's career in a university. Persistence, as an emotional disposition as well as a habit of mind, is built on our experiences in the past, and directed toward imagined possible futures. At our Writing Center, we understand that, when a writer comes to the writing center, we are working with that person at one moment on their journey as a writer that began long before the person entered the writing center and will continue long after they leave. Experiences are vital to whether we think we can meet a challenge. If we have what psychologists term an authentic mastery experience where we meet a challenge successfully, we not only can feel more confident in meeting subsequent similar challenges, but also be more willing to expend more effort and resilience in doing so (Pajares and Schunk; Wilson). The more people believe in the possibility of change, the more they are willing to struggle toward it, and the more they are able to regulate feelings of anxiety (Bandura). Yet memory does more than link us to the past. Researchers of the mind point out that memory is intimately connected into how we imagine the future, both in terms of identity and actions (Fernyhough; Kahnemann). A vital function of memory is to help us both draw on experience to plan for the future, as well as to determine how successful we are in reaching our goals. In addition to considering, and asking about, a writer's experiences in the past, we also consider, and ask about, the imagined future of the writer. We may ask, when appropriate, what the writer not only hopes to achieve in an assignment or course, but what kind of writer they may hope to be in five or ten years. Such questions are sometimes met with silence but provoke thought and productive conversations that range well beyond the draft on the table. As we talk about the future, we also can engage in positing alternative paths to the writer, based on different writing habits—and habits of mind—

that allow the writer to imagine more opportunities for success. More than simply the "power of positive thinking," research indicates that the more imaginative effort that goes into creating a scenario of the future, the more plausible that scenario seems and the more likely the person is to put more effort into making the outcome possible (Fernyhough). Research on self-efficacy (Bandura; Pajares and Schunk) indicates, unsurprisingly, that confidence leads to perseverance and positive results while doubt and anxiety lead to poor performance or abandoning a project. Persistence, as an emotion and habit of mind, develops in a mixture of memory and imagination. We regard our writing consultations as an opportunity to mediate those moments and offer both strategies, and perspectives, which can help writers imagine a future where persistence has allowed them to meet successfully the challenge before them.

METACOGNITION AND RESPONSE

The *Framework* defines metacognition as, "the ability to reflect on one's own thinking as well as on the individual and cultural processes and systems used to structure knowledge." Reflecting on thinking is never disconnected from emotions. The reflection inevitably evokes memories of the emotions that took place at the time, even if those were unremarkable or if they are discounted. The act of reflecting is also connected to the emotions evoked by the response or context of the situation. Reflection on jubilant success is certainly different than reflection on discouraging failure, and such differences can influence the efficacy of reflection and metacognition (Aarts et al.; Ekifides). Reflection and response are, of course, at the center of much of what happens in a writing center consultation. Typically, such consultations begin with questions that ask for reflection (For example, "Where are you with this draft? What concerns do you have? How do you feel it's going at this point?") and often progress to other reflection-focused questions ("How have you approached an assignment like this in the past?" "How do you understand what your instructor wants you to learn through this assignment?"). Like many writing centers, we typically end consultations with explicit debriefing and planning conversations that include asking the writers to reflect on what they learned from the appointment as well as their plans for revision.

In addition to these conventional ways of engaging in reflection during appointments, we are sensitive to the pressure students feel about grades. The moment of receiving a grade can have a deleterious effect on both the writer's perception of agency, as well as the perception of what was actually learned during the assignment (Adams; Blum; Klapp). When writers receive disappointing grades, along with discouragement or resentment, they can discount or question what they actually learned during the process of writing the essay (Alm and Colnerud; Blum; Chory et al.). We take the time, then, to ask writers in the writing center to reflect on what they have learned in the process of completing the assignment. Before a grade has been assigned, writers are often able to articulate a great deal they have learned. It's a metacognitive moment that focuses on learning as a process, not just an outcome, and, we hope, may help develop habits of mind that reinforce such an understanding about learning. After all, we say to writers, regardless of the grade, no one can take away what they have learned.

Our understanding of long timelines also means that, sometimes, we do ask questions about past experiences or imagined futures that involve reflection that stretches past the draft in question. We draw from techniques developed by psychologists to help people reflect on and reimagine narratives about their identities and the social world in which they live. Timothy Wilson calls such reflection "story editing," in which people are asked to consider a powerful narrative or event and imagine how the future might change that narrative. Such an approach is not a matter of discounting experiences, but to think about how they might be reframed in ways that allow a person to successfully navigate similar circumstances in the future. When writers come in with an existing narrative about their inability to write, we may use more informal forms of "story editing" that encourages them to understand that previous experiences do not define their future identities as writers, who will experience writing as an ongoing process of learning that continues throughout their lives. During consultations we also share, when appropriate, our own stories of struggles as writers and how we eventually met those challenges. Our stories not only can help establish empathy, but also model metacognitive reflection about writing with the emotions of uncertainty and anxiety many writers feel.

FLEXIBILITY AND REVISION

Writing center consultations are dialogic and, as such, require flexibility from the writer and the consultant. Through listening and thoughtful response (Newman), the two people involved in the consultations typically "adapt to situations, expectations, or demands." If either person insists on trying to maintain unyielding control over the consultation, the result can be frustration on both sides. Flexibility, like many of the habits of mind in the Framework, is predicated on dealing with other people. We are only required to be flexible when we have to adapt our goals and actions in response to others. We learn to be flexible, then, through conversing with others, receiving responses to our ideas, and shifting our responses, based on what we hear, to communicate more successfully. Writing center consultations offer, over and over again, intense practice in navigating relationships in flexible ways.

Any relationship with another person involves emotion; and any identifying and feeling of an emotion is always dependent on the social context, and often the response of another individual person. As Margaret Wetherell notes, an interaction between two people can rarely be described accurately through a single term, such as "friendly" or "sad" or "angry." Instead, in such interactions, emotions develop, and are negotiated and interpreted, through movement, response, intonation, and so on. Wetherell describes these as unfolding emotional experiences that are dependent on both of the people involved. It is "a joint, coordinated, relational activity" (83). As consultants, we work to be attentive to how the emotions are developing and unfolding during a consultation, and to think about ways we can further develop positive emotions, or, when necessary, step back from and reframe our responses in ways that might reset a negative emotional response from a writer to something we have said. Sometimes this involves naming an emotion and checking in with the writer, "You seem frustrated with that suggestion, can you tell me what you're thinking?" or "To me you're sounding a lot more confident than when you came in. Is that right? How are you feeling about the revisions you have to do?" Such moments also offer the writer permission to acknowledge emotions in that moment—or correct our perceptions. In the give-and-take of writing center consultations, we model a flexibility about learning and dialogue that helps shape the writer's emotional experience of receiving response and engaging in revision.

CONCLUSION

Bring up emotion in an academic setting and, even today, some people will scoff and others will squirm. Talk about constructive emotional experienced in the university gets dismissed as happy talk or as introducing a potential lack of rigor that can't be graded. After talking about this for a number of years, I'm not convinced that those who worry about being gritty enough, serious enough, or not paying enough attention to negative emotions, will ever be convinced of the importance of understanding learning as ongoing emotional experiences. Yet, if we think about our own learning experiences, our own motivations, our abilities to successfully surmount a challenge, we know that emotion has played, and continues to play, an essential role in our learning and cognition. Clear-eyed critique, difficult conversations, and hard reflection can still be done in ways that attend to control, meaning, and relationships of emotional experiences past and present. I ground my work in that of feminist scholars and scholars of color who have argued that when we deny the knowledge created by emotion, we miss out on important ways of understanding the world (Delgado; Kirsch; Ronald and Roskelly; Young). Emotional experiences and the dispositions that are built from them have a significant impact on how students perceive and understand agency. Yet, even as emotions are formed through repeated, sedimented experiences, new experiences, positive as well as negative, can shift or even fracture these sediments and create contexts where students can learn to write more effectively.

Although I think all writing teachers are capable of creating constructive emotional experiences for writers, I believe that writing centers are distinctly well positioned to have this impact. The things that are central to much of the pedagogical identity of a writing center—being radically dialogic, working on long timelines, teaching collaboratively, refusing to grade—are also approaches that contain the possibility for emotional experiences that offer writers a greater sense of control, meaning, and simply being heard. I also believe, then, that writing centers should make the constructive emotional experiences an explicit part of their identity (Williams, "Making Sense"), both in terms of how they teach tutors, as well as how they construct institutional identities within the larger university (Williams, "Writing Centers"). We can create, and advocate for, a different model of learning than what often happens in traditional classrooms. The approaches I mention above are just some of the ways we work, in our University Writing Center, to respond to the emotional contexts of the consultation and try to create a positive experience for the writer—even when we might be explaining there is a great deal of work ahead in a draft. (And, though not the focus of this chapter, attending and responding to the emotional experiences of consultants is also essential in how we do our work.)

The goals of the *Framework* are goals that I want to see writers develop, both in the classroom and throughout their lives. I hope that we can imagine and experience these goals and habits of mind as emotional, as well as critical and metacognitive. I hope we can help students recognize that the great joy in learning, as we all know, emerges from a cognitive *and* emotional process composed of various measures of struggle, frustration, surprise, reflection, curiosity, and inspiration.

Works Cited

Aarts, Kristein, et al. "Erroneous and Correct Actions Have a Different Affective Valence: Evidence for ERPs." *Emotion*, vol. 13, no. 5. 2013. pp. 960–73.

Adams, Jeffrey B. "What Makes the Grade? Faculty and Student Perceptions." *Teaching of Psychology*, vol. 32, no. 1, 2005, pp. 21–24.

Alm, Fredrik, and Gunnell Colnerud. "Teachers' Experiences of Unfair Grading." *Educational Assessment*, vol, 20, no. 2, 2015, pp. 132–50.

Ariely, Dan, et al. "Man's Search for Meaning: The Case of Legos." *Journal of Economic Behavior and Organization*, vol. 67, nos. 3–4, 2008, pp. 671–77.

Baas, Matthijs, et al. "A Meta-Analysis of 25 Years of Mood-Creativity Research: Hedonic Tone, Activation, or Regulatory Focus," *Psychological Bulletin*, vol. 134, no 6, 2008, pp. 779–85.

Bandura, Albert. *Self-Efficacy: The Exercise of Control*. W. H. Freeman, 1997.

Barrett, Lisa F. "Variety Is the Spice of Life: A Psychological Construction Approach to Understanding Variability in Emotion. *Cognition and Emotion*, vol. 23, no. 7, 2009, pp. 1284–306.

Belli, Jill. "Why Well-Being, Why Now?: Tracing an Alternate Genealogy of Emotion in Composition." *Composition Forum*, vol. 34, 2016, compositionforum.com/issue/34/why.

Blum, Susan. *I Love Learning; I Hate School: An Anthropology of College*. Cornell UP, 2016.

Boquet, Elizabeth. *Noise from the Writing Center*. Utah State UP, 2002.

Chory, Rebecca M., et al. "Justice in the Higher Education Classroom: Students' Perceptions of Unfairness and Responses to Instructors." *Innovative Higher Education*, vol. 42, no. 4, 2017, pp. 321–36.

Council of Writing Program Administrators, National Council of Teachers of English, and National Writing Project. *Framework for Success in*

Postsecondary Writing. CWPA, NCTE, and NWP, 2011, wpacouncil.org/aws/CWPA/asset_manager/get_file/350201?ver=505. Accessed 18 Jan. 2020.

Daniels, Lia M., et al. "A Longitudinal Analysis of Achievement Goals: From Affective Antecedents to Emotional Effects and Achievement Outcomes." *Journal of Educational Psychology*, vol. 101, no. 4, 2009, pp. 948–63.

Davis, Mark A. "Understanding the Relationship Between Mood and Creativity: A Meta-Analysis." *Organizational Behavior and Human Decision Processes*, vol. 108, no. 1. 2009, pp. 25–38.

Delgado, Richard. "Storytelling for Oppositionists and Others: A Plea for Narrative. *Michigan Law Review*, vol. 87, no. 8, 1989. pp. 2411–41.

Dweck, Carol. *Self-Theories: Their Role in Motivation, Personality, and Development.* Taylor and Francis, 2001.

Ellis Henry C., and Patricia Ashbrook. "Resource Allocation Model of the Effect of Depressed Mood States on Memory." *Affect, Cognition and Social Behavior*, edited by Klaus Fiedler and Joseph Forgas, Hogrefe International, 1988, pp. 25–43.

Efklides, Anastasia. "Affect, Epistemic Emotions, Metacognition, and Self-Regulated Learning." *Teachers College Record*, vol. 119. 2017. pp. 1–22.

Eodice, Michele, et al. *The Meaningful Writing Project: Learning, Teaching, and Writing in Higher Education.* Utah State UP, 2017.

Fernyhough, Charles. *Pieces of Light: The New Science of Memory.* Profile Books, 2012.

Geller, Anne Ellen, et al. *The Everyday Writing Center: A Community of Practice.* Utah State UP, 2007.

Goetz, Thomas, et al. "Academic Emotions from a Social-Cognitive Perspective: Antecedents and Domain Specificity of Students' Affect in the Context of Latin Instruction." *British Journal of Educational Psychology*, vol, 76, 2006. pp. 289–308.

Haswell, Richard, and Janis Haswell. *Hospitality and Authoring: An Essay for the English Profession.* Utah State UP, 2015.

Isen, Alice M. "Some Ways in Which Positive Affect Influences Decision Making and Problem Solving." *Handbook of Emotions*, 3rd ed., edited by Michael. Lewis, et al., Guilford P, 2008, pp. 548–73.

Kahnemann, Daniel. *Thinking, Fast and Slow.* Farrar, Straus, and Giroux. 2011.

Kirsch, Gesa. "Friendship, Friendliness, and Feminist Fieldwork." *Signs*, vol. 30, no. 4, 2005. pp. 2163–72.

Klapp, Alli. "Does Grading Affect Educational Attainment? A Longitudinal Study." *Assessment in Education: Principles, Policy and Practice*, vol. 22, no. 3, 2015. pp. 302–23.

Kurtyka, Faith. "Settling In To Genre: The Social Action of Emotion in Shaping Genres," *Composition Forum*, vol. 31, 2015, compositionforum.com/issue/31/settling-in.php.

Leake, Eric. "Writing Pedagogies of Empathy: As Rhetoric and Disposition," *Composition Forum*, vol. 34, 2016, compositionforum.com/issue/34/empathy.php.

Micciche, Laura. *Doing Emotion: Rhetoric, Writing, Teaching*. Boynton/Cook, 2007.

McConnell, Meghan, and Kevin W. Eva. "The Role of Emotion in the Learning and Transfer of Clinical Skills and Knowledge." *Academic Medicine*, vol. 87. 2012, pp. 1316–22.

Newkirk, Thomas. *Embarrassment and the Emotional Underlife of Learning*. Heinemann. 2018.

Newman, Jessica. "Writing Center Pedagogy, Affective Labor, and Fostering Engaged Centership." International Writing Center Association Conference. 13 Oct. 2018. Atlanta. GA. Conference presentation.

Norton, Michael, et al. "The IKEA Effect: When Labor Leads to Love." *Journal of Consumer Psychology*, vol. 22, 2011, pp. 453–60.

Pajares, Frank, and Dale H. Schunk. "Self-Beliefs and School Success: Self-Efficacy, Self-Concept, and School Achievement." *Self-Perception*, edited by Richard Riding and Stephen Rayner, Ablex, 2001, pp. 239–66

Pekrun, Reinhard, et al. "Achievement Emotions and Academic Performance: Longitudinal Models of Reciprocal Effects." *Child Development*, vol, 88, no. 5, 2017, pp. 1653–70.

Postareff, Liisa, et al. "The Complex Relationship Between Emotions, Approaches to learning, Study Success and Study Progress During the Transition to University." *Higher Education*, vol. 73, 2017. pp 441–57.

Reddy, William. "Say Something New: Practice Theory and Cognitive Neuroscience." *Arcadia: International Journal for Literary Studies*, vol. 44, 2009, pp. 8–23.

Ronald, Kate, and Hephzibah Roskelly. "Learning to Take it Personally." *Personal Effects: The Social Character of Scholarly Writing*, edited by Deborah Holdstein and David Bleich, Utah State UP, 2001, pp. 253–66.

Ryan, Richard M., and Edward Deci. "Self-Determination Theory and the Facilitation of Intrinsic Motivation, Social Development, and Well-Being." *American Psychologist*, vol. 55, no. 1, 2000, pp. 68–78.

Scherer, Klaus. "The Dynamic Architecture of Emotion: Evidence for the Component Process Model." *Cognition and Emotion*, vol. 23, no. 7, 2009, pp. 1307–51.

Wegner, Etienne. *Communities of Practice: Learning, Meaning, and Identity.* Cambridge UP, 1998.

Wetherell, Margaret. *Affect and Emotion: A New Social Science Understanding.* Sage, 2012.

Williams, Bronwyn T. "Making Sense of How Things Feel: Attending to Emotional Experiences in Writing Programs" *Sensemaking in Writing Programs and Writing Centers*, edited by Rita Malenczyk, Utah State UP, Forthcoming.

—. *Literacy Practices and Perceptions of Agency: Composing Identities.* Routledge, 2018.

—. "Writing Centers, Enclaves, and Creating Spaces of Pedagogical and Political Change within Universities." *European Association for the Teaching of Writing*. June 2017. Unpublished Conference Paper. Royal Holloway University. London. 2017.

Wilson, Timothy. *Redirect: The Surprising New Science of Psychological Change.* Penguin UK, 2011.

Wrzesniewski, Amy, et al. "Multiple Types of Motives Don't Multiply the Motivation of West Point Cadets." *Proceedings of the National Academy of Sciences,* vol. 111, no. 30, 2014, pp. 10990–95.

Young, Morris. *Minor Re/Visions: Asian American Literacy Narratives as a Rhetoric of Citizenship.* Southern Illinois UP, 2004.

Afterword: Considering Whiteness in the *Framework*'s Habits of Mind

Asao Inoue

For this afterword, I thought about highlighting themes and interesting ideas about cognition (and metacognition) that are present in this collection's chapters, but I don't want to do that. I think, if you're reading this afterword, you likely have read the chapters, so you know what's in this collection. You've heard or seen the themes, things that likely will help you reconsider your pedagogy, writing program, or writing center practices. There's lots of good stuff in this collection, and it doesn't require me to point it out or validate it.

Instead, let me focus on a theme I do not see or hear very clearly in this collection, one that the editors bring up in their introduction, and from my reading only two chapters reference directly (D'Angelo and Maid; Beavers, Bogan, Brown, James, and Rankins-Robertson), but none address it substantively. I'm referring to my own critique of how the *Framework for Success in Postsecondary Writing* is used in writing courses and programs uncritically, or without much attention to the ways the *Framework* might reproduce white supremacy. I discuss this in my 2019 Conference on College Composition and Communication Chair's Address (360–62).

The center of that critique is about the ways that white racial habits of language can travel with good ideas and our judgments of language. The center of the *Framework* itself is a set of descriptions of dispositions, habits of mind that lead to success in college writing courses. These habits are ones that do not just make for success but make for ways we judge things, people, and language. I'll put aside in this discussion my criticisms of the absence of many bodies of color and the overabundance of white bodies as writing teachers, scholars, or administrators, and the unintended effects those white bodies can have on people of color. I talk about those things in my address. Here, I focus on white habits of language and judgment. My argument is that most of the time when writing teachers or programs invoke or use the *Framework*, they do so through white racial dispositions toward language, white habits of language and judgment, that further translate the habits of mind in the *Framework* when used or assessed in writing courses.

In my address, I ask: "Do you still have a standard next to the *Framework*? Is the *Framework* being used as a method to get students to write White, but not used to attend to an ever-widening universe of reflective discourses?" (361). I'm referring to the habit of metacognition, and it's central to this collection's discussions. As I read through these smart chapters, most of which focus on habits of mind in the classroom in creative ways, I wondered about the unsaid ways judgment happens when a teacher or a program uses the *Framework* to center pedagogy or program goals, to assess students' progress or development. I wondered how judgment circulates when we encourage a particular habit such as persistence. I wondered how teachers and students in particular classrooms address the ways that people come to understand those habits of mind through their unique but patterned material conditions in the world?

The *Framework* offers this definition for persistence: "the ability to sustain interest in and attention to short- and long-term projects" (5). It almost sounds like this "ability to sustain interest" is separate from one's relations to whatever project is put in front of our students, or separate from the past conditions that clothed school literacy projects for our students. The grammatical subject here, "the ability to sustain interest," is abstracted from the conditions and bodies in which it always exists, and there's no attention given to this fact, no caveat about how this ability to sustain interest may look quite different in different populations of students. It is almost as if we can see persistence outside of those things we are being asked to persist through, as if persistence and the conditions I persist through are not related. Do some conditions or writing projects encourage some students to persist and others not to? Are college writing teachers working from unexamined notions of persistence that we think are universal, or universally in reach by all our students? Why would we think this? Why think that all students have the same access to our (teachers') private notions of persistence?

It may sound like I'm suggesting something deeply un-American and undemocratic. It may sound as if I'm suggesting that some students, like those students of color who do not persist in our writing classes, just don't have much of the persistence gene. I'm not saying this. It is the conditions, and bodies that get conditioned in different places and ways, that I'm trying to call our attention to. Just as our students do not all work under the same conditions, the same conditions in our classrooms are not experienced as the same conditions by all students. We usually assume an idealized, white, middle-class, monolingual student persisting when we call on habits of mind as just habits of all minds, like a decontextualized, disembodied habit called persistence. Whose bodies and conditions for persisting or being open-minded have created the *Framework*, not just the document we have now, but the institutional memory of those habits of mind that the *Framework* identifies? White, middle class, monolingual, English speaking academics.

In school, I was a brown kid in remedial reading classes. Those classes presented us with shorter books to read that had shorter words to decipher. If my reading practices were left up to my schools, I might still be reading those short books, but they weren't. On my own, I searched out longer books, with long words I didn't know. I purposefully ignored the age recommendation on the stacks in my library. I will read whatever book I damned well pleased, I thought. I kept a dictionary near me as I read for years, even into college. How did I learn to persist like this? Where did I get the willingness to do the things that the *Framework* says teachers can do to encourage students to persist, things like, "commit to exploring, in writing, a topic, idea, or demanding task," or "grapple with challenging ideas, texts, processes, or projects." These are things one might see my younger self doing on my own. No teacher asked me to do them. But why did I do them? Was it something innate in me, or was it my need to escape the poverty that I lived in as a child, the way in which I saw literacy as a ticket on the bus out of the ghetto, or was it the way I saw it attached to the only male role model I knew as a child, or maybe it was in watching my mom read boxes of books each weekend, thinking how amazing she was, how that made her better and grown up? These are conditions related to economics, race, location, and other social structures in my life—my life—that have twisted my dispositions, shaped my habits of mind and body into what I am and do today.

Let's look at a habit of mind closer to the center of this collection. The *Framework* defines and helps describe ways to encourage metacognition in writing classrooms. It states:

> Metacognition—the ability to reflect on one's own thinking as well as on the individual and cultural processes and systems used to structure knowledge.
>
> Metacognition is fostered when writers are encouraged to
>
> - examine processes they use to think and write in a variety of disciplines and contexts;
> - reflect on the texts that they have produced in a variety of contexts;
> - connect choices they have made in texts to audiences and purposes for which texts are intended; and
> - use what they learn from reflections on one writing project to improve writing on subsequent projects. (5)

I appreciate this definition. I hear in the "cultural processes and systems" that "structure knowledge" a very meaningful set of terms that most students new to such epistemological framing might be able to use. What is metacognition? It's the act of thinking about my own thinking, how it is structured by mine and other white cultural processes and systems around me, like schools, curricula, the disciplines I engage in, and the books I've read. Those systems might also be the economic systems that paid women like my mom, a single parent with two kids, less than her male counterparts. It could be the systems of government subsidized housing I lived in as a child, which was located in a poor African American community in North Las Vegas, which today still has a very low average household income of $26K a year. These histories, systems, and contexts surely would affect how and what I think about when I think about my thinking, right? But I wonder, is this how the habit of mind of metacognition is presented and used in most writing classrooms? I hope so, but this nice definition isn't helping draw out the importance of specific systems and cultures. It actually does the opposite. It erases them.

The definition, however, has some space to acknowledge a rich, diverse array of processes and systems that determine one's thinking. My guess is that most or all writing teachers would say that it ain't just elite, white, monolingual men's thinking or ways of reflecting on that thinking that are acknowledged as key to this habit of mind. So we all do or can do this habit. The question is: Can a teacher discern this habit in students' labors or the products of those labors if that teacher and student do not share the same conditions for building such a habit of mind? And since conditions are racialized in the US, we might also ask: Can a white teacher recognize a Black or Latinx student's metacognitive moves? Will all those moves be in writing, or should they be? How do we really know when our students are doing metacognition? What markers of metacognition is the teacher using to judge the existence or degree of such a habit, how do we assure ourselves that we are not simply demanding that our students think about their thinking as white people have thought about theirs? If we can do metacognition in a number of ways with a number of cognitive practices or processes, and these cognitive processes can be cultural, then how are we certain that we are not using unacknowledged, white racial habits of metacognition as universal habits when we look for and judge such things in our diverse classrooms? Beyond the good intentions of writing teachers who have taken on white racial habits of language and judgment, what proof do we have?

This question becomes all the more problematic when I read the ways that the *Framework* says teachers might encourage it in all students. Each of the five ways writing teachers or classrooms are offered to see metacognition in action are presented as universal and do not acknowledge the ways that they may be more closely associated to a white, middle-class, monolingual language user. The academy is a white cultural system, and those who make a living in it will be inhabitants of that white cultural system, taking on the habits that structure that system. It will be difficult for any articulated habits of mind for success in postsecondary writing to not be deeply white in nature. How else is one to be successful in a white supremacist system if not to take on white habits of mind? Even so, we can be more critical and more self-aware of such structural dispositions that we all have. We can fight back, revolutionize the *Framework*.

From research on whiteness, critical race studies, and critical whiteness studies, I offer in another place six habits of white language in English. These are habits that may often be used to understand and judge students' performances of metacognition. Perhaps the most important habit of white language and judgment is an "Unseen, naturalized orientation to the world—an orientation (or starting point) of one's body in time and space that makes certain things reachable" ("Writing Assessment" 399). This comes from the good work of Sara Ahmed, in which she argues that whiteness is phenomenological and often is an orientation to the world that is unexamined and assumed to be universal, but of course, it is not (154). We all do not inhabit the same bodies, places, or perspectives in the world, so we cannot have the same starting points. Not everything is reachable to everyone in the same ways, but it is often easy for white people to assume this because there is a history, written by them, from their orientation in the world, that affirms their orientation as the only one possible, or as the best one possible, the ideal. This orientation to the world affirms that what is reachable by them is reachable by all. If a teacher shares in this unseen, naturalized orientation to the world and its languages, then we may use it to read and make judgments on students' writing and reflections. We might think of it as the way in which the habits of mind in the *Framework*, such as metacognition, get translated and used to assess all students, as if all students were assessable in the same ways. But make no mistake, if we do not closely examine our pre-cognitive impulses, our habits of language and judgment for the stamp of whiteness, then we will unwittingly perpetuate the white supremacist conditions in our classrooms and schools we try desperately to stop.

I have been guilty of this myself. Think of the times we ask students for more details or to attach something real, an experience, to their reflections on their learning. Our orientation to their thinking about their thinking is to have as much of it as possible accessible to us as the teacher. This is a whitely move, a move that assumes that our students must submit to us and our evaluative gaze no matter what. Why should we believe that we can have all or most of a student's learning in our reach? Because whitely teachers before us expected that? Because we cannot trust our students when they say that they've learned something but give no evidence of it in their reflections? Because they don't say something about their learning in an explicit way, or a way we think is explicit enough?

Yes, there is a paradox here. If we don't have access to students' learnings, then we cannot know they've learned, or we cannot judge that learning, grade it, evaluate it. We cannot know that we've done what we were supposed to do as teachers. But this is a version of the first white habit of language and judgment above. We expect our own orientation to the world to be primary, to be in proximity of what a student is learning. We expect everything that is of consequence to be in our reach or sight because we must teach and evaluate. That's a very whitely assumption to make. It's also a paradox. Teachers have to assess something to know that metacognition is happening, right? Students should be able to explain and support their ideas about their thinking and learning.

It isn't that I think these habits of mind are bad, that they deceive us. It is that I think not naming them as coming from a particular white racial history of education and educators, who have mostly been educated in particular conditions that make certain manifestations of these habits of mind possible, is dangerous. It's dangerous not just because it can harm many students who do not exhibit metacognition in the ways that white or whitely teachers of writing ask of them, regardless of the personal conditions that made those students different, but because it also harms the academy. Not examining and naming the racialized, gendered, and economic conditions that make our habits of mind possible and constitute their natures, limits our classrooms, limits the ways we can know any habit of mind. It turns teachers' surprise and wonder at the unexpected or unknown in student performances into anger and disappointment at what is not done correctly.

So my criticism is partly one about how the *Framework* articulates the habits of mind as an unexamined set of white habits of mind, and partly one about the absence of much needed discussions of how such habits are always habits of mind of particular people who have cultivated their habits of mind in particular histories, structures, and experiences that likely are quite uneven in any group of students. Because of who administers these habits of mind in classrooms, that is, teachers who have taken on white habits of language and judgment because of the generalized conditions that create writing teachers and their habits of mind in the first place, this unevenness usually hurts students of color most. How do we stop this? I think, it begins with writing teachers first examining the ways that white habits of language and judgment are already a part of the way they understand the *Framework*, then find ways to not use their private notions of what any habit of mind may look like as a universal standard in their courses. If we can do this, the academy and our classes will become a better place, one with more room for more minds with a colorful variety of habits that foster success in languaging in life, and not just postsecondary education.

Works Cited

Ahmed, Sara. "A Phenomenology of Whiteness." *Feminist Studies*, vol. 8, no. 2, 2008, pp. 149–68.

Inoue, Asao B. "2019 CCCC Chair's Address: How Do We Language So People Stop Killing Each Other, or What Do We Do about White Language Supremacy?" *College Composition and Communication*, vol. 71, no. 2, 2019, pp. 352–69.

—. "Classroom Writing Assessment as an Antiracist Practice: Confronting White Supremacy in the Judgments of Language." *Pedagogy*, vol. 19, no. 3, 2019, pp. 373–404.

Council of Writing Program Administrators, National Council of Teachers of English, and National Writing Project. *Framework for Success in Postsecondary Writing.* CWPA, NCTE, and NWP, 2011, wpacouncil.org/aws/CWPA/asset_manager/get_file/350201?ver=505. Accessed 1 Aug. 2020.

Contributors

Melvin Beavers is the first-year writing director in the Department of Rhetoric and Writing at the University of Arkansas at Little Rock. Dr. Beavers teaches courses in first-year composition, persuasive writing, and research methods. His recent dissertation research examined the professional development practices and approaches writing program administrators use to help further develop contingent faculty teaching first-year writing online. Additionally, he has presented at several national conferences, including conferences for the Council of Writing Program Administrators and the Association of Rhetoric and Writing Studies.

Subrina Bogan is an adjunct professor in the Department of Rhetoric and Writing at the University of Arkansas at Little Rock. She teaches a variety of courses, including Composition Fundamentals and Composition. Ms. Bogan spent three years as a writing instructor for the Charles W. Donaldson summer bridge program. In 2018, she served as co-director for the composition portion of the program. She is a composition instructor at Philander Smith College, an HBCU.

Harold Brown is a professional who splits his time between rolling burritos and delving into scholarship on identity, language, and power. As a student, Harold found his passion for writing and helping students when he became an intern at the university writing center. From his passion for seeing students succeed, Harold became an instructor for the Charles W. Donaldson Scholars Academy, a summer bridge program offered on the campus of the University of Arkansas at Little Rock. Now, he lends his voice to helping students entering college navigate and own their collegiate experience.

Christine Peters Cucciarre is a professor of English at the University of Delaware. She is the director of composition and directs the post-doctoral program on the teaching of writing. She works across campus and across the state to promote writing and the teaching of writing. She also chairs the Teacher to Teacher event held annually during the Conference on College Composition and Communication.

Barbara J. D'Angelo is Clinical Professor of Technical Communication at Arizona State University (ASU). She earned her MSLIS from the University of Illinois, Urbana-Champaign and her PhD from Texas Tech University. She teaches courses in technical communication, business communication, proposal writing, and health communication. She has coordinated a multi-section course on communication in healthcare. Barbara's work on information literacy spans two decades as both librarian and professor of technical communication, with a focus on the relationship between IL and writing. Her current research interests include information literacy, threshold concepts, writing assessment, and writing analytics. She has presented and published book chapters and articles on information literacy, writing assessment, and business communication, and health communication.

Gita DasBender is a language lecturer at New York University's Expository Writing Program and Fulbright advisor at NYU's Office of Global Awards. Prior to joining NYU, she was the coordinator of second language writing at Seton Hall University where she also served as the director of Prestigious Fellowships and Scholarships. She is the author of *Language: A Reader for Writers* (Oxford University Press, 2013) and her research interests include second language writing theory and practice, assessment, writing transfer, and writing in global settings. She is also the assistant editor for the *Journal of Writing Assessment*.

Tonya Eick is a first-year composition instructor at Arizona State University and Chandler-Gilbert Community College, as well as a PhD student in the Linguistics and Applied Linguistics program at ASU. From 2015 to 2017 she served as the assistant then associate director of Second Language Writing in ASU's Writing Programs. Her research focuses on TESOL curriculum and teacher development, World Englishes, English for Specific Purposes (ESP), and second language learner cognition. Over the past fifteen years she has worked with second language learners from preschool-aged all the way to graduate students and workplace professionals in the United States and Japan.

Gregg Fields earned his doctorate in Writing, Rhetorics, and Literacies from Arizona State in 2019. He is Lead Faculty for FYC at Chandler-Gilbert Community College. Other recent book chapters include "Advanced rhetoric and socially-situated writing" and "An integrative pedagogy of affirmation and resource sharing" focused on fostering translingual practices, his scholarly research is highly focused on re-imaging the writing discipline more systematically and holistically while maintaining close ties between composition pedagogy and theory. The professional, emotional, and spiritual support of his wife and three daughters make it possible to continue work in these areas.

Morgan Gross is the associate director of the Academic Resource Center at Loyola Marymount University in Los Angeles where she oversees the writing center. Kelsie Walker is the grants and programs coordinator at the Academy of Model Aeronautics. Their chapter in this collection was written when they worked as graduate assistant directors of the writing program and writing center, respectively, at Ball State University.

Jessica Harnisch is an instructor in first-year composition Writers' Studio at Arizona State University. She has extensive experience teaching and designing online courses in first-year writing, literature, and business writing. Her current research interests are in online course design and best practices in online writing instruction including online classroom climate and culture.

David Hyman is an associate professor of English at Lehman College/City University of New York. Before his career in postsecondary education he taught for several years in the New York City public school system. His scholarship and teaching range from composition studies, the Bible as literature, classical Greek, comics, film, and popular music. His book *Revision and the Superhero Genre* (Palgrave)was nominated for the 2018 Comics Studies Society Book Prize and the 2018 Eisner Award for best Scholarly/Academic Work.

Asao B. Inoue is Professor and Associate Dean of Academic Affairs, Equity, and Inclusion for the College of Integrative Sciences and Arts at Arizona State University. He is a past member of the Executive Board of CWPA and the CCCC Executive Committee, and the 2019 Chair of CCCC. He has published many articles and chapters on writing assessment and race and racism, as well as two edited collections and two books on writing assessment and race. He has won the CWPA's 2014 Outstanding Scholarship Award, their 2015 Outstanding Book Award, and the NCTE/CCCC Outstanding Book Award in 2014 and 2016.

Caleb James is an assistant professor of English at the University of Maine at Augusta, where he teaches courses in first-year composition and professional writing. His past research explores how writing teachers develop their teaching philosophies and classroom practices and how those might evolve. In an effort to identify practical strategies for faculty to support the missions of academic tutoring centers on their campuses, his current research looks to administrators of academic tutoring centers for insight on their experiences with receiving support from campus stakeholders.

Peter H. Khost (pronounced *coast*) is an associate professor and the associate director of Stony Brook University's Program in Writing and Rhetoric, where he is also founding co-principal investigator of the Writing Research Lab. His book *Rhetor Response: A Theory and Practice of Literary Affordance* (Utah State University Press) has been nominated for the Conference on College Composition and Communication's (CCCC) 2020 Outstanding Book Award and Modern Language Association's 2020 Mina P. Shaughnessy Prize. Peter coedits the *Journal of the Assembly for Expanded Perspectives on Learning* and has won research grants from CCCC and the Council of Writing Program Administrators.

William J. (Bill) Macauley, Jr. is a professor of English at the University of Nevada, Reno, where he has directed the writing center, directed the WAC/WID program, the development of the university's new core curriculum, and participated in multiple areas and levels of department and university assessment. Bill has been studying the roles and responsibilities of students in academic writing for twenty years, most recently studying the Oxford Tutorial. He continues to be fascinated by how students make decisions about their writing and what supports those decisions in higher education.

Heather MacDonald is an instructor of first-year composition in the Arizona State University Writers' Studio. She has taught various transfer-level writing courses in both Southern California and the Phoenix Metro Valley, including surveys of literature, critical thinking, argumentation, success strategies, creative writing, and freshman composition. Her current research interests include online education, instruction of writing courses in hybrid or "blended" formats, and research writing in the era of "fake news."

Barry Maid is a professor and founding head of the technical communication program at Arizona State University. He led that program for ten years. Previously, he taught at the University of Arkansas at Little Rock where, among other things, he helped in the creation of the Department of Rhetoric and Writing. Along with numerous articles and chapters focusing on technology, outcomes assessment, information literacy, independent writing programs, and program administration, he is a co-author, with Duane Roen and Greg Glau, of *The McGraw-Hill Guide: Writing for College, Writing for Life*.

Susan Miller-Cochran is Professor of English and Director of General Education at the University of Arizona. She formerly served as director of the writing programs at the University of Arizona and North Carolina State University. Her scholarly work has appeared in over 40 journal articles and book chapters, and she is a co-editor of *Composition, Rhetoric, and Disciplinarity* (Utah State, 2018); *Rhetorically Rethinking Usability* (Hampton, 2009); and *Strategies for Teaching First-Year Composition* (NCTE, 2002). She is also a co-author of *An Insider's Guide to Academic Writing* (Macmillan, 2019), *The Cengage Guide to Research* (Cengage, 2017), and *Keys for Writers* (Cengage, 2016). She is a past president of the Council of Writing Program Administrators.

Courtney Patrick-Weber is an assistant professor of Rhetoric and Composition at Bay Path University. She teaches first-year writing composition courses with a focus on writing as a way of healing, as well as introductory literature and technical writing courses. Her work has been published in *Technoculture* and *Computers and Composition Online*. Currently, she is working on a book project about pregnancy and trauma in horror films that is under contract with Lexington Books.

Patricia Portanova is Associate Professor of English at Northern Essex Community College where she teaches writing and communication and serves as the coordinator of the Liberal Arts Program and Creative Writing Program. She currently co-chairs the Cognition and Writing Special Interest Group at CCCC. Her research focuses on cognition and writing, civic inquiry, and public rhetoric with scholarship appearing in *Social Writing/Social Media: Publics, Presentations, and Pedagogies* and *Linguistically Diverse Immigrant and Resident Writers: Transitions from High School to College*. She holds a doctorate in Composition Studies from the University of New Hampshire and has taught at several colleges in Massachusetts.

Sherry Rankins-Robertson is Professor of Writing and Rhetoric at the University of Central Florida where she serves as department chair. Her research has appeared in *Kairos, Computers and Composition*, and the *Journal of Writing Assessment* along with diverse edited collections. She has served as co-editor of the *WPA journal*. With Nicholas Behm and Duane Roen, she edited *The Framework for Success in Postsecondary Writing: Scholarship and Applications*. Her recent co-edited collection is *Prison Pedagogies: Learning and Teaching with Imprisoned Writers*. Sherry is a co-author of *McGraw Hill Guide to Writing 5th edition*. She is an officer for CWPA and serves as a member of the executive committee for CCCC.

J. Michael Rifenburg, Associate Professor of English at the University of North Georgia, serves a Co-Director of First-Year Composition and Senior Faculty Fellow for Scholarly Writing with UNG's Center for Teaching, Learning, and Leadership. He authored *The Embodied Playbook: Writing Practices of Student-Athletes* (Utah State University Press, 2018) and co-edited *Contemporary Perspectives on Cognition and Writing* (WAC Clearinghouse, 2017). His next book, *Drilled to Write: A Longitudinal Study of a Cadet at a Senior Military College*, is currently under contract.

Duane Roen, Professor of English at Arizona State University, serves as the dean of the College of Integrative Sciences and Arts, vice provost of the Polytechnic campus, and coordinator for the Project for Writing and Recording Family History. His publications and presentations have focused on a wide range of topics in writing studies—pedagogy, curriculum, cognition and writing, audience awareness, the history of CCCC, writing across the curriculum, portfolio assessment, and community engagement.

Airlie Rose is the STEM writing specialist at the Amherst College writing center. She was a doctoral candidate in biology when she discovered writing center pedagogy at Duke in 2002. Since then, she has supported students, faculty, and fellow tutors in writing and the teaching of writing, earning a doctorate in composition-rhetoric from UMASS Amherst in 2015 and an MFA in poetry. Airlie's exploration of voice in writing is informed by her interest in neuroscience, psycholinguistics, and cognitive poetics. Her current mixed-methods study of freewriting was vetted at the Dartmouth Summer Seminar for Composition Research in 2018.

Wendy Ryden is Professor of English at Long Island University Post where she teaches courses in writing and literature, including creative nonfiction and writing and healing, and oversees the WAC program. She is co-author of *Reading, Writing, and the Rhetorics of Whiteness* (Routledge) and co-editor of *Haunting Realities: Naturalist Gothic and American Realism* (University of Alabama). She co-edits the *Journal of the Assembly for Expanded Perspectives on Learning*.

Thomas Skeen is Associate Professor of English at Grand Canyon University, where he teaches in the first-year writing program and in the professional writing program. He also teaches graduate courses on rhetoric, writing pedagogy, and grant writing in GCU's master's degree program. Some of his previous work has appeared in *Computers and Composition* and *College English*, and his current research interests include writing pedagogy, cognitive psychology, and learning transfer.

Michelle Stuckey is a clinical assistant professor at Arizona State University and the writing program director for the Writers' Studio, a fully online writing program housed in the College of Integrative Sciences and Arts. The Writers' Studio serves over three thousand students a semester. She also oversees a course-embedded tutor program of more than fifty writing mentors who provide additional instructional support to online students.

Sean Tingle is an instructor of first-year composition in the Arizona State University Writers' Studio, a fully online writing program housed in the College of Integrative Sciences and Arts. They have taught and designed various online English and Humanities courses at both the university and community college level. They have a strong interest in examining human nature, creation, interaction, and communication. Their current research interests include online education, compassion and empathy in education, gender in language, and student engagement.

James Toweill is an instructor of first-year composition in the Arizona State University Writers' Studio. His research interests include research methods and transfer in college writing courses. He has many years of experience in designing and teaching courses in first-year composition, creative writing and literature at two-year and four-year academic institutions.

Martha (Marty) Townsend is Professor Emerita of English at the University of Missouri. Townsend's scholarship has played a central role in the conceptualization and development of writing-across-the-curriculum (WAC) programs in the United States and abroad. She is a former literacy consultant to The Ford Foundation and consults widely on WAC program implementation, development, and assessment. From 1991 to 2006 she directed the University of Missouri's internationally renowned Campus Writing Program. She holds the BA (1983) and MA (1985) in English from the University of Utah and the PhD (1991) in English from Arizona State University.

Bronwyn T. Williams is a professor of English and director of the University Writing Center at the University of Louisville. He writes and teaches on issues of literacy, identity, digital media, writing center theory and practice, and popular culture. His books include *Literacy Practices and Perceptions of Agency: Composing Identities*; *Shimmering Literacies: Popular Culture and Reading and Writing Online*; *Identity Papers: Literacy and Power in Higher Education*; and, with Amy Zenger, *New Media Literacies and Participatory Popular Culture Across Borders* and *Popular Culture and Representations of Literacy*.

Index

ACT, 22, 236
Adler-Kassner, Linda, vii–viii, 7, 46, 48–49, 77, 111, 180, 191–192, 251
Advanced Placement, 25, 176
affect, 30, 62, 67, 110, 127, 213, 218, 254, 273, 279, 306, 326
agency, 5, 8, 12, 21, 28, 30, 35, 69, 137, 151, 189, 191, 193–194, 201, 216, 258, 267, 281–298, 303–305, 309, 316, 318
Ahmed, Sara, 327
Alderson-Day, Ben, 54, 62, 65
Alexander, Jonathan, 4, 252–253, 266
Angelou, Maya, x
Anzaldúa, Gloria, 85–86, 103–104
Aristotle, 3, 24
Arizona State University, 12, 46, 152–153, 157
Association of American Colleges and Universities, 23, 36
Atwill, Janet M., 31

Bacon, Francis, 4
Bain, Alexander, 4
Baker-Bell, April, 211
Bakhtin, Mikhail, 114, 116–117, 122
Bandura, Albert, 287, 288, 296, 314–315
Bartholomae, David, 222
Bartlett, William, 289

Bawarshi, Anis, 114, 207
Bazerman, Charles, 55, 97, 113
Beavers, Melvin E., 12, 323
Beaufort, Anne, 160
Behm, Nicholas, 8, 13, 177
Bereiter, Carl, 43
Bergen, Benjamin, 29
Bey, Hakim, 283
Beyoncé, 116
BIPOC, 210
Bitzer, Lloyd, 27–28, 85, 89–90, 103–106
Blaauw-Hara, Mark, 10, 13
Black Lives Matter, 210
Blackman, Lisa, 30
body, 4, 21, 28, 31, 36, 56, 245, 325; awareness of, 32; human, 4, 238
Bogan, Subrina, 12, 224, 323
Boondocks, The, 223–224
Boquet, Elizabeth, 282
Bowden, Darsie, 251
Brand, Miles, 233
Breen, Mara, 62
bricolage, 34
Brown, Harold, 12, 323
Bruning, Roger, 297
Buddhism, 33
Bueller, Ferris, 25

Calhoon-Dillahunt, Carolyn, 251
Campbell, George, 4
Carillo, Ellen, 228

339

340 *Index*

Carr, Nicholas, 85–86, 103–104
Cass, Jeffrey, 296
CCCC Guidelines for Ethical Conduct of Research in Composition Studies, 237
Cheville, Julie, 238
Cicero, 284, 296, 298
Clifton, Chuck, 62
CNN, 233
Cochran, Stacey, ix
code-switching, 224; cognition, 30, 44, 48, 55, 149, 169, 180, 218, 264, 311, 318, 323; classroom, 190; in community-focused writing, 150–151; emotions in, 305, 308, 311; etymology of, 4; linguistic, 27; model of, 28; role of, 6; for student-athletes, 239; teacher, 195; view of, 29; in writing pedagogy, 304, 307
cognition and composition, 13
cognition and writing, 6–11, 13, 305–306
Cognition and Writing Standing Group, 9
cognitive, 4, 22, 110–111, 120, 146, 163, 195, 201, 286, 292, 328; activity, 27, 29, 44, 48, 55–56, 218; approaches, 149; behaviors, 48; bridge, 8, 189; choices, 46; dimension, 30; habits, 252, 285; load, 308; moves, 5 ; models, 5–7, 11, 57, 63; patterns, 307; practices, 150, 327; processes, 304, 319; psychology, 108–109, 112, 122, 128; reserves, 246; rhetoric, 9; science, 10, 55, 296; skills, 119, 182; steps, 140; system, 190, 192, 205; theory, 10–13, 28, 55, 135, 137
collective learning, 282

College English, 7
college-ready, 10, 23, 175, 177, 183
colonialism, 10
Columbia University, Embodiment Lab, 238, 245
Common Core State Standards Initiative, viii, 7, 22, 176, 179
community college, 32
community writing, 12, 150–151, 155, 169
Compass Education Group, 214
composition, 7, 116–117, 169, 193–194; classrooms, 71, 100, 145, 211, 214, 223, 226, 239; cognitive approaches to, 11; course, 78, 83, 90, 110, 199; discipline of, 77; field of, 82; heuristics of, 24; instructor, 220; multimodal, 155; researchers, 238–239; scholars, 53, 77, 145–146, 252; specialists, 195; studies, 79; theory, 134, 215
composition and rhetoric, 53, 55–56
Composition Forum, 109
Conference on College Composition and Communication, 10, 13, 77, 145, 210, 255, 323, 210–211, 221–222, 225, 229, 237, 330
Contemporary Perspectives on Cognition and Writing, 6, 9, 53, 55, 149
Cook, Tim, 116
correctness, 283
Council of Writing Program Administrators, vii, 6, 9, 150–155, 251, 272
Cousin, Glynis, 82
Coutinho, Maria Antonia, 115-117
Cox, Anicca, 215
creativity, viii, ix, 7, 160, 252, 264, 272, 278

Delaware's use of, 184; emotions in, 308–309, 312–313; in FYC curricula, 188, 190, 198; student's reflection on, 159, 162; students', 224; in writing centers, 294,
Creswell, John W., 255
Crowley, Sharon, 4
Cucciarre, Christine, 12, 229
curiosity, viii, ix, 7, 105, 110, 160, 169, 252, 268, 272, 278, 291, 319
compassionate, 53; Delaware's use of, 184; emotions in, 308–310; in FYC curricula, 188, 191, 193–196, 206–207; in information literacy, 42; student's reflections on, 164; in writing centers, 293–294

DasBender, Gita, 11, 49, 129, 265
Davidson, Cathy, 245-246
Davis, Josh I., 238
Davis, Mark A., 312
De Ridder-Symoens, Hilde, 281
decision-making, 257, 284–285, 290, 294–295
design problem, 112, 119–124, 126–130
Dew, Debra, 112
Dewey, John, 25, 161
dialogic learning, 304
dialogue, 106, 181, 282, 311, 317
differentiated instruction, 281
direct instruction, 81
dispassionate analysis, 306
Downs, Doug, 77–78, 82, 112, 160
Doyle, Terry, 245
Dr. Phil, 291
Driscoll, Dana Lynn, 253
Dryer, Dylan, 53, 180
dual enrollment, 25, 176, 179–180

dualities, 285–286
Dweck, Carol, 245–246, 286, 289, 307, 313

education research, 83
Efklides, Anastasia, 110, 309
Eick, Tonya, 12, 187, 189
Elbow, Peter, 52–53, 56, 60, 62, 67, 71, 127, 227
Elon Research Seminar, 9
Elon Statement on Writing Transfer, 9, 128
embodiment, 11, 229, 235, 238–239, 306
embody, 169, 239
Emdin, Christopher, 224, 226
Emig, Janet, 290–291
emotion, 168, 253, 285, 303–309, 315, 317–319
engagement, viii, ix, 7, 252; in community focused writing, 12, 154–155, 159, 170; in consultant training, 262–263, 272, 278; Delaware's use of, 182, 184; emotions in, 306, 308; in FYC curricula, 188, 191, 193–196, 199, 202, 206; with online learning, 150, 156; part-time contingent faculty teaching, 216–220, 228; for readiness, 28, 30, 32; with revision, 97; for student-athletes, 240; student's reflections on, 156–157; teaching, 32; in threshold concepts, 81; in transfer, 79, 90, 101, 207; in writing assignments, 88, 160, 217; in writing centers, 281, 288, 293–294
English Studies, 6
epimeleias, 239
Europe, 281
executive function, 71

expertise, vii, 43, 44, 84, 111–114, 122, 130, 193–194, 260, 282

failure, 23, 35, 245, 252, 266, 282, 309, 312, 315
Farris, Christine, 176
Fernyhough, Charles, 54–55, 65, 314–315
Fields, Gregg, 12
first-year composition, 82–83, 133, 150, 154, 157, 160, 188–189, 194–196, 199, 204, 229, 285, 287, 292, 295
first-year writing, 12, 44, 77–78, 81, 83–84, 89, 101, 135–137, 140, 142, 150, 160, 178–179, 215, 298, 310
Fitzgerald, Lauren, 263
Flanagan, Michael, 81
Flavell, John, 8
Fleckenstein, Kristie, 56, 238
Fleischer, Cathy, 7
flexibility, viii, ix, 7, 35, 41–42, 110, 160, 184, 252, 263–265, 273, 278, 294, 308, 316–317
Flower, Linda, 4, 6–7, 9, 55, 71, 154, 189, 194–196, 291
Floyd, George, 210
fNIRS, 5
Framework for Information Literacy for Higher Education, 41, 44, 47–48
Framework for Success in Postsecondary Writing, 11, 23, 36, 55, 109, 110–111, 129; in community-engaged writing, 151; in consultant-training, 251–254, 256-57, 269–271; critiques of, 10, 35, 221, 225–226, 280, 297, 323–330; Delaware's use of, 178, 181–185; drafting of, vii–viii, ix; emotion in, 304–305, 308–312, 315, 317, 319; in

FYC curricula, 188, 196–197, 206; part-time contingent faculty teaching, 211–214, 216, 218–219; reactions to, 6–9, 177, 181, 228–229; in trauma theory, 137; for student-athletes, 240; in writing centers, 281–295, 298, 310–312, 315, 317
Frere-Jones, Sasha, 115–117, 122
Frost, Robert, 53–54
Fulwiler, Toby, 57–58, 63, 67–68

Galen, 4
Ganim, Sara, 233
Geertz, Clifford, 53
Geller, Anne Ellen, 264, 304
genre, 4, 29, 32, 84, 111–120, 122–130, 135–136, 142, 162, 194, 201, 313
Geva, Sharon, 62
Gillham, Bill, 236
Good News, 233
Gore, Al, 85–86, 92, 103–104
Gross, Daniel M., 252–253, 266,
Gross, Morgan, 12, 187, 240, 270
Grutsch McKinney, Jackie, 253
Guba, Egon, 236–237

habits of mind, 6, 9, 36, 213–214, 224, 228–229, 285, 288; attitudes as, 213; Black students and faculty reacting to, 211–212; in consultant training, 12, 251-54, 257, 263–272, 277–279; in community-engaged writing, 151, 154, 159–160, 169–170; critiques of, 10, 35, 212, 216, 226, 280, 324–325; drafting of, viii, ix; definitions of, 7–8, 181, 187, 252, 323; Delaware's use of, 183–185; disposition as, 31; emotions in, 305, 308–312, 314, 316–317, 319, 327–329; in

FYC curricula, 188–189, 191, 193, 195–196; in ill-structured problems, 110, 160; instructor's reflecting on, 216, 219–220, 227; modeling of, 217–218; in online learning, 154, 163; for student-athletes, 240; student's reflections on, 156, 158, 162–163, 165, 168; in writing centers, 281-282, 286, 290-95
habitus, 35
Hacker, Douglas, 8
Hall, Anne-Marie, 7
Hand, Brian, 5, 10
Hanson, Kristine, 176
Harnisch, Jessica, ix, 12
Hawhee, Debra, 30–31, 35–37, 238–239
Hayes, John, 4, 6–7, 43, 55–57, 63, 71, 149, 291
Herman, Judith, 138–139, 144–145
hexeis, 31
higher-order, 216, 283
Historically Black Colleges and Universities, 213
hooks, bell, 143, 220, 221; Teaching to Transgress, 221
Horning, Alice, 228
hospitality, 311–312
How People Learn, 42, 113, 130
Huckleberry Finn, 223
Huot, Brian, 97
Hurlburt, Russell, 54, 56, 59, 60
Hyman, David, 11, 175, 212

Ianetta, Melissa, 263
Indianapolis Resolution: Responding to Twenty-First-Century Exigencies/Political Economies of Composition Labor, 215
information literacy, 41, 47–49

Inoue, Asao, 9–10, 13, 35–36, 185, 225–226, 286
institutional research board, 58, 83, 189, 235, 237, 252, 254, 309
International Writing Centers Association, 253
iTunes, 116

James, Caleb, 12, 323
Jamsen, Kirsten, 251
Jaschik, Scott, 233
Johnson, Kristine, 7, 252
Jonassen, David H., 112, 119–124, 126–129

Kahnemann, Daniel, 308, 314
kairos, 30–31, 34–36
Kalish, Katie, 215, 229
Keener, Matt, 8
Kezar, Adrianna, 215
Khost, Peter, 11, 21, 24, 27, 175, 212
Kircher, John, 8
Knight Commission on Intercollegiate Athletics, 232
Kroll, Keith, 32–33
Kuhlthau, Karen, 42

labor, 10–11, 35, 185, 215–216
Lamb, Richard L., 5, 10
Land, Ray, 40–41, 47, 50–51, 77, 79, 80–81, 84, 101–103, 131, 141, 163
Lawless, Elaine J., 237
Lerner, Neal, 253, 281–282, 284
Levelt, Willem, 56–57, 71
Lévi-Strauss, Claude, 34
Library Information Science, 11, 40–42, 44, 47–48
Lincoln, Yvonne, 236–237
literacy, 30, 84–85, 90, 145, 176, 213–314, 325; academic, 136; community, 154; courses, 212;

digital, 155; experiences, 83, 100, 305; department of, 7; development, 12, 214; instruction, 178; practices, 12, 239, 305; prior, 81, 82; projects, 324; skills, 177, 296
Literate Lives, 235–237
Lloyd, Annemaree, 47
locus of control, 286
Louisiana State University, 234

Macauley Jr., William J., 12, 56, 187, 258, 267, 283
MacDonald, Heather, ix, 12
Machlin, Tzvi, 234
Maid, Barry, ix, 11, 40, 45–46, 49, 323
Males, Michael, 285, 292
Maxey, Daniel, 215
McComiskey, Bruce, 7
McGruder, Aaron, 225
memory, 56, 59, 124, 137–139, 146, 192, 202, 314–315, 325
Merriam, Sharan, 236
metacognition, viii, ix, 7, 161, 175, 183, 252, 288, 293, 295, 323; in community-focused writing, 12, 151, 154; in consultant training, 268, 273, 278 critiques of 324, 326–329; emotions in, 304, 306, 309–10, 315; in mindfulness, 32–33, 35; for student-athletes, 235, 238, 240; in threshold concepts, 83; in transfer, 6, 8–9, 11, 40–48, 82, 128, 149, 159 ; in writing pedagogy, 22, 28, 185, 190, 206–207, 216–220
metanoia, 34–35
metis, 30–31, 33
Meyer, Jan, 40–41, 47, 77, 79–81, 84, 101, 163
Meyer, Kelly A., 34–35

Mickelson, Nate, 33
Miller, Carolyn, 117–118
Miller, Michael D., 296
Miller, Nicole, 156
Miller, Richard, 234
Miller, Susan, 24, 156, 251
Miller-Cochran, Susan, 11, 13
mind, 52, 63–64, 68, 205, 219, 238, 245, 284–285, 295; in rhetoric and writing studies, 4; in writing pedagogy, 5; rhetorical presence of, 21, 28; in memory, 314; in emotions, 307; of students, 190, 241, 290–291
mindfulness, 32
mindset, 69, 183, 233, 245, 286, 289, 291
Miranda, Florencia, 115–117
monolingual, 325–327
MRI, 3
multimodality, 239
multiplicity, 115, 285

Naming What We Know, 41, 44, 180
National Collegiate Athletic Association, 232–233, 235, 237
National Council of Teachers of English, viii, 6, 150, 251
National Geographic, 3
National Writing Project, viii, 6, 251
Nelson, Cary, 215
neuroscience, 5, 10, 56, 304–306
New Yorker, 115–116, 118
Newcomb, Matthew, 252
Nicklay, Jennifer, 263
North, Stephen, 281–282

one-to-one attention, 281
openness, viii, ix, 7, 36, 41, 110, 137, 160, 164, 169, 182, 184, 216, 219–220, 226, 228,

252, 277–278, 294, 308–309, 311–312
oppositional thinking, 285

Pajares, Frank, 288, 295–296, 314–315
Patel, Leigh, 11
Patrick-Weber, Courtney, 12
Peary, Alexandra, 30, 33
Penrose, Ann, 211
Pentecostal, 224
performative act, 220
Perkins, David, 25, 79–80, 86
Perl, Sondra, 4–5, 53, 56
Perloff, Richard, 214
persistence, viii, ix, 7, 110, 150, 156–157, 164, 182, 188, 221, 252–253, 278, 281, 293–294, 308, 313, 315, 324–325
personal narrative, 32, 135, 137, 141–142, 145–146
Peterson, Christopher, xi
Peterson, Todd, 217
Pflugfelder, Ehren, 30–31, 34
phenomenological, 53, 327
phrenology, 10
Plato, 4, 284, 296
Porter, Roy, 4
positivism, 10
problem solving, 108–112, 114, 119, 120–123, 128–130, 160, 189, 219
psycholinguistics, 52–53, 56–57
psychology, 4, 8, 12, 52–54, 108–109, 111–112, 122, 128, 141, 149, 244–245, 275, 285, 304–306, 312

Quintilian, 284

Race to the Top, viii
racism, 10, 35, 223

Rankins-Robertson, Sherry, 8, 12, 177, 323
Ratcliffe, Krista, 219
readiness, vii, viii, 7, 11, 21–25, 27, 29–36, 153, 176–177, 181, 211–214, 252
reciprocity, 237, 312
Reiff, Mary Jo, 114, 207
Reitman, Walter, 108
relativism, 285
remediation, 22–23, 178, 282
resilience, 221, 229, 307, 314
responsibility, viii, ix, 7, 182, 188; in consultant training, 252, 254–263, 265–269, 277–279; in FYC curricula, 188, 195, 207; in online writing classes, 153; part-time contingent faculty teaching 216–222, 225; for readiness, 35; student's reflections on, 159; in trauma theory, 137; in writing centers, 280–281, 288, 293, 295
rhetoric and composition, 215, 252, 269
rhetorical listening, 219
Rifenburg, J. Michael, 8, 238–239
Robertson, Liane, 9, 43–44, 82, 102, 112, 161, 193
Roen, Duane, 3, 8, 38, 177
Roozen, Kevin, 90, 103, 238–239
Roth, David Lee, 115–116
Rotter, Julia, 286–288
Rowe, Steven, 289
Royster, Jacqueline, 225
Russell, David R., 53
Ryden, Wendy, 11, 175, 212

Sasson, Remez, 291
SAT, 83, 176, 178, 236
Scardamalia, Marlene, 43, 50–51
schemas, 119–122, 156, 285
Schoem, David, 32
Schwitzgebel, Eric, 54, 60

Scogin, Joseph, 236
self-efficacy, 12, 143–144, 281, 283–285, 287–289, 291, 293–298, 315
self-reactivity, 287, 295
self-reflectivity, 287
Selfe, Cynthia L., 145
Selfe, Richard, 251
Seligman, Martin, ix
Severino, Carol, 177, 182, 218
Skeen, Thomas, ix, 12, 21, 160
Smith, Linda Tuhiwai, 10
Soja, Edward, 283
Soliday, Mary, 34
Stake, Robert E., 236
Steinbach, Rosanne, 43
STEM, viii
Stern, Yaakov, 245
Stevens, Wallace, 234
Stuckey, Michelle, ix, 12, 129, 149
Sullivan, Patrick, 183, 229, 252

Taczak, Kara, 9, 43–44, 112, 161, 193
Takaku, Seiji, 297
Teaching for Transfer, 9, 112, 130
techne, 30–32, 34
TedX, 224
temporality, 283
temporary autonomous zone, 283, 298
think-aloud protocol, 291
think-aloud protocols, 4
threshold concepts, 11, 40–44, 46–49, 77–85, 89–90, 92, 94, 97, 100–101, 118, 129, 163
time management, 243
Tinberg, Howard, 26, 37, 39, 44, 48, 51, 97, 102, 177
Tingle, Sean, ix, 12, 149
Toweill, James, ix, 12
Townsend, Martha, 12, 182, 235, 265

Trainor, Jennifer Seibel, 34
transfer, 6, 11, 111, 114, 119, 122; cognitive psychology's view on, 109; of course content, 207; critiques of, 32; in ill-structured problems, 129; metacognition's role in 8, 42, 48, 159, 185; of knowledge, 265; student's reflections on, 162, 243; teaching for, 21, 43, 112, 128; writing, 9, 11, 77, 79, 83, 101, 110, 130, 150; learning, 25, 40, 44, 86, 149, 160–161, 170; of threshold concepts, 82; in workplace learning, 47, 49
Trickster, 264–265
Tugend, Alina, 286
tutor-training, 12

U2, 116–117, 131
Uehling, Karen, 26
Ueland, Brenda, 290
Usher, Ellen L., 288, 295

Valiante, Giovanni, 296
Van Halen, 115, 117
Van Halen, Wolfgang, 116
Van Halen, Alex, 116
Van Halen, Eddie, 116
voice, 11, 52–54, 57–59, 60, 62, 65–69, 70, 211, 224–225
Vygotsky, Lev, 55

WAC Clearinghouse, 217
Waddington, C. H., 56
Walker, Clay, 30
Walker, Guy, 80
Walker, Kelsie, 12, 39, 187, 240, 270
Warburton, Elizabeth, 62
Wardle, Elizabeth, 48–49, 77–78, 109–110, 112, 114, 160, 180, 211

Wenger, Christy, 32
Wetherell, Margaret, 306–307, 317
White, Edward, 42
White, Mary Jane, 297
whiteness, 9, 13, 35–36, 327–328
wicked problems, 280
Williams, Bronwyn, 12, 253, 305, 308, 311, 318
Williams, James, 297
Wilson, Timothy, 308, 314, 316
WPA Outcomes Statement for First-Year Composition, vii, viii, 7, 47–48, 151, 160, 165, 167, 169, 227, 252, 280
Writing About Writing, 103, 112
Writing Across Contexts, 9, 17, 51, 133, 161, 172
writing centers, 6, 12–13, 56, 251–254, 256, 258–259, 262–263, 265–268, 271–272, 275–278, 281–287, 292, 295, 297, 303–305, 310–318, 323

writing center tutoring, 251, 254–255, 263, 265–267, 271–272, 277, 279, 282
writing curricula, 21, 47, 176, 282
Writing Studies, 6, 41, 48, 50–51, 102–103, 131, 291
writing-centered, 283
Written Communication, 7

Yagelski, Robert, 33
Yancey, Kathleen Blake, 9, 4–244, 46, 56, 82, 112, 130, 145, 160–161, 191, 193–194, 205
yoga, 32
Yoon, Sae Yool, 5, 10
Young, Morris, 318
Young, Vershawn Ashanti, 210, 222–223

Zakrajsek, Todd, 245
Zimmer, Carl, 3
Zimmerelli, Lisa, 263, 284
Zuberi, Tukufu, 10

www.ingramcontent.com/pod-product-compliance
Lightning Source LLC
Chambersburg PA
CBHW030302240426

43673CB00040B/1037

CATCHING THE WIND

Penang in a Rising Asia

Edited by
Francis E. Hutchinson & Johan Saravanamuttu

Institute of Southeast Asian Studies
Singapore

First published in Singapore in 2012 by
ISEAS Publishing
Institute of Southeast Asian Studies
30 Heng Mui Keng Terrace
Pasir Panjang
Singapore 119614
Email: publish@iseas.edu.sg
Website: http://bookshop.iseas.edu.sg
For distribution in all countries except Malaysia

First published in Malaysia in 2012 by
Penang Institute
10 Brown Road
10350 Penang
Malaysia
Website: www.penanginstitute.org
For distribution in Malaysia

All rights reserved. No part of this publication may be reproduced, stored in a retrieval system, or transmitted in any form or by any means, electronic, mechanical, photocopying, recording or otherwise, without the prior permission of the Institute of Southeast Asian Studies.

© 2012 Penang Institute

The responsibility for facts and opinions in this publication rests exclusively with the authors and their interpretations do not necessarily reflect the views or the policy of Penang Institute, ISEAS or their supporters.

ISEAS Library Cataloguing-in-Publication Data

Catching the wind : Penang in a rising Asia / edited by Francis E. Hutchinson & Johan Saravanamuttu.

    1. Pulau Pinang—Economic conditions.
    2. World Heritage areas—Malaysia— Pulau Pinang.
    3. Pulau Pinang —Social life and customs.
    I. Hutchinson, Francis E.
    II. Saravanamuttu, J. (Jayaratnam)

HC445.5 Z7P4C35   2012
ISBN 978-981-4379-87-8 (soft cover)
ISBN 978-981-4414-35-7 (e-book, PDF)

Printed by The Phoenix Press Sdn Bhd

CONTENTS

Foreword
K. Kesavapany, Director of the Institute of Southeast Asian Studies ... VII

Foreword
Liew Chin Tong, Executive Director of Penang Institute ... IX

Acknowledgements ... X

About the Contributors ... XI

Introduction
Johan Saravanamuttu and Francis E. Hutchinson ... XV

1. Situating Penang in Asia and Malaysia ... 1
Francis E. Hutchinson

2. George Town, Penang: Managing a Multicultural World Heritage Site ... 20
Khoo Salma Nasution

3. Heritage as Knowledge: Time, Space, and Culture in Penang ... 42
Goh Beng Lan

4. Heritage Conservation and Muslims in George Town ... 55
Syed Muhd Khairudin Aljunied

5. Investment Opportunities in Penang ... 68
Lee Kah Choon, Wein Siew Wei and Sherine Loke

6. Penang in the New Asian Economy: Skills Development   84
& Future Human Resource Challenges
Poh Heem Heem and Tan Yin Hooi

7. PBA Holdings Bhd: The Road to Privatisation,   116
Corporatisation and Beyond
Jaseni Maidinsa

8. Penang's Technology Opportunities   128
Yoon Chon Leong

9. Building a Temporary Second Home: 160
Japanese Long-stay Retirees in Penang
Mika Toyota and Mayumi Ono

10. Medical Tourism in Penang: A Brief Review of the Sector   179
Su-Ann Oh

11. Penang's Halal Industry   192
Rosalind Chua

References   204

FOREWORD

In 2009, the Institute of Southeast Asian Studies (ISEAS) co-organized the inaugural Penang Outlook Forum with the Socio-Economic and Environmental Research Institute (SERI). The inaugural Forum, with a focus on "Restructuring and Reshaping Penang", was held in George Town, Penang on 1-2 June 2009. I am pleased to note that this inaugural Penang Outlook Forum resulted in the joint publication of *Pilot Studies for a New Penang* by the two research institutions in 2010.

It was therefore with great pleasure that ISEAS decided to host the second Penang Outlook Forum with the focus on "Penang in Asia". In the event, I was most encouraged by the enthusiastic response from the Singapore community to the forum and pleased that the forum has resulted in a second joint publication. I would like to congratulate the editors and the paper writers for their sterling effort.

As I understand it, the book aims at positioning Penang, and its primary city, George Town, in context of the rise of Asia as the new growth hub of the world economy. George Town is not a capital city or a megalopolis, yet it has still managed to carve out a niche for itself in a range of sectors. Second-tier cities, such as George Town, are clearly emerging as important sites for innovation, as their smaller size and pro-active policy-making has enabled them to attract or nurture a range of new industries. Specialized industries and services must also be served by efficient infrastructure, well-planned townships, functioning public transport as well as the proper management of basic resources such as water.

We in Singapore are of course happy to share with Penang our experience in areas such as economic efficiency, in public transport, housing and infrastructural development. But I hasten to add that the two cities have developed quite differently over time although they shared a common history as Straits Settlements under the British.

It was from Penang that Sir Stamford Raffles set sail to found Singapore in 1819. It is therefore most appropriate today for Singapore and Penang to think about each other's new Asian connectivity. I am confident that the two cities can re-connect in many meaningful ways in this age of globalization to enhance their economic, social and cultural ties. Singapore's more global connectivity could surely help to enhance Penang's own regional connectivity. In short, I believe that the two cities can mutually help each other improve their respective statuses as unique cities in the new global environment of a rising Asia.

Ambassador K. Kesavapany
Former Director
Institute of Southeast Asian Studies, Singapore
(November 2002 - February 2012)

FOREWORD

Since the conference co-organized by ISEAS and SERI took place in June 2010 from which the papers that constitute this book, the latter think-tank has undergone a major organizational transformation.

Most significantly, SERI became Penang Institute in August 2011. This name change proclaimed a consolidation of research initiatives aimed at strengthening institutional competence in selected fields; helping the state and federal government in key policy areas; and positioning the institute within the growing regional context with the conviction that economic growth must immediately involve new thinking about emerging issues affecting East Asia in order for its impact to be broad and responsible.

The ideas discussed in this volume are in line with this ambition, following as it does on the earlier publication in the Penang Studies Series, *Pilot Studies for a New Penang* (ISEAS and SERI 2010). More volumes are in the making, geared towards turning Penang Studies into a discipline that not only discusses the finer points of sub-national development and its connection to national and regional well-being, but also illustrates the regionalism that has always informed Penang's culture, politics and economy.

We are thankful to ISEAS and its former Director, Ambassador K. Kesavapany, for his cooperation in our projects, and to all the scholars and friends of Penang who have contributed in various ways to bring this second volume to completion.

We live in exciting but difficult times. Such times throw forth new challenges that are best met by the region's best minds working together, constructing new concepts and ideas and bringing these to public attention. National perspectives need to be complemented by sub-national and regional ones at the same time if we are to have a good chance of breaking the back of the serious problems troubling our times, such as shortages involving water and food, crises involving urban sprawl and poverty; and climate change and global warming.

Liew Chin Tong
Executive Director
Penang Institute

ACKNOWLEDGEMENTS

Most of the papers in this volume were first presented at the second Penang Outlook Forum, with the theme "Penang in Asia", which was held at the Institute of Southeast Asian Studies (ISEAS), Singapore, on 3 June 2010. The Forum was jointly organized by ISEAS and the Socio-economic and Environmental Research Institute (SERI), now renamed the Penang Institute. We would therefore like to thank both research institutions for making the Forum not just possible but also a major success.

Second, we would like to thank all the paper presenters for their participation and efforts in writing the papers and revising them for publication, along with several others who were commissioned to write chapters for the book. Our heartfelt thanks also go to all the chairpersons and discussants for their involvement and active participation in the Forum.

Our thanks go to the Parkway Group for generously contributing to the conference expenses and to Ms Janick Vatikiotis of JVB Consultants, representative of InvestPenang in Singapore, for her organizational assistance. On the ISEAS side, our sincere thanks go to Amb. Tan Keng Jin and Ms Hafidzah Ikbar of the Public Affairs Unit of ISEAS for their constant organizational assistance. And many thanks go to Ms Betty Kwan of ISEAS, who assisted the editors from start to finish of the project.

Finally, our thanks go to Mr Lim Guan Eng, the Honorable Chief Minister of Penang, and Ambassador K. Kesavapany for gracing the occasion and giving their keynote addresses.

The Editors

ABOUT THE CONTRIBUTORS

Editors:

Francis E. Hutchinson is a Fellow at the Institute of Southeast Asian Studies. His research focuses on governance, decentralization, and economic policy-making at the sub-national level in the Southeast Asian region. He is currently writing a sole-authored monograph on the influence of institutions on economic outcomes in Malaysia, with specific reference to the states of Penang and Johor. He has a PhD in Public Administration from the Australian National University, and degrees in Social and Political Sciences and Development Studies from the Universities of Cambridge and Sussex, respectively. He is also a Visiting Senior Research Fellow at the Penang Institute.

Johan Saravanamuttu is Visiting Senior Research Fellow at the Institute of Southeast Asian Studies, Singapore and was formerly professor of political science at Universiti Sains Malaysia (USM) in Penang where he served as Dean of the School of Social Sciences (1994-1996). In 1997, he was the Visiting Professor in ASEAN and International Studies at the University of Toronto. He recently authored *Malaysia's Foreign Policy, the First 50 Years: Alignment, Neutralism, Islamism* (ISEAS, 2010) and edited *Islam and Politics in Southeast Asia* (Routledge, 2010).

Chapter Writers:

Khoo Salma Nasution is President of the Penang Heritage Trust (2009-2011). She writes on the local history and heritage of Penang and is the author or co-author of nine books. She pioneered the idea of cultural tourism in Penang through her book *Streets of George Town* (1993) and various heritage trails. In 2006, she co-founded the Little Penang Street Market. Through Lestari Heritage Network, she has been involved in convening heritage meetings in Asia. She is the custodian of the Sun Yat Sen Penang Base at 120 Armenian Street, a historic house associated with the founder of the modern Chinese Republic. The Sun Yat Sen Penang Base was one of the organisers of the Penang Conference 100th

Anniversary Celebrations in November 2010. She and her husband run the Penang-based publishing company Areca Books.

Goh Beng Lan is an Associate Professor and Head of the Southeast Asian Studies Program at the Faculty of Arts and Social Sciences, National University of Singapore. She is trained in anthropology and her research interests revolve around the issues of modernity, urbanism, and knowledge production in Malaysia and wider Southeast Asia. She is the author of *Modern Dreams: An Inquiry into Power, Cultural Production, and the Cityscape in Contemporary Urban Penang, Malaysia* (Cornell SEAP, 2002), a co-editor of *Asia in Europe, Europe in Asia* (IIAS, Leiden and ISEAS, Singapore, 2004), and editor of the volume on *Decentering and Diversifying Southeast Asian Studies: Perspectives from the Region* (ISEAS, 2011).

Syed Muhd Khairudin Aljunied is Assistant Professor at the National University of Singapore. His research interests include Colonial History, the History of Ideas, Ethnic Minorities and Social Identities in Southeast Asia. Among his recent publications are *Colonialism, Violence and Muslims in Southeast Asia* (Routledge, 2009 and 2010), *Reframing Singapore*, co-editor (Amsterdam University Press, 2009), *Singapore in Global History*, co-editor (Amsterdam University Press, 2011) and *Melayu: The Politics, Poetics and Paradoxes of Malayness*, co-editor, (Singapore University Press, 2011). He is currently working on a monograph on Malay anti-colonialism in British Malaya.

Lee Kah Choon was the Chairman of the Executive Committee of "InvestPenang" and a Director of the Penang Development Corporation. Lee served as the Parliamentary Secretary of the Ministry of Health from 2004 to 2008, and the Member of Parliament for the Jelutong Constituency from 1999 to 2008. He was the Seberang Perai Municipal Councillor from 1997 to 1999. He was a practicing lawyer with his own private legal practice from 1987 to 2004, after being called to the Bar of Malaysia in 1987 and Bar of England & Wales in 1986. Lee holds an LLB from the Southampton University UK and an MA from the City University, London. He is an alumnus of the Royal Military College Kuala Lumpur and Chung Ling High School Penang.

Poh Heem Heem is the Senior Manager for Special Projects and Consultancy at the Penang Skills Development Centre (PSDC). She is also the writer for the People Economics segment of the Penang

Economic Monthly. Prior to joining the PSDC in 2006, she was the Senior Economist at the Socio-Economic & Environmental Research Institute (SERI), Penang.

Tan Yin Hooi is the Senior Executive for Special Projects and Consultancy at the Penang Skills Development Centre (PSDC). She was a Research Officer and subsequently an Economist at the Socio-Economic & Environmental Research Institute (SERI) Penang before moving to the PSDC in 2006.

Yoon Chon Leong obtained his degree in Electrical Engineering from Monash University, Melbourne in 1973. Yoon went on to spend 30 years working with Hewlett-Packard and Agilent Technologies (a spin-off of Hewlett-Packard) in various capacities, of which 20 years was in Research & Development. Over the years, Yoon acquired a wide spectrum of experiences, including high technology manufacturing, process development, equipment development, Research & Development to IT. Yoon retired from Agilent Technologies in January 2006 and started a management consulting practice focusing on strategic business development, R&D management and entrepreneur incubation, with special emphasis on electronics, advanced materials, software and agriculture. In 2010, Yoon established a collaborative relationship with SERI as an external associate to work on the development of industry in Penang.

Jaseni Maidinsa is Chief Executive Officer of PBA Holding Bhd (PBAHB) and General Manager of Perbadanan Bekalan Air Pulau Pinang Sdn Bhd (PBAPP). He holds a Diploma in Civil Engineering from Universiti Teknologi Malaysia (1979); a BSc. (Hons.) Civil Engineering degree from University of Glasgow (1984); a Diploma in Management (Merit) from the Malaysian Institute of Management (1991); and a Masters Degree in Business Administration from Universiti Sains Malaysia (2001). Ir. Jaseni Maidinsa has been serving in PBAPP, and previously in Pihak Berkuasa Air (PBA), for a total of 25 years. He was the Distribution and Workshop Engineer for Penang Island, PBA Penang (1985 – 1987), Consumer Engineer for Penang Island, PBA Penang (1987 – 1991), Senior Executive Engineer for Planning & Development for Penang Island, PBA Penang (1991 – 2001) and Development Manager, PBAPP (2001 – 2007).

Mika Toyota was Assistant Professor in the Department of Sociology, National University of Singapore. She obtained her PhD at the University of Hull, UK in 2000. She lectured at the University of Hull (2000-2002) before taking up a Postdoctoral fellowship at the Asian Meta Centre for Population and Sustainable Development Analysis (2002-2004), and Research Fellowship at Asia Research Institute (2004-2008), National University of Singapore. Her current work examines retirement industry development and Japanese retirees in Southeast Asia, ageing, care and globalization, and transnational migration of health care workers in Asia and beyond. Dr Toyota has extensive field research experience in both Japan and Southeast Asia, and has published more than 30 refereed journal articles and book chapters in English and Japanese.

Mayumi Ono is a Ph.D. candidate at the department of cultural anthropology, the University of Tokyo. Her research focuses on global human mobility, especially with reference to international tourism and transnational migration. Her regional interest is with Southeast Asia, particularly Malaysia, Thailand, and Japan. She was affiliated with the Universiti Kebangsaan Malaysia from August 2006 to January 2008 and conducted fieldwork in Malaysia (Kuala Lumpur, Penang, Cameron Highlands, and Kota Kinabalu) on long-stay tourism and international retirement migration with the case of Japanese retirees in Malaysia. She recently published "Long-stay Tourism and International Retirement Migration: Japanese Retirees in Malaysia" *Senri Ethnological Reports* 77, 2008.

Su-Ann Oh is a sociologist specialising in education and forced migration, and is a Visiting Research Fellow at the Institute of Southeast Asian Studies (ISEAS), Singapore. She is also a co-director of Room to Grow Foundation, a charity based on the Thai-Burmese border, which provides basic necessities to migrant and refugee children living in camps and in migrant areas.

Rosalind Chua is the deputy editor of *Penang Economic Monthly* and the founder of Clarity, a copywriting/contract publishing agency.

INTRODUCTION

Johan Saravanamuttu
and Francis E. Hutchinson

Since its establishment in 1786, Penang has had to consistently reinvent itself. Originally conceived of as a port-of-call on India-China trading routes, Penang lost out to the better-located Singapore in the 1820s. Subsequently, it had to reinvent itself as a regional entrepôt, catering to southern Thailand, northern Sumatra, and Kedah in order to survive. Following the opening of the Suez Canal in 1869 and the age of steamships, Penang established itself as a conduit between the riches of Peninsular Malaya and the world (Chuleeporn, 2009: 105-06). European and Chinese businessmen linked the Settlement with tin mines and rubber plantations in Perak, southern Thailand, and beyond.

These periodic reinventions, along with Penang's historic openness to migration, led to an enviable cultural mix. At the apogee of the British period, the Settlement was a regional educational hub for Islamic, English, and Chinese education. Penang's polyglot society of diverse groups, cultures and ideologies proved potent enough to result in two secession movements in 1948 and 1953. Economics was no doubt a factor behind the challenges to Penang's incorporation in the emerging Federation of Malaya. The Penang Chamber of Commerce - the representative of European business interests - led the movement but secessionists also included the Penang Eurasian Association, the Chinese and Indian Chambers of Commerce and the Penang Clerical and Administrative Union (Mohd. Noordin Sopiee, 1973). However, the movement failed to gather momentum, or Penang's modern history may well have been different.

In the immediate post-independence era, Penang as a state within the Federation of Malaya (and Malaysia) saw its economic fortunes decline, especially after the Korean War, the withdrawal of its free port status, and increasing competition from other ports on the peninsula. However, in the 1970s, under the direction of Chief Minister Lim Chong Eu, the aging entrepôt transformed itself into an offshore manufacturing hub for the electronics industry and a well-known tourist site. This outward-looking model of economic growth has underpinned Penang's economic development up until the present.

The issue that now arises is whether Penang's present mode of development will continue to be effective. Some of the current questions that face the state are the following:

First, Malaysia in general, and Penang in particular are caught in a middle-income trap. Rising wage levels coupled with middling progress in productivity have seen the country and the state progressively losing ground to economies with higher skill levels on one hand, and lower labour costs on the other.

Second, while the evolving weight of the global economy is shifting towards Asia, many of the emerging powers are competing with Penang in areas where it formerly excelled. China and India offer Penang competition, but also potential partnerships and rapidly-expanding consumer markets.

Third, Penang is a state within a federation, and its capital, George Town, is a secondary city. While George Town cannot rival Kuala Lumpur in sheer size or facilities, it can offer investors an enabling environment for business due to its comparatively unburdened infrastructure, pleasant urban environment, and skilled workforce. Effectively leveraging these attributes will require far-sighted planning, positioning, and agile policy-making.

In order to address these issues, the Penang Institute, in partnership with the Institute of Southeast Asian Studies, has organized yearly Forums to share up-to-date information and research on key issues facing the state. The first Penang Outlook Forum entitled 'Restructuring and Reshaping Penang' was held in April 2009. The Second Outlook Forum was held in June 2010 at the Institute of Southeast Asian Studies in Singapore. Its theme was 'Penang in Asia', and it drew together a range of papers that examined aspects of the state's economy, cultural heritage, and living environment.

This volume draws on many of the papers presented at the Forum and complements them with a number of articles that were commissioned to cover specific subjects. Building on the original theme, this book asks and seeks to address the fundamental questions that lie before Penang as it seeks to position itself in a changing global environment. These include:

- How can Penang and its primary city, George Town, meet the challenges and opportunities resulting from the increasing economic importance of Asia?
- What niche industries and investment opportunities can Penang offer investors in the region and beyond?
- How can Penang proactively manage and preserve the benefits that come from its status as a UNESCO World Heritage site?
- How can Penang reconcile the pursuit of economic growth with the conservation of its natural and urban environments?

To this end, the book has four distinct sections, all of which deal with the issue of how best to position Penang to 'catch the wind' in the evolving economic context. The first section, which includes this introduction, examines the implications for Penang's economy in terms of: Asia's growing economic importance; the new technological imperatives for maintaining competitiveness; and the challenges facing firms in Penang in their pursuit of innovation. Hutchinson's chapter provides the overall context for this book, as it looks at structural shifts in the global economy, Malaysia's evolving economic framework, and what these mean for Penang.

The second section of the book focuses on Penang's new status as a World Heritage Centre. It explores the notion of heritage itself, what the status entails for the state, and what needs to be done for an active and responsible stewardship of Penang's rich multicultural heritage. Chapter Two by Khoo Salma Nasution delves into George Town as a World Heritage site and how it should be managed. Taking this line of argument further, the next chapter by Goh Beng Lan interrogates the very notion of heritage as local knowledge and historical memories which are not just embedded in physical forms such as buildings but in societal values, movements and social consciousness. The final essay in this section by Syed Muhd Khairudin Aljunied examines heritage conservation in Penang from the perspective of the Muslim community.

The chapters in the third section offer various perspectives of Penang's economy in terms of investment opportunities, skills development and infrastructural support. Chapter Five by InvestPenang – the state government's investor liaison agency – puts forward an overall perspective of the current investment opportunities that the state offers, as well as a discussion of the role of various governmental and private sector organizations. The chapter by the Penang Skills Development Centre (PSDC) focuses on the current and foreseeable skills requirements of the state's manufacturing sector. The final chapter in the section by Jaseni Maidinsa provides an in-depth view of the agency charged with water provision. The Pihak Berkuasa Air Holdings Berhad (PBA), formerly-known as the Penang Water Authority, is a crucial part of the state's competitive advantage.

The fourth set of essays looks at some of the niche industries or 'green shoots' that have emerged in Penang. The chapter by Yoon Chon Leong of Bizwise Consulting, examines Penang's electrical and electronics sector in great depth, seeking to identify unique capabilities. Drawing from a survey of 600 companies, the author lays out a range of core competencies where firms in the state can make a unique value proposition. In Chapter Nine, Mika Toyota and Mayumi Ono present an in-depth study of Japanese long-stay retirees in Penang, which stands out as a primary destination for this age-group for retirement and as a gateway to Southeast Asia. The next chapter by Su-Ann Oh looks at the growth of medical tourism in Penang, which represents one-third of the visitors to Malaysia for this purpose. The final chapter of this section looks at the Malaysian halal industry, and the development, opportunities and challenges faced by this industry in Penang.

The time has come to take stock, evaluate strengths and weaknesses, and to chart the course ahead for the state. While Penang cannot change the direction of the wind, it can adjust its sails accordingly to best ride the waves. It is hoped that these papers and the discussion that they will generate will form part of a continuous discussion by Penangites and others as to the course and direction the state will chart in the years to come.

Chapter 1

Situating Penang in Asia and Malaysia[1]

Francis E. Hutchinson

INTRODUCTION

Penang, like many other small, land- and resource-poor territories, has had to survive by being externally-oriented. For much of the past two centuries, its growth model has been outward-looking, fluctuating between catering for regional markets and acting as a conduit between Malaysia and global markets. And, since 1826, as a constituent unit of a larger entity – be it the Straits Settlements or Federation of Malaysia – it has always had to weigh up collective and individual needs.

A good reading of developments on these two planes has always been imperative for formulating strategies for Penang to best position itself. To this end, this chapter will provide an overview of the regional and national context. Of particular relevance are the large-scale and far-reaching structural changes taking place as the global economy shifts towards Asia – which conveys opportunities and threats. Of equal importance is the policy framework being put into place at the national level – which may map imperfectly onto Penang's localized attributes and strengths.

This chapter is comprised of four sections. The first asks what is happening in Asia economically and what implications this has for Penang. The second explores what is happening at the policy level in Malaysia in response to

---

[1] *This chapter draws on elements of Chapters 2 and 3 of the Penang Blueprint to which this author has contributed.*

this. The third section assesses what this implies for a constituent state such as Penang in a relatively centralized federal system. The fourth and final section summarizes this chapter's main arguments.

GLOBAL ECONOMIC TRENDS: THE SHIFT TO ASIA AND ITS IMPLICATIONS FOR PENANG

As economies, consumer tastes, and production networks the world over become more sophisticated, levels of competition are rising. This shift has been classified by some as a shift from the production or 'P' Economy to the knowledge or 'K' Economy, where successful competition is based on the acquisition and use of knowledge, as opposed to the undifferentiated physical production of goods and services (Machlup, 1962).

This shift in economic structures in end-markets such as the United States and Western Europe, coupled with accentuating economic globalization, has led to a dramatic increase in levels of competition. As such, even domestically-focused manufacturing and service operations in far-off countries are no longer immune from these 'gales of creative destruction'.

East Asia, with its export-oriented economies and increasingly sophisticated global production networks, is no exception. Local firms are facing competition in their domestic markets from overseas companies, and established international clients are demanding: increased technological sophistication; modern accounting and management standards; and regional – if not global – reach (Yusuf and Nabeshima, 2004: 9-10).

In addition, a new group of countries are emerging that are predicted to account for more of the world's economic weight as well as its manufacturing and innovative potential. The World Bank argues that the world economy is becoming 'multi-polar' with a group of countries comprised of China, India, Indonesia, Russia, Brazil, and South Korea becoming 'growth poles'. By 2025, these countries will, collectively, account for more than half of global growth (World Bank, 2011).

The emergence of these countries constitutes a challenge to Malaysia's economic model. The country and – by extension – Penang are poised to lose jobs to nations such as China and India in many areas where they currently excel, thus requiring an honest appraisal of their comparative advantage (Betina, Ianchovichina, and Martin, 2006: 92). Penang, with its well-developed manufacturing and services sectors, is particularly vulnerable to these challenges.

However, this new panorama also presents significant advantages. In addition to constituting important sources of competition, these countries will also represent important end markets. It is likely that the bulk of the world's new consumers will come from Asia's burgeoning cities and middle class – estimated at one billion people living in urban areas. In contrast, the growth in the U.S. and, especially, European markets will level off and lose relative weight (Kharas, Zeufack and Majeed, 2010: 12). The region's sustained growth rate and level of sophistication means that the bulk of consumers and, consequently, markets will be found closer to home.

In addition to the shift of the weight of the global economy to Asia, a significant portion of economic activity will be carried out by multinational corporations from emerging economies who will, in turn, invest in other emerging markets. These firms will consolidate themselves as key players in establishing new trade links and production networks (World Bank, 2011: 74).

Within this context, Penang is arguably in a good position to benefit from this growth, given its export orientation, integration into international firm networks, and cultural links with the biggest potential markets – China, India, and Indonesia. However, a reorientation to this new opportunity requires a commitment to questioning established business practices, as Penang will need to branch away from established export markets in mature economies such as the United States and Western Europe.

This means seeking to understand more about tastes, needs, and wants in Asia – and cultivating contacts for this purpose. *An East Asian Renaissance* argues that one of the strengths of Asia is its inter-connectedness, as firms in countries around the region collaborate in a variety of sophisticated production networks. That said, many of these networks are targeted to mature industrial economies that are not growing as quickly as their Asian counterparts. This requires reconstructing and reorienting business relationships (Gill and Kharas, 2007).

In addition, distance still matters. While China seems, at first blush, a particularly desirable market, it actually is a little bit too far away for Penang-based firms to cater to effectively. Rather, recent surveys argue that Penang should re-discover its historic role as a regional entrepot, catering to markets in northern Indonesia and southern Thailand.

Given its location facing the Bay of Bengal, the state will be well-placed to cater to the Indian market when its cities grow enough to constitute attractive end-markets (Kharas, Zeufack and Majeed, 2010: 53). This positioning towards Indonesia and Thailand will be helped by the ASEAN Free Trade Agreement, which will reduce barriers to trade with countries in the region. A regional focus of this nature may be more feasible for Penang than seeking to take on the Chinese manufacturing sector.

However, the geography of these regional markets is also changing in important ways. Sustained economic expansion, population growth, and increasing urbanization entail a wider range of potential sites or untapped markets. The Philippines and Malaysia have more than 60% of their populations living in urban areas, and Indonesia's urbanization rate is above 40% (Asian Development Bank, 2010: 32). The international consultancy firm McKinsey predicts that India's urban population will grow from 340 million in 2010 to some 590 million by 2030 (McKinsey Global Institute, 2010: 37).

But this growth will not all be concentrated in capital cities, as secondary urban centres will grow in number and in relative wealth. According to *An East Asian Renaissance*, during 2005-2015 more than half of all growth in urban areas will be in cities with less than 500,000 people (Gill and Kharas, 2007: 240). Greater wealth, expenditure on infrastructure, and changing tastes mean that these dispersed markets are one front where the economic battles of tomorrow will be won or lost (The Boston Consulting Group, 2010: 6).

Thus, instead of establishing ties with individual countries, Penang will need to build relationships with a wide range of urban centres in these countries. Gone are the days when commercial delegations could focus on capital cities. In the next years, growth will be urban, but largely driven by smaller cities. While contacts in Jakarta will be increasingly important, those in Makassar, Balikpapan, and Padang will be as or more important.

This will require an openness on the part of policy-makers and business people to question traditional approaches, networks, and products in response to an evolving economic landscape.

MALAYSIA'S ECONOMIC POLICY FRAMEWORK

It is worth examining how Malaysia's economic policy framework is evolving in response to some of these changes.

While the impact of the recent global economic crisis on Malaysia was moderate and the prospects for growth over the short to medium-term are quite good, it is clear that the country's growth model is under question. The World Bank, in the Malaysia Economic Monitor of 2009, states that even though the Malaysian economy has made remarkable progress over the past few decades, it has lagged behind other economies in Asia. It has become trapped in a middle-income manufacturing-production economy, as it is 'unable to remain competitive as a high-volume, low-cost producer, yet unable to move up the value chain and achieve rapid growth by breaking into fast growing markets for knowledge- and innovation-based products and services' (World Bank, 2009: 53).

This middle-income trap is not unique to Malaysia, but escaping it is far from easy. While growth rates remain positive, the fear is one of a gradual decline in competitiveness vis-à-vis countries with cheaper labour and better skills sets. As aptly articulated by Yusuf and Nabeshima:

> The Southeast Asian Tigers feel threatened. Even though their growth rates have remained above the average for the world and also above the average for developing countries, their economic performance falls short of that in the first half of the 1990s. The underlying worry is that is presages the beginning of a downward trend, the harbingers of which are lower rates of investment, persistently low rates of total factor productivity, and low levels of innovativeness (Yusuf and Nabeshima, 2009: 3).

Largely to address this issue, Malaysia's economic policy framework has evolved considerably over the past two years, with important implications for the country as a whole as well as its constituent states. The following paragraphs will set out the key differences and departures in policies contained in the Northern Corridor Economic Region, the 10th Malaysia Plan, as well as the New Economic Model and associated Economic Transformation Programme.

The Northern Corridor Economic Region

In the past, development planning as pursued by the Economic Planning Unit (EPU), involved the assembly of a five-year plan defining social and economic policy objectives – the well-known 'Malaysia Plans'. On the social side, these included a wide range of goals, ranging from the eradication of poverty to restructuring of society to overcome imbalances, and community development to education and training. On the economic side, this encompassed important transport, communication, and energy items.

All countries have intra-national disparities in social and economic outcomes. In the case of Malaysia, state- or regional-level plans were given coverage in dedicated chapters in the Malaysia Plans. However, the treatment of this issue centred on an analysis of regional imbalances of output by different sectors that were mostly attributed to geographical differences. In response, a variety of spatial strategies, such as the development of urban growth centres, was proposed as early as the Fifth Malaysia Plan (1986-1990).

In mid-2008, the EPU, in preparation for the Tenth Malaysia Plan (2011-2015), identified the need for a more comprehensive regional strategy. While Kuala Lumpur had been consolidated as Malaysia's primary economic hub – contributing eight times more to the growth of the country's domestic product than any other urban centre in the country – there had been little concerted effort to develop alternative economic centres (National Economic Advisory Council, 2010: 117). Patterns of public spending concentrated in the Klang Valley, accompanied by the economies of scale that Kuala Lumpur offered, led to an increasing concentration of economic activity. By the 1970s, secondary centres of economic activity such as Penang began to fade, due to economic nationalism and political centralization, as well as the proliferation of customs procedures and trade barriers (Rimmer and Dick, 2009: 100).

In light of this, the concept of growth corridors was developed, and a number of such entities were proposed for various parts of Malaysia outside the Klang Valley. The idea behind such corridors was that they would work as an integrated whole, with a primary urban hub or city driving its development and supplying manufacturing or service expertise, global connections, and export-oriented infrastructure. These hubs would tap labour, land, and natural resources available from the hinterland.

The basic premise of this strategy is not sector specialisation, as traditionally emphasised. Instead, regions are best developed by identifying and developing their comparative advantage in a holistic sense, recognizing that what works today may not fit into tomorrow's global economy. The strategy of positioning is therefore one of knowing what one has, in terms of location, and how this inventory of spatial qualities is best deployed and matched up against external trends.

The Northern Corridor Economic Region (NCER) is the expression of this new strategy for four northern states of Peninsular Malaysia: Perlis, Kedah, Penang and northern Perak. The aim is to approach these four states as a single economic region, so that the NCER will develop into a "world–class economic region and a choice destination for investment, work and living" (Northern Corridor Implementation Authority Act 2008 (Act 687)). The focus is not exclusively on economic issues, but also seeks to promote social development, arts, culture and heritage, as well as human capital development.

The Northern Corridor Implementation Agency (NCIA) is the organization responsible for the coordination of development strategies between the four states. It also provides investor liaison services, and is in charge of expediting the approval of permits and incentives for investments in its area.

In line with the NCER strategy, the federal government has committed to investing in a range of important infrastructure projects such as: the expansion of the Penang Bridge; construction of a second bridge; the upgrading of the port and supporting infrastructure; double tracking of the railway; establishing Butterworth as the northern transport hub; upgrading public transportation; housing development; sewerage treatment; broadband infrastructure; industrial estate expansion; and improved air links and sea routes with the surrounding region.

The Tenth Malaysia Plan (2011-2015)

Consistent with the thinking advanced by the NCER, the 10th Malaysia Plan also focuses on fostering a high-income economy that it is based on concentrated growth accompanied by inclusive development policies. This is to be achieved by supporting greater specialization of economic activity in chosen areas, encouraging increases in productivity through innovation, and cultivating and attracting high quality human resources. The Tenth Malaysia Plan also incorporates the concept of growth corridors. It is designed bottom-up to direct growth in areas which will contribute most to the economy and to build urban agglomerations, corridors and clusters.

The Tenth Plan lists five corridors: three in the peninsula (Northern, Eastern, and Iskandar) and two in East Malaysia (Sabah and Sarawak). The government has appointed a dedicated agency to oversee the development of each of the respective corridors (EPU, 2010: 119-123). These corridors are meant to serve as the new 'engines' of the economy, as they specialize in one or more of the national key economic areas (NKEAs), which include activities with a large potential for productivity- and innovation-driven growth. These range from oil and gas to palm oil, and from electrical and electronics production to agriculture (EPU, 2010: 123-25).

This focus on strategic economic areas is to be facilitated by: a series of 'smart' partnerships with the private sector; liberalization of more sectors of the economy accompanied by regulatory reform; and a reinvention of government through adopting modern management principles.

The New Economic Model (NEM) and the Economic Transformation Programmes (ETP) I and II

The goal of the New Economic Model (NEM) is to transform Malaysia into a high-income inclusive and sustainable nation by 2020 with a per capita income above USD 15,000. The country's economy will be market-led, well-governed, regionally integrated, entrepreneurial and innovative. Like the Tenth Malaysia Plan, the idea is for Malaysia to break through the middle income trap to advance into high income status with investment as the main driver of economic growth. The approach to economic development will be based on growth through productivity (and high value-added goods and services), private sector-led growth, localised autonomy in decision-making, cluster and corridor-based economic activities, the favouring of technologically capable industries and firms, and orientation towards Asia and the Middle East, and retaining and attracting skilled professionals.

The NEM aims to provide the framework and environment for entrepreneurial energies to be unleashed, and for the development and use of advanced technology to generate high value-added products and services. The government's role will be to facilitate the private sector's endeavours and to promote accountability in its own work. Sustained growth will be supported by fiscal prudence and a further reduction of the fiscal deficit.

This will be supplemented by a focus on inclusiveness to prevent marginalization of any communities. The idea is to design effective measures that strike a balance between the special position of the Bumiputra and the legitimate interests of different groups. Transparent and market-friendly affirmative action programmes will target assistance to the bottom 40% of households, as well as ensuring access to state resources based on needs on one hand and merit on the other. Small and medium enterprises are also singled out for particular mention, specifically with regard to technologically-intensive areas (NEAC, 2010: 19).

The economic and social thrusts of the NEM are complemented by a focus on the environment. The rationale is to seek sustainable growth that meets the ongoing needs of the population without compromising future generations by effective stewardship and preservation of the natural environment and non-renewable resources, particularly the management of water and oil and gas resources.

The goals of the NEM are to be achieved through the Economic Transformation Programme (ETP), which is the government's economic agenda. Much as with the 10th Malaysia Plan, the ETP focuses on 12 key growth engines - National Key Economic Areas (NKEAs) - which are expected to make substantial contributions to Malaysia's economic performance and will receive prioritised public investment and policy support. Those selected are: oil, gas and energy; palm oil; financial services; tourism; business services; electronics and electrical; wholesale and retail; education; healthcare; communications content and infrastructure; agriculture; and Greater Kuala Lumpur/ Klang Valley (NEAC, 2010: 19).

The rationale behind this strategy is that focusing on a small number of sectors generates economic benefits because it: aligns policies coherently; avoids sub-scale investment; develops a clear value proposition; provides leadership focus; and allows for higher quality monitoring (NEAC, 2010: 13).

It is expected that these NKEAs will transform Malaysia into a high-income economy. The four largest NKEAs – oil, gas and energy, financial services, palm oil and wholesale and retail - are projected to generate 60% of the incremental GNI growth from the 11 NKEA sectors.

According to the ETP, more than 90% of the funding will come from the private sector. The public sector will provide seed capital as well as talented staff and Prime Ministerial attention as regards implementation. Policy reforms such as removal of barriers to competition and market liberation will be targeted at the NKEAs. The implementation mechanisms include 131 Entry Point Projects (EPPs) in the 12 NKEAs that have been identified and developed through collaboration between the public and private sectors.

PENANG AND THE NATIONAL ECONOMIC POLICY FRAMEWORK

Despite its prodigious growth record over the past four decades, Penang – like Malaysia – is also caught in the middle-income trap. In large part, these challenges reflect issues that the national economy is facing. The paragraphs above laid out the emerging policy framework at a national level. As mentioned, it is important to recognize that there is a wider macroeconomic policy context which shapes the parameters within which a high income economy may come about in Penang (and the rest of Malaysia).

What, then, does this overall policy framework mean for Penang?

First, it is clear that national-level policy has been influenced by much of the latest thinking on the relationship between economic growth, distance, technology, and human capital. Rather than seeing cities and urban areas exclusively as magnets for labour from the country-side, they are seen as sources of innovation, dynamism, and creativity – particularly in high-technology areas. Rather than seeking to combat the drift of people from rural to urban areas, this strategy seeks to harness the innovative and efficiency-enhancing properties of urban areas.

This approach bodes well for the state of Penang - as well as all states that are not in the Klang Valley. To date, federal funding under the Malaysia Plans has tended to favour the Kuala Lumpur Federal Territory, reinforcing the concentration of economic activity there (Table 1). This has been to the detriment of secondary urban centres throughout the country that have seen their importance wane. A renewed interest in urban areas outside the capital city will, hopefully, translate into increased resources and attention for these areas.

Table 1: Per Capita Expenditure by State under the 9th Malaysia Plan

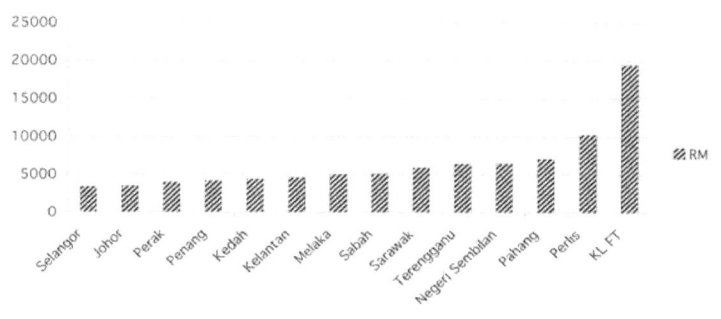

Source: Calculated from the 9th Malaysia Plan

In addition, the 10th Malaysia Plan and New Economic Model are cognizant of the importance of fostering the growth of greater value-added activities in the country. This also is a good omen for Penang, which currently houses a great deal of technology-intensive manufacturing as well as some promising business process outsourcing, medical tourism, and software activities. Given that Penang accounts for almost one-half of the country's E&E exports, it should, in theory, receive a considerable financial and infrastructural boost under these plans.

Furthermore, these plans all make explicit mention of the need to provide support to small and medium enterprises, particularly those active in technologically-demanding sectors. This is of vital importance to Malaysia in general, whose industrial policy has been traditionally targeted to large domestic corporations, and whose policy framework towards SMEs has been dispersed (Abdullah, 2000: 66). This change in focus is of crucial importance to Penang, whose economic viability will hinge on the ability of its SMEs, particularly those active in the electronics sector as well as those in fledgling sectors such as software and business process outsourcing, to offer unique, value-added solutions.

Last, these plans all make an explicit commitment to enhancing links between industry and universities. This has been a stumbling block to attempts to foster innovation in Penang. Industry surveys have reported that the three most voiced complaints are: a shortage of skilled workers; a weak government research structure; and a lack of public technical services (PSDC, 2007: 55). Concerted action by federal authorities to more fully integrate Universiti Sains Malaysia into Penang's economic and social structure would be greatly welcomed.

However, it is important to remember that these focuses on urban areas, agglomeration, and economic corridors may not provide all answers from Penang's perspective.

First, it is worth asking if – the discourse on growth corridors aside – the New Economic Model and the other plans still focus a little too much on Kuala Lumpur. As mentioned above, federal funding has tended to favour the Kuala Lumpur federal territory, reinforcing the concentration of economic activity there and in the surrounding state of Selangor. One can argue that there is too much of a good thing. After a certain size, urban centres begin to suffer from diseconomies of scale, notably pollution, congestion, and labour shortages. This is a lesson that has been painfully learned by South Korea and Thailand, who have struggled against the run-away growth of Seoul and Bangkok, respectively.

Second, it is worth asking if these plans are not a little too heavy on infrastructure. Actually, Malaysia already has good 'hard' infrastructure in the form of highways, ports, airports, and telecommunications. A look at the most dynamic 'hotspots' of the global economy such as Silicon Valley in California and the Emiglia-Romagna region in Italy shows us that while 'hard' infrastructure is important, so too is 'soft' infrastructure. Firms in these and other regions operate in contexts where there is a great deal of communication between firms, business associations, research institutes, and credit providers. Malaysia has many of these organizations too, but available evidence suggests a lack of communication between them.

In addition, some of the goals put forward by the 10th Malaysia Plan and NEM are quite ambitious and constitute a very formidable challenge. This is seen in the sheer number of national key economic activities to be pursued by the country. Penang is listed as having NKEAs in 10 out of the relevant 11 economic areas (PEMANDU, 2010: 19). The McKinsey 2010 report *How to Compete and Grow: A Sectoral Guide to Policy* argues that, unlike middle-income countries, high-income countries do not rely on large, diverse manufacturing sectors. Rather, as they become more sophisticated, they specialize in a few key sectors. The manufacturing sector as a whole shrinks, but retains a key number of high value-added niches that are very efficient and dynamic.

Thus, if Malaysia wants to move forward and higher up the value chain, it needs to specialize more, rather than seeking to attain excellence in a wide range of new areas. Recent research done bears this out with reference to Penang. The 2009 World Bank publication *Can Malaysia Escape the Income Trap: A Strategy for Penang* states the following about Penang's prospects (Yusuf and Nabeshima, 2009: 35-36):

- George Town is a medium-size city with limited urbanisation economies to trigger diversification and support upgrading

- Although statistical analysis suggests that electronics has emerged as the city's strong suit, this is belied by the evidence of relatively weak industrial deepening and rising value added in electronics
- The local innovation system is not strong
- There is an absence of local firms that could play a lead role in moving up the value chain
- There is little demand from local companies for 'innovation'
- Current salaries and lifetime earnings for researchers are not high enough to attract the best and brightest
- Innovation in electronics generally require large research teams led by experienced research managers which neither USM nor local Malaysian firms can easily mobilise
- Furthermore, product space analysis does not support the case for high-tech development other than in electronics

In essence, this report stresses that Penang's small human resource base will only allow it to specialize in a very limited number of high-end activities. As it is, there are serious shortages of high-end personnel in established sectors. So, while few would argue with deepening capabilities in areas such as electronics and tourism, the findings from this report urge for caution in seeking to cultivate a wide range of new sectors.

Regarding implementation, the focus of the 10th Malaysia Plan and the NEM bear re-examination. For example, much is made of the potential role of the Northern Corridor Implementation Agency in enabling decision-making to take place locally. However, the NCIA will still use existing federal, state, and local government bodies for execution – in effect constituting a fourth administrative layer.

The Khazanah/World Bank publication *Cities, People, and the Economy: A Study on Positioning Penang* refers to Barcelona and Bologna as inspiring examples of smaller, dynamic, and high-tech focused cities that Penang should emulate (Kharas, Zeufack, and Majeed, 2010: 6). It is worth examining this city's governance arrangements. In fact, Barcelona's city council is given more responsibility than other city governments in Spain. It is responsible for city planning, traffic regulation, dispensing social services such as health and education, and it even has its own police force. In certain circumstances, the city council can even veto central government directives.

Delegating a wider range of responsibility to Malaysia's 13 state governments, along with suitable fiscal incentives for performance, would greatly encourage policy innovation. At present, Penang keeps a minuscule percentage of the income it generates for the federal government. In contrast, grouping Penang with two other states and part of a fourth under an intermediate administrative layer between the federal and state governments does not seem to be the most obvious manner of unleashing its potential.

In sum, recent national policy developments have positive implications for Penang. The greater awareness of the need to generate and support economic activity outside of Kuala Lumpur is a welcome development. The appreciation of the need to support higher-value added activities as well as create and maintain liveable and dynamic urban centres also bodes well for George Town and Penang. Greater emphasis on the needs of small and medium enterprises as well as greater university-industry links would be most beneficial. However, the desire to pursue world-class competitiveness in a wide range of areas needs to be tempered with a real appreciation of the scale, resources, and time required to attain this. In addition, the proposed implementation measures do not seem to constitute the most efficient method of encouraging innovation and efficiency.

A ROLE FOR THE STATE GOVERNMENT?

What scope does the above-mentioned context leave for local agency? In fact, concerted attention by the state government in partnership with the local and international private sector affords significant potential for addressing some of Penang's key challenges.

At first blush, the Penang State Government does not seem to be well-positioned to be an agent of change. Malaysia is a federation, with a central government and thirteen state counterparts. However, despite its formal structure as a federation, state governments do not have a great deal of revenue or responsibilities.

The Constitution lays out the responsibilities of each level of governance with a list each for the federal and state governments and a concurrent list with shared responsibilities. The federal government is responsible for public goods such as finance, defence, as well as services such as education, health, and transport. In contrast, states are given residual responsibilities consisting of land, forestry, Islamic affairs, and local government. Local government, for its part, includes local public services such as water supply, waste collection and disposal, drainage, and parks (Ninth Schedule, Constitution of Malaysia).

Resources are similarly apportioned, with the bulk of revenues accruing to the federal government. States receive established amounts from the federal government as well as a small range of taxes including: revenue from land sales; natural resources such as mines and forests; an Islamic tax; and a duty on entertainment (Tenth Schedule, Constitution of Malaysia).

Thus, Penang is a small state with few resources in a centralized political system and an increasingly competitive environment. That said, the State Government has the opportunity and the means to be an effective agent of change. The key challenge, however, is to distinguish between power and influence.

Public administration literature talks about the beneficial effects of subsidiarity. This argues that government institutions that are closer to the end-users are better-placed to deliver services that provide localized benefits. This is because the level of government closest to the target group will have more information on their needs. Thus, reliable and up-to-date information can enable initiatives to be carefully targeted, maximizing scarce resources (Musgrave and Musgrave, 1989: 455-56).

Given its relationships with citizens, firms, business associations, and multinational corporations that have been nurtured over decades, the Penang State Government is in an ideal position to engage in the intense social and contact-work required to foster high-technology sectors. Given how quickly windows of technological opportunity open and close, it is preferable to have a small, agile agency with small pockets than a remote and disconnected bureaucracy with deep pockets.

Second, despite its formal list of its responsibilities being confined to land, natural resources, and religion, state governments can, and do, exercise influence in many other areas. For example, state governments can take the lead in economic planning. While the 1970 Nathan Report was carried out by an international consultant, the subsequent planning and implementation that put Penang on another growth trajectory was carried out by the Penang State Government.

The State Government has also exercised leadership in other areas that are not constitutionally-mandated. It was the first to perceive the opportunities afforded by the electronics sector in the early 1970s, travelling overseas to market itself, a notable step in becoming one of the most successful manufacturing centres in the country (Hutchinson, 2008: 227). Another important example was the establishment of the Penang Skills Development Corporation, the industry-oriented training institute that was key in retaining a core of MNCs in the state, and has subsequently been replicated in almost all states in the nation.

Third, the NEM and ETP have long lists of big-ticket infrastructure to be funded by the federal government in Penang, which is sure to play a part in helping the state's economy develop. While important, 'hard' infrastructure is only part of the story. 'Soft' infrastructure also matters for business, and issues such as transparency, accountability, and consistency are vital for investor confidence. From this point of view, the important strides made by the Penang State Government in balancing the budget, establishing an electronic tendering system, and more clearly defining the lines between politics and business are also a vital part of building a dynamic urban setting. Through its actions as an employer and a consumer, the Penang State Government can have an important effect on the local business context.

Fourth, many of the most pressing issues facing manufacturing and service operations in the state are not concerned with large-scale infrastructure investments. On a daily basis, they are concerned with: obtaining secure and consistent supplies of water and electricity; getting building permits and licences; meeting new clients; and learning about market and technology trends. The successful acquisition of new technological capabilities is a long-term and piece-meal process that is supported through building an environment conducive to innovation and learning. This environment is largely social in nature, and is dependent on: accessible government at the local level; a business environment characterized by trust, and an enabling context for everyday operations (Storper and Scott, 1995: 512). These factors are as, if not more, important than highly visible facilities such as airports and highways.

At present, Malaysia is in a crucial period. Civil servants in a growing number of state governments must now adapt to receiving instructions from a different set of elected representatives. Public administration, as defined by Woodrow Wilson, should be run by apolitical career civil servants (Wilson, 1887: 209). In Malaysia, issues of overlapping jurisdictions also need to be sorted out, as servants at the highest level of the state governments of Penang, Melaka, and Selangor – to name a few – are appointed by the federal government, yet answerable to the Chief Ministers of their states (Yeoh, 2011: 39).

Given the importance for Malaysia and Penang to emerge from the middle-income trap, it behooves both levels of government to establish a working relationship.

CONCLUSION

This chapter has set out the international and national context within which Penang and its citizens must formulate their strategies for encouraging sustainable economic growth. Structural changes in the global economy constitute both threats and opportunities for the state. While the economic weight of the world is shifting to Asia, and Penang has links to its major markets, many of these emerging powers challenge the state's growth model directly. Many of the new opportunities and growth markets will lie off Penang's radar, in smaller provincial cities in nearby countries. This will require local firms to question and reconfigure their existing business approaches and relationships.

At the national level, many of the policy changes herald much that is positive for Penang. In sum, these are: greater attention paid to urban centres out of the Klang Valley; an appreciation of the value of technology-intensive activities for the long-term future of the country; an awareness of the need to offer targeted support to small and medium enterprises; and a commitment to improve the interface between university and industry. However, this must be tempered by a sense of realism with regard to the possibility of attaining excellence in such a wide range of areas. It is a stretch for Malaysia in general and Penang in particular to successfully produce goods and services across all NKEAs. Available research on

Penang argues for a very focused strategy to deepen capabilities in a very limited range of areas, given the state's limited human resource base.

While the challenges facing Penang are formidable, the state can fruitfully hark back to its past, when its long-term vision, perceptive targeting of promising sectors, commitment to trying new things, and ability to listen to the private sector enabled it to re-invent its economic model.

Chapter 2

George Town, Penang: Managing a Multicultural World Heritage Site

Khoo Salma Nasution

INTRODUCTION

In the eyes of the world, it is the multicultural character of George Town and Melaka that sets them apart from other World Heritage Sites. The historic centres of the two cities are cultural sites in Malaysia, jointly listed as a World Heritage Site in July 2008 for their histories of trade and civilizational encounter, their living traditions and intact townscapes, all of which reflect a confluence and co-existence of diverse cultures.² An obvious manifestation of the cities' multiculturalism is the clustering of various religious sites - George Town and Melaka each has a "street of harmony", where mosque, church and temple have stood side by side for hundreds of years. This tradition of religious pluralism was apparently a factor which persuaded the UNESCO World Heritage Committee to include them in the prestigious list.

---

2 It could be argued that since Singapore belongs to the same historical-cultural group, the nomination should have logically consisted of the 'former British Straits Settlements'. However, a transboundary serial nomination would probably have been impeded by the on-off political tensions and controversies between Malaysia and Singapore, but since Singapore was not a state party of UNESCO at the time of submission, this was a moot point. Nonetheless, as Singapore has finally rejoined UNESCO in late 2007 after a 22 year absence, the idea has sparked interest among Singapore heritage circles.

George Town, capital of Penang, has not always been celebrated for its historic qualities. Over the last fifty years, the processes of nation-building, local place-making and economic globalization have influenced the public estimation of this former British colonial port city. Its reputation is now greatly enhanced by the recent UNESCO inscription, even though the process of getting listed took almost ten years. Furthermore, this recognition was only possible with the new thinking of UNESCO and its partner ICOMOS (International Council on Monuments and Sites) in terms of cultural sites. Since the creation of the 1972 World Heritage Convention, the World Heritage Committee has gradually (some say too slowly) enlarged its purview beyond monumental sites to acknowledge the value of intangible heritage and historic communities.

The story of the "Historic Cities of the Straits of Malacca", it could be said, started in Melaka and continued in George Town. The river port of Melaka dates back to 1400, when it was established by the precursors of the first Malay Sultanate on the Peninsula. It became an illustrious port on the maritime silk route and a stopover on the Zheng He voyages, before being occupied by the Portuguese, Dutch and British in succession. As such, the history, culture and urban fabric of Melaka beautifully encapsulates the historical layering of successive empires in the Southeast Asian region.

The history of George Town as a seaport dates back to 1786, when Penang island, then part of the kingdom of Kedah, was secured by the East India Company as a trading post. Penang was upgraded to the Fourth Presidency of India, and then a member of the Straits Settlements which came under colonial rule in 1867. The port became an outpost of British imperialism and a principal centre for the expansion of Nanyang Chinese trading networks in the region. From the late 19th century onward, Penang grew as a regional port, a gateway of migration and a hub of capital for the development of the rich hinterland.

In 1957, boasting a population of 250,000, Penang became a city by royal charter. Local pride peaked and civic engagement flowered. However, after Merdeka, Penang's strident labour politics alienated it from the powerful federal mainstream. The decline of the free port in the late 1960s sparked massive unemployment, leading to an outflow of Penang's young generation and educated elite. Bread and butter issues came to dominate the political-economic agenda. The Tun Lim Chong Eu era saw economic recovery through the promotion of manufacturing and resort tourism. For many years, Penang led in Malaysia's industrial development. The Penang Development Corporation also undertook urban renewal, producing the monolithic KOMTAR. But on the whole, the former port area of George Town was left to decay. A new breed of developers saw economic opportunities in constructing high-density downtown office space, but their ambition was bridled by the rent control act which kept the tenants in place and impeded wide-scale redevelopment.

The Penang Heritage Trust, formed in 1986, initially sought to preserve a few public structures and millionaires' mansions and later became concerned with the fate of shophouses and inner city neighbourhoods. The urban conservation approach was introduced through a workshop organised by the northern branch of the Pertubuhan Akitek Malaysia, as well as through German expertise which came in to advise the municipal council. Singapore had just undertaken its pilot restoration project at Armenian Street and the Urban Redevelopment Authority began its first-generation conservation projects, proving to the region that heritage could attract tourists and that tourism could be a raison d'etre for heritage preservation by allowing heritage buildings to generate economic benefits. In Penang, the first heritage trails were designed, and state tourism began to market the city to tourists. In 1993, Penang undertook its first state-led pilot restoration project involving the municipal-owned Syed Alatas Mansion which was, coincidentally, like a similar pilot restoration in Singapore, also located at Armenian Street and advised by the same consultant architect, Didier Repellin. However, the heritage training centre established within the Syed Alatas Mansion premises was short-lived as the need for restoration expertise and transmission of skills was not widely appreciated.

Dr. Richard Engelhardt, Regional Adviser for Culture in Asia and the Pacific, arrived in Penang in 1998 and experienced the Chinese New Year and Thaipusam celebrations which overlapped in that year. During his walking tour, he witnessed a Thaipusam ritual in which Chinese kavadi-bearers stopped to pray in the forecourt of the Goddess of Mercy Temple and remarked, "This is more than a layering of cultures; it is cultural fusion". Engelhardt's visit was pre-arranged by the Penang Heritage Trust but hosted by the Penang State Government. As the Malaysian government was anxious to get Melaka listed as a World Heritage Site, Engelhardt apparently advised the federal government to include George Town in order to strengthen the Malaysian bid. This was the starting point of Malaysia's "serial nomination" for World Heritage. Starting with the landmark nine-day conference entitled "Economics of Heritage" conducted in Penang and Melaka in 1999, the UNESCO regional office helped build capacity for heritage management in Malaysia over the years.

In reality, the progress of the Malaysia nomination also depended on federal initiative, as the nomination had to be officially submitted to UNESCO by the "state party". To pave the way, the Malaysian government reconstituted the Culture, Arts and Heritage Ministry (2004) and gazetted the National Heritage Act (2005). The National Heritage Department was thus established with a Heritage Commissioner, as provided for under the Act. The agency for the nomination and management of the World Heritage Site has endured changes under the regimes of three prime ministers (Mahathir, Badawi and Najib).[3] However, the heritage agenda has yet to be mainstreamed in other relevant ministries such as tourism, education, local government and public works.

In the meantime, the heritage movement in Penang began to spread beyond the elite and middle-class. New groups came into existence in response to the repeal of rent control. The first was SOS, a housing rights group that represented tenants affected by rental hikes and evictions. The other two were cultural groups. The Nanyang Folk Culture (NYFC) started to capture the "spirit of the place" by staging photography exhibitions and street festivals with a strong appeal for, but not limited to, the Chinese-educated public. The group's Chinese New Year street festival was the precursor and prototype for the massive annual street extravaganza organized by the clan youth today. Through an organization called Arts-Ed, founded in 1999, performing arts lecturers from Science University of Malaysia (USM) created initiatives to promote the heritage city as a learning site. Young artists brought new energy to the scene,

---

3 *The preparation of the dossier was formerly the responsibility of the Department of Museums and Antiquities, but the responsibility has subsequently passed to the newly-formed National Heritage Department, now under the Ministry of Information, Communication and Culture created in 2009. Malaysia's World Heritage Natural Sites, Kinabalu and Mulu, come under the Parks Departments of Sabah and Sarawak respectively, and are overseen by the Tourism Ministry.*

and translated the idea of heritage for new audiences. Workshops and performances involving schoolchildren were staged in heritage settings. In the last few years, Arts-Ed also served as the secretariat for the Cultural Heritage Advisory Team (CHAT), a loose coalition of heritage practitioners which included members of PHT and NYFC. The Penang Heritage Trust, together with a media partner, organized the Penang Story conference, in 2001-2002, and encouraged diverse community groups to get involved in local history. Through a series of colloquia, local historians presented how their communities, both indigenous and migrant, had a role in building the city. These stories were reported in both English and vernacular presses, thus broadening social identification with the heritage city. By the time George Town was listed in 2008, the local heritage movement already had working experience in issues of historical recovery, community revitalization and living heritage.

OLD ISSUES, NEW GOVERNMENT

In the March 2008 Malaysian elections a "political tsunami" swept the opposition coalition into power in Penang and several other states. When the listing was announced four months later, it seemed as though the result of ten years' effort put in by the former state government had fallen into the lap of the new Pakatan Rakyat state government. On the other hand, the latter also inherited many existing contradictions which had remained unresolved up to this point. Hence the current Chief Minister Lim Guan Eng has had to tackle many old problems in the course of establishing a more consistent framework for heritage management in order to maintain World Heritage status for George Town.

Lim's first act was symbolic. The municipal administration had long misspelt the city's name as one word, "Georgetown", while the previous state administration even failed to admit its status as a city; this was a symptom both of the contentious politics within the then state government as well as a compromised local government. As a result, the name "George Town" was lost for two decades or so, and the name "Penang" came to be equivocally applied to the city and the state. In celebrating the listing, Lim pronounced the reinstatement of George Town's name and city status to great public acclaim. He also expressed his vision of transforming Penang into an "international city" or world-class city, which means doing what it takes to ensure that George Town retains its World Heritage status. Two women have been entrusted with these vital twin missions - Patahiyah Ismail, the first woman president of the local council (equivalent to mayor) and Maimunah Mohd Sharif, the first general manager of the newly-established World Heritage Incorporated.

The first alarm bell for George Town sounded only five months after the UNESCO inscription, and the issue became a test of state-federal cooperation. In November 2008, UNESCO's World Heritage Centre was alerted to four high rise hotel development projects in George Town - two within the core zone and two in its buffer zone - which would breach the 18 metre height limits stipulated in the heritage guidelines. The scale of these projects would potentially have had a negative impact on the heritage zones. Responding to UNESCO concerns, the Ministry of Unity, Culture, Arts and Heritage of Malaysia, as chair of the Management Committee for the World Heritage Sites of Melaka and George Town, commissioned two independent experts, Dr. Augusto Villalon of the Philippines and Professor Yukio Nishimura of Japan, to assess the proposed projects and to prepare Heritage Impact Assessment (HIA) reports. In April 2009, a joint World Heritage Centre-ICOMOS mission arrived in Penang "with a mandate to clarify the process that had led to the approval of the four projects in question, to assess their impact on the outstanding universal value of the site and to strengthen the conservation and management system at the site." After intense negotiations, both developers in the buffer zone consented to reduced building heights - one ongoing construction in the buffer zone was brought down from 17 to 15 floors although the original plan had been approved for 28 floors, while another's overall façade design would be amended to harmonize with surrounding heritage buildings. The two developers in the core zone agreed to keep to the 18 metre height limit; one developer resubmitting a new plan, and the other limiting the construction in progress but reserving legal rights. All parties reached a compromise apparently satisfactory to UNESCO, while the state government promised to tighten the approval process. Upon the mission's recommendations, the World Heritage Committee, at its 33rd Session in 2009 (Seville, Spain), decided not to raise the "yellow flag" which would have placed George Town on the list of World Heritage sites in danger. The threat of delisting turned out to be a mere slap on the wrist as the mission subsequently "praised the spirit of genuine cooperation and the positive attitude demonstrated by the State Party in trying to address the issues, and also commended the valuable contributions made by the representatives of the four developers" (Ghafar Ahmad, 2010: 29).

How such planning travesties could have been allowed in the first place can be simply explained by the fact that there is, as yet, no Local Plan for George Town or Penang island, although its preparation is authorized by the Town and Country Planning Act of 1976. In the meantime, to avert the threat of inappropriate new developments, the Municipal Council of Penang Island (MPPP) has established a Technical Review Panel to screen development applications for properties located within the World Heritage Site core and buffer.

While most World Heritage Sites, especially those in Europe, are meticulously maintained, urban management standards of the two Malaysian cultural properties fall below par. It is no surprise that the UNESCO inscription came as a "referred listing" with strict conditions, paraphrased as follows. In order to enhance the conservation of the cultural properties, a comprehensive plan must be designed and implemented for both cities. This plan must especially take into account the proper conservation of all buildings, especially shophouses, and adequate techniques of intervention. It should also include measures for decreasing motor traffic and control of tourism pressures. The monitoring system should be improved by establishing comprehensive indicators for the whole range of urban and architectural heritage components. These conditions have to be met through the creation of a comprehensive management plan and special area plans for each of the cities by February 2011.

Funding for work on the World Heritage Site remains a concern. The previous Prime Minister and Finance Minister Abdullah Badawi declared in his budget speech of August 2008 that UNESCO listing "reflects a global recognition of our rich and diversified cultural heritage." In delivery of an earlier promise, he also announced a RM50 million allocation for conservation works of heritage sites in Malacca and Penang "to support activities undertaken by non-governmental organisations (NGOs) and private sector".[4] Not surprisingly, this promised allocation became a bone

---

4 Interestingly enough, this text appears under the budget strategy 'strengthening the nation's resilience' and the subtitle 'promoting tourism'. (Full text of PM's Budget speech, Friday, 29 August 2008, archived in www.malaysianbar.org.my)

of contention between the under-financed opposition state government and the federal government, which decided to channel a RM 20 million allocation to Khazanah Nasional, the investment holding arm of the federal government. Khazanah has incorporated a special purpose vehicle called "Think City Sdn Bhd" to implement the George Town Grants Programme, starting from early 2010. In order to "kick-start the urban rejuvenation of the George Town World Heritage Site (WHS)", Think City's strategy is to build on the momentum of civil society and private sector initiatives by spurring private-public partnerships. It aims to build capacity for the protection and development of the living heritage, culture and architecture, as well as encourage a sustainable, livable environment.

In taking a developmental approach to stimulate economic growth, Malaysia has long neglected to foster a finely-tuned culture of maintenance. New institutional partnerships have to be forged to overcome the many structural problems underlying the mainstreaming of heritage conservation at federal, state and local levels. Due to the complicated nature of federal-state-local government relations post-2008, the responsibility for setting up a heritage management office for the World Heritage Sites involved more than a year's negotiation. "World Heritage Incorporated" (WHI) was eventually constituted at the end of April 2010, with an initial grant from the state. The WHI general manager Maimunah liaises directly with the National Heritage Department, the Town and Country Planning Department, the Penang state government as well as the local government in approaching the heritage management of the site. Under-resourced and under-staffed, WHI taps on the strengths of a working committee made up of government representatives, academics from the Penang-based university, as well as heritage advocates and practitioners from civil society groups such as the Penang Heritage Trust and CHAT. This committee had been meeting and working long before WHI's formal incorporation.

Rather belatedly, the drawing up of a Special Area Plan was outsourced to Kuala Lumpur-based consultants and the latter is engaging Penang experts to provide inputs in specific areas. The Special Area Plan vision espouses an idea of an 'intelligent and sustainable city.' On the whole, the historic district's problems are being tackled by a loose consortium of government, academia and community groups. Within the current social environment of weak planning controls, they realize that it is critical to engage with communities.

URBAN MANAGEMENT

The George Town World Heritage Site is a cultural property covering a total of 259.42 ha, including 4,665 buildings, streets, amenities and open spaces. It is surrounded on two sides by the sea. It consists of a core zone of 109.38 ha containing 2,344 buildings and a buffer zone of 150.04 ha, containing 2,321 buildings. This makes the George Town World Heritage Site significantly larger than Melaka, both in terms of size and number of buildings. In terms of land-ownership, public buildings and land are mainly concentrated in the civic-cultural area along the northern and eastern waterfront. Major institutional land owners include schools and historical religious charities. In the past, old Penang families also had large property holdings, but one by one these trusts are being broken up. The ownership of vernacular shophouses in the World Heritage Site is largely in private hands; a large proportion of residents and businesses are tenants, rather than owner occupiers.

In order to inform policy and programmes for the World Heritage Site, Think City commissioned a baseline survey. The George Town Land Use and Population Survey 2010 yielded useful facts and statistics. For example, it enumerated 2,900 businesses, a high proportion of them consisting of the self-employed. In addition, 830 hawkers operate in the heritage zone. As many as 10,500 people actually live in the city, but the population is aging.

George Town has always served as a place to live and work. Lifestyle change began in the period just before, during, and after the Second World War, when the new middle-class started the flight to the suburbs. After the war, rentals were suppressed by the authorities to prevent profiteering due to housing shortages. The inner city became a largely working-class enclave. Then the younger, more educated, prosperous and socially mobile segment of the population began to move out, leaving behind their parents as well as less educated and lower income relatives. After several decades rent control, which placated working class voters but irked the landlords, was finally repealed with a window period (1997-2000). A sudden rent hike accelerated the demographic change by displacing many tenants to the low-cost housing areas in the urban periphery. Local businesses closed down and community resilience was eroded. Having driven out their tenants, many property owners found that they could not get new tenants at the price they anticipated. Due to the poor infrastructure and sanitation, as well as inadequate open spaces and community amenities, the World Heritage Site was hardly attractive to residents and businesses who had no reason to be there.

Once the civic and commercial centre of the city, old George Town has become a backwater compared to other more dynamic parts of the state. The thinning out of its economic functions started with the decline of Penang's trading function from the late 1960s, following the loss of its free port status and the development of a container terminal on the Prai mainland. In the 1970s and 1980s, government functions moved from the crammed administrative offices in the City Hall and Town Hall to fill up the KOMTAR tower. Major banks and offices in Beach Street shifted out to better serve the middle-class clientele. The decantation of the inner city population after rent control repeal as well as the relocation of the important Prangin Market further reduced the city's vibrancy.

The loss of George Town's centrality can also partly be blamed on the gradual deterioration of public transport over the decades, accompanied by the incoherent and fragmented spatial development of the state, resulting in chronic traffic congestion. Suburban centres and regional townships such as Pulau Tikus, Ayer Itam and Bayan Baru have subsequently swelled and become self-sufficient with their own shopping malls and other facilities. As a result, the George Town historic centre has lost its importance for much of the larger Penang population.

Nevertheless, George Town does retain some functions that cannot be easily duplicated. Foremost among them are the old and established houses of worship, especially the Goddess of Mercy Temple, the Kapitan Keling Mosque and the Maha Mariamman Temple, which continue to attract visitors from out of town. These icons help sustain a number of their respective supporting businesses such as joss-stick sellers, flower sellers, jewellery shops, pelikat shops and food shops. The court house is another major institution, anchoring the lawyers' offices, and consequently stationers and pubs. The two remaining wet markets, namely, the Campbell Street Market and Chowrasta Market, are still important for the inner city residents, but the Chowrasta's diverse produce also attracts customers from the suburbs. Around the two markets are a myriad of stores selling women's clothes, household sundries, dried foods and so forth. Upper

Beach Street is still the premier banking hub of Penang, though not as exclusive as before. The wholesale shops along Beach Street, the hardware shops, metal-smiths and recycling trades are still important to the local economy. Due to its longstanding role as port and travel destination, George Town also maintains a well-established service industry, which includes food outlets, souvenir shops, travel agencies, money changers and a range of visitor accommodation from budget to five star.

Ten years after the repeal of rent control, 15-20% of properties within the WHS are vacant and, of these, approximately half are in derelict physical condition. In 2010, the local government released a list of 180 derelict properties. Uninhabited properties quickly deteriorate in tropical weather, and their state of decay is a deterrent for would-be tenants, especially those who are used to modern housing and amenities. Due to unrealistic expectations fuelled by property speculation, the rental market remains irrational, and it is difficult to find cheap rentals or long-leases being offered in return for repairs.

With an abundance of vacant properties, a lucrative but polluting industry has taken root. This is the use of heritage houses as cave-like homes for swifts, harvesting the saliva for a Chinese delicacy known as bird's nest soup. In the last few years, a hike in demand from newly prosperous China consumers has stimulated the proliferation of swift-farming in Southeast Asia. Swift farming in populated urban areas causes problems of noise pollution and a potential threat to public health. A proposed ban in the city was postponed year after year, during which time new swift-farms increased several fold. In line with the new national swift farming guidelines and federal heritage policy, the state government has now declared its intention to remove swift-farming in the World Heritage Site over a period of three years. Implementation will take strong political will and enforcement.

MULTICULTURAL TOWNSCAPE

Of the three "Outstanding Universal Values" (OUVs) possessed by Melaka and George Town, that which is easiest to understand refers to the site as "an outstanding example of a type of building, architectural or technological ensemble or landscape" which illustrates a significant stage in human history. The nomination showed that Melaka and George Town "reflect a mixture of influences which have created a unique architecture, culture and townscape without parallel anywhere in East and South Asia. In particular, they demonstrate an exceptional range of shophouses and townhouses".

In order to conserve the city, Penang has to prove the viability and contemporary relevance of the traditional shophouse. The shophouse typically refers to its dual function as a place of residence and trade, although the term shophouse is also generically applied to all prewar terrace "dwelling houses". As the street front could easily be converted into a shopfront, some units which were originally built as residential have since been converted to shops and offices, thus blurring the distinction.

The shophouse has long been lauded for many reasons. Designed for comfort while relying only on natural ventilation through its internal air wells which resemble Roman atriums, the traditional shophouse is a superb example of climatically appropriate architecture. With long windowless side walls, the shophouse provides highly adaptable and flexible space. George Town used to be a hive of family businesses. The shophouse was suited for family business, as the family or extended family was able to live upstairs, and work downstairs, thus ensuring security for the shop and store. Offices and cottage industries were also easily accommodated in terraced "dwelling houses". Rows of shophouses form the perimeter block, and a townscape made up of such blocks offered maximum social networking between neighbours, hence providing the basis for a strong sense of community. Although average family sizes have decreased, and lifestyles have changed, the shophouse is still ideal for young entrepreneurs and can serve as a business incubator. A challenge for Penang is to re-establish the shophouse model of living and working among a new generation of Penangites and Malaysians. As cities will be challenged to wean themselves from car and carbon-dependency, the potential of this urban patterning for low-energy consumption lifestyles are even more desirable when framed within the new goals of environmental sustainability.

In order for the George Town built townscape to be sustainably conserved and maintained, several major strategies are necessary. The first is an economic strategy to ensure that the buildings are optimally used and economically viable, the second is to regenerate communities by improving livability, and the third is to build expertise and capacity for architectural conservation.

Swift-farming and many illegal and destructive building works have left George Town in need of large-scale rehabilitation. In terms of physical conservation, the most critical problem is the lack of conservation know-how within the building industry and weak public enforcement. This know-how has to be expanded at several levels. The public sector needs conservation professionals who are involved in conservation policy, planning and management, as well as trained officers who carry out site inspections, monitoring and enforcement. Conservation is a meticulous process requiring a sound knowledge of building history, traditional building methods and traditional materials. It also requires a multi-disciplinary understanding of cultural significance with an appreciation of genius loci, or "the spirit of the place".

Finally, the work involves a laborious process of constant investigation, detailed analysis and informed application. Heritage impact assessments are required for larger projects and conservation specialists are essential for the restoration of significant buildings. However, as most property owners normally engage small scale contractors, roofers and odd-job workers for maintenance and small-scale repairs, it is necessary to reform the existing industry from the bottom-up as well as top-down.

In short, a system has to be in place to ensure that owners and tenants maintain their sites and carry out sensitive renovations and conversions which respect the original character of the buildings, and entail minimal, reversible changes to the fabric. In a multilingual society with a low standard of legal literacy, the lofty intentions of heritage legislation and guidelines can simply be "lost in translation". In the last few years, CHAT played a critical role in establishing heritage monitoring and working out processes within the local government machinery as well as creating an interface between local government and NGOs. CHAT's experience shows that the best way to reduce the incidence of illegal unsympathetic renovation works, is to having friendly, flexible but firm on the ground roving advisors, at least until such a time when improved monitoring mechanisms, more rigorous enforcement and a culture of heritage compliance are in place. George Town needs a new generation of builders who value the original qualities of traditional ways of building, the science of natural ventilation and natural materials such as lime plaster and lime concrete, terracotta roof and floor tiles, recycled timbers and other recycled materials. In urban rehabilitation, opportunities to introduce new sustainable technologies, for example, in renewable energy and recycling should not be missed.

Although a lot of work has gone into the preparation of the dossier for UNESCO, the "referred listing" implies that there is much more to do. Heritage properties need to be adequately surveyed and inventorized. Existing heritage guidelines need to be reviewed and extended to cover all building types, not just shophouses. The government itself must make it a priority to inventorize, maintain and restore its own heritage assets, and to draw up conservation plans for major public monuments such as the Fort Cornwallis. A fine-grain development plan has to be worked out for the eastern waterfront area, where commercial buildings like shipping godowns, elongated mixed use wholesale shop-warehouse entities and small-scale industrial uses are found. Existing reclaimed land can be transformed from wasteland to public open space. The authorities have to ensure that infill development in the buffer zone is controlled by an envelope plan and that the "buffer of the buffer" is also constrained. Otherwise, as Aga Khan experts who conducted a workshop in Penang in May 2010 warned, the World Heritage Site might be imminently walled in by "fifty mini-KOMTAR towers".

The George Town WHS marks the end of a chapter of contestation between conservationists and developers who complain of "density suppression", but the saga continues well beyond the WHS. With no Local Plan, redevelopments are still approved in an ad hoc manner. In the recent past, heritage bungalows have been conveniently disposed of through illegal demolition for the fine is small enough to be factored into the cost of development. The architecturally important prewar mansions and bungalows along the northern coast and the suburban "green belts" are being replaced one by one with office blocks and condos, transforming the hinterland of the World Heritage Site into a veritable concrete jungle, without adequate provision for sustainable transport and open space. In public infrastructure projects, the problem usually stems from lack of public consultation in the push for big contracts. Penang Botanic Gardens and Penang Hill are two important cultural landscapes which are potentially eligible for annexation to the George Town World Heritage Site. However, due to lack of heritage appreciation and public consultation, two federal tourism projects to "improve" them ended up compromising their historical integrity.

Within the World Heritage Site, local government will have to prioritize improvements to the public realm, including open spaces and infrastructure. For instance, in anticipation that George Town will become a "restaurant city", the infrastructure for food industry, including the better management of hawkers, al fresco dining, and waste disposal should be worked out. Examples of successful cities all over the world show that raising the standards of urban management is a straightforward challenge that can be answered with professional expertise backed by adequate financing and political will. The only difference is that in a cultural heritage site which is layered with history and heritage, cultural values and community need to be fully taken into account when planning for urban improvements.

In a workshop held in June 2010, the cultural landscape expert Ken Taylor advised that George Town should be interpreted as a Historic Urban Landscape (HUL), which has been and continues to be shaped by human processes. The city has to be understood as more than just an agglomeration of buildings within an urban settlement; it is just as important to consider the public realm, the vistas, the waterfront landscape and the surrounding sea buffer which provides the context for the trading port. The southern part of the eastern waterfront is characterized by the famous clan jetties, perhaps the most densely populated part of the World Heritage Site today. These villages built over the sea with their lively traditional waterfront communities are a charming anachronism in modern-day George Town. However, the clan jetties have a long legacy of infrastructure and tenure issues, and conventional planning approaches do not apply. As such, the conservation of the jetties and their living heritage present a unique challenge.

MULTICULTURAL TRADITIONS

The second of the three OUVs refers to the site as bearing "exceptional testimony to a cultural tradition or to a civilization which is living"; the dossier proved that Melaka and George Town are "living testimony to the multi-cultural ... tangible and intangible heritage expressed in the great variety of religious buildings of different faiths, ethnic quarters, the many languages, worship and religious festivals, dances, costumes, art and music, food, and daily life."

As the UNESCO Convention on intangible heritage (2003) is relatively more recent compared to that on cultural heritage (1972), specialists have fewer tools for conserving intangible heritage. Furthermore, the challenges and the solutions differ so much from one society to another, that there are few prescribed methods to deal with this. In George Town, some living traditions show signs of good health. The tradition of Penang food is flourishing due to its large following, while self-appointed "foodies" happily play a role in feedback and quality control. In terms of traditional festivals, many are still carried on by community groups with little or no government funding or interference, yet flourishing by the year.

Much attention has been drawn to "endangered trades". These are trades and crafts which used to be common but are now continued by a few practitioners. The most celebrated of these traditional trades is represented by a Chinese lantern marker, the only surviving practitioner of his trade, who for years was making his bamboo and paper lanterns in a condemned house. He is one of the master artisans and performers recognized by the Penang Heritage Trust as "Living Heritage Treasures" and granted a small annual stipend. Those who have been similarly honoured include cultural performers, a batik painter, a kebaya designer, a signboard carver, puppet troupe owners, a jewellery artisan, a traditional cane furniture maker and a chef.

Ordinary practitioners are dwindling as many of these traditional trades simply suffer from a lack of demand due to the availability of cheaper replacement goods or changing lifestyles and consumer trends. The chain of transmission is easily broken when practitioners do not pass on their trades. After years of mounting concern, the Penang Heritage Trust with its partner Arts-Ed has formulated the Penang Apprenticeship Programme for Artisans (PAPA) to train apprentices. However, not all practitioners are natural pedagogues. At the same time, students may learn the craft as a hobby but not as a trade as they cannot see a good stable income, or a future career. A bumiputra tourism cooperative called KOPEL is building capacity for the repair and maintenance of trishaws among the Malay operators in order to make the trade more sustainable.

Tourism and an emerging creative industry could offer a new market for certain endangered trade. The Little Penang Street Market, a monthly arts, crafts and culture market established in 2006, attracts the sort of cultural entrepreneurs who could make it happen.

MULTICULTURAL HISTORY

The third Outstanding Universal Value refers to the site as exhibiting "an important interchange of human values" over a span of time; the dossier gave evidence that Melaka and George Town "represent exceptional examples of multi-cultural trading towns in East and Southeast Asia, forged from the mercantile exchanges of Malay, Chinese, and Indian cultures and three successive European colonial powers for almost 500 years, each with its imprints on the architecture and urban form, technology and monumental art". This criterion reflects relatively recent UNESCO thinking which emphasizes "living" and "intangible" heritage in addition to built heritage, and acknowledges a contemporary global appreciation of the significance of a long period of multicultural, multi-religious co-existence.

At the same time, this OUV has to be understood within the cultural contestation that is taking place in Malaysia today. In a country in which political parties are identified by race, the Malaysian nomination and UNESCO listing has helped to open up a new discourse on religious and cultural diversity. While the Melaka story of the Malay Sultanate has been the central narrative of Malaysian official history and nation-building, it could be said that the significance of George Town and Penang has largely been cast outside the scope of Malaysia's cultural vision. This imbalance is being countered by a popular social history movement in Penang. In 2002, the Penang Story Conference explored how George Town represents an "interchange of human values" between various cultures from East and West over a span of time. By doing so, it helped to re-energize a plurality of social memories among Penang's diverse communities.

Like many places in the world today, George Town today faces systemic threats to its character, integrity and authenticity as a historic urban site. The conservation of the OUVs of a trading centre that is multicultural, historically layered, and encouraging of cultural exchange requires an in-depth understanding of the forces that forged[5] the city and continue to shape its society today. A landmark document on this issue is the Nara Document on Authenticity (1994), which states that the respect due to all cultures requires that heritage properties must be considered and judged within the cultural contexts to which they belong. The Hoi An Protocols emphasize the need to draw from different sources of authenticity and overlay various dimensions to understand the historic palimpsest.[6] The maintenance of George Town's OUVs will in itself require a multi-disciplinary, multi-lingual and multicultural team. As a prerequisite, the World Heritage Site needs to build up its cultural institutions, such as library, museum and archives, through long-term documentation projects. As historic communities can still be found in situ, and their social and genealogical networks remain strong and within a largely intact historic setting, George Town is an exciting place for social historians. At the same time, programmes in local history, cultural literacy, arts, heritage and so forth, should be part of an ongoing effort to realize the potential of a richly diverse multicultural society.

URBAN REGENERATION

The most obvious way to jumpstart urban regeneration is through cultural tourism. With a large number of historic attractions within a compact city, George Town could be developed as a showcase of Asian architectures, communities and food, with an ambience of an open-air museum or "museum without walls". The experience of individual heritage sites can be integrated through a variety of heritage trails, and enriched by visual arts, performance, community interaction and forms of "intangible heritage". Through a recent upgrading of its cruise ship terminal, George Town now has a ready tourist market. In 2010, cruise ships have brought an estimated 890,000 passengers to the city's doorstep. Typically half these passengers pre-booked their tours, while another half are "free and easy" tourists. Tourism could help to stimulate the economy by creating service sector jobs, providing a market for entrepreneurs, catalyzing the growth

---

5 Nara Conference on Authenticity in Relation to the World Heritage Convention. Nara, Japan. (1994) [http://www.international.icomos.org/icomos/nara.htm]
6 Hoi An Protocols for Best Conservation Practice in Asia: Professional Guidelines for Assuring and Preserving the Authenticity of Heritage Sites in the Context of the Cultures of Asia. Bangkok: UNESCO Bangkok, 2009.

of cultural industries and crafts, and helping to finance restoration and maintenance.

However, the growth of tourism can be a double-edged sword and the benefits of tourism to the local community are not automatic. Links have to be made between the consumers and the target beneficiaries. The lack of infrastructure planning and provision for tourism is already being felt. Large tourist busses that come into the World Heritage Site overwhelm the heritage surroundings with congestion, pollution, noise, and ground vibrations. Tourism could encourage the growth of touts, souvenir peddlers and rogue transport providers. The proliferation of restaurants and eating places, many of them resulting from illegal conversions and not being equipped with grease traps, will put the strain on inadequate sewage facilities and exacerbate the rodent problem. The hurry to create low-budget hotels and boutique hotels has resulted in renovations that are more concerned with expediency and glamour than authenticity and sustainability. New guidelines for budget hotel conversions are urgently needed to uphold standards and address issues of safety, security and legality. There are already projects which tend towards Disneyfication. The Hoi An Protocols warn of loss of authenticity when cultural assets are modified and homogenized, or when traditional rituals and performances are decontextualized (Hoi An Protocols for Best Conservation Practice in Asia 2000, revised 2005).

The success of tourism may also lead to a takeover by outside players. In Phuket and Bali for example, tourism has attracted investments by foreigners or national players, leaving the lower-level service jobs to the locals and ultimately leading to the repatriation of profits. In a project which looks at Housing in Historic Asian Cities (Alexander, 2006), André Alexander has shown that in newly-conferred World Heritage Sites, visitor numbers increase, the local economy improves and the service industry begins to form. Then major local and international players invest in the local economy, edging out small local players. As the tourism scene matures, the environmental, social and infrastructure costs begin to set in, together with inflation. This is followed by a period of stability in visitor numbers, or decline. However, by this time, local culture has been replaced by sanitized culture for visitors, traditional local jobs have largely vanished, and land prices are now too high for low-income communities.

Tourists in the mean time, start to opt for new competing destinations that are still "unspoilt". From this and other similar studies, it appears that World Heritage Site will predictably be blighted by the tourism industry if the numbers are uncontrolled, proper safeguards are not in place and the impacts are not understood and minimized.

The George Town World Heritage Site offers opportunities for property investment. However, a few foreign buyers paying unrealistic prices are enough to attract speculators, edging out genuine local buyers and local community. Alas, the slightest interest shown by potential investors in tenanted properties is sometimes enough to prompt existing owners to evict their tenants. It is better to direct investors towards derelict sites as their investments are more likely to prove a net gain to the city. While small-scale and slow gentrification may actually improve old neighbourhoods, rapid gentrification may distort the local market, cause displacement of marginalized communities and irrevocably alter their character. There are, however, examples of investors who have supported the creation of extra value. In one case, the owner of a property being converted into a boutique hotel is also financing research into building materials and techniques, and the results are published on a blog. In another case, the prospective operators of a boutique hotel have allocated a choice part of the building for the original business tenant, a medical hall, to remain on the premises.

Policy makers should be aware that local community is part of an eco-system of sustainable tourism. The Outstanding Universal Values will be better served by higher standards of urban management which seeks to retain existing community and bring more people back to live and work in the World Heritage Site. In order to advance the idea of livable, affordable housing in George Town, it will be necessary to create a pilot project which promotes the old principle of "mixed use" – living above the shop. The long-term plan should be a systematic urban rehabilitation programme addressing the need to repair and upgrade heritage buildings, possibly having specific programs for roofs, electricals, kitchens, toilets, and the improvement of neighbourhood amenities and urban waste management. George Town's dynamic entrepreneurial sector should be encouraged to play a role in growing the heritage industry.

The old city of George Town now needs to find a strong role within the context of the larger Penang metropolis. Instead of focusing unduly on foreign investors, it is better to strengthen the local economy and develop the local market by restoring George Town's central role. Business strategies are required to boost business clusters which are rooted in George Town. Steps should be taken to bridge WHS with other parts of Penang, partly through better public transport, as well as through campaigns and programmes that bring Penangites back to the old city centre. In all this, it is good to keep in mind a vision of preserving "old Penang" for Penangites and the Penang diaspora. Strategically located in an economically vibrant region, George Town can also renew its role as hub of the northern corridor and the Indonesia-Malaysia-Thailand growth triangle.

Indeed, the novel challenge of sustaining living heritage calls for general urban revitalization as well as specific interventions to improve quality of urban environment and stimulate new businesses and creative industries. "George Town by night" can bring visitors into the World Heritage Site during non-peak traffic hours. Another strategy for George Town would be to draw young people, for example, by attracting a university with creative industries to locate its city campus in George Town. A student population would not bring in too many cars, and could also help balance the existing aging residential population. For years, arts groups have been calling on the government to create a cultural hub by integrating cultural venues like the Fort Cornwallis, Town Hall and Dewan Sri Pinang under professional management. The George Town Festival, which grew out of the commemoration of World Heritage listing in July, has grown into a month-long festival in 2010. It has given a boost to the local arts scene and cultural entrepreneurs and demonstrated how a combination of arts subsidies and the activation of under-utilized government assets venues could help to realize George Town's potential.

Conservation together with the improvement of urban quality are the means towards achieving a stronger urban cohesion and improved livability. A pilot greening project along Carnarvon Street has met with good public response. Another good pilot project would be the urban regeneration of Prangin Canal, on the edge of the World Heritage Site, involving the creation of a green park for surrounding residential and business district, as well as the rehabilitation of shophouses for mixed use. There are opportunities here to demonstrate new green technologies.

CONCLUSION

The listing of George Town and Melaka in July 2008 as UNESCO cultural properties galvanized various sectors – government, business, community groups and even the Penang diaspora – into focusing on the potential of the George Town World Heritage Site. On the other hand, the attention attracted by World Heritage listing has also accelerated the rate of rash or illegal works and gentrification. Although a small number of refurbishments give the impression that the World Heritage Site is on the upturn, the net decay of infrastructure, careless destruction of heritage and loss of community continues on an alarming scale.

The transformation of the George Town World Heritage Site into a vibrant and livable capital of Penang, is now understood as an important strategy in making Penang more attractive to talent, and thus facilitating the metropolis's transition to a post-industrial economy. But in order to accomplish this, Penang as a whole needs to make a paradigm shift from real-estate based development to heritage value-based development. Regenerating the World Heritage Site requires a micro-planning approach and a finely crafted vehicle for careful urban renewal. Funding has to be less ad hoc and institutional weaknesses have to be overcome.

George Town itself is an interesting example of a Historic Urban Landscape which continues to be shaped by community with their living traditions and cultural memories. Among World Heritage experts, George Town has a reputation for innovative bottom-up approaches. Today, the George Town World Heritage Site is in a unique position to pioneer culturally-based urban regeneration strategies in a plural society. Creative partnerships that bring together multicultural stakeholders from state, business, NGOs and community will be the key to success.

Chapter 3

Heritage as Knowledge: Time, Space, and Culture in Penang

Goh Beng Lan

INTRODUCTION

George Town's new status as a UNESCO World Heritage City has heightened the importance of heritage as a means to turn Penang into a major tourist destination and revitalise its economy. The commodification of heritage is however closely entwined with Malaysian nationalist discourses as heritage is often synonymously understood as "tradition", a central narrative in the reconstructions of national identity. Against this background, heritage pursuits in the inner city of George Town have been characterised by claims on ethno-religious legacies and a call for the preservation of their associated buildings, sites, objects, skills and/ or ways of life in order to ensure their survival into the future. In these pursuits, state, semi-quasi-state agencies, and capitalists often act together to impose heritage imaginations along the lines of mainstream ethnic distinctions between Malay, Chinese, Indian, and other communities. Affected civil and community groups have responded by invoking a myriad of multi-layered ethnic identities and/or shared cultural dimensions between ethnic groups as resistant culture. These dynamics have produced a wide array of imaginaries that not only reinforce but also challenge and complicate official ethnic categories in Malaysia. It is evident that both hegemonic and counter-hegemonic forms of heritage imaginations are deeply encumbered by nationalist ethnic categories, the very forces which threaten to tear Malaysian society apart. There is hence an imperative to expand the meaning, goals and repercussions of heritage practices in Penang beyond ethnic legacies.

In this paper I wish to explore the promise of heritage in the hope of providing alternative pursuits to those driven by nationalist and market interests. In particular, I am interested in heritage as a mode of knowledge production that creates critical consciousness about time and society. For this, I draw on the conceptualisation of heritage as a practice which creates new forms of knowledge via re-assembling time and space or architecture. I begin with theoretical discussions to approach heritage as a mode of knowledge production with recourse to the past but which produces new ideas. The capacity to generate knowledge makes heritage an "interpretive interface" (Kirshenblatt-Gimblett, 1995: 377) which enables the imagination and the mobilization of life in the past for contemporary social transformations. I suggest that the turn of the 20th Century in Penang - a colonial and interwar era associated with quests for new ideas and ideals about humanity, society, and politics - is a good starting point for rethinking heritage. I will draw on critical legacies left by the Hu Yew Seah during the early decades of the 20th century as grounds to create empowering heritage practices. In particular I will call for new strategies of showcasing historical sites and a need to turn heritage spaces into civic and not merely tourist spaces.

HERITAGE AS A MODE OF PRODUCTION OF NEW CONSCIOUSNESS

Academic debates on heritage have presented us with frameworks which attempt to conceptualise heritage either within or outside the framework of capitalist commodification.

Studies adopting a commodification approach have provided us with a mixture of instrumentalist, meaningful, and contested understandings about heritage. Some studies view heritage as a manipulation of history for consumption and production, especially for the tourist market (MacCannell 1976; Cohens 1988). Others have tried to carve more nuanced understandings by recovering meaningful dimensions in heritage "transactions" which reconstitute and transform cultural practices and meanings. Picard's (1996) work on the impacts of the tourist cultural industries on the transformations of Balinese identity is one example of this latter approach. Other studies have instead pointed to the contested nature of heritage highlighting class and cultural politics that shape the heritage industry. These analyses often focus on struggles between powerful and marginal actors such as state and/or capitalists versus civil society and community groups.

Shifting away from a market focus, others have instead highlighted heritage's entwinement with nation-building politics (Picard & Wood 1997; Hitchcock et al 2003). In particular, postcolonial states have been singled out for efforts to monopolize heritage in the course of national identity making. Heritage is seen as a means for the state to impose unified collective pasts. Inevitably this makes heritage an arena of contestations over national identity and meanings of nationhood.

Yet others have departed from the market versus state frameworks. They have instead approached heritage as a mode of cultural production which produces new ideas about time and space. These approaches overthrow assumptions about heritage as something "authentic" from the past which can be rescued, conserved, and so on. Rather, they argue that heritage is a new invention; that heritage is a mode of knowledge production that draws on the past but which produces new meanings (Kirshenblatt-Gimblett 1995; Hobsbawm & Ranger 1983). Here I find Abidin Kusno's (2010) work which approaches architectural/spatial practices as devices that produce both disciplined and empowering forms of identities useful to our discussions. Kusno (2010.: 9-18) argues that by bringing time into architectural/spatial practices, the interconnections between past and present are not only better revealed but can create new imaginations which can liberate and also constrain human action. Borrowing from this perspective, we can therefore treat heritage as potent manipulations of space and architecture as well as social-cultural imaginings which can shape society either for the better or the worse. It is therefore imperative that the drives behind and the consequences of heritage visions and pursuits are considered seriously and not left alone to the dictates of nationalist and capitalist agendas. Here civil society can help redirect heritage pursuits to re-inscribe other inspiring ideas about self, community and society onto urban space which can counterbalance the narrow preoccupation with ethnic identifications in current pursuits. Hoping to contribute to such efforts, this paper explores empowering alternatives which can supplement current heritage practices.

PRESENT LIMITATIONS AND CHALLENGES

As pointed out earlier, heritage enterprises in contemporary Penang appear incapable of leaving behind official ethnic categories created by the Malaysian state. The combination of market interests and preoccupation with nationalist categories has confined heritage pursuits to a mere celebration of ethnic diversity. Heritage pursuits have tended to revolve around the recovery of "authentic" ethnic legacies. Such quests suggest prior conceptions about ethnicity. Yet the agents of such heritage discourses, whether they represent the state, capital or communities, are often un-reflexive about their own prior conceptions. It is precisely because of un-reflexivity about encumbrances with official definitions of ethnicity in the Malaysian context that leads to the valorisation of authenticity despite inherent ambiguities and contradictions within ethnic identifications. By operating within predetermined conceptions of ethnic identity and heritage the cart is put before the horse in these pursuits of heritage. Ethnic identities become end goals to be reached, creating a sense of foreclosure instead of openness when thinking about heritage. Not surprisingly, heritage conservation has created spectacles of quaint, diverse yet harmoniously plural Penang for the tourist market. This rosy image of ethnic authenticity and plurality is however distinctly remote from the realities of heightened ethnic tensions and social-class differences in contemporary Malaysia (Jenkins and King, 2003: 45-46).

If heritage wants to take on a transformative role, it has to shed its complacency with given knowledge and take up new imaginative horizons and ambitions which have relevance to the present. Heritage pursuits will have to go beyond the dictates of national visions and capitalist commoditisation of ethnic heritage. It must strive to think about how it can inscribe, reveal, and bring together interconnections between past and present so as to stimulate new cultural, intellectual, and ethical imaginations which can transform society for the better. I suggest that heritage expands its visions to consider critical consciousness as also a form of cultural heritage. Heritage should try to create social and spatial environments which can provoke critical thinking about contemporary society. The progressive visions about culture, society, and politics that emerged at the turn of the 20th century in Penang provide us with a good starting point to rethink heritage practices. The critical consciousness of this era provides alternatives to the politics of sectarianism and ethno-religious intolerance in contemporary Malaysian society. Using the case of Hu Yew Seah, a cultural-literary group, I will show how inscribing critical consciousness produced in this era onto heritage pursuits can empower imaginations about the future.

MODES OF CONSCIOUSNESS AS HERITAGE

As a late colonial port city and cosmopolitan centre of immigration, trade, and press, Penang was a site of experimentation with the new and the modern (Lewis 2009). Inevitably, a variety of social, cultural, artistic, and political organizations were formed during this period alongside the rise of new cultural, artistic, and political imaginations as local society grappled with colonial and interwar history. The pluralism of this era took multiple forms and shapes. Different groups were participating in modernity and producing new conceptions of self, culture, and society. It was a time of great openness to ideas. Humanity was not defined by any singular terms let alone ethnic identity. Rather what was valued at the turn of the 20th century was new knowledge which led to efforts of translation and experimentation with foreign ideas in the quest to create locally relevant meanings. Within Southeast Asia, this was a time when people were beginning to see themselves as agents of change. James Seigel has pinned down the emergence of the conceptions of "saya" or "I" in Malay, the lingua franca of the region, to this era (1997: 13-26). The search for self began to lead people to see themselves as agents of social and political change in their fight against colonial domination. Anthony Milner has termed this as the rise of "new mode of public discourse" and the "invention of politics" in Malaya (1995: iv). The new modes of human experiences had spurred people to rethink their identity, desires, and awakened them to take on new social and political roles. Independent spirit and critical thinking were the hallmarks of pluralism in this era as different people interacted and competed over different visions of society and modernity.

Yet the inspiring visions of this era have not been fully captured by heritage efforts. Much of this period is remembered only by its tangible legacies. Contemporary heritage practices have tended to focus either on preserving architecture, cultural objects, artifacts, ways of life, and so on, or remembering personalities or organisations associated with this era. Less is however remembered of the significance of the critical ideas and the new meanings of humanity and society during this time. Yet the multiple forms of imaginations about self, society, and politics generated during this period can provide us with important lessons to rethink the problem of pluralism in contemporary Malaysia.

If cultural conservation is to create new knowledge, consciousness from this period can be a source of inspiration to change social outlooks today. Conservationists have to strive to bring these memories back into contemporary spatial reality and create thought provoking experiences from them. Inheritances of ideas, attitudes, and thinking about humanity, culture, and society are forms of heritage as well. Here, the ideas and ideals associated with the Hu Yew Seah, a cultural-literary group, during the early decades of the 20th century may provide an example for us to explore alternative heritage practices and imaginations of Penang/ Malaysian society. The history of Hu Yew Seah calls for new heritage strategies which seek not just to inscribe its current site but also the trail left behind in George Town as the Association shifted headquarters over time as well as relocated the school that it ran several times. It also calls for a need to turn heritage sites into civic rather than tourist spaces. I will use a brief survey of the rise and fall of the illustrious history of the Hu Yew Seah to make my points on the need to re-inscribe forgotten social visions associated with this Association onto George Town's landscape.[7]

Today the Hu Yew Seah is commonly known by the Art Décor style building with Shanghai plaster finish that stands on 43 Madras Lane, George Town. This double storey building completed in 1928 has all the hallmarks of sleek and minimalist elegance associated with the Art Décor Style. The Hu Yew Seah is no more than a recreational club for its members and little known to many younger Penangites today. Yet the history of this Association is once charged with creativity and imagination and which leaves inspirational social legacies within George Town. A visit to the building today tells little about its glorious past. Only a

---

7 *Information on the Hu Yew Seah is obtained from the Association's 50th Anniversary Magazine (1964) during a visit in January 2003. I would like to thank the then President of Hu Yew Seah, Mr Eric Lim Khen Guan, for providing me with the magazine.*

small marble plaque mounted on a wall in the main hall of the building provides a clue to its splendid past. The plague marks the foundational stone laid by Nobel laureate poet and philosopher Rabrindranath Tagore who inaugurated the building on 14 August, 1927. This plague is a tell tale sign of the Hu Yew Seah's status as a cultural-literary association at the forefront of social-cultural life in Penang during the early decades of 1920s. Throughout the 1920s and 1930s, the Hu Yew Seah was a centre of intellectual and social activity. By the 1930s the role of the Association had expanded into areas of Chinese cultural and martial arts, sports - in particular badminton - and education via the establishment of the Hu Yew Seah Girls' school.[8] By 1950s, the Association had gone into national language education by running the biggest Malay Night School to teach Malaysians the national language. The narratives behind the history and aspirations of this Association have remained a kept secret to many Penangites. It is the task of conservationists to exploit the progressive visions of this Association so as to motivate Penangites to think beyond current confines of self, identity and society.

The Hu Yew Seah, or literally the "League of Helping Friends", was established as a cultural literary association on 17 July, 1914. The name of the Association is derived from a phrase from the Confucian Analects which states that, "The superior man associates with his friends by means of literary studies and pursuits, and by this friendship helps his own virtue" (Lim 1964: 88). In an age prior to Foucauldian thought, the Association's motto was "Knowledge is Power" (Choy, 1964: 10). The idea to set up this Association came from a casual afternoon "tiffin" gathering amongst four friends in Market Street Penang (Hu Yew Seah, 1964: 14). These were Mr Choong Thiam Poe and his friends, all of whom were English-educated Straits Chinese elites, many of whom were also members of the underground resistance movement, Tung Meng Hooi, a party set up by the leader of Chinese nationalist revolution, Dr Sun Yat Sen (Khoo, 1993: 123).[9] Given their political affiliations to Chinese revolutionary politics, these English-speaking Straits Chinese wanted to set up a literary association so as to provide Chinese Language and Literature classes for the English educated Straits Chinese in Penang. A Special General Meeting held on 17 July, 1914, led to the establishment of the Association.

8 A Hu Yew Seah Orchestra was formed in 1930 (Hu Yew Seah 50 Anniversary Magazine, 1964: 17).
9 Penang was the headquarters for the Southeast Asian Tung Meng Hooi from 1909-1911 (Khoo, 1993: 34).

The Association first took residence on 40 Church Street before moving to 72 Love Lane in 1917. It was in 1926 that the Association acquired its current premise and built its own building which was completed in 1928. The move to this new premise and Tagore's visit marked the height of the Association's achievements. Although its founding members were linked to the Tung Meng Hooi, the Hu Yew Seah clearly developed into an organization concerned about local belonging and community-building. Throughout the 1920s and 1930s, the Hu Yew Seah served as a centre for intellectual and social activities in Penang. This was a time where local society was beginning to fight for their interests against the colonial government and forge a sense of local identity. The Hu Yew Seah was a venue for public debates where many political leaders and cultural visionaries spoke at its premise. Leaders of the Hu Yew Seah included several renowned members of the Penang community who were also active in other organisations such as the Straits Chinese British Association, the Chinese Recreation Club, the Penang Chinese Town Hall and so on during this era. Amongst past Presidents was Dr Lim Chwee Leong,[10] the father of former Chief Minister of Penang, Dr Lim Chong Eu and the architect who designed KOMTAR, Lim Chong Keat. Not surprisingly the Hu Yew Seah rendered its voice to various political and social causes of the time. In 1933, the Association lent support to Mr Lim Cheng Ean's appeal to the colonial government to reduce school fees in English schools (Tan, 1980: 94).[11]

In the same year, the then President, Mr Koh Sin Hock and other intellectuals, politicians, and journalists including the prominent Manicasothy Saravanamuttu formed a discussion group called "Lost Souls". The name conveys the spirit of a deep desire to search for meanings of humanity. The hunger for knowledge was so strong that several members of the discussion group travelled regularly from Taiping in order to attend its meetings.

Yet, the search for meaning during this time was not a narcissistic or parochial enterprise. Self was not merely conceived in terms of personal welfare and ambition as is common today. Rather it was accompanied by strong moral conscience and consciousness about a sense of belonging

---

10 Dr Lim Chwee Leong was President of the Hu Yew Seah from 1915-18.
11 Lim Cheng Ean eventually lost his appeal and walked out of the Straits Settlements Legislative Council.

to a wider society and even a regional world beyond Penang. This was manifested in charity work taken up by the Hu Yew Seah when it collected funds to help relief work after natural disasters within Penang (such as the Influenza Epidemic in 1918 and Ayer Itam Fire in 1935) but also in China (such as the Canton Flood in 1915 and the Swatow and Amoy Earthquake in 1918) (Hu Yew Seah 1964: 17). The Association's concern for social advancement also saw it making generous donations to the Penang Asiatic Unemployment Fund in 1932 and providing meals to coolies stationed in Pulau Jerejak when they became unemployed in the great economic slump during this period.

As part of protecting the social and moral welfare of its own members, the Association also provided lessons in Chinese martial arts and encouraged badminton as a sports activity. During the 1930s the Association had such a strong badminton team that it was known as the "premier badminton club" in Malaya (ibid, p. 16).

In 1930, the Association became a serious patron of education when it first took over the management of a primary school located on Macalister Road (on the present site of the St Paul Anglican Church) which was running into financial difficulties.[12] The Association first relocated the school to Dato' Keramat Road (on where now stands the Hock Aun hotel) but renamed it the Hu Yew Seah School when it was officially opened in 1931. The school expanded and eventually moved to where now the Hu Yew Seah Girls' School stands adjacent to Association's building on Madras Lane.

In anticipation of Malaysia's impending Independence, the Hu Yew Seah took upon itself to establish a Malay Night School in 1956 with the aim of offering national language classes to Malaysians from all walks of life. With Independence, the Hu Yew Seah was quick to change its membership rules in 1962 (Hu Yew Seah, 1964: 8). Originally the Association only opened its membership to the Chinese community but allowed for honorary members from other races. Amongst the honorary members included the figures of N. Raghavan and Dr N.K. Menon who had facilitated Tagore's visit (Tan, 1980: 93). However by 1962 membership was opened to all races in order to reflect the multi-racial composition of newly independent Malaysia. Stepping up to take up the

---

12 This school was called Chinese Kindergarten.

challenge of nation-building, the Hu Yew Seah actively expanded its night school in order to teach Malaysians the national language. By the 1960s some 23,000 Malaysians had studied in this night school making it the "biggest private national language school in the country" (Lim, 1964: 4). The school also marked the Association's link to the Sultan Idris Teachers' Training College in Tanjung Malim as its first teacher, Mr Ismail Bin Said, came from this college (Tan, 1964: 40).

By the 1970s, the Association focused solely on promoting the learning of the national language and appeared to have given up on its role as transformative agent of social change. Working with the state towards achieving nationalist education is not necessarily a bad thing. However, it is the abandonment of its role as critical transformative agent that led Hu Yew Seah to lose its social role when national education no longer became an issue by the 1980s, as most Malaysians became conversant in the national language.[13] Without alternate visions and purposes, the Hu Yew Seah soon declined into a mere recreational club for its members, who are still predominantly English-speaking Chinese from the middle classes and above in Penang. The story of Hu Yew Seah's magnificent past and its decline into a recreational club reminds us of the importance for civil groups to strive towards critical coalition with rather than succumb to state discourses. In the pursuit of heritage, it is important for the state, capitalists and civil groups to work together to counterbalance and constrain each other's action. There has to be space for the constant deconstructing and re-constructing of heritage categories and meanings in order to allow for alternative imaginations that could actively countervail the powers not only of the state and capital, but also civil society, especially when the latter is no longer the exclusive domain of tolerant and democratic interests in contemporary Malaysia.

REFLECTIONS AND WAY FORWARD

The critical visions about self, society and community advocated by the Hu Yew Seah, its rise and fall as a cultural-literary association, from between the 1920s until the 1980s, provide us with important lessons as we think about the future of Malaysian society. In line with the spirit of the time, the pursuits of the Hu Yew Seah during the 1920s display an

---

13 By the 1980s, the Hu Yew Seah School was also taken over by the Ministry of Education.

openness to learn from outside ideas and reflexivity of self and one's own cultural traditions. Tradition such as language and literature was not a hindrance but viewed as necessary knowledge for progress. The desire for knowledge and new ideas was translated into efforts to go beyond oneself, to transform oneself and one's old ways of life by gaining knowledge about language, culture, and society and reflecting upon one's relationship with others and wider society. To be new during this time was a quest to learn how not to be one's self which is a sharp contrast to the preoccupation with how to arrive at one's self in current heritage imaginations. What is inspiring is the progressive, open and forward-looking nature of the quests for self, identity, and social meanings when compared to the insular, closed, chauvinistic, and backward frameworks of identifications today. The self-reflexivity produced in this era should be recaptured and used to provoke a rethinking of contemporary society and identity for both Penangites and perhaps members of the Hu Yew Seah itself.

As we see, the history of the Hu Yew Seah is connected to several sites in George Town, not to mention the Association's interconnections with several other institutions of its time. Heritage as we know today tends to associate history with singular sites or buildings. Yet the evolution of the Hu Yeah Seah from a cultural-literary association to one which was engaged in welfare, sports, and educational activities has left several spatial footprints in George Town. Attempts to map the history of the Association should really begin with Market Street, in the core heritage zone today. It was from an innocuous everyday activity such as having afternoon tea with friends on this street that the idea for the establishment of the Association was hatched. The growth of the Association leaves a trail from Church Street to Love Land and finally Madras Lane where the Association currently stands. Yet if we were also to include its visions on education, the track would extend to Macalister Road and Dato Kramat Road, revealing the multilayered and overlapping nature of Penang's spatial, institutional, and social histories. A trail for the history of the Hu Yew Seah could be established and sites along this tract could be commemorated with small plagues to spur curiosity amongst visitors and Penangites to find out more about the Association and what it symbolised. Similarly, the linkage between the Hu Yew Seah and Tagore, one of the most inspiring thinkers and anti-colonial figures of the 20th century, is little-known. Equally signs can be put up in front of the Hu Yew Seah building to provide information on this inspiring historical event in order to better publicise this knowledge. Such strategies can be easily be adopted by conservationists. They can even be commoditised as tourist attractions. The means can be varied but the aim is to convey the broad-minded imaginations of society and community to the present generation.

Inevitably there are limitations in using space to convey history. Like other modes of instructions, one can never be sure that intended consequences can always be achieved. While heritage pursuits can establish a walking trail denoting Hu Yew Seah's history in Georgetown, we can never be certain that the lessons from its history can be effectively conveyed to visitors. However, there can be other interventions to better convey the social aspirations once held by the Hu Yew Seah. An effective way is to turn the current Hu Yew Seah building into a civic space beyond a tourist destination. Here a network of concerned individuals called, Saya Anak Bangsa Malaysia (SABM),[14] has already paved the way on 21 November, 2009. This network used the Hu Yew Seah as a site to kick start a nation-wide road show to foster inter-ethno-religious dialogue and instil the spirit of "One People, One Nation" in Malaysia.[15] This event turned the Hu Yew Seah into a civic space as youths, religious leaders, lawyers, film makers, human rights activists, and other civil society actors freely debated on various thorny issues plaguing Malaysian society. The discussions covered a range of subjects such as inter-faith dialogue, ketuanan Melayu (Malay supremacy), crisis of the nation, as well as current disputes over the interpretations of the Federal Constitution and Malaysian history.[16] During this event participants discovered the illustrious history of the Hu Yew Seah and were able to draw on parallels between the Association's progressive visions and their current mission to liberate the minds of Malaysians from political and cultural chauvinisms.

14 *SABM was formed as a result of an article written by a young Malaysian, Jayanath Appudurai, entitled, "Break the shackles of 'Tribal Think" in a popular Malaysian blog site (http://harismibrahim. wordpress.com /2007/07/26/break-the-shackles-of-%E2%80%9Ctribal-think%E2%80%9D/ (accessed 19/9/2010)). The article sparked off such an earnest discussion in cyberspace that it motivated a group of concerned individuals to form this network on 25 August, 2007.*

15 *http://www.sayaanakbangsamalaysia.net/index.php?option=com_content&view=article&id= 69:background-to-sabm&catid=43:sabm-initiative&Itemid=56*

16 *KOMAS, a partner of SABM, was instrumental for this workshop in Penang. Komas is the Malaysian Popular Communications and Human Rights Centre, an organization formed in 1993. It is modeled after the concept of Popular Communications (PC) which was originally developed in Latin America whereby educators and community organisers use popular channels of communications to create and organise participatory participation at the grassroots level. For details see http://www.komas.org/.*

In fact, another civil group had initiated the effort to bring civic activities into heritage sites in Penang, just a couple of months ahead of SABM's effort. This was the "Bangun- Penang Clan Jetty Community Arts Project" by an artist collective based in Kuala Lumpur, The Lost Generation, which brought multi-media art to communities living in the jetty area on 12 September 2009. This activity brought two important legacies together: Penang's place as a major centre for the beginnings of modernist art in Malaya during the 1920s; and the distinctive cultural history of the clan jetty. Through the Bangun project, the artists brought art into the everyday life of ordinary people creating a departure from art's usual association with "high" cultural activities, an elitist audience and the art gallery. Such an event democratises the access to Penang's artistic heritage by making it reachable to the common people. It is precisely initiatives that not only connect the past and present but make their interconnections relevant that can turn heritage into an experience which can inspire future imaginations. Such developments pose us with the challenge of turning heritage sites/practices into arenas of civil societal engagement with social issues. Such a direction may help free heritage from merely following state discourses to instead endeavour to work in critical coalition with the state, interrogating and revising official narratives and the interests of elites and the market as and when necessary.

To conclude, heritage pursuits must learn to inscribe social memory and consciousness instead of official history in order to create empowering possibilities for the future. It must depart from conventional definitions about history and culture and take on a new ambition to deploy heritage as a means of creating experiences which can spur a cognitive or intellectual change. To do so, heritage has to take on new imaginative horizons, strategies, and goals. It must be open to the possibilities of representing multilayered and overlapping narratives which cannot be easily subsumed into any coherent category or singular flow of time/influences. Such narratives may require spatial and architectural imaginations which can better illuminate interconnections between space and time and make relevant the past and present so as to provoke new imaginations. Heritage sites should strive to become civic spaces where people can engage with the past and present to better understand the legacies that shaped them. Only by venturing into such directions can heritage empower Penangites to create a more integrated and viable future.

Chapter 4

Heritage Conservation and Muslims in George Town

Syed Muhd Khairudin Aljunied

INTRODUCTION

Much has been spoken in the recent years about efforts to conserve George Town's long standing heritage in ways that may seem unprecedented to the outside observer. The terms of debate between state and federal governments, and between them and civil society organizations have been couched within a set of parameters that could be characterised as "personal and advocatory" on the one hand, and narrowly as "political and instrumentalist", on the other. For many heritage enthusiasts, to conserve sites and buildings that define George Town's landscape is to relive a part of their own collective memories of living within these nostalgic spaces. The social and personal dimensions of life thus become the raison d'être for change and this has been made the project of advocacy groups such as the Penang Heritage Trust and the Lestari Heritage Network. But the struggle for George Town's heritage has its political dimensions as well, especially upon the conferment by UNESCO of World Heritage Site status in 2008. Here, governments and political parties take centre stage, lobbying and garnering for support and muscling their way towards ends that are essentially instrumentalist, that is, to maintain their grip in the corridors of power and on the chests of the treasury. In the debates and battles to conserve and promote George Town's heritage, what tends to get lost are the voices of common folk and the landless class that are effaced by the more influential discourses of the state and power brokers - and not pottery and artefacts, heritage trails and museums. This makes it plain that the processes of heritage conservation are, in many instances, elite enterprises (Lowenthal, 2000: 419).

This effacement of the voices of the common folk and stakeholders is not limited to 'talk' and 'politicking' over heritage conservation by contending groups. It has permeated the terrain of scholarship and the work of researchers and practitioners located within George Town and outside. A cursory survey of the literature suggests that much scholarship has been concerned largely with the processes, structures and mechanisms of heritage conservation to the neglect of the human and everyday experiences of individuals and groups. Wherever and whenever terms such as 'pro-development groups', 'heritage lovers', 'Penangites' and 'tenants' are used in scholarly and policy-driven publications, they are often couched in generalities and vagueness leaving the reader to second guess whether these personae truly represent the actual views and anxieties on the ground (cf. Ho 2009).

There are, of course, exceptions to this order of things. Khoo Salma, Gwynn Jenkins and Goh Beng Lan are a few notable examples of scholar-activists who have brought to the fore the everyday struggles of the common folk while explaining the wider ranging processes that had impacted heritage conservation in George Town. I use the term 'scholar-activist' here in the manner in which Asata Zerai (2002: 206) has conceptualized it, as a person who participates in scholarly and grassroots struggles and, in doing so, contributes to the process of improving the conditions of a group of people. As a case in point, Salma and Jenkins' (2002) study of community responses to urban development strategies provides edifying insights into the attitudes and responses of community leaders, activists and laymen towards the efforts by state and civil society bodies to preserve Penang's heritage.

In the same vein, Goh (2002) examines the Kampung Serani redevelopment project in the 1980s and 1990s and the attendant effects of power politics and economic modernization upon a Portuguese Eurasian community in their endeavour to preserve their heritage and *habitus*. Adopting an eclectic methodology that combines discourse analysis with ethnographic practice and modernization theories, Goh gives agency and voice to kampong dwellers who had been evicted from their age-old homes. Her study shows how "the experience of modernity in Malaysia begins with the everyday processes of urban eviction and the accompanying upheavals of social, political, and economic behaviour, which unfolds within a complex intertwining of local, national and global dynamics" (2002: 201).

This chapter builds upon the existing corpus of works about the realities, and by implication, the politics of heritage conservation in Penang. It seeks to present how state-linked heritage conservation programmes could, at times, be driven by civil society actors, as seen through the perspective of a public listed company, Think City, and how such efforts can nonetheless be limited by a given community's perceived marginality and the polarization. The community of concern here are the Muslims of George Town. More than two dozen of whom I have spoken to are above thirty years of age and see themselves as "Malay", "Indian" and/or "Arab" while acknowledging that what binds them together as a "community" are the facts of being "Muslim" and "minorities" within a largely non-Muslim, Chinese-dominated city. We will return to these two forms of identifications later. Suffice it to state here that although my sample of interlocutors is relatively small and, in many ways, problematic for the purposes of generalizations, I would argue that the following *excursus* can provide us with a new pathways, albeit partial, into an understanding of the nature of the Muslim community in George Town and what structures the manner by which they have made sense of the rapid changes that are occurring around them. In so doing, I hope to offer a counterpoint to the prevailing perception of politicians and analysts and to illuminate some blind alleys about efforts to conserve George Town's heritage.[17]

It is crucial to mention here that the following study was conducted at a time of rapid transformations and upheaval following the March 2008 election and the installation of non-Barisan Nasional government in Penang. The fall from grace of the Malay-dominated BN coalition in Penang also ushered in a change in thinking among Muslims there of their presumed pre-eminent place in Malaysian society. Lagging behind economically even after more than three decades of the implementation of the New Economic Policy, Muslims residing in Penang are now faced

---

17 I have left the names of persons and their organizational affiliations anonymous although some insisted that they should be quoted at length and that their identities be made public.

with a new set of realities. Foremost amongst these is that their over-reliance upon the BN government to manage their way of life and heritage has become untenable. For some influential leaders in the community, 'scapegoating' is used to dissimulate their personal failings and abortive schemes.[18]

The implications of this study of heritage conservation in George Town extend beyond its empirical specificity. What I hope to show is that heritage conservation may not necessarily see the active participation of the 'common folk' especially in cases where state intervention is not met with genuine and wide ranging strategies to gain the trust and to empower the people. Heritage conservation projects that are solely directed by governments and/or state-linked companies – common in sites that have been conferred by the World Heritage status by the United Nations – will be confronted with pessimism and indifference from amongst the local inhabitants who would logically perceive such efforts as driven less by the will to sustain and preserve long-standing legacies than to generate income for the coffers of governments and private businesses. Left unaddressed, this dissonance between state/private profiteering motives and the common people would cause disillusionment and feelings of estrangement and generate conditions for conflict, mutual aggrandizement and even violence. Alternatively, through enlightened assistance given by the state, its agencies and willing partners, common folk could become more empowered and optimistic about heritage conservation and this would yield positive outcomes for the benefit of all parties concerned.

PERCEPTIONS AND REALITIES OF HERITAGE CONSERVATION IN GEORGE TOWN

One of the more persuasive efforts at heritage conservation in Penang is that driven by Think City, a subsidiary of a government linked company, Khazanah Nasional Berhad. In August 2009, I was approached to be an 'historian-consultant' for the company's project aimed at rejuvenating the Muslim enclave in George Town; a heritage site which is considered by the inhabitants themselves as unabashedly neglected. I agreed to become a part of this ambitious project only after having been impressed by the

---

18 Personal Conversation with Dr Maznah Mohamad, Former Vice-Dean of Universiti Sains Malaysia.

company's mature approach in reviving the urban rejuvenation efforts in George Town. Towards achieving that end, Think City sought to build partnerships between civil society organizations and private companies thereby strengthening local capacity and capability for the conservation of heritage. In the long run, the company hopes to encourage sustainable development and the creation of a livable environment in George Town. The means by which they seek to achieve these objectives were by establishing intra-community solidarities and networks as well disbursing grants to interested personalities and groups.[19]

Through the 'interactive process' approach, local communities are encouraged by one or two coordinating agencies to participate in heritage management. To ensure long-term protection of their homes and heritage, representatives of local communities in turn elect and/or employ professionals and experts from within the community itself to oversee and coordinate conservatory work (Robertson, 2008: 149). Seen in this light, the role of Think City is as a mere catalyst, facilitator and financial backer for long-term projects run by the local Muslim community.

No attempt at preserving heritage is free from interference from politicians. Examples from different parts of Southeast Asia abound and what comes out most clearly in each of these cases is that the struggles between politicians and other participants in the heritage conservation business have tended to become all the more raucous when the issue at stake involves the distribution of state funds to bodies that are deemed by oppositional groups as complicit partners in the project of hegemony and political domination (Delafons 1997; Ismail, Shaw and Ooi 2009). It does not come as a surprise then that Khazanah Nasional Berhad, and by implication Think City, has been criticized by state politicians for delving into areas that are "not within their expertise" and that the "handing over RM20 million of funds" to the government-linked company to develop heritage sites is "discriminating" and "punishing" Penang.[20] Above and beyond the conflict over funds, such statements are symptomatic of the ongoing tensions between the federal and state governments and the tenuous place that Penang as an opposition-led state is in at the present

---

19 See: http://www.thinkcity.com.my/index.php/gtgp
20 'Guan Eng questions Khazanah handling Penang heritage cash', http://www.themalaysianinsider.com/malaysia/article/guan-eng-questions-khazanah-handling-penang-heritage-cash/

moment within the Barisan Nasional political chimera. Granted that there may be a grain of truth in this claim of discriminatory treatment by the federal government towards Penang, a closer and grounded view of Think City's activities presents a more complex state of affairs.

The composition of the company's staff members and board of directors is one key aspect that complicates the view that all monies that have been given to Think City would serve to "punish" Penang. These personalities belonged to second, third or even fourth or fifth generation Penangites and are actively involved in community-based efforts, mass movements, policy advocacy work and publishing; activities that have at times run contrary to the state aims and legitimation of authoritarianism. Their involvement in civil society activities and in Think City concurrently knowing full well of its linkages to the federal government cuts through the state-civil society dichotomy prevalent in many writings about Malaysia. Rather, what these figures seek to achieve is to mediate, if not, influence state policies by participating in government linked bodies to bring about social change and initiate reform in local societies. Muthiah Alagappa has described this as "the deep penetration and influence over the state by certain civil society actors" (2004: 37). By this, he is referring to the creative ability of civil society actors to enter into various arms of the state apparatus and take up strategic positions to gain access to a range of resources. This will allow them to push for mobilization efforts that were previously made impossible by the restrictions by the reigning state. In the case of Think City, this "deep penetration" has brought about some important strides in the realm of heritage conservation for reasons that the active participation of civil society activists in the company has been complemented by a revitalized oppositional movement in Penang upon Anwar Ibrahim's arrest in 1998 (Saravanamuttu 1998; Nagata 2001).

Partly due to the deep penetration of civil society activists in the company, since August 2009, Think City has managed to organize several meetings with Majlis Agama Islam Pulau Pinang (MAIPP), Dewan Perniagaan and many other civil society bodies to allow the company to play a more concerted role with them to upgrade the Muslim enclave. Think City also met with the Urban Planning Authority (UDA), of which MAIPP has outsourced the marketing and the management of the Muslim Enclave to. Closer working partnerships between Universiti Sains Malaysia (USM) and the Dewan Perniagaan have also been forged through Think

City's arrangement. The two bodies will be submitting a joint proposal to document the history of the Muslim community in Penang as content material for the Malay Museum in Hutton Lane. This document will also provide a framework for the revamping of the Museum Islam in Acheen Street and spark community activities in the enclave. Aside from these meetings, four physical conservation projects are now underway which includes the Kapitan Keling Mosque, facade upgrading at the Liga Muslim, refurbishing the Islamic Park and Kapitan Keling Mausoleum as well as repair works at Himalayathul Anjuman. Thus, Think City had been able to reach out and bring into concert all of the main players in the Muslim communities.

And yet, Think City's 'achievements' must not be taken uncritically for they mask the deeper apprehension that hangs over the Muslim community in George Town. It is this apprehension or 'a climate of pessimism' (as I would like to term it) about the longevity of the heritage conservation efforts that piqued me most throughout my involvement in the project. The more time I spent on discussions at restaurants and homes of mosque committee members, leaders and members of community organizations, retired individuals and lay observers who are still based in George Town or have migrated to other parts of Malaysia whilst maintaining close relations with kith and kin through occasional visits, the more I was made to believe that what lies beneath the public show of support for Think City's efforts are a subtle, sometimes invisible, sense of disempowerment and of being overwhelmed by factors that Muslims felt they have little control of.

One does not have to have any special powers to discern the climate of pessimism among Muslims in George Town. We can unravel this and other sentiments when we are sensitive to the analogies, metaphors, metonymies, stray comments, reflections, expressions and gestures employed by Muslims in Penang in narrating, often lamenting, about their current conditions and about their heritage. James Scott (1990), in what is now regarded as a classic in the study of subalterns and subordinated peoples, describes these practices as 'hidden transcripts' that exist within a social site. They are hidden because they take place 'offstage', that is, beyond the perceptual grasp of those in positions of authority. These practices are 'transcripts' because they are marked by a high degree of consistency which confers them the position of records, even if unspoken, can be easily detected and understood by the social actors that share common affiliations and concerns. I would argue that the ensemble of these hidden transcripts produces a climate which would ultimately affect all efforts at conserving the Muslim Heritage in George Town. I will discuss two hidden transcripts and their social and historical roots.

HIDDEN TRANSCRIPT 1: 'WE ARE FEW AND 'THEY' DO NOT TREAT US AS EQUALS'

There have been no reliable censuses of Muslims in George Town or of Muslims in the island of Penang as a whole. The reason for this is that the available censuses are often framed within the Chinese, Malays, Indians and Others nomenclature, which is based on categories that were constructed and imposed upon by the preceding colonial state. Used as an instrument of disciplining ethnicity, such categories have now acquired a logic of their own throughout present-day Malaysia. They are used by state and federal governments to facilitate developmentalist projects in accordance with the progress and needs of different communities. Although problematic, especially at the everyday-defined level, all four categories are seldom put to question because they serve to maintain the dominance of elites and scholars who associate themselves with a given majority ethnic group; the strength of numbers and the reification of identities enable the larger group to influence policy and practice (Shamsul 2005; Milner 2008; Department of Statistics 2010).

Even so, from the anecdotal evidence that have come down to us, it is said that Muslims constitute less than 20 per cent of the 220,000 strong population located in various parts of George Town. Even if this estimate is inaccurate, the fact remains that Muslims on the island perceive themselves as "minorities" within a non-Muslim dominated state. "*Kita orang Islam tiada kuasa di sini. Orang kita terlalu sedikit* (We Muslim people have no authority here. Our people are too small in numbers)" is one transcript that is imbricated within the general feeling of pessimism among my respondents. Moreover, the sense is that Muslims could do little to institute wide-ranging reforms so as to improve the sorry state of their built heritage. At operation here is the demarcation of who belongs to the minority group and who does not, which gets entangled with the issue of heritage conservation. This is consistent with the observation made by Fiona Mclean that 'identity is central to heritage (2006: 6).' For this select group of Muslims in George Town, religion is one facet of their identity that is grafted into their conceptions of heritage, thereby differentiating themselves from the larger non-Muslim populace. Added to this reasoning is the suggestion that differences in religious identities and heritage are contributing factors to their marginalization by non-Muslims.

It can be argued that this hidden transcript is an upshot of a host of historical, social and political factors, shaped primarily by the cultural distance maintained by Muslims and non-Muslims in George Town and accentuated by media propaganda sponsored primarily by the dominant political coalition. Still, to the Muslims I spoke to, it is clear that their unequal status is manifested in the practice of everyday life and that discriminatory practices are far from mere perceptual biases. For example, at the level of politics, it is said that the non-Muslims are given the mandate to make or break any plans or initiatives spearheaded by Muslim civil society groups. At another level, persecution is seen as coming in the form of discriminate employment which meant that most Muslims are unable to work in non-Muslim companies. Muslim businesses and private companies, even if they are regularly featured in the mainstream media and that they provide alternative forms of employment, have no prospect of expansion nor to offer career advancement opportunities because of their inability to penetrate into a tightly closed Chinese dominated market. Other cases of discrimination that were cited include the alleged cancellation of public processions such as the Prophet's Birthday celebration and the assault against Malay petty traders, both of which took place in 2010.[21] The recent raid of an Indian-Muslim shop by a KOMTAR assemblyman and political secretary of the Chief Minister of Penang, Ng Wei Aik, worsened the state of affairs.[22] Indeed, despite the attempts by the Chinese-led Democratic Action Party to clarify that these isolated incidents had nothing to do with discriminatory attitudes against Malay-Muslims, many of my interviewees reasoned that these and other incidents bore testimony to the government's callous disregard of their heritage, way of life and occupations.

21 http://www.igeorgetownpenang.com/news/486-penang-government-besieged-over-malay-muslim-issues
22 http://thestar.com.my/columnists/story.asp?col=joceline&file=/2011/1/16/columnists/joceline/7810820&sec=Joceline c=joceline

The circulation and amplification of alleged discriminatory practices against Muslims has led to the out-migration of some George Town Muslims to Seberang Perai, Kedah, Perlis, Kuala Lumpur and other parts of Malaysia. *Tanah, rumah lagi murah di sini. Tanjung tempat orang kaya. Orang dialah* (Land, houses are cheaper here. Tanjung (local Malay term for George Town) is a place for the rich. Their kind)" is one comment made by a sixty-year-old Arab-Muslim lady who was born and bred in George Town. Research on the out-migration of Muslim Penangites is more than wanting though there have been allusions to the uprooting of Jawi Peranakans from Penang to the capital city (Halimah and Zainab, 2004: 9). Suffice it to state here that 'the flight of the creative class' – to borrow from Richard Florida (2005) – has meant that Muslims who remained on the island tend to find it hard to work hand-in-hand with the non-Muslim majority towards preserving their heritage. Wherever working partnerships are established, it is done with some measure of caution and a certain expectations of impending failure or collapse.

HIDDEN TRANSCRIPT 2: 'WHOSE HERITAGE IS IT? MUSLIM? MALAYS? INDIANS? ARABS OR...?'

The perception of being treated unequally by virtue of religiosity and other markers is but one hidden transcript that has had repercussions upon the formation of the climate of pessimism towards heritage conservation. The other unspoken yet omnipresent transcript pertains to the fragmented nature of the Muslim community. In other words, at the same time as Muslims in George Town seek to mark out differences between themselves and non-Muslims, another process of differentiation was taking place within the 'Muslim' community itself. These cleavages emerge out of many factors ranging from personal choices, to class positions, to cultural diversity and political interests. It would be erroneous to argue that these divisions are unique to George Town or that it is a recent phenomenon. Rather, such divisions have become more salient than ever throughout Malaysia upon the advent of what Joel Kahn has termed as a 'culturalization process'. This involves the reworking of cultural landscapes to fit in with the state-sponsored projects, such as in promoting tourism, which impose its own brand of "Malayness" on the Muslim community. In the case of George Town, this culturalization process has meant that relics and sites that were previously regarded 'Arab' or 'Indian' in origins must now be refashioned and inscribed to display a more Bumiputera, Malay outlook that is appealing to the tourist gaze. More often than not, the groups that stand to gain from this process are those who identify themselves with the larger 'Malay majority' and, more crucially, with the middle classes in that community who rode on the wave of urbanization (Kahn 1997).

Tamil-speaking Muslims in George Town are most affected by these developments. Having resided for more than two hundred years in George Town, Tamil Muslims experienced two distinctive yet convergent set of changes which affected their place in the wider Muslim community. On the one hand, there developed the growth of a Jawi Peranakan group mentioned above who were descendants of Indians that married Malay women and adopted, in a variety of ways and manners, the Malay culture and language. This group of Muslims, as Judith Nagata observes,

> ...may make use of different self-ascriptions to suit the occasion, by identifying with the community most appropriate to the situation at hand. Thus where a question involving Malay constitutional privileges arises, as in qualifying for certain kinds of loans, scholarships or shares, that identity will naturally come to the fore. In matters of business contacts and networks, an Indian affiliation may be more advantageous, and even reinforced by membership in the Indian Chamber of Commerce (Nagata, 2006: 522-523).

On the other hand, a segment of the community sought to maintain their cultural roots by maintaining links with the home countries and inter-marrying with persons from the parental society. This second group have now become a minority within the minority Muslim community and it is suggested by recent studies that they suffer from stigmatization and stereotyping from their Malay counterparts and also faced the dilemma of being Muslim, Indian and members of a given communal political party all at once (Stark 2006; Saidatulakmal 2010).

During one of my meetings with members of this minority within a minority, mention also was made about first, the lack of acknowledgement given to the contributions of their forebears and second, the attempts made by Arabs and Indians to eradicate their own traditions so as to gain the acceptance of the Malay majority. To the Tamil-speaking Muslims in George Town, their history has been effaced by the larger Malay narrative, which, to them, is not only an act of historical amnesia; it is also an attempt by the Malays to lay claim over achievements that are not truly theirs.

'Siapakah orang Islam pertama yang datang sini? Caudeer Mohudeen. Dia orang Melayukah? Ini semua dia orang tiada sebut. Tapi kita tahu sejarah kita. Kita ingat. Mereka yang ada di Lebuh Acheh. Orang Melayukah? Arab tapi panggil diri Melayu. Sekarang banyak orang India pun ikut cara gitu. Bahasa Tamil tak tahu cakap. Mereka nak jadi macam orang Melayu. (Who is the first Muslim who came here? Caudeer Mohudeen. Is he Malay? They don't mention all these facts. But we know our history. We remember. Those people who are at Lebuh Acheh. Are they Malays? Arabs but they call themselves Malay. Now many Indians are taking that route. They don't know the Tamil language. They want to be Malays).'

To be a Tamil-speaking Muslim in George Town is thus to perceive oneself as placed in the periphery of the overall heritage conservation schemes determined by Malays. One of the reactions of members of this minority group to this internal marginalization and fragmentation is to assert their rights in protecting their unique identities. They have done so through language courses and cultural events. Another reaction comes in the form of active participation in Malay-dominated platforms such as political parties and civil society organizations. Indeed, many Indian-Muslims have risen to become leaders of the Malay Chambers of Commerce and the UMNO Tanjung branch on the island and, in doing so, have tried to push for the preservation of their cultures and heritage. However, this deep penetration (recall Alagappa above) of Malay precincts has yielded contradictory outcomes in that Tamil Muslims were pressured to assimilate themselves into the larger Malay community and to place their sub-ethnic interests at bay (Brown, 2006: 237-265). This has, since the last decade, led to Tamil Muslims in George Town to be suspicious or even defensive about the conservation efforts by Malays, which may include Tamils and Arabs. Such a hidden transcript which may well be shared by other sub-ethnic groups such as the Sumatrans and Hadramis will worsen the climate of pessimism that is already in place. Efforts at rejuvenating the Muslim enclave, thus, are at the risk of being stunted especially when one minority begins to perceive that they are marginalized by their own kindred.

CONCLUSION

What makes a study of heritage conservation in the Muslim enclave in George Town interesting is that it informs us of the wider issues affecting, and the forces at play in, Malaysian society in general. At one level, we are witnessing an attempt by a fairly weakened political coalition to regain lost ground by engaging in the business of heritage. This stratagem may just work to their advantage but it is clear that such moves have not been left to their own devices. Civil society actors get activated as and when claims are laid upon conservatory projects, pressuring from within and without, making "the State porous, destabilizing its dictatorial powers or rather 'reabsorbing' them within the expanding hegemony of civil society" (Hardt, 1998: 27). Some qualifications are necessary here. While there is indeed an "expanding hegemony of civil society" in George Town, such expansion is rife with ethnic fragmentations which limit the ability of civil actors to promote and promulgate heritage programmes as well as conservation efforts.

Further, by taking on a more grounded view and by tilting the observations from the eventful to the ordinary, what this study has done is to uncover some of the long-standing cleavages and divisions, anxieties as well as fears shared by those very persons affected by the dynamics of heritage conservation in George Town – the hidden transcripts, so to speak. I hope readers of this essay will take heed of this neglected angle of vision. When we listen more to the voices of small people and the marginalized, we will realize that the conservation of George Town's heritage, or any heritage for that matter, is not contingent upon funds and trained personnel per se. What is urgently needed is a conscious endeavour at winning the hearts and minds of the common folk and to set off a change in societal mindsets beyond ethnic jingoism. This in itself requires an act of fine diplomacy, a high degree of empathy and a deep knowledge of cultures and problems inherent within disparate communities for all parties concerned.

Chapter 5

Investment Opportunities in Penang

Lee Kah Choon, Wein Siew Wei and Sherine Loke

With a population of 1.6 million and approximately 1,000 square kilometers of land, Penang is a state in northern Malaysia that has earned a reputation as the "Silicon Valley of the East". Despite its small size and population base, it houses a sizeable cluster of electronics firms. In 2010, Penang attracted more foreign direct investment than any other state in Malaysia and over the past thirty years has consistently ranked among the top four states in the country.

However, the story behind Penang's deep and rapid economic transformation is less well-known. Traditionally a prosperous entrepôt economy dependent on trade, shipping, finance, and tin smelting, the state's economic model was called into question in the late 1960s. In 1968, the state's GDP per capita was 12 percent below the national average, and its unemployment rate of 15 percent was more than double the national average (Penang Chinese Chamber of Commerce 1968:9, Nathan Associates 1970:85).

In 1970, the Penang state government launched an ambitious economic program aimed at revitalizing the economy through promoting manufacturing and tourism. In 1972, the first multinational corporations set up their operations in the state. These companies - which are still in the state today - include: Advanced Micro Devices; Agilent Technologies (came in as Hewlett Packard); Clarion; Fairchild Semiconductor (came in as National Semiconductor); Intel; OsramOpto Semiconductors (came in as Litronix); Renesas (came in as Hitachi) and Robert Bosch.

Over the next four decades, the growth of the state's manufacturing sector was consistent and rapid. In 1970, manufacturing accounted for a mere 12.7% of the state's gross regional product (GRP). Today, manufacturing accounts for 48.2 per cent of the state's GRP, followed by the services sector, which represents 47.9 per cent. Within the manufacturing sector, electronics is the main growth engine, accounting for 54.5 per cent of all employment in 2006 (InvestPenang, 2008: 13). Similarly, the workforce in the manufacturing sector increased from 15 per cent of the total in 1970 to 32.2 per cent in 2010 (SERI, 2010: 6).

Figure 1: Penang's GDP by sector, 1970-2009

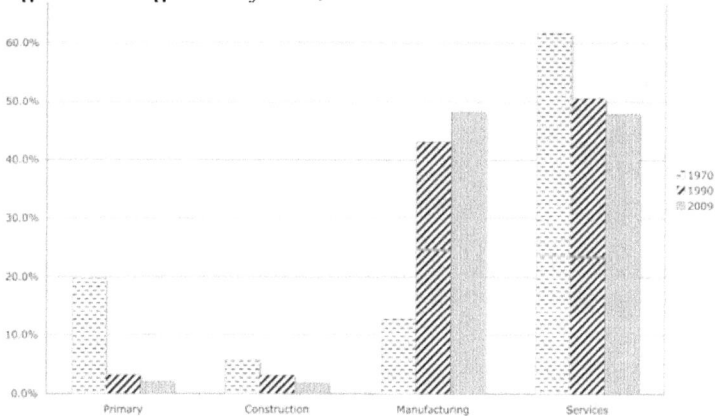

Source: Department of Statistics, Malaysia; Second Penang Strategic Development Plan, Tenth Malaysia Plan

A significant portion of this dynamism is due to the state's external orientation. Table 1 depicts Penang's contribution to Malaysia's electronics and total exports for 1995, 2000 and 2007. Despite the state housing some six percent of the country's population, it accounts for a vital and increasing proportion of the country's exports. In 2007, Penang produced 31 percent of Malaysia's exports and almost 50% of the country's electronics exports.

Table 1: Penang's Share in Malaysia's Total Exports

	1995 (%)	2000 (%)	2007 (%)
Penang's exports as a percentage share of Malaysia's exports	23.6	27.7	31.0
Penang's electronics exports as a percentage share of Malaysia's electronics exports	35.8	36.1	49.0

Source: Kharas, Zeufack, and Majeed, 2010: 33

Following manufacturing, tourism is the second key contributor to Penang's economy. The state registered 5.96 million tourist arrivals in 2009 compared to 6.3 million in 2008. This figure excludes tourists who visited Penang via sea cruises, on day trips, or who stayed with friends and relatives. Contrary to expectations, in 2009 tourist arrivals recorded a growth of 5.9 per cent compared to year 2008. With George Town's inscription as a UNESCO World Cultural Heritage Site, there is huge potential for economic growth in the tourism sector and Penang targets 10 million tourist arrivals by 2014 (The Star, 24 May 2009).

However, while the state's economy has been growing, its relative well-being is declining vis-à-vis the national average. In 1980, the state enjoyed a GRP per capita 28 per cent above the national level. Today, the figure is only 12 percent.

This decline in relative well-being may be due to the state's export-oriented model. While offering great potential for expansion, it means that the state is vulnerable to swings in the global economy. As seen in Figure Two, Penang was disproportionately affected in 2009, registering a contraction of more than 10 percent when the global manufacturing sector slumped. In contrast, the corresponding contraction for Malaysia as a whole was under 2 percent. However, looking forward, the panorama is positive for Penang, as while national GDP is forecast to grow by 4.5 to 5.5 per cent in 2010, the State's GRP is projected to grow by 7.9 per cent.

Figure 2: Economic Growth in Penang and Malaysia, 2007-2010 (2000 Constant Prices)

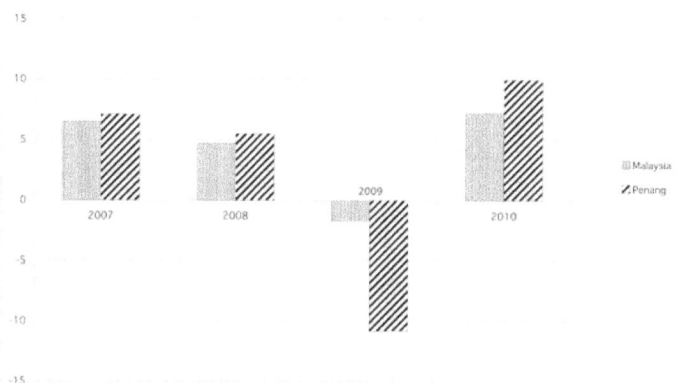

Source: Department of Statistics, Malaysia.

Consistent with its focus on manufacturing and tourism, Penang consistently performs well relative to other states in Malaysia. Figure Three shows the figures for total capital investment for the period 1980-2010 for Malaysia's principal centers of industry, namely Penang, Selangor, Johor and Kuala Lumpur. Penang topped the four destinations in 1999 and most recently in 2010. The results for 2010 are particularly encouraging, as Penang registered RM 12.2 billion in investments, a record for both the state and country. Figure Four shows that, in per capita terms, Penang garners a substantially higher amount of investment than other centres of industry in the country.

However, the nature of investment is also important. Penang is seeking to move from traditional 'high volume, low mix' production to 'low volume, high mix' operations. In addition, it is seeking to host more technology-intensive tasks such as research, design, and development. The state's transition from a greenfield site to a mature industrial sector is seen in the increasing importance of investment from existing investors (Figure Five). This shows that the state has been able to retain existing investors and convince them to expand their initial investments.

Chapter 5 | **Investment Opportunities in Penang**

Figure 3: Total Capital Investments in Penang, Selangor, Johor and Kuala Lumpur Federal Territory, 1980-2010

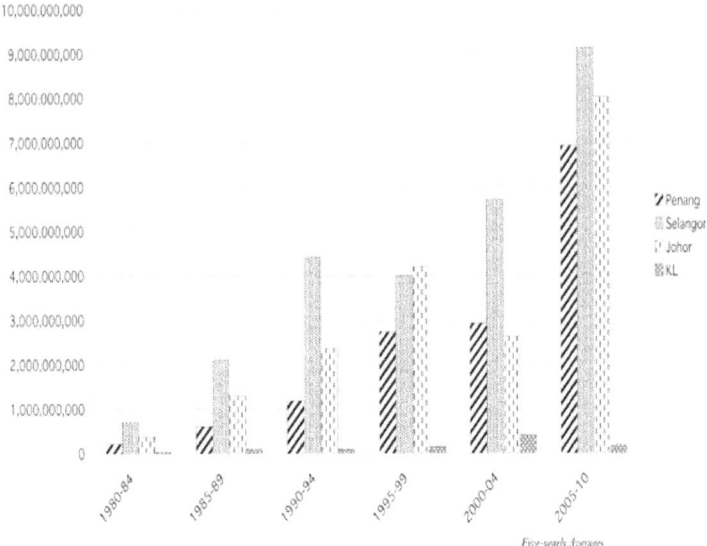

Source: Economic Planning Unit, MIDA, Department of Statistics Malaysia

Figure 4: Total Capital Investment per capita, 1980-2010

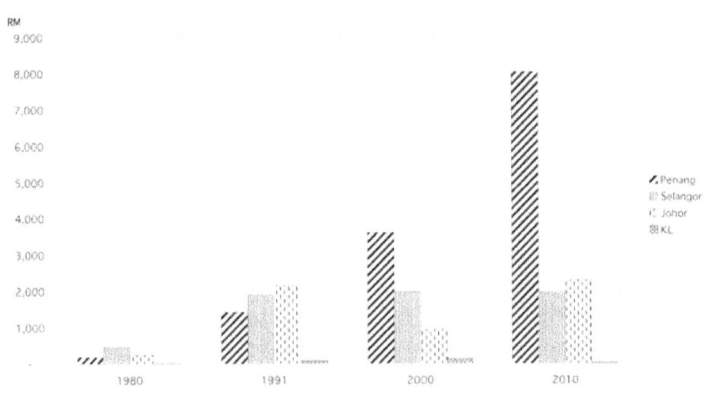

Source: Economic Planning Unit, MIDA & Department of Statistics Malaysia

Figure 5: Source of Total Capital Investment in Penang, 1981-2010

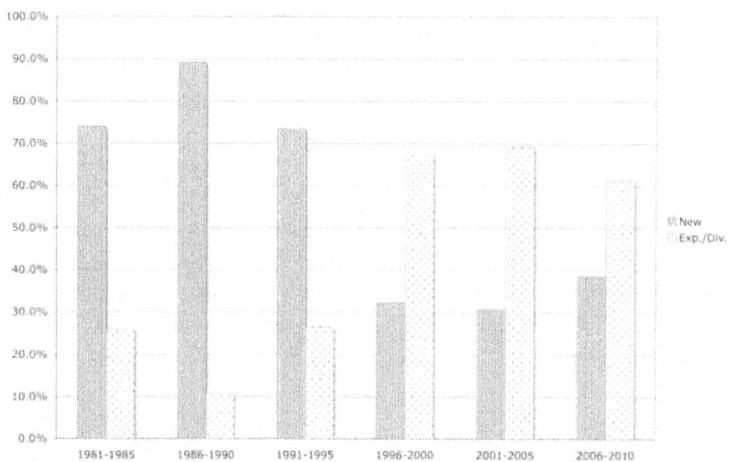

Source: Economic Planning Unit, MIDA & Department of Statistics

What, then, is the basis of Penang's competitive advantage, and what does the state offer potential investors? The remainder of this article will analyze and put forward the key elements of Penang's competitive advantage.

STRATEGIC LOCATION

Situated between the large and growing Indian and Chinese markets, Penang is ideally located for investors seeking to learn about and cater to these populations. Historically, the state was established for this very purpose, serving as a port for ships plying the route between these two nations. In addition, Penang bolsters its strategic position in the Indonesia-Malaysia-Thailand Growth Triangle (IMT-GT) and Northern Corridor Economic Region (NCER).

IMT-GT is a sub-regional cooperation initiative formed in 1993 by the governments of Indonesia, Malaysia and Thailand to accelerate economic transformation in less developed provinces and to develop closer collaboration between both public and private sectors. The Growth Triangle is composed of 14 provinces in southern Thailand, 8 states in Peninsular Malaysia, and 10 provinces in Sumatera, Indonesia.

Due to its central location within the IMTGT, Penang serves as the gateway to Southern Thailand and Northern Indonesia. The Penang State Government is actively collaborating with nearby provinces such as Aceh and Surabaya in Indonesia to promote investments in sectors such as tourism, real estate, education, transportation, and agriculture.

The Northern Corridor Economic Region is strategically located within the IMT-GT. The NCER is a government initiative to accelerate economic growth and elevate income levels in the northern region of Peninsular Malaysia, encompassing the states of Perlis, Kedah, Penang and the northern part of Perak. The Northern Corridor Implementation Authority (NCIA) has been established and given authority to initiate this development project.

Penang is at the heart of the NCER. This is due to the state's strong manufacturing backbone and its key logistics facilities such as Penang International Airport and Penang Port. One of the NCER initiatives is to build on this to enable firms in Penang to access raw materials, services, land, and labour in other states in the north, such as Perlis, Kedah, and Perak. Penang, in turn, can offer investors an environment conducive to business characterized by the protection of property rights, low transaction costs, and spillover effects from existing investments in the manufacturing and services sectors.

HARD INFRASTRUCTURE

The state's strategic location is complemented by extensive and efficient infrastructure, i.e. roads, highways, seaports and airports. The road and rail systems link Penang to other states in peninsular Malaysia, South Thailand and Singapore. The iconic Penang Bridge connecting the island to the mainland has been expanded. As of August 2009, the bridge can now accommodate 155,000 vehicles a day, compared to 120,000 before the expansion. The Second Penang Bridge is presently under construction and is scheduled for completion by 2013. The 24 km bridge will link Batu Kawan on the mainland to Batu Maung, which is adjacent to Bayan Lepas Industrial Park on Penang Island. Upon its completion, the Second Penang Bridge is expected to be the longest bridge in Malaysia and Southeast Asia. It will ease the traffic flow on the present Penang Bridge by at least 20 per cent.

The Penang International Airport (PIA) is the main airport for the northern region of Peninsular Malaysia. It is located at Bayan Lepas, about 16km from George Town, on the southeastern part of Penang Island. The airport was awarded the Best Emerging Airport (Asia) in the 23rd Annual Asian Freight and Supply Chain Awards 2009 (AFSCA). It was also selected as Airport of the Year (for below 15 million passengers annually) in the 2009 Frost and Sullivan Asia Pacific Aerospace and Defense Awards.

Presently, PIA serves domestic flights and direct international flights to Singapore, Indonesia, Thailand, India, Macau, Guangzhou, Hong Kong and Taipei. It is the main air facility for the northern part of the country, handling 3 million passengers between January and September 2010. At present, the airport is undergoing expansion and upgrading, which is expected to be completed by the end of 2011.

The Penang Port is a regional sea port which caters to the Northern Region of Malaysia and Southern Thailand. Currently, the Port captures more than 90% of the market share of the four northern states in peninsular Malaysia and more than 50% of the market share of the southern Thailand region (New Straits Times, 30 March 2010). Currently, the Port is able to handle 1.0 million TEU containers at one time and it can accommodate vessels with a capacity of up to 4,400 TEUs. Penang Port handled a total of 920,100 TEU containers from January to September 2010.

Upgrading the Penang Port is prioritized under the 10th Malaysia Plan (The Edge, 1 April 2010). Dredging works will enable the Port to accommodate larger vessels with a capacity of up to 7,000 TEUs and the cargo handling capacity will be increased to 1.8 million TEUs by 2011. In addition, the Penang Port is the first port in Malaysia to be certified by SIRIM under the MS1900:2005 Quality Management System, which will enable it to be the gateway for Halal products and services.

Other infrastructure upgrading plans include a transport hub in Butterworth on the mainland, upgrading public transport with the expansion of the RapidPenang bus service, and offering free wireless broadband services across the state.

While Penang is a small state, the State Government ensures a consistent supply of land for investors. Industrial parks in Penang developed by the Penang Development Corporation (PDC) are: Bayan Lepas Industrial Zone; Prai Industrial Park; Seberang Jaya Industrial Park; Bukit Tengah Industrial Park; Bukit Minyak Industrial Park; Penang Science Park; and Batu Kawan, a new area under construction.

The State Government also offers the Penang Science Park for investors in high-tech sectors such as solar energy, aerospace, and biotechnology. The Park comprises approximately 300 acres of industrial land in the Bukit Minyak Industrial Park on the mainland. In addition to excellent infrastructure, the Park also offers investors a community of innovative firms who are already on site. Firms such as Progenix Research, Alpha Biologics, Ibiden Co Ltd and Ixmation Sdn Bhd are in various stages of implementation and operation in PSP. Other tenants include a pharmaceutical manufacturer, an aerospace manufacturer, and a fitness equipment manufacturer. There is also a site allocated for the Halal industry within the park, where three companies are currently setting up their plants.

SOFT INFRASTRUCTURE

In addition to an extensive array of hard infrastructure, Penang also offers investors an environment conducive to business. This is comprised of a range of proactive government agencies, a set of well-developed business associations, as well as an extensive range of supplier firms.

Key government agencies that investors will have contact with include: InvestPenang, which handles investor liaison in the state; the Penang Development Corporation, which is the state government's agency for real estate development; and the Penang Skills Development Centre, which handles human resource development and training.

In addition, other specialized agencies take care of: job placement (Career Assistance and Training (CAT) Centre); small and medium enterprise support (SME Market Advisory Resource and Training (SMART) Centre); Halal promotion and development (PIHH Development SdnBhd); heritage (George Town World Heritage Incorporated); and tourism (Penang Global Tourism (PGT)).

Regarding the state's supplier base, Penang has a strong supply chain in various disciplines, including precision engineering, automation, plastic injection moulding, packaging and software development. These local suppliers are also able to maintain their competitive advantage through continuously enhancing of their skill sets, expertise and technological capabilities. Some of the local SMIs have grown and became well known entities. They include Eng Teknologi Holdings Bhd, South Island Packaging Sdn. Bhd., Rapid Precision Engineering Technologies Sdn. Bhd., Micro Carbide Engineering Sdn. Bhd. and Atlan Holdings Bhd (The Star, 7 April 2008). Currently, Penang has around 3,000 local SMEs which provide network support for international firms in Penang (The Star, 25 January 2010).

This depth of firms is complemented by a range of well-established business associations. Some are found throughout the country, such as the Federation of Malaysian Manufacturers, and others are local, having arisen out of complementarities between firms. Examples of these include the Software Consortium of Penang (SCoPe) as well as the Free Industrial Zone, Penang, Companies' Association (FREPENCA).

Having set out Penang's competitive advantage, the next section will turn to the state's current opportunities and challenges.

INVESTMENT OPPORTUNITIES

Regarding the manufacturing sector, Penang has attained global recognition in the electrical and electronics industries. While this sector will remain a growth pillar for the state, several 'green shoots' are emerging in sub-sectors such as light emitting diodes, medical devices, and the photovoltaic sector. Thus, in addition to generating jobs and investment directly, Penang's electronic manufacturing foundation has also become an incubator for the development of other industries.

Light Emitting Diodes (LED)

The LED industry is poised to grow substantially in the near future, driven by an increase in LED penetration rates in mobile handsets, LED

TVs, notebooks, LCD (liquid crystal display) indicators, machine vision systems, backlit displays, architectural lighting and general lighting. From 2008 to 2013, the LED market is expected to grow at a Compound Annual Growth Rate (CAGR) of 24%, reaching $14.9 billion in 2013 (Strategies Unlimited 2009).

Malaysian exports of LED products, totaling RM1.81 billion in 2009, are projected to increase by 20 per cent by 2010 (The Star, 28 April 2010). Today, Penang has the presence of three of the 2009 world's top five LED makers. Osram has its wafer fabrication, assembly and test operations while Lumileds has its assembly and test operations in Penang. Other key LED players which are located in the state are Globetronics Technology, DSEM Technology, Rubicon Technology, Avago, SILQ and CS Opto.

As a result of the established LED packaging and component making industries, Penang has also attracted the LED system integration industry. Ledzworld Technology, a Dutch company, started up operations in Penang in 2008, focuses on LED solutions.

Medical Devices & Equipment

In 2009, the manufacture of medical devices ranging from masks to disposable medical electrodes and orthopaedic implants received the highest investments in Penang with each investment project valued at more than RM100 million (Penang Economic Monthly, March 2010).

Penang is home to key medical devices manufacturers such as B.Braun, Ambu, Symmetry Medical and Vigilenz Medical Devices. One of the recent investors in the state is St. Jude Medical Inc, the world-renowned cardiovascular medical devices manufacturer. The planned products for its Penang facility include pacemakers, pacemakers, implantable cardioverter defibrillators and leads. This will be St. Jude Medical Inc's first pacemaker manufacturing facility in Asia.

B.Braun has invested RM 300 million for a plant to manufacture intravenous catheters. This will position the firm to be the world's largest intravenous catheter manufacturing centre. B.Braun will be also investing RM 1.75 billion to expand its needle, surgical instruments and pharmaceutical solution manufacturing facilities by 2013. Meanwhile, the world's largest orthopaedic product outsourcing firm, US-based Symmetry Medical Inc, also plans to invest RM30 million over the next two years for the design and development of medical devices for the endoscopy industry. In addition, US$ 5-10 million a year will be allocated to expand its facility in Bayan Lepas over 5 years (The Star, 1 May 2010).

The Photovoltaic (PV) Industry

Due to the increasing demand for renewable energy, the photovoltaic industry has advanced significantly in recent years.

Presently, there are packaging companies in Penang that meet the requirements of PV companies. One such example is Ire-Tex, which focuses on packaging material for the solar power, automotive, and aerospace industries. It invested RM 5 million to increase its output of packaging materials for solar panels to serve a major US solar power customer. Cable manufacturing companies in Penang such as P.I.E Industrial Bhd has invested RM30 million to make solar panel cables has also diversified their products service the PV industry.

First Solar, is a United States-based firm and the dominant player in the thin film market specializing in Cadmium Telluride (CdTe) technology. It has set up its first Asian manufacturing plant in Kulim, Kedah which is 30 minutes away from Penang. This lead investment offers downstream opportunities in supporting industries such as equipment providers, system integrators for solar modules, system components, R&D, installation and services.

SERVICES

In addition to the state's manufacturing base, the service sector also offers a range of opportunities for investors.

The ICT Sector

The Multimedia Super Corridor (MSC-Malaysia) is Malaysia's focus and initiative to support the global information and communication technology (ICT) industry. The MSC-Malaysia is host to a thriving and vibrant ICT industry with home grown as well as foreign-owned companies focusing on: creative multimedia; software & e-solutions encompassing R&D; D&D and Internet business; as well as shared services and outsourcing and communications.

Penang is the number two outsourcing location in Malaysia after Cyberjaya and was awarded with the MSC-Malaysia Cybercity status in 2005. Officially known as the Penang Cybercity (PCC), it provides a hi-tech growth platform for industries and businesses. As of September 2010, there were 196 MSC-Malaysia status companies in Penang. The breakdown by cluster is shown in Table 2 below.

Table 2: Breakdown Clusters for MSCs in Penang

Clusters	As of September 2010
Software & e-Solution	178
Creative Multimedia	7
Share Services Outsourcing	7
Institute of Higher Learning (IHLs) & Incubators	4
Total	**196**

Source: Derived from www.mscmalaysia.my

The consulting firm KPMG named Penang as one of the 31 outsourcing hubs of the future, citing the availability of a trained, skilled and multilingual workforce.[23] Penang's strength as a BPO hub has attracted MNCs such as Intel, Motorola, Dell, Jabil, Citicorp, Echo Broadband, Penang Seagate and IBM to set up facilities in the state.

---

23 http://www.the-outsourcing.com/feature/Issue11/penang.html and http://limguaneng.com/index.php/2009/02/24/penang-listed-as-one-of-the-31-outsourcing-hubs-by-kpmg/

Tourism

Penang as a tourist destination was ranked third out of the top three Asian islands by the *Travel & Leisure's 2008 World Best Award*, a world's leading travel magazine. The state's attractiveness is under-pinned by its natural attractions, living culture, medical facilities, and well-developed real estate sector.

George Town, the state's capital, was awarded World Heritage Status by UNESCO in 2008. The uniqueness of George Town lies not only in its heritage and colonial buildings but also in the living culture arising from the state's numerous immigrant communities. The buildings in George Town were influenced by both Asian and European designs. The infrastructure in George Town constitutes a unique architectural and cultural townscape without parallel anywhere in East and Southeast Asia. As such, this offers investors in the food and beverage as well as hospitality sectors a range of potential opportunities.

With regard to medical tourism, Penang has contributed two-thirds of the RM 250 million revenues from medical tourism nationwide (Penang State Tourism Official Website). The state has a range of well-established hospitals that offer services at an attractive cost/quality ratio.

In addition, Penang offers a wide selection of properties for acquisition and investment, and these include condominiums, resort homes by the sea, bungalows and terraced houses. The residential property sector remains the dominant driver in the property market on the island and Seberang Perai. In spite of the economic crisis in 2009, numerous projects were launched by developers. In addition, the Malaysia My Second Home (MM2H) programme, enables third-country nationals to purchase retirement properties. Despite competition from destinations like Singapore, Bangkok and Kuala Lumpur, Penang fares well.

KEY CHALLENGES

While Penang offers investors a range of opportunities, the state must also successfully manage a series of challenges – many of which have arisen from its success at attracting and retaining investment.

Scarcity of Land

While demand for industrial land has increased tremendously, the land bank in Penang is limited, especially on the island. To mitigate this issue, the Penang State Government is exploring coastal land reclamation and land acquisition. In addition, the Penang Development Corporation has allocated approximately 1,000 acres of land in Batu Kawan for investments in the industrial sector.

In line with Malaysia's vision to transform from the production-based economy (P-economy) to the knowledge-based economy (K-economy), the State Government is pro-actively promoting investments in high-end technology industries and activities, such as research, design and development (RD&D) which require relatively smaller land space or built-up area. The State Government also offers investors a range of ready-made facilities for purchase or lease to enable investors to move in immediately.

Shortage of Skilled Workers

Over the past five years, investment flowing into Penang has been more targeted to product development and design as well as more complex manufacturing activities. This has led to a greater demand for skilled workers and shortages have emerged in a range of areas.

In order to meet this challenge, the Penang State Government has implemented a range of measures. The Penang Skills Development Centre provides a range of training and workforce development courses. Over the past 20 years, PSDC has grown significantly from its initial set-up phase of providing certificate and diploma courses to bachelor and even master degree courses. The Penang Career Assistance and Training (CAT) Centre, was set up to resolve human resources issue during the recent recession and has now expanded its role to include promoting Penang and encouraging people to come, work and live in the state. The Penang Science Council was established to foster science and mathematics education.

CONCLUSION

The experience accrued over the past four decades in the electrical and electronics sector and the presence of a large number of E&E players in the state has established Penang's reputation as the Silicon Valley of the East. While the electronics industry is still the main engine of growth for the state, there are new areas of promise. Sub-sectors such as LED, medical devices & equipment, and photovoltaic equipment offer investors interesting and unique opportunities.

In addition, Penang offers promise in a substantial range of service sectors. These include software and business process outsourcing as well as tourism and its downstream sectors. These same characteristics offer investors and skilled workers a lively, cosmopolitan, and historic living environment.

These attributes are underpinned by Penang's: strategic location; well-developed hard and soft infrastructure; and committed State Government.

Chapter 6

Penang in the New Asian Economy: Skills Development & Future Human Resource Challenges

Poh Heem Heem and Tan Yin Hooi

INTRODUCTION

From world-class industrial giants to globally-renowned IT leaders, Penang hosts a wide range of companies. From less than 10 MNCs in the 1970s, it has more than 1,000 MNCs and local SMEs today and was the first state in Malaysia to establish export processing zones. By the early 90s, it had earned itself the title of the "Silicon Valley of the East." The state's pursuit of competitiveness has paid off as companies present in Penang have chosen to locate higher value-added activities in the state, changing much of the manufacturing landscape. The Penang Skills Development Centre has played a key part in this transition through its role in liaising with industry to identify key skill gaps in the state's workforce and moving to address them through practical and focused training interventions.

SKILLS DEVELOPMENT IN PENANG: THE UNIQUE ROLE OF THE PSDC

The Penang Skills Development Centre (PSDC) is a player critical to the evolution of the state's manufacturing industry. The Centre is a unique organization that has helped in the transformation of Penang's E&E sector. Established in 1989 as the first skills development centre in Malaysia, the PSDC is an industry-led, non-government, non-profit oriented human resource development centre. First in the country, it is built upon a tripartite partnership between industry, academia and government. This synergistic relationship has allowed the PSDC to evolve along with the changing needs of the economy and produce industry-relevant students and trainees which are of international standard.

The establishment of the PSDC came at a time when Penang needed to ensure a ready supply of appropriately skilled labour to support the needs of existing and potential investors. The State Government of Penang, through its then investment and trade promotion arm, the Penang Development Corporation (PDC), initiated discussions with three of the state's leading multinational corporations – Hewlett Packard, Motorola and Intel – to set up a skilled manpower training centre in Penang.

At start-up, the PSDC received support from the Penang State Government in the form of subsidized rental of premises and an annual operating grant. From 1993, the PSDC received capital grants from the Federal Government to assist with its capacity building expenditure such as equipment and machinery. Today, the Centre has a core of 88 staff, including its own academic team, and is self-sustaining operations-wise. While it no longer receives operating grants from the State Government, it continues to receive capital grants from the Federal Government.

The PSDC invites membership from firms, agencies, and associations active in the manufacturing and related sectors. As at December 2010, the Centre has a member base of 154 companies, comprising MNCs, local companies and government institutions. A large majority of PSDC members are from the E&E subsector. The PSDC is managed by a Management Council, comprising 11 elected and 4 appointed office bearers and 6 ex-officio members; which meets at least 4 times a year. The Council members are senior representatives from corporations and government agencies.

While basing its policies on a reading of the state's economy, the PSDC also aligns itself with federal government policies. Table One depicts the relationship between federal government priorities and the Centre's activities.

Table 1: PSDC Focus in Alignment with National Policies

Phase 1: The Early Years

National Policy: First Outline Perspective Plan (OPP1) Year 1971-1990
Identified Thrusts: • Eradicating poverty and restructuring society
 • Structurally transforming the economy towards modernization and diversification

Second Outline Perspective Plan (OPP2) Year 1991-2000
Identified Thrust: Promoting human resource development

PSDC Focus: Creating a productive and disciplined labour force with the necessary skills to meet the challenges of industrial development, while sustaining a culture of merit and excellence

---

Phase 2: Growth of the PSDC

National Policy: Industrial Master Plan 2 (IMP 2) Year 1996-2005
Identified Thrust: Developing the global orientation of the Malaysian economy

PSDC Focus: • Recognizing changing trends within the global market
 • Driving the manufacturing industry to compete internationally
 • Increasing the participation of Malaysian-owned companies within the national, regional and global markets
 • Adopting information-intensive and knowledge-driven processes

---

> **Phase 3: Breaking Away: Progressing with Time**
>
> *National Policy: Industrial Master Plan 3 (IMP3) Year 2006-2020*
> Identified Thrusts: • Sustaining the manufacturing sector's contribution towards growth
> • Positioning the services sector as a major source of growth
>
> *PSDC Focus:* Facilitating the development and application of knowledge-intensive technologies and nurturing creative and innovative human capital.

For more than 20 years, the PSDC has provided the workforce with cutting-edge programs and, through collaboration with its industry partners, has developed and spearheaded many industry-workforce initiatives that address the needs of SMEs and MNCs for both school leavers and those already in the workforce. It also works closely with relevant federal government agencies such as SME Corporation to develop training programs and initiatives aimed at encouraging the growth of local industries. The nature of these programs and their funding structure are modified and tailored to suit the needs of the given sectors. The ultimate goal is to raise the educational level of the workforce and to prepare workers for future occupational competence.

The PSDC orients its programs to three main target groups. The specific needs of each target group evolve over time, and programs and curricula are adapted in consultation with PSDC board members.

The first target group is comprised of school leavers, who have on average 5 years of secondary education. Two main program categories exist for this group. First is the Malaysian Skills Certificate Program in technical skills (Precision Machining) which is awarded at five different levels of competency. Second are PSDC Diploma Programs in various sub-disciplines in Engineering which fulfill the Malaysian Qualification Agency (MQA) requirements. The MQA provides the standard quality measure for Malaysian Universities. Students can then build on these qualifications and pursue a degree in either electrical or mechanical engineering. This is done in conjunction with partner universities. At present, the PSDC has agreements with 18 universities.

The second target group is comprised of fresh graduates, many of whom are seeking to make a first entry into the workforce. Feedback from industry has shown that most graduates are lacking industry experience and technical skills. As such, the INSEP and FasTrack programs are 6 to 12 month intensive programs which serve as a bridge between university and the working world. These courses are intensely practical and offer students an opportunity to work with PSDC member firms.

The third target group is the existing workforce. Given the rapid evolution of the manufacturing sector, employees are constantly in need of upgrading. As a result, the PSDC offers a series of corporate training programs in 'soft' and 'hard' skills such as leadership and IT, respectively. It also has a series of Masters' Programs that offer advanced education in a range of new sectors such as photonics, telecommunications, and microelectronics, as well as Business Administration.

Table 2: PSDC Programs

Target	Programs
School Leavers	Applied Engineering Certificate Programs Precision Machining Technologies – Level 1 to 3 Engineering Diploma Programs Electronic Engineering Mechatronic Engineering Computer Engineering Telecommunication Engineering Information Technology Engineering Degree Programs (in collaboration with partner institutions) Electrical & Electronics Mechanical
Fresh Graduates (Degree-holders)	Industrial Skills Enhancement Program (INSEP)

Existing Workforce	PSDC Corporate Training Programs Specialized Technical Skills Leadership, Management and Language Information Technology Master Programs (in collaboration with partner institutions) Master of Engineering in Microelectronics Master of Engineering in Photonics Master of Engineering in Telecommunications Master of Business Administration

THE PSDC'S MAIN ACHIEVEMENTS AND KEY ENABLING FACTORS

The PSDC today conducts close to 700 various training courses per year and has trained more than 150,000 participants throughout its 21-year history. It has been awarded Training Provider of the Year by the Ministry of Human Resources twice, once in 2000 and again in 2005. The PSDC business model was held up as relevant to and potentially replicable in other developing nations by agencies such as UNIDO, UNCTAD and the World Bank. To date, PSDC has consulted for countries such as Madagascar, Bangladesh and Brazil through its affiliation with these international agencies. Given its success in addressing key skill gaps in Penang, the PSDC has since been replicated in 11 other Malaysian states by their respective state governments.

Table 3: Skills Development Centres in Malaysia

State	Skills Development Centre		Establishment
Penang	PSDC	Penang Skills Development Centre	1989
Selangor	SHRDC	Selangor Human Resource Development Centre	1992
Negeri Sembilan	NSSDC	Negeri Sembilan Skills Development Centre	1993

Kedah	KISMEC	Kedah Industrial Skills and Management Development Centre	1993
Perak	PESDC	Perak Entrepreneur and Skills Development Centre	1993
Johor	PUSPATRI	Johor Skills Development Centre	1993
Terengganu	TATI	Terengganu Advanced Technical Institute	1993
Sarawak	PPKS	Sarawak Skills Development Centre	1994
Melaka	MISDC	Malacca Industrial Skills Development Centre	1994
Pahang	PASDC	Pahang Skills Development Centre	1996
Terengganu	TESDEC	Terengganu Skills Development Centre Berhad	1996
Sabah	SSTC	Sabah Skills and Technology Centre	2000

Regarding the factors that have enabled the Centre's effective action, its success is based on strong ties with the state's industry. This enabled the PSDC to be positioned to assist Penang's industry to cope with evolving needs as regards skills and capabilities. The Centre leverages on its strong ties with the industry to:

i. keep abreast of the changing trends in the skills development industry;
ii. identify workforce development issues as they arise;
iii. identify the skill sets needed in the marketplace and thus train and re-skill the workforce through the appropriate intervention programs;
iv. tap the industry for highly experienced trainers; and
v. formulate viable HRD action plans and to design and deliver industry relevant training programs.

PSDC is an operationally viable organization that is able to demonstrate:

i. Industry Support – PSDC is a neutral and reputable platform for idea and material share. Industry leaders give direction and input to the Centre via the Management Council. PSDC Members contribute training material to the Centre, which are then re-worked and adapted for general audience.

ii. Efficient and Effective Use of Operating Capacity – Its existing 230,000 sq. ft. facility is fully utilized to house training labs and conduct training programs; and it maintains full transparency and accountability of government funds disbursed for expansion projects.

iii. Proven Track Record – PSDC has a good understanding of the challenges faced by the manufacturing industry. It has successfully utilized government grants and industry contributions to set up lab facilities and to pioneer industry relevant training programs. Table 4 shows the keys statistics regarding the Graduate Re-Skilling Scheme (GRS), the Industrial Skills Enhancement Program (INSEP), and the Workforce Transformation Technical Program (WTTP) which is targeted at school-leavers.

Table 4: PSDC – GRS & INSEP Track Record

Program	Year	Total Funds Received (RM)	Total Candidates	
			GRS/ INSEP	WTTP
GRS (Economic Planning Unit)	2001 – 2004	10,416,300	442	0

	2005	4,942,000	158	60
INSEP & WTTP (Ministry of Finance)	2006	5,115,400	145	113
	2007	8,542,400	409	72
	2009	21,276,200	647	275
	2010	6,000,000	223	0
			2,024	520
		56,292,300	2,544	

MANUFACTURING IN PENANG: THE SHIFT, PRESENT AND FUTURE

The changing economic environment has brought much change in the core activities of the manufacturing industry in Penang. From the earlier focus on test and assembly activities, the MNCs have shifted their emphasis to Design & Development (D&D) and Research & Development (R&D) activities. Today, Penang is not only a hub for global operations but is also a centre for high-level design and development activities for these companies. In keeping abreast of its members needs, the PSDC adjusted its programs accordingly, complementing basic workplace training to also include higher-end capabilities in microelectronics, photonics, and telecommunications. Table 5 lists some of Penang's anchor firms and the capabilities that they house.

Table 5: Global Role and Responsibilities of Penang-Based MNCs

Company	Global Roles and Responsibilities
Intel Corporation *Leading semiconductor chip maker.*	Intel Penang is one of the Corporation's 3 Global Design Centres. In 2001, the MNC established its Global Shared Services Centre here. Penang is also Intel's single largest international site.

Company	Global Roles and Responsibilities
Advance Micro Devices (AMD) *Leading semiconductor chip maker.*	AMD set up its Penang Design Centre in 1997 and subsequently its Global Shared Services Centre here in 2001. Both Intel and AMD account for 50% of the world microchip shipments.
Altera Corporation *First inventor and manufacturer of programmable logic devices*	Penang is the group's largest offshore R&D Centre and is involved in designing the next generation of Field-Programmable Gate Array (FGPA) chips. Currently, 94% of their total employees are engineers
Agilent Technologies *Designer and manufacturer of electronic and bio-analytical measurement instruments and equipment for measurement and evaluation*	Agilent Technologies conducts R&D, supply chain management and global shared services in its Penang facility which account for more than 50% of its turnover.
OSRAM Opto Semiconductors *Leading lighting manufacturers*	Osram's Asia R&D hub is based in Penang. Its new wafer fabrication plant here is set to produce 50% of the group's LEDs.
Motorola *Manufacturer of wireless telephone handsets. Designs and sells wireless network infrastructure equipment such as cellular transmission base stations and signal amplifiers.*	Motorola Penang is the world's largest facility for R&D and manufacturing of its 2-way communication devices (more than 50% of market share)
Dell *Develop, sell and support home, small business and enterprise computing products and services*	Dell Penang supplies 95% of lap tops computers to North America, which are air-freighted and delivered in less than 4 days after order. It is responsible for the supply of all computers to ASEAN, India and Australia.

Source: Individual Company Websites

The Electrical and Electronics (E&E) subsector remains as the main cluster and driver of the manufacturing industry in Penang. A strong ecosystem has emerged and led to the rise and growth of Malaysian companies involved in design and Original Design Manufacturing (ODM). These companies are contracted to design and manufacture products with their own intellectual property for another company that typically has a higher brand value. While not the end goal of having firms with their own brand name, these activities are an important indicator of the evolving technical capabilities of Penang-based firms. Table 6 highlights several examples of local companies that are involved in ODM and design activities in Penang.

Table 6: Local Large and Emerging Companies in Design and ODM in Penang (Selected Companies)

Companies	Year Established in Malaysia	Core Business
Eng Teknologi	1974	Supplier of hard disk drive components, tape drives and other industrial products and devices.
Pentamaster Corporation	1991	Provider of manufacturing automation solutions and services.
Zoomic Technology	1992	Supplier of integrated automation solution, precision machining components, electronics design and sub-assemblies.
SRM Integration	1996	Supplier of integrated circuit test handlers.
Vitrox Technologies	2000	Provider of automated vision inspection system solution and equipment for the semiconductor and electronic packaging industries.

Aemulus Corporation	2004	Manufacturer of automatic test equipment (ATE) and test & measurement instruments (T&MI)
CeedTec	2005	Provider o complete one-stop engineering, turnkey design, OEM and ODM services
Myreka Technologies	2006	Developer of products and solutions for the electronics test & measurement industry

Source: Individual Company Websites

With the rise in the demand for medical implants and surgical instruments, there is also an emerging cluster of companies involved in the medical devices manufacturing in recent years. Medical devices can include instruments, appliances, implants, machines, software, materials, calibrators, apparatuses, in vitro reagents and other related articles.[24] It is estimated that there are approximately 180 small to large healthcare manufacturing players in Malaysia that generate a total revenue of approximately RM 7 billion. The industry is estimated to be growing at 8 % per annum.[25]

Precision engineering and machining companies in Penang are very well-positioned to play a major role in this industry as they are able to leverage on their existing core talent and high level of machining skills. These companies are globally recognized for their capability to produce quality components and are expected to have little problems in meeting the regulatory requirements of the medical devices industry.

Industry players that have been predominantly involved in the electronics subsector are also seen to be progressing to the area of life sciences and biotechnology. Examples of existing companies operating in Penang with such interests include the following:

---

24 Praxiom Research Group Limited, (http://www.praxiom.com/iso-13485-definitions.htm, retrieved 1 August 2011).

25 Association Of Malaysian Medical Industries (AMMI), Presentation on 'Global Scenario and Opportunities in Medical Devices Industry' at seminar on 'Opportunities For Medical Devices and Surgical Instruments Manufacturing', 29 October 2009

Table 7: E&E Companies in Biotechnology and Life Sciences

Company	Biotechnology Activities
Agilent Technologies	Instrumentation, data systems and compliance services designed to meet the requirements of the GMP/GLP-regulated lab.
Altera	Programmable Logic Devices with optimized IP cores, hard and soft microprocessors, design software and development kits for medical equipment manufacturers
Flextronics	Provides design, manufacturing and logistics solutions to medical device and equipment companies
Plexus	Provides design, manufacturing and logistics solutions to medical device and equipment companies

Source: Khazanah Nasional Berhad

These new sectors will require initiatives to ensure that the labour-force is adequately trained to cope with the new and emerging skill requirements.

CHALLENGES FACED IN SKILLS DEVELOPMENT

While the transition is apparent, the rate of progress is dependent upon the availability and skills of the talent pool. For Penang to become a centre for high-level design and development activities, it needs access to an available and appropriately skilled human resource talent pool. According to the 2009 Graduate Tracer Study by the Ministry of Higher Education (Table 8), Penang has the highest employment rate amongst fresh graduates in the Northern Region (comprised of the states of Penang, Perlis, Kedah and Perak). Out of the total number of fresh graduates from Penang, 25% have not been employed.

Table 8: Status of Graduates from Northern States of Malaysia, 2009

States	Total	Working	Furthering Studies	Upgrading Skills	Waiting for Job Placements	Not Working
Kedah	13,218	41.3%	16.8%	2.2%	8.2%	31.4%
Perak	15,584	44.4%	18.4%	1.9%	7.4%	27.9%
Perlis	1,726	39.2%	19.6%	2.3%	9.0%	29.9%
Malaysia	155,278	45.1%	18.4%	2.2%	7.6%	26.7%

Note: Survey was conducted 6 months after completion of studies.
Source: 2009 Graduate Tracer Study System, Ministry of Higher Education, Malaysia

Despite being a leading state in the Northern Region, Penang is still struggling to provide a sufficient skilled and innovative workforce for industry. While the industry is progressing, skill sets remain stagnant and, therefore, companies are unable to upgrade employees' salaries. Employee wages and productivity within the state are relatively low. The calibre of the future talent pool is not able to meet industry level requirements and the existing talent pool needs to be consistently upgraded through training and re-skilling.

PSDC: SHAPING THE HUMAN CAPITAL OF MALAYSIA

In its role to address the human resource issues, the PSDC undertakes a two-pronged strategy to enable the industry ecosystem to grow. It targets human resource development initiatives as well as identifying and ensuring that the enabling infrastructure required to support the former is established.

Table 9: Two-Pronged Strategy of PSDC to Grow Industry Ecosystem

Human Resource Development Initiatives	Enabling Infrastructure
iLEAP Initiative: To enhance and accelerate the learning process of fresh graduates and the existing workforce to personify effective and productive talent	• Shared Services Centre • Set-up of the: -Centre of Engineering Excellence (CEE) -Medical Technology Centre (MedTech Centre)
Core Objectives • Acceleration of Talent Development • Talent Development - for SMEs in R&D Involvement - for MNCs in R&D Expansion Creation of a Larger Talent Pool	**Core Objectives** • To enable D&D activities through facilities for the industry to design and test new applications and products, technical training laboratories to train new engineers in related fields and incubation facilities. • Provision of a platform and access to knowledge transfer and infrastructure for local industries at a nominal cost • To spark the interest of local industries to embark into new services and technologies

HUMAN RESOURCE DEVELOPMENT INITIATIVES

The PSDC will focus on the creation of a larger talent pool and up-skilling of the existing workforce through the following initiatives:

iLEAP

The objective of the iLEAP initiative is to enhance and accelerate the learning process of fresh graduates and the existing workforce within identified core technology areas. The iLEAP is expected to:

i. Accelerate and develop engineering talent
ii. Transform human capital
   • increase employability of fresh graduates
   • upgrade skill sets of existing knowledge workers

The iLEAP initiative will target three key segments: fresh graduates, the existing workforce, and school leavers.

Table 10: PSDC i-LEAP Initiative

Fresh Graduates	Existing Workforce	School Leavers

FasTrack Program
• Medical Technology
• Radio Frequency
  - Electrical
  - Mechanical
  - Software
• Computer & Embedded Systems
	Workforce Transformation[a]
	• Technical Development
	• Medical Technology
	
	i-Workforce Transformation[b]
	• Leadership Development
	  - Breaking Boundaries Program
		School2Work Program
		• Diploma in Engineering
		• Precision Machining Technology

End-In-Mind		
Provision of a sufficient pool of employable talent to support the growth of local industries and the creation of a viable industry ecosystem.	Transformation of the existing worker pool to support higher value-added manufacturing activities; and the creation of the next generation of adept, creative and innovative leaders.	Provision of a complete education pathway where post SPM students pass through college and/or university and into permanent job placements.

a *Workforce Transformation Programs are targeted at the skills upgrading of operator and technician levels.*
b *i-Workforce Transformation Programs are targeted at the skills upgrading of middle to senior level employees.*

Chart 1: PSDC i-LEAP Initiative

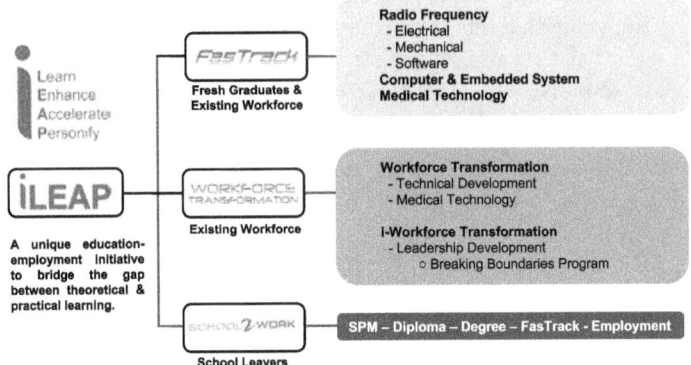

PSDC FASTRACK PROGRAM

The PSDC FasTrack Program is a skills upgrading program to equip Diploma and Degree graduates with skills required for future employment. Jointly developed by MNCs and PSDC, the FasTrack Program will fine-tune and enhance the fundamental skills sets acquired to the level of industry expectations.

Chart 2: PSDC FasTrack Program

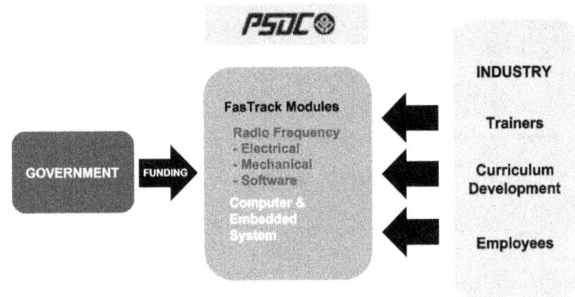

The 'FasTrack' Training Programs will:

- Raise the level of work experience of fresh graduates from 0 to the equivalent of 3 working years
- Upgrade the technical competencies of current workforce to promote more transfer of R&D to companies in Malaysia
- Provide an immediate solution to the knowledge worker shortage especially in R&D.

The curriculum of the FasTrack program is identified by the Industry and co-developed with the PSDC. As the trainers under this program are also from the Industry, it guarantees the relevance of the Program to both the graduates and the employers. The PSDC FasTrack training commenced in June 2010 and, as at end of 2010, 124 participants have been trained under this program.

PSDC 'SCHOOL 2 WORK' PROGRAM

The PSDC currently provides world-class engineering and technical diploma courses to SPM school leavers. The Centre started off with the Business Technology Education Council (BTEC) Higher National Diploma (HND) in Engineering program from UK in 1993 to address the shortage of technicians in Penang in the 1990s. In 2006, the PSDC began to offer its own Diploma programs which are accredited by the Malaysian Qualifications Agency (MQA) instead of the BTEC HND. The PSDC also has articulation agreements with 18 well-known universities, both private and public from Malaysia, Australia, Ireland and the United Kingdom and is also involved in strategic partnerships with other local institutions such as Multimedia University (MMU) to provide post-graduate programs. The universities are selected based on their track record and suitability with the PSDC's education mapping system for its students. The introduction of the PSDC 'School 2 Work' Program is to complement and provide a complete education-to-employment pathway for school leavers.

COLLABORATION WITH INDUSTRY

Collaborative Research in Engineering, Science and Technology Centre (CREST)

Co-initiated by Khazanah Nasional Berhad and the Northern Corridor Implementation Agency, the Collaborative Research in Engineering, Science and Technology Centre (CREST) is a knowledge hub within the Northern Corridor to enable the advancement of scientific knowledge in the Electrical & Electronics sector through collaborative basic and applied research between academia and industry.

The PSDC is one of the training and human capital development partner to CREST.

Collaborative Research in Engineering, Science ad Technology Centre (CREST)					
Solid Foundation	Retain & Strengthen	Dynamic Environment	Grow & Proliferate	Fertile Ground	Nurture & Develop
	Identify 25-30 MNCs in Penang and enable them to become Global Strategic Impact Centres		Develop industry clusters through integration using connectivity (both physical and virtual)		Establish an enabling environment and identify new business opportunities & markets

The Medical Technology Centre (MedTech Centre)

The MedTech Centre is a collaboration centre between the government and industry to provide services related to manufacturing and assembly, computer-aided design and manufacturing, production equipment, automation and controls, packaging materials and machinery, medical device software and validation solutions in the medical technology industry.

The PSDC launched its first MedTech training program, which is the Competency Development Program in Medical Technology, in late September 2010 and 25 people have been trained so far.

Chart 3: PSDC MedTech Centre of Excellence Ecosystem & Functions

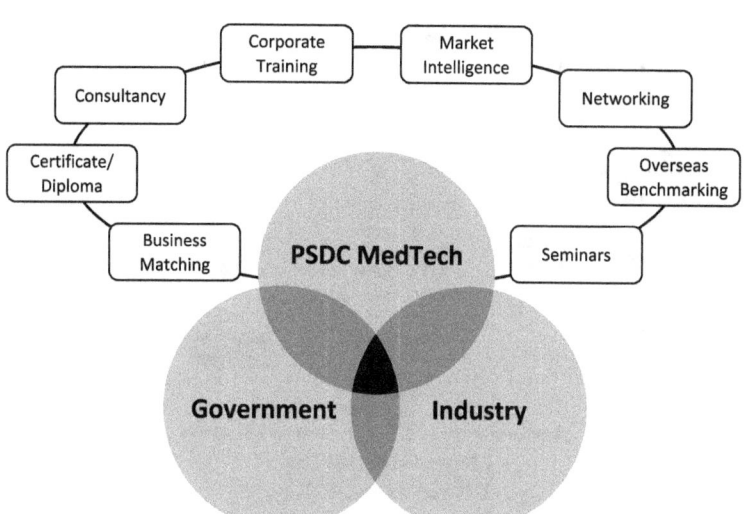

ENABLING INFRASTRUCTURE: PSDC SHARED SERVICES FACILITIES

Adequate infrastructure is required to support and complement the human resource development initiatives designed to maintain and promote industrial investments. The PSDC has benefited from Federal Government funding which has enabled growth and expansion to its current 230,000 square feet of operating capacity. The existing operating premises houses the highly successful certification and diploma programs in machining and engineering; and the workforce intervention programs which keeps the PSDC financially viable and self-sustaining.

As PSDC moves to cater to the emerging needs of high technology and value-added activities, enabling infrastructure which will include land acquisition for building expansion and investments in labs and equipment are required.

Chart 4: PSDC 3.0 - Enabling Infrastructure

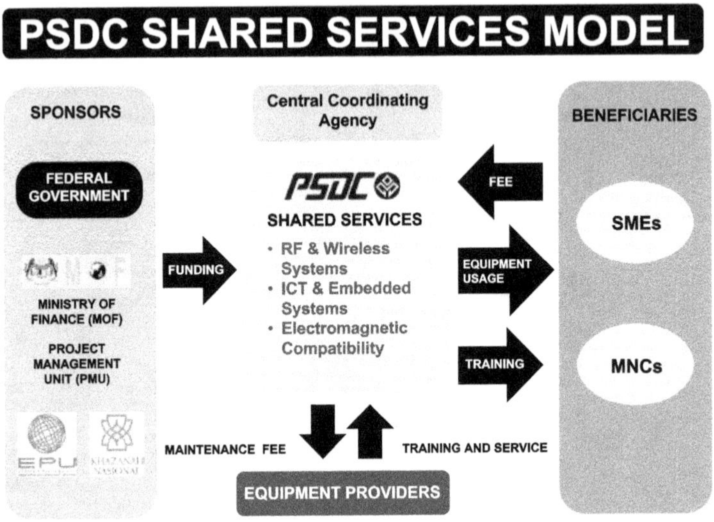

PSDC SHARED SERVICES MODEL

SPONSORS	Central Coordinating Agency	BENEFICIARIES
FEDERAL GOVERNMENT	PSDC SHARED SERVICES • RF & Wireless Systems • ICT & Embedded Systems • Electromagnetic Compatibility	SMEs
MINISTRY OF FINANCE (MOF)	FUNDING → ← FEE EQUIPMENT USAGE → ← TRAINING	MNCs
PROJECT MANAGEMENT UNIT (PMU)		
EPU	MAINTENANCE FEE ↓ ↑ TRAINING AND SERVICE EQUIPMENT PROVIDERS	

The PSDC currently provides Shared Services facilities for Industry (especially E&E) to design and test new applications and products. This includes technical training laboratories to train new engineers in RF Technology & Wireless Systems, Computer & Embedded Systems and Electromagnetic Compatibility (EMC) as well as incubation facilities for new business set up in designing and new application field. The labs were initiated based on the concerns and needs raised by the industry through various dialogues and RM30 million funding to build the labs were provided through the Federal Government. The Shared Services Centre was officially launched in 30 October 2010 and at least 6 companies have already started to actively utilize the labs since.

In the near future, the PSDC plans to expand its shared services centre to house extended areas of:
  i. compatibility testing and biocompatibility evaluation for the medical devices industry
  ii. inspection services in failure analysis
  iii. rapid prototyping and rapid manufacturing solutions for precision machining

ROLE OF STAKEHOLDERS

In order for the strategy to work, the PSDC requires commitment from the Industry, Government and Academia to play their role in supporting the development of the various projects.

Table 11: Role of Stakeholders

Project	Industry	Federal Government	Academia
Expansion of Shared Services Centre	Identify services and technology required Support through usage on a nominal cost basis	Financial investment of the set up Liaise with government agencies such as SME Corp, MIDA regarding grants and training funds	Assign lecturers and facilitators to provide expertise Provide opportunities to university students access to state-of-the-art industry relevant technologies
Setting up of Centre of Engineering Excellence	Provide opportunity to embark into new technology at affordable cost Platform for industry expert to share knowledge	Financial investment to set up facility	Platform for academicians to share knowledge and expertise
Setting up of the Medical Technology Centre	Provide opportunity to embark into new technology at affordable cost Platform for industry expert to share knowledge	Financial investment of hardware and software related to designing medical parts and components	Collaborate on incorporating post-graduate certificates and diplomas

PSDC 3.0: SUPPORTING THE FUTURE OF THE MANUFACTURING INDUSTRY

The next step for the PSDC is to support a new era of human capital development in high-technology and value-added activities within and beyond the field of manufacturing. The objective is to grow the industry ecosystem to encourage design and development activities to:
- Support the New Economic Model (NEM) for Malaysia
- Support new emerging industry areas stifled by acute labor shortage
- Address immediate and future industry needs

Beyond 2010, the PSDC foresees an increased demand for engineering talent especially in Design & Development (D&D) as more and more MNCs pursue the expansion of more higher-end activities here. With that, Penang will also require the establishment of a healthy SME ecosystem to support the MNCs in this endeavour. With this in mind, the PSDC conceptualized the PSDC 3.0 Roadmap. The implementation of the Roadmap will complement the NEM in developing a quality workforce as well as support the building of a knowledge based infrastructure.

Chart 6: PSDC's Value Roadmap

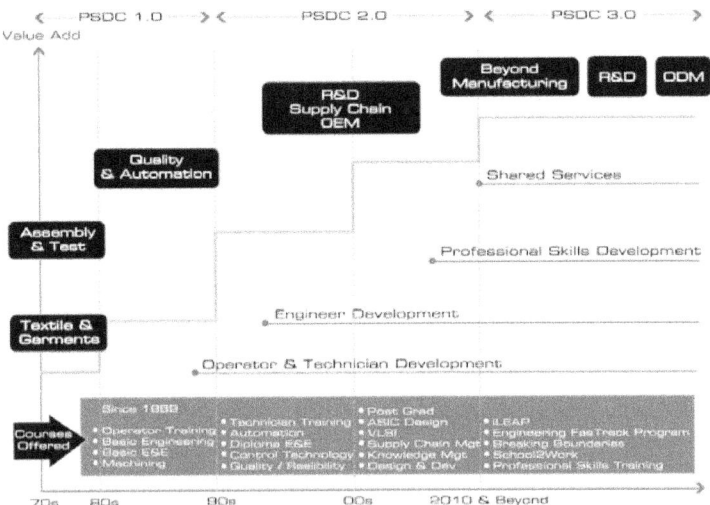

8.0 KEY MESSAGE

In recent times, the changing landscape of the E&E sector highlights the critical shortage of appropriately skilled engineers which hinders the industry and the nation in its pursuit of higher value-added industrial activities and ultimately achieving 'high income nation' status. The PSDC has become a critical pillar of support for the human resource development for Penang and Malaysia. It assumes the role of framing the context for a new level of human capital development in the "K"-economy as Penang leads the Northern region to move beyond manufacturing. The Centre will continue to play its role in harnessing industrial synergy and stakeholder commitment to accelerate the rate of talent creation and regeneration and drive the economy.

APPENDIX A

PSDC: COLLABORATION WITH INDUSTRY & OBJECTIVES ACHIEVED

Collaborative Partner	Objectives
1990 Hewlett Packard	Computer Lab Set-up Training for HP employees and the public
1991 Motorola	Programmable Automation Literacy (PAL) Lab Set-up Training for Motorola employees and the public
FESTO	Automation Technology Lab Set-up Industrial automation training
1992 Conner Peripherals	Electronics Lab Set-up Basic electronics training
Poi Huat Machine Tools, Numac Machinery, Nippon Machine Tools, Mikron, Charmilles Technologies, Ohmi	Precision Machining Workshop Set-up Precision machining training for school leavers and employees
1993 Motorola	Development of Project Mutiara, a Workforce Transformation program
Intel	Microprocessor Lab Set-up Training for Intel employees and the public

1994 Hewlett Packard	Computer Lab upgrade Training for HP employees and the public
Mecomb Malaysia, Fuji Machine and Nichimen Corporation	Surface Mount Technology (SMT) Lab Set-up
Komag and Penang Seagate	Vacuum Technology Lab Set-up
Penang Seagate	Establishment of a Teambuilding Park Experiential training to improve teambuilding
1995 Hewlett Packard	Set-up of the second computer lab
AMD	Construction and set-up of a Technical Library
IDEMA	The PSDC and IDEMA co-organize Malaysia's 1st Technical Conference on Disk Drive and Components
1996 PACE	Asia Pacific's 1st PACE Repair and Soldering Lab is set-up Provision of basic repair and soldering training
1997 Excel Precision	Advanced Manufacturing Technology Lab Set-up Flexible manufacturing line training is provided

1998 Malaysian Plastics Manufacturers Associations (MPMA)	Management and operations of plastics technology training
Institute of Precision Moulds (IPM)	Management and operations of mould making and design training
Agilent, Astec, Eng Teknologi, Robert Bosch, Fairchild Semiconductor, Komag, Intel, Motorola and Penang Seagate	Joint development of the Global Supplier Program (GSP) to develop capability of local companies to become global suppliers.
2000 Intel	Upgrade Microprocessor Lab
2002 Mitutoyo	Metrology Lab Set-up
Agilent, Altera, Intel and Motorola	Joint development of the Graduate Reskilling Scheme (GRS) in Design and Development
2004 Eng Teknologi	Establishment of the Dato'Teh Ah Ba Scholarship
2005 Motorola	Radio Frequency Lab Set-up Fastrack training is made available for engineers
2007 Penang Water Supply Corporation (PBAPP)	Establishment of the Penang Water Services Academy (PWSA) to provide water supply technologies training

2008 Gold and Jewellery Federation	Co-development of the Jewellery Design Program to formalize training and apprenticeship for gold and jewellery designers.
2010 Association of Malaysian Medical Industries (AMMI)	Joint development of Competency Development Program in Medical Technology (MedTech Program) to produce talent to support the requirement of the medical devices industry

APPENDIX B

PSDC: COLLABORATION WITH ACADEMIA & GOVERNMENT ORGANIZATIONS AND OBJECTIVES ACHIEVED

Collaborative Partner	Objectives
1993 BTEC (Business & Technology Education Council), UK	Provision of pre-employment training for school leavers. This was the pre-cursor for all future PSDC diploma programs.
1995 Autodesk	To offer AutoCAD training programs through the set up of the Certified Autodesk Training Centre.
Microsoft	To offer Microsoft application training programs as the Certified Microsoft Authorized Training Centre.
1996 Penang State Government	The PSDC conducted training and seminar sessions on ICT awareness under PenangNet
1997 NIIT, India	To conduct Applied IT Training programs, the first in Malaysia
SMIDEC	The PSDC was designated as an official training centre for SMEs in the Northern Region

1999 MMU and JICA	The Networked Multimedia Education System was set-up
APEC (Asia Pacific Economic Cooperation)	Co-organized the Seminar on Best Practices for Public-Business Sector Partnership in Skills Development
Sabah State Government	The PSDC assisted in the institutional set up of Sabah Skills and Technology Centre (SSTC)
2001 Yayasan Majudiri PGRM	Machining training was offered to needy students
APEC	A learning portal, NetSDC was developed to facilitate continuous exchange of information on skills development across Asia Pacific Economic Countries
2002 CISCO	To set up the Cisco Networking Academy and Lab, the first in Northern Region
2003 Ministry of Women and Family Development	Co-launched the 'Program ICT untuk Wanita', which aimed to educate women in use of Internet, email and Microsoft Office Applications
University of Hull, UK	PSDC Partner University offering articulation programs for PSDC diploma holders to pursue degrees
Multimedia University	PSDC Partner University
2004 University of Herfordshire Northumbria University University of Plymouth University of Sunderland	PSDC Partner Universities

2005 Dublin Institute of Technology London Southbank University University of Kent University of Leeds University of Strathclyde University of Wolverhamton	PSDC Partner Universities
AK Khan Foundation and Telekom Malaysia International	PSDC Consultancy to spearhead the set-up of an industry-led skills development centre in Chittagong, Bangladesh. The Chittagong Skills Development Centre (CSDC) was successfully established in 2006
World Bank and the Government of Madagascar	PSDC Consultancy was engaged to assist in the set up an industry-led skills development centre in Madagascar
2006 Japan Bank for International Cooperation (JBIC)	PSDC Consultancy was engaged to assist in the set up an industry-led skills development centre in Manaus, Brazil
2007 Wawasan Open University	The PSDC as a partner to promote life-long learning to working adults
Rotary Clubs of Penang and Balwyn, Australia	Establishment of the Rotary Tsunami Scholarship Fund for needy students at the PSDC
Penang State Government	To support children with learning difficulties through the establishment of Pusat BOLD-PSDC (Bureau of Learning Difficulties)

2008	Manchester Metropolitan University	PSDC Partner University
2009	Northern Corridor Implementation Authority (NCIA) & Kulim Industrial Tenants Association (KITA)	The PSDC was appointed to manage and operate a pilot training program for human capital skills enhancement in front end technology for the semiconductor and wafer fabrication industry to fast track the skills acquisition of new graduates, and existing engineers and technicians in Northern Corridor Economic Region (NCER).
	Malaysian Biotechnology Corporation (BiotechCorp)	The PSDC was appointed to manage and operate the Biotechnology Entrepreneurship Special Training (BeST) program in Northern Region.
	Khazanah Nasional Berhad	Establishment of a Shared Services Centre at the PSDC to house the Electromagnetic Compatibility (EMC) lab with a 10 m Semi-Anechoic Chamber, an RF and Wireless Technology Training Lab, and an Embedded Systems Training Lab

PSDC Consultancy was engaged to assist in the set up of a centre to provide specialized courses in post-basic nursing, and continuous professional development programs for allied health professions. The Allied Healthcare Centre of Excellence was successfully set up and operationalized in Penang in 2010. |

Chapter 7

PBA Holdings Bhd: The Road to Privatisation, Corporatisation and Beyond

Jaseni Maidinsa

Often taken for granted, water is a necessity for life, and potable water, in particular, is a critical factor for the development and evolution of a community. The public provision of water began in Penang in 1805, when the island was administered by the East India Company. In response to complaints from residents as well as traders using the port, Governor Farquhar built an aqueduct system made of ceramic pipes running from waterfalls at the base of Penang Hill to George Town (Barber, 2009).

Since that time, the state's population and water needs have expanded significantly. From a sparsely settled trading outpost, Penang has become the industrial centre for Northern Malaysia. In particular, since the 1970s, the state has witnessed rapid development in the manufacturing, tourism, and international trade sectors.

As such, the organizational capabilities of Penang's water management bodies have had to evolve to meet these challenges. In 1968, water was provided to the state's residents by two different agencies, one run by the

George Town City Council and the other by the State Water Department. Following recommendations made by the Asian Development Bank, this was streamlined and, in 1973, the Penang Water Authority was established as one of Malaysia's first statutory bodies charged with water supply.

The Authority built its reputation as one of the best water supply operators in Malaysia. A rapid introduction of a computerized billing system in 1975 enabled more effective revenue management. This, coupled with commitment to improving water supply and an efficient connection system, enabled the Authority to expand coverage and lower levels of non-revenue water.

However, there was a price for Penang's progress. As it prospered, the state became increasingly water-stressed due to its geographical limitations and a growing population. Water consumption increased by almost four-fold, from 59,663,636 m^3 in 1975 to 285,583,785 m^3 in 2010. With catchments totalling only 6% of its total land area of 1,031 sq. km., the state needed a forward-thinking and result-driven organisation that could effectively manage its water demand.

CORPORATISATION

In 1999, the Penang State Government took the decision to corporatise water management through the establishment of Perbadanan Bekalan Air Pulau Pinang Sdn.Bhd. (PBAPP) - or the Penang Water Supply Corporation Pte. Ltd. PBAPP's scope of activities encompasses the: extraction of raw water; treatment of raw water; distribution and supply of treated water; and billing for water supply services.

Following corporatisation, the next step in PBAPP's evolution was the establishment of PBA Holdings Bhd (PBAHB), a public company to serve as a vehicle for public listing on the Main Board of Bursa Malaysia. PBAHB was successfully listed on 18 April 2002 with PBAPP as its 100% owned subsidiary.

Since water supply is an essential service, SSI Incorporated, an investment arm of the Penang State Secretary's Office, was (and still is) the majority shareholder in PBAHB. Moreover, SSI also holds a "golden share" to further ensure the protection of public interest. The allocation of "pink forms" to PBAPP employees allowed them to own shares in their water supply company. As of 2010, the principal equity holders of PBAHB were: the Penang State Government (55%); the Penang Development Corporation, which is a state government-owned statutory body (10%); and the public and PBAPP employees (22%).

At present, the Penang State Government controls the direction of PBAPP via its majority holdings in PBAHB. This arrangement ensures a good balance of public and private interests as it ensures good supply coverage, accountability, and fair tariffs, while at the same time promoting efficiency and productivity.

This process of organizational change has required long-term planning. The PBAPP's precursor, the Penang Water Authority, employed 999 civil servants. The majority were absorbed into the PBAPP, but the corporatisation process required the introduction of a new work culture governed by performance for pay, efficiency and productivity. To acclimatise all employees and establish a professional corporate culture, PBAPP embarked on a series of management initiatives as part of its "managing change" strategy.

This involved a concerted effort to conceptualize the organization's vision, mission, and commitment, which were defined as:

Vision: Meeting all your water supply needs

Mission: PBAPP will be the leading organisation in water supply.

Commitment: We will be environmentally sensitive, responsible, professional, innovative and committed to excellence and sustainable development.

In 2000 and 2001, the vision, mission statement, and key corporate objectives were used as key reference points in a corporate restructuring programme. Following this re-structuring, five departments - Operations, Production, Strategic Planning, Development and Quality, Safety and Health (QSH) - were empowered to address engineering challenges. Meanwhile, administrative functions were entrusted to five other departments: Corporate Services; Human Resource; Finance; Information Technology (I.T.); and Internal Audit. In 2008, two new departments were introduced, namely Facilities and Customer Care. As a result, the company now operates with 12 departments reporting to the General Manager.

As at 31 December 2010, there were 1,147 employees in PBAPP. The company offers average salary packages as compared to the open market and has employed a significant number of professionals from the private sector over the last decade. Today, PBAPP is regarded as one of the best water supply companies in Malaysia. In 1999, PBAPP's employee to customer ratio was 1:339. In 2010, the ratio was 1:442, reflecting a higher scale of operational efficiency.

CORPORATE CULTURE

As a private sector company, PBAPP has been focusing on enhancing customer and employee relationships by cultivating a "21st century corporate culture". The essence of this new corporate culture is the "PBA Way" as in "People we motivate" (in reference to PBAPP personnel, "Best we deliver" (in reference to systems) and "Aim for excellence" (with regard to customer satisfaction)). Workshops were also staged for all executives and supervisory staff to promote the internal "core values" of Accountability, Communication, Teamwork, Integrity, On-going learning, and New ways for improvement ("ACTION"). In 2009, the PBA Group launched its "Friendly, Caring, Responsive", or FCR, customer care campaign, featuring the iconic hand sign for 'okay'.

The forging of a corporate culture has enabled PBAPP to secure 100% urban and 99.7% rural supply coverage as well as 91.3% bill collection efficiency for 2010. At the same time, this corporate culture has also been instrumental in helping the company to achieve high customer acceptance and approval ratings in independent public opinion polls that are conducted bi-annually by the company as part of its ISO 9001 commitment to continuous improvement.

In line with its mission to serve as a leading organisation in water supply that is professional and result-driven, PBAPP sought accreditation for its management systems. In May and June 2003, PBAPP received multi-site ISO 9001:2000 certifications for continuous improvement from UKAS of the United Kingdom and DAR of Germany. PBAPP was the first Malaysian water supplier to receive international ISO 9001 certifications with a scope encompassing "treatment and supply of water with the provision of customer services." In 2009, PBAPP successfully "migrated" to the latest ISO 9001:2008 standards for continuous improvement.

In February 2005, the corporation received ISO 14001:2004 environmental certification for the "management and treatment of raw water and the supply of potable water" at the Batu Ferringhi Treatment Plant and the Teluk Bahang Dam. In 2007, the Waterfall Treatment Plant received its ISO 14001:2004 certification as well. The latest PBAPP facility to receive its environmental-friendly certification in March 2010 is the Air Itam Water Treatment Plant.

In March 2006, PBAPP received the OHSAS 18001:1999 certification from SGS International, with accreditation to Swiss Certification, for its occupational health and safety management system. The certification is for the "treatment and supply of water with provision of customer services." In 2009, the company successfully migrated to the OHSAS 18001:2007 standards.

Consistent adherence to these international certifications requires PBAPP to operate in accordance to international guidelines for excellence. The accreditations also serve as a useful tool that drives the company to operate professionally and innovatively, while benchmarking its performance to global standards.

SERVICE PROVISION

Since PBAPP's incorporation, the number of registered water consumers in Penang has increased by 49.8%, from 338,523 consumers in 1999 to 506,989 consumers in 2010. Despite this rapid increase, the Corporation has sustained 100 percent urban supply coverage and 99.7% rural supply coverage throughout the state.

At the same time, PBAPP has managed to sustain relatively low tariffs to all domestic and trade category water consumers. Water bills for 80 percent of Penang's registered domestic water users are subsidized in accordance to PBAPP's commitment towards corporate social responsibility. Water tariffs in Penang are structured such that domestic consumption is subsidized while trade tariffs generate earnings for the PBA Group. To illustrate, Singaporeans pay an average of RM 3.55 per 1,000 litres for the first 35,000 litres consumed every month while Hong Kong residents pay RM 1.82 for this level of domestic consumption. In comparison, PBAPP bills domestic water consumers in Penang an average of RM 0.31 per 1,000 litres for the first 35,000 litres every month. Table A shows a comparison of Penang's domestic tariffs based on a National Geographic Magazine report in 2010. Penang trade tariffs for business-related consumption of up to 500,000 litres per month also compares well with that of a selection of Asian cities (Table B).

Table A: Comparison Of International Domestic Water Tariffs 2010

	Cities	Average Tariff in RM (USD) per 378 litres for consumption of approx. 15,120 litres per month
1	Berlin	7.69 (2.52)
2	Sydney	4.91 (1.61)
3	Newcastle (UK)	4.45 (1.46)
4	Helsinki	3.72 (1.22)
5	New York City	2.44 (0.80)
6	Tokyo	2.26 (0.74)
7	Madrid	1.89 (0.62)
8	Singapore	1.86 (0.61)
9	Rio de Janeiro	1.04 (0.34)
10	Moscow	1.01 (0.33)
11	Jakarta	0.85 (0.28)
12	Seoul	0.67 (0.22)
13	Hong Kong	0.64 (0.21)
14	Beijing	0.61 (0.20)
15	Manila	0.49 (0.16)
16	Penang	0.06 (0.02)

Source: National Geographic Magazine, April 2010 / USD to RM conversions as at Feb 2011

Table B: Comparison Of Asian Trade/Business Water Tariffs 2010

	Cities	Average Tariff in RM (USD) per 1,000 litres for consumption of the first 500,000 litres per month
1	Jakarta	4.33 (1.42)
2	Singapore	3.55 (1.16)
3	Manila	2.52 (0.83)
4	Tokyo	2.35 (0.77)
5	Kuala Lumpur	2.27 (0.74)
6	Hong Kong	1.82 (0.60)
7	Beijing	1.70 (0.56)
8	Macau	1.70 (0.56)
9	Seoul	1.45 (0.48)
10	Ventiane (Laos)	1.38 (0.45)
11	Bangkok	1.24 (0.41)
12	Penang	1.19 (0.39)

Source: International web postings / USD to RM conversions as at Feb 2011

As a wholly-owned subsidiary of PBA Holdings Bhd, PBAPP helped to generate a total revenue of RM 198.54 million for the public listed company for the year ended 31 December 2010 and a profit after tax (PAT) of RM 26.23 million.[26]

Meanwhile, PBAPP continues to implement an "Uninterrupted Water Supply Programme" (UWSP) as part of its service package in Penang. Targeted at maximising customer satisfaction while minimising the adverse effects of mishaps, the key elements of this programme include:
- Continuously replacing outdated pipes prone to bursting or that may cause murky water;
- Scheduling supply interruptions to facilitate water works from midnight to the early hours of dawn;
- Establishing a 24-hour Call Centre and committing to completing all emergency repair work within 24 hours;
- Utilising technology (where possible) to fit and join pipes without interrupting supply; and
- Establishing a materials committee to review materials for use in water supply networks.

---

26 See PBA Holdings Bhd, Annual Report 2010, (Penang: PBA Holdings Bhd).

Reducing water loss

Regarding water loss, Penang's non-revenue water (NRW) – the amount of water that is lost through leakages, pipe bursts, maintenance works, water theft and fire-fighting - of 18.2% was amongst the lowest in the country in 2010. In comparison, the national average is 36%, and in some states this figure reaches 50%. (Quah, 2011: 12).

To achieve a low NRW percentage, PBAPP continues to implement a NRW management programme that includes:
- Monitoring and ensuring speedier pipe repairs;
- Ensuring accurate measurements of production outputs;
- Introducing district metering for new housing schemes;
- Zone metering for measurement and analysis of base night flows;
- Managing an active leakage control program;
- Controlling materials for use in water supply systems; and
- Initiating a meter replacement programme to ensure accuracy of water meters.

PBAPP has also developed proactive supporting control systems such as: a pipe burst leakage reporting system; licensing of plumbers; establishment of a materials approving technical committee; and licensing specific pipe-laying contractors. In 2008, PBAPP was able to repair 97% of burst pipes in 24 hours.[27] This low level of water loss translates into cost savings that can be passed on to consumers.

Geographical Information Systems

Proactive water management is also facilitated by the usage of a Geographical Information System. With on-line integration of engineering data, consumer data, aerial photography and a catchment area plan into a "strategic network model", PBAPP's GIS system is able to support analysis of water demand, the distribution network, leakages, supply interruptions, water source tracing and water quality modelling. Data from the system is also being used to manage and conserve gazetted catchment areas and safeguard raw water sources. PBAPP monitors water catchments in Penang by superimposing satellite photographs of land lots gazetted as catchments to detect encroachments or any illegal activities.

27 See PBA Holdings Bhd, Annual Report 2010, (Penang: PBA Holdings Bhd).

Revenue Management System

One of the key developments in information technology (IT) for PBAPP following corporatisation is the successful transformation of the PWA's computerised billing system into a proprietary integrated revenue management system (iRMS). Today, the iRMS has become an online system that integrates data from the IT, Corporate Services, Operations and Finance databases for accurate status reviews and on-line updating of every single customer account. It also supports the success of PBAPP's Customer Care Centres, 24-hour Call Centre, an online payment facility and a pre-payment facility. In 2010, the iRMS helped PBAPP to achieve a bill collection efficiency of 91.3%.[28]

Customer Service

PBAPP has actively sought to improve its customer care with the dual aims of improving service and facilitating the rapid identification of issues and repair needs.

In 2002, PBAPP became the first water supply company in Malaysia to set up a 24-hour Call Centre. The Centre offers customers the option of calling in to seek assistance, or to file a report, request or complaint.

As of 2010, nine customer care centres have been established in strategic locations throughout the state, including on the island and mainland. Equipped with computer systems with links to the databases of the Finance, I.T., Operations and Corporate Service departments, PBAPP personnel can handle 20 types of customer transactions on-the-spot.

PBAPP has also established One-Stop Office Complexes that are similar in form and function to district police stations and post offices. Each Complex is a self-contained "nerve centre" which can provide a range of comprehensive services. Each houses a Customer Care Centre, an Operations Centre, store facilities and quarters in one convenient location. To date, PBAPP operates four such centres, which has enabled response times to be lowered significantly.

---

28 See PBA Holdings Bhd, Annual Report 2010, (Penang: PBA Holdings Bhd).

To monitor its performance in accordance to the requirements of ISO 9001:2008 certification, PBAPP's customer care division commissions independent surveys to audit public perception of its performance every two years. The following are some of the key results of the most recent poll in December 2010:

Topic	Domestic category acceptance rating (%)	Trade category acceptance rating (%)
Water Quality	82	98
Services	95	98
Tariffs	94	74

OTHER MILESTONES

In 2004, PBAPP helped the Penang State Government to gazette eight water catchments on Penang Island and three catchments in Seberang Prai on the mainland. Gazetting effectively provides legislative protection for these precious resources. Penang's neighbouring states of Kedah and Perak have been advised to do the same for their own benefit.

In 2005, the company embarked on a study to recycle industrial water for non-potable use at factories in the Bayan Lepas Industrial Park. The study revealed that while it is technically possible to re-process the wastewater for non-potable use, the costs of doing were higher than that of supplying conventionally treated potable water.

PBAPP has also installed Streaming Current Detectors (SCDs) in five water treatment plants. This SCD system is very effective in optimising chemical dosing and further enhancing the performance of these plants.

In April 2006, PBAPP commissioned the first ultra filtration (UF) water treatment plant in Malaysia for potable water. The pilot 5MLD (million litres/day) plant at Bukit Pancur employs membrane filtration technology to remove 99.99% of all water-borne pathogens. It serves as a research and development facility for future applications.

PBAPP is also planning to reduce Penang's heavy dependency on the Muda River as an indispensable raw water resource. The company has initiated a study to look into means of ensuring sufficient water supply until the Year 2050. The study has identified an alternative source of raw water in Perak. If approvals are given to tap this alternative resource, it is projected PBAPP can sustain sufficient water supply for the State of Penang until 2050.

Plans are underway to expand the Mengkuang Dam, and land acquisition is underway. The project is scheduled for completion in 2015 to increase Penang's in-state raw water storage capacity by 3.3-fold, from 22 million m^3 to 73.5 million m^3. This project will help to ensure sufficient in-state storage to meet demand until 2020.

PBAPP is also working with the State Government, non-government organisations and the mass media to urge domestic water consumers in the State to use water wisely. The target is to reduce domestic consumption from 286 litres per person/day to 233 litres per person/day.

Building on the Corporation's water sector as well as organizational expertise, its parent company, PBAHB, has embarked on a number of strategic initiatives. These include: establishing a water treatment plant in China's Yi Chun city in a joint venture; creating a bottled drinking water company; and setting up the Penang Water Services Academy with the Penang Skills Development Centre. In 2010, the Academy successfully launched a Malaysian Skills Certificate programme for school-leavers that is recognized in Malaysia and signed agreements with the Council of Trust for the People (MARA), the Malaysia Water Association and PERPAMSI (the Indonesia Water Association) to jointly accredit, market, organise and conduct water industry related training courses in Malaysia and Indonesia.[29]

CONCLUSION

As at 2010, Penang continued to offer vibrant economic prospects and a healthy lifestyle to an estimated population base of 1.6 million people.

---
29 See *PBA Holdings Bhd, Annual Report 2010, (Penang: PBA Holdings Bhd).*

Penang has PBAPP which exists to serve the state as a holistic water operator that can support its continuing development and evolution in the 21st Century.

As the licensed water operator for Penang that is in full compliance with Malaysia's National Water Services Re-structuring Initiatives with effect from 1 June 2011, PBAPP will continue to strive towards meeting all of the state's water supply needs in the future. As Penang is a water-stressed state, the primary focus will be on managing sustainable water supply in the face of global climate change and increasing water demand.

Chapter 8

Penang's Technology Opportunities

Yoon Chon Leong

INTRODUCTION

Over the last 40 years, the technology landscape of Penang has been gradually transformed, from a commodity-trading centre into the vibrant high-technology electronics hub we see today. The driver for this transformation has been the government's ability to construct and communicate a compelling business case based on cost as well as the quality of its human resources to attract serious multinational companies in the technology sector to set up manufacturing branch operations in the state. This seed enabled Penang's subsequent transformation into a high technology-based industrial economy.

In the early 1970s, the first electronics component multinationals established operations in Penang. Over the course of the next 20 years, these firms were joined by other component manufacturers as well as consumer and industrial electronics producers, who all sought to capitalize on the state's good infrastructure and relatively well-educated labor. By the end of the 1980s, the state had established a reputation as the "Silicon Island" of the East.

In the 1990s, a large cluster of component producers, particularly in the semi-conductor sector, reached maturity stage with Penang becoming one of the major exporters for the industry. This core of firms was effectively complemented by a large cluster of local suppliers in the automation, contract manufacturing, and piece-part sectors.

Because of the close proximity of the clusters to each other and the possibilities for learning and innovation that this provided, Penang quickly became one of the well-known leaders in the global quality and productivity revolution. The reason for this is somewhere in the mid 1990s, the industrial world became increasingly aware of Japan's manufacturing methods that differentiates that country's products in terms of consistent quality through statistical quality controls and automation.

At that time, Penang's fledgling manufacturing sector took the brave step to embrace these principles and started to make manufacturing-in-Penang as a strategic business advantage for investors. Of particular importance was the rapid development of the local process automation equipment industry which became well known for its back-end (particularly in the molding and final test) process improvement and automation innovations. This was achieved by leveraging and enhancing the capabilities of the existing local tooling and machine shops to find ways to automate the labor intensive practices of that time. The focus, as guided by the Japanese experience, is not only to reduce cost, but to improve quality by reducing errors that follow with manual operations.

Around the mid-1990s, the rapid adoption of Information and Communication Technologies (ICT), together with the deployment of an effective telecommunications network, allowed companies to construct very effective and globalized operating business structures. In addition, the rapid economic expansion of the Chinese and Indian economies, hence attractive large markets, made it necessary for multi-national companies to be more geographically diverse in order to optimize cost and market leverage. The net result for Penang was the gradual break-up of the established manufacturing cluster as multi-nationals re-engineered their operations to become more geographically diversified. By 2000, most of the lower value-added operations which relied on high-volume and low-mix manufacture had – or were in the process of being – moved out of Penang. Many MNCs present in Penang began altering their existing operations towards higher value activities, such as research and development (R&D), supply chain management, customer support centers, or sales and marketing branches.

In theory, the timing of this global business model (where MNCs start to consider Penang as a candidate for higher value-added activities) should be very welcomed. As a result of the growth of the local industry and resulting higher cost of people and infrastructure, they gradually became less competitive against other regional competitors, particularly in serving the high-volume and cost-sensitive manufacturing markets. This should have, in turn, created the impulse for the local industries to turn towards re-engineering their value propositions to better align to the MNCs move towards higher value activities such as R&D. This would have led to an evolution in Penang's industrial landscape towards a higher income activity landscape.

Unfortunately, this re-engineering towards higher value-added activities has proved to be a much more difficult challenge, especially for Penang's local industries. As a result, Penang's high technology industry base has experienced gradual loss of its competitive advantage that it enjoyed from the 1980s through to the mid-1990s. There are many reasons for this, but a major factor is the industry's inability to leverage its learning base to create increasingly higher value-added products and services in a timely manner to satisfy the higher end needs of a fast changing market.

This paper will take a deeper look at this situation by carrying out an assessment of the technology competencies of the firms in the E&E sector that are currently based in Penang. This will be done by mapping their combined core competencies and then seeing to what extent they are aligned with current and future trends in technology. From there, the transitions needed in company competencies can be identified as can key market segments for priority focus. From a scoping standpoint, this paper is part of a bigger project to develop an industrial blueprint for Penang beyond 2010. This report represents the first section of that blueprint which is still in progress. Some changes will be expected as new information comes in and hence will be updated as the project progresses.

The article is divided into four sections. The first will look at the reasons behind Penang's decline in competitiveness; the second will discuss the competency assessment of Penang's E&E firms, including locally-based multinational corporations, the automation cluster, as well as providers of supporting services; and the third will identify technology opportunities that are already well-aligned with Penang's existing learning base. The final section will present conclusions.

The data used generally comes from the following sources: two studies carried out by BizWise Consulting for the Penang Technology Roadmap; a survey of 600 companies of various sizes to understand their operations, difficulties, and competitiveness; and extensive informal interviews with a wide range of people within the industry in Penang.

PENANG'S DECLINE IN COMPETITIVENESS

Figure 1 shows the evolution of the E&E industry in Penang focusing on the capabilities of multinational corporations and local, small and medium enterprises (SMEs).

Figure 1

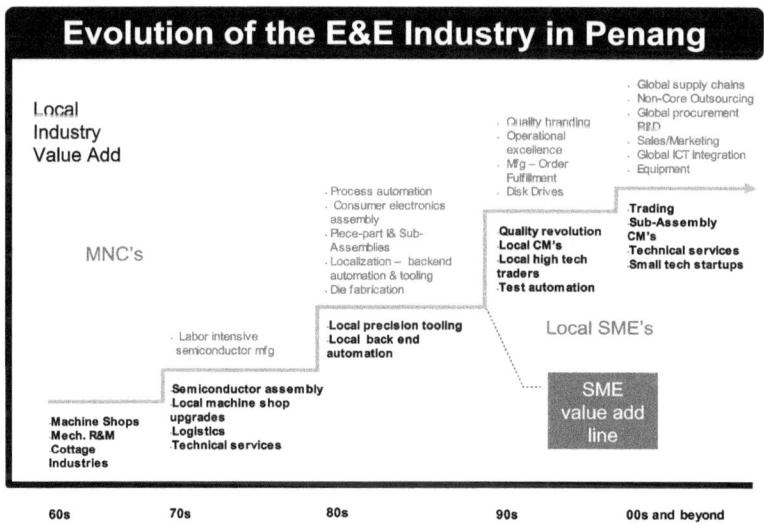

Source: Yoon, 2010: 8.

While the competencies of local SMEs have continued to improve over time, the challenges to the viability of Penang's manufacturing sector come from several sources. Key informal interviews with local and foreign business leaders over the last two years highlighted several issues regarding changes in the E&E market as well as the Malaysian context.

With regards to the trends in the local E&E market, the gradual marginalization, that is, the moving away of lower-end manufacturing activities, particularly of high-volume, low-mix, and cost-sensitive manufacturing which was the mainstay of Penang-based contract manufacturers began approximately fifteen years ago. Local contract manufacturers that used to command the bulk of business from multinational companies operating in Penang began losing their capacity to foreign competitors who were now physically closer to the relocated operations of these MNCs. This is especially the case in China. To make matters worse, these foreign competitors, in turn, started their own local downstream sourcing activities within their local environments, which caused further degradation to the established Penang supply chains.

At the initial stages, Penang-based automation equipment makers continued to supply equipment to these new overseas facilities. However, over time, automation equipment providers with regional operations began to effectively compete with the Penang-based firms by taking advantage of their better access to customers who had overseas operations. Some of these resorted to copying some of the existing designs and produced lower-cost equivalent machines. Today, these competitors have become a very serious challenge for Penang.

With regard to Penang-based MNCs, they began their transformation towards higher value-added activities around 2000. At that time, manufacturing began to move towards the more knowledge-based "low-volume and high-mix" type of work. They began by installing aggressive workforce transformation programs to upgrade their employee competencies to accommodate activities such as R&D, Order Fulfillment, Marketing, Shared Services and Applications Development. Some examples of such competencies can be seen in integrated circuit design, industrial design, product test and characterization, software development, marketing and supply chain management. While this is encouraging, these transformations began to create a significant demand

and supply competency gap between the MNC and the Penang-based local suppliers which continues to this day. In addition, the new foreign competitors (such as those in China) have been aggressively investing in moving up their value chains, even while lower-end businesses are moving to them. Some examples are high precision machining services, industrial automation equipment and the plastic molding industry.

This move towards higher value-added activities places local firms in a quandary, as they do not have the financial strength and global reach to achieve the desired transformation as quickly and effectively as their multinational customers. In addition, many of these firms do not fully comprehend the structural changes that the market has undergone over the last three decades. During the 1980s, the business environment was shaped by government incentives, cost, and geographic proximity. This helped the emergence of Penang's base of supplier firms. Today, the market is significantly different as re-engineered MNCs seek more knowledge-based and flexible suppliers. In addition, there is a growing need for value-added suppliers with global reach to service MNC affiliates regardless of location. This means that Penang companies now need to be much more competitive globally, both in terms of competencies, information systems, and physical reach. Current assessment of the readiness of local companies to compete under these new realities indicates that most neither possess the required learning base, reach, nor brand, to win. Most have simply not invested to upgrade themselves to take advantage of current opportunities. They were, in effect, lulled into complacency by the easy markets that the MNCs provided until they moved away.

In the domestic context, local operations are affected by several structural issues. According to conventional wisdom, the development of the E&E industry has been hampered by the lack of skilled human resources. While this is true to a certain extent, our research also shows that the quality of the top segment of graduates from local universities is at par with top graduates from foreign universities (Penang Skills Development Centre, 2007). The problem stems from the remainder which show capabilities that are much lower than their grades indicate. This unique bi-modal distribution perhaps is the cause of the lack of trainable technical resources for the industry.

Penang's E&E industry has also developed without the benefit of a significant local domestic market. Unlike firms in China, who were able to develop and test their products through their domestic customers, Penang companies tested their offerings in a much more stringent export market. This harsher environment meant that fewer firms were able to survive the early stages of birth and growth, with the resulting effect of having a much smaller core of viable firms.

In addition, the market for high-technology items is a competitive one. The development of competitive technology-based products requires time, funding and talent to realize and success generally does not come immediately. Failures are to be expected, but the resulting learning base needs to be nurtured so that future success is guaranteed. Discussions carried out with fund managers continue to indicate that local funds remain too risk averse to nurture world class ideas (interviews). In addition, feedback from entrepreneurs shows that grants remain elusive and take too long to conclude to be able to keep ahead of the competition. While there is no formal paper written to summarize this feedback (many stories concerning why funds are approved or not approved), the general trend is that local fund managers tend to invest mainly on growth companies rather than start-ups due to the inherent lower risk of the former.

Looking forward, the great dependence of Penang firms on locally-based multinational customers in the electronics sector can be considered to be an unusual case insofar as traditional business models are concerned. The positive element is that suppliers can capitalize on an attractive but narrow customer base and focus on growth. The negative element is complacency, resulting in insufficient effort to develop their unique value propositions, products and markets.

CAN PENANG STILL BE COMPETITIVE?

In the "Electronics Century", change is one of the few things we can be certain of. Every decade since the 1950s has seen quantum leaps in technological achievements and revolutionary changes in business models.

Penang's economy grew in tandem with technological developments of the E&E industry from the 1970s to the 1990s. This meant that local industries kept pace with the requirements regarding the sophistication of manufacturing operations made by local based MNCs. However, with the increasing trend towards globalization, while the multinationals responded to these new realities by initiating actions to create value-added "eco-systems" – particularly in R&D – to continue to justify their own value preposition to their headquarters, the local supplier base was not able to keep pace. The result is a competency gap that MNCs in Penang are moving up the ladder much faster than their local suppliers. It is true, however, that the learning base of some local firms did continue to improve and diversify to fill the demand gap that multinationals created – but not many. As part of the solution, in 2005, the Malaysian government decreed that the key industrial areas of Penang possessed Multimedia Super-Corridor status, providing firms with a less regulated environment as well as an array of incentives to upgrade operations. Together, these actions created an environment for a new type of technical entrepreneur start-ups that are more IP- and product development-based.

Figure 2 uses the technology life-cycle framework for technology driven products to analyze the evolution and convergence of mobile communications, internet and computers. This set of curves is a popular chart used by technology companies to map their technology roadmaps, particularly for large MNCs. The next revolution will be triggered by the further convergence of this integrated paradigm with a new one that combines electronics with biology and advanced materials. The expectation from this technological revolution will further embed electronics into the very way we live. In the meantime, as seen by the green curve, innovation will continue to optimize the value creation of existing technologies and offer a range of products that will serve as a bridge before the final convergence.

The following paragraphs will focus on the green innovation curve, as it is unrealistic to assume that Penang's current technology learning base will play a significant role in the yellow curve to revolutionize the industry.

While this means that Penang is not at the technology forefront, there still is continual demand for products and services on the green innovation curve and the meeting between the successive green and yellow curves will not occur for at least the next 5 years, and then be superseded by the new paradigm.

Figure 2

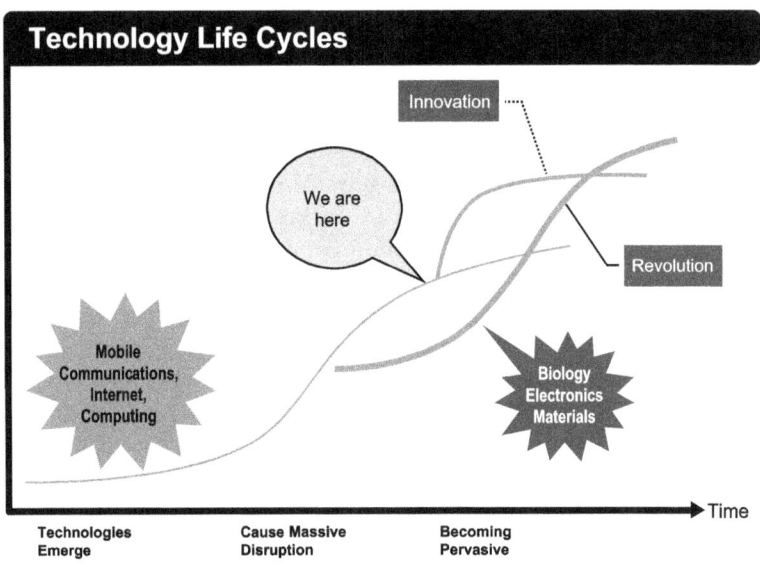

Source: Bizwise Consulting

Figures 3 and 4 give an indication of the specific technologies and their impact to the way we live based on an analysis from Anton, Silberglitt, and Schneider published by the US National Defense Institute.

Figure 3

Key Technology Trends over the next 10 years		
Past	Present	Future
Trend Paths		
Metals and traditional ceramics Separate Engineering and Biology Selective Breeding Small-scale Integration Micron plus lithography Main Frame Stand alone computers	Composites and polymers Biomaterials Genetic Insertion Very large scale integration Sub-micron lithography Personal computer Internet connected machine	Smart materials Bio/Genetic engineering Genetic Engineering Ultra/giga-scale integration Nano-assembly Micro-appliances Appliances and assistant networks
Meta Trends		
Single discipline Macro-systems Local Physical	Dual/hierarchically discipline Micro-systems Regional Information	Multi-Discipline Nano-systems Global Knowledge
Tickets to Technology Revolution		
Trade schools General University Locally resourced products Capital $	Highly specialized training Specialized degree Locally resourced components Increased capital $$	Multi-disciplinary training Multi-disciplinary degrees Products tailored to local resource Mixed

Source: US National Defense Institute.

Source: Anton, Silberglitt, and Schneider, 2001: 46.

Figure 3 summarizes the major trends in technology development, its associated meta-trends (i.e. trends about the technology trends), and the necessary tickets or competencies that are required to play in these future environments. In a nutshell, what it says is that enabling components are getting smaller and smarter, giving rise to the development of very small scale systems to replace individual components wired together on a large board. An example is the "lab on a chip" technology that performs an entire function from measurement to analysis on a single micro-chip platform. Finally, from a competency standpoint (tickets to play), the trend is to move from single competency training as in the case today for university students to one that is multi-disciplined where graduates can have one or multi specialties in order to perform well in a world where integrated knowledge is a critical driver.

Figure 4

Effects of this Technology Revolution

Smart materials →	Integrated Micro-Systems →	Information Tech →	Life sciences
Enabled pervasive systems	Wide, multi-mode Integration	Continued explosion	Extensive genome manipulation
Continuous body function monitoring Targeted, non-invasive drug delivery Pervasive sensor and displays (wearable/structural) Weather responsive shelters	Lab analysis on a chip Pervasive sensors (biological/optical/chemical etc.) Micro and Nano-satellites Micro-robots	Photonics: Bandwidth, computation Ubiquitous computing Pervasive sensors Global information utilities Nano-scale semiconductors Natural language translation and interfaces	GM plants and animals for food and drug production, organs, organic compounds Gene therapy
Effects	Effects	Effects	Effects
Improved quality life span Improve life quality and health Increased energy efficiency and reduced environmental effects Continued growth of entertainment industries	Facilitate drug discovery, genomic research, chemical analysis and synthesis Chemical and biological weapons detection and analysis. Huge device cost savings Proliferation of controlled processing capabilities. (nuclear isotopes separation etc.)	E-commerce dominance Creative destruction of industry Continued globalization Reduced privacy New digital divides	Longer life span Improved life quality and health Improved crop yields and drought tolerance Reduced pesticides and deforestation for farming. Possible eco-system changes Possibility of eugenics

Source: US National Defense Institute.

Source: Anton, Silberglitt, and Schneider 2001: 37.

Figure 4 complements Figure 3 by describing the effects of these technology trends in terms of products and their effects on the way we live. Briefly, the appearance of smart materials and system level integration will give rise to major disruptions via quantum leaps in ICT capabilities that will now connect the world (especially with ubiquitous sensors) in a way that will cause constructive destruction of existing economic and social orders. In addition, the development of micro-systems will enable a revolution in the way we think about life sciences as biology start to converge into electronics. An example is in the science of Biomimetics (or Bio-mimicry) that studies biological systems and processes and models them into physical machines.

By taking advantage of the fast changing nature of the electronics industry, it is possible for the industries in Penang to wake up, accelerate and rejoin the battle through careful selection and focussing on some of these winning technologies, discarding those that are no longer as relevant. Penang industries should first look at products on the green innovation curve while investing in integrated research to become a fast adopter of new research from industrialized countries and become a fast follower along the yellow curve.

LEVERAGING ON PENANG'S STRENGTHS

It is important for Penang to carefully pick the right battles to fight, as the electronics industry is characterized by a very wide spectrum of products and technologies. Picking the wrong combinations that do not provide leverage from existing established local core competencies can be disastrous, especially in an extremely time-sensitive and internationally competitive environment. The margin for error is quite narrow.

From this perspective, it is important that a deeper analysis be made to more clearly define Penang's industrial core competencies, as well as the competitiveness of its learning base. Figures 5 and 6 show a high-level description of the products that are already in the market from Penang technology companies.

Figure 5

Source: Bizwise Consulting

Figure 6

Source: *Bizwise Consulting*

The above two charts depict the current level of sophistication of the Penang industry landscape. As can be seen, Penang local industries today are no longer just supplier of parts and services to their MNC customers. They have grown to produced value-added products – mostly in the form of sub-assemblies for machines and, in some cases, have become full original equipment suppliers themselves.

From a high level standpoint, these are the types of competencies that are extremely relevant for the E&E industry, both for manufacturing as well as for higher value activities such as R&D. The conclusion we can make from these two illustrations is that Penang already has the basic capabilities to compete in a globalized environment. For example, Penang's automatic testing machines for semiconductors are competitive with world class players, and in some instances, already have created stronger brands than much more established players. As also indicated in the two charts, there is a beginning in the creation of electronic products and advanced materials, especially in the field of advanced polymers. These can be considered to be very positive trends indeed.

The challenge is the size and rate of growth of these fledgling industries. They remain very small at this time relative to the MNCs. Even the largest local based companies are achieving revenues of a few hundred million ringgits per year. They have yet to become true MNCs. The challenge is how to leverage on these existing competencies and build a competitive portfolio of industries that will propel the economy forward in a global environment where everyone else is trying to do the same.

The above figures point to five pillars in Penang that can be considered as part of the state's industrial learning base. These are:

- Existing multinationals
- Local process automation companies
- Local engineering technology providers in the following sub-sectors:
  - Precision machining
  - Plastic molders
  - Sheet metal
  - Advanced materials
- MSC-status companies
- Global logistics service providers

With regard to each of these pillars:

Existing multinationals

These companies can be divided into three general categories of products:

- Semi-conductors
- Equipment
- Contract manufacturers

Semiconductors comprise the largest and most diverse of the five pillars. This includes some of the largest and most technically advanced companies in the world, such as Intel, AMD, Altera, Osram, Phillips, Renesas, Avago and others. Their key competencies include the following:

- LED wafer fabrication - Osram
- Digital integrated circuit development - Intel

- Analog microwave chip development - Avago
- High frequency micro-circuit development - Agilent and Mini Circuits
- Microprocessor and ASIC chip applications - Altera, Renesas and Intel
- IC package development - Intel, Altera, AMD
- LED package development - Phillips, Osram, Avago
- IC test development - Intel, AMD, Avago, Altera, Agilent
- Low-volume, high-mix and high-pin count semi-conductor package manufacturing –widespread.
- High bright LED package manufacturing – Widespread.

Regarding the development and manufacture of electronics equipment, there is growing competency gradually being established in this sector in Penang. Below are some of the competencies available within locally-present MNCs:

- System level design up to entry level instrument grade functionalities - Agilent, Motorola
- Microprocessor based equipment development - Intel, Dell
- Equipment level mechanical design - Agilent, Motorola
- Design for regulatory compliance - Agilent, Motorola, Dell
- Software and firmware development - Agilent, Intel, Altera, Dell, AMD

There are also contract manufacturers who are present in Penang to cater to the needs of locally-based MNCs. Also, among the multi-nationals are the global contract manufacturers who have invested here because of the needs of the locally based multi-nationals. Their global reach, whilst enabling them to win business, also requires them to invest in regions where their customers are located. Some key competencies associated with these companies are:

- PCB assembly
- PCB manufacturing
- Electronics manufacturing services
- Global procurement
- High-volume manufacturing process development

From the above analysis, we can conclude that there is still significant depth in Penang's technology learning base residing inside the multinationals. However, a few multinationals should not be viewed as constituting the desired scale necessary to make a difference in moving the economy up the value chain. There is an urgent need to incentivize them to duplicate these competencies in local companies via the development of mutually beneficial eco-systems and local clusters to help scale up these critical competencies at state or national level.

Local process automation companies

As described earlier, this group of companies has, over time, developed capabilities that enable them to effectively compete in the international business environment. The problem is that there are only a few such companies that have the scale required to be effective. Regardless of their technical competencies, these firms face serious questions as to their viability in today's market context. Issues associated with scale such as the breadth of their product portfolio, the resources to carry out marketing on a regional or global scale, and the ability to offer after sales service are formidable requirements. It is probably accurate to state that local automation companies are still participating in a very niche market centered on board assembly, test and final packaging automation for semiconductor manufacturing.

Core competencies from this group can be generally divided into two main groups:

- Automated production equipment design and manufacturing
- Semiconductor test systems design and manufacturing

Competencies in automated production equipment design and manufacturing niche markets are well developed. Local products have seen adoption in large scale manufacturing factories all over the world. Competitive cost, customization and almost-free after sales service models are the market differentiators for Penang firms. The revenue streams from these companies normally come from equipment sales, spare parts, and customization. A list of the key competencies from these companies is described below:

- Growing library of reference designs for high speed automation mechanisms
- Growing library for machine control operating software and firmware electronic and electrical control boxes
- Electro-mechanical system integration

In this category, companies such as Pentamaster, LKT, MMSV, SRM and ATI are representative of these competencies.

In the semiconductor test systems design and manufacturing category, we see a different set of players such as Elsoft and Vitrox. Although still considered to be part of the process automation grouping, companies such as these have chosen to focus on the electronic test processes which include electronics hardware design as well as the associated software test managers. In a manner of speaking, these companies have already started along the path of becoming full-fledged test and measurement companies. At this stage, they remain essentially system integrators with capabilities to design and develop complementary integration hardware. Below is the list of competencies associated with companies in this sub-category:

- Design and development of test strategies and measurement methods
- Design and development of companion connectivity hardware to link test instruments together into a system
- Design and development of SMUs (Source Measure Units) as customized test drive sources for semi-conductor product testing
- Design, development and manufacturing of high performance vision systems for machine inspection and positioning
- Design and development of test management software
- Design, development and manufacture of integrated test systems, including the mechanical test heads and probes

Figure 7 shows a table of the key players and how they compare with internationally competitive companies.

Figure 7

Major players that are globally competitive

Major International companies	Major Local Malaysia Companies	
Applied Material (US)	LKT (Now Singapore Owned)	Antcorp
Ermanco (US)	Eng Hardware Technology	ACM
iXMation (US)	Pentamaster Corporation	Quest Adaptations
Yokogawa (Japan)	AT Systematization	UBCT
Kardex (Switzeland)	MMS Berhad	Walta Engineering
Komax (Switzeland)	SRM	Wanjun
ASM (Switzeland)	Vitrox Berhad	Zengyi
Daifuko (Japan)	Precede	YGL
Hirata (Japan)	Soft Fix	Softphix
Nihon Garter (Japan)	Elsoft	Comdev
Delta (US)	Flexmove	Exabytes
MicroVision (US)	Prodelcon	Smart-Ed
Ismeca (Switzeland – with presence in M'sia)	DSEM	Akeetoons
Agilent (US – with presence in M'sia)	ValuesFirst	Dignersys
Ismeca (Switzeland – with presence in M'sia)	CeedTec	Mobiweb
ATS Automation (Canada – with presence in M'sa)	Policom	Mobif
MultiTest (Germany – with presence in M'sia)	CSVT Vision	

Source: *Bizwise Consulting*

Local engineering technology providers

This group represents a much larger base of companies offering a wide spectrum of components and services. The target markets are the multinationals (including disk drive companies), as well as to a larger extent, the local process automation companies. For the latter group, their manufacturing model is more cluster-based than that seen among the multinationals. In general, it can be said that these local engineering technology providers are intimately embedded in the overall equipment design and make-up of the final piece of equipment. It is this leveraging that plays a key role in reducing cost, as well as leveraging on diversity of design ideas.

In a macro way, we can sub-divide this group of companies into four further sub-categories:

- Precision machining
- Plastic molding
- Sheet metal
- Advanced polymers

The precision machining group comprises very large local companies such as Engtek and Prodelcon that design and manufacture high-volume precision metal components for a wide range of industries, ranging from disk drives, micro-circuits, medical and automated equipment.

A list of key competencies for this sub-group is described below:

- Wide spectrum of sophisticated high precision machining equipment
- Precision mechanical measurement
- Sophisticated mechanical design tools

This is an extremely capital intensive industry. There is very high dependency by customers on their suppliers to maintain a very high level of quality for the machined parts. The barrier to entry is funding and availability of top-level technical resources, including machinists.

Penang has a reasonably large precision machining capacity, with many smaller companies upgrading themselves to more sophisticated production equipment as automation companies move more of these activities to them. In addition, our analysis also shows that these smaller companies are actively clustering together to share capacity and leveraging on their diversity of competencies to meet customer demands.

The demand for precision machined parts will continue to grow in volume and performance. The existing competencies in this area will certainly be beneficial to Penang's future plans.

The plastic molding industry is relatively less developed compared to precision machining. Traditionally, because of the dominance of the semiconductor industry, molding was limited to basic level extrusion technology where plastic components are molded at high speed, mainly to function as casing and optical components for LED devices, as well as for the few consumer electronics factories present in the state. Over time, as plastics started to play a mainstream role in all sorts of applications, these companies diversified to acquire competencies to produce more complex shapes, colors, and surface textures. This industry continues to face enormous competition, especially from China.

Some key competencies from this sub category are described below:

- Mold design
- Relatively high tonnage for large sized products
- Large range of materials including lenses

Conversely, the sheet metal industry is relatively well developed here in Penang. There are significant competencies in the design and production of a wide variety of shapes using different metals ranging from small form factor devices to very large integrated systems. Companies such as UWC, Power Choice and many others are good examples of companies that are already producing these equipment frames and housings, both for the domestic as well as for the export markets.

The advanced polymer industry is at the fledgling stage, particularly for semiconductor manufacturing processes. We have found suppliers that have successfully won contracts with major multinational companies against established international players. However, this sector remains very small and needs to be expanded, especially in an environment where LEDs and photo-voltaic packages are becoming increasingly relevant. In addition, the rapid development of nano-technology and their associated implications to advanced materials development makes this sector a prime candidate for downstream innovations.

This industry is highly dependent on cost and customization. For Penang, while it is still possible to compete on cost due to highly mechanized nature of the operations, there will not be a geographical advantage as very high-volume and low-mix factories are no longer here. The key is to utilize this set of competencies to create higher value offerings in highly customized niche markets.

Multimedia Super Corridor (MSC) status companies

This group of young companies was formed as a result of government incentives to technology entrepreneurs to realize their ideas and business vision. The history of this group is fundamentally different from those of their predecessors. In the past, local companies started with one market - the multinationals. In contrast, MSC companies started with no markets - just an idea and a vision. However, there are a few of these companies that were spawned as extensions or subsidiaries of established local companies. The drivers are the MSC incentives associated to R&D investments. In essence, these companies became as entrepreneurial as they spawned new start-ups.

Most of these are software-based companies, as the MSC started as a focal point for the ICT industry. This was unfortunate as this initial strategy left out the critical hardware-based entrepreneurs that typifies Penang's technology base. Subsequently, the focus was realigned to reflect the realities in Penang by the inclusion of E&E hardware development as part of the MSC supported industries. The net result is a growing number of hardware-based MSC companies, although at the time of writing, there is still only a sprinkling of such companies in the state.

Listed below is a summary of core competencies associated with the Penang MSC or equivalent technology start-up companies:

- Business process software development
- Customized software solutions
- Embedded firmware development
- Electronics hardware design and manufacturing:
  - Product test systems
  - Application specific cards
  - Electronic instrumentation
  - System integration
  - RFID solutions
  - Mobile broadband solutions
  - Digital wireless applications
  - Electronic vision systems
  - Advanced polymers
  - Remote access solutions

In general, the depth of technology is at the low- to mid-level stage but growing quickly. The problem is the lack of a sophisticated local market for firms to test and improve their products. Export markets are not as easily accessible for software firms to penetrate as they require brand development, reach and economic size. All these factors are still at the infancy stage for these companies at the moment, and hence they remain fairly vulnerable to external competition.

Global logistics service providers

In addition to the process automation group, logistics service providers constitute another business segment that has grown in sophistication along with the continual upscaling of multinational companies. Over the years, large multinational logistics companies such as DHL have set up local operations to meet the demands of an increasingly sophisticated supply chain. This has resulted in the creation of many locally-based logistics companies offering similar services, although more on a regional – as opposed to global – scale.

In addition to providing transport logistics, these companies also created additional value by offering services such as smart warehousing, inventory management, accessory purchasing and order configuration. The larger multinational companies in this category have adopted sophisticated IT systems that are directly connected to those of their customers to allow seamless operations. Unfortunately, local equivalents are not at this stage yet.

Listed below are some of the key core competencies of this group:

- Global networks, in and out of the country
- Turn-key warehouse outsourcing.
- Order management
- Shipment configuration logistics
- Virtually managed inventory hub

THE POTENTIAL FROM THESE ESTABLISHED COMPETENCIES

From an electronics industry standpoint, Penang possesses the necessary competencies to create a platform to propel its E&E industry forward and start competing with more developed economies such as Taiwan, Korea and India, for high value-added products and services. The key question is how public policy can help create an environment that will expand the depth of this platform and nurture the necessary competitive innovations to happen. Listed below are some of these key technological opportunities that will align well with the established competencies described above:

1. Automation technology
2. High speed broadband equipment
3. Solar power
4. Optoelectronics
5. RFID
6. Automotive
7. Medical electronics
8. Web 2.0
9. Technical Outsourcing

These nine possible business segments are not exclusive. The electronics market segments are highly overlapped, and there are frequent examples where players from one segment cross to another and become extremely successful.

Below is a brief description to expand upon the above set of technological opportunities that Penang can leverage on.

1. Process automation

Semiconductor upstream and chip-scale automation
Current products are narrowly focused into the areas of PCBA and final test/packaging sections of the semiconductor packaging processes. This industry did not upgrade to compete in the much higher precision front end processes such as Die Attach, Wire-bonding, Die and Wafer fabrication automation equipment. With the emerging trend towards chip-scale packaging and manufacturing, the front end producers will be in an advantageous position compared to the local producers in terms of precision high density processes. However, local producers can counter by leveraging on their core for integrated automation. Moving upstream in this direction will be appropriate for Penang.

Agricultural automation
Although there are already many players in this industry, there is a market space in automation of "environmentally sustainable agriculture" processes which require a very much higher level of control and land optimization. The concept of labor independent smart greenhouses with automated soil and climate management systems that deliver very high crop yields are emerging

technology areas for local companies to diversify into. As an extension to this strategy are also opportunities to apply the existing competencies towards environmental monitoring and recycling technologies.

Medical automation
Life science testing is moving towards the high volume environment. Medical practitioners are increasingly dependent on intensive testing in order that diagnosis can be as accurate enough to quickly identify root causes and resulting medical treatment. At this time, turnaround times from analytical labs are considered to be too long to enable significant productivity improvements in disease treatment. There is a fast growing market to provide automated sample handling solutions to support the analytical processes both to improve diagnostic productivity as well as to significantly improve expensive equipment utilization.

2. Broadband Deployment

Wireless Broadband Network Management
Currently, this technology is externally sourced. For full mobile broadband deployment, it is necessary for the country to develop base station technologies based on current 3.5G, 4G and Wimax platforms. SMEs are already offering downstream customer premise equipment in the market and we need to upgrade their capabilities to bring wireless broadband network management solutions into play and perhaps even go upstream to be closer to the base station. Current clusters should be capable of creating these solutions.

Outdoor and Customer Premise Equipment
To offer "last mile" wireless connectivity either in fixed or mobile applications. Technology already exists (although limited) in the country and effective clusters can be formed to deliver these solutions. This should be part of the solution for ubiquitous broadband deployment in Malaysia. In tandem with the above mentioned broadband network management solutions, it is possible to create commercially viable complementary hardware solutions to enable network operators to deploy wifi everywhere. These solutions can subsequently be exported to foreign markets.

Cloud Computing
Development of commercially viable ubiquitous broadband deployment will further drive downstream web based business growth. The concept of "cloud computing" while experiencing great interest in developed countries, is still relatively unknown locally. Most software providers continue to develop the traditional "software in a box" products. The deployment of ubiquitous broadband availability will signal the decline of such solutions in favor of the more cost effective cloud systems and begin the process of creating mobile virtual organizations and communities. The fast growing software industry in Penang is well positioned to take advantage of this emerging market, especially due to the fact that the local software adoption base is still small. Introducing the new cloud platform at this point in time will enable rapid adoption as customers do not need to migrate from their investments into the more traditional systems.

3. Solar Power

Home based power units
This includes the development of home solar power generation kits that can work seamlessly with the existing power grids. Malaysia is already has an established manufacturing base in solar panels that can be leveraged upon as a key supply chain partner for this industry segment. The value add elements for the local SMEs will be in the development and commercialization of the optical, storage, inversion, grid synchronization and control systems necessary for individual consumption as well as for power sharing with the existing electricity grids. Elements of all these competencies already exist in Penang's industrial base.

Large solar power farms
The electronics, optics, control and software required to enable such facilities can either be sourced internationally or be developed and built domestically. The industry can collaborate with Tenaga Nasional Berhad which is the leader for this large scale solar power initiative to develop a technology roadmap to create a local solution that can be used domestically as well as for the export markets. Currently, the competency gap to make this happen is in the field of power electronics which the Penang industries do not participate in. All other competencies, including mechanical systems are already available.

Off grid lighting and security monitoring
Solar powered or off-grid lighting products are rapidly finding a niche within the public infrastructure as well as security lighting markets. The need for small geometry solar power engines is a market that Penang industries can benefit from to address a very wide range of applications. Such products will include the power engine, sensor systems, wireless connectivity as well as network control systems. The market is currently position at the "emerging technology" phase and is a perfect place for Penang's industries to adapt and compete with innovative products and solutions.

4. Optoelectronics

LED based lighting
To deploy LED technology and place the country in the forefront for this green technology. It is possible to leverage on the deep knowledge of LED applications available within the Malaysian cluster to develop and deploy the technology effectively for commercial lighting, street lighting, traffic lighting and large format displays. Although Malaysia does not have the necessary wafer fabrication plants, significant technology value-add can be achieved with such downstream applications.

Automotive lighting
Deploy LED technology into Malaysia's local cars in the form of signal lights, instrument cluster backlighting and in-car courtesy lighting using locally developed solutions. Successful adoption will result in competitive products for the locally assembled cars as well as the export markets. LED technology is a core competency in Penang and it is not good strategy to favor imports over local solutions.

Architectural and Decorative Lighting
The LED driven Solid State Lighting technologies will create huge potentials in the field of aesthetic lighting both at the architectural as well as in the indoor/outdoor environment enhancement markets. These will come in the forms of mood lighting, wall washing, color changing as well as a wide range of decorative lighting fixtures. From a competency standpoint, the Penang industrial landscape is prepared to deliver the light engines but will fall short in decorative or industrial design. Effort must be put into this area to bridge the gap so that products in this category are

not only best in class performance, but also extremely desirable from an aesthetic design standpoint.

5. RFID (System and Hardware without tags)

Asset tracking
The market for RFID in the asset tracking market segment is rapidly growing as the cost to performance ratio of this technology continue to improve. The precision required for accurate 3D tracking of high volume assets has reached a point that it can enable a very wide spectrum of applications. Some of the key application that companies in Penang can effectively participate are:

(i)	Warehouse management
(ii)	Fleet management
(iii)	Logistics tracking
(iv)	Product warranty and maintenance systems
(v)	Library systems
(vi)	Baggage tracking

Door access and employee tracking
The growing maturity of the SME market in Malaysia is creating a market for security access and employee tracking in order to optimize people productivity. This technology can be bundled with HR management systems to provide an end to end solution to customer needs. From a competency standpoint, the skills to develop the scanners and readers for deployment around the customer premises exists – especially when the shared RF laboratories are set up for validation and later verification testing for performance and compliance. This market will also be attractive for software developers to provide cost effective tracking systems.

Perishable products tracking
RFID is one of the remote tracking technologies that fit very well with

products that depend on time critical logistics. Agricultural products such as perishable foods will need to be placed into market shelves within a very short time after harvest. Interviews with industry players show that the unnecessary losses incurred because of delayed logistics are very significant. Together with ubiquitous mobile broadband, it is now feasible to develop RFID solutions that will track these products throughout the delivery chain and allow managers to create solutions quickly when problems arise. From this view point, Malaysia has a large agricultural sector that can be modernized via RFID technology using local solutions.

6. Automotive electronics

Instrumentation clusters
The relatively established instrumentation, consumer electronics and embedded software competencies in Penang should be sufficient to participate meaningfully in this industry considering the fact that there is a relatively large local automotive business segment. Other than aesthetic design, it is entirely possible to develop world class instrument clusters as well as in-vehicle management systems. The key is the lack of a brand to put these solutions in the international markets. However, with a large domestic manufacturing market, it is possible to create the solutions and launch these into this market before moving into the international environment.

Sensor clusters
This sub-assembly market segment will be more challenging to develop. There will be a need to source the appropriate analog chip sets and build the filters, amplifiers and appropriate measurement modules to create the products that will be competitive in the global market place. Sensor systems in the automotive environment will probably represent the most challenging task because of the harsh environment these sensors are subjected to. The ability to build such sensors to meet these standards will differentiate Penang's products from the competition. With the exception of the analog chip sets, the technology exists within the Penang industrial landscape. For the analog chips, it is possible to source these from international fabricators. However, it will be a great advantage if the Malaysian government were to provide the support to build a dedicated analog sensor fabrication facility to provide this upstream component as part of this cluster.

Vehicle infotainment
Developing in-vehicle information such as sensor data, entertainment, vehicle settings, external environmental monitoring, communications that are currently only available in the high end models into lower cost cars can become a significant market opportunity for Penang companies. Again, the technologies are there in the forms of digital circuits, measurement modules, analog circuits, embedded firmware, display technologies. The key is branding and compliance certification.

7. Medical Electronics

Patient monitoring
Create a line of critical first line medical monitoring equipment for public medical care givers to increase patient throughput. Modern hospitals are increasingly network- connected via a common patient database for monitoring, management and test information. It is possible to replace foreign developed systems for a local version given sufficient support to the cluster because of its experience in networked testing and software. Locally made portable analysis machines can be used to equip remote hospitals and clinics for quick tests with connectivity features to larger hub hospitals.

Consumables
Recycling and cleaning of medical consumables such as gloves, dialysis filters, syringes, catheters etc. Automated equipment for the effective processing of these consumables can be developed to optimize cost.

Medical infrastructure equipment
Precision and Semi Precision equipment such as beds, trolleys, clean rooms (operating theaters), fixtures, mobility aids can be designed and constructed by local precision machine suppliers to replace imports. Local competencies in precision tooling and machine making, together with control and measurement electronics will be able to produce these to meet international regulatory standards.

8. Web 2.0

Tourism
Use world class interactive websites to promote integrated tourism for

Malaysia. Service providers, shops, attractions need to be better integrated to attract and bring tourists to the appropriate spots and services with the objective of encouraging visitors to spend extended time in the country.

Trade
Construct interactive trade portals with E-Exhibitions to optimize opportunities for local suppliers of goods and services. This is a critical market segment that will create revenue via advertisements, especially from products and services coming out of the Penang industries as well as the upstream and downstream international cluster members.

Cloud Computing Applications
Software developed on the Linux platform and delivered as web based "Cloud Applications" are rapidly taking market share from traditional business software products. This is due to the fast evolution of high data rate wireless broadband that is causing companies to migrate towards outsourced and remotely hosted systems and software and eliminating the need keep their their own expensive IT systems and infrastructure. This is especially true for SMEs who cannot afford large and expensive business software. By using this platform, SMEs will be able to benefit from the productivity offered by the large traditional systems at a fraction of the cost. Examples of such applications can be found in ERP, CRM, Order Management, Finance and HR solutions.

9. Technical Outsourcing Centers

Design
As MNCs upgrade their technology core, there is a trend that they want to have close proximity design eco-systems in order to diversify their design effectiveness. Local design houses, particularly around IC, Hardware, Firmware and System integration will find attractive markets in this sector. There is also opportunity to invest in proprietary designs that can be private label candidates for MNCs.

Training
The market for technology training, especially for focused skill acquisition is expanding rapidly. Companies are depending on strong technical training providers to solve many of their skill gaps that limit their ability

to diversify and be competitive. These types of training must now evolve beyond theory and include a significant portion of practical work to give trainees a "design experience".

Technical support and technical writing
Shared service outsourcing is already progressing in Penang. However, there is a good market for technical support outsourcing. This market is expected to grow very fast as consumers embed more technology into their lifestyles. In addition, there is a market for technical writing outsourcing to provide customers with the appropriate literature both on-line as well as in physical form.

Both the public and private sectors will need to take a deep look into the technology and business intelligence details of these markets and construct the necessary strategic frameworks to create the environment for these types of innovations to happen.

The details of this strategic framework is currently being worked on and will be published together with a more detailed version of this report targeted to be completed by the end of 2010. At a high level, the most critical elements that need to come together are:
- The establishment of a market intelligence unit to support entrepreneurial opportunity development. Effective dissemination of such information will help trigger innovative thinking among entrepreneurs and help them justify their investments and new directions.
- Setting up of a funding consulting unit to guide entrepreneurs to source and justify their funding needs.
- The establishment of public shared laboratories that will enable extensive prototype and product testing at affordable cost.
- An educational infrastructure that teaches industry relevant subjects both at graduate and undergraduate level.
- Setting up of an industry cluster development framework to encourage complementary industries to form complete supply chains around a specific technology, a product and associated services.

The end objectives of all these infrastructures should be to encourage entrepreneur activity by offering opportunities, financial support, shared technical services and collaborations in order to optimize development and go-to-market investments.

CONCLUDING COMMENTS

When the competency maps of the Penang Electrical and Electronics industry are analyzed this way, we find them to be in reasonably good alignment with some of the fastest growing industries in the global market-place.[30] Penang's 40 years of experience in the electronics industry remain an area of relative strength at this time even though innovation has slowed down significantly, especially among local companies, in recent years for reasons mentioned earlier. In fact, there is evidence that some local companies have indeed started the process of re-engineering themselves to remain competitive in this fast-moving industry. In addition, most multinational companies with operations in Penang have not relocated, but rather are in the process of re-engineering themselves to make Penang a hub of higher value-added activity in Asia. However, this positive situation will not last long as competing countries upgrade themselves and close the gap. It is time for the country to act.

In conclusion, it is time to act quickly to bridge the competency gaps that were created as a result of the various reasons mentioned and retain the E&E industry's attractiveness in Penang, particularly for activities that is located on the higher portions of the value chain. In order to achieve this, it will be necessary to take a deep dive into Penang's current industrial blueprint and update it to reflect current realities and future forces and come up with a set of meaningful tactical strategies to facilitate the development of this industry.

---

30 One additional key competency that would be highly desired as an enabling factor for these recommended industries is the fab-less IC design group of competencies. At the initial phase of innovation and development, companies tend to use generic catalog chipsets to create their hardware solutions. This approach is very relevant for products that are highly customized for niche markets, which require lower volumes and higher product mixes. Here, the use of generic chipsets will leverage on the economies of scale as a result of standardization. However, especially for consumer products, well-designed products tend to gain mass adoption very quickly and at that time, volume and cost becomes a dominant business success factor. Our findings indicate that many local companies face this challenge of reducing chip cost, which dominates their cost structures in order to be competitive in the mass market. To solve this problem, there will be a need to design an ASIC package that will integrate many of the designed functions into a single low chip, both to improve cost, as well as to allow better form factor flexibility. To do this will require deep fab-less IC design competencies, as well as long term funding to support the necessary "tape out" iterations to optimize each design. At this present time, there is no example of a company that had overcome this problem in the country. This is a major cause for the inability to scale-up good designs.

Chapter 9

Building a Temporary Second Home: Japanese Long-stay Retirees in Penang

Mika Toyota and Mayumi Ono

INTRODUCTION

Penang has recently become a popular destination for Japanese long-stay retirees. Although more Japanese tourists are reported to visit Thailand (1,146,633 in 2008) than Malaysia (433,462), the latter country has constantly been voted by Japanese retirees as "the most desirable destination" overseas for long-stay since 2007. In Malaysia, Penang stands out as the primary destination city for the Japanese. Furthermore, thanks to Penang's strong reputation and well-developed facilities, it serves as a gateway to Southeast Asia for many Japanese retirees in their exploration of the region. Many Japanese come to Penang first, and then move on to various places in order to choose an ideal place for their retirement life.

Why do an increasing number of Japanese elderly choose to live overseas after retirement? What kind of retirees come to Southeast Asia, and, why Penang? This chapter aims to provide a broad overview about this emerging Japanese migration trend and its implications for the new development dynamics of Penang. We will first provide background information about the "super ageing" process in Japan and explain why Japanese retirees are heading to Southeast Asian countries. Secondly, we will trace the historical evolution of Japanese retirement migration, a process which is related to the development of tourism, government policies as well as business interests. Thirdly, we will describe how Malaysia and Penang emerged as important destinations for the long-stay retirees. Finally, we call attention to the phenomenon of outflows of Japanese from Penang, and attribute this to gaps between Japanese retirees' life strategies on the one hand, and the expectations of the Malaysia government and "retirement industry" developers on the other. By "retirement industry" we refer to a wide spectrum of businesses that target retirees as customers, including care homes, elderly-friendly real estate properties, travel agencies and the like.

PUSH FACTORS IN JAPAN

Japan has become a "super ageing" society where 23.1 per cent of the total population in 2010 was sixty-five years old and above (Ministry of Home Affairs, cited in Yomiuri Newspaper, 20 September 2010). It is estimated that the percentage will steadily increase to 30.8 per cent by 2030, and further up to 37.8 per cent by 2050.[31] This "super ageing" society has resulted from two major modern demographic trends. Firstly, total fertility rate declined from 1.99 from the year 1960-1965 down to 1.30 for the year 2000-2005 (WHO). Secondly, life expectancy has been increasing steadily, with the 2009 figure being 79.59 years old for men and 86.44 for women.[32]

But demographic ageing alone does not necessarily lead to the outflow of retirees. What we should pay attention to are specific socioeconomic effects of ageing that are discernable in Japan since the 1980s, which constitute direct reasons for the retirement migration. At least four such structural reasons can be identified. First, although inter-generational ties among family members still remain critical in care provisional arrangements and a relatively high percentage of elderly live with or near their adult children as compared to other developed countries,[33] Japanese families are arguably in the situation of 'transition' (Ochiai, 1997) or even 'crisis' (Hayahsi, 2002). Japanese families and inter-generational relations in particular, are

---

32 Ministry of Health, Labor, and Welfare, "Regarding on the Current Status Simplified Life Table in Heisei 21"

33 The rate of household residing with adult children has decreased from 52.5% (1980) to 23.3% (2005).

becoming more heterogeneous in both forms and functions (Rebick and Takenaka, 2009). Currently two thirds of the elderly (translated into 8.5 million households) live independently from their children; they instead either live alone or live with spouses, forming "elderly households". The number of such elderly household is estimated to increase to 11,600,000 in 2015 and to 12,700,000 by 2025. These independent elderly obviously have to be concerned with the question how they can survive their later life with limited pensions. Therefore, it is not surprising that some of them consider the possibility of living abroad, where the cost of living is lower than that of Japan. A survey conducted by the Research Institute for Senior Life indicates that a significant number of pensioners are motivated to move overseas precisely in order to stretch the purchasing power of their pension (Zaidanhôjin Shinia Puran Kaihatsu Kikô, 2005: 107).

Second, demographic ageing in Japan is characterized by a relatively large number of senior singles, which is in turn caused by the growing trend of late marriage and non-marriage. These people are more likely to migrate after retirement than those with families in Japan partly because of their less complicated family obligations in Japan, and partly because their greater need for care. The 2005 Population Census shows that in the age cohorts of 45-49 years old, 8.3 percent of women and 17.6 percent of men were single.[34] The 2010 population statistics indicates that 8 percent of Japanese women and as many as 16 percent of Japanese men are never-married at the age of 50. Even more strikingly, it is estimated that by 2030 the never-married rate at the age of 50 may increase up to 29 percent for male and 22 percent for female.[35] Since the cultural norm of the filial obligations is widely perceived as a basis for care provision for the elderly, the increased numbers of single elderly persons understandably raises new anxieties for the elderly. It is thus not surprising that a book (2007) by the feminist sociologist Chizuko Ueno, titled "Ohitori Sama no Rogo" (Retiring as Singles), has become a bestseller. The book provides a guide on how to prepare to survive alone in the old age, and how to cope with life after one's retirement. Though the book does not highlight overseas

---

34 Statistics Bureau, Director-General for Policy Planning (Statistical Standards) & Statistical Research and Training Institute, Ministry of Internal Affairs and Communications, "The 2005 Population Census," http://www.stat.go.jp/english/data/kokusei/kihon1/00/03.htm, retrieved on 2010/07/21.

35 National Institute of Population and Social Security Research, "Population Statistics of Japan 2008," http//www.jpss.go.jp/syoushika/tohkei/Popular/Popular2010.asp?chap=0, retrieved on 2010/07/21.

long-stay, the option of moving abroad has become a common strategy for an increasing number of retirees.

Third, the Japanese super-ageing trend has created a peculiar phenomenon of what we may call "cross-generational ageing". An increasing number of relatively "young" elderly (60-74 years old) have found themselves to be in the position of care provider for the older elderly (80 years old and above). Around the time when these "young" elderly retire, they have to become full-time care providers for their parents instead of themselves being care recipients. They thus have to be concerned with the care arrangement for their elderly parents as well as with their own long-term financial security for the next twenty years or more. In our field research on retiree migration in a number of Southeast Asian countries, we came across quite a few of such two-generation elderly who migrate together. By doing so the "young" elderly hire helpers (which they are not able to do in Japan) for their parents, and enjoy life as much as they can.

Fourth and finally, retirees opt to move overseas also because of the shortage of care labor and increasing doubt about the sustainability of the pension scheme in Japan. While achieving the world's highest longevity should be celebrated, ageing raised a serious question: who is going to support the rapidly increasing aged population at the household level as well as at the national level? Age dependency (the ratio of older dependents—people older than 64 – to the working-age population – those aged 15-64) in Japan increased from 17.17 (1990) to 25.29 (2000) and further up to 32.85 in 2008. While the recent free trade agreement admitted a limited number of incoming foreign care providers (nurses and care givers from the Philippines and Indonesia) it is far from solving the serious labour shortage of care for the elderly. The possibility of hiring domestic helpers at the destination countries is one of the important incentives for some elderly to live abroad after retirement. The very high age dependency rate also poses serious challenges to the national pension scheme. People are increasingly skeptical towards the current pension system and social welfare policies for elderly people in Japan. While the pension income remains limited, individuals' medical expenses are growing. The government White Paper on Ageing Society 2008 reported that 37.8% of the Japanese elderly (above the age 65 years old) feel financial insecurity, and about 60 % of Japanese elderly household earn less than 3,000,000 yen per year as income. More households are relying on state welfare than before.[36] These generated financial as well as welfare insecurity amongst Japanese new elders, making migration a feasible alternative.

But this certainly does not mean that every Japanese retiree is driven away from the country as an "economic-care refugee", as some of our informants have dubbed themselves. The super-ageing society has produced not only elderly who need care, but also relatively young elderly people who are actively seeking to build a second life. These "wealthy, healthy, older people"— called "whoopies"[37]—are interested in investing their 'second life' to attain a sense of satisfaction. Although Japan has been experiencing economic stagnation in the last twenty years or so the senior generation had a chance to benefit from the remarkable economic growth in the past. As a result it is reported that senior citizens (those over 50 years old comprise 42.7 per cent of the total population) hold 75 percent of individual wealth in Japan (2008). Indeed, we are observing a widening economic gap among Japanese senior population,[38] and migration overseas seems a feasible option for people across the income levels.

The increasing life expectancy means that elderly now have unprecedentedly long post-retirement life during which period active retirees face the problem of having too much "surplus time". Self-realization or pursuing "ikigai", which an anthropologist Gordon Mathews (1996) translated as "what makes a life worth living" in their retirement life is increasingly becoming key concern for Japanese elders. Before retirement, work and/ or raising children are the typical "ikigai" for Japanese people. After retirement, people start searching for something that can provide them alternative "ikigai" such as leisure activities, hobbies, and volunteer work which was not possible during the pre-retirement life. This self-conscious individualistic pursuit of "ikigai" in their 'second life' made retired elders important consumers of the emerging 'silver market'. These new generation of retirees are willing to consume products and service to fulfill their retirement lives by maximizing their savings and retirement fund.

36 Cabinet Office Japan, "White Paper on Ageing society in Heisei 20" http://www8.cao.go.jp/kourei/whitepaper/w-2008/zenbun/20index.html, retrieved on 2010/07/16

37 The term "whoopie" is mentioned as a person aged 58 by retired World Bank agricultural economist in the column "ecotourists: a personal profile" in the chapter on a new tourist class by Mowforth and Munt (1998: 131)

38 Cabinet Office Japan, "White Paper on Ageing society in Heisei 20" http://www8.cao.go.jp/kourei/whitepaper/w-2008/zenbun/20index.html, retrieved on 2010/07/16

Travelling abroad is one of such activities for retirees as it provides fresh socio-cultural experiences. The Long-Stay Foundation claims that long-stay tourism is effective for self-realization and creating "ikigai" (Long stay foundation 2005: 18). According to the Social Life Basic Survey, 10 percent of the senior population (60-69 years old) travels abroad at least once a year.[39] (See Table 1 for further details) Traveling abroad for Japanese retirees, therefore, not only reflects the socio-economic anxiety of an ageing society but is also a cultural phenomenon. Very often, the retirees became long-stay residents as a result of shorter trips. For example quite a few retirees decide to stay in Penang for a long time after visiting the place as tourists, or because they had worked in Malaysia for Japanese companies before retirement. In this sense we should understand long-stay as part of a wider spectrum of activities that consist of typical tourism visits at one end, and typical migration (permanent relocation) at the other.

Table 1: The number of Japanese seniors who went abroad (2008)

Age group	Numbers
50-54	1,357,514
55-59	1,490,023
60-64	1,318,517
65-69	824,878
70+	683,745
All senior age groups	5,674,677

39 Statistics Bureau, Director-General for Policy Planning and Statistical Research and Training Institute of the Ministry of Internal Affairs and Communications, "Heisei 18th Basic Survey on Social Life 2006 "http://www.stat.go.jp/data/shakai/2006/index.htm.

THE HISTORICAL EVOLUTION OF JAPANESE RETIREMENT MIGRATION

Although international retirement migration is a recent and rapidly developing phenomenon in Japan, the retirees' long-stay should be understood in a longer historical context. International outbound tourism, for which Japan is well known, is attributable to the recent development of retirement migration. The Japanese government de-regulated overseas travel of the Japanese nationals in 1964, and since then the number of Japanese overseas travel has been increasing. According to the Japanese Ministry of Justice (MOJ), more than 17 million Japanese traveled overseas in 2007 whereas only about 5 million did so in 1985.[40] This shows that in two decades the number of Japanese tourists traveling abroad has increased more than three-fold. Furthermore, according to the Ministry of Foreign Affairs (MOFA), the number of Japanese nationals residing overseas has been increasing and has surpassed one million since 2005.[41]

In terms of destinations, there was a clear "looking East" shift in the early 1990s. When Japan was hit by the economic downturn, Asian destinations became much more popular. The White Paper on Tourism shows that the number of Japanese tourists visiting PRC has more than doubled since the late 1990s whereas those visiting USA, Hawaii, Italy, and France are declining. According to the Ministry of Land, Infrastructure, Transport, and Tourism, Southeast and East Asian destinations constituted more than 50 percent of all destinations for Japanese outbound tourists in 2005.[42] The Japan Travel Bureau (JTB) reported that Southeast Asian destinations amounted to 17.5 percent of the market share for Japanese overseas tourism, the second largest market after the East Asian region (JTB 2009: 16). In 2008, according to the statistical data of Japan National Tourism Organization, the top 10 destinations for Japanese tourists consists of PRC, South Korea, USA, Hong Kong, Hawaii, Thailand Taiwan, Guam, France and Germany. (See Table 2 for further details).

---

40 See Ministry of Justice: http://www.moj.go.jp/PRESS/090108-1.html, retrieved 2009/06/30).

41 Ministry of Foreign Affairs, "Annual Report of Statistics on Japanese Nationals Overseas":http://www.mofa.go.jp/mofaj/toko/tokei/hojin/08/pdfs/1.pdf, (accessed 2009/06/30).

42 See Ministry of Land, Infrastructure, Transport, and Tourism: http://www.mlit.go.jp/ hakusyo/mlit/h16/hakusho/h17/index.html (accessed 2009/06/30).

Table 2: Top 10 destinations for Japanese tourists

Destinations in the East	Number	Destinations in the West	Number
P.R.C	3,446,117	U.S.A	3,249,578
South Korea	2,378,102	Hawaii	1,175,198
Hong Kong	1,324,797	Guam	850,034
Thailand	1,146,633	France	674,000
Taiwan	1,086,691	Germany	597,655
Singapore	571,040	Australia	457,232
Indonesia	546,713	Canada	287,198
Malaysia	433,462	Italy	283,819
Vietnam	392,999	Switzerland	277,657
Macau	366,920	U.K.	238,910

Source: Japan National Tourism Organization

The shift to Asia as the main overall destination also suits the needs of the Japanese elderly well. In choosing destinations, Japanese retirees are primarily concerned with warm climate, physical distance, familiarity and social networks. The difference in cost of living between the destination and Japan has significant weight in choosing destination including the possibility of hiring domestic helpers. Some Japanese retirees bring their own elderly old parents along to the destinations (Toyota 2006) where live-in care givers are available. In this regard, Japanese retirees are expecting to meet various demand of their life strategy by residing in Southeast Asian countries ranging from financial security, care provisions, as well as spiritual fulfillment in a later stage of life.

Compared to their European counterparts, Japanese international retirement migration, especially that to Southeast Asian countries, is a relatively new. Retirees from Western Europe such as British and German started to move to the Mediterranean in the 1970s (King, Warnes and Williams, 2000). In the case of international retirement migration within Europe, its growth has been shaped by three major factors: knowledge of and familiarity with foreign destinations; transport and accessibility; and legal and institutional barriers (King et al, 2000: 30). After the establishment of the European Union, international retirement migration has become intensified within the EU. The international migratory movement of citizens within the EU is facilitated by the Treaty on European Union (TEU) and the freedom of movement has long been central to the very idea of EU citizenship (Ackers and Dwyer, 2002: 1), whereas in Asian countries international mobility remains tightly restricted. While some states have developed policies to encourage foreign tourists they carefully guard against immigration.

The development of international retirement migration from Japan however followed a quite different trajectory. The movement was originally initiated by a government-led project, called the "Silver Columbia Plan '92". It was launched by the former Ministry of International Trade and Industry in 1986, reportedly after the Japanese government was inspired by foreign retirement communities in Spain. The project aimed to build a Japanese overseas retirement village somewhere with a lower cost of living, nicer climate, and better living environments (MITI, 1986). The plan, however, was criticized as a plan of the government to "export" its elderly. Subsequently the private sector took charge to establish the Long-Stay Foundation in 1992 to reform the plan and proposed not as "migration" of older people but as "long-stay" encouraging a new style of leisure activity for a wider variety of people. In the beginning the preferred destinations used to be western destinations such as Hawaii, Canada, Australia, West Coast of U.S., and New Zealand. However, the preference has shifted from Western to Asian countries. In 2007, Malaysia was voted the most desirable destination followed by Australia, Thailand, Hawaii, and New Zealand.[43]

Japanese international retirement migration to Southeast Asia has been increasing since the late 1990s due to new national development strategies of the destination countries. The new policies – issuing special visas for foreign retirees such as "non-immigrant 'o-a' (long stay)" and "non-immigrant 'o' (pension)" in Thailand, 'Special Resident Retiree's Visa (SRRV)' in the Philippines, and "lansia or lanjut usia (retirement)" in Indonesia – enabled the new form of transnational mobility. Both Thailand and Malaysia have also been receiving international flows of

---

43 The annual survey was conducted by Long-Stay Foundation

patients by promoting health/medical tourism (cf. Chee, 2007, Toyota 2007). In the case of Malaysia, although the current linkage between the medical tourism industry and the overseas retirement program does not appear strong, each could potentially gain from the other (Chee, 2007:17). Whereas in case of Thailand, many retirees noted that the internationally recognized medical facilities made them feel at ease in choosing the country as a long stay destination. In the Philippines, large scale facilities, such as nursing homes and retirement villages at resorts, are being developed, specifically targeting Japanese elderly as customers (Toyota 2008).

As a result, a "retirement industry" is being developed fast. The emerging industry has three key components: 1) the tourist industry that was the pioneer by initiating "long-stay tourism" targeting foreign retirees; 2) the real estate industry that has identified the so-called Retirement and Second Home (RSH) purchasers as increasingly important customers and promote second home ownership by foreign retirees; and 3) the medical service industry providing medical care services for foreign consumers. Issuing long-term residential visas for affluent foreign retirees facilitates the mobility of foreign retirees to the destinations. The exact scale of the industry is difficult to estimate but the expectation of the growth is high due to the general global trend of ageing populations. Across the region, Japanese retirees are one of the prime targets of this emerging retirement industry. For example, Japanese comprise 17 percent of the total number of medical tourists in Thailand in 2007, compared to 136,000 from U.S.A. (9.9%), 110,000 from U.K. (8.0%), and 169,000 from Middle East (12.4%) in 2007. Thus, in order to understand the Japanese retirement migration phenomenon, we have to examine government policies and industry initiatives in the host country. The next section will be devoted to this issue.

PENANG CALLING: PULL FACTORS IN MALAYSIA

In a landmark event for the post-war connections between the two countries, Malaysian Airlines launched a direct flight between Kuala Lumpur and Tokyo when Tourism Malaysia opened a branch office in Tokyo in 1974. Malaysia was actively marketed as tourism destination for Japanese tourists for the first time in 1980 when the Japan branch office of the Pacific Asia Travel Association (PATA) held a seminar on "Malaysia and Singapore for women and honeymooners" in Japan. The governments of Japan and Malaysia agreed in 1983 to mutually exempt citizens of either country from visa requirements for a stay up to three months. This policy was crucial for making Malaysia a long-stay destination firstly under the Silver Hair Programme and then under the Malaysia My Second Home Programme (MM2H). By availing themselves of the visa exemption policy, Japanese elderly could move to and stay in Malaysia as tourists to try out the place. They could then commit themselves to the MM2H Programme if they were convinced that Malaysia was a suitable place for their retirement life.

The Malaysian government has played a critical role in attracting foreign expatriates and residents. The government launched the 'Silver Hair' program, an inbound migration policy for foreign retired people above fifty years old, in 1988. Under this program, applicants were not allowed to work or earn income inside Malaysia, and were required to deposit a certain amount of money (RM 150,000) in Malaysian banks. It aimed to increase the income from tourism and to stimulate the economy by active foreign investment and earning foreign currency. Although the Malaysian government anticipated 20,000 applications, by 2000 they have received less than 900 (New Straits Times, 14 February, 2002). Consequently, the government shifted the authorization of the program from the Immigration Department to the Ministry of Tourism in 2002, renamed it as the 'Malaysia My Second Home' (MM2H) program, and reformed the visa system so that MM2H applicants would get a 10-year multiple entry social visit pass. The terms and conditions of the program have been revised several times since 2002. For example, limitations based on nationality and age have been abolished, and applicants are now allowed to bring their spouses, unmarried children (below the age of 21) and parents above the age of 60 as dependants. Foreign applicants need to show that they have liquid assets worth more than RM 350,000 and some form of a monthly income, such as a pension, if they were above 50. For applicants aged 50 and below, they have to show they have liquid assets worth RM 500,000 when applying and a monthly income of RM 10,000. The authorities have also tightened the procedure as they suspect the inflow of illegal workers disguised under MM2H, which led to a decrease in the numbers of entrants from the PRC and Bangladesh between 2005 and 2007 (See Table 3). Upon approval, the applicant will have to keep

RM300,000 in a fixed deposit account in a bank in Malaysia. He or she will be able to withdraw up to RM 150,000 from the second year onwards if he/she wishes to use the money. As of November 2010, 14,675 participants from more than 75 countries registered under MM2H (See Table 3 for further details).

Table 3: Top 10 countries of participants in MM2H programmes (2002-2010)

Country	2002	2003	2004	2005	2006	2007	2008	2009	2010 Nov	Total
PRC	241	521	468	502	242	90	120	114	120	2418
Bangladesh	0	32	204	852	341	149	68	86	67	1799
UK	108	159	210	199	209	240	208	162	129	1624
Japan	49	99	42	87	157	198	210	169	189	1200
Iran	0	2	8	7	9	59	227	212	200	724
Singapore	96	143	91	62	94	58	48	61	70	723
Taiwan	38	95	140	186	63	31	16	36	45	650
India	45	123	118	80	51	46	32	35	44	574
Indonesia	88	118	104	54	63	25	27	53	24	556
Pakistan	9	55	82	104	36	31	65	103	70	555
Others	144	298	450	482	464	576	491	547	400	3852
Total	818	1645	1917	2615	1729	1503	1512	1578	1358	14675

(Source: Ministry of Tourism, Malaysia)

Japanese retirees are seen as one of major client groups for the MM2H Programme. The Ministry of Tourism and its counterpart body representing the tourist industry, Tourism Malaysia, organized large promotion events for several times in Japan. It released MM2H promotional DVDs in English, Japanese, and Korean so as to provide them to potential applicants for free. It also published a free guidebook and newsletters on MM2H especially for the Japanese market by collaborating with Japanese associations. In addition, the Malaysian government has recently aired a TV commercial on MM2H in England, Japan, and Korea. The Ministry of Tourism set up the one stop center where MM2H licensed agents bring in application forms and it also functions as information desk for international tourists regarding MM2H. One Japanese female staff and one Korean female staff were hired to liaise with these client groups. According to the interview conducted by NNA, the Secretary General of the Ministry of Tourism Malaysia, Dato Ong said, "MM2H has grown up to occupy one of the important positions in tourism policies." Malaysia aims to reach 1700 approvals in 2010 and wants to increase them by 10 % every year from next year.

According to the latest statistics provided by the Malaysian Ministry of Tourism, Iran, Japan and UK constituted the top three nationalities of participants in the MM2H programme for first eleven months of 2010. As a result of the marketing efforts made by the Malaysian authorities, 47 participants from the Republic of Korea have joined MM2H, moving Korea to 9th spot in terms of participants (See table 4). Malaysia aims to receive more upper and middle class people as targeted groups.[44] Malaysia will continue to see Japan as important market and promote MM2H more to Japanese people. The increase of the frequency of direct flights between Malaysia and Japan may also make the MM2H popular among the Japanese. Malaysia Airlines now operates regular flights from KL International Airport to Osaka and Narita. By the end of 2010 both Malaysia Airlines and AirAsia would start direct flights to Haneda, near Tokyo.

Table 4: Top 10 countries of participants in MM2H programmes (Jan-Nov 2010)

	Country	Number
1	Iran	200
2	Japan	189
3	UK	129
4	PRC	120
5	Pakistan	70
5	Singapore	70
7	Bangladesh	67
8	Australia	59
9	Rep. of Korea	47
10	Taiwan	45
	Others	362
Total		1358

44 NNA, 25 June 2010, "The Ministry of Tourism improved long-term visa system, attracting more Japanese etc.", http://news.nna.jp/free/news/20100625myr002A.html, retrieved on 2010/07/20

While the MM2H is open to any age groups, most Japanese applicants are retirees in their 50s and 60s. For example, in 2007 the total number of Japanese MM2H approved applications was 349. The number of applicants aged in their 60s was 152 (99 male and 53 female) and in their 50s was 124 (54 male and 70 female).[45] This is an interesting contrast to Korean MM2H applicants, who are mostly in their 30s and 40s who bring their unmarried children below the age of 21 as dependents. Conversely, some Japanese retirees bring their elderly parents above the age of 70 as dependents. The different motivation in joining the MM2H Programme between Japanese and Koreans is observed from the characteristics of the applicants. Obviously the MM2H Programme needs to be modified in order to accommodate the different needs of diverse populations. Simply translating the same promotional materials into different languages may not be sufficient. For this purpose, it may be necessary for the Ministry of Tourism to collect more detailed data about the MM2H applicants, differentiated by age and gender. The current statistics collected by the Ministry of Tourism are rather confusing as it counts by household instead of individuals, which means that an application collectively lodged by three members of a family (e.g. a couple with a child) is counted as "one" in the same way as an application by a single person. This explains the discrepancy between our data and the official statistics: for instance, a total of 349 Japanese persons joined the MM2H scheme in 2007, whereas the Malaysian official data recorded 198 applications (See Table 3).

Besides the Ministry of Tourism of Malaysia, there are various other key players that are actively involved in the MM2H programme. In the case of the Japanese market, it seems a self perpetuating mechanism has been developed as some of the pioneer individuals who are Japanese retirees themselves play a critical role in promoting the country and encouraging further migration to Malaysia. For example, Mr Sakamoto published a handbook titled "Rewarding life in Malaysia: Shall we live in Malaysia after retirement?" that asserts that Malaysia is the best place for retirement life. In his book, Sakamoto (2006) explains the economic benefit of living in Malaysia, such as the low cost of living and relief from dual taxation. He declares that he intends to stay in Malaysia for the rest of his life. This handbook and his website are widely read, and he is a popular information resource person for the newcomers. Other books have also appeared in Japan recently. Like Sakamoto's most of them are based on the experiences

45 Data received at the one stop center during fieldwork in 2008.

and advices from individual retirees who are already residing in Malaysia. The Long-stay in Malaysia calls the country a "retirement heaven" (Rashin 2004). Some of the typical appealing descriptions of Malaysia include: a relatively safe country with political stability; cost of living within the pension budget (e.g. average monthly rent for two bedrooms at RM1500) is one third of that in Japan; English is widely spoken by locals; distance from Japan and time difference (only one hour); rich in nature with beautiful beaches and rain forests; warm winter and cooler summer than that in Tokyo and Osaka; variety of food (Japanese food and ingredients are available); friendly locals; and finally, of course, the "golf heaven":

Such discursive depictions of the image of the destination are particularly important for retirement migration, as the retirees usually start preparing their retirement life a few years in advance and spend considerable time collecting information by attending seminars, reading books and joining some kind of information network group. The fact that Malaysia was voted as "the most desirable destination" since 2007 was widely known among our informants. Japanese retirement migration to Malaysia, in this regard, may be called "life-style migration", whereby the stylization of migration has been created through various media, including guidebooks (Ono 2009). These media materials create the impression that Japanese elderly can enjoy life in Malaysia without having to speak any foreign language. Our fieldwork data show that the foreign language proficiency of Japanese retirees is considerably lower than that of MM2H participants from other countries. It is not uncommon that some Japanese retirees who had never lived abroad before retirement expected that life in Malaysia would be just as secure and convenient for them as it was in Japan. Inevitably some of them faced difficulties in everyday matters, such as in communication with taxi drivers, or became easy targets of petty crimes. Their limited ability in communicating in local languages also hindered them from making local friends and getting involved with the local community, despite a strong desire to do so as indicated in our interviews. Assistance from the local authorities and community would be crucial to establish psychological bonding and a sense of belonging for these retirees.

The statistical data of Japanese Embassy in Malaysia shows that 5,358 Japanese nationals live in Selangor (inclusive of Kuala Lumpur and Petaling Jaya), 1,665 in Penang, and 74 in Pahang state in which the

Cameron Highlands is located.[46] However, due to the seasonal pendulum of mobility patterns it is extremely difficult to estimate the actual number of Japanese retirees residing in Malaysia (Toyota et al. 2006). Some long-term retirees may be holding tourist visas without taking up the MM2H visa, and thus do not register with the Japanese embassy in Malaysia. Others may be frequently moving back and forth – e.g. staying in Malaysia during the winter time for three months or so to avoid the cold weather in Japan but returning during the cherry blossom season, and again coming back to Malaysia during the summer etc. It is therefore not surprising that the estimated number differs from various sources. Japanese nationals who reside in Malaysia and have registered with the Embassy of Japan in Malaysia numbered 701 in 2009[47] whereas the number of Japanese registered under MM2H is 1011 in 2009.[48] On the other hand, one of the MM2H agents estimated that there are about 200 to 300 MM2H Japanese retirement settlers in Kuala Lumpur, 300 to 400 in Penang and about 30 in the Cameron Highlands, where the number can be up to 300 during the peak season. It is estimated that there are twice as many seasonal long-stayers as settlers.

Among the four popular destinations for Japanese retirees in Malaysia - Kuala Lumpur, Penang, the Cameron Highlands, and Kota Kinabalu - Penang has been the first prime retirement destination. This certainly has something to do with Penang's economic position. Penang has also been known as a commercial center in Southeast Asia and holds the second largest population of Japanese nationals inside Malaysia. More than 150 Japanese multinational corporations have their factories and branch offices in Penang and their expatriate workers and their families stay for extended periods. The population of Japanese nationals who reside in Penang has kept growing from 1,432 in 1999 to 1,632 in 2008 in spite of the fact that the number of Japanese nationals in all Malaysia has declined due to the gradual shift of production bases of Japanese multinational corporations to neighboring countries. We have reason to speculate that it is precisely the increase in the number of Japanese long-stay retirees that offsets the declining number of Japanese corporate expatriates.

---

46 Japanese Embassy in Malaysia
47 Embassy of Japan in Malaysia, http://www.my.emb-japan.go.jp/Japanese/ryoji/census/2010. htm retrieved 2010/07/20
48 Ministry of Tourism, Malaysia.

Penang has been consciously developed to be one of the prominent long-stay destinations for Japanese retirees since the mid-1990s. Three MM2H agents—private companies accredited by the MM2H programme to provide relevant services to foreign customers—in Penang have all specifically targeted Japanese clients. Two of them are Japanese married to Malaysians and are living in Penang permanently, and the third is a Malaysian who speaks fluent Japanese. The Malaysian agent's business was booming, he had accumulated more than 350 Japanese customers since he started the business. They have contributed greatly reaching out to the Japanese market by providing customized services in Japanese. These agents not only provided pre-departure services but also helped them to settle down. They have facilitated creating Japanese associations, such as the Japan Club of Penang and an exclusive salon based on membership, where Japanese retirees can mingle with each other. These social networks help to ease the anxiety of Japanese retirees who often face language barriers at the destination.

What are Penang's attractions for the Japanese retirees? The ethnic component of Penang, Chinese being the majority ethnic group, is said to make the Japanese feel comfortable. The issue of race hardly surfaced in our interviews, what stands out as a more important concern is general lifestyle, specifically about food. Although there is a Japanese store where Japanese products and ingredients imported are available, some retirees frequently eat out and the ubiquitous Chinese food makes this an easy solution. One retiree told us: "My husband and I dine out every night with our friends. I appreciate it because I do not have to cook. We have more fun to eat out because we go many different restaurants in a group so that we can taste many different things, especially Chinese food. Someone call us or we call someone to meet up for dinner every day" (Female/63 years old living in Penang for four years).

One of the MM2H agents explains that sea view and beach is the biggest attraction for Japanese retirees in choosing Penang for long-stay or retirement settlement. Penang as the "Pearl of the Orient," has been known among Japanese as one of the prominent beach resorts in Southeast Asia since the 1980s. Residing next to seaside evokes the image of a tropical paradise, which matches the popular image of an ideal retirement life. Such images are repeatedly projected by Japanese TV programs, newspapers and guide books which publicize long stay retirement life in

Penang. The image that Penang is a "cultured" place is another draw. After George Town was registered as a world heritage site in 2008, Penang has started being recognized not just a beach resort but a historical site with colonial/historical architectures and has attracted educated middle class, well-educated Japanese retirees.

But there is still a clear difference between long stay and permanent settlement. At the same time as new comers arrive in Penang constantly, we also observe outflows of Japanese retirees. Many cited the inconvenience in everyday life as a main reason. For example, insufficient public transport in Penang forces Japanese retirees either to purchase their own cars or to leave Penang for elsewhere. Some long stay retirees complain that taxis do not charge by the meter, which means that Japanese retirees have to negotiate the price with taxi drivers with limited English. This can be not only bothersome but often causes trouble and summon a sense of unfairness and "being cheated because we are Japanese." Once they start feeling negative about the destination, they are quick in moving on to other places because they are committed to searching for a fulfilling retirement life which can be anywhere. This explains why not so many Japanese retirees are interested in purchasing the property at the destination. While property development is an integrated part of the MM2H Programme, Japanese retirees prefer renting instead of purchasing and prefer a simple (or humble) rather than sumptuous lifestyle after retirement.

The Japanese retirees' nostalgia for rural life is another important reason why some of the retirees decided to leave Penang. Some retirees who have stayed in Penang for a few years under the MM2H moved to Ipoh, Cameron Highlands, or Kota Kinabalu to seek a "rural" and natural environment. For them, Penang is losing its attraction due to many high rise condos. Excessive urban development destroys the city's charm and scenery. It is ironic that the very purpose of the MM2H Programme, particularly property development, is undermining the popularity of the destination for MM2H customers.

DISCUSSION

Penang's history, population and especially its sea view with beach and blue skies have made the island a top overseas long-stay destination for

Japanese retirees. But in order to understand the underlying dynamics of the flows, this paper has examined how specific socioeconomic effects of population ageing in Japan, policies in the destination countries, and private sector have all played important part in the making of the transnational flows of Japanese retirees. The role of the public media, individual and corporate intermediary agents, and last but certainly not least, the retirees' personal life strategies and desires, should not be ignored. The migration of Japanese retirees to Penang should thus be best understood as a social phenomenon that emerges from the interaction of an assemblage of various actors located in different places and at different levels (Toyota 2008).

Using this analytical lens, we have observed two somewhat contradictory dynamics in the migration to Penang. On one hand, a self-perpetuating mechanism of the flows is discernable. A few early-comers actively published their experiences as that of "successful" cosmopolitan retirees who enjoy fulfilling, and even a glamorous retirement life in a foreign land. With the development of the Japanese community in Penang and networks spanning across Malaysia and to Japan, more retirees became interested in moving to Penang.

On the other hand, some Japanese retirees moved out of Penang. Although each individual has different reasons for doing so, it seems that a gap between the expectations of Malaysian policy makers and retirement industry and Japanese retirees' needs and desires was a main cause for this. Most notably, the Malaysian government and industries strived to develop and sell properties to MM2H customers, while the majority of the Japanese retirees are planning to stay in Malaysia temporarily. The retirees cherish the freedom and flexibility of being a temporary resident and see mobility between different places as to their advantage. This explains their relatively low level of interest in purchasing property — only 10 percent of Japanese MM2H retirees in Malaysia purchased a property. The retirees are neither tourists nor immigrants but "transit" residents. The quality of their retirement life can be achieved only by constantly seeking desirable destinations. They are willing to pay for their leisure activities such as golfing and traveling, but are unwilling to take risks in making a financial and psychological commitment to the temporary second home.

Chapter 10

Medical Tourism in Penang: A Brief Review of the Sector

Su-Ann Oh

INTRODUCTION

Medical tourism is being developed as a priority area in the Malaysian tourism industry. Of all the cities and towns in the country offering medical services to visitors seeking treatment, Penang generates the most revenue, receiving around a third of the visitors who travel to Malaysia for this purpose. This chapter presents basic information available on medical tourism in Penang, and situates this information within the context of tourism in Malaysia and the region.

The discussion begins with a brief description of medical tourism in Malaysia and the region as a backdrop to the trends in Penang. The focus then narrows to a consideration of medical tourism in the state, looking first at the number of visitor patients in the state over the past few years and then at the revenues generated. Information on visitor patients' country of origin, the type of procedures that are commonly sought, and their preference for Penang is summarised. Following this, the efforts of the state and federal governments as well as the corporate sector in developing the medical tourism sector in Penang and Malaysia are discussed. The effect of medical tourism industry on the domestic population's access to quality healthcare is also highlighted. Finally, some policy recommendations are made based on the discussion on medical tourism in Penang.

The terms medical tourism and health tourism are often used interchangeably. However, the former is mostly used to describe the range of medical treatments that are necessary for diagnosing and treating illness, such as tests, surgical procedures and recovery treatment. In contrast, the term health tourism often includes wellness and wellbeing programmes along the lines of therapeutic treatments in spas. In this chapter, the discussion pertains to medical tourism unless otherwise specified.

MEDICAL TOURISM IN MALAYSIA AND THE REGION

In Southeast Asia, governments and hospitals in Malaysia, Singapore and Thailand embarked on a marketing campaign to cater to the medical needs of visitors after the financial crisis of 1997 (with Singapore starting a little earlier). In fact, the governments of these countries have been directly involved in promoting medical tourism in their respective countries (Chee, 2007: 3). These three countries compete with one another for medical tourism revenue.

Quoting Frost & Sullivan's Dr. Pawel Suwinski in 2009, the International Medical Travel Journal reported that medical tourism in Malaysia grew at a rate of 25.3 percent a year since 1998, with revenues growing at a rate of 37.9 percent during the same period (IMTJ, 2009: 1). Revenue per patient grew 2.5 fold from 1998 to 2008. Estimates of private hospital receipts for members of the Penang Health Association were RM 156.53 million in 2007 and RM 166.15 million in 2008. About 15% to 30% of their patients are medical tourists (The Star, 14 February 2009). This means that between RM25 million (USD 8.2 million) and RM 50 million (USD 16.4 million) of revenue reported by these hospitals came from medical tourists.

The figures for medical tourism in Thailand come from Bumrumgard Hospital in Bangkok, which is usually taken to reflect trends in the medical tourism industry. In 2003, 800,000 foreign visitors went to Bumrumgard for medical treatment, paying more than 19 billion baht (USD 618 million) (The Straits Times, 19 March 2005).

Singapore is the only country of the three which has comprehensive and updated statistics. Medical tourism receipts amounted to SGD 732 million (USD 571 million) in 2009, with the bulk of patients coming from Indonesia, Thailand, Malaysia and the Philippines (83.6%). This is a fall from SGD 1,025.4 million in 2008, but still higher than SGD 561.3 million in 2005 (Singapore Tourism Board, 2010:10).

In 2007, nearly 75% of medical tourists arriving in Malaysia were from Indonesia (SERI, 2009: 15). The Malaysian government extended the visa period for health tourists from one month to six months allowing visitors to stay for longer periods. Major hospitals in Malaysia are also targeting patients from new markets in Vietnam and Cambodia. There have also been reports of Africans going to Malaysia because it is cheaper to do so rather than to travel to Europe as some did in the past (IMTJ, 2009: 8).

MEDICAL TOURISM IN PENANG: SOME FACTS

Numbers and scale
The number of visitors seeking medical treatment in Penang from 2003-2007 is shown in Table 1.

Table 1: Number of visitor patients to Penang and receipts

Year	Inpatient	Outpatient	Total patients	Receipts (RM mil)
2003	NA	NA	102,946[a]	58.9[a]
2004	NA	NA	174,189[a]	104.98[a]
2005	NA	NA	232,161[a]	150.92[a]
2006	NA	NA	296,687[a]	203.66[a]
2007	NA	NA	341,288[a]	253.84[a]
2008	17,271[b]	209,020[b]	226,291[b]	183.65[b]
2009	15,700[b]	187,050[b]	202,750[b]	164.68[b]
Jan-Mar 2010	4,870[b]	56,273[b]	61,143[b]	53.54[b]

[a] *Source: adapted from Association of Private Hospitals of Malaysia (APHM) as cited by SERI. "Medical Tourism – A New Growth Frontier for Penang in 2009 and Beyond." Penang Economic Monthly. Vol.11 No. 4. 2009, p. 11.*

[b] *Penang Global Tourism as cited in SERI. "Penang Blueprint 2010" draft. 2010c, p. 11.*

Table 1 shows that the number of patients increased steadily and threefold between 2003 and 2007. Revenue from visitor patients increased by slightly more than four times between 2003 and 2007.

The figures for 2008-2010 are available from a separate source, Penang Global Tourism.[49] There was a decrease in the number of visitor patients from 2008 to 2009. This fall has been attributed to both the financial crisis and the outbreak of the H1N1 virus in 2009. The table also shows that the overwhelming number of visitor patients underwent outpatient treatment. Recent figures estimate revenue from medical tourism in Penang reaching RM 230 million in 2010 (Visit Penang, 2011).

Taking into account the inconsistencies in the figures in Table 1, a rough estimate of the percentage of visitors who sought medical services in Penang out of all visitors is listed in Table 2. These figures have to be taken with some caution, since the base numbers are neither consistent nor accurate.

---

49 In using these figures, it is important to take into account possible inconsistencies and inaccuracies. First, the figures for Tables 1 and 2 are not comparable because the data were collected by different agencies; they may not have used the same conventions and definitions. For example, there may be inconsistencies in the use of terms such as medical and health tourism. The sources of information cited in this chapter do not make this clear. Further, the figures for visitor patients may not distinguish between 1) tourists who fall sick or are injured during their visit and require medical attention, 2) foreign patients who travelled to Malaysia expressly for the purpose of medical treatment and care and 3) foreign residents in the country. Second, the figures may be incomplete, particularly in the earlier years because not all hospitals provide statistics to the body collecting these figures, such as the Ministry of Health (Chee 2007). There are few other sources of information. The Visitor Profile Survey, previously conducted by the Penang Tourism Action Council in collaboration with Socio Economic and Environmental Research Institute (SERI) was discontinued three years ago. The result is that there are no accurate figures for the number and type of visitors to Penang over the last three years (SERI 2010a).

Table 2: Penang medical tourism visitor numbers as percentage of tourists in Penang

	2005	2006	2007	2008	2009	2010 (Jan-May)
Estimated number of visitors seeking medical treatment	232,161[a]	296,687[a]	341,288[b]	226,291[b]	202,750[b]	61,143[b]
Estimated Total Visitor Arrivals for the State	3.09 mil[c]	3.08 mil[c]	3.44 mil[c]	N/A	N/A	0.865 mil[c]
Estimate of visitors who are medical tourists	7.5%	9.6%	9.9%	N/A	N/A	7%

a Source: adapted from Association of Private Hospitals of Malaysia (APHM) as cited by SERI. "Medical Tourism – A New Growth Frontier for Penang in 2009 and Beyond." *Penang Economic Monthly*. Vol.11 No. 4. 2009, p. 11.

b Penang Global Tourism as cited in SERI. "Penang Blueprint 2010" draft. 2010c, p. 11.

c SERI. Penang Statistics Quarter 3, 2010. Penang: Socio-Economic and Environmental Research Institute, 2010b, p. 1.

Table 2 shows that approximately seven to 10 percent of visitors to Penang were recorded as seeking some form of medical treatment.

Revenue

In an article on the Visit Penang website, the state was hailed as the leading medical tourism provider in Malaysia, earning the lion's share (two-thirds) of the RM 250 million profit in the industry nationwide (Visit Penang, 2009). In the same article, Yang Bhg Dato' Dr Chan Kok Ewe, chairperson of the Penang Health Association was quoted as saying that Penang recorded RM 171 million in revenue from medical tourism in 2008 and it was expected that the figure would increase to RM 180 million in 2009. The figure in Table 2, at RM 164,685,351, shows that revenues in 2009 actually fell short of his expectations.

The figures in Table 2 show that the revenue from medical tourism in Penang grew between 2003 and 2007 with a dip in 2008 and 2009. This follows the national trend. According to data from the Association of Private Hospitals Malaysia (APHM), the number of foreign patients in Malaysia grew at an average annual rate of 21.4% from 2004 to 2008 (Chee, 2010: 343). The revenue generated in 2008 was RM 299.1 million (USD 90.5 million), bringing the average growth rate of revenue for that time period to 30.3%.

An average growth rate of 45.3% in revenue from medical tourism in Penang was recorded between the years 2003 and 2007, according to the figures in Table 1. Looking more closely at the figures though, we see that the growth rate is actually falling from year to year. Since 2008 and 2009 are not included, the fall cannot be attributed to the financial crisis or to the H1N1 virus. Readers are cautioned about the accuracy and validity of the base figures.

Table 3 uses figures from Table 1 for a crude analysis of revenue figures.

Table 3 Estimated revenue per visitor patient in Penang

Year	No. of patients	Receipts (RM mil)	Revenue per patient
2003[a]	102,946	58,900,000	572.14
2004[a]	174,189	104,980,000	602.68
2005[a]	232,161	150,920,000	650.07
2006[a]	296,687	203,660,000	686.45
2007[a]	341,288	253,840,000	743.77
2008[b]	226,291	183,653,563	811.58
2009[b]	202,750	164,685,351	812.25
Jan-Mar 2010[b]	61,143	53,548,602	875.79

[a] *Source: adapted from Association of Private Hospitals of Malaysia (APHM) as cited by SERI. "Medical Tourism – A New Growth Frontier for Penang in 2009 and Beyond." Penang Economic Monthly. Vol.11 No. 4. 2009, p. 11.*

[b] *Penang Global Tourism as cited in SERI. "Penang Blueprint 2010" draft. 2010c, p. 11.*

This rough average of revenue earned per patient shows that the amount has been increasing every year. This could mean that 1) there has been a rise in the price of treatments and/or 2) over the years, foreign patients have sought costlier treatments. The reason(s) for this trend may be discerned from data on the cost of treatment across the years and the types of treatment sought by foreign patients.

Invest-Penang reported that, after manufacturing, tourism is the biggest contributor to the Penang economy, although no actual figures were presented (Invest-in-Penang Berhad, 2010). Figures showing the revenue from medical tourism as a percentage of overall tourist receipts and of the economy in Penang would provide us with a picture of the significance of medical tourism to the tourism industry and the GDP of Penang.

Patient demographics
In 2007, nearly 75% of medical tourists arriving in Malaysia were from Indonesia (SERI, 2009:15). Citing figures provided by APHM, SERI reported that about 70% of the patients and revenues from medical tourism came from Indonesia, followed by those from Singapore at roughly 10% (SERI, 2009: 11). The rest were from Japan, India, Europe and other countries. Estimates vary, but it is clear that the overwhelming majority of visitors seeking medical treatment come from Indonesia (Chee, 2007: 343). In Penang, about 90 to 95% of all medical tourists are from Indonesia (SERI, 2009: 15).

Visit Penang reported that medical tourists, made up mostly of Indonesians, rose from 202,000 patients in 2009 to 250,000 patients in 2010 (Visit Penang, 2011). The increase was also attributed to the newly introduced Penang-Surabaya air route by AirAsia.

In 2007, the majority of medical tourists going to Malaysia were the middle and upper classes from countries where 'quality' healthcare services are not available – Indonesia, Vietnam, China, Burma and Cambodia (Chee, 2007:15). The other group of patients consists of visitors from developed countries where waiting lists are long and private services are costlier. This is in direct contrast to the foreign patients in Thailand. While Thailand has a similar medical tourism market profile as Malaysia, most overseas patients in that country are from Japan, the US, the UK, China and Indochina. Considering the global economic upheavals of 2008 and

2009, it would be interesting to see if the composition of medical tourists has changed in both countries.

While it is commonly assumed that the rich are the ones who travel overseas for medical treatments, there have been reports that those in the middle income bracket in western Europe and Northern America have also found cost benefits to seeking medical treatment in countries such as Malaysia and Thailand (SERI, 2004).

SERI warned of the risks to the medical tourism sector in Penang of relying on patients from one particular country, arguing that a more diverse client base would counter possible country-specific (or rather Indonesia-specific) risks. To address this, the Penang Health Association was quoted as calling for more concerted marketing and promotion in the Middle East (SERI, 2009:14).

Type of procedure
According to Datuk Dr K Kulaveerasingam, who headed the health tourism committee of the Association of Private Hospitals of Malaysia (APHM) in 2004, the procedures sought by foreign patients going to Malaysia were for coronary heart disease, plastic surgery, hip and knee implants, dental implants and high end diagnostic services (Chee, 2007:15). In Penang, the services most in demand by foreign patients are: cardiology, cardiothoracic surgery, general surgery, orthopaedic, eye, and obstetric-gynaecologist services and general medical screening (SERI, 2004). In 2004, Penang was labelled as a prime destination for cosmetic surgery which accounted for about 23 percent of the treatment sought in 2001-2003 (Chee, 2007:15).

This information is consistent with the type of procedures usually sought after by medical tourists. While medical tourism may theoretically include all medical treatments, it is traditionally known for hip replacements, cardiac, orthopaedic, cosmetic, and dental procedures because of the constraints of medical travel (The Star, 2 May 2010). First, patients need to be able to travel safely by plane without complications. The second consideration is the time constraints faced by visiting patients. They need to be able to undergo assessments, complete tests or treatments, and recover at the destination to be fit enough to travel home within a certain period of time.

Preference for Penang
The Visit Penang website attributes visitor patients' preference to the advanced medical facilities, good service, competitive cost, and general infrastructure in Penang. According to the website, the cost of medical treatment and services in Penang is five times lower than in the US and European countries (Visit Penang, 2009).

While there is a combination of reasons why Penang is selected, cost seems to be considered a significant factor in media reports. Without a doubt, this is one of the advantages that Malaysia has over Singapore. However, low cost as a competitive edge has to be taken in the context of the competition in the region. Although the cost of health treatments in Singapore is on average 40% higher than in Malaysia, Singapore manages to attract a large number of foreign patients based on its reputation as a 'leading medical hub and its impressive supporting infrastructure' (SERI, 2004: 7). In addition, despite an accelerated growth rate in Malaysia's foreign patient numbers between 2004 and 2008, its revenue from foreign patients was only about one-eighth of Singapore's earnings in 2008 (Chee, 2010: 343).

The medical tourism industry in Singapore is distinctly different from that in Malaysia. Singapore has been catering to the medical needs of the upper-middle classes Indonesians and Malaysians since the 1980s. Since the Asian financial crisis in 1997, the number of Indonesians and Malaysians, while still making up the majority of foreign patients, has fallen. Patients from the US, Canada, the UK, Brunei and South Asia have increased.[50]

THE DEVELOPMENT OF MEDICAL TOURISM IN PENANG

According to Chee, the 1997 Asian financial crisis marked the beginning of Malaysia's focus on developing medical tourism as a growth industry. The Malaysian state has been directly involved in promoting medical tourism in the form of tax incentives to support the development of healthcare corporations, the creation of institutional infrastructure and directly leading in the marketing and promotion of medical tourism overseas (Chee, 2007: 25 and Chee, 2010: 345).

---

50 Khoo, 2003 cited in Chee, 2007: 20.

In the early 2000s, the Malaysian government appointed 35 private hospitals country-wide to promote as key players in medical tourism (Chee, 2007: 12). The majority of these hospitals are situated in Kuala Lumpur and Selangor, followed by eight in Penang and two in Melaka. Moreover, there have been reinforced and regular initiatives to encourage growth in this sector. In June 2010, the Ministry of Health set up the Malaysian Healthcare Travel Council to promote the country's healthcare services abroad (The Star, 25 June 2010). At the same time, dentists have been urged to participate in the medical tourism industry and there has been a further relaxation on the conventions on advertising for health care (The Star, 15 November 2010).

Some of the reasons that have been cited for promoting medical tourism in Malaysia (and Penang) as a growth industry are that it is a sustainable growth sector and that it is considered relatively recession-proof (SERI, 2009:12). However, there are also other reasons: it provides close linkages to the presence of manufacturing capabilities in Penang such as the production of medical devices, automation and electronics, thereby providing a strong foundation for future economic growth (Kharas, Zeufack, and Majeed, 2010: 35); it generates employment for skilled workers; and it feeds into other initiatives put forward by the state government, such as the Penang Medical College.

In the beginning of 2010, the Penang State government, as part of efforts to enhance Penang's strength in medical tourism, announced the development of Pulau Jerejak as a medical tourism centre. The 362 hectare island off the east coast of Penang island will be developed into a medical tourism centre for the region. It was reported that incentive packages would be provided to develop the medical tourism industry.[51]

Despite government efforts, private hospital executives have expressed disappointment in the lack of supporting infrastructure provided by the state government, such as transportation and public safety (SERI, 2004: 22). In addition, they flagged the lack of coordination among hospitals in Penang, and between the state government and the hospitals as stumbling blocks to ensuring a joined approach to improving the quality of medical tourism and in marketing it to other countries, particularly when compared

---

51 Penang State Government, "Penang to undergo transformation into major logistics, transportation hub", 19 January 2010.

to Singapore (SERI, 2009:14). The Penang State government was criticised for not taking full advantage of promoting Malaysia's capacity to offer medical services and infrastructure in line with Muslim practices and conventions, particularly to patients from the Islamic Middle East (SERI, 2004: 2).

The issue of coordination for promotion purposes has moved forward though. The Penang Health Association, consisting of seven major private hospitals in Penang, was launched in the beginning of August 2010. One of their aims is to work collectively to promote Penang as a destination for medical tourism. The hospitals are: Gleneagles Medical Centre, Lam Wah Ee Hospital, Island Hospital, Loh Guan Lye Specialist Centre, Mount Miriam Hospital, Pantai Hospital Penang and Penang Adventist Hospital (The Star, 14 August 2010). The other private hospitals in Penang - Mertajam Specialist Centre and Tanjung Medical Centre – are not members of the association.

Some commentators have expressed concern over the shortage of medical expertise for medical tourism and for the healthcare sector as a whole. In 2004, concerns about the shortage of medical doctors and paramedical staff were raised (SERI, 2004: 20). While this has implications for the sustainability and growth of the medical tourism industry in Penang, it also poses serious challenges to the provision of medical services to the local population. In fact, according to Chee, this is the most serious problem. Medical tourism makes private hospitals more lucrative to work in, thus exacerbating the long-standing problem of doctors switching from the public to the private sector (Chee, 2010: 348).

In an article about the economic potential of the medical tourism industry, Health Minister Datuk Seri Liow Tiong Lai was reported as saying that the Ministry of Health would not abandon its core purpose of providing health services to the domestic population, and that the ministry had put in place a set of key performance indicators to gauge the efficiency of its services (The Star, 25 June 2010). Chee warns that '[i]n order to match the high incomes of private sector specialists and other personnel, either the government will have to commit ever greater resources, or users will ultimately have to pay more' (Chee, 2010: 20). Given these concerns, a study of the impact of corporatisation and the development of medical tourism on the domestic population's access to quality healthcare in the public sector would be useful and timely.

POLICY RECOMMENDATIONS

While the medical tourism sector already has the infrastructure in place to provide good quality medical treatment to visitor patients and an existing industry-led grouping, there are areas that may be improved. The state government can play a facilitating role in the following areas:

Collecting more comprehensive, reliable and valid data
There is a lack of valid, reliable, and accessible data. Sources of information on Penang medical tourism tend to quote newspaper articles or speeches made by officials. The statistics cited by these sources may be accurate, but there is no way of substantiating them. A more nuanced and in-depth understanding of this sector can only be gained if there are reliable and valid data which can provide some way of forecasting trends. This would, in turn, benefit the stakeholders, visitor patients, the corporate sector and the state government.

The state government needs to ensure that reliable information on medical tourism is available so that it can view the trends in numbers, procedures, length of stay, preference for Penang, and visitor patients' home countries to tailor its service provision and promotion accordingly.

Knowing the reasons why foreign visitors choose Penang over other cities in Malaysia and neighbouring countries would go a long way to targeting and improving the services and products that foreign patients expect. Stakeholders would be in a better position to know if they can actually provide them and/or which areas they need to give more attention to.

Providing platforms
The state government can further assist by providing a common platform between hospitals and other supporting services such as hotels and tour agencies to further strengthen and brand the product.

Coordinating in branding and promotion
The state government needs to continue to work in coordination with industry stakeholders and the federal government to strengthen branding and promotion efforts to the Middle East and other markets.

Another issue that was highlighted was the risk of relying on patients from one country, namely Indonesia. To this end, efforts to promote Penang and Malaysia in other countries are underway. Corporate organisations in Penang have taken the initiative to do so. At the same time, the federal government has stepped up its game in this area.

Tying medical tourism to existing manufacturing and service sectors
Making links between medical tourism and existing manufacturing and service strengths and capabilities in Penang would make use of economies of scale. For example, the production of medical devices, automation and electronics, as well as university-industry-hospital links would be a 'pathway to growth via technological upgrading that harnesses the resources of several key drivers' (Kharas, Zeufack, and Majeed, 2010: 44).

CONCLUSION

Penang contributes roughly two-thirds to medical tourism receipts in Malaysia. The information presented in this chapter has shown that there has been growth in the medical tourism sector in Penang showing that it is a significant niche in the state's tourism industry. The 'hard' infrastructure is in place; what needs to be further strengthened is the 'soft' infrastructure, which includes skilled medical and service staff, coordination amongst stakeholders and a better link between the medical tourism sector and the rest of Penang's key economic drivers.

Chapter 11

Penang's Halal Industry

Rosalind Chua

INTRODUCTION

International industry experts place the global halal industry in the region of USD3 trillion[52] and the concept of halal goods and services is fast gaining ground in non-Islamic countries that have a substantial Muslim population. For instance, Europe's halal market is estimated to include over 50 million Muslim consumers with a substantial spending power of nearly USD66 billion a year.[53] In the UK alone, the halal meat market is estimated to be worth up to £2 billion a year.[54]

The food industry is the traditional mainstay of the wider halal industry and is centered around how food is prepared and whether animals have been slaughtered according to age-old Muslim practices (the word halal means 'permissible' in Arabic). Today's international halal industry comprises goods and services as diverse as pharmaceuticals, finance, logistics and bio-technology. The halal industry is more than just how livestock is prepared, it is the integration of many separate industries linked by a unique set

---

52 This figure is based on the world's 1.6 billion Muslim population and 1 billion non-Muslim consumers spending the equivalent of USD 0.50 a day.

53 http://halalfocus.net/2010/04/02/brussels-great-potential-to-develop-halal-market-in-europe/ (accessed 6/6/2011).

54 http://www.meatinfo.co.uk/news/fullstory.php/aid/11161/Feature:_Halal_here_we_come.html (accessed 6/6/2011).

of Islamic-based guidelines. This growing awareness of halal is creating new commercial possibilities much as what green development and the organic movement have done.

This chapter presents a brief overview of the global and Malaysian halal industry, and the development, opportunities and challenges faced by the halal industry in Penang.

HALAL IN MALAYSIA

Malaysia has been a key player in this global phenomenon, leading the way in certification, Islamic finance and food production. Two of the world's most established halal expos take place in Malaysia, including the World Halal Forum and the Malaysia International Halal Showcase (MIHAS) which promotes itself as the 'world's largest platform for halal products and services.' Concerted efforts and strategies to transform Malaysia into a global halal hub and to further develop the local halal industry have been outlined in various federal government plans including the Second Industrial Master Plan, 1996 - 2005, the National Agriculture Policy, 1998 - 2010, the Ninth Malaysia Plan (9MP), 2006 - 2010, and the Third Industrial Master Plan (IMP3), 2006 - 2020.

One important initiative of the 9MP was the establishment of the Halal Industry Development Corporation (HDC), tasked with developing and reviewing halal standards, encouraging investment in the halal industry, promoting halal products and services internationally and providing the necessary infrastructure to facilitate investment (i.e. developing halal parks). The 15-year Industrial Master Plan (IMP3) released in 2006, identified the development of the halal industry as one of the priority areas for the nation, with 11 strategic thrusts identified to develop Malaysia as a global halal hub for the production and distribution of halal products, halal service providers, reference on the halal standards and R&D on halal matters.

Malaysian halal certification by the Department of Islamic Development Malaysia (JAKIM) was established under the Islamic Affairs Division of the Prime Minister's Department. The Malaysian Halal Standard launched in August 2004 was created within the framework of the Malaysian

Standards Development System. The Malaysian Halal Standard's compliance to Good Manufacturing Practices (GMP) and Good Hygiene Practices (GHP) further cements Malaysian halal certification as one of the most recognized halal logos in the world.[55] Malaysia works closely with the Organization of Islamic Conference (OIC) countries to promote the Malaysian Halal Standard as the international benchmark for halal products. This is expected to further contribute to the acceptance of Malaysia's halal food products globally.[56]

The religious authorities of each state are responsible for halal certification and certification issued by the private sector is not recognized by the federal government. Active Islamic money market channeling about RM30 - RM40 billion monthly has created a critical mass of diversified players – Islamic banks, investment banks, takaful (Islamic insurance) companies, development financial institutions, savings institutions, fund management companies, stock brokers and unit trusts.[57] By the end of 2009, takaful assets comprised 8.0% of total assets in insurance, Islamic banking assets comprised 19.6% of total assets in the banking industry and some 62% of total global sukuk (Islamic bonds) originated in Malaysia (Tenth Malaysia Plan, 2011-2015, 2010).

There are nearly 3,200 manufacturers involved in the food manufacturing industry in Malaysia, and the industry accounts for nearly 10% of the country's manufacturing output. According to the Malaysia External Trade Development Corporation (MATRADE), Malaysia's exports of processed food products in 2010 accounted for close to RM12 billion, an increase of 12% over the previous year with major export markets including Singapore, US, Indonesia, Thailand, Australia and China. Big corporations such as Nestle and Tesco are known to work hand-in-hand with the government to achieve the halal hub goal. With more than 30% of Nestle Malaysia's exports heading for the Middle East, and a large portion going to markets with substantial Muslims population such as Indonesia, Singapore and Philippines, Nestle has picked Malaysia as their global halal food production centre and currently exports over USD100 million

---

55 http://www.standardsmalaysia.gov.my/v2/images2/strategic/S%20&%20H%20JAKIM.pdf (accessed 6/6/2011).
56 http://www.foodexport.org/Resources/CountryProfileDetail.cfm?ItemNumber=1029 (accessed 6/6/2011).
57 http://www.pwc.com/my/en/issues/islamic-finance-malaysia.jhtml (accessed 6/6/2011).

annually. Meanwhile, Tesco Malaysia has announced its plan to export USD2.7 million worth of halal products from Malaysia to Britain by 2011.

While Malaysia enjoys definite strengths in certain aspects of the halal industry, it is difficult to assess the extent to which the country could be called a global halal hub. In the area of global Islamic finance, Malaysia is a leader; however in terms of the value of Malaysia's exports of halal products, the country lags behind some of its ASEAN neighbours. One industry expert recently expressed his concerns, "I think that Malaysia's halal initiative started very well in 2004, say until 2007, at which point it lost focus...so, even now in 2011, if you are to ask people in the halal sector what Malaysia's halal agenda is, no one can really give you a clear answer, either from the public or the private sector...I think Malaysia has yet to recognize its own real strengths and weaknesses in the halal sector. After so much publicity about halal coming out of Malaysia, all the competitors have developed their own plans and there is a danger that Malaysia may become slightly marginalised unless there is a revitalised strategy and implementation to go along with that."[58]

OVERVIEW OF PENANG'S HALAL INDUSTRY

Penang's halal industry has been driven by the well-established food industry. The state is a major exporter of processed seafood products accounting for a significant proportion of Malaysia's processed food exports valued at RM2.6 billion (exact figures are difficult to obtain and verify). There are 185 halal-certified food processors located in Penang according to the latest Penang International Halal Hub directory. The directory also lists over 100 F&B service providers i.e. hotels, restaurants and seven livestock organisations.

In 2006, MATRADE figures extracted from the 'Malaysia Exporters of Halal Products, Directory' showed that there were only 21 exporters of halal food products from Penang, by the first half of 2011, this figure had risen to 40 exporters. Major export destinations are Europe, ASEAN nations, US, Middle East, Australia and New Zealand (Lim and Mohd Rizal, 2006). The number of firms that obtained Halal certification from

---

58 *World Halal Forum director, Abdalhamid Evans, interview in Chan, C.T. "Making it Halal" SME News March 26 – April 8 2011.*

the State Department of Islamic Affairs Pulau Pinang (JAIPP) has increased from 170 in 2003 to 277 in 2010. Halal certification was issued for products, catering services, restaurants, hotels, and abattoirs.

It may not be accurate to attribute the steady rise in halal certification to increased demand for halal products as there are still many Muslim-owned F&B providers that do not have recognized halal certification. Rather, these figures may reflect an increasing awareness of halal certification, especially by Muslim consumers.

Table 1: Firms that obtained halal certification from Jabatan Agama Islam Negeri Pulau Pinang (JAIPP), 2003 – 2010

2003	2004	2005	2006	2007	2008	2009	2010	Up to March 2011
170	230	270	311	-	257	296	344	349

Source: Jabatan Agama Islam Negeri Pulau Pinang (JAIPP) and PIHH

Despite the federal government's concerted efforts to promote the halal industry nationwide – with the development of new halal parks and incentives – little concerted action was taken by the previous Penang state government. The current state government appears to have been inspired by the potential of the halal industry, establishing the Penang International Halal Hub (PIHH) or Halal Penang in 2009, with its development spearheaded by the state EXCO for Religious Affairs, Domestic Trade and Consumer Affairs. By establishing a new government agency dedicated to the development of the halal industry in Penang and placing a senior member of the state EXCO in charge, the Penang state government high-lighted the potential of the halal industry.

Unlike the eight other halal parks in Malaysia, the PIHH encompasses the entire state of Penang. Rather than simply creating halal parks for investors to set up manufacturing facilities, PIHH offers would-be investors an integrated approach similar to what the Penang Development Corporation (PDC) did with the E&E manufacturing industry in the 1970s. Penang already enjoys a business-friendly environment for investors, R&D facilities, good connectivity by air and sea and support services. PIHH aims to tap into this existing infrastructure to leverage the halal industry.

PIHH has identified ten clusters that make up a holistic and integrated halal supply chain, namely, manufacturing, agro-based industries, logistics, human capital, hospitality and tourism, entrepreneur development, marketing and promotion, finance, R&D and life sciences. PIHH currently employs eight staff involved in promoting Penang as a location of choice to local and international investors. Each of the ten clusters is led by a steering committee comprising local industry insiders. According to YB Haji Abdul Malik Kassim, state EXCO for Religious Affairs, Domestic Trade and Consumer Affairs and chairman of PIHH, "Halal Penang's (PIHH) approach is about marketing and branding Penang as a gateway to world halal markets and creating an interest in halal, rather than just selling industrial land.

Manufacturing
To complement its industrial promotion activities, PIHH established the dedicated Penang Halal Industrial Park – a 100 acre park located in the Bukit Minyak Industrial Estate on the mainland close to the North-South Highway. The Industrial Park was awarded HALMAS status in 2011, indicating that PIHH has successfully complied with all the guidelines for halal parks established by the HDC. This is the state's first Halal Park and PIHH has already made a request to the Penang state government for a further 100 acres of land in Batu Kawan for another park.[59] To date, there are eight companies in the Halal Park (seven food manufacturers and one pharmaceutical company) with a combined investment worth RM258 million.

Food products and services continue to dominate Penang's halal industry and the existence of numerous hypermarkets and supermarket chains (including Sunshine, Tesco and Carrefour) in the state offers local food processors good opportunities. Leading hypermarkets in Penang "have indicated halal compliance is part of their business expansion plans and highlighted that halal products have a promising future as these products have gained increasing appeal from both local and foreign Muslim and non-Muslim customers" (Lim and Mohd Rizal, 2006).

59 Interview with YB Malik 12 May 2011.

Not only do these chains source for local halal products for their Malaysian operations, the chains also source locally for halal products which can then be exported to their international operations, where there is demand for halal products. To date, the publicised Juru beef project (halal high quality beef similar to Kobe beef) has not moved, and currently, PIHH is in discussions with a Pakistan-based company to develop high quality corn based animal feed in a new dedicated Halal Agro Park. PIHH is negotiating with the Kedah state government to identify and acquire suitable agricultural land in Kedah for the Agro Park. PIHH is also assisting a new Malaysian-China JV seafood company source for a suitable aquaculture site on mainland Penang.

Logistics is an important link in the halal value chain, from agricultural or farming activities, processing and manufacturing, transportation and shipping, to retail and consumption. Halal certified logistics plays a necessary role in ensuring that halal integrity is actually in place from 'farm to fork.' As Penang's Free Industrial Zones (FIZs) have existed for over 30 years, the island already has an integrated logistics system that covers land, sea and air transport. PIHH played a key role in 'matchmaking' the Port of Rotterdam (the world's first halal-certified port) with Penang Port and today, Penang Port is Malaysia's first and only halal certified port[60] opening up opportunities for exporters of halal goods.

PIHH has now turned its attention to establishing Malaysia's first halal air logistics hub at the Penang International Airport. PIHH is exploring the possibility of partnership with International Halal Integrity Alliance (IHIA) to establish a halal auditors programme. As the halal accreditation process is so crucial to the halal industry the creation of a professional body of halal auditors will help to enhance skill sets and streamline the accreditation process further.

Penang attracts many Middle Easter tourists each year and July to September is the peak travel period for Arab travellers escaping the summer heat. Currently, most of Penang's more established 4-5 star hotels offer halal dining, however these establishments are not fully syariah-compliant as they serve alcohol and have non-segregated swimming

---

60 Penang Port is the first port in Malaysia to achieve the MS1900:2005 "Quality Management Systems - Requirements from Islamic Perspectives" for the provision of container handling services and dedicated warehouse services within Penang Port.

pools. It is difficult to establish whether there is significant demand for fully syariah-compliant hotels in Penang – currently there are only two in existence, with a further two in the pipeline.[61] To assist Muslim visitors to get the most out of their trips to Penang, PIHH will be releasing a 'Muslim Travel Guide for Penang' in the later part of 2011. PIHH is also looking into the feasibility of establishing a dedicated area in Penang, outside of the Batu Ferringhi tourist belt, for family concept hospitality which focuses on universally accepted values.

For the time, being entrepreneur development is focussed on assisting local food processors to obtain the necessary accreditation/certification for them to export; and familiarising them with US and European FDA requirements, including BTEC and HACCP. All food processors that apply for halal certification are currently advised to comply with GMP and HACCP guidelines.[62] This is an ongoing process that focuses on raising awareness of halal and halal certification within the state as well as promoting Penang as a potential investment destination. PIHH attempts to make halal-related information freely available and accurate and publishes the Penang Halal Directory every three months (this is made available free of charge). PIHH has also recently streamlined the process of halal accreditation by setting out SOPs that include inspection of premises seven days after the submission of application forms and approval/rejection one month after submission.

Finance is a sector where PIHH is unlikely to have much impact given the strict regulation of banks and financial institutions in Malaysia. As Kuala Lumpur is globally recognized as an Islamic financal hub it would be unrealistic to expect Penang to compete. However, syariah-compliant financing is widely available in Penang. World-class R&D in halal products and services is essential if Penang's halal industry to progress. Universiti Sains Malaysia (USM) which is located in Penang is already highly involved in R&D for halal pharmaceuticals and has recently innovated halal mouthwash, halal food grade collagen and halal meningitis vaccine.

---

61 Interview with YB Malik 12 May 2011.
62 FDA (Food and Drug Adminstration of the US), BTEC (Business and Technology Education Council), HACCP (Hazard Analysis & Critical Control Points), GMP (Good Manufacturing Practice).

During the Penang International Halal Expo & Conference (PIHEC) 2011, PIHH brought together five of the region's leading universities with expertise in halal research including: Chulalangkorn University, Prince of Songkla University, Universiti Sains Malaysia (USM), International Islamic University Malaysia (IIUM) and Universiti Putra Malaysia (UPM). PIHH are currently in negotiations with USM to establish and lead a halal R&D cluster that includes the five universities.

Some attempts at B2B matchmaking have taken place; PIHH has identified a producer of non-swine based enzymes for the production of halal insulin (especially pertinent given the high incidence of diabetes in Malaysia). To further promote Penang's halal capabilities to international and Malaysian organisations and government agencies, PIHH organised the inaugural Penang International Halal Expo & Conference (PIHEC) in 2010 which has since become an annual affair. Although a relatively small trade fair (PIHEC 2011 recorded 94 exhibiting booths and 40 kiosks during the three-day event), over time it will help to enhance Penang's global branding as a one-stop Halal location.

PIHEC 2011 attracted participation from Russia, Iran, Pakistan, Indonesia, the World China Muslim Association, Kyrgystan and Korea; as well as a 56-member trade delegation of business leaders and senior corporate officers from Thailand. The Expo was jointly organised by PIHEC in collaboration with the Islamic Religious Department of Penang (JAIPP), Penang Development Corporation (PDC) and Indonesia-Malaysia-Thailand Growth Triangle (IMT-GT) - signifying the state government's commitment to promoting halal in Penang.

CHALLENGES

In spite of its growing success, a number of factors hamper the growth of the halal industry in Penang. Although PIHH has attracted investment into the new Halal Park, Abdul Malik believed that there is a long way to go to before Penang's full potential in the halal industry is realised, "Currently I can't see the private sector overtaking us (Penang state government). The private sector seems to be in a 'comfort zone' and does not appear to be enthusiastic to invest in halal." This apparent lack of interest may be due to Penang's relatively late foray into the halal industry (beyond halal food products) compared to other states in Malaysia. As PIHH is less than three years old it will take time for the organization to reap the fruits of its intensive local and international marketing and promotions.

Bureaucratic red tape is another challenge. According to Lim (Lim & Mohd. Rizal, 2006: 10), although halal industry players have access to financial assistance, the speed in processing the SMEs' loan applications, particularly by government-linked financial institutions is not fast enough. The slow approval of loans has impacted SMEs and prevented these from quickly expanding their production capacities to meet export demand. World Halal Forum director, Abdalhamid Evans noted, "There are various incentives, grants and soft loans that are all available to Malaysian SMEs that are all listed on various government websites. However, in my experience talking to local SMEs, there seems to be a lack of connection between the government incentives and the needs of the SMEs. Thailand has been very successful in developing SMEs for the international market, and I think there is sometimes a slight complacency in Malaysia that needs to be overcome in order to be really competitive in the market."[63]

Related to this is regional competition. Penang's position in the Indonesia-Malaysia-Thailand Growth Triangle (IMT-GT) offers the state many advantages e.g. easy access to markets with demand for halal products and services, access to halal raw materials and the like. However, the potential of halal products and services has also attracted strong regional contenders into the industry, including Thailand, Indonesia and Brunei. Thailand in particular has a competitive, export-oriented food industry and as of 2009 was the world's fifth largest halal food exporter with a market share of 5.6%[64]. Thailand's attempt to brand itself as 'The World's Halal Kitchen' is especially worrying for Malaysian food exporters. In a report in The Star March 12, 2010, International Trade and Industries Deputy Minister Datuk Mukhriz Mahathir noted that Malaysia had not been able to produce enough halal food for export despite strong demand from the Middle East countries and that local producers could not even meet the volume for the first consignment. Despite carrying a premium halal brand, Malaysia lacked the capacity to produce adequate volume for export.

---

63 *World Halal Forum director, Abdalhamid Evans, interview in Chan, C.T. "Making it Halal" SME News March 26 – April 8 2011.*
64 *http://www.daganghalal.com/HalalNews/HalalNewsDtl.aspx?id=862 (accessed 6/6/2011).*

Mukhriz said this had resulted in Thailand taking the lead in halal food production and penetrating the Middle East countries.[65]

There are also continuing issues regarding certification. While the Halal Malaysia certification may be recognized worldwide, not all potential halal food exporters have the necessary certifications needed to export to the US, UK and EU. While PIHH assists local SMEs by familiarising them with various certifications, the actual certification process is a long and expensive one that may deter potential halal product exporters. Local SMEs may benefit from more guidance and assistance in exploring new export markets.

Another problem is the lack of raw materials. It is estimated that up to 70% of the raw materials for the Malaysian food processing industry are imported and that there is a lack of local halal raw materials, particularly meat, as pointed out in the Third Industrial Master Plan, 2006 – 2020. As a small, industrialised state, Penang lacks the land mass necessary for large-scale agriculture meaning that it faces a competitive advantage with regards to the food processing industry. Rather than continuing to focus on importing raw materials and processing/manufacturing these in Penang, PIHH is actively encouraging companies to venture beyond the state/national boundaries and to develop upstream activities at the source. This approach will require substantial investment as well as a long-term commitment which may be beyond the capabilities of all but the largest, more established food processors.

Finally, a set of issues revolve around the limited understanding of halal. Traditionally the scope of the halal industry has been confined to halal food and food-related products, yet the concept of halal is far more encompassing and touches all aspects of a Muslim individual's life. Local manufacturers and service providers need to familiarise themselves with a holistic understanding of halal to create unique halal certified products and services. The PIHH works in tandem with various agencies and organisations of the State/Federal government such as investPenang, Penang Development Corporation (PDC), Penang Islamic Religious Department (JAIPP), Malaysian Department of Islamic Development (JAKIM), Halal Industry Development Corporation (HDC),

---

65 *http://thestar.com.my/news/story.asp?file=/2010/3/12/nation/5850074&sec=nation (accessed 6/6/2011).*

MATRADE, MIDA and SME Corporation. While the model of federal and state agencies working closely to attract FDI has been successful for Penang over the past four decades, the presence of so many different agencies involved in promoting halal may actually hinder rather than promote the industry's growth.

CONCLUSION

In the two years since its inception, PIHH has arguably had some success in promoting Penang as a potential investment destination to Malaysian and international investors. It has clearly identified 10 clusters or sectors that build on Penang's existing strengths and takes a long-term view of developing an integrated halal industry in the state. The state's halal infrastructure is already in place and in synchrony with federal government initiatives, notably the IMP3 which aims to position Malaysia as an international halal hub. Backed by federal and state government initiatives and incentives, it is now up to the private sector to make the most of these opportunities.

REFERENCES

Abdullah, M.A., 2000. 'Myths and Realities of SMEs in Malaysia', in M.A. Abdullah and M.I.B. Bakar (eds), *Small and Medium Enterprises in Asia-Pacific Countries*, Vol I, Nova Science Publishers, Huntington NY, pp. 59-74.

ACHR, 2006. *Asian Heritage Project: Visit to Luang Prabang, Laos*, mission report by André Alexander, with input from Maurice Leonhardt.

Ackers, Louise and Peter Dwye, 2002. *Senior Citizenship?: Retirement, Migration and Welfare in the European Union*. Bristol: The Policy Press.

Alagappa, Muthiah, 2004. "Civil Society and Political Change: An Analytical Framework", in Muthiah Alagappa (ed.), *Civil Society and Political Change in Asia: Expanding and Contracting Democratic Space*. Stanford: Stanford University Press, pp. 25-60.

Anton, Philip S., R. Silberglitt, and James Schneider, 2001. *The Global Technology Revolution: Bio/Nano/Materials Trends and their Synergies with Information Technology by 2015*. Arlington VA: RAND.

Asian Development Bank, 2010. *Key Indicators for the Asia-Pacific 2010: The Rise of Asia's Middle Class*. Manila: Asian Development Bank.

Association of Malaysian Medical Industries (AMMI), 2009. Presentation on 'Global Scenario and Opportunities in Medical Devices Industry' at seminar on 'Opportunities for Medical Devices and Surgical Instruments Manufacturing', 29 October 2009.

Barber, Andrew, 2009. *Penang under the East India Company 1786-1858*. Kuala Lumpur: AB&A.

Brown, Rajeshwary Ampalavanar, 2006. "The Contemporary Indian Political Elite in Malaysia", in K.S. Sandhu & A. Mani (eds.) *Indian Communities in Southeast Asia* (Singapore: ISEAS), pp. 237-265.

Chee, Heng Leng. 2007. "Medical Tourism in Malaysia: International Movement of Healthcare Consumers and the Commodification of Healthcare". Working Paper in National University of Singapore's Asia Research Institute Working Paper Series No.83, January.

Chee, Heng Leng, 2010. "Medical Tourism and the State in Malaysia and Singapore". *Global Social Policy*, Vol 10: 3, pp. 336-357.

Choy, C.Y. 1964. "Message from the Mayor City Council of Georgetown, Penang". *Hu Yew Seah 50th Anniversary Magazine*.

Chuleeporn Virunha, 2009. "From Regional Entrepot to Malayan Port: Penang's Trade and Trading Communities, 1890-1940", in *Penang and Its Region: The Story of an Asian Entrepot*, Yeoh Seng Guan, Loh Wei Leng, Khoo Salma Nasution, and Neil Khor (eds), Singapore: NUS Press, pp. 103-130.

City Council of George Town, 1966. *Penang Past and Present, 1786-1963, An Historical Account of the City of George Town since 1786.* Penang: City Council of George Town.

Cohens E, 1988. "Authenticity and Commoditization in Tourism". *Annals of Tourism Research*, Vol 15: 3, pp. 371- 86.

Constitution of Malaysia, 2008. Northern Corridor Implementation Authority Act 2008. Parliament / Acts & Bills. Parliament

Delafons, John, 1997. *Politics and Preservation: A Policy History of the Built Heritage, 1882-1996.* London: E & FN Spon.

Department of Statistics, 2010. *Basic Population Characteristics by Administrative Districts*. Department of Statistics: Putra Jaya.

Dimaranan Betina, Elena Ianchovichina, and Will Martin, 2006. "Competing with Giants Who Wins, Who Loses?" in Yusuf, S. and Alan Winters, *Dancing with Giants: China, India and the Global Economy*. Washington D.C.: World Bank.

Florida, Richard, 2005. *The Flight of the Creative Class: Why America is Losing the Competition for Talent*. New York: HarperBusiness.

Geografia, 2010a. *George Town Transformation Programme: Baseline Survey, Population & Land Use Census, and Conurbation Spatial Strategy*. Progress Report, prepared for Think City Sdn Bhd, by Geografia, www.geografia.com.au. 10 January 2010.

Geografia, 2010b. *George Town Land Use and Population Survey: Method, Results and Implications*. Prepared for Think City Sdn Bhd, by Geografia, www.geografia.com.au. May 2010.

Ghafar Ahmad, 2010. "Melaka and George Town, Historic Cities of the Straits of Malacca: the challenge to retain the status", in *World Heritage*, No. 55 (Feb 2010), pp. 22-29.

Gill, Indermit and Homi Kharas, 2007. *An East Asian Renaissance: Ideas for Economic Growth*. Washington D.C.: International Bank for Reconstruction and Development.

Halimah Mohd Said and Zainab Abdul Majid, 2004. *Images of the Jawi Peranakan of Penang: Assimilation of the Jawi Peranakan Community into the Malay Society*. Tanjong Malim: Universiti Pendidikan Sultan Idris.

Hardt, Michael, 1998. 'The Withering of Civil Society', in Eleanor Kaufman & Kevin Jon Heller (eds.) *Deleuze & Guattari: New Mappings in Politics, Philosophy, and Culture*. Minnesota: University of Minnesota Press.

Ho, Richard, 2009. "George Town's UNESCO World Heritage Status: Implications and Challenges in the Road Ahead", *Penang Economic Monthly*, 11, 3 (2009), pp. 1-9.

""Hitchcock, Michael and King, Victor T, 2003. "Discourses with the Past: Tourism and Heritage in South-East Asia". *Indonesia and the Malay World*, Vol 31, 89, pp. 3-15.

Hobsbawm, E., and Ranger, T, eds., 1983. *The Invention of Tradition*. Cambridge: Cambridge University Press, 1983.

Hutchinson, F. E, 2008. "Developmental States and Economic Growth at the Sub-National Level: The Case of Penang" in *Southeast Asian Affairs 2008*, edited by D. Singh and M.M.T. Tin. Singapore: Institute of Southeast Asian Studies, pp. 223-246.

International Medical Tourism Journal (IMTJ), 2011. "Malaysia: Tracking Medical Tourism Statistics", http://www.imtjonline.com/news/?entryid82=155988 (accessed 15 February 2011).

Invest-in-Penang Berhad, 2010. "Investment Opportunities in Penang". Paper prepared for: Penang Outlook Forum 2010 Socio-Economic and Environmental Research Institute, 2010.

InvestPenang, 2008 "2007 Penang Industrial Survey Report". Penang: InvestPenang.

Jenkins, Gwynn, 2009. *Contested Space: Cultural Heritage and Identity Reconstructions, Conservation Strategies within a Developing Asian City*. Zürich: Lit Verlag.

Jenkins, Gwynn and King, Victor T, 2003. "Heritage and development in a Malaysian city: George Town under threat?", *Indonesia and the Malay World*, Vol 31: 89, pp. 44-57.

JTB Report. 2009. *All About Japanese Overseas Travelers*. Tokyo: Japan Tourism Marketing Co.

Kahn, Joel S, 1997. 'Culturalizing Malaysia: Globalism, Tourism, Heritage, and the City in Georgetown', in Michel Picard and Robert E. Wood (eds.) *Tourism, Ethnicity, and the State in Asian and Pacific Societies*, Honolulu: University of Hawaii Press, pp. 99-127.

Kharas, H., Zuefack, A. and Majeed, H, 2010. *Cities, People and the Economy: A Study on Positioning Penang*. Kuala Lumpur: Khazanah Nasional Berhad and The World Bank.

Khoo Salma Nasution and Jenkins, Gwynn, 2002. "George Town, Pulau Pinang, Malaysia: Development Strategies and Community Realities", in Logan, William S. (ed.), *The Disappearing Asian City: Protecting Asia's Urban Heritage in a Globalization World*. Oxford: Oxford University Press, pp. 208-228.

Khoo Su Nin, 1993. *Streets of George Town Penang: An Illustrated Guide to Penang's City, Streets & Historic Attractions*. Penang: Janus Print & Resources.

Khoo Salma Nasution, 2008. "George Town: The Challenge of World Heritage Listing", *Heritage Asia*. Vol 5 No. 3 (Oct-Dec 2008), pp. 26-28.

King, Russel, Tony Warnes and Allan Williams. 2000. *Sunset Lives? : British Retirement Migration to the Mediterranean*. Oxford and New York: Berg.

Kirshenblatt-Gimblett, Barbara, 1995. "Theorizing Heritage". *Ethnomusicology*, Vol 39: 3, (Autumn), pp. 367-380.

Lewis, Su Lin, 2009. "Cosmopolitanism and the Modern Girl: A Cross-Cultural Discourse in 1930s Penang". *Modern Asian Studies*, 43: pp. 1385-1419.

Lim San Hai,1964 ."President's Preface". *Hu Yew Seah 50th Anniversary Magazine*.

Lim San Hai, 1964 "A Short History of the Hu Yew Seah Girl's School". *Hu Yew Seah 50th Anniversary Magazine*.

Lim, W.S. & Mohd Rizal b. Abd Wahab, 2006. "The Potential of Halal Industry in Penang" *Penang Economic Monthly*, Vol 8, Issue 11.

Lowenthal, David, 2000. *George Perkins Marsh, Prophet of Conservation*. Seattle: University of Washington Press.

MacCannell, D, 1976. *The Tourist: A New Theory of the Leisure Class*. New York: Schocken Books.

Mathews, Gordon, 1996. *What Makes Life Worth Living? : How Japanese and Americans Make Sense of Their Worlds*. Berkeley and Los Angeles: University of California Press.

Machlup, F, 1962. *The Production and Distribution of Knowledge in the United States*. Princeton: Princeton University Press.

McKinsey Global Institute, 2010. *How to Compete and Grow: A Sector Guide to Policy*. Boston: McKinsey Global Institute.

McKinsey Global Institute, 2010. *India's Urban Awakening: Building Inclusive Cities, Sustaining Economic Growth*. Boston: Mckinsey Global Institute.

McLean, Fiona, 2006. "Introduction: Heritage and Identity", *International Journal of Heritage Studies*, Vol 12, 1, pp. 3 – 7.

Milner, Anthony, 2008. *The Malays*. Oxford: Wiley-Blackwell.

Milner, Anthony, 1995. *The Invention of Politics in Colonial Malaya: Contesting Nationalism and the Expansion of the Public Sphere*. Cambridge, New York: Cambridge University Press.

Mohd. Noordin Sopiee, 1973. "The Penang Secession Movement, 1948-1951", *Journal of Southeast Asian Studies*, Vol. 4, No. 1, pp. 57-71.

Mowforth, Martin and Ian Munt. 1998. *Tourism and Sustainability: New Tourism in the Third World*. London and New York: Routledge.

Nagata, Judith, 2001."Heritage as a Site of Resistance: From Architecture to Political Activism in Urban Penang", in Maznah Mohamed & Wong Soak Konn (eds), *Risking Malaysia: Culture, Politics & Identity*. Bangi: UKM Press, pp. 179-201.

_____, 2006. 'Religion and Ethnicity among Indian Muslims of Malaysia', in K.S. Sandhu & A. Mani (eds.) *Indian Communities in Southeast Asia*, Singapore: ISEAS, pp. 513-540.

Nara Conference on Authenticity in Relation to the World Heritage Convention. Nara, Japan. 1994. [http://www.international.icomos.org/icomos/nara.htm]

Nathan Associates, 1970. *Penang Master Plan*. Robert R. Nathan Associates Inc., Penang.

National Economic Advisory Council, 2010. *New Economic Model for Malaysia Part I: Strategic Policy Directions*. Putrajaya: National Economic Advisory Council.

Ochiai, E. 1997. *The Japanese Family System in Transition: A Sociological Analysis of Family Change in Postwar Japan*. Tokyo: LTCB International Library Foundation.

Ono, Mayumi. 2008. "Long-stay Tourism and International Retirement Migration: Japanese Retirees in Malaysia," in S Yamashita, M. Minami, D. Hains, and J. Eades (eds), *Transnational Migration in East Asia: Japan in a Comparative Focus* (Senri Ethnological Reports 77). The National Museum of Ethnology, Osaka, pp. 151-162.

Ono, Mayumi. 2009. "Japanese Lifestyle Migration/Tourism in Southeast Asia," in *Japanese Review of Cultural Anthropology*, Vol. 10, pp. 43-52.

PBA Holdings Bhd, 2011, *Annual Report 2010*. Penang: PBA Holdings Bhd.

PEMANDU, 2010. *Economic Transformation Programme: A Roadmap for Malaysia*. Malaysia: PEMANDU.

Penang State Government. "Penang to Undergo Transformation into Major Logistics, Transportation Hub", 19 January 2010. <http://www.penang.gov.my/index.php?websiteId=1&ch=14&pg=90&ac=651> (accessed 19 December 2010).

Picard, M. Bali, 1996. *Cultural Tourism and Touristic Culture*. Singapore: Archipelago Press, 1996.

Picard, M., and Wood, R.E., eds., 1997. *Tourism, Ethnicity, and the State in Asian and Pacific Societies*. Honolulu: University of Hawai'i Press, pp. vii-xi.

Praxiom Research Group Limited, 2011. (http://www.praxiom.com/iso-13485-definitions.htm)

PSDC, 2007. "Technology Roadmap for the Electrical and Electronics Industry of Penang". Business Wise Consulting, PSDC, SERI.

PSDC, 2007. "Technology Road for the Electrical and Electronics Industry of Penang". Penang: Penang Skills Development Centre.

Quah, Jeffrey Hardy, 2011. "Keeping Penang Watered". *Penang Economic Monthly*, Issue 03.11, pp. 8-15.

Rahil Ismail, Brian J. Shaw, Ooi Giok Ling, eds., 2009. *Southeast Asian Culture and Heritage in a Globalising World: Diverging Identities in a Dynamic Region*. Burlington: Ashgate.

Rashin, Ed, 2004. "Mareshia de Rongusutei (Long-stay in Malaysia)", Tokyo, Ikarosu.

Rebick, Marcus, and Ayumi Takenaka (eds.), 2009. *The Changing Japanese Family*. London and Newyork. Routledge.

Robertson, Iaim J.M, 2008. "Heritage from Below: Class, Social Protest and Resistance", in Brian Graham and Peter Howard (eds.) *The Ashgate Research Companion to Heritage and Identity*. Burlington: Ashgate, pp. 143-158.

Saidatulakmal Mohd, 2010. 'Ethnic Identity Dilemma – A Case Study of the Indian Muslims in Penang', International Review of Business Research Papers, Vol 6:3 (August), pp. 70-82.

Sakamoto, Yasuhiko, 2006. "Gohobi Jinsei Mareishia (Rewarded life in Malaysia)," Tokyo: Ikarosu Shuppan.

Saravanamuttu, Johan, 1998. "Mobilizing for Change: Civil Society, State and Market" paper delivered at Roundtable on Popular Participation, Sustainable Penang Initiative, Penang, 19–20 September, 1998.

Scott, James C, 1990. *Domination and the Arts of Resistance: Hidden Transcripts*. New Haven: Yale University Press.

SERI, 2004. "Health Tourism in Penang", *Economic Briefing to the Penang State Government* Vol. 6: 11.

SERI, 2009. "Medical Tourism – A New Growth Frontier for Penang in 2009 and Beyond." *Penang Economic Monthly*. Vol.11: 4. <http://www.seri.com.my/v3/files/econ_brief/2009/EconBrief2009-4.pdf> (accessed 1 December 2010).

SERI, 2010a. *Penang Economic Outlook 2010*. Penang: Socio-Economic and Environmental Research Institute.

SERI 2010b. *Penang Statistics Quarter 3, 2010*. Penang: Socio-Economic and Environmental Research Institute. <http://www.seri.com.my/v3/files/quarterly_penang_statistics/2010/Q3_Jul-Sept_2010_21Dec2010.pdf> (accessed 1 December 2010).

Shamsul, A.B, 2005. "History of Identity, an Identity of a History: the Idea and Practice of 'Malay identity' in Malaysia Reconsidered", in Timothy P. Barnard (ed.), *Contesting Malayness: Malay Identity Across Boundaries*. Singapore: Singapore University Press, pp. 135-48.

Shiraishi, Takashi, 1990. *An Age in Motion: Popular Radicalism in Java, 1912-1926*. Ithaca: Cornell University Press, 1990.

Siegel, James T, 1997. *Fetish, Recognition, Revolution*. Princeton: New Jersey: Princeton University Press, 1997.

Singapore Tourism Board, 2010. "Annual Report on Tourism Statistics (2009)" Singapore: Singapore Tourism Board. https://www.stbtrc.com.sg/images/links/X1Annual_Report_on_Tourism_Statistics_2009.pdf (accessed 15 February 2011).

Stark, Jan, 2006. "Indian Muslims in Malaysia: Images of Shifting Identities in the Multi-ethnic State", *Journal of Muslim Minority Affairs*, 26:3, pp. 383 – 398.

Tan Siew Inn, 1980. "Koh Sin Hock – "Anak Pulau Pinang". *Malaysia in History*, 23, pp 91-100.

Tan Teik Lim, 1964. "Sekolah Malam Bahasa Kebangsaan Hu Yew Seah". *Hu Yew Seah 50th Anniversary Magazine*.

Taylor, Ken, 2009. "Cultural Landscapes and Asia: Reconciling International and Southeast Asian Regional Values", *Landscape Research*, 34:1, pp 7-31.

The Boston Consulting Group, 2010. "Winning in Emerging-Market Cities: A Guide to the World's Largest Growth Opportunity", Report, September 2010.

The Economic Planning Unit, 2010. *10th Malaysia Plan 2011-2015*. Putrajaya: EPU, Prime Minister's Department.

The Long Stay Foundation (Zaidanhôjin Rongusutei Zaidan), 2005. Rongusutei Chôsa Tôkei 2005 (Statistical Report on Long-Stay 2005). Tokyo: Zaidanhôjin Rongusutei Zaidan (the Long Stay Foundation).

The Long Stay Foundation (Zaidanhôjin Rongusutei Zaidan), 2007. Rongusutei Chôsa Tôkei 2005 (Statistical Report on Long-Stay 2007). Tokyo: Zaidanhôjin Rongusutei Zaidan (the Long Stay Foundation).

The Ministry of International Trade and Industry. 1986. Silver Colombia Plan '92: A Support Project for Affluent Second Life Abroad (Sirubā-Koronbia Keikaku '92: Yutaka na Daini no Jinsei wo Kaigai de

Sugosu Tameno Kaigai Kyôjyû Shien Jigyô)

The New Straits Times, "Silver Hair Programme Conditions Relaxed". 14 February, 2002.

The Research Institute for Senior Life (Zaidanhôjin Shinia Puran Kaihatsu Kikô) 2005. Kaigai Chôki Taizaisya no Seikatsu to Ikigai ni Kansuru Chôsa (Survey on life and ikigai of overseas sojourners). Tokyo:

The Star. "Malaysian Medical Tourism Growing". 14 February 2009. http://biz.thestar.com.my/news/story.asp?file=/2009/2/14/business/3245091&sec=business (accessed 15 February 2011).

The Star. "Healthcare Beyond Borders". 2 May 2010. <http://thestar.com.my/health/story.asp?file=/2010/5/2/health/6152063&sec=health> (accessed 15 December 2010).

The Star. "Healthcare can Bring RM10bil to Economy, says Liow". 25 June 2010. <http://thestar.com.my/news/story.asp?file=/2010/6/25/nation/6540862&sec=nation> (accessed 15 December 2010).

The Star. "United to Draw Medical Tourists". 14 August 2010. <http://thestar.com.my/metro/story.asp?file=/2010/8/14/north/6853770&sec=north> (accessed 15 December 2010).

The Star. "Care for the Sick is Still the Main Aim". 26 September 2010. <http://thestar.com.my/news/story.asp?file=/2010/9/26/focus/7102997&sec=focus> (accessed 19 December 2010).

The Star. "Get a Share of the Health Tourism Industry, Dentists Urged". 15 November 2010. <http://thestar.com.my/news/story.asp?file=/2010/11/15/sarawak/7425840&sec=sarawak> (accessed 15 December 2010).

The Straits Times. "Sick? Get some Five-star Treatment". 19 March 2005.

The Third Industrial Master Plan, 2006 – 2020, 2006. Putrajaya Government Printer, 2006.

Toyota, Mika, 2006. 'Pensioners on the Move: Social Security and Trans-border Retirement Migration in Asia and Europe' IIAS Newsletter no.40

Toyota, Mika, 2006. "Ageing and Transnational Householding: Japanese Retirees in Southeast Asia" *International Development Planning Review* Vol.28, no.4, pp. 515-531.

Toyota, Mika, 2007. "Medical tourism in Asia: the Cases from Singapore and Thailand" in *Cultural Anthropology of Tourism*. Tokyo: Shinyo Publishing Co. Ltd. Chapter 17 (in Japanese), pp.153-158.

Toyota, Mika 2008. 'Creating Transnational "Retirement Industry": a Political Economy of Ageing, Migration and Development in Asia', paper presented at the American Anthropological Association Annual Conference (19-22 Nov. San Francisco, USA).

Traphagan, John W, and John Knight (eds.), 2003. *Demographic Change and the Family in Japan's Aging Society*. Albany: State University of New York Press.

Ueno, Chizuko. 2007. *Retirement of the Singles* (Ohitori Sama no Rogo). Hoken.

UNESCO, 2009. *Hoi An Protocols for Best Conservation Practice in Asia: Professional Guidelines for Assuring and Preserving the Authenticity of Heritage Sites in the Context of the Cultures of Asia*. Bangkok: UNESCO Bangkok.

Visit Penang. "Penang Medical Tourism on CNBC". 2009. <http://www.visitpenang.gov.my/portal3/medical-tourism.html> (accessed 15 December 2010).

Visit Penang, 2011."Penang Medical Tourism Increases in Revenue Monday". 2011. < http://www.visitpenang.gov.my/portal3/penang-tourism-news/1297-pg-medical-tourism-increaserevenue.html?

(accessed 15 February 2011).

Von Grunsven, L, 2007. "New Industries in South East Asia's Late Industrialization Evolution versus Creation. The Automation Industry in Penang (Malaysia) Considered". *Penang Economic Monthly* Vol. 9, No. 5.

Watanabe, Akihito, 2000. *Penang: The Retirement Paradise*. (Chuchokisya no Tame no Penan Seikatsu Gaido.) A.P.Press (M) SDN. BHD, Kuala Lumpur.

Wilson, Woodrow, 1887. "The Study of Administration" *Political Science Quarterly* Vol. 2 No. 2, pp. 197-222.

World Bank, 2009. *Malaysia Economic Monitor: Repositioning for Growth*. Bangkok, Thailand: The World Bank.

Yeoh Seng Guan, Loh Wei Leng, Khoo Salma Nasution, and Neil Khor, (eds.) 2009. *Penang and Its Region: The Story of an Asian Entrepot*. Singapore: NUS Press.

Yeoh, T, 2011. "What the Selangor State Secretary Issue Teaches Us", *Penang Economic Monthly*, February, issue 2.11, pp. 38-40.

Yoon Chon Leong, 2010. "Penang Industrial Blueprint 2010". Penang: Bizwise Consulting, 2010.

Yusuf, S. M. Anjum Altaf and Kaoru Nabeshima, (eds.) 2004. *Global Production Networking and Technological Change in East Asia*. World Bank and Oxford University Press.

Yusuf, S. and Nabeshima, K, 2009. "Can Malaysia Escape the Middle-Income Trap? A Strategy for Penang". Policy Research Working Paper 4971. The World Bank Development Research Group Director's Office.

Zerai, Assata, 2002."Models for Unity between Scholarship and Grassroots Activism", *Critical Sociology*, Vol 28:1-2 , pp. 201-216.

www.ingramcontent.com/pod-product-compliance
Lightning Source LLC
Chambersburg PA
CBHW062021220426
43662CB00010B/1423